EXAMINING
HEISEI JAPAN

EXAMINING HEISEI JAPAN

ECONOMY

Supervised by
KITAOKA Shinichi

Edited by
KOMINE Takao

VOL. III

Japan Publishing Industry Foundation for Culture

Publisher's Note

This book follows the Hepburn system of romanization, and with few exceptions long vowels are indicated by macrons. The tradition of placing the family name first has been followed for Japanese, Chinese, and Korean names. All essays featured in this compilation are from academic sources and were written during the Heisei period (1989–2019). With permission, adjustments have been made to each essay for purposes of style and readability.

Examining Heisei Japan, *Vol. III: Economy*
Supervised by Kitaoka Shinichi. Edited by Komine Takao.

Published by
Japan Publishing Industry Foundation for Culture (JPIC)
2-2-30 Kanda-Jinbocho, Chiyoda-ku, Tokyo 101-0051, Japan

First edition: March 2023

This publication is the result of a collaborative effort between the Japan Institute of International Affairs (JIIA) and Japan Publishing Industry Foundation for Culture (JPIC).

Book design: Miki Kazuhiko, Ampersand Works

Printed in Japan
hardcover ISBN 978-4-86658-227-6
ebook (ePub) ISBN 978-4-86658-228-3
https://www.jpicinternational.com/

CONTENTS

FOREWORD

This volume is based on a suggestion made by Dr. Kitaoka Shinichi, special advisor to the president of the Japan International Cooperation Agency (JICA) and a member of the steering committee for the territory, sovereignty, and history studies project that the Japan Institute of International Affairs (JIIA) undertook under a contract with the Japanese government.

Compiled here are English articles published during the Heisei years (1989–2019) by leading scholars and academic figures in various fields. This publication is intended, through these articles, to reexamine the features characterizing the Heisei era that extended over three decades of postwar Japanese history, and to make their insights more broadly available to the world.

The Heisei era, which started in 1989, was a period of turmoil both in Japan and internationally, contrary to the meaning of its name. Up until its end in 2019, the era was consistently characterized by unpredictability. By examining the writings of the leading scholars of the time, we can come to know how they regarded the era they lived through and, by sharing their thoughts in English with a global readership, we can provide important insights to better understand the Heisei era and to chart Japan's future path as we move forward in the Reiwa era.

The first volume in the series addresses foreign and security policies; the second will be on politics. This volume, the third in the series, looks back on economic developments during the Heisei years. Edited by Professor Komine Takao of Taisho University, it brings together essays and speeches by leading economists, policymakers, and practitioners. By touching on the relationship between the economy and society during that time, it offers a broad-ranging reflection on the Japanese economy throughout the Heisei era. The fourth volume will revisit culture and society in Heisei Japan.

In closing, I would like to express my profound gratitude to Dr. Kitaoka, who suggested this program and guided it through to fruition; our editor, Professor Komine; the outstanding scholars who supported the project's objective and so generously donated their time, insights, and writings; and all those who contributed so much to make this publication possible.

Sasae Kenichiro

President, JIIA

February 2023

PREFACE

Komine Takao

This volume brings together representative essays written by experts on the Japanese economy during the Heisei era. Japan's Heisei era comprises the thirty years between 1989 and 2019. There is, of course, no theoretical basis for delimiting a period of time by the era name selected to mark the accession of a new Japanese emperor. The economy of Heisei Japan, however, has sufficient meaning to demarcate that portion of time as subject matter for discussion. Japan's experience during that time is also likely to be recalled and used as a reference when something similar happens or is about to happen in other countries in the years to come. Sharing with an international audience the experience of the Japanese economy during the Heisei era is therefore very meaningful, making this volume highly significant.

For an overview of the Heisei economy as a whole, please refer to my essay "A Retrospective View of the Heisei Economy" in part I, which should provide a sense of the major trends in the domestic economy during the Heisei years. Here, I would like to foreground three key points to be considered in any discussion of the Heisei economy.

First, during the Heisei years, the Japanese economy was confronted with a multitude of uncharted challenges that caused it considerable difficulty. Japan's economic bubble began to collapse during this time, and the huge fluctuation in asset prices accompanying the bubble's formation and collapse created a major headache in dealing with financial institutions' nonperforming loans. Around the year 2000, plummeting commodity and service prices triggered deflation, an issue that was to plague Japan throughout the Heisei era. In 1997, the Asian currency crisis saw stock prices dive, which in turn created a financial crisis in Japan as major banks collapsed. Eye-watering amounts of public capital were injected into the economy in an effort to escape the crisis. The growth rate slowed, and the economic turmoil known as the "lost decade" dragged on to become the "lost twenty years." In 2005, Japan's population began to decline, and birthrates have since remained low.

Japan is often ironically described as the "advanced nation of problems" in the sense that it was the first to experience issues that came later to other countries, or even as the "department store of problems," as it has experienced such a wide range of challenges. The Japanese economy of the Heisei era in particular certainly presented a whole series of new and difficult economic issues.

Second, policy responses to these issues took the form of an ongoing process of trial and error, sometimes so experimental that they were implemented without any clear idea as to the outcome. This was arguably unavoidable given the unprecedented nature of the issues faced.

Fiscal stimulus was used repeatedly to address the protracted economic downturn. The financial crisis removed the option of the amalgamation of financial institutions and other schemes previously used by the financial authorities to prop up the economy. Instead, massive amounts of public funds were injected and major financial institutions and securities firms were allowed to collapse. Perhaps the most experimental effort was monetary policy aimed at shaking off deflation. The initial policy response to deflation was a textbook interest-rate cut, but eventually the authorities turned to quantitative easing, using zero interest rates to expand the monetary base. In 2013, the most radical measures to date were adopted as part of the "Abenomics" program. These included wholesale expansion of the monetary base, a negative interest-rate policy, and yield curve control.

Third, many Heisei-era policy issues have been carried over to the current Reiwa period. The basic economic growth rate has not improved, and the need for a growth strategy is still being touted. The fiscal deficit continues to grow, while the social security system has yet to be rebuilt.

There has also been no end to the string of new problems. The COVID-19 pandemic began in 2020, prompting Japan to issue a series of state-of-emergency declarations. Due to restrictions placed on eating out, travel, and other face-to-face services over this period, the economy has experienced a succession of pendulum swings, forcing the government to adopt emergency policies such as providing small- and medium-enterprise financing and household subsidies. The year 2022 has presented more new challenges for the Japanese economy, with Russia's invasion of Ukraine causing import prices to skyrocket and disrupting international supply chains.

In terms of the deflation situation, rising import prices pushed consumer price inflation over the 2 percent target in April 2021, but the Bank of Japan and many experts predict that it will drop back below that mark once the impact of higher import prices has been absorbed. As a result, the exceptional measure of monetary easing remains in place. In addition, with Japan's birthrates falling still further, particularly since the start of the pandemic, Japan's population policy framework needs to be revisited.

These economic experiences may provide a reference for other countries as well. Japan's nonperforming loan experience, for example, shows that once an asset bubble has occurred, financial institutions will almost inevitably see a buildup of nonperforming loans, and tackling the issue early on, even by spending public funds, will ultimately benefit the economy. Japan's experience with deflation reveals that once the inflation rate slips into negative territory and the expectation of low inflation takes hold, it is almost impossible to restore normality using financial policy alone. Further, some Asian countries are already beginning to struggle to deal with falling birthrates, and more countries will join their number in the years to come. Japan's population experience demonstrates how difficult it is, amid the inevitable socioeconomic shift toward gender equality, to raise birthrates and halt population decline.

These are just a few of the lessons and insights which I believe that the analyses of economic issues in this volume offer to an international audience. Because the aim is to present the analyses and corresponding recommendations made by experts on the Japanese economy and its many issues, essays written back when these issues first emerged have been reproduced here as they were at the time of initial publication. My heartfelt thanks go to the authors and publishers for allowing them to be reproduced in this manner.

Part
I

The Heisei Economy

Part I of the book addresses the Heisei economy as a whole.

In "A Retrospective View of the Heisei Economy," Komine Takao gives an overview of the changes in the Japanese economy during the Heisei era and the policies adopted accordingly. He divides the era into five phases. The first phase, from 1989 to the early 1990s, saw the collapse of the economic bubble, which caused stock and land prices to tumble and ushered in Japan's "lost twenty years." The second phase was in the late 1990s, when the Asian currency crisis triggered a financial crisis in Japan along with deflation. The third phase, in the early 2000s, saw Koizumi Junichirō's cabinet explore structural reform, with progress made on dealing with nonperforming loans. In the fourth phase, which ran from the late 2000s to the early 2010s, a Democratic Party of Japan (DPJ) administration took power and policy turmoil ensued. This phase was also affected by the global financial crisis triggered by the collapse of the Lehman Brothers global financial services firm. The fifth phase, beginning at the end of 2012, marked Abe Shinzō's introduction of a series of economic measures dubbed "Abenomics."

Yoshikawa Hiroshi, author of "Japan's Lost Decade: What Have We Learned and Where Are We Heading?" discusses the background of Japan's economic slump in the 1990s. He identifies the failure of conventional macroeconomic thought in this case, which he describes as an "uncertainty trap." He argues that the lack of innovation designed to create demand was a major factor in Japan's lost twenty years. This observation still holds true for the Japanese economy today.

In "Explaining Japan's Unproductive Two Decades," Fukao Kyōji analyzes the reasons for Japan's productivity growth rate remaining low for so long. He focuses on Japan's slow accumulation of information technology-related capital and intangibles, suggesting that small and medium-sized enterprises (SMEs) in particular have been slower to invest in these areas than large companies, which in turn has slowed the increase in SME total factor productivity.

I-(1) A Retrospective View of the Heisei Economy

Komine Takao

Asia-Pacific Review, 2018

The Nakasone Yasuhiro Peace Institute (formerly Institute for International Policy Studies) marks its thirtieth anniversary this year in June 2018. The three decades that the institute has existed coincide almost perfectly with the length of the Heisei period, as the fact that this is Heisei year thirty indicates. Therefore, in the present article, "Heisei economy" will be the term used in this review of developments in the Japanese economy over the past three decades.

Introduction

The Heisei economy traced a history that unfolded in a very different way from the Shōwa economy (1926–1988) that preceded it. The Japanese economy during the Shōwa era—particularly in the years after World War II—did have to confront numerous difficult problems, but on the whole, it overcame them with an almost surprising smoothness and developed in ways that most people did not expect.

The high levels of growth that it achieved (from the mid-1950s to early 1970s), as indicated by 10 percent average annual growth rates, dramatically improved the country's economic power and standard of living. At one point, observers at the time believed that various changes in the international environment—including the "Nixon Shock" and the shift to a floating exchange-rate mechanism (1971) in the United States, the two oil crises (1973 and roughly 1982), and the rapid appreciation in the value of the yen following the signing of the Plaza Accord (latter half of the 1980s)—would have a major impact on the Japanese economy. However, it ultimately weathered them relatively smoothly. The years of the Shōwa economy concluded with an era of prosperity known as the "bubble economy" period (the latter half of the 1980s).

In contrast, the Heisei economy that marked its start in January 1989 has faced a series of trials. One problem after another has arisen, many of which are of a sort that has never been seen before: the collapse of the bubble economy and the nonperforming loan problem, the Asian currency crisis and the more general financial crisis, ongoing deflation and an unprecedented "new phase of monetary easing," and the country plunging into a state of population decline.

Furthermore, the policy responses to these various issues have been far from satisfactory. The nation has been forced to pursue a series of experimental, trial-and-error approaches to deal with these various unprecedented problems. These ad hoc approaches have not met with much success, and the country continues to need policy responses to deal with the problems of deflation, population issues, and public finances and social security.

With this perspective in mind, I believe it is crucial that we look back at the various issues Japan's economy and society have confronted in the Heisei era and the policy responses to them as a means of laying the groundwork for future policy responses.

The Collapse of the "Bubble" Economy and the Start of the "Lost Decades" (1989 to Mid-1990s)

The formation of the bubble economy and its collapse

The "Heisei economy" began (in January 1990) with the collapse of the bubble economy. On December 29, 1989, stock prices set a record for the Nikkei average of ¥38,915 in the final session of the year for the Tokyo Stock Exchange. It was not understood until many years afterward, but that marked the peak for stock prices on the Nikkei. As of this writing (March 2018), that record remains untouched. Stock prices began a precipitous decline with the start of the following calendar year. In October 1990, they fell below ¥20,000.

As to land prices, on March 27, 1990, the Ministry of Finance (MOF) issued a circular limiting total bank lending to the real-estate sector. This move is seen as the biggest reason for the collapse in land prices.

Japanese asset prices (stock and land prices) fluctuated wildly, with a dramatic rise in the late 1980s followed by a dramatic decline. These developments comprise the "birth of the bubble" and "collapse of the bubble." Economically, the scale of these asset price fluctuations was quite large. This fact can be seen most clearly in the workings of reconciliation accounts in the system of national accounts. A "reconciliation account" records the fluctuating portion in asset values that are not dependent on investment—that is to say, the change in asset values arising from changes in asset prices. They are equivalent to so-called capital gains.

Both land and stock prices continued rising to quite high levels from 1985 to 1989. This resulted in the generation of enormous capital gains in stocks and land. In contrast, after 1990, the prices of both fell, resulting in massive capital losses. The scale of these gains and losses in each of these years was such that in some cases the amount exceeded that of one year's worth of nominal GDP. One might say this is a surprisingly enormous sum.

These sharp rises and falls in asset prices and the enormous capital gains and losses that they produced caused enormous fluctuations in Japan's economic performance. First, during the bubble years of the late 1980s, the economy's performance took a surprising turn for the better.

The development of the bubble improved the growth rate through several routes. First was the demand stimulus effect (the so-called "asset effect") produced by those capital gains. The existence of an asset effect has been confirmed with respect in particular to consumer durable expenditures in household budgets, even based on an empirical analysis using the consumption function. Consumer durable expenditures swelled in the first half of the 1980s, and despite their subsequent reactionary decline, it is thought that this asset effect made an impact.

Second was the increase in home investment activity. The rise in the security value of real estate held by landowners was due to the ease of procuring financing. This is thought to be the reason that the late 1980s saw an increase in condominium building, particularly around the Tokyo area, as well as the sharp spike in the building of "resort" condominiums.

Third was the upsurge of capital expenditures. The rise in land prices improved the ability of corporations to borrow from financial institutions, while the increase in stock prices facilitated the procurement of financing through such measures as issuing warrant bonds (bonds that can be converted to stocks at a fixed price). This caused capital expenditures to swell in the latter part of the 1980s.

In this way, the Japanese economy from 1986 to 1989 posted high annual growth rates of around 5 to 6 percent, and on that basis was able to resolve a series of problems that it had faced up to that point. First, tax revenues increased, and the balance of public finances turned for the better due to the nominal growth rate rising to the 5 to 8 percent level. Even the special public bonds issued in FY 1983 with a total value of around ¥7 trillion at long last amounted to zero in FY 1990 (initial budget base level). Also, the upsurge in the growth rate increased imports, and the current account surplus that had been a major issue for the Japanese economy decreased. The nominal GDP rate for the current account surplus fell from 4.4 percent in 1986 to 1.1 percent in 1990. The employment situation also improved. The unemployment rate of 2.8 percent posted in 1986 fell to 2.1 percent in 1990, while the effective job opening ratio rose from 0.59 to 1.43 over the same period.

However, when the economic bubble collapsed as the 1990s began, a mechanism completely opposite to that seen in the late 1980s began to operate, with the result that economic performance turned for the worse. The stagnant 1990s came to be referred to as the "Lost Decade," and, as they stretched out over twenty years, as the "Lost Decades." Concrete examples of how economic performance worsened include the following.

First was the stagnation in economic activities. The economic growth rate slumped for a long time. The average growth rate for the early 1990s stood at 1.5 percent, while for the latter half it was 1.0 percent. The deflationary aspect (a fall in commodity and service prices) grew stronger from the mid-1990s onward, and nominal wages fell.

Second was the worsening of the employment situation. The lifetime employment system was preserved in Japan until the 1980s, and employment itself was usually stable. However, as the 1990s began, employment conditions became strikingly worse. The unemployment rate in the 1980s stood at 2.5 percent on average, but in concert with the economy going stagnant, it gradually rose and hit 5.4 percent by 2002. This was the worst level since statistics started being kept.

Third was the consequent worsening of the state of public finances. The balance of general public finances in Japan stood at a surplus through 1992, ranking it among the highest worldwide. However, after the bubble collapsed—owing to an increase in annual expenditures applied as a stimulative measure to address the decline in tax revenues brought about by economic stagnation—the balance instantly went into the red. The size of this deficit grew rapidly, with the result that by around 1997 Japan came to have the largest such deficit among any of the world's leading industrialized countries.

Fourth, the financial intermediation capabilities of financial institutions became paralyzed, and there was a loss of trust in the banking sector. The outstanding balance of loans from all of the country's banks had increased by 6 to 12 percent year on year during the latter half of the 1980s. However, that growth began to ebb in the 1990s, and starting in 1997 the decline became a continuous one. In autumn 1997, Hokkaido Takushoku Bank and Yamaichi Securities collapsed, and concerns over credit risk grew stronger. It was not until 2006 that the amount of loans made began to increase.

Fifth, various structural problems with the Japanese economy began presenting themselves one after another. Any number of systems in Japan that had functioned well prior to this began to show some fraying around the edges. These included Japan's regulatory, management, employment, health care, and social security systems. There came to be demands for so-called structural reform as a result. Previous ways of doing things gradually came to be negated, and Japan as a whole lost confidence in itself.

The emergence of the balance sheet adjustment problem

The aforementioned economic performance decline was deeply connected with the fall in asset prices due to the bubble's collapse. In particular, it had a severe impact on the emergence of the balance sheet adjustment problem. This developed in the following way.

First, during the bubble years when corporations and households had increased their assets without any trouble, they were increasing their liabilities at the same time that they were stepping up high-risk investment activities such investing in stocks and real estate. They increased their assets and liabilities in a hedging fashion. Under these circumstances, when the bubble collapsed and asset prices fell, the monetary value of their assets dropped in a flash. However, since their liabilities did not fall, their ratio against assets inevitably increased. Accordingly, the balance sheet for companies and households worsened.

The effort to get this worsened balance sheet back to its starting point was referred to as a "balance sheet adjustment." This balance sheet adjustment problem can truly be said to be a negative legacy of the bubble. That is due to the fact that even if the bubble itself disappeared, the impaired balance sheet that resulted from it would remain for a long time.

What typically results from a balance sheet adjustment problem is a nonperforming loan problem for financial institutions. The fact that liabilities became excessive on the side of procuring financing and repayments fell into arrears represented nothing less than the deterioration of assets for financial institutions. The nonperforming loans that accumulated at financial institutions impaired the financial intermediation functions of credit transactions and the ability to supply risk moneys to economic circles. They became a major factor behind economic stagnation.

Thus, the slump in the Japanese economy continued, and it slid into the situation described as the "Lost Decade" and "Lost Decades."

The Financial Crisis and the Genesis of Deflation (Latter Half of the 1990s)

To cope with the economic stagnation that developed after the bubble's collapse, the government attempted to buoy the economy through both public finances and credit transactions. However, these measures had no significant effect, and the economy on the whole continued to flag. The effects of the nonperforming loans that had accumulated at financial institutions lay behind this. As this was unfolding, the Asian currency crisis occurred in the summer of 1997. Its repercussions were felt in Japan, and that autumn the country experienced its own financial crisis.

The transformation of economic policy

In the early 1990s, when the bubble economy started to collapse, many people were still arguing for directing energies toward crushing the bubble, and there was a delay in implementing full-blown measures to stimulate economic growth.

With respect to financial policy, a series of Keynesian strategies was worked out after 1992 that focused on increasing public investment. The first of these comprised the comprehensive economic measures (a ¥10.7 trillion program) adopted in August 1992. Practically each of the next three years through 1995 also saw economic measures put into play. However, although demand may have increased, and the economy may have been propped up when such economic measures focused on concerted joint investments were put into effect, in the final analysis the effects were temporary. It was not possible to lift the economy's fundamental potential for growth through them.

As to fiscal policy, the government shifted to one of monetary easing starting in July 1991 and made a series of drops in the official discount rate, going from 6.0 percent to 0.5 percent by September 1995.

An increase in nonperforming loans stifles the economy

The reason that the growth rate of the Japanese economy flagged, regardless of the cumulative economic stimulus packages, at root is thought to have been—unlike during a normal economic downturn—because it was weighted down with a millstone in the form of nonperforming loans.

"Nonperforming loans" refers to the portion of the funds that banks and other financial institutions lend out for which recovering the original principal and interest becomes difficult or impossible. When the bubble economy collapsed as the 1990s began, the number of nonperforming loans held by financial institutions skyrocketed. However, at first it was not possible to determine exactly how much those loans amounted to. To begin with, no definition existed as to what a nonperforming loan was. This was because neither financial institutions nor the government (the Ministry of Finance) actively attempted to make explicit the reality of the situation.

People also had misplaced optimism at the initial stage about their potential economic impact. For example, the white paper on the economy for 1993 showed that the value of delinquent loans that had stopped paying interest for more than six months as of the end of March 1992 stood at around ¥7 to ¥8 trillion. Of that, some ¥2 to ¥3 trillion worth were not covered by either security or guarantees. After presenting these figures, the paper then went on to say: "When comparing this to the assets of all banks, delinquent loans account for only a portion of the ¥351 trillion in total loans. Given that they account for only a small portion of banking assets, and furthermore given that the unrealized profits of negotiable securities are on the scale of ¥17 trillion, it is apparent that the problem of nonperforming loans is not a critical one for bank management." It continued, "It is believed that several years will be required to recover and consolidate the nonperforming loans.

During that period, it appears that this will be a factor that squeezes profits. However, when considering the fitness of the banks, it is thought that they will have enough leeway to dispose of them. Based on this, we do not believe that the business foundations of the banks will be shaken, and no problems from a trust perspective will arise."

Based solely on this text, we can see that the government at the time underestimated the impact of the nonperforming loans in a number of ways, including (1) it was understated in its view of the scale of the nonperforming loans; (2) it believed that the existence of unrealized profits from stocks would provide a buffer; and (3) it thought that the business foundations of the banks were stable.

The definition of nonperforming loans and the rules on making them public were set down in March 1999. In terms of amounts, the total value of nonperforming loans peaked in March 2002 at an amount in excess of ¥40 trillion. The ratio of nonperforming loans (the percentage of the total amount of loans accounted for by such bad loans) likewise peaked at just under 9 percent that month. We can see just how naive the thinking at the start of the 1990s was.

This increase in the amount of nonperforming loans continued to function as a weight on the economy by generating a credit crunch that restrained banks from lending. In short, during the bubble years of the late 1980s, banks were able to proactively engage in lending without covering the costs or going through the effort of doing screening because they used land that had risen in price as security. However, when land prices slumped, they were no longer able to use this approach. Conversely, after the 1990s, banks that had seen a deterioration in their financial affairs started to avoid risk as a way to ward off any further such deterioration, and became circumspect about lending.

Structural reform under the Hashimoto administration and its breakdown

Turning to look at the political situation of the time, in January 1996 Socialist prime minister Murayama Tomiichi announced his resignation, and a cabinet took shape that was headed by Hashimoto Ryūtarō. Starting at the end of 1996, the Hashimoto cabinet devoted some energy toward structural reform. It touted reforms in six areas: administrative reform, fiscal structural reform, economic structural reform, financial system reform, social security reforms, and education reforms. Administrative reform entailed a massive reorganization of government ministries and agencies, and economic structural reform saw an easing of various regulations such as in the transportation sector, while financial system reform meant carrying out the so-called financial big bang (a major easing of regulations in the financial field).

Prime Minister Hashimoto also persisted when it came to rebuilding public finances. Debate began in March 1997 over the draft Fiscal Structural Reform Law, and the consumption tax rate was increased from 3 percent to 5 percent the following month. At the same time, ¥2 trillion worth of special tax cuts that had been in force since 1994 were eliminated. These had been in place from the cabinet of Hosokawa Motohiro to that of Murayama Tomiichi, and had been compensated for by the future consumption tax. The Fiscal Structural Reform Law was passed that November, and the budget for FY 1998 was a major austerity budget.

However, as I will discuss later, the path toward rebuilding public finances broke down due to the Asian currency crisis that began around July 1994 and the great chaos in Japanese finance that followed. In December 1997, the government was forced to put together special tax cuts totaling ¥2 trillion to deal with the worsening economy. The following April, it cut taxes by another ¥4 trillion and increased public expenditures for programs on the order of ¥16.65 trillion. The purpose of the Fiscal Structural Reform Law had been to encourage steady progress toward rebuilding public finance by setting down the program for doing so in a law, but its enforcement was brought to a stop under the Obuchi cabinet that succeeded Hashimoto's administration.

The Asian currency and financial crises

The Asian currency crisis started in Thailand. Most East Asian countries at the time had pegged their exchange rates for all intents and purposes to the dollar. They pursued economic growth by accepting large amounts of short-term financing from foreign countries and applying it toward long-term investments in their own country.

It was against this backdrop that hedge funds took advantage of the overvaluation of the Thai baht to launch a currency attack (baht selling) on it. Furthermore, the country had also just seen a real-estate bubble collapse. Dollar financing all at once drained out of Thailand, and at long last, in July 1997, the baht was moved to a floating exchange rate regime. The value of the Thai currency dropped, making it difficult to repay dollar debts, and the country wound up receiving aid from the International Monetary Fund (IMF) and other such bodies. Similar developments occurred in Indonesia and South Korea, resulting in the situation referred to as the Asian currency crisis.

Stock prices fell in Japan as a result of this crisis, and the economy also worsened due to the decline in exports. As a result, financial institutions that had already been struggling with massive numbers of nonperforming loans saw their financial condition worsen further. First, the brokerage company Sanyo Securities saw its business come to a dead stop due to the excessive capital expenditures it had made during the bubble period, and the loans that had been made in connection to real estate for non-bank subsidiaries went bad. That November it filed a bankruptcy reorganization plan. As a result of the failure of Sanyo Securities, the first default in the postwar era occurred on the interbank call market (the lending market among banks for short-term financing). This invited further bankruptcies among such other financial institutions as Hokkaido Takushoku Bank and Yamaichi Securities.

Given this situation, as an emergency measure in February 1998, the government passed two laws related to financial stabilization, and also took such steps as injecting public funds. However, in the end these measures were inadequate. That October, the Long-Term Credit Bank of Japan collapsed, followed in December by the Nippon Credit Bank. Taking this in, the government then prepared two more laws and came up with a scheme that would make it possible to temporarily nationalize the failed banks and inject large amounts of public funds into financial institutions before they collapsed. With these emergency measures in place, two of the failed banks were nationalized, and in March 1999 approximately ¥7.5 trillion in public funds was injected into fifteen major banks. These moves were just barely in time to avert crisis conditions for Japanese finance, but at this point the nonperforming loan problem still had not been fundamentally resolved.

Koizumi's Structural Reforms and the Disposal of Nonperforming Loans (First Half of the 2000s)

Koizumi Junichirō's cabinet took office in April 2001. Prime Minister Koizumi made the most of the framework provided by the Council on Economic and Fiscal Policy (CEFP) to establish a prime minister–led style of policy management and took on so-called structural reform.

The content of the Koizumi reforms

The objectives of structural reform under the Koizumi cabinet were to stimulate the economy, to ensure the public's peace of mind, and to establish a system of public finances that could handle its responsibility for future generations. It moved forward with these under such slogans as "from the public to the private" and "from the government to the regions."

The specific details of these reforms covered such areas as (1) regulatory reform and the institution of special deregulation zones; (2) channeling of finances and financial and industrial revitalization; (3) tax-system reforms; (4) buttressing of employment and "people's vitality" (*ningenryoku*); (5) social-security system reforms; (6) reforms in the relationship between the national government and local authorities; and (7) reforms to the budget-drafting process.

Even some within Koizumi's Liberal Democratic Party (LDP) were opposed to the postal privatization drive to which he was particularly attached, and the House of Councillors voted the privatization bill down in August 2005. Koizumi took advantage of this to dissolve the victory in the general election that followed. With public opinion on his side, as the results showed, the bill was approved that October, and the postal service privatization program was put into effect.

Progress on disposing of nonperforming loans

Japanese finance had to face two major issues from the end of the 1990s through the mid-2000s. One was the need to dispose of the nonperforming loans and return financial intermediary functions to normal, while the other was the matter of how to counter deflation in the form of falling commodity prices. Greater progress was made under the Koizumi cabinet on dealing with the nonperforming loans.

In October 2002, Minister of Finance Takenaka Heizō—who concurrently served as minister of state for economic and fiscal policy—set down his "Program for Financial Revival." The program was a severe one that aimed at reducing the percentage of nonperforming loans held by major banks to half of their then-current levels by the end of March 2005, and called for such measures as stricter asset assessments, emphasis on the adequacy of equity capital, and strengthening governance at these institutions.

Progress was made on the disposal of nonperforming loans under these policies, with the percentage of such loans falling from 8.7 percent (at fifteen major banks) at the end of March 2002 to 2.9 percent (at thirteen major banks) by the end of March 2005. At the same time, banks were proactive in increasing capital and worked to augment their equity capital. In this way, the issue of the nonperforming loans that had been a drag on the Japanese economy was finally and largely resolved.

From zero interest rates to quantitative easing

As the twenty-first century began, the issue afflicting the Japanese economy was the continued advance of deflation (an ongoing drop in prices). Up to that point, the price problem that Japan had faced was how to avoid inflation—that is, how to stabilize an excessive rate of price increases. The country had no experience with a continuous decline in prices, and accordingly it was similarly inexperienced when it came to policies aimed at increasing those prices.

A glance back at the course of the policies attempted shows that the BOJ lowered the official discount rate nine times from the 6.0 percent figure of July 1991 to reach the previously unprecedented low level of 0.5 percent by September 1995. However, these traditional monetary policy moves did not improve the deflationary conditions. As a consequence, the BOJ decided in February 1999 to set the overnight unsecured call loan rate to 0.25 percent. Also that month, it further reduced the target rate to 0.15 percent, gradually bringing the levels down. The result was that the call rate stood at around 0.03 percent after March, making it for all intents and purposes a zero interest rate. This marked the start of the so-called zero interest-rate policy.

The policy was briefly lifted in August 2000 in brazen disregard of the government's opposition, but the economy continued to lag and the pressure pushing down prices grew. Consequently, in March 2001 the BOJ implemented a quantitative easing policy as a measure that went even farther beyond the zero interest-rate policy. This changed the operational objective of monetary policy from call rates, as it previously had been, to the BOJ's current account balance. It served to increase the amount of those current accounts to around ¥5 trillion through the purchase of long-term government bonds, among similar steps. Furthermore, this market adjustment would stay in place until the rate of increase in the consumer price index remained stable at not less than zero. Thus, what the government committed to during this period of monetary easing was an attempt to create expectations in the market that the zero interest rate would continue through the policy's application. This was referred to as the "time-axis effect" (*jikanjiku kōka*).

Furthermore, starting in October 2010 the BOJ also responded with a comprehensive easing policy. This policy lowered interest rates as its predecessors had done and laid out a rate of increase for prices (1 percent this time) that would stand as the target for ongoing monetary easing. Furthermore, it also called for the purchase of exchange-traded funds (ETF) and real-estate investment trusts (J-REIT).

Traditionally, the BOJ had provided capital through such measures as purchasing debentures like government bonds, commercial papers (CP), and corporate debentures from the market. This new step meant it would also purchase stocks, as well as land and other real estate. Increasing the kinds of financial assets subject to purchase not only promoted further quantitative easing but also reduced the credit risk premium (the interest rate differential produced by differences in creditworthiness). In short, the comprehensive engagement with quantitative and credit easing explains the BOJ at this point in time. Previously, the financial authorities had regarded intervention in the prices of assets such as stocks and land as something that would distort price formation on the market. Now, however, that limitation had been surmounted.

Thus, monetary policy had entered unprecedented realms, but deflation showed no signs of abating. As I will discuss later, monetary policy would step even further into unknown realms under the Abenomics policies pursued by the Abe cabinet starting at the end of 2012. We know that when an economy slides into a deflationary state, however briefly, escaping from it is extremely difficult. This would later serve as an important lesson for handling monetary policy in other advanced countries.

The Birth of the DPJ Government and the "Lehman Shock" (Late 2000s to Early 2010s)

The Democratic Party of Japan (DPJ) scored a major victory in the general election of August 2009, while the LDP suffered a major defeat. The newly launched DPJ government would have to deal with ordeals in the form of the economic stagnation that followed the Lehman Shock and the Great East Japan Earthquake.

The start of DPJ rule and its collapse

Prime Minister Hatoyama Yukio, under DPJ rule, would attempt to put into action the election manifesto as presented that had served as a campaign pledge, but it did not go well in the end. The specifics of what happened are as follows.

First, the election manifesto called for a shift from bureaucratic initiative to political initiative. Grounded in the criticism that the LDP had acted as one with the bureaucracy in pursuing various policies, Diet members attempted to take the lead in administration in their roles as minister, vice-minister, and parliamentary secretary at each of the ministries. Another reform carried out was the abolishment of the administrative vice-ministers' conference. However, this meant that politicians simply tried to take on work for which bureaucrats should have been appointing responsibility. The result was that administration became more inefficient.

Second, the Hatoyama government attempted to implement the policies it had promised in its election manifesto as presented without securing the financial resources needed. The DPJ had made an array of pledges in its election manifesto, such as providing allowances for children, creating a system for protecting individual farmers, and making highways toll-free, but when it came to the necessary financial resources, the only decision reached was to put something together by "eliminating wasteful uses." The end result was that the government could not guarantee sufficient financial resources, and it wound up accumulating a considerable deficit.

Third, the DPJ did not have any specific growth policies. At the outset, the DPJ government lacked a clear vision when it came to macroeconomic policy, merely touting the abstract slogan "from concrete to the people" (*konkuriito kara hito e*). The party had the idea that if it could achieve its touted platform of cutting public investments and increasing allowances for children, it would eventually be able to achieve the desired levels of economic growth. The plan had been for the newly launched National Strategy Office to craft a vision statement, but this, too, failed to work out as planned. In response to criticisms that the government lacked a growth strategy, at the end of 2009 it presented one titled "New Growth Strategy (Basic Policies)" (*Shin-seichō senryaku* [*kihon hōshin*]). However, the policy objectives it set were based not on gross domestic product but rather on "levels of happiness," which meant it did not work as a pillar for economic policy.

The Hatoyama cabinet faced other problems,

including vagaries induced by the issue of relocating the US Marine Corps' Futenma Air Station in Okinawa and surfacing of issues involving political financing. In the end, it resigned in June 2010. It would be followed by governments led first by Kan Naoto and then by Noda Yoshihiko.

The Lehman Shock and the downturn in the Japanese economy

Starting in the second half of the 1990s, the US saw an ongoing phenomenon of rising housing prices and declining long-term interest rates. The number of so-called subprime housing loans exploded during this period. These were thought to be a means of providing housing loans to borrowers with poor credit ratings. The borrowers could refinance the loans and reduce the interest rate, and if worse came to worst and they could not repay the loans, they would be able to sell the housing to make up for it. On the other hand, lenders were able to get rid of their risk and disperse it through sales of debentures to investors at high yields. They managed this by subdividing multiple debts and combining them with other debentures.

However, this mechanism gradually ceased to function. When the US economy began to improve, the Federal Reserve Board (FRB) implemented an ongoing rise in interest rates starting in June 2004. Meanwhile, housing prices hit their peak around mid-2006 and began to decline. This rise in interest rates and fall in housing prices delivered a heavy blow to subprime loan borrowers, and many in succession found themselves unable to repay their loans. By mid-2007, many actors were dumping subprime-loan–related securities and terminating funds. This chaos spread to financial institutions, and in September 2008 it ultimately led to the collapse of the fourth-largest investment bank in the US, Lehman Brothers Holdings. This was the trigger for simultaneous stock drops around the world and massive turmoil in the financial markets. This international crisis was known in Japan as the "Lehman Shock."

When the Lehman Shock first occurred, it was thought that its impact on Japan would be limited. This was because Japanese financial institutions had almost no involvement with subprime-loan–related investing. However, the fall in growth rates that occurred in Japan was considerably larger than that which had occurred in the country most directly involved; i.e., the US. This was due to the fact that the global financial crisis blunted world trade, which in turn caused a major downturn in Japanese imports and exports.

The Great East Japan Earthquake and its economic impact

The Great East Japan Earthquake occurred on March 11, 2011. With an epicenter off the Tohoku region's Sanriku coast, it caused an enormous tsunami in which many people lost their lives.

The earthquake and disaster also had major economic effects, the most striking of which was the severing of supply chains. Symbolic of this were supply chains related to microcomputers for automobile components. The factories of a major company that manufactured these devices were damaged in the disaster. This created a bottleneck, with the result that the manufacturing of automobiles themselves had to be halted. The impact of this is said to have extended even to overseas production. Against a backdrop of technological innovations and globalization, the supply of parts to manufacturers had become highly specialized, and they were produced in locations that were optimal from a global perspective. The disaster wound up reinforcing how the global economy has constructed highly interdependent relationships through the division of labor.

From a macroeconomic perspective, signs could be seen that Japan's balance of trade would go into the red due to a major slump in industrial production and an expansion in energy imports. However, production recovered after several months, and the trade deficit likewise gradually shrank. For that reason, the impact of the Great East Japan Earthquake was not sufficient to cause a major setback to business activity in Japan.

The Introduction of Abenomics (from the End of 2012)

The LDP was victorious in the general election held at the end of 2012, and took up its old position in power. Prime Minister Abe Shinzō promoted his economic policy as the most crucial issue. That policy came to be referred to as "Abenomics," and while it has gradually changed shape, it remains in place today.

The "three arrows" and their effects

The Abe cabinet made overcoming deflation its overriding imperative. To accomplish this task, the prime minister came up with "three arrows" in the form of "bold monetary policy," "flexible management of public finances," and "a long-term strategy for stimulating private investment."

"Abenomics" scored some major successes in its early stages. This is apparent even from a glance at the major economic indicators. For example, the real growth rate of the GDP climbed from a 0.9 percent rise for FY 2012 to 2.0 percent for FY 2013, while the nominal growth rate for the same period went from 0 to 1.7 percent. A glance at employment conditions likewise shows that the unemployment rate fell from 4.2 percent for the October–December 2012 period to 3.6 percent for the January–March 2014 period, while the effective job opening ratio rose 0.82 to 1.05. Consumer prices (general, excluding fresh produce) likewise rose from -0.1 percent in October–December 2012 to +1.3 percent in January–March 2014. The growth rate was higher, employment conditions improved, and prices rose from the negative range.

Why, then, did Abenomics work so well at the start? Four reasons may be offered. First, when the Abe cabinet took office, the market expected that it would be easier to get financing and the government would pursue a growth-focused economic policy. This would lead in fact to a rise in stock prices, and the yen would weaken. Second, the ongoing weakening of the yen would push up prices through an increase in import prices, and in turn profits for export-oriented companies would rally through the rise of export prices in yen terms. Third, and in particular, FY 2013 saw public investment increase by 8.6 percent (based on GDP, in real terms), which brought about an expansion in demand. And fourth, in FY 2013 the government staved off raising the consumption tax (from 5 percent to 8 percent) in FY 2014, ending the year with a massive last-minute rise in demand.

However, given that all of these factors were rather temporary, their impact wore off post-2014, and the upswing in economic performance came to a halt.

The story of "unprecedented" monetary easing

Monetary policy was the centerpiece of Abenomics. With the deflationary trend maintaining pace, policymakers continued to go beyond previous frameworks in monetary policy as they implemented ever more detailed programs. Many of these attempts stepped into heretofore unknown domains and could not help being "experimental" in nature.

I will trace some of those efforts here. The first of those was the application of "inflation targeting." In January 2013, shortly after Abe formed his administration, the government and the BOJ issued a joint statement declaring an inflation target of a 2 percent rate of increase in the consumer price index.

The second effort was the so-called unprecedented monetary easing plan that began in April 2013 under the new BOJ governor, Kuroda Haruhiko. This was an attempt at monetary easing of a different order both quantitatively and qualitatively. With its objective of achieving a 2 percent rise in consumer prices as quickly as possible, though with a two-year time frame in mind, it targeted doubling the monetary base and the retained amount of both long-term government bonds and ETFs over that two-year period, and extending the average current maturity of long-term government bond purchases by double the length or more.

The announcement of the policy had a considerable impact, between Governor Kuroda's very self-confident explanation of it in easily comprehended terms and the strong commitment that was presented in the form of language about not hesitating to do whatever would be necessary to achieve the 2 percent goal in two years.

Given how difficult it subsequently became to achieve the 2 percent in two years goal, in October 2014 the BOJ enacted a further monetary easing measure by increasing the amount of its monthly purchases of government bonds by ¥10 trillion.

Third was the negative interest rate policy

adopted in January 2016. This is what led the BOJ's monetary policy to be referred to as "quantitative and qualitative easing with negative interest rates."

Prior to this, the BOJ's policy had rather single-mindedly been focused on easing. After this, it would be adjusted to pursue a more multidimensional track. After carrying out "comprehensive verifications" with respect to the monetary easing policy that had been in place, in September 2016 the BOJ settled on a new monetary policy framework based on its predecessor.

The new framework called for (1) purchasing government bonds so that the long-term interest rate would float around 0 percent; (2) letting the negative interest rates stand; and (3) continuing to increase the funds in circulation until the rise in prices remained stable at over 2 percent. For these reasons, the monetary policy would subsequently be described as one of "quantitative and qualitative monetary easing with long-term interest-rate controls."

The reasons why such verifications were necessary is clear. They include the facts that (1) the unprecedented monetary easing policies had not produced any actual effects and were unable to obtain the objective of "2 percent in two years"; (2) the massive purchases of government bonds would reach their limit in two years; and (3), as noted earlier, the negative interest rates had not had much of a positive effect, while their adverse effects were noticeable.

It should be noted that this policy transformation is still ongoing, making evaluation difficult. Given (1) the change in policy from controlling volume to controlling interest rates; (2) the fact that no further progress has been made with pushing forward on negative interest rates; and (3) the fact that it is unlikely that there will be any reduction in the amount of government bonds purchased in order to achieve the goal of ultra-low interest rates, it would be natural to assume that Japanese monetary policy has begun to change course. In the future, the biggest policy issues will be working out how to avoid falling back into sustained deflation while moving toward an exit that leads to ordinary management of monetary policy.

A continually expanding Abenomics

Since then, the policy scope of Abenomics has continued to expand further. In June 2016, the Abe government settled on its "Japan's Plan for Dynamic Engagement of All Citizens" (*Nippon ichioku sōkatsuyaku puran*), and as part of this worked out its "new three arrows."

The first of these was to have "a robust economy that gives rise to hope" by setting the objective of attaining a nominal GDP of ¥600 trillion. Second was to have "dream-weaving childcare supports," with a more concrete objective of attaining "the desirable birthrate of 1.8." Third was to have "social security that provides reassurance," expressed in concrete terms by guaranteeing that "no one [would be] forced to leave their jobs for nursing care."

Furthermore, the government would also make an effort to deal with the cross-cutting issue of "work-style reform." The main pillars of this are achieving equitable levels of compensation for equitable levels of work and relieving long working hours. In March 2017, the government settled on an action plan for work-style reform. This plan called for setting upper limits on working hours that would not be permitted even if there were agreements between labor and management or special provisions in place. As for the issue of equal pay for equal work, it would forbid any unreasonable discrimination between how regular and non-regular employees were treated, not just in terms of wages, but also in awarding bonuses and in offering benefits packages.

Conclusion: Remaining Issues

This completes a brief sketch of the course of the Heisei economy. As noted before, numerous issues remain and will persist into the post-Heisei era. The main issues are as follows.

First is escaping from deflation and improving the Japanese economy's potential for growth. Thanks to having pursued a radical monetary easing policy for a long period, the economy is finally in a state that may be termed "not deflation." However, it has not been able to achieve the targeted 2 percent rate of increase in the consumer price index.

As of early 2018, Japanese economic

conditions have continued to recover in a comparatively smooth fashion. However, an export increase due to the stability of the global economy has played a major role in this. Domestic demand in the form of corporate capital expenditures and household consumption as before remains somewhat flat. It will be necessary to set aside the anxieties corporations and households have about the future, improve labor productivity, and achieve self-sustaining growth in the economy.

Second are public finance and social security reforms. Most people know that the balance of Japan's public finances is deteriorating to a critical degree. Many economists fear that if this is left to take its own course, economic chaos of some sort will result, and at that point public welfare will seriously break down. However, Abenomics has put off any rebuilding of public finances. The increase in the consumption tax to 10 percent that had been planned for October 2015 has been postponed twice. Furthermore, the sources of revenue that had been obtained from tax increases were set aside to provide support for childrearing and early childhood education. Rebuilding public finances is becoming all the more remote.

If we think about the future of public finances, we see that social security reform is developing into urgent business. If we simply look on as the population ages, social security–related costs for such things as healthcare, nursing, and pensions are naturally going to swell. Social security needs to be reformed, and annual expenditures ought to be rationalized, but, fearing a backlash from senior citizens, politicians have not set their hands to the task.

Third is responding to the declining birthrate. The government has set a population of 100 million as its policy target, and is engaged in measures to cope with the declining birth rate. However, in order to halt the population decline at 100 million, it will be necessary to increase the fertility rate to 2 or higher by around 2040. Japan's fertility rate has been increasing somewhat in recent years, but the most recent (2016) figure showed it to be 1.44. It simply does not seem like it is going to reach 2.

The government's expenditures related to this issue are no more than half to one-third (relative to GDP) of those made by such countries as the UK, France, and Sweden that have brought this problem under control. The first thing that needs to be done is to vastly increase the financial resources used to overcome this problem.

Fourth is the promotion of free markets around the world. The trend toward free markets that had once been making progress has greatly abated, owing to the appearance of US president Donald Trump. The US has even stepped away from the already-concluded Trans-Pacific Partnership (TPP) agreement for which it had once taken the initiative. In response, Japan demonstrated strong leadership in pushing forward on a TPP without the US (TPP-11). This has reached the point where the broad outlines of an agreement have been secured. Japan will need to work together with the countries of Europe and Asia to protect the global free-market system.

Originally published in *Asia-Pacific Review* 25, no. 1 (2018): 19–37. The table from the original entitled "Main Events in the Heisei Economy Years" has been omitted at the author's request and integrated into the full chronology at the back of this volume.

I-(2) Japan's Lost Decade

What Have We Learned and Where Are We Heading?

Yoshikawa Hiroshi

Asian Economic Policy Review, 2007

The lost decade has provided us a number of lessons. One of them is the limit of standard macroeconomics. This paper attempts to show that uncertainty plays a much more important role in the macroeconomy than most economists recognize. Once the economy is caught in an uncertainty trap, the effectiveness of standard policy necessarily weakens. The zero interest rate may well be a consequence of an uncertainty trap. In fact, whether or not the economy is caught in such an uncertainty trap distinguishes a depression from the normal cyclical recession. The significance of demand-creating innovation is another point I emphasize in this paper. In my view, a lack of demand-creating innovation is a part of the explanation for the lost decade. At the same time, this paper offers prospects for the future of the Japanese economy.

1. Introduction

As of the year 2007, Japan's "lost decade" has become something of the past. Thanks to vigorous exports and corporate investments, the Japanese economy has sustained sound growth for more than four years. The average annual growth rate of real gross domestic products (GDP) from 2003 to 2006 was 2.1 percent. For comparison, the corresponding figures for the USA and European Union were 3.2 percent and 2.1 percent, respectively. The current expansion that began in February 2002, in fact, surpasses the cyclical expansion during the late 1960s in its length, and is the longest in postwar history.

Overall, the lost decade is now a thing of the past. Nevertheless, it was a historical event, and it left scars not only on the economy, but also on Japanese society. To glimpse its effects, we can observe the number of suicides (see figure 1). Suicides dramatically rose during the late 1990s, when the financial system was on the verge of collapse and a storm of restructuring was raging. The legacy of the lost decade is still with us. As a result of the restructuring of Japanese firms during the decade, the number of non-regular workers as compared to regular workers has doubled to one-third by 2005. The once-celebrated "lifetime employment" of the Japanese firm appears to have disappeared. Now, inequality, symbolized by a rising number of part-time workers, is the top political issue in Japan.

Thus, the lost decade remains a very important topic to study, and challenges economists. Specifically, we can ask ourselves why the bubble preceding the long stagnation was not avoided, why stagnation lasted so long, what policy mistakes were made, what structural changes or adjustments have occurred (and not occurred), what the current challenges facing Japan are, and what the potential growth rate under declining

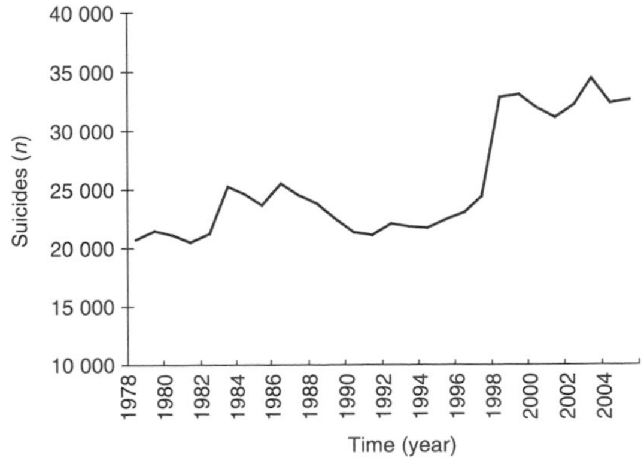

Figure 1. Number of suicides in Japan, 1978–2004
Source: National Police Agency.

population may be. It is impossible to address all these issues in this paper. In fact, I wrote a book entitled *Japan's Lost Decade* (Yoshikawa 2002) in which I offered my own explanations for some of these problems. In the present paper, I briefly review the lost decade and then focus on two issues.

First, I address the question of why the economy did not revive despite the sizable fiscal and monetary policy measures implemented. In this quest, among the fundamental difficulties Japanese policymakers faced during the late 1990s, I take up and stress the importance of *uncertainty*. To mimic the "liquidity trap," I advance a proposition that Japan was caught in an "uncertainty trap." True, uncertainty did *not* trigger the long stagnation. However, it seriously hindered the economy from normal recovery. The importance of uncertainty is a lesson we learned from the lost decade. To make my argument concrete, as an example, I discuss monetary policy in detail. However, the basic point is general, and is not confined to monetary policy.

The second issue I discuss is the potential growth rate of the Japanese economy in the face of a declining population. Despite a decline in the population, Japan's potential growth rate is expected to be about 2 percent. The reason is that in the modern economy, technical progress and capital accumulation play a much more important role in economic growth than an increase in the workforce. I emphasize the role of demand-creating innovation as the key concept. Before I address these issues, I first briefly survey the Japanese economy during the 1990s.

2. The Japanese Economy during the 1990s

In the buoyant 1980s, when some even suggested "Japan as Number One," who would have imagined such gloomy 1990s? As it turned out, amid the worldwide IT revolution, Japan suffered from a decade-long stagnation during the 1990s and up until 2002. After a series of recessions, the interest rate had fallen to zero by the late 1990s. Notwithstanding this, the economy did not revive. Far from it, the economy lapsed into deflation, Irving Fisher's curse! (Fisher 1933). The average growth rate of Japan during 1992–2002 turned out to be a mere 1 percent. During the same period, the US economy enjoyed 3 percent growth, hailing the "New Economy." Even the European Union, suffering from high unemployment, outperformed Japan.

The important question, of course, is why the Japanese economy was trapped into such a long stagnation. In particular, which was the source of the growth slowdown: the demand side or the supply side? Hayashi and Prescott (2002) advance a hard-core supply-side explanation. According to them, the source of Japan's trouble is simply a fall of total factor productivity (TFP). However, it is well known that the measured TFP is highly procyclical, and a substantial decline in TFP may well be merely a reflection of the long stagnation (see, for example, Mankiw 1989; Basu 1996). Fukao (2003) indeed took issue with the thesis of Hayashi and Prescott (2002) based on the real business cycle theory, and argued that the fundamental cause of the long stagnation is on the demand side. I basically share Fukao's demand-side explanation, but put off discussing my own argument to the end of this section.

In any case, a sensible way to get an overview of the Japanese economy during the lost decade is to look at the demand decomposition of the growth rate of real GDP. Table 1 presents the contributions of demand components such as consumption, investments, and exports to the growth of GDP. The contribution is defined here as the growth rate of each demand component—for example, investments—multiplied by its share in real GDP. By construction, the figures sum up to the growth rate of GDP.

Table 1 shows that fixed investments are by far the most important factor to account for cyclical fluctuations during the period, namely the 1992–1993 recession, the 1994–1996 recovery, and also the 1997–1998 recession.[1] In fact, investments are the most important explanatory variable for the Japanese business cycles throughout the postwar period (see Yoshikawa 1993). This stylized fact applies to the 1990s. When the growth rate fell from 2.2 percent to -1.0 percent during 1991–1993, for example, the contribution of investments fell from -0.2 percent to -2.4

Table 1. Contribution of demand components to gross domestic product (GDP) growth (%)

Fiscal Year	GDP growth	Consumption	Housing investment	Fixed investment	Inventory investment	Public consumption	Public investment	Net exports	Exports	Imports
1990	6.0	2.6	0.3	2.2	-0.1	0.5	0.3	0.2	0.5	-0.3
1991	2.2	1.7	-0.5	-0.2	0.2	0.5	0.3	0.3	0.4	0.0
1992	1.1	1.0	-0.2	-1.0	-0.6	0.4	1.1	0.4	0.3	0.1
1993	-1.0	1.0	0.2	-2.4	-0.7	0.4	0.7	-0.1	-0.1	0.0
1994	2.3	1.3	0.3	-0.2	0.6	0.5	-0.2	-0.2	0.4	-0.6
1995	2.4	1.3	-0.3	0.5	0.4	0.6	0.6	-0.7	0.4	-1.1
1996	2.8	1.4	0.6	0.8	0.0	0.3	-0.2	-0.1	0.7	-0.8
1997	-0.1	-0.6	-1.0	0.5	0.3	0.1	-0.5	1.1	0.9	0.2
1998	-1.3	0.2	-0.5	-1.1	-0.5	0.4	0.1	0.2	-0.4	0.6
1999	0.6	0.7	0.1	-0.1	-0.8	0.6	0.0	0.0	0.6	-0.6
2000	2.8	0.5	0.0	1.0	1.0	0.7	-0.6	0.1	1.0	-0.8
2001	-0.8	0.7	-0.3	-0.3	-0.4	0.5	-0.3	-0.5	-0.8	0.3
2002	1.1	0.8	-0.1	-0.4	0.0	0.4	-0.3	0.7	1.2	-0.5
2003	2.3	0.5	0.0	0.9	0.2	0.5	-0.6	0.8	1.1	-0.3
2004	1.7	0.9	0.1	0.8	-0.3	0.3	-0.7	0.5	1.4	-0.9
2005	3.2	1.3	0.0	1.1	0.2	0.3	-0.1	0.5	1.2	-0.8
2006	2.1	0.4	0.0	1.2	0.0	0.2	-0.5	0.8	1.2	-0.4

Source: SNA (National Accounts of Japan).
Compiled by the Cabinet Office.

percent, accounting for nearly 70 percent of the fall in the growth rate. Similarly, when growth accelerated from -1.0 percent to 2.8 percent during 1993–1996, the contribution of investments rose from -2.4 percent to 0.8 percent, again accounting for 84 percent of the recovery.

Besides fixed investments, depressed consumption is notable. For 1997, we even observe an unprecedented decline in consumption. Contrary to common belief, however, the fall in asset prices had a relatively small effect on consumption. One might expect that the negative wealth effect depressed consumption after the bubble burst in the early 1990s. Altogether, during the bubble period of 1986–1990, households enjoyed almost ¥1,200 trillion worth of capital gains on their assets (¥200 trillion on stock, and ¥1,000 trillion on land), but subsequently suffered ¥400 trillion worth of capital losses during 1990–1992. The analysis of consumption by type of household reveals that capital losses on stock did exert a negative wealth effect on the consumption of aged retirees, as well as a portion of the self-employed who were the major stock owners. The share of these types of households, however, is only 12 percent.

The major capital gains and subsequent losses accrued on land. As one would expect, most land that households own is indivisibly tied to housing. Therefore, to the extent that housing service and other consumables are weak substitutes, and that land and housing are indivisible, it is not irrational that sizable capital gains and losses on land left most households to keep their houses and their consumption basically intact. Capital gains and losses on stock and land affected household consumption only marginally. Bayoumi (1999), using a vector autoregression-based analysis, found that the effects of land prices on output largely disappear once bank lending is added as an explanatory variable, and concluded that the "pure" wealth effect was quite limited.

Among the factors to explain unprecedentedly depressed consumption, we can point to job insecurity. It is well known that the unemployment rate in Japan was very low by international standards. During the 1980s, when the unemployment rate reached 10 percent in many European Union countries, it remained at 2 percent in Japan. The unemployment rate had been traditionally low in Japan for several reasons. Thanks to bonus payments and the synchronized economy-wide wage settlements called the *shuntō* (spring offensive), wages in Japan were believed to be more flexible than in other countries.[2] In addition, the necessary adjustments of labor were once achieved through changes in working hours per worker rather than changes in the number of workers. On the supply side, cyclical fluctuations in the labor-force participation rate were large.

In recessions, the "marginal" (typically female) workers who had lost jobs often left the labor force rather than remaining in the labor force and searching for jobs. These factors once kept the unemployment rate from rising (Yoshikawa 1995, chapter 5). Even during the 1992–1994 recession, the unemployment rate, although rising, did not reach 3 percent.

The long stagnation during the 1990s, however, thoroughly changed the structure of the Japanese labor market. Most importantly, with the slogan of "restructuring," firms were ready to discharge workers. The number of involuntary job losses more than tripled between 1992 and 1999. In 1999, the unemployment rate in Japan finally became higher than its US counterpart. Nobody had expected that this would ever happen. The unemployment rate finally reached its peak of 5.5 percent in 2002. It was not until 2007 that the unemployment rate fell below 4 percent, the socially acceptable level by Japanese standards.

In the autumn of 1997, large financial institutions such as the Hokkaido Takushoku Bank and Yamaichi Securities went bankrupt. These events made an unmistakable announcement that the celebrated lifetime employment in Japan was over. Understandably, job insecurity depressed consumption.[3] In 1998, consumption actually fell. In summary, households faced an unprecedented rise in uncertainty, which depressed consumption during the late 1990s.

From another angle, McKinnon and Ōno (1997) attributed the stagnation of the Japanese economy to the appreciation of the yen. They advanced the argument of what they called "fear of an ever-higher yen" as being the fundamental cause of the long stagnation of the Japanese economy, and that the introduction of an adjustable peg was the key solution. Their argument rests on the premise that fluctuations in exchange rates were the basic cause of the troubles. They even attribute the fall in the growth rate in the early 1970s to the end of the Bretton Woods system and the introduction of floating exchange rates. However, the contribution of net exports to growth was actually much higher in the 1970s and 1980s, when exchange rates were floating, than in the 1950s and 1960s, when the exchange rate was fixed (see Yoshikawa 1995, chapter 2).

McKinnon and Ōno (1997) emphasized the possibility of misalignment (deviations from purchasing power parity) under the floating exchange rate regime. Misalignment does occur. However, for the Japanese economy, the most important misalignment was the overvaluation of the dollar or the undervaluation of the yen under the Reagan administration in the 1980s. This misalignment is, therefore, not consistent with "fear of an ever-higher yen." McKinnon and Ōno (1997) also argue that, in responding to the appreciation of the yen, the Bank of Japan (BOJ) initially eased money policy, but in the medium run, the BOJ was prone to tighten money to produce deflation. This simply contradicts the facts. The BOJ did not implement an easy money policy in response to the yen appreciation, not only in the short run, but also in the medium run.

More fundamentally, the appreciation of the yen from 240 per dollar (1985) to 120 (1988) was actually caused by high productivity growth in the Japanese export sector, and broadly followed purchasing power parity with respect to tradables (see Yoshikawa 1990). Thus, it is not plausible to regard the appreciation of the yen as the major cause of the long stagnation of the Japanese economy. Table 1 shows that net exports were fairly stable throughout the 1990s except for two years; the first was 1995, when the yen was highly overvalued at ¥96 per dollar, and the second was 2001, when the US economy was in recession after the IT boom was over.

In conclusion, the key variables for understanding the lost decade are corporate investments,[4] and, to a lesser extent, consumption. I will document in the next section that the credit crunch significantly affected investments during the 1997–1998 recession. This fact casts serious doubt on the hard-core supply-side explanation for depressed investments, and consequently, for the long stagnation of the Japanese economy.

The episode of vigorous recovery that began in 2002 and put an end to the lost decade also suggests strongly that demand shocks play a decisive role in the ups and downs of the macroeconomy. That is, there is no denying that a significant positive demand shock, namely the "China Shock," saved the Japanese economy from the long stagnation. Beginning in 2002, a surge of exports, particularly to Asia, triggered a recovery (see table 1). This export-led recovery changed itself into sustained growth and put an end to the lost decade. From the ending of the lost decade, we learn that the Keynesian principle of effective demand, our old friend, is still alive and well (Yoshikawa 2000). Although TFP is important for economic growth, it is difficult to explain the Japanese economy during 2002–2006 by way of TFP alone. Plainly, the principal factor is an increase in exports, a pure demand shock. Again, this casts serious doubt on the hard-core supply-side story based on the real business cycle theory such as that of Hayashi and Prescott (2002). Plainly, the demand side is important for any explanation of the lost decade.

3. Macroeconomic Policies

How did macroeconomic policies respond to the long stagnation? Throughout the lost decade, both the government and the BOJ were deeply concerned with the bad-loan problem. As early as 1993, Prime Minister Miyazawa well recognized the seriousness of the problem and thought of a possible injection of public money into the banking sector, although the idea was then regarded as premature and turned down. In any case, we cannot properly understand Japan's fiscal and monetary policies during the lost decade separately from the bad-loan problem that afflicted the financial system.

Now, during the 1990s, in order to revive the economy, the government compiled altogether nine fiscal packages, the first under Prime Minister Miyazawa in August 1992 and the last by Prime Minister Obuchi in November 1999. These packages totaled ¥130 trillion. The packages included tax cuts and purchases of land; therefore, the figure, ¥130 trillion, does not correspond to government expenditure or *G* in economics textbooks. Still, it is fair to say that the government exerted a sizable fiscal expansion. As a result, the debt outstanding more than doubled during the period from 1990 to 2000, reaching almost ¥400 trillion. Yet, in the light of the fact that during the 1990s the economy never recovered sustainable growth, the consensus view is that expansionary fiscal policies were by and large failures.

Some economists criticize Japan's fiscal policies during the 1990s, saying that they were too little and too late. Whether or not they were too little is a matter of judgment depending on how we assess the seriousness of the mounting debt for a rapidly aging economy like Japan's. As for timing, many criticize the fiscal tightening—raising the consumption tax rate from 3 percent to 5 percent and a substantial cut in public investments—implemented by Prime Minister Hashimoto in 1997 as a mistake. I concur with this majority view. The Ministry of Finance overestimated the strength of the brief recovery during 1995–1996. The fiscal tightening then was ill-advised, chiefly because the bad-loan problem had not been solved at all, and the financial crisis was about to come.[5]

The Koizumi administration during 2001–2006 changed the basic stance of fiscal policy. It stopped fiscal expansion, which had been pursued during the preceding decade, and cut public investment. However, it would not be quite true to say that the Koizumi administration really exerted a fiscal tightening. After all, the annual deficits during 2002–2004 were ¥35 trillion, the second largest in history. Public investments were cut, but more than ¥50 trillion of public money was used for clearing up the bad loan that had afflicted Japan's banking system for a decade. It is the consensus view that the bad-loan problem and the instability of the banking system had been finally overcome with the injection of public money into Risona Bank in 2003. This paved the way for an export-led recovery that turned into sustained growth. The role of fiscal policy was changed under the Koizumi administration.

So much for fiscal policy. I next turn to monetary policy. Monetary policy is often said to be responsible for the asset-price bubble during the late 1980s and the subsequent long stagnation during the 1990s. According to this view, during the 1980s, low interest rates produced the asset-price bubble, and high land prices, in turn, allowed liquidity-constrained firms to make excessive investments through increases in the value of collateral. For the same reason, but now in the opposite direction, the collapse of the asset market entailed the stagnation of investments during the 1990s.

Although the "standard" view contains an element of truth, it does not actually stand up to careful analysis. There are a number of studies that demonstrate a significant relationship between real variables such as investments and real GDP on the one hand, and asset prices—in particular, land prices—on the other. Since asset prices and GDP went up and down broadly in tandem, these findings are not surprising. The problem is causality. Most of these analyses interpret their findings as indicating that changes in asset prices affected investments by financially constrained firms through changes in their collateral values. Ogawa and Suzuki (1998), for example, found land prices significant in their investment functions, and concluded that financial constraints were significant. Bayoumi (1999) also found in his vector autoregressions that land-price changes were an important factor behind the rise in the output gap over the bubble period and the subsequent decline.[6]

However, this is not exactly what happened in Japan during the late 1980s and the 1990s. During the bubble period, it was believed (falsely, in retrospect) that land-intensive sectors, such as holiday resorts and office space in Tokyo, would command high profits in the near future. These (false) expectations made land prices explode, and at the same time induced firms to make land-intensive investments. Firms purchased land with money borrowed from banks, and banks, based on their expectations of higher land prices in the future, often allowed more than 100 percent (!) collateral values for the land that firms had just purchased. Therefore, theoretically, firms could borrow money from banks without any collateral in advance to purchase land. This is very different from the standard story explained earlier, according to which an increase in the price of land that firms had owned in advance made it possible for the liquidity-constrained firms to borrow more money to make investments. In fact, the ultimate cause of both the rise in land prices and the extraordinary surge in land-intensive investments was false expectations regarding the future profitability of holiday resorts and office space in Tokyo.

After the bubble burst, asset prices collapsed, and at the same time, investments also fell. However, it is once again not self-evident that this fact suggests that the fall in asset prices cut investments by way of a fall in the value of collateral held by firms. For example, investments by large firms and by small firms both fell during the 1992–1994 recession by roughly the same magnitude. Large firms do not finance their investments by borrowing from banks, but rather by issuing bonds and new equity in the capital market. They are not financially constrained; therefore, the collateral story does not hold true for large firms at the outset. Yet, not only small firms but also large firms cut their investments.

Thus, the popular collateral story is doubtful. Meltzer (2001) and Hayashi and Prescott (2002) also expressed skeptical views on the significance of financial constraints. Whatever the reasons, investments stagnated. Monetary policy responded to the stagnation of the economy. The BOJ cut the discount rate from 6.0 percent to 5.5 percent in July 1991. Through five successive cuts within a year, the discount rate was reduced to 3.25 percent by July 1992.

Despite further cuts in interest rates during 1993–1994, the economy hardly revived. The annual growth rate of the money supply (M2 + CD), which was 12 percent in 1990, had fallen to zero by 1992. The major cause of a sharp decline in bank lending, which was responsible for the fall in monetary growth during 1991–1993, appears to have been a fall in demand for bank lending on the part of nonfinancial firms (Gibson 1995; Bayoumi 1999; Woo 1999).

Meanwhile, the fall in stock prices created a serious problem for Japanese banks to meet the Bank for International Settlements (BIS) capital adequacy standards. New legislation in April 1996 allowed the authorities to intervene if a bank was likely to fail to meet the BIS requirement. This new policy regime was to start in April 1998. In March 1997, the Ministry of Finance clarified the new capital adequacy requirements. Very unfortunately, this basically correct policy action was taken at the worst possible time. Desperate to raise their capital/asset ratios within a short period of time, banks squeezed their assets by cutting lending. In the autumn, the bankruptcy of big financial institutions such as Yamaichi Securities and the Hokkaido Takushoku Bank triggered a real credit crunch. The BOJ's Tankan diffusion index for the "lending attitude of financial institutions" abruptly worsened during this period, despite the BOJ's efforts to ease monetary policy. It should be noted that the Tankan diffusion index for the lending attitude of financial institutions normally deteriorates when money is tight, whereas it improves when money is easy. Using the Tankan data, Motonishi and Yoshikawa (1999) estimated that the credit crunch, by way of depressing investments by financially constrained firms, lowered the growth rate of real GDP by 1.3 percent during 1997–1998.

I maintain that the credit crunch not only depressed investments by financially constrained firms, but also significantly raised the degree of uncertainty in the economy as a whole. Arguably, the economy was caught in an "uncertainty trap" during the 1997–1998 financial crisis. The consumer price index started falling in 1999. The Japanese economy lapsed into deflation. Amid the credit crunch, the BOJ was forced to lower interest rates further. The call rate became 0.3 percent in 1998, and finally 0.03 percent in 1999. Taking into account transaction costs, a rate of 0.03 percent effectively means a zero interest rate, the absolute minimum for the nominal interest rate.

At the zero interest-rate boundary, the BOJ apparently lost the use of its instrument for traditional monetary policy. The "liquidity trap" (Keynes 1936) was once considered a mere theoretical possibility. However, amid the long stagnation, Japan literally faced this problem. When the short-term policy rate is at zero, the conventional means of effecting monetary ease is no longer feasible. Economists then started discussing how monetary policy could possibly affect the economy with a zero interest rate. Krugman (1998) was one of the first economists who proposed an alternative policy. Based on his theoretical model, he argued that all the BOJ must do is just persuade the public that the future money supply will increase enough to raise the future price level. If the BOJ could succeed in this endeavor, it would create inflationary expectations, and thereby lower the real interest rate today. This would save the economy from the liquidity trap.

Following Krugman's lead, many economists made similar, but slightly different, policy recommendations. This array of proposals included announcing a price-level target path; reducing long-term interest rates via a commitment to keep the short-term rate at zero for substantial periods in the future; depreciating the currency through foreign exchange intervention; introducing negative interest on the currency (Gessell's solution); and, finally, a policy of combining a price-level target path, a currency depreciation and a crawling peg, and an exit strategy that would constitute Svensson's (2001) "foolproof way" to escape from a liquidity trap. These are all different policies. However, for my present argument, the technical differences between the various theoretical models and policy recommendations are secondary. The crucial point is that none of them takes into account the potential instability of the financial system or uncertainty in our sense.

In these models, inflationary expectations stimulate demand by reducing the real interest rate. Here, demand is assumed to be interest elastic, of course. In micro-data models, this interest elasticity is linked to a parameter of the representative consumer's utility function, and is assumed to be constant. That is, the standard analysis takes it for granted that the individual elasticity derived theoretically from a microeconomic analysis of the representative agent can translate itself into elasticity for the economy as a whole. This assumption is not correct, however. The interest elasticity in the economy as a whole is not constant, but depends crucially on the degree of uncertainty. Specifically, when the degree of uncertainty rises, this elasticity necessarily diminishes, and at the zero lower bound, it approaches zero.[7] Therefore, when the degree of uncertainty rises, the effectiveness of macroeconomic policy is necessarily weakened, and, at the zero lower bound, it becomes ineffective. This proposition is theoretically derived in a model in which there is a heterogeneity of many economic agents, and the combinatorial aspect of the macroeconomy is explicitly taken into account. The reader interested in theoretical analysis is referred to chapter 4 of Aoki and Yoshikawa (2007). Indeed, in the Japanese economy during the 1990s, particularly after the credit crunch in 1997–1998, a major problem facing monetary policy was the low interest elasticity of demand.

Beyond that, in Krugman's model, the "future" is not in a liquidity trap, and the simple quantity theory of money is assumed to hold in the future; that is, prices are proportional to the money supply in the future. Thus, in theory, it is easy for the central bank to generate expected inflation despite the absence of current actual inflation. The only thing the central bank must do is to persuade the public now to believe that the money supply will increase enough to generate inflation in the future. However, in reality, the most important factor determining the expected inflation is the current actual rate of change of prices. Whatever the policy actions of the central bank, who would believe in inflation so easily when the economy is actually facing deflation? As long as we believe in the Phillips curve wisdom—namely, the story that only high pressure in the real economy produces inflation—then we are likely to be caught in a catch-22 situation in our efforts to cure a recession by generating inflationary expectations.[8] In fact, deflation as measured by the consumer price index finally ended in 2006 after four consecutive years of 2 percent growth accompanied by a steady decline in the unemployment rate. The Phillips curve wisdom appears to have survived the lost decade.

Meanwhile, a large increase in the supply of money coupled with inflation targeting was a popular solution to the problems facing the Japanese economy around the year 2000. Proponents of this policy solution included Krugman (1998), Bernanke (2000), Blanchard (2000), Rogoff (2002), Eggertsson and Woodford (2003), Bernanke et al. (2004), and Auerbach and Obstfeld (2005). In some circumstances, inflation targeting may indeed be a useful framework to conduct monetary policy. A number of central banks have already adopted inflation targeting, which, in some cases, is said to be instrumental in reducing inflation (see Bernanke and Woodford 2005). Having acknowledged that, I question the efficacy of inflation targeting as a remedy for deflation in a liquidity-trapped economy. The reason is that in an uncertainty-trapped economy such as Japan's during the lost decade, the fundamental problem may not have been really deflation and the zero interest rate per se, but rather great uncertainty. Such uncertainty reduces the (interest) elasticity, theoretically, to zero at the lower bound. This makes all the policy proposals in the existing literature for generating inflationary expectations ineffective.

Not only being ineffective, such policies may well have contributed toward mounting uncertainty, and, therefore, been harmful. That is, the central bank, by "credibly promising to be irresponsible," may confuse the public, and actually prolong the uncertainty trap rather than rescuing the economy from the liquidity trap. King (2004) made the important point that, in some circumstances, expectations of monetary decisions within a given policy regime may be less important than expectations of changes in the regime itself, and, therefore, an ordinary policy may not work.[9] To repeat, the "enemy number one" in the uncertainty trap is not deflation or the zero interest rate per se, but rather the low (interest) elasticity and the ensuing policy ineffectiveness. Despite all of their technical sophistication, the policy proposals for generating inflationary expectations miss this essential point. The apparently impeccable inflation targeting will not work in an economy facing great uncertainty.

The BOJ did not adopt inflation targeting. However, on top of the zero interest-rate policy, it introduced a quantitative easing policy (QEP) in March 2001 that was brought to an end in March 2006. The main operating target changed from the overnight call rate to money balances at the BOJ, while at the same time, the BOJ made a commitment that an ample money supply would continue to stay in place until the "core" consumer price index registered stably at 0 percent. There is a good deal of empirical analysis of the effects and efficacy of the QEP, which lasted

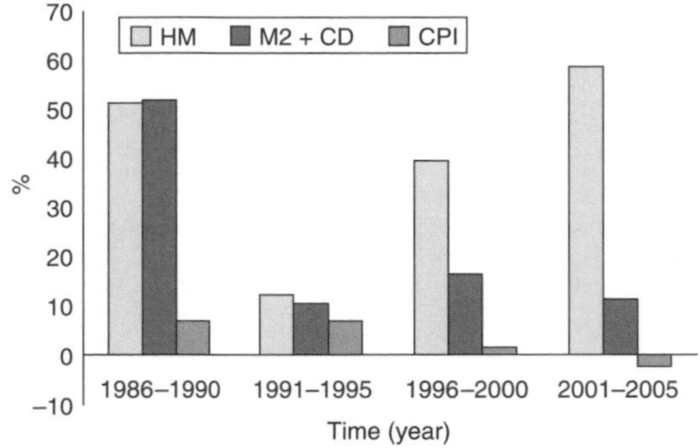

Figure 2. Money supply and prices (five-year cumulative change), Japan

five years (see Ueda 2005a, b; Ugai 2007). The consensus view is that the primary effect of the QEP was to stave off financial institutions' funding uncertainty, and, thereby, financial market instability. In this sense, the QEP contributed to mitigating uncertainty in the economy as a whole. However, it contributed little to inflationary expectations, on which many economists place much importance. In fact, there is virtually no relationship between money supply and prices during that period (see figure 2).

An important lesson we learned from Japan's lost decade is that the effectiveness of policy necessarily weakens as the degree of uncertainty rises. We can call this problem the "uncertainty trap." Whether or not the economy is caught in such an uncertainty trap distinguishes a depression from the normal cyclical recession.

Before we leave this section, I will mention some evidence which suggests that the degree of uncertainty has, in fact, risen in the Japanese economy during the 1990s. We have already referred to the increased job insecurity facing households. Deflation was also a wholly new experience for both households and firms. Arguably, the credit crunch in 1997–1998 pushed the economy into an uncertainty trap. The amount of cash held by the public had, in fact, doubled from ¥35 trillion in 1994 to ¥70 trillion by 2001. Even bank deposits were not perceived as being safe. This indicates extreme risk perceived by the public. The same story basically holds true for firms as well. The net savings of corporate firms had been negative throughout the postwar period up to 1997. It turned positive in 1998, so that nonfinancial firms became net savers!

Finally, figure 3 shows the coefficient of variation (standard deviation divided by the mean) of the quarterly GDP growth rates for five years (twenty quarters). For the sake of comparison, we also show the same coefficient of variation for the USA. We observe that the coefficient of variation has, in fact, risen extraordinarily in Japan during the 1990s, especially in the latter half. Figure 3 suggests that the degree of uncertainty has, in

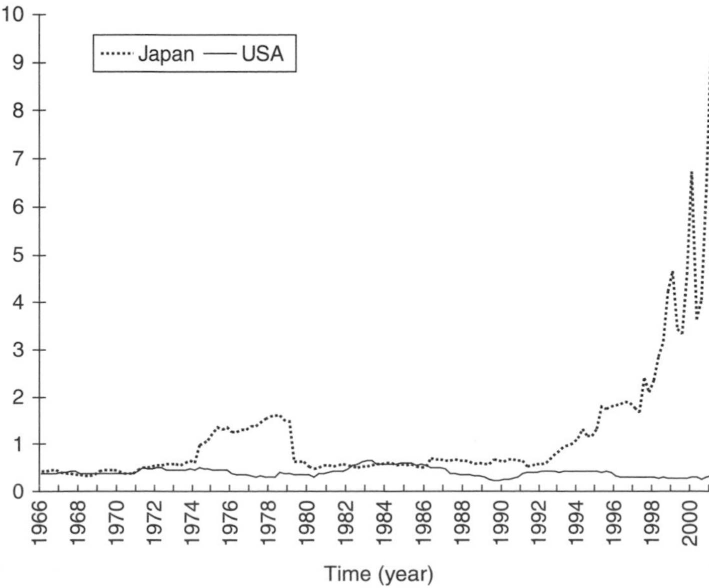

Figure 3. Coefficient of variation of growth rate of gross domestic product (GDP) for Japan and USA

Note: CV = Standard deviation/mean of quarterly GDP growth rates over the past five years.

fact, risen in the Japanese economy. I surmise that in the case of Japan's lost decade, the ultimate factor responsible for the great uncertainty was the instability of the financial system caused by the bad-loan problem.

Once the economy falls into this uncertainty trap, textbook macroeconomic policies, including monetary policy, become ineffective. Tobin (1975), in his article entitled "Keynesian models of recession and depression," suggested that "the system might be stable for small deviations from its equilibrium, but unstable for large shocks." The same point was also made by Fisher (1933) a long time ago. In our view, uncertainty is another key factor. When uncertainty is insignificant, the economy will fluctuate around the (unique) "natural" equilibrium, and macroeconomic policies are effective. However, when the degree of uncertainty rises above a critical level, the economy may be trapped, and standard policies become ineffective. This is an important lesson we learned from the lost decade.

4. Japan's Potential Growth: The Importance of Demand-Creating Innovation

So much for the lost decade. Now, where are we heading? It is well known that Japan's population is declining. The recent official estimate is that the 2005 population of 128 million will decline to 90 million by 2055. Although the labor participation rate is not constant,[10] it is a necessity that the labor force will also shrink in tandem with the decline of the population. In fact, a decade ahead of a decline in population, the labor force has already declined by 0.6 percent each year for ten years. In any case, the population of those aged fifteen to sixty-four years is 84 million in 2005, which is estimated to decline to 46 million by 2055. At the same time, aging will proceed rapidly.

An important question, then, is what the potential growth rate of the Japanese economy is as it faces a declining labor force. Many laymen and even businesspeople are pessimistic about our future. Their pessimism seems to be heavily influenced by the lost decade. Contrary to common perceptions, standard growth accounting tells us that the direct contribution of labor to growth is, in fact, much smaller than those of capital deepening and total factor productivity. For example, Jorgenson and Motohashi (2004) present projections of the Japanese economic growth for the period 2002–2012. Their "base-case" projection of the average annual growth rate is 2.4 percent per annum, despite the assumption that labor hours shrink by 0.5 percent each year. Capital deepening and TFP are projected to contribute to growth by 1.6 percent and 1 percent, respectively. I take it that 2 percent growth is a consensus projection of Japan's potential economic growth.

Now, realizing the consequences of a shrinking

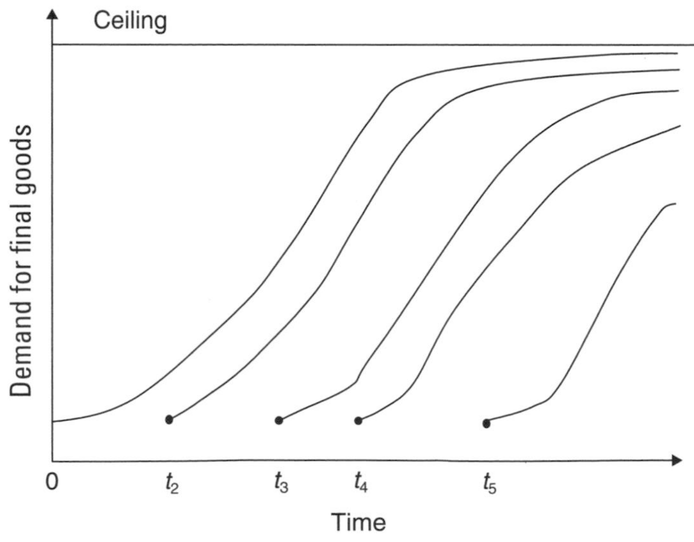

Figure 4. Saturation of demand and emergence of new goods and services

Note: t_i is the date of birth of the *i*th good/industry.

population and labor force, more and more economists attach importance to technical progress and TFP for the growth of the Japanese economy. No doubt technical progress and innovation play a key role in modern economic growth, but TFP is an amalgam, and not a perfect measure of technical progress or innovation (Wright 1997). The economy always mobilizes resources and accumulates capital whenever it finds goods or sectors for which demand grows rapidly.

In the standard growth models, whether old or new, the fundamental factor restraining economic growth is diminishing returns on capital in production or research and development technology. As an alternative, Aoki and Yoshikawa (2002) present a model in which the factor restraining growth is saturation of demand for old products and services. The model provides new perspectives on several important problems addressed by the economics of growth. A particularly important point is the nature of technical progress or innovation. In the standard analysis, technical progress brings about higher value added given the same level of inputs. It is basically equivalent to an "upward shift" of the production function. In the Aoki–Yoshikawa model, saturation of demand constrains capital accumulation and leads to a deceleration of growth. Innovation or technical progress in this model creates a major new product or industry, which commands high growth of demand and thereby elicits capital accumulation, and so sustains economic growth (figure 4).[11] Demand-creating innovations are most likely to entail changes in industrial structure. Yoshikawa and Matsumoto (2001) indeed demonstrate that changes in industrial structure and economic growth are positively related for Japan.

Following Hayashi and Prescott (2002), many economists attribute the lost decade to a decline in TFP during the 1990s, and the decline in TFP, in turn, to a misallocation of resources (Fukao and Kwon 2006). They tend to take the misallocation of resources as a cause of low productivity growth. I suggest that a lack of demand-creating innovations, which is basically equivalent to a lack of leading sectors, leads to a misallocation of resources. Resources do not flow into high-productivity sectors because demand does not grow enough in such sectors.

For example, it is a commonly held belief that the construction industry, which is supported heavily by notorious public investments, is a low-productivity sector. During the 1990s, resources wrongly flowed into such industries, and this contributed to the long stagnation. So the argument goes. It is probably true that the construction industry is a low-productivity sector. However, by international comparison, the share of the construction industry was extraordinarily high in Japan not only during the 1990s, when the economy stagnated, but also during the 1970s and 1980s, when the average growth rate was above 4 percent and the highest among the advanced economies (Shinohara 2006).[12] It is unlikely that productivity in Japan's construction industry was high during the 1970s and 1980s, but fell during the 1990s. By the same token, misguided land-intensive investments, which brought about the bubble during the late 1980s, simply reflected a lack of demand-creating innovation in those years. To repeat, I suggest that the fundamental problem is a lack of demand-creating innovation, particularly in the service industries.

Finally, let us look at the bright side. Japan faces rapid aging and environmental problems. They are not unique to Japan, but are global issues. They are opportunities as well as challenges. Good technology and a large market provide Japan with an advantage in this respect. If Japan succeeds in producing innovations to overcome these problems, they certainly will form a basis for the future of the Japanese economy. The best current example would be energy-efficient Japanese cars.

5. Conclusion

The lost decade has left us with a number of lessons. Although TFP is important, it is hard to maintain that we can reasonably explain Japan's experiences—the lost decade (1992–2002) and the recovery thereafter (2003–2007)—by supply-side factors alone. Demand, for example, a fall in investments due to the credit crunch, and a surge in exports to China played a decisive role.

This paper attempts to show that uncertainty

plays a much more important role in the macroeconomy than most economists recognize. Uncertainty did not trigger the long stagnation after the bubble burst in the early 1990s. The lost decade began as investments fell as a kind of stock adjustment after the long boom. However, once the economy lapsed into severe recession, uncertainty seriously hindered a normal recovery, particularly after the 1997–1998 financial crisis. In my judgment, the instability of the financial system was the ultimate source of uncertainty. Indeed, we cannot properly understand both fiscal and monetary policies during the lost decade separately from the bad-loan problem. In any case, once the economy is caught in an uncertainty trap, the effectiveness of standard policy necessarily weakens. The zero interest rate may well be a consequence of an uncertainty trap.

The significance of demand-creating innovation is another point I emphasize in this paper. In my view, a lack of demand-creating innovation is a part of the explanation of the lost decade, and, at the same time, it offers prospects for the future of the Japanese economy.

Courtesy of Japan Center for Economic Research (JCER).

Originally published in *Asian Economic Policy Review* 2, no. 2 (2007): 186–203.

Notes

1. The recession that started in May 1997 officially ended in January 1999. According to the government, the Japanese economy subsequently entered an expansionary phase during February 1999–October 2000. Then, another recession started in November 2000, which ended in January 2002. An expansion that started in February 2002 is still continuing as of April 2007.
2. Taylor (1989), for example, emphasized the role of the *shuntō* as means of wage flexibility in Japan.
3. Nakagawa (1999) demonstrated that uncertainty surrounding the public pension system also depressed consumption.
4. Ueda Kazuo in his comments reminded me of the fact that depressed housing investments also played an important role (see table 1).
5. In the autumn of 1997, the Asian currency crisis also occurred, and hit the Japanese economy. However, this was largely unpredictable, and, therefore, may be regarded as a bit of bad luck for the Japanese policymakers.
6. Kiyotaki and Moore (1997) offer a theoretical model that suggests this kind of interpretation.
7. Dixit and Pindyck (1994) convincingly argued that uncertainty by way of increasing the option value lowers the interest elasticity of irreversible investments. Specifically, they showed that a reduction in the real interest rate makes the future more important compared to the present, but this increases not only the present value of the stream of profits, but also the value of waiting (the ability to reduce or avoid the prospect of future losses). The net effect is weak and sometimes even ambiguous. In other words, greater uncertainty lowers the interest elasticity. Their analysis pertains to the behavior of an individual firm or a consumer. Our analysis is for the economy as a whole.
8. Blanchard (2000; pp. 190–193) states that "the Phillips curve wisdom remains largely true in modern treatments of the determination of prices, wages, and output: If output is above its natural level, then we are likely to see inflation increase." Despite his belief in the Phillips curve wisdom, he is very optimistic in that the BOJ can easily generate inflationary expectations to lower the real interest rate: "All that is needed is to convince markets that money growth will be cumulatively higher over the next ten years by 20 percent." He notes that monetary policy affects long-term interest rates "mostly—entirely?—through its effects on expectations," and continues that "the only thing specific to Japan today is that emphasis is not on changes in future expected nominal interest rates, but on the expected future price level. This is not an essential difference." There is an essential difference in the role of expectations in the determination of prices in goods and financial markets, however.
9. As an example of such a case, King (2004; p. 6) showed that interest rate policy did not work to defend exchange rates under the target zone regime in Brazil (1998–1999) and the UK (1992). "In the literature on target zones for exchange rates, it is assumed that raising interest rates is a successful method for supporting the exchange rate because of uncovered interest parity. But this ignores the possibility that raising interest rates to defend a fixed-exchange-rate regime will simply call into question the durability of the regime itself and raise the probability that the peg or target zone will be abandoned. In such circumstances an increase in interest rates may lead to a fall in the exchange rate."
10. In fact, to mitigate a decline in the labor force, the government is now targeting a rise in the labor participation rate. For example, the target seeks to raise the labor participation rate of married

women aged twenty-five to forty-four from 57 percent to 71 percent by 2017.

11. Schumpeter (1934), in his famous book, distinguished five types of innovations: (i) the introduction of a new good; (ii) the introduction of a new production method; (iii) the opening of a new market; (iv) the conquest of a new source of supply of raw materials; and (v) the new organization of an industry. His first and third types of innovations as an engine for growth seem to be most naturally interpreted in terms of the kind of model presented in Aoki and Yoshikawa (2002).

12. Shinohara (2006) showed that the share of Japan's construction industry had risen from below 5 percent in 1955 to above 9 percent by 1980, and has stayed at that level since then. By comparison, the share is about 5 percent in the USA and the UK.

References

Aoki Masanao, and Yoshikawa Hiroshi. 2002. "Demand Saturation-Creation and Economic Growth." *Journal of Economic Behavior and Organization* 48 (2): 127–154.

———. 2006. *Reconstructing Macroeconomics: A Perspective from Statistical Physics and Combinatorial Stochastic Processes*. New York: Cambridge University Press.

Auerbach, Alan J., and Maurice Obstfeld. 2005. "The Case for Open-Market Purchases in a Liquidity Trap." *American Economic Review* 95 (1): 110–137.

Basu, Susanto. 1996. "Procyclical Productivity: Increasing Returns or Cyclical Utilization?" *Quarterly Journal of Economics* 111 (3): 719–751.

Bayoumi, Tamim. 1999. "The Morning After: Explaining the Slowdown in Japanese Growth in the 1990s." *Journal of International Economics* 53: 241–259.

Bernanke, Ben S. 2000. "Japanese Monetary Policy: A Case of Self-Induced Paralysis?" In *Japan's Financial Crisis and Its Parallels to U.S. Experience*, edited by Mikitani Ryōichi and Adam S. Posen, 149–166. Washington DC: Institute for International Economics.

Bernanke, Ben S., Vincent R. Reinhart, and Brian P. Sack. 2004. "Monetary Policy Alternatives at the Zero Bound: An Empirical Assessment." *Brookings Papers on Economic Activity* 35 (2): 1–100.

Bernanke, Ben S., and Michael Woodford, eds. 2005. *The Inflation-Targeting Debate*. Chicago: University of Chicago Press.

Blanchard, Olivier J. 2000. "Discussions of the Monetary Response: Bubbles, Liquidity Traps, and Monetary Policy." In *Japan's Financial Crisis and Its Parallels to U.S. Experience*, edited by Mikitani Ryōichi and Adam S. Posen, 185–193. Washington DC: Institute for International Economics.

Dixit, Avinash K., and Robert S. Pindyck. 1994. *Investment under Uncertainty*. Princeton: Princeton University Press.

Eggertsson, Gauti B., and Michael Woodford. 2003. "The Zero Bound on Interest Rates and Optimal Monetary Policy." *Brookings Papers on Economic Activity* 34 (1): 139–233.

Fisher, Irving. 1933. "The Debt-Deflation Theory of Great Depressions." *Econometrica* 1 (4): 337–357.

Fukao Kyōji, and Kwon Hyeog-ug. 2006. "Why Did Japan's TFP Growth Slow Down in the Lost Decade? An Empirical Analysis Based on Firm-Level Data of Manufacturing Firms." *Japanese Economic Review* 57 (2): 195–228.

Fukao Mitsuhiro. 2003. "Chōki fukyō no shuin wa juyō fusoku ni aru" [The Fundamental Cause of the Long Stagnation Is on the Demand Side]. In *Ushinawareta jūnen no shinin wa nanika* [What Are the True Causes of the Lost Decade?], edited by Iwata Kikuo and Miyagawa Tsutomu, 17–20. Tokyo: Tōyō Keizai Shinpōsha.

Gibson, Michael S. 1995. "Can Bank Health Affect Investment? Evidence from Japan." *Journal of Business* 68 (3): 281–308.

Hayashi Fumio, and Edward C. Prescott. 2002. "The 1990s in Japan: A Lost Decade." *Review of Economic Dynamics* 5 (1): 206–235.

Jorgenson, Dale W., and Motohashi Kazuyuki. 2004. "Potential Growth of the Japanese and U.S. Economies in the Information Age." ESRI Discussion Paper Series, no. 88, Economic and Social Research Institute, Tokyo.

Keynes, John Maynard. 1936. *The General Theory of Employment, Interest, and Money*. London: Macmillan.

King, Mervyn. 2004. "The Institutions of Monetary Policy." *American Economic Review* 94 (2): 1–13.

Kiyotaki Nobuhiro, and John Moore. 1997. "Credit Cycles." *Journal of Political Economy* 105 (2): 211–248.

Krugman, Paul. 1998. "It's Baaack: Japan's Slump and the Return of the Liquidity Trap." *Brookings Papers on Economic Activity* 29 (2): 137–203.

Mankiw, N. Gregory. 1989. "Real Business Cycles: A New Keynesian Perspective." *Journal of Economic Perspectives* 3 (3): 79–90.

McKinnon, Ronald, and Ōno Kenichi. 1997. *Dollar and Yen: Resolving Economic Conflict between the United States and Japan*. Cambridge, MA: MIT Press.

Meltzer, Allan H. 2001. "Monetary Transmission at Low Inflation: Some Clues from Japan in the 1990s." *Monetary and Economic Studies* 19 (S-1): 13–34.

Motonishi Taizō, and Yoshikawa Hiroshi. 1999. "Causes of the Long Stagnation of Japan during the 1990s: Financial or Real?" *Journal of the Japanese and International Economies* 13 (3): 181–200.

Nakagawa Shinobu. 1999. "90-nendai irigo mo Nihon no kakei chochiku-ritsu wa naze takai no ka?: Kakei zokuseibetsu ni mita 'risuku' no henzai ni kansuru jisshō bunseki" [Why Has Japan's Household Savings Rate Remained High from the 1990s: Empirical Analysis on the Uneven Distribution of 'Risk' by Household Attributes]. *Nippon Ginkō Chōsa Geppō* [Bank of Japan Monthly Review] (April), 69–101.

Ogawa Kazuo, and Suzuki Kazuyuki. 1998. "Land Value and Corporate Investment: Evidence from Japanese Panel Data." *Journal of the Japanese and International Economies* 12 (3): 232–49.

Rogoff, Kenneth. 2002. "Stop Deflation First for the Revival of the Japanese Economy." *Nikkei Shimbun*, October 7, 2002.

Schumpeter, Joseph. 1934. *Theory of Economic Development: An Inquiry into Profits, Capital, Credit, Interest, and the Business Cycle*. Cambridge, MA: Harvard University Press.

Shinohara Miyohei. 2006. *Seichō to junkan de yomitoku Nihon to Ajia: Nani ga seichō to teitai o umidasu no ka* [Japan and Asia in Terms of Growth and Cycles: What Causes Growth and Stagnation?]. Tokyo: Nihon Keizai Shimbun Shuppansha.

Svensson, Lars. 2001. "The Zero Bound in an Open Economy: A Foolproof Way of Escaping from a Liquidity Trap." *Monetary and Economic Studies* 19 (S-1): 277–312.

Taylor, John B. 1989. "Differences in Economic Fluctuations in Japan and the United States: The Role of Nominal Rigidities." *Journal of the Japanese and International Economies* 3 (2): 127–144.

Tobin, James. 1975. "Keynesian Models of Recession and Depression." *American Economic Review* 65 (2): 195–202.

Ueda Kazuo. 2005a. *Zero kinri to no tatakai : Nichigin no kin'yū seisaku o sōkatsu suru* [The Fight against the Zero Interest-Rate Bound: A Review of the BOJ's Monetary Policy]. Tokyo: Nihon Keizai Shimbunsha.

———. 2005b. "The Bank of Japan's Struggle with the Zero Lower Bound on Nominal Interest Rates: Exercises in Expectations Management." *International Finance* 8 (2): 329–350.

Ugai Hiroshi. 2007. "Effects of the Quantitative Easing Policy: A Survey of Empirical Analyses." *Monetary and Economic Studies* 25 (1): 1–48.

Woo, David. 1999. "In Search of 'Capital Crunch': Supply Factors behind the Credit Slowdown in Japan." IMF Working Papers, no. 99/3.

Wright, Gavin. 1997. "Towards a More Historical Approach to Technological Change." *Economic Journal* 107 (444): 1560–1566.

Yoshikawa Hiroshi. 1990. "On the Equilibrium Yen-Dollar Rate." *American Economic Review* 80 (3): 576–583.

———. 1993. "Monetary Policy and the Real Economy in Japan." In *Japanese Monetary Policy*, edited by Kenneth J. Singleton, 121–159. Chicago: University of Chicago Press.

———. 1995. *Macroeconomics and the Japanese Economy*. Oxford: Oxford University Press.

———. 2002. *Japan's Lost Decade*. Translated by Charles H. Stewart. Tokyo: International House of Japan. Originally published as *Tenkanki no Nihon keizai* (Tokyo: Iwanami Shoten, 1999).

———. 2003. "The Role of Demand in Macroeconomics." *Japanese Economic Review* 54 (1): 1–27.

Yoshikawa Hiroshi, and Matsumoto Kazuyuki. 2001. "Sangyō kōzō no henka to keizai seichō" [Change in Industrial Structure and Economic Growth]. *Ministry of Finance Financial Review* 58:121–138.

I-(3) Explaining Japan's Unproductive Two Decades

Fukao Kyōji[1]

Asian Economic Policy Review, 2013

1. Introduction

Following the burst of the "bubble economy" in 1991, productivity growth in Japan declined notably and has remained at a relatively low level for more than twenty years. This decline, which has been well documented in many studies,[2] must have reduced the rate of return on capital and exacerbated economic stagnation. Since Japan's working-age population will continue to shrink rapidly and the capital–labor ratio is already high, improving total factor productivity (TFP) represents the only way for Japan to accomplish sustainable economic growth. This paper examines why Japan's productivity growth has been slow for such a long time and how it can be accelerated in the future.

The low rate of TFP growth and the low rate of return on capital are of considerable relevance in the debate on Abenomics, the policy mix pursued by the present government. Japan has been suffering from a lack of final demand for the last two decades. Even now, Japan has a negative gross domestic product (GDP) gap of 2.3 percent, according to estimates by the Cabinet Office. The government is implementing policies to get out of deflation and seems to be planning to stimulate private investment through a reduction in real interest rates. However, since investment opportunities are limited and the rate of return on capital is very low, extremely low or negative real interest rates are required, but maintaining very low or negative real interest rates, a positive inflation rate, and full employment without causing bubbles is likely to be extremely difficult to achieve. Therefore, for sustainable growth, it is necessary to raise the rate of return on capital through productivity growth, and to stimulate private consumption through job creation and higher wage incomes.

The analysis in this paper has three characteristics that set it apart from preceding studies on Japan's productivity slowdown since the 1990s. First, the paper examines Japan's TFP not only at the macro level but also at the sectoral, firm, and establishment levels. Using industry-level data makes it possible to examine in what sectors TFP growth has slowed down and to make inferences on the main causes of the slowdown. Moreover, using microdata, it is possible to examine productivity dynamics and Japan's market selection mechanism. Second, utilizing recently developed cross-country databases such as the EU KLEMS database, to which the author has contributed, this paper compares Japan's sectoral productivity growth with that of other developed countries. Third, in order to fully understand the stagnation of Japan's productivity, this paper examines the Japanese economy from a long-term perspective by comparing Japan's productivity performance at the sectoral and micro level since the 1990s with that of the 1970s and the 1980s.

The structure of the paper is as follows. The next section provides an overview of Japan's TFP growth at the macro and industry levels and compares Japan's performance with that of other developed countries. In the case of the USA, it has been pointed out that the information and communication technology (ICT) revolution and the increase in intangible investment have contributed to the acceleration of TFP growth since the mid-1990s (Inklaar et al. 2007; Corrado et al 2012). Section 3 examines this issue in greater detail. Specifically, it compares Japan's ICT and intangible investment in the 1990s and 2000s

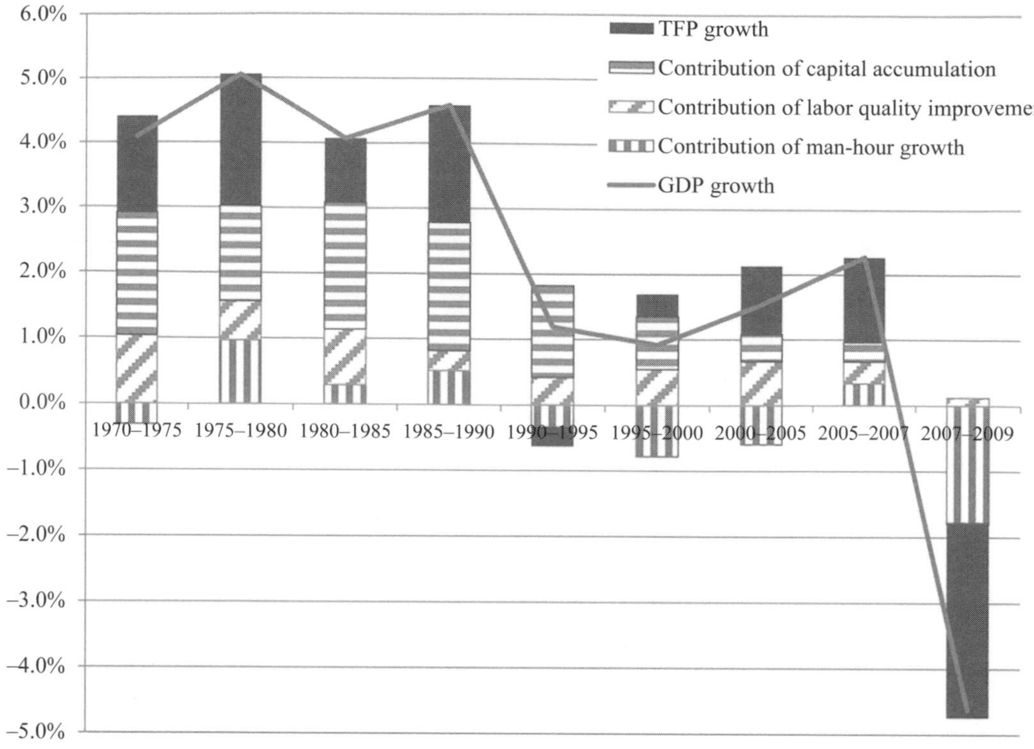

Figure 1. Growth accounting for Japan's macroeconomy

Source: Japan Industrial Productivity (JIP) database, 2012.
Note: GDP, gross domestic product; TFP, total factor productivity.

with that of other developed countries. Section 4 then examines whether the natural selection mechanism works in Japan's economy or not, and if not, why it does not work. Finally, section 5 presents some policy implications of the findings and concludes the paper.

2. Japan's TFP Growth at the Macro and Sectoral Levels

Let us start by examining the sources of Japan's macroeconomic growth from the supply side by conducting a growth accounting analysis. Assuming a smooth constant-returns to scale-production function for the macroeconomy and perfect competition in factor markets, GDP growth can be broken down into the contribution of capital and labor input growth and the residual (TFP growth). The result of the growth accounting analysis is reported in figure 1. As for many other countries, after the Lehman Shock of September 2008, Japan's TFP dropped sharply because of labor hoarding and the idling of capital stock caused by negative GDP growth.[3] In order to focus on the long-term trend before this exogenous shock, the growth accounting result for the period after 2007 is shown separately in the figure.

Figure 1 shows that after 1990, all three sources of economic growth—capital accumulation, labor input growth (man-hour input growth plus labor improvement), and TFP growth—diminished substantially and contributed to the slowdown of GDP growth. Comparing the 1970–1990 period and the 1990–2007 period, the annual contribution of capital accumulation, labor input growth, and TFP growth declined by 1.0, 1.0, and 1.1 percentage points respectively. In the 2000s, TFP growth gradually recovered until 2007, but the average annual TFP growth rate during the 2000–2007 period, 1.1 percent, was still only about two-thirds of the TFP growth rate during the 1970–1990 period, which was 1.6 percent.[4]

It has been argued that deflation (Hamada and

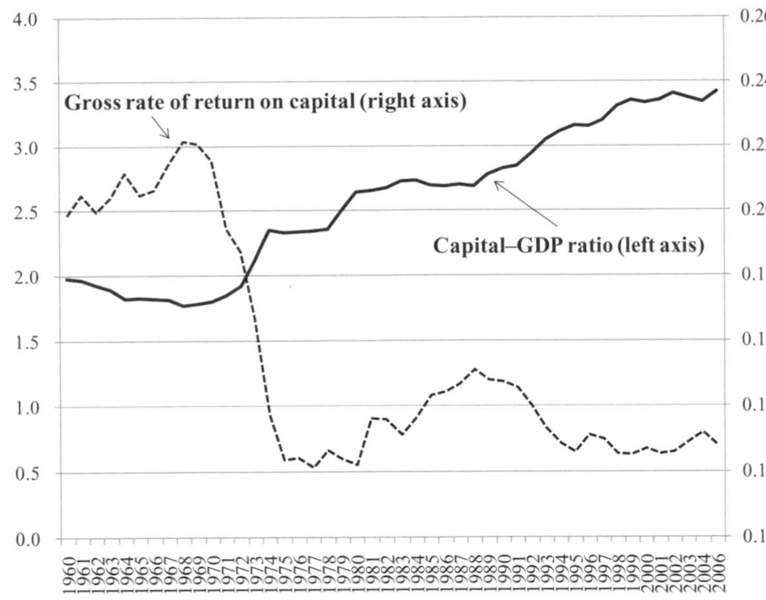

Figure 2. Capital coefficient and gross rate of return on capital in Japan. GDP, gross domestic product

Source: Fukao (2012). The original data for 1975–2006 are taken from the EU KLEMS database, November 2009.

Notes: Capital–GDP ratio = gross capital formation deflator × real capital stock / nominal GDP.
Gross rate of return on capital = gross operating surplus / (gross capital formation deflator × real capital stock).

Horiuchi, 2004) and damage to firms' balance sheets (Koo, 2003) reduced capital accumulation, and that these were the main cause of Japan's stagnation.[5] In fact, however, as figure 2 shows, capital accumulation continued apace after 1990, especially when taking the slow rate of GDP growth and the decline in the working-age population into account. According to the EU KLEMS database for November 2009, Japan's capital–GDP ratio (gross capital formation deflator × real capital stock / nominal GDP) increased by 21.2 percent during the sixteen years from 1990 to 2006, which is even slightly greater than the 21.1 percent increase in the capital–GDP ratio during the twenty-five-year period from 1975 to 1990. This increase in the capital–GDP ratio must have contributed to the continuous decline in the rate of return on capital in Japan by decreasing the marginal productivity of capital (figure 2).[6]

In contrast with Japan, the USA has experienced a continuous decline in the capital–GDP ratio and an increase in the rate of return on capital (measured as gross operating surplus / (GDP deflator × real capital stock)). It seems that these stark differences in the capital–GDP ratio and the rate of return on capital between Japan and the USA are mainly due to differences in the main engines of economic growth between the two countries.

That Japan's growth has been led by capital accumulation can be seen by comparing the main engines of labor productivity growth in the two countries. In both countries, annual labor productivity (real GDP / man-hours) growth from 1990 to the Lehman Shock was 2.0 percent (the rate for Japan is for 1990–2007, and that for the USA is for 1990– 2006). Using growth accounting, labor productivity growth can be broken down into the following three factors: increases in the capital input–labor input ratio, improvements in labor quality, and TFP growth. In the case of Japan, the contribution of each of these was 0.8, 0.7, and 0.5 percentage points respectively, while in the case of the USA, their contributions were 0.8, 0.2, and 1.0 percentage points respectively. Thus, Japan's labor productivity growth was mainly accomplished by physical and human capital deepening, not by TFP growth. On the other hand, the main engine of labor productivity growth in the USA was TFP growth. This difference is responsible for the increase of the capital–GDP ratio and the decline of the rate of return on capital in Japan.[7]

Although the rate of return on capital stagnated in the 1990s and early 2000s, Japan's capital–GDP ratio continued to increase. The prolonged zero interest-rate policy and public sector investment as part of the fiscal stimulus measures are likely to have contributed to this increase. However, because of the decreasing marginal productivity of capital, it is impossible to permanently maintain investment-led growth in the presence of a declining labor force and low TFP growth. As figure 1 shows, the contribution of capital accumulation to economic growth rapidly declined in the 2000s. It appears that investment-led growth in Japan is coming to an end.

Next, let us analyze Japan's TFP growth at the sectoral level. Figure 3 shows how TFP (on a value-added basis) in Japan's manufacturing and nonmanufacturing sectors has changed over time. Since inter-temporal changes of TFP in nonmarket activities, such as public administration, education, and health and social services, are difficult to measure, our data for the nonmanufacturing sector cover only the market economy.

In the case of the manufacturing sector, TFP growth declined sharply after 1991. The dotted line in figure 3 shows the TFP level of the manufacturing sector, assuming that the TFP growth rate from 1992 onward remained the same as the average annual TFP growth rate in the 1970–1991 period. TFP growth in the manufacturing sector accelerated again after 2002. However, since the stagnation of TFP growth in the 1990s and early 2000s was so pronounced, there is a huge gap between the past trend line and the actual TFP level. If Japan's manufacturing sector had been able to maintain TFP growth as high as that in 1970–1991 after 1991, the manufacturing sector's real value added now would be more than two-thirds larger (without increasing factor inputs) than the actual current level.

In the case of the nonmanufacturing sector, TFP growth in Japan, like in other countries, has been much lower than that in the manufacturing sector. Nevertheless, there is also a distinct difference between before and after 1991. Until 1991, the nonmanufacturing sector achieved slow but steady TFP growth, and the TFP level in 1991 was 29 percent higher than that in 1970. However, after 1991, there was almost no TFP growth in this sector.

Comparing the 1970–1991 period with the 1991–2007 period, the average annual TFP growth in the manufacturing sector declined by 1.94 percentage points, from 3.70 percent to 1.76 percent, while the average annual TFP growth in the nonmanufacturing sector (market economy) fell by 1.16 percentage points, from 1.20 percent to 0.04 percent. Since the nominal value-added share of the nonmanufacturing sector (market economy) is more than twice as large as that of the manufacturing sector (in 1991, the shares were 54 percent and 26 percent, respectively), the contribution of the slowdown of TFP growth in the nonmanufacturing sector (market economy) to the slowdown of TFP growth in the macroeconomy (approximated by multiplying the TFP growth decline by the value-added share) was

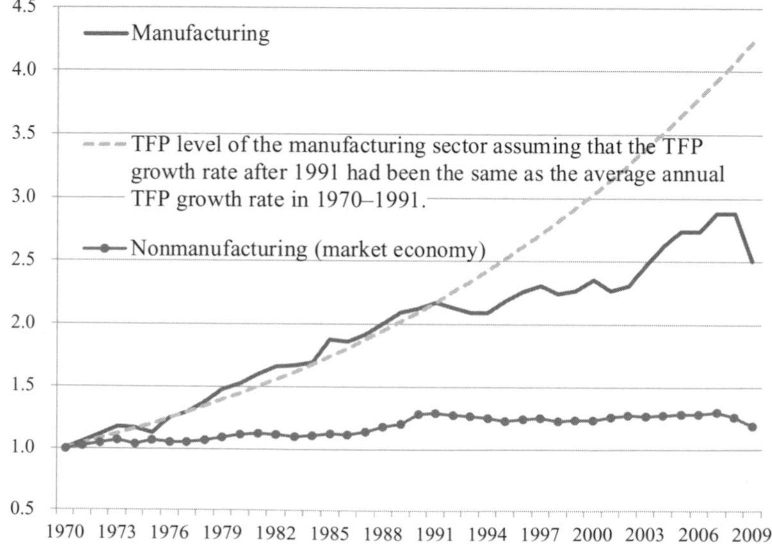

Figure 3. Total factor productivity (TFP) level of the manufacturing and the nonmanufacturing sector, 1970–2009 (1970 = 1)

Source: JIP database, 2012.

Notes: TFP values are on a value-added basis. The nonmanufacturing sector (market economy) does not include imputed rent for owner-occupied dwellings.

slightly greater than that of the manufacturing sector. Overall, it seems fair to say that both the manufacturing and the nonmanufacturing sector almost equally dragged down macro TFP growth after 1991.

Before 1991, Japan was rapidly catching up with the USA. After 1991, both the slowdown in productivity growth in Japan and the acceleration in productivity growth in the USA reversed this trend. In 1991–2007, Japan's TFP level relative to that of the USA declined by 19 percent in the manufacturing sector and 8 percent in the nonmanufacturing sector. Why has TFP growth in the USA accelerated? And why was Japan left behind? As already mentioned, one important factor is the ICT revolution in the USA. This can be confirmed by comparing Japan's TFP growth with that of the USA and other developed countries at a more disaggregated level. In figure 4, the market economy is divided into six sectors, and the average annual TFP growth rates in each sector before and after 1995 are compared across six major developed economies.

Figure 4 shows that the USA experienced an acceleration of TFP growth not only in the ICT-producing sector (electrical machinery, post and telecommunications), but also in the ICT-using sectors such as distribution services (retail, wholesale, and transportation) and in the rest of the manufacturing sector (i.e., excluding electrical machinery).[8] Japan also experienced relatively high TFP growth in the ICT-producing sector. The problem for Japan, however, is that TFP growth in the ICT-using service sectors, such as distribution services and the rest of the manufacturing sector, declined substantially after 1995.[9] Moreover, these ICT-using sectors are much larger than the ICT-producing sector: the average labor input share (hours worked) of the ICT-producing sector in Japan's total labor input in 1995–2007 was only 4.1 percent (similar to the corresponding share in the USA of 3.8 percent). On the other hand, the labor input shares of distribution services and the rest of the manufacturing sector in 1995–2007 were 22.8 percent and 16.5 percent, respectively.

Figure 6 also shows that most of the major European countries did not achieve a productivity acceleration in the ICT-using sectors like the USA after 1995, although their performance was not quite as bad as that of Japan.

3. ICT and Intangible Investment in Japan

Why did an ICT revolution of the magnitude observed in the USA not occur in Japan and in major European countries? This question was one of the core themes of the EU KLEMS project supported by the EU Commission. Figure 5 shows the project's main answer to this question.

In Japan and some of the European countries, such as Germany, the ICT investment–GDP ratio in IT-using service sectors, such as distribution services, is very low in comparison with the USA. This result was obtained after a careful compilation of internationally comparable data of fixed capital and software investment by detailed categories of capital goods. It appears that the ICT revolution did not happen in Japan simply because Japan has not accumulated sufficient ICT capital.[10]

The next question that needs to be addressed is why ICT investment in some sectors is so small in Japan. It is interesting to note that Japan's ICT investment in these sectors has been low in comparison with other countries since the 1970s. It therefore cannot be argued that the economic slump after 1991 has been the main cause of Japan's low ICT investment. Several structural impediments to ICT investment in Japan can be pointed out.

First, one of the main contributions of the introduction of ICT is that it allows firms to save on unskilled labor input. However, because of the high job security in Japan, it may be difficult for firms to actually cut jobs.

Second, in order to introduce ICT, firms need to incur certain initial fixed costs, such as those associated with the revision of organizational structures and the training of workers.[11] Some of these expenditures are one-shot, and it seems that once firms have adjusted their organizational structures to new ICT and have accumulated a certain mass of ICT-literate workers, they can expand their scale later without substantial additional costs. Probably because of this

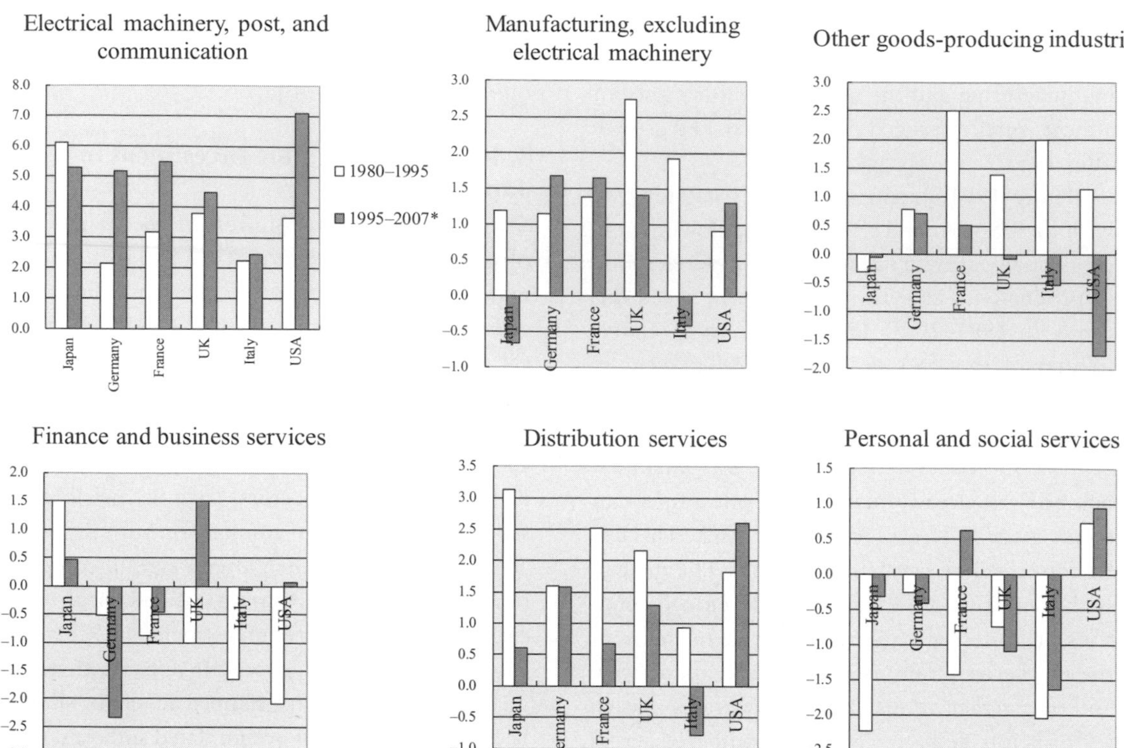

Figure 4. Total factor productivity growth in the market sector: by sector and by country, 1980–1995 and 1995–2007* (annual rate, %)

Source: EU KLEMS database, November 2009.
*Growth accounting for Japan is for the period 1995–2006.

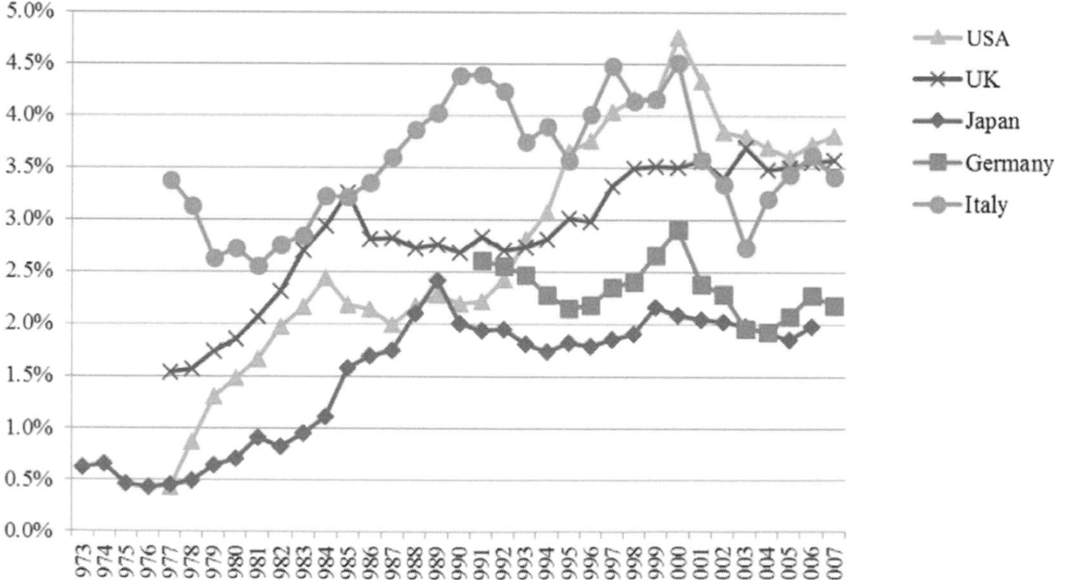

Figure 5. ICT investment–GDP ratio in major developed economies: distribution services. GDP, gross domestic product; ICT, information and communication technology

Source: EU KLEMS database, November 2009.

characteristic of ICT technology, younger and growing firms tend to be more active in ICT investment. Using microdata from the Ministry of Economy, Trade and Industry's *Basic Survey of Japanese Business Structure and Activities*, Fukao et al. (2012) find that, in Japan's nonmanufacturing sector, after controlling for firm size, industry, etc., younger firms have a significantly higher software stock/sales ratio. However, because of the low entry and exit rates in Japan, firms that have been around for forty-five years or more have a majority of the market share in all industries except transportation, communication, and public services (Fukao et al. 2012). This low metabolism has probably impeded ICT investment in Japan.

Third, Japan's retail sector is characterized by small shops, whereas the US retail sector is characterized by large chain stores (Haskel et al. 2007). Moreover, in the service sectors, Japanese-listed firms are of a much smaller scale on a consolidated basis than their counterparts in the USA (Fukao and Miyagawa 2010), and these smaller firms in Japan probably have found it more difficult to introduce ICT because of their small scale.

It is also important to note that in order to avoid changes in corporate structure, employment adjustment, and training of workers, Japanese firms tend to choose customized software rather than packaged software, making ICT investment more expensive and network externality effects smaller, because each firm uses different customized software.

The impediments to ICT investment mentioned above may be closely related to intangible investment in Japan. Intangible investment is defined as expenditures by firms for future production and profits, and includes the training of workers and the revision of firms' organizational structures. ICT capital and intangible assets may be close complements, as highlighted in the 2007 Economic Report of the President, which states that "[o]nly when they made intangible investments to complement their IT investments did productivity growth really take off" (p. 56).

Using the perpetual inventory method and intangible investment data, it is possible to estimate how intangible assets have accumulated over time. Moreover, using this result, it is possible to conduct a new type of growth accounting in which capital services from intangible assets are treated as one of the factor inputs. In the present system of national accounts, most categories of intangible investment are still treated as firms' intermediate inputs, not as capital accumulation. Therefore, in this new approach, it is also necessary to estimate a new "GDP" in which goods and services used for intangible investment are regarded as final goods and services, and not as intermediate inputs.

Using this type of framework, which was first proposed by Corrado et al. (2009), new growth accounting has been conducted for many developed countries. According to Corrado et al. (2012) and Miyagawa and Hisa (2013), in 1995–2007, the contribution of intangible investment to labor productivity growth in Japan was the lowest among the major developed countries. When conducting growth accounting without taking account of intangible asset accumulation, the derived "TFP" growth will contain the contribution of intangible asset accumulation to economic growth. Therefore, the low "TFP" growth in Japan since 1990 that we observed in figure 1 must have partly been caused by the slow growth of intangible assets in Japan (Fukao et al. 2009).

In the case of the USA, the contribution of intangible asset accumulation to labor productivity growth has been very large. In fact, it has been larger than the contribution of TFP growth in the USA and the largest among all the countries compared (Corrado et al. 2012). It thus can be said that the "TFP" resurgence of the USA after 1995 that we observed in figure 3 was partly caused by active investment in intangibles.[12]

Why has intangible asset accumulation in Japan been so small? In the framework of Corrado et al. (2009), intangible assets consist of three categories: innovative property (science and engineering research and development [R&D], mineral exploitation, copyright and license costs, other product development, design, and research expenses), computerized information (software and databases), and economic competencies (brand equity, firm-specific human capital, and organizational structure).

Looking at intangible investment in detail and comparing Japan with other countries shows that, reflecting the huge R&D expenditures by manufacturing firms, Japan invests a lot in innovative property but relatively little in economic competencies. Moreover, since around 2000 in particular, investment in economic competencies and computerized information has stagnated (Chun et al. 2012 and JIP database 2011).

It seems that the decline in the accumulation of economic competencies was caused by the harsh restructuring resulting from the long-term economic stagnation. For example, many firms increased the percentage of part-time workers in total workers and did not provide intensive training in the case of part-time workers. This change reduced training expenditures substantially.[13]

Why is the percentage of part-time workers increasing so rapidly in many industries in Japan? In sectors where individual proprietorships used to dominate, such as retail and eating and drinking places, one factor is that as individual proprietorships are replaced by corporations, family employees are replaced by part-time workers. However, this explanation does not apply to many other sectors, such as most manufacturing industries.

Another possible factor is that firms are increasing the number of part-time workers in order to maintain the flexibility of employment levels. Given the decline in the size of the working-age population and economic stagnation, most firms cannot expect their need for employees to steadily increase, as was the case during the high-speed growth era. At the same time, areas in which individual firms have a competitive advantage over their rivals are changing quickly, and Japan's comparative advantage as a whole is also changing over time. Given the high job security provided under traditional employment practices, increasing the reliance on part-time workers is almost the only way for firms to keep both the level and the mix of employment flexible.

Providing a theoretical model to capture these aspects, Matsuura et al. (2011) empirically show that firms that face greater uncertainty in their sales tend to have a higher percentage of part-time workers. They conjecture that globalization and the increase in international competition have raised sales uncertainty for manufacturing firms, and that this factor has contributed to the increase of part-time workers in Japan's manufacturing sector.

In order to examine whether firms employ part-time workers simply to take advantage of lower wage rates or to gain more flexibility in their workforce, Fukao et al. (2006) estimate both the marginal productivity of part-time workers in comparison with that of regular workers and the compensation of part-time workers in comparison with that of regular workers, using employer–employee-matched data at the factory level. They find that the productivity gap between part-time workers and regular workers is larger than the wage gap between them. This means that firms pay a premium to part-time workers in order to obtain flexibility of employment.

Such behavior by firms is quite rational in the context of slow economic growth and Japan's system of high job security. However, at the same time, it may also be creating a huge economic loss by reducing human capital accumulation, and this loss seems to be greater than the observable wage gap between part-time workers and regular workers. In order to resolve this problem, Japan's labor market needs to be reformed.

4. Has the Natural Selection Mechanism Been Working in Japan's Economy?

Sector-level TFP growth is equal to the weighted average of the TFP growth of firms or factories in that sector. Since productivity levels differ considerably across firms and factories within each sector, resource allocation across firms and factories is bound to have a large impact on TFP growth. If the economic natural selection mechanism works, more productive firms would be expected to enter and expand, and less productive firms would be expected to shrink and exit. The slowdown of Japan's TFP growth may have partly been caused by deterioration of this mechanism.

Several studies have already examined this issue. For example, using data on listed firms, Ahearne and Shinada (2005) and Caballero et al. (2008) have shown that, since the 1990s, in bad-loan–infested sectors such as real estate and construction, profitless and highly indebted (zombie) firms tended to survive, probably because of lender banks' continuous support. Using data from the *Basic Survey of Japanese Business Structure and Activities*, which covers not only large firms but also small- and medium-sized enterprises (SMEs), Nishimura et al. (2005) examined productivity dynamics in the manufacturing and nonmanufacturing sectors from the mid-1990s onward and observed negative exit effects (productive firms exit and less productive firms survive) in some industries such as commerce. On the other hand, using factory-level data from the Ministry of Economy, Trade and Industry's *Census of Manufactures* from the beginning of the 1980s onward, Fukao and Kwon (2006) examined productivity dynamics in the manufacturing sector and found that the market selection mechanism already did not work very well in the 1980s, so that entry and exit effects made a much smaller contribution to TFP growth than in other countries. They further found that the slowdown in TFP growth in the 1990s was mainly due to a slowdown in TFP growth within factories.

This section revisits the issue of productivity dynamics using recent empirical results. In addition, the results of the analysis of productivity dynamics will be compared with the results of the sectoral and macro-level analysis in section 2.

In figure 6, TFP growth (on a gross output basis) in Japan's manufacturing sector is broken down into entry, exit, reallocation, and within effects. Microdata from the *Census of Manufactures*, which covers all factories with four or more employees, were used. Factories are classified into fifty-four industries, and following Good et al. (1997) and Aw et al. (2001), within each industry, each plant's TFP level in comparison with the industry average TFP level was measured.

Figure 6 shows that from 1990 onward, the within effect steadily declined and the negative exit effect expanded (i.e., productive factories were shut down, while less productive factories remained). Taken together, these two trends reduced TFP growth in the manufacturing sector substantially. On the other hand, the positive entry effect and the reallocation effect expanded and partly mitigated the decline in TFP growth.

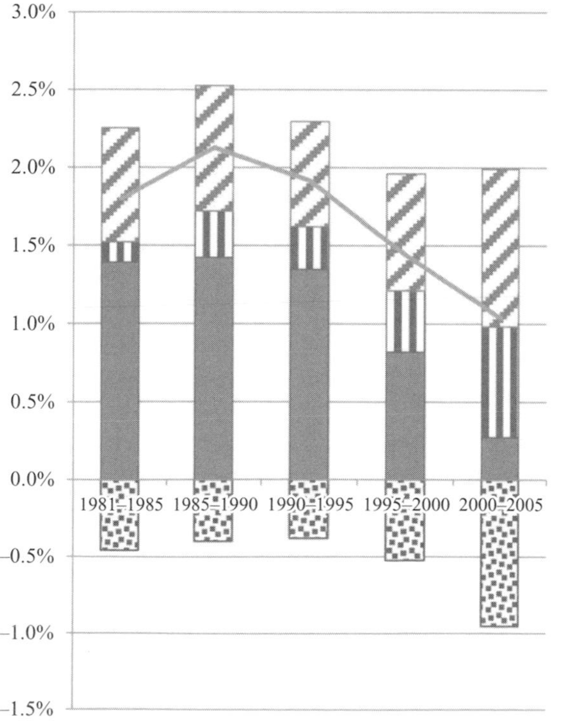

Figure 6. Breakdown of total factor productivity (TFP) growth in the manufacturing sector (annual growth rate)

Source: Ahn et al. (2012).

Why did the negative exit effect increase over time? Comparing the survival rates of factories shows that less productive factories have a higher probability of being shut down. However, some large and productive factories have also been shut down, as a result of which the weighted average of the TFP level of factories that are closed has been higher than the average TFP level of surviving factories (Kim et al. 2007).

As figure 7 shows, there is a statistically significant negative correlation between the industry-level exit effect and industry-level gross output growth by Japanese multinational enterprises (MNEs) in Asia. MNEs have higher productivity than non-MNEs (Fukao 2012), and many of them have relocated, or are relocating, production activities abroad, meaning that as they reduce production within Japan, only unproductive non-MNEs are left behind. It seems that this is the main cause of the negative exit effect.

Another important fact we can point out from the microdata is that the productivity gap between large firms and SMEs has increased in the 1990s and 2000s. Employing the data used for figure 6, Kim et al. (2010) examined the TFP growth of stayers by factory size for five-year intervals from 1980 to 1999 (the final period is 1995–1999). They subdivided factories into four groups according to factory size at the beginning of each period for each industry. The grouping is conducted so that the total sales of each group in each industry are equal to one-quarter of the total sales of that industry. They then calculated the weighted average of the TFP growth for each group of factories of different sizes. They found that in the manufacturing sector, the TFP growth of large factories, most of which are owned by large firms, actually accelerated in the 1990s, while small- and medium-sized factories, most of which are owned by SMEs, were left behind. Thus, there was no lost decade in the case of large manufacturing firms. Using microdata from the Ministry of Finance's *Financial Statements Statistics of Corporations by Industry*, it can be

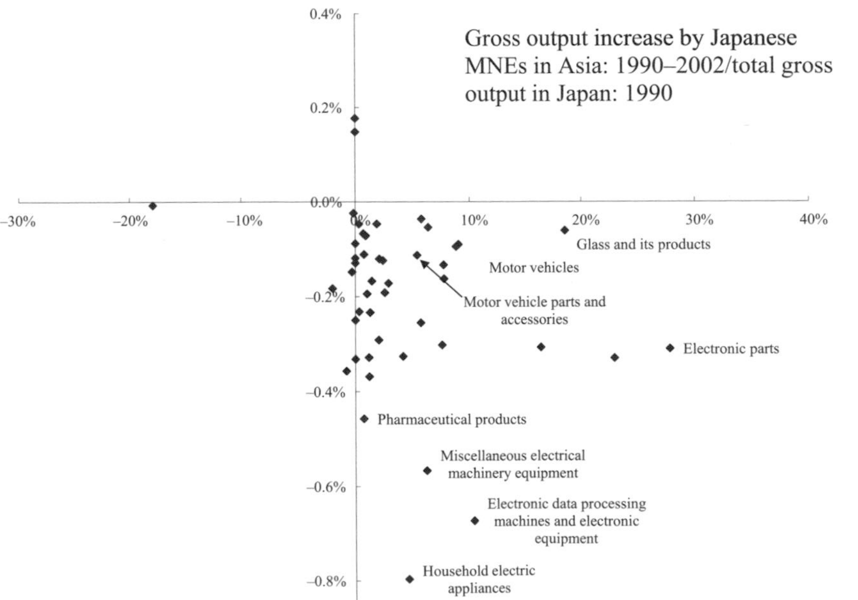

Figure 7. Overseas production and the exit effect at home (1990–2003)

Source: Gross output data of Japanese multinational enterprises (MNEs) in Asia were taken from the JIP database.

further confirmed that the TFP gap between large firms and small firms in the manufacturing sector continued to expand in the 2000s (Fukao 2012).

One possible explanation for this divergence is that SMEs were left behind in R&D. In the 1990s and 2000s, the R&D expenditure–gross-value-added ratio of the Japanese manufacturing sector continued to grow. However, in Japan, R&D expenditures are mainly confined to large firms, which conduct the bulk of R&D. According to the *1999 White Paper on Small and Medium Enterprises in Japan*, the average R&D–sales ratio of Japanese firms is higher than that of US firms in the case of firm groups with 5,000 or more employees, but it is lower in the case of firm groups with fewer than 5,000 employees. Moreover, according to the *Report on the Survey of Research and Development 2011*, total R&D (including sponsored research) by firm groups with 300 or more employees amounted to 13 trillion yen, while total R&D by firm groups with fewer than 300 employees was only 1 trillion yen.

Japanese SMEs probably enjoyed R&D spillovers from large firms through tight supplier–purchaser relationships and geographic proximity within Japan before the 1990s. However, as large firms expanded their supply chains globally and relocated their factories and even their R&D activities abroad (Belderbos et al. 2009), spillovers from large firms seem to have declined.

Using matched microdata from the *Census of Manufactures* and the Ministry of Education, Culture, Sports, Science and Technology's *Survey of Research and Development* from the 1980s to the 2000s, Ikeuchi et al. (2013) examine R&D spillover effects through geographic and technological proximity and supplier relationships. They find that R&D spillover effects have declined since the 1990s, partly because of a decline of geographic proximity through the closure of factories in industrial districts by R&D-intensive firms. In recent years, SMEs have started to become more active in R&D (Fukao et al. 2012), probably in order to respond to this decline of spillover inflows. However, it will take some time for SMEs to catch up.

It should further be noted that only a limited part of the decline in the TFP growth of SMEs can be explained by the weakening of spillover effects (Ikeuchi et al. 2013). Another factor contributing to the decline in TFP growth probably is the stagnation of investment by SMEs in ICT and intangibles (Fukao et al. 2012). However, further research is needed on this issue.

Next, let us examine the slow TFP growth in the nonmanufacturing sector. It is difficult to conduct an analysis that is as detailed and rigorous as that for the manufacturing sector because of a lack of sufficient microdata. That being said, figure 8 shows the results of breaking down the TFP growth of listed firms in the nonmanufacturing sector using data from their financial reports. Since the data cover only listed firms, "entry" refers to firms that were newly listed, while "exit" refers not only to firms that went bankrupt, but also to firms that were delisted.

Figure 8 shows that the sharp drop in TFP growth from 1985–1990 to 1990–1995 was mainly caused by the decline of the within effect. On the other hand, although the contribution of the entry effect declined, there was some improvement in the reallocation and the exit effect in the 1990–1995 period. Therefore, when looking at all listed firms in the nonmanufacturing sector as a whole, it seems difficult to argue that the "zombie" firm problem was the number one cause of the decline in TFP growth from 1985–1990 to 1990–1995.

Figure 8 also shows that after the bad performance in 1990–1995, TFP growth steadily increased after 1995. The main engine of this TFP growth resurgence was the increase in the within effect. In the case of the TFP growth acceleration from 1995–2000 to 2000–2005, both the increase in the reallocation effect and the reduction of the negative exit effect also contributed to the TFP acceleration. These two factors may be related to the fading of the "zombie" problem.

As in the manufacturing sector, listed firms in the nonmanufacturing sector, most of which are large firms, enjoyed an acceleration in TFP growth in recent years. Therefore, figure 8 does not really help explain the extremely low TFP growth in the nonmanufacturing sector in the 2000s seen in figure 4. Figure 8 covers only listed firms, which make up only a relatively small proportion of the

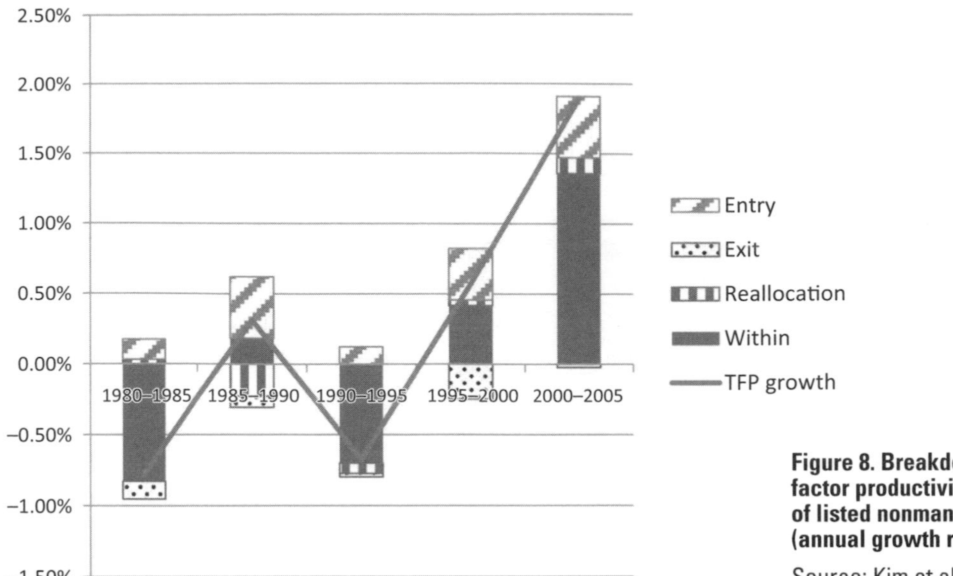

Figure 8. Breakdown of total factor productivity (TFP) growth of listed nonmanufacturing firms (annual growth rate)

Source: Kim et al. (2010).

firms in the nonmanufacturing sector. Comparing data on listed firms and data from the *Financial Statements Statistics of Corporations by Industry*, Kim et al. (2007) suggest that in the case of the nonmanufacturing sector, the value-added share of listed firms among all firms in the sector was only 22 percent in 2000.

To examine the TFP performance of firms in the nonmanufacturing sector by firm size, Inui et al. (2011) classified firms within each of the seventeen nonmanufacturing industries into four groups by firm size, and found that the gap between the average TFP level of the group of largest firms and the group of smallest firms was 14 percent in 1982–1990, 18 percent in 1991–2000, and 21 percent in 2001–2007. In other words, the TFP gap between large and small firms has increased substantially over time. According to Fukao and Kwon (2011), larger, older, and more productive firms in the nonmanufacturing sector are very slow to increase their capital and labor input. As in the case of the manufacturing sector, it seems that the natural selection mechanism does not work well in the nonmanufacturing sector. More analyses are needed on why SMEs have been left behind in terms of productivity, and why the natural selection mechanism does not work in the nonmanufacturing sector.

5. Conclusion

Using industry- and micro-level data, this paper examines why Japan's productivity growth has been slow for such a long time and how it can be accelerated in the future. Our findings yield the following policy implications.

First, as explained in section 1, the present government is implementing policies to overcome deflation and appears to be planning to stimulate private investment through a reduction in real interest rates. However, since investment opportunities are limited and the rate of return on capital is very low, extremely low or negative real interest rates are required, but maintaining very low or negative real interest rates, a positive inflation rate, and full employment without causing bubbles is likely to be extremely difficult to achieve. Therefore, for sustainable growth, it is necessary to raise the rate of return on capital through productivity growth.

Second, more empirical analysis is needed to judge for certain whether Japan's low growth rates of ICT capital and intangible assets are suboptimal. However, if it is indeed desirable to enhance ICT and intangible investment, labor-market reforms (such as improving the social safety net, enhancing labor-market flexibility, and reducing the unfair gap between regular and part-time workers) and support for ICT and intangible investment by SMEs will be important issues. Labor-market reform is also important from the perspective of human capital accumulation. Firms pay a premium to part-time workers in order to obtain flexibility of employment. Such behavior by firms is quite rational in the context of slow economic growth and Japan's system of high job security. However, at the same time, it may also be creating a huge economic loss by reducing human capital accumulation.[14]

Third, to raise TFP growth, the natural selection mechanism of the economy needs to be enhanced. To achieve this in the case of the manufacturing sector, it is important to enhance the start-up of domestic establishments by Japanese and foreign multinationals through the improvement of regional logistics, the establishment of free trade agreements, the reduction of corporate taxes, etc. In the case of the nonmanufacturing sector, this is still overregulated in Japan, and regulatory reforms are required. For example, the government could relax regulations preventing the entry of private firms in agriculture and medical services. It could also revise the Large-scale Retail Stores Law and facilitate the entry of large retail stores. When the government supports SMEs, it should refrain from supporting all SMEs uniformly. Such support harms the market selection mechanism. Instead, the government needs to introduce a scheme that enhances the growth of promising small firms. For example, the government could promote the diffusion of technology to innovative SMEs by revising the Japanese version of the Bayh–Dole Act (Article 30 of the Law on Special Measures for Industrial Revitalization and Innovation). The government could also increase its procurements from SMEs. Labor-market reform is another important element to enhance the natural selection mechanism, because the expected high closure cost of firms decreases the incentives for entrepreneurs and investors to set up new businesses. In sum, there is a wide range of steps that the government could take to address the fundamental cause of Japan's economic stagnation—low TFP growth—and boost the economy's growth potential.

Courtesy of Japan Center for Economic Research (JCER).

Originally published in *Asia-Pacific Review* 8, no. 2 (2013): 193–213.

Notes

1. I am grateful to Lee Jong-wha, the editors of the journal, and other conference participants for their helpful comments on an earlier draft.
2. See, for example, Hayashi and Prescott (2002), and Fukao and Kwon (2006).
3. Because of the steep decline in Japanese exports, Japan's real GDP growth during the period 2008–2009 was much lower than that of the USA, which was the epicenter of the Lehman Shock. This drop in GDP, the decline of capacity utilization, and serious labor hoarding, which was partly caused by the high job security in Japan, resulted in a larger TFP decline in Japan than in the USA. Specifically, the seasonally adjusted capacity utilization rate of Japan's manufacturing sector declined by 38 percent from September 2008 to February 2009 (Indices of Industrial Production, Ministry of Economy, Trade and Industry). On the other hand, man-hour input in Japan declined by only 2.7 percent from 2008 to 2009, whereas in the USA it fell by 5.2 percent (EU KLEMS database, March 2013). In the USA, the average annual growth rates of real GDP and TFP during this period were 1.9 percent (Economic Report of the President 2012) and 0.9 percent (Conference Board Total Economy Database), respectively.
4. Because of labor hoarding and the idling of capital stock, there is a risk of underestimating TFP growth in recessionary periods, such as the period from 1990 to 1995. Using the capacity utilization rate of the JIP database, which covers both the manufacturing and nonmanufacturing sectors, it is possible to examine this issue. After taking changes in the capacity utilization rate into account, the estimate of annual TFP growth in 1990–1995 becomes 0.2 percentage points higher than that shown in figure 1 (see Fukao 2012). However, this adjustment does not change the overall picture. On the other hand, making adjustments in order to take labor hoarding into account is more difficult. It is possible to assume, though, that when the GDP gap is zero or positive, the problem of labor hoarding is probably not very serious, and when comparing the TFP level of years with a zero or positive GDP gap over time, a similar declining trend in TFP growth can be observed. Thus, it seems safe to say that the decline in TFP growth seen in figure 1 is not simply an artifact created by labor hoarding and the idling of capital stock.
5. On the main causes of Japan's economic stagnation, see also Saxonhouse and Stern (2004), Itō et al. (2005), and Caballero et al. (2008).

6. The gross rate of return on capital in Japan declined markedly in the first half of the 1970s, probably because of the first oil shock and the substantial yen appreciation following the end of the adjustable-peg exchange-rate system.

7. The analysis here is based on the following reasoning. Assume a Solow-type constant returns to scale macro production function, $Y=F(q_K K, Aq_L H)$, where Y, q_K, K, A, q_L, and H denote GDP, the quality of capital, the capital stock, the Harrod neutral productivity index, labor quality, and man-hour input, respectively. Then, the capital input–GDP ratio, $q_K K/Y=1/F(1, Aq_L H/q_K K)$, will be an increasing function of the capital input–labor input ratio, $q_K K/q_L H$, and a decreasing function of the productivity index, A. Moreover, the marginal productivity of capital input, $\partial Y/\partial q_K K=\partial F(q_K K/q_L H, A)/\partial(q_K K/q_L H)$, will be a decreasing function of the capital input–labor input ratio, $q_K K/q_L H$, and an increasing function of the productivity index, A. Further, TFP growth is equal to the growth rate of A times the cost share of labor. In figure 2, the capital stock–GDP ratio, K/Y, and not the capital input–GDP ratio, $q_K K/Y$, is used. However, similar results are obtained when using the capital input–GDP ratio in place of the capital stock–GDP ratio.

8. During the 2000–2006 period, the average percentage of ICT investment in total fixed capital formation in each of the six sectors in the USA and Japan was as follows: electrical machinery, post and telecommunications, 51 percent and 25 percent, respectively; manufacturing, excluding electrical machinery, 28 percent and 8 percent; other goods-producing industries, 10 percent and 6 percent; finance and business services, 47 percent and 36 percent; distribution services, 39 percent and 20 percent; personal and social services, 11 percent and 10 percent (EU KLEMS database, November 2009). For details on the industry classification of each sector, see O'Mahony and Timmer (2009).

9. We should note that the TFP growth in Japan's finance and business services, which is an ICT intensive sector, was higher than that of the finance and business services in the USA. The reason probably is Japan's relatively active ICT investment in this sector (see footnote 7).

10. Total fixed-capital formation in the market economy can be classified into three categories: ICT investment (computing and communications equipment and software), investment in other equipment (transportation equipment and other machinery and equipment), and investment in nonresidential structures and other fixed capital assets (nuclear fuel, cultivated assets, etc.). During the period 2000–2006, the shares of these categories of investment in Japan were 17 percent, 40 percent, and 43 percent, respectively. For the USA, the corresponding shares were 34 percent, 36 percent, and 30 percent (EU KLEMS database, November 2009). This comparison shows that Japan invests much more in nonresidential structures and other fixed capital assets and much less in ICT capital than the USA.

11. On this issue, see Bloom et al. (2012). Using firm-level data for Japan and the USA, Atrostic et al. (2008) find that computer network use has a much larger positive impact on firms' performance in the USA than in Japan.

12. It should be noted that both the ICT investment in figure 5 and intangible investment include software investment.

13. According to the JIP database 2012, Japanese firms' total off-the-job-training expenditures (including the estimated opportunity cost for trainees' time) declined from 2.5 trillion yen (annual average of 1991–1995) to 0.8 trillion yen (annual average of 2004–2008). At the same time, the number of employees in their twenties declined from 13.9 million (average of 1991–1995) to 11.0 million (average of 2004–2008), and the percentage of part-time workers among these employees increased from 11 percent to 20 percent. Therefore, it seems that not only the decline in the number of young full-time workers, but also other factors, such as cost-cutting by firms in response to the prolonged economic stagnation, contributed to the reduction in off-the-job training.

14. We should note that labor-market flexibility might impede accumulation of firm-specific human capital as workers change their jobs. In a flexible labor market, non-firm-specific general skills will become more important. The government can implement several policies to promote the accumulation of general skills. For instance, the government could help workers develop their careers by reforming the present "job card" system. The government could also support vocational training at high schools and universities.

References

Ahearne, Alan, and Shinada Naoki. 2005. "Zombie Firms and Economic Stagnation in Japan." *International Economics and Economic Policy* 2 (4): 363–381.

Ahn Sanghoon, Fukao Kyōji, Kim Young-gak, and Kwon Hyeog-ug. 2012. "Productivity Dynamics: A Comparison of the Manufacturing Sector in Korea and Japan." PowerPoint presented at the Korea-Japan Workshop on Productivity, Seoul National University, December 7, 2012.

Atrostic, Barbara, Motohashi Kazuyuki, and Sang Nguyen. 2008. "Computer Network Use and Firms' Productivity Performance: The United States vs. Japan." US Census Bureau, Center for Economic Studies Paper, no. CES-WP-08-30.

Aw Bee-yan, Chen Xiaomin, and Mark J. Roberts. 2001. "Firm-Level Evidence on Productivity Differentials and Turnover in Taiwanese Manufacturing." *Journal of Development Economics* 66 (1): 51–86.

Belderbos, René, Fukao Kyōji, and Iwasa Tomoko. 2009. "Foreign and Domestic R&D Investment." *Economics of Innovation and New Technology* 18 (4): 369–380.

Bloom, Nicholas, Raffaella Sadun, and John Van Reenen. 2012. "Americans Do IT Better: US Multinationals and the Productivity Miracle." *American Economic Review* 102 (1): 167–201.

Caballero, Ricardo J., Hoshi Takeo, and Anil K. Kashyap. 2008. "Zombie Lending and Depressed Restructuring in Japan." *American Economic Review* 98 (5): 1943–1977.

Chun Hyunbae, Fukao Kyōji, Hisa Shōichi, and Miyagawa Tsutomu. 2012. "Measurement of Intangible Investments by Industry and Its Role in Productivity Improvement Utilizing Comparative Studies between Japan and Korea." RIETI Discussion Paper Series, no. 12-E-037, Research Institute of Economy, Trade and Industry (RIETI).

Corrado, Carol, Jonathan Haskel, Cecilia Jona-Lasinio, and Massimiliano Iommi. 2012. "Intangible Capital and Growth in Advanced Economies: Measurement Methods and Comparative Results." IZA Discussion Paper Series, no. 6733, Institute for the Study of Labor (IZA), Germany.

Corrado, Carol, Charles Hulten, and Daniel Sichel. 2009. "Intangible Capital and U.S. Economic Growth." *Review of Income and Wealth* 55 (3): 661–685.

Fukao Kyōji. 2012. *"Ushinawareta 20-nen" to Nihon keizai: Kōzōteki gen'in to saisei e no gendōryoku no kaimei* [The Structural Causes of Japan's "Two Lost Decades": Forging a New Growth Strategy]. Tokyo: Nihon Keizai Shimbun Shuppansha.

Fukao Kyōji, Kambayashi Ryō, Kawaguchi Daiji, Kwon Hyeog-ug, Kim Young-gak, and Yokoyama Izumi. 2006. "Deferred Compensation: Evidence from Employer-Employee Matched Data from Japan." Hi-Stat Discussion Paper Series, no. 187, Hitotsubashi University.

Fukao Kyōji, Kim Young-gak, and Kwon Hyeog-ug. 2012. "Intangible Investment in Japan." PowerPoint prepared for the OECD Workshop on Productivity, OECD Conference Centre, Paris, November 5–6, 2012.

Fukao Kyōji, and Kwon Hyeog-ug. 2006. "Why Did Japan's TFP Growth Slow Down in the Lost Decade? An Empirical Analysis Based on Firm-Level Data of Manufacturing Firms." *Japanese Economic Review* 57 (2): 195–228.

———. 2011. "Nihon keizai seichō no gensen wa doko ni aru ka: Mikurodēta ni yoru jisshō bunseki" [Sources of Future Economic Growth in Japan: An Empirical Analysis Based on Micro-Data]. RIETI Discussion Paper Series, no. 11-J-045, Research Institute of Economy, Trade and Industry (RIETI).

Fukao Kyōji, and Miyagawa Tsutomu. 2010. "Service Sector Productivity in Japan: An Analysis Based on the JIP Database." In *The Service Sector Advancement: Issues and Implications for the Korean Economy*, edited by MoonJoong Tcha, 92–109. Seoul: Korea Development Institute (KDI).

Fukao Kyōji, Miyagawa Tsutomu, Mukai Kentarō, Shinoda Yukio, and Tonogi Konomi. 2009. "Intangible Investment in Japan: Measurement and Contribution to Economic Growth." *Review of Income and Wealth* 55 (3): 717–736.

Good, David H., M. Ishaq Nadiri, and Robin C. Sickles. 1997. "Index Number and Factor Demand Approaches to the Estimation of Productivity." In *Handbook of Applied Econometrics, Volume 2: Microeconometrics*, edited by M. Hashem Pesaran and Peter Schmidt, 14–80. Oxford: Wiley-Blackwell.

Hamada Kōichi, and Horiuchi Akiyoshi. 2004. "*Sōkatsu komento: Chōki teitai wa naze okotta noka*" [Wrap-Up Comments: Why Prolonged Stagnation Occurred]. In *Ronsō Nihon no keizai kiki: Chōki teitai no shin'in o kaimei suru* [Discussions on Japan's Economic Crisis: An Investigation into True Causes of Japan's Prolonged Stagnation], edited by Hamada Kōichi, Horiuchi Akiyoshi, and Economic and Social Research Institute, Cabinet Office, 289–340. Tokyo: Nihon Keizai Shimbun Shuppansha.

Haskel, Jonathan, Ron S. Jarmin, Motohashi Kazuyuki, and Raffaella Sadun. 2007. "Retail Market Structure and Dynamics: A Three Country Comparison of Japan, the U.K. and the U.S." Harvard Business School Working Paper, Harvard Business School, July 9.

Hayashi Fumio, and Edward C. Prescott. 2002. "The 1990s in Japan: A Lost Decade." *Review of Economic Dynamics* 5 (1): 206–235.

Ikeuchi Kenta, Kim Young-gak, Kwon Hyeog-ug, and Fukao Kyōji. 2013. "Seizōgyō ni okeru sangyōsei dōgaku to R&D supiruōbā: Mikurodēta ni yoru jisshō bunseki" [Productivity Dynamics and R&D Spillovers in the Japanese Manufacturing Industry: An Empirical Analysis Based on Micro-Level Data]. *Economic Review* 64 (3): 269–287.

Inklaar, Robert, Marcel P. Timmer, and Bart van Ark. 2007. "Mind the Gap! International Comparisons of Productivity in Services and Goods Production." *German Economic Review* 8 (2): 281–307.

Inui Tomohiko, Kim Young-gak, Kwon Hyeog-ug, and Fukao Kyōji. 2011. "Sangyōsei dōgaku to Nihon no keizai seichō: 'Hōjin kigyō tōkei chōsa' kōhyō dēta ni yoru jisshō bunseki" [Productivity Dynamics and Japan's Economic Growth: An

Empirical Analysis Based on the Financial Statements Statistics of Corporations by Industry]. RIETI Discussion Paper Series, no. 11-J-042, Research Institute of Economy, Trade and Industry (RIETI).

Itō Takatoshi, Hugh Patrick, and David E. Weinstein. 2005. *Reviving Japan's Economy: Problems and Prescriptions*. Cambridge, MA: MIT Press.

Kim Young-gak, Fukao Kyōji, and Makino Tatsuji. 2010. "'Ushinawareta 20-nen' no kōzōteki gen'in" [The Structural Causes of Japan's Two Lost Decades]. *Economic Review* 61 (3): 237–260.

Kim Young-gak, Kwon Hyeog-ug, and Fukao Kyōji. 2007. "Kigyō, jigyōsho no sannyū, taishutsu to sangyō reberu no seisansei" [Entry and Exit of Companies and Establishments, and Productivity at the Industry Level]. RIETI Discussion Paper Series, no. 07-J-022, Research Institute of Economy, Trade and Industry (RIETI).

Koo, Richard C. 2003. *Balance Sheet Recession: Japan's Struggle with Uncharted Economics and Its Global Implications*. Singapore: Wiley.

Matsuura Toshiyuki, Satō Hitoshi, and Wakasugi Ryūhei. 2011. "Temporary Workers, Permanent Workers, and International Trade: Evidence from Japanese Firm-Level Data." RIETI Discussion Paper Series, no. 11-E-030, Research Institute of Economy, Trade and Industry (RIETI).

Miyagawa Tsutomu, and Hisa Shōichi. 2013. "Estimates of Intangible Investment by Industry and Productivity Growth in Japan." *Japanese Economic Review* 64 (1): 42–72.

Nishimura Kiyohiko, Nakajima Takanobu, and Kiyota Kōzō. 2005. "Does the Natural Selection Mechanism Still Work in Severe Recessions? Examination of the Japanese Economy in the 1990s." *Journal of Economic Behavior and Organization* 58 (1): 53–78.

O'Mahony, Mary, and Marcel P. Timmer. 2009. "Output, Input and Productivity Measures at the Industry Level: The EU KLEMS Database." *Economic Journal* 119 (538): F374–F403.

Saxonhouse, Gary R., and Robert M. Stern, eds. 2004. *Japan's Lost Decade: Origins, Consequences and Prospects for Recovery*. Oxford: Blackwell.

Part
II

The Formation and Collapse of the Bubble

Part II comprises essays on the background of the dramatic rise in asset prices known as the bubble economy and the bubble's subsequent collapse, along with the economic impact of that event.

Noguchi Yukio, the first economist to analyze Japan's bubble economy, published his pioneering results in *Baburu no keizaigaku* (The Economics of Bubbles) in 1992. The essay included here, "Closing the Books on the Bubble Years," is an excerpt from that work, with the author looking at asset-price fluctuations and breaking down the economic background and economic impact thereof, as well as discussing policies for preventing future bubbles.

Itoh Motoshige's "Lessons of Japan's Bubble Economy" considers the formation and collapse of the bubble economy from a long-term perspective. The author notes that the bubble emerged after strong growth and suggests that mistakes were made in the policy response to the bubble's collapse. He identifies commonalities between these observations and the issues being faced by many other countries.

Takenaka Heizō is an economist who became minister of state for economic and fiscal policy when Koizumi Junichirō came to power in 2001. He is particularly well-informed about issues such as the handling of nonperforming loans, as he grappled with these directly as part of his portfolio. "The Reality of Financial Reform: The Burden of Bad Loans" is excerpted from his book on his experiences with the Koizumi cabinet's structural reforms entitled *Kōzō kaikaku no shinjitsu* (The Structural Reforms of the Koizumi Cabinet). It is an invaluable record of his work engaging in financial reconstruction as a cabinet member.

II-(1) Closing the Books on the Bubble Years

Noguchi Yukio
Japan Echo, 1994

From the latter part of the 1980s through the early 1990s the Japanese economy went through an unprecedented experience. First, asset values surged to great heights, and then they came tumbling down. The assets I am referring to here are objects that store economic value, mainly stocks and land. In a phenomenon sometimes called "asset-price inflation," stock and land prices skyrocketed dramatically in the first part of this period. What made this inflation unusual was that while the price of assets went up, the price of regular goods and services remained stable.

The long-term trends in stock and land prices are illustrated in figure 1. As can be seen, the start of the sharp climb came around 1986. The Nikkei index, an average of 225 selected shares on the Tokyo Stock Exchange, recorded a threefold increase from around 13,000 points in January 1986 to around 39,000 points at the end of 1989. Similarly, the price of commercial land in the six largest cities roughly tripled.

Under normal conditions, stock and land prices tend to go up in step with the economy's growth. To judge the degree of deviation from normal, accordingly, we need to compare changes in aggregate stock and land values with changes in gross domestic product. Figure 2 traces the ratio of these values to nominal GDP, using the market prices of the stocks listed on the first section of the Tokyo Stock Exchange and of residential land in Tokyo.

In the middle of the 1980s, the total value of these stocks and of Tokyo's residential land were both equal to approximately half of Japan's GDP. As of mid-1985, the values were ¥169 trillion for stocks and ¥176 trillion for land, compared to ¥324 trillion for the GDP. By the end of 1986, however, the value of residential land had risen above the figure for the GDP, and a year later it was about 1.5 times as large as the latter. In other words, in a period of less than three years the value of this land grew by an amount equal to the GDP. The stock-price explosion lagged somewhat behind this trend, but the total value of shares reached the size of the GDP in 1988 and grew yet larger in 1989. Obviously, these trends were abnormal. In economic theory, a financial bubble is the portion of a price increase that is in excess of overall trends in the economy. In the second half of the 1980s, the Japanese economy experienced a classic example of bubble inflation.

The Bursting of the Bubbles

During the boom years, many people expected stock and land prices to continue their climb indefinitely. But bubbles inevitably burst. The first to be punctured was the one in the stock market. After peaking close to 40,000 at the end of 1989, the Nikkei index plummeted to about 24,000 points in December 1990, stripping stocks of nearly 40 percent of their value. Share prices remained relatively stable in 1991, but they resumed their precipitous decline the next year. By mid-August 1992 the Nikkei average had fallen to the 14,000 level, roughly 30 percent below its position at the beginning of the year. Measured in terms of the total value of first-section stocks, the drop was from ¥590 trillion in December 1989 to ¥260 trillion in July 1992. This means that more than ¥300 trillion had vanished into thin air. Thereafter the market rebounded in response to the announcement of a comprehensive package of economic stimulus measures, but share prices remain below the 17,000 level as of this writing at the end of October 1992.

Land prices in the Tokyo area held steady at a high level during 1990, and prices in major regional cities continued to climb. In 1991, however, a marked decline set in. According to prefectural land surveys, in the year from July 1991 to July 1992 residential land prices fell by 15 percent in Tokyo, 24 percent in Osaka, and 28 percent in Kyoto. Compared with the decline in stock values, the contraction of Tokyo's residential land market has thus far been modest, but it has nonetheless wiped out about ¥100 trillion in assets. In the period since World War II, the pattern has been for land prices to increase steadily every year; only in 1975 was a decline recorded. The steep drop that began in 1991 is thus a new experience for the Japanese economy.

At present the ratios of aggregate stock and land values to GDP are headed back toward where they were in the mid-1980s. From today's vantage point, it is patently clear that the high ratios of the late 1980s were signs of enormously inflated speculative bubbles. When we also take into account recent trends in interest rates, moreover, we find that asset prices have been deflating in parallel with a downturn in interest rates. Ordinarily, asset prices increase when interest rates are in decline. From this perspective, as well, the only way we can explain the falling prices is by postulating the puncturing of bubbles.

But while it has now become clear to everybody that speculative bubbles became inflated, this was not widely understood while asset prices were rising. On the contrary, the idea that there might be excessive speculation in either the stock market or the real-estate market was generally denied in the second half of the 1980s.

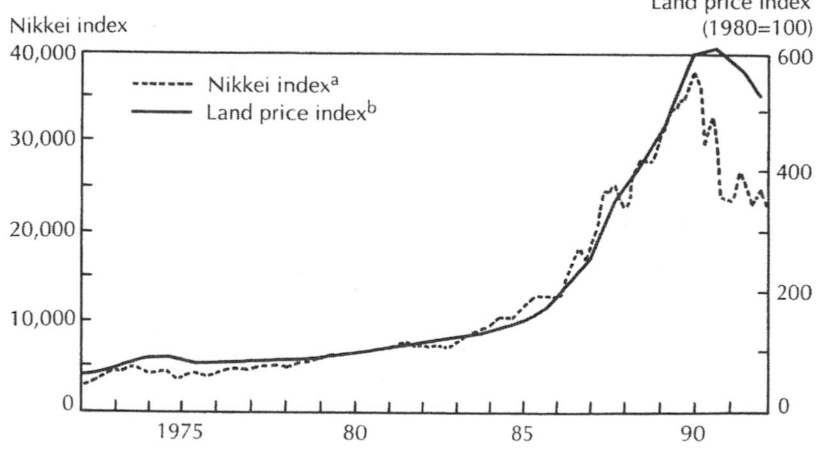

Figure 1. Trends in stock and land prices

Notes: a. Nikkei average of 225 selected shares on the Tokyo Stock Exchange
b. Commercial land prices in the six largest cities.

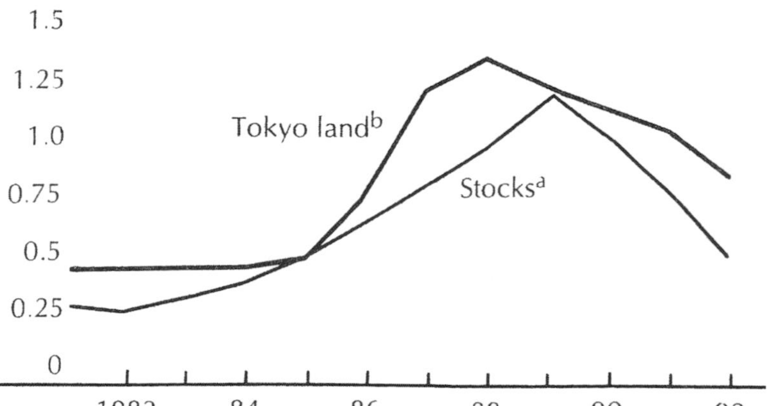

Figure 2. Ratio of the total value of stocks and Tokyo residential land to GDP

Notes: a. Ratio to nominal GDP of the market value of all shares listed on the first section of the Tokyo Stock Exchange as of June each year.
b. Ratio to nominal GDP of midyear residential land values calculated as arithmetic averages of year-end figures from national accounts statistics through 1990; the 1991 and 1992 figures are extrapolations based on the 1990 figure and Tokyo metropolitan government surveys.

An advertisement that Nomura Securities—Japan's largest broker—ran in newspapers and magazines around the world at the end of 1988 captured this viewpoint eloquently. The ad said that perceiving Japanese stock prices as being too high was like clinging to the Ptolemaic theory of the earth as the center of the universe; it urged anybody holding this antiquated view to make a Copernican revolution in thinking. In effect, the message was that the new age required a whole new way of thought, and in this new paradigm, rising share prices should be considered natural.

Not just securities houses and real-estate companies, but even economists were trumpeting similar views. Among the academic arguments, one was that Tokyo's land prices were rising because of easy credit and the extreme concentration of people and businesses in the city, and another was that share prices were riding high in anticipation of the future growth of the Japanese economy.

Much the same point can be made by a count of the number of articles in the business daily *Nihon Keizai Shimbun* and its sister publications in which the word *bubble* appeared in the sense of a financial bubble. The number of such articles was only three in 1986, one in 1987, four in 1988, and eleven in 1989, and generally the subject was not inflated stock and land prices, but bubbles in currency markets. But the number rose to 194 in 1990 and then jumped all the way to 2,546 in 1991; so far in 1992 (as of the end of October) there have been 3,475 such articles. In other words, during the period when stock and land prices were exploding, these phenomena were not being called bubbles. At the time, it was hard for most people to imagine that prices would fall back down. Indeed, this is precisely why the bubbles inflated. As is always the case, it was not until the bubbles began to deflate that their existence came to be recognized.

Did the Bubbles Contribute to Growth?

That the bubbles produced desirable results is not something people say these days—at least not in public. This was not the case while asset prices were rising, however. The unprecedented profits raked in by securities and real-estate firms were not the only benefits people talked about. Arguments to the effect that rising asset prices were desirable for the economy and for the public were put forth from a variety of perspectives. One view was that the only real problem created by the rising asset values themselves was the fact that most people were not sharing in the profits. Such was the argument advanced by the economist Miyao Takahiro, who characterized the period as follows:

> What is occurring [in Japan in the 1980s] is none other than a paradigm shift from a "flow" economy to a "stock" economy. . . . When reality is examined through the lens of the new paradigm, one can correctly perceive what is truly normal and what is an irregular change that deviates from the norm. . . . With the new way of thinking, the beneficial aspects of rising land prices can be properly appreciated. [In such a world,] the optimum way to invest the family's assets may be to purchase and rent out a condominium in a regional city with good real-estate opportunities and to live in a rented apartment in central Tokyo, where many high-paying jobs are found.[1]

Similarly, the group of economists calling themselves the Forum for Policy Innovation advanced a proposal for the "securitization of real estate." In their view, problems at home and abroad were being caused by the scarcity of investment opportunities to effectively utilize the assets being accumulated in Japan; they urged the creation of a market for new financial products giving small investors with limited funds a way to participate in the real-estate market.[2]

There was widespread support for the view that rising asset prices contribute to economic growth. In fact, even orthodox economic theory acknowledges that such price increases can speed up growth for a number of reasons. For one thing, they may have a "wealth effect" on consumer spending, which means that as the value of stocks and other assets go up, the propensity to consume moves to a higher level. For another, they bring down corporate fundraising costs and can thereby spur investment in plants and equipment.

Rising stock prices facilitate the raising of funds through equity financing; that is, the issue by companies of stocks, convertible bonds, or warrant bonds. Economists also pointed out that because land is often used as collateral for loans in Japan, companies owning land can, when its price appreciates, borrow more money, using these funds for new facilities or overseas investments.

As if in confirmation of points like these, the asset inflation was accompanied by a vigorous expansion. After the economy overcame the *endaka* (strong yen) recession of 1986—a slump triggered by the yen's rise—it grew at a relatively fast 5 percent clip from 1987 to 1990. As shown in the table, a capital spending boom began in FY 1988 (April 1988 to March 1989), and for three consecutive years investments in plants and equipment recorded double-digit growth. Such a high level of investment was reminiscent of the economy's performance during the rapid-growth era of the 1960s. Meanwhile, automobile sales, which normally run at about 3 million cars a year, surged to 5 million in 1989 and 1990.

When we consider the inflation of asset prices with trends like these in mind, it seems quite possible that the higher prices made a major contribution to economic growth. Actually, however, the precise causal relationship between these phenomena is not all that clear. The authors of the 1989 economic white paper carried out an empirical analysis of the wealth effect's impact on consumer spending, and using the results of their study, one can calculate that in the latter half of the 1980s, the effect accounted for 10 percent of the average annual growth in private final consumption. While this figure might be considered a fairly large contribution, it also tells us that the wealth effect was not the sole cause of the spending spree during this period. More than that, it is doubtful whether the escalating land prices had much of a wealth effect at all.

A more important issue is whether the asset inflation played a role in the capital-spending boom. It is clear that rising share prices did indeed contribute to an increase in equity financing, which lowered corporate fundraising costs. (It is said that the cost of raising funds through equity financing was 2.0 to 2.5 percent.) But the evidence indicates that most of the funds raised in this manner were allocated to financial investments, not to plants and equipment. They were funneled via financial institutions into speculative real-estate investments, and when land prices then rose further, adding to the unrealized capital gains of landowning corporations, share prices moved yet higher. As this money game continued, stock and land prices spiraled upward.

As this brief review suggests, the rising asset prices gave a boost to the economic growth rate, but their impact was not that significant. One cannot assert that the sustained expansion of the late 1980s would not have occurred in the absence of asset inflation. But one *can* state with confidence that the bubbles had powerful negative effects, as I will now discuss.

Ill-Fated Gamblers and Lucky Homeowners

The first problem was the spread of the gambler's mentality. Inflated asset prices enabled quite a few investors to amass vast fortunes. When people playing money games can rake in profits that are an order of magnitude larger than those from ordinary income flows, their sense of values is thrown out of kilter. If it becomes advantageous to devote oneself to these games rather than to live by the sweat of one's brow, the will to work will be seriously undermined. And when companies can earn portfolio profits exceeding the returns from their main lines of business, research and development and other low-profile activities will be neglected. Such conditions cannot be considered healthy. The increases in the aggregate value of land and stocks between 1986 and 1989 equaled or exceeded nominal GDP. If this situation had persisted, the entire nation would probably have fallen captive to the gambler's mentality.

As the bubbles began to burst, the deleterious effects of this mentality were manifested in even more dramatic fashion. To many speculators, the collapse in prices meant ruin, especially if they had been funding their speculation with borrowed money. This was clearly demonstrated by the fate of the "bubble companies" that had gone too far in taking out loans to finance real-estate deals. After the bubbles began to burst at the

Major Economic Indicators, Fiscal Years 1985–91

FY	Annual growth rates (percent)			Current account balance ($ billion)
	Gross national expenditures	Plant & equipment investment	Housing investment	
1985	4.8	12.2	2.7	55.0
1986	2.9	3.0	10.6	94.1
1987	4.7	8.6	26.3	84.5
1988	6.0	16.8	4.9	77.2
1989	4.4	14.6	1.0	53.4
1990	5.7	12.1	4.9	33.7
1991	3.5	3.0	-11.3	90.2

Source: Economic Planning Agency data.

start of the 1990s, various scandals were exposed to the public eye. The scandal- and debt-ridden Itoman Shōji, a medium-sized trading company, saw a variety of its shady dealings come to light; Fuji, Tokai, and other banks were revealed to have engaged in improper lending activities; the big securities houses were caught compensating their favored clients for stock-market losses; and various shady deals involving speculator groups and gangsters came to light. The corruption was so extensive that it became difficult to find a financial institution that had not been tainted.

In the case of shares, nobody suffers injury as long as a price climb continues. In the case of land, however, a trend of appreciation can be quite damaging. Land is, after all, a vital resource for economic activity and human life. The biggest problem caused by the land-price spiral of the 1980s was that housing in large cities grew so expensive that families became unable to buy homes using income earned solely from work. With the price of real estate skyrocketing, the relationship between the "haves" and the "have-nots" began to display peculiar aspects. Among the stories that people came to tell, one was of executives of major corporations who could not afford to buy housing, even though some of their subordinates were in possession of homes worth hundreds of millions of yen.

The increase in land prices was not evenly distributed across Japan. Different rates of increase further widened the existing price disparities between cities and the countryside and between centrally located and peripheral urban districts. As a result, huge differentials emerged even among the "haves" in the value of their homes. Although buying a home or inheriting one has nothing to do with gambling, the possibility of acquiring a home came to depend on two factors in which luck is involved: whether one had made the purchase before housing prices spiraled out of reach, or whether one was in a position to acquire a home through inheritance. In this context, the worth of the urban worker's labor became a much smaller factor in home acquisition.

As long as increases in land prices properly reflect changes in the economy, they send accurate signals on how to achieve the optimum distribution of resources. But when prices are bloated by a bubble in the land market, they cause an undesirable resource distribution.

A China Syndrome in the Financial System

If the damage from the speculative investments that failed when asset prices collapsed had been limited to the real-estate industry and to those companies that had engaged in *zai-tech*—the fancy "financial technology" that portfolio managers were applying in search of easy profits—the overall economy would not have suffered seriously. The problem was that financial institutions had become deeply entangled in the excesses. Because banks had provided most of the funds used for speculation, they were saddled with bad debts when the investments turned sour.

A precise estimate of the total amount of nonperforming loans cannot be made. Disclosure requirements for banks are inadequate, and in any event not even the bankers know the full extent of their losses, since their problems have only just begun. Based on a few assumptions, however, I would estimate the total debts to be in the vicinity of ¥30 trillion, of which perhaps ¥10 trillion cannot be recovered by selling collateral. Compared with the net operating profits of all Japanese banks from their principal businesses (¥3.7 trillion in fiscal 1991), these are enormous sums. Considerable time will be needed to write off the uncollectable loans using profits.

Financial institutions used to be protected from bad loans by the unrealized capital gains in their vast stock portfolios. In September 1989, for instance, the total of these capital gains at Japan's "city banks" (big commercial banks with branches nationwide), long-term credit banks, and trust banks was approximately ¥62 trillion. These latent profits have been disappearing with the stock market crash, however, and it is said that if the Nikkei average drops to 13,000 points, the unrealized capital gains of the city banks will turn into losses. This would pose serious problems for the management of banks, and some might even go under. The financial order is strong enough to withstand the bankruptcy of some individual banks, but it would be endangered if depositors became so nervous that runs on banks began. And even the fear of this sort of development might drive share prices down, further weakening banks. Back in mid-August, when the Nikkei average was sliding toward the 14,000 level, the Japanese economy was probably not far from just such a vicious circle.

The financial system serves as the foundation of a country's economy. If we liken it to the core of a nuclear reactor, its collapse can be compared to a meltdown. It is said that the consequences of a genuine meltdown would be far more devastating than people imagine. In the phenomenon known as "China syndrome," chunks of extraordinarily hot nuclear fuel would burn their way through the reactor's floor and continue on down, melting even the rocks in the ground. Similarly, a collapse of the financial system would have ramifications going far beyond what people imagine. Especially in Japan, which has not experienced the total collapse of a single bank in the years since World War II, the consequences would be serious.

The response to the bad-loan problem has just begun. Over the next several years the Japanese economy will be paying a huge price to put banks back on their feet.

The Role and Responsibility of the Bankers

When we inquire into the causes of the bubbles, we come first to the issue of bankers' morals. Bank managers are being severely criticized for not having conducted strict screenings of loan projects and for having rushed to engage in a loan competition in order to reap fat profits. While banks are private businesses, they also perform a public function by serving as clearing institutions. Given this public side of their character, they cannot duck the charge that they went overboard in focusing their management on generating profits. It goes without saying that banks must be called to task for those instances in which they broke their own rules by, for instance, extending improper loans. In a similar vein, real-estate firms that engaged in reckless land speculation and companies that became engrossed in money games need to reflect on their actions. All of this was clearly problematic.

Much of such behavior can be condemned only with the benefit of hindsight, however. People cannot easily exercise self-restraint when an opportunity to earn huge profits comes knocking. The actors in all of history's financial bubbles have exhibited this weakness. Bankers were desperately trying to find borrowers in the latter half of the 1980s, as corporations were doing more of their financing by themselves at a time when the authorities were implementing an ultra-easy money policy. From the viewpoint of each individual bank, it may have been only natural to promote real-estate deals, which promised handsome returns. Within companies as well, financial personnel would have been considered incompetent had they failed to look into the merits of equity financing at a time when stock prices were rising.

Granted, the management philosophies of the time deserve to be criticized, and businesspeople must reflect on their mistakes. That alone will not resolve the problems, however. Viewed from the perspective of economic theory, our need is to clarify the macroeconomic conditions and economic mechanisms that caused the bubbles to form.

Major changes in money flows were at work in the background. Since the bullish stock market had greatly lowered financing costs, big businesses became enthusiastic about equity financing, and they made active use of the capital market. Between 1985 and 1990 Japan's corporations raised as much as ¥91 trillion on the capital market, mostly in the 1987–89 period (¥58 trillion). They also borrowed ¥185 trillion from banks and secured ¥130 trillion using other means, bringing their fund-raising total over these six years to more than ¥400 trillion. But they did not invest the bulk of this money in plants and equipment. On the contrary, 64 percent of the total (¥258 trillion) was put into financial investments, such as time deposits, the discretionary investment accounts known as *tokkin*, and trust funds.

At the same time, many companies were weaning themselves off their heavy reliance on bank financing. This trend was particularly evident among large corporations in the manufacturing sector, which reduced the share of bank loans in their total financing from 59 percent to 34 percent. The total amount of their borrowing from banks also went down. With the loss of this business, the banks found themselves with an excess of funds on hand, forcing a shift in their lending away from big businesses, especially manufacturers, and toward small businesses and the real-estate industry.

The increase in real-estate loans was pronounced. As of the end of 1984, Japan's financial institutions had ¥23 trillion out on loan to the real-estate business, but between 1985 and 1990 they increased this figure by ¥33 trillion. In addition to this direct financing, indirect lending through so-called nonbank financial institutions was also channeled into real estate. The amount of these loans from 1985 to 1990 is estimated at ¥11 trillion, bringing the total increase to ¥44 trillion.

Drawing on these fund flows, the real-estate industry invested an estimated ¥28 trillion in land during this period. In addition, it invested a cumulative total of ¥11 trillion in fixed assets (such as buildings) and ¥9 trillion in securities. There was much talk at the time about "land sharks," who put together large tracts by badgering reluctant homeowners into selling their houses and moving out, and about "land churners," who sold and resold single plots to rake in commissions. The speculative nature of the era was also evident in the enthusiasm for developing resorts throughout Japan and for erecting buildings housing tiny condominiums, which were presented to the public as offering an excellent investment opportunity.

The Beneficiaries of Financial Liberalization

The government's moves to liberalize financial markets were an important cause of the altered money flows. These moves began with the introduction of certificates of deposit in May 1979. Then, in the 1980s, interest rates on large deposits were deregulated by stages. The first deposits with market-linked interest rates were introduced in March 1985, and in October of that year the rates on large time deposits of ¥1 billion or more were freed from control.

Financial institutions set the interest rates on deregulated products above the rates on regulated products, giving those companies with the wherewithal to use the deregulated instruments an opportunity to earn greater financial returns. This incentive marked the opening phase in the use of *zai-tech* strategies. According to a study by the Japan Development Bank, the rate of return on the financial assets of large corporations reached nearly 8 percent around 1986.[3] Against this, the cost level when raising funds through equity financing was in the vicinity of 2 percent. What this meant was that companies could rake in financial profits simply by moving funds from one place to another. The fact that firms came to neglect their core businesses in their infatuation with money games was undeniably problematic. But where the problems really began was in these sorts of abnormal financial conditions.

From the vantage point of banks, the deregulation of interest rates raised the cost of acquiring funds. Nevertheless, banks did not move the interest rates on their loans to a higher level. To offset the higher fundraising cost, they opted instead to shift their focus to loans promising higher rates of return. This decision, coupled with the desertion of their big corporate clients, contributed to the stepped-up financing of the real-estate industry.

In the meantime, the phased deregulation of interest rates was slow to work its way down to small deposits. Interest on the small accounts of household depositors remained controlled, preventing most people from earning the kind of interest they could have earned in a deregulated market. Corporations were thus doubly blessed. Not only could they put their own money into products with market interest rates, but through the banking system, they could acquire at low cost the funds that households were putting into regulated deposits. All this enabled companies to implement capital-spending programs inexpensively and, by accumulating debts as well as assets, to record huge profits on their balance sheets.

Easy money was another cause of the new fund flows. As shown in figure 3, the monetary authorities left the official discount rate at 5.0 percent for slightly longer than two years starting from October 1983, then cut the rate by steps until it reached a record low of 2.5 percent in February 1987. This virtually rock-bottom rate was left in place until May 1989.

The unprecedented loosening of the monetary reins was thought to be necessary for curbing the rapid appreciation of the yen in and after 1985. Changes in the yen–dollar rate inherently should cause a clash between the interests of producers (that is, exporters) and of consumers. When the yen goes up, producers are hurt by a slump in exports, but consumers should be helped by lower prices on imported goods. Nevertheless, many companies did not object to the yen's steep rise, and that was because they were in a position to siphon off the exchange-rate gains on imports before they reached retail outlets. At the time, Japan lacked an adequate system for passing the benefits of the rising yen on to the consumer. Herein we find another of the structural distortions that inflated the bubbles.

The economic mechanisms here might be put in the following terms: The yen appreciates as a result of elevated productivity rates. Ordinarily one result should be lower prices for imported products, which would reward workers for their hard labor, but in fact producers and distributors snare the gains, thereby earning fatter profits and becoming encouraged to participate in money games. Seeing the large profits companies are earning, players in the stock market bid up the prices of these companies' shares, and this makes equity financing increasingly attractive to corporate managers. The fundraising on the securities market generates more money for *zai-tech* investment, much of which is funneled via banks into speculative real-estate deals. Land prices then follow share prices up, and both receive a further boost from an easy money policy designed to curb the yen's climb.

In such ways the hard-working and frugal

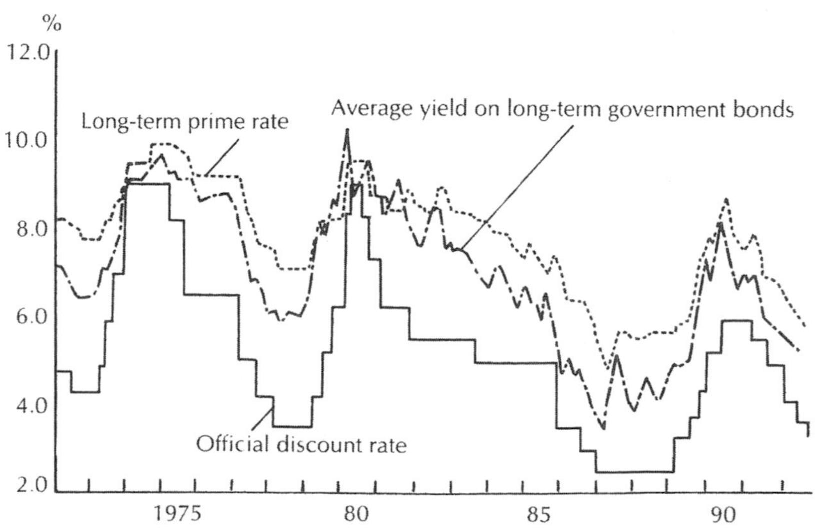

Figure 3. Trends in interest rates

individual Japanese were prevented from enjoying either lower prices or higher interest rates on their savings; all they got for their labors was a land-price spiral. And because extraordinary financial measures will be needed for disposing of the bad debts banks are saddled with, the public will be forced to bear additional burdens for some time to come.

A New Type of Recession?

What effects have plunging asset prices had on the real economy, which went into a slump early in the 1990s? The general assumption is that these effects have been disastrous. One development that has received much comment is a credit crunch, which is said to have resulted from the stock market crash coupled with the capital-adequacy requirements stipulated by the Bank for International Settlements. The BIS requirements obligate major banks to maintain their capital-to-assets ratio above a certain level. Among the components of capital, banks can include a certain percentage of their unrealized capital gains on stocks, and for many Japanese banks, this component was pivotal. But when share prices went into free fall, the value of this capital diminished. It is said that banks were left in a position where, in order to meet the BIS rule, they had no choice but to cut back on lending and thereby compress their assets. And this credit crunch is thought to have curbed capital spending and other economic activities.

Commentators have also been saying that the asset deflation has damaged the real economy through a reverse wealth effect, higher fundraising costs, and other such routes. Needless to say, the mechanisms involved here are the opposite of those that were being discussed when asset prices were inflating. Building on points like these, some even argue that the current recession is of a new type; in addition to being a regular downturn in the business cycle, it has been aggravated by long-term structural shifts. The economist Miyazaki Yoshikazu, a proponent of this view, has labeled the ongoing slump a "combined recession."[4]

Certainly, growth in the money supply has been feeble. In fact, the money supply contracted by 0.4 percent in the year up to September 1992. And equally obviously, asset prices have undergone an unprecedented decline. At first glance, accordingly, it seems reasonable to conclude that constraints on the supply of funds are holding down corporate spending and other activities. Furthermore, it is probably true that the plunge in stock prices has reduced consumer spending and that corporate fundraising costs have increased because equity financing is no longer an option.

Still, it is hard to believe that these factors were the fundamental causes of the recession. After all, powerful cyclical factors have also been present, and they have cooled off investment demand. As noted above, the second half of the 1980s witnessed a spectacular expansion, and outlays for plants and equipment, consumer durables, and housing were going strong. As a result, holdings of all these items rose to high levels. A period of inactivity in investment is to be expected until these stocks return to normal. What is involved here is the economy's "stock adjustment mechanism." There is nothing novel about this mechanism as such, but insofar as the scale of the adjustments needed is extremely large, considerable time will be required before the downturn runs its course.

In this way it seems soundest to conclude that demand-side factors, notably the slowdown in both capital investment by companies and purchases of durables by consumers, have lowered the demand for funds, and this in turn has caused the money supply to contract. Rather than saying that banks are cutting back on lending, we should say that conditions are preventing them from loaning out more money even if they want to. Even when other factors are taken into account, it is difficult to believe that the negative consequences of plunging asset prices are having a profound impact on the real economy. While the collapse of the bubbles has undeniably caused serious problems in the financial sector, its direct effects on the real economy have been limited.

We should not overlook the fact that the punctured bubbles will also be having positive effects on economic growth. For example, housing investment will begin to increase as land prices return to a more normal level. The same observation applies to plant investment that requires land purchases.

Furthermore, there are a number of areas where it would have been impossible to sustain normal economic activities over the long term had the bubbles persisted. In this regard, since land acquisition accounts for a considerable percentage of infrastructure expenditures, the sky-high land prices were obstructing the installation of social overhead capital, particularly in large cities.

It would be incorrect to assert that the bursting of the bubbles will lead to the collapse of the economy. On the contrary, the prospects for a sound post-bubble economy will brighten only after the bubbles have been completely deflated.

Steps to Prevent Future Bubbles

The tales of the incidents of financial euphoria throughout history all bear close resemblance. And with hindsight, most appear quite foolish. Nonetheless, bubbles continue to appear time and again because as long as the speculation continues, those who engage in it can make money. This is the essential character of the bubble phenomenon. The possibility that bubbles will swell again in Japan cannot be ruled out. At the very least, it will be difficult to totally prevent prices in the stock market from inflating abnormally.

Insofar as land is such a vital resource for human life, though, we should make every effort to prevent it from again becoming an object of speculation. Deterring another land-price spiral will be an important issue in future economic policy.

This time around, the initial measures adopted to curb rising land prices were primarily directed at the symptoms rather than the causes. A classic example is the system of designating districts for the close monitoring of land prices. Introduced in 1987, this system relied on government intervention and guidance to prevent land sales at inflated prices. Had the measures involved been imposed at an earlier stage, they would probably have been more effective in cooling down the speculative fever. Even so, they were not designed to eliminate the causes of rising prices, and thus were nothing more than stopgap measures. Judged in terms of their worth in preventing a future bubble in the land market, they must be deemed insufficient and inappropriate.

Land serves as a vehicle for speculation in Japan because of distortions in the tax system. In this light, rationalizing the tax system is the most essential step for preventing another land-price bubble. Early during the last bout of asset-price inflation, the authorities slapped a higher capital gains tax on those who sell land after holding it for only a short period of time. But there is a risk that the burden of this tax could be transferred to the buyer, in which case it would tend to push up prices. Furthermore, this tax might have the effect of freezing sales in the land market. The problem in the tax system is that because property taxes and other levies on land are too low, people are motivated to hold land as an asset. Recently a tax on landholding was introduced to remedy this defect, and it marks a step in the right direction. But because the new tax has a low rate and limited scope, it cannot serve as a bulwark against the recurrence of bubbles.

Monetary policy has great influence over trends in asset prices. The recent bubbles were triggered by an easy-money policy, and they were punctured by steps taken to tighten money and impose a ceiling on the total amount of real-estate-related loans. The lesson to be learned from this is that appropriate management of monetary policy will be indispensable for preventing bubbles. In the past, the monetary authorities set targets in relation to the volume of economic flows, keeping their eyes on indicators like the price of goods and services and the level of capital investment. Henceforth they must also make the prevention of excessive fluctuations in asset prices one of their targets.

In addition to this rethinking of measures to prevent future speculative excesses, we should engage in a broad review of Japan's economic structure. Earlier I suggested that the lack of an adequate system for passing the strong yen's benefits on to the consumer played a role in the bubbles. If this is correct, reforms in this area will be helpful. Such structural adjustments may seem a roundabout way of treating the problems before us, but they are nonetheless important.

On observing Japan's slump and the aftereffects of the asset-price deflation, some Westerners have been declaring that the "Japanese age" has ended. They assert that what seemed to be a strong phase of economic growth in the second half of the 1980s was actually an illusion built upon bubbles, and they assume that Japan's prosperity has come to an end now that the bubbles are no more.

I disagree. As discussed earlier, the period of sustained growth was no doubt spurred on by rising asset prices, but it was basically caused by factors in the real economy. More than that, the performance of the Japanese economy rests fundamentally on such factors as the country's advanced level of technology, its well-educated and diligent work force, and its high savings and investment rates. Such aspects of the real economy's structure have not changed much. Admittedly the savings rate is gradually declining, but it remains at a high level. These conditions are likely to persist at least until the end of this century. The challenge we face is one of unleashing the latent potential of the economy in order to achieve a number of goals.

First, we must actively promote projects to improve the everyday environment. As is widely recognized, the area where Japan is lagging the furthest is in infrastructure to upgrade the quality of life in large cities. The degree of crowding on commuter trains and subways has reached inhumane proportions, and the quality of housing and related facilities remains lower than in North America and Europe despite recent improvements. Japan today has sufficient overall resources and economic might to carry out the massive investments needed to improve such conditions. Soaring land prices placed a major obstacle in the way of infrastructure investments, but as these prices return to earth, spending should be greatly increased.

Second, we must see to it that Japan plays the roles expected of it in the new international setting. From an economic perspective, probably its most important role is as a supplier of capital. In this regard, the gigantic external surpluses Japan has been registering are not temporary aberrations related to the bubbles. The black ink in the current account represents a structural trend underpinned by the high level of savings. In fact, to the extent the surpluses were brought down by the investment boom in the late 1980s, they will probably swell again. The task before us is one of determining how our country's economic power can best be used to build a new international order. While continuing to supply capital to developing countries and the United States, Japan must also channel funds to the former communist countries, where the demand for capital is on the rise. Various difficulties will be encountered in pursuing objectives like this, and we will need a sound global strategy.

Third, we must prepare for the coming of a graying society. Recently the percentage of the elderly in Japan's population has been increasing, but it is still below the level in Europe. This is a basic cause of Japan's excellent economic performance. In the years to come, however, the share of the elderly will rapidly expand. It is projected that by around the year 2020, Japan will have surpassed every European country to become the nation with the oldest society in the world. This graying process will have serious repercussions in many economic areas. In particular, it will lower the savings rate and thereby markedly diminish Japan's economic power. At the same time, taxes and social security contributions will have to be hiked in order to pay the growing bill for welfare. In these and other areas, we should start preparing our response now.

English version originally published in *Japan Echo* 21, Special Issue (1994): 8–18.

Translated from "Baburu no sōkessan" [The Sum Total of the Bubble], in *Baburu no keizaigaku* [Bubble Economics] (Tokyo: Nikkei Business Publications, 1992), 21–48; slightly abridged.

Notes

1. Miyao Takahiro, *"Sutokku keizai" no jidai: Yutakasa kakutoku e no shohōsen* [The Age of the "Stock Economy": A Prescription for Acquiring Affluence] (Tokyo: Nihon Keizai Shimbunsha, 1989), 49–52. The author goes on to discuss corporate portfolio management in these terms: "Unlike in the flow age, a managerial approach focused narrowly on the company's core business

and aimed at simple objectives for economic flows is no longer viable. No matter whether it is a main business or a side business, what is important is to utilize the total power of managerial resources centered on economic stocks effectively, thereby aiming to maximize total returns" (p. 55).

2. Forum for Policy Innovation, *Sutokku keizai ni okeru yutakasa no jitsugen no tame ni: Fudōsan no shōkenka ni yoru nozomashii toshi kikai no sōshutsu o* [For the Realization of Affluence in a Stock Economy: Creating Desirable Investment Opportunities through the Securitization of Real Estate] (Tokyo: Forum for Policy Innovation, 1990).

3. Japan Development Bank, "80 nendai no manē furō to kongo no kigyō kin'yū" [Money Flows in the 1980s and Corporate Finance in the Future], *Chōsa,* no. 162 (July 1992).

4. Miyazaki Yoshikazu, *Fukugō fukyō* [Combined Recession] (Tokyo: Chūōkōronsha, 1992).

II-(2) Lessons of Japan's Bubble Economy

Itoh Motoshige

Discuss Japan—Japan Foreign Policy Forum, 2010

Two decades have passed since Japan's bubble began to burst in 1990, and throughout this period the economy has been in poor health. It has encountered successive financial crises, experienced price deflation for the first time since World War II, and seen the public debt mushroom, all the while limping along at a very slow growth rate. This has been a bewildering change for a nation that until then was registering spectacular growth. After all, over a period of more than forty years after the war's end, Japan's economy had grown into an entity so weighty that it was even said to have become a threat to the economy of the United States.

Why did a speculative bubble with so much destructive power inflate in the second half of the 1980s, and why has the impact of its deflation lasted so long? These are questions that many economists are still trying to answer. Without doubt, a variety of factors were involved. It is said that a failure in macroeconomic policy management was the cause of the bubble economy, and that when the bubble burst, policymakers again bungled their response. And it is also said that there was basically nothing the government could have done to weather the nation's first full-blown financial crisis of the postwar period. Arguments like these deserve to be carefully examined one by one, but treating all of them would take up more space than is available.

In the following I will instead place the changes in the Japanese economy in a long-range perspective and seek to shed light on where and how, within the historical flow, a bubble inflated in the second half of the 1980s and stagnation set in starting in the 1990s. As I develop this argument, it will become evident that it is useful not just for looking at Japan but also for clarifying points in common with the problems many countries have encountered.

In 1990, when the bubble began to collapse, the baby boom generation's older members were reaching the age of forty-five. Subsequently, large numbers of nonperforming loans accumulated, quite a few financial institutions failed, and Japan got its first taste of price deflation in the postwar period. As the 1990s drew to a close, the baby boomers were moving into their fifties. This was a time when the bubble's collapse ushered in a period of falling prices, and it was also when the Japanese economy moved beyond the stage of fast growth with a youthful population. Japanese society had matured, and the assorted problems associated with an aging population and a declining number of children had to be tackled. This huge shift in demographic structure was intimately related to the nation's experience during the age of the bubble and falling prices.

Actually, quite a few industrially advanced countries are going through a similar transition. Many are countries with their own baby boom generation, and many are experiencing a declining birthrate, with the result that they also have a population growing top-heavy from the swelling ranks of senior citizens. The changes in Japan, though, have been more dramatic. The Japanese economy grew faster during the years of high-tempo growth, and the Japanese population has been aging faster since early in the 1990s, with the birthrate falling further. The speediness of the changes is reflected in the severity of the bubble and the downward trend in prices. In this light, a study of Japan's experience during this period should yield lessons that will be of interest to people in other developed nations.

The High-Growth Model's Bubble Effect

The creation of the bubble economy was not unrelated to Japan's high-tempo postwar development. When we examine the companies that acquired a heavy debt load during the bubble's formation, such as distribution firms and property-related businesses like general contractors, we find that they had been busily acquiring real estate with the help of extensive borrowing from banks. In the case of the distribution industry, chain stores bought land to build new outlets, and if this property rose in value, they used it as collateral for borrowing more money and buying more land. Even at times when the profits from distribution were slim, rising property prices would push up the corporate value of the chains.

As long as property prices continued to climb, this business model offered a very effective method of increasing corporate scale over a short period of time. To be sure, it should have been apparent that the model would break down if property prices stopped rising. The Japanese economy had been enjoying fast growth for a long time, however, and we may say that this threw corporate behavior off course.

Distortions in Japan's financial markets were another key cause of the bubble's formation. Inherently, it is not normal for a big business in distribution or a property-related industry to go calling on a bank when it wants to raise a large chunk of cash. As a financial system grows more sophisticated, major corporations become able to raise all the funds they need by issuing corporate bonds and other types of securities, which permit them to cut back on bank borrowing. Unfortunately, Japan in those days still had the financial markets of a newly industrialized country, and the weight of bank borrowing in financing remained large.

When the purpose of financing is to complete a real-estate deal, companies ordinarily need to utilize the methods provided by securitization. They raise funds broadly, collecting money from numerous investors. This makes it unnecessary for firms whose main business is in distribution or real estate to provide excessive padding to their balance sheets. General investors, meanwhile, gain the opportunity to put some of their funds into property-related businesses. In the 1980s, however, there were practically no arrangements available in Japan for securitizing real estate, and even large corporations had no choice but to rely on banks for financing property transactions.

A particularly explosive bubble formed as the combined result of the myth of fast growth and financial markets of the emerging-country type. The problem of the bubble was then compounded by a monetary policy that was unable to respond properly. When the bubble was growing in the second half of the 1980s, consumer prices in general were not rising very rapidly, even though property and stock prices were skyrocketing. Orthodox monetary policy teaches that, in the absence of fast inflation of ordinary prices, there is no need to pull back on the monetary reins. In this respect, Japan's situation was like the one the United States encountered midway through the twenty-first century's first decade, when moves to tighten credit were put off despite a boom in property prices. The delay came about because US consumer prices were not rising very rapidly at that time.

Mishandling the Bubble's Collapse

Looking back from today's perspective, we can see that the Japanese government's response to the collapse of the bubble created numerous problems. By 1998, eight years after the bubble started to deflate, several major financial institutions had gone bankrupt, including Yamaichi Securities, Hokkaido Takushoku Bank, and the Long-Term Credit Bank of Japan. This was a period when a mountain of bad debts cast a shadow over the economy. The government failed to come to grips with the problem, however, and the financial crisis of the late 1990s was the result. It was not until the 2002–2003 period, during the administration of Prime Minister Koizumi, that work on clearing away the bad debts began to make substantial progress. More than ten years had passed with little being done.

This was Japan's first postwar encounter with such a huge pile of nonperforming loans, and the government did not have arrangements in place for the disposal of the debts. It was quite some time after the bubble began to deflate that the authorities worked out systems for using the power of the state to recover nonperforming assets (the Resolution and Collection Corporation) and support the reconstruction of companies buried under bad debts (the Industrial Revitalization Corporation of Japan). Furthermore, Japan was short of the human resources required for writing off bad debts, recovering assets, and putting companies back on their feet.

As I noted, the Japanese financial system continued to rely excessively on banks for collecting deposits and providing financing. Reforming this financial setup became a crucial task after the bubble burst, but struggling financial institutions were foundering, banks were engaged in realignment through mergers, and arranging a reform paving the way for the introduction of market-based financial methods, as symbolized by property-backed securities, took time. It is fair to say that because such changes and reforms were slow to make progress, the bad debts turned into a veritable quagmire.

To deal with the slump that ensued as the bubble lost air, the government relied on conventional fiscal and monetary tools. On the fiscal front, the authorities applied a stimulus by cutting taxes and stepping up spending on public works, and on the monetary side, they made cuts in the policy interest rate. While such macroeconomic policies were needed, in themselves they were inadequate for getting to the root of the problems. Fundamental changes in financial markets and systems were also required. It was, in other words, a half-baked stimulus program, and it had a damaging effect. It persuaded financial institutions and debt-ridden firms to postpone radical restructuring. We should further note that the government debt ballooned as a result of the fiscal stimulus, and this placed a severe constraint on policy management over the ensuing years.

Is Fiscal Stimulus the Answer to Deflation?

At the end of the 1990s, in the midst of the prolonged slump and bad debts, Japan found itself stumbling into a period of deflation. None of the major countries, not just Japan, had experienced such a situation during the years following World War II. For the government and the corporate sector, which were carrying a heavy debt load, the deflation had the effect of further swelling the size of their debts. When it became evident that prices were likely to continue on a downward path for some time, a deflation mindset proliferated, and this outlook had a depressive effect on consumer spending, real-estate investment, and plant and equipment investment.

It is by no means easy to bring deflation to a stop through the use of monetary tools. The policy interest rate had already been lowered almost all the way to zero, leaving no room for bold action to push interest rates down. In a situation of virtually zero nominal interest rates coupled with deflation, real interest rates rise at the speed of the price decline. Such is deflation's negative impact on economic activity.

Viewed from the vantage point of classical Keynesian economics, Japan had fallen into a "liquidity trap" in which cuts in interest rates were not possible. Only vigorous fiscal stimulus can rescue an economy caught in a liquidity trap, we are told. The government began to implement a rescue effort of this type around 1998, during the administration of Prime Minister Obuchi, but it had only a limited effect. Worse than that, it wound up further enlarging the government debt and narrowing the scope of fiscal policy freedom.

In order to understand why prices began to deflate in the first place, we need to examine the macroeconomic supply-demand gap during the period after the bubble burst. For more than ten years starting from around 1992, aggregate supply was larger than aggregate demand in Japan, creating what is called a deflationary gap. (Statistics for 2010 show that the gap is still present. With the exception of the few years of global overheating around 2005, it has persisted from 1992 to the present day.) A deflationary gap means that the economy has an excessive supply (demand shortage), which produces deflationary pressures and can initiate or perpetuate a downward trend in prices. Bad-debt problems and financial crises can spur the formation of deflationary conditions, but the primary cause of

Japan's falling prices was without doubt the long-term presence of this deflationary gap.

Why should the gap have persisted for so long? The graying of Japanese society is one of the factors involved, and another is the declining birthrate. Despite the massive changes in the structure of the Japanese economy, many companies continued on as before. Because they had too many facilities and too much production capacity, the economy was left with a tendency toward excessive supply. Many Japanese people, meanwhile, were conscious of their advancing years, and they were inclined to hold back on spending. We should see these as structural factors behind the deflationary gap.

On giving thought to the gap's background, we can appreciate that it could not be easily closed through the continued application of fiscal stimulus. Stepped-up government spending can offset a demand shortage over the short term, but the government cannot continue to run up fiscal deficits year after year to cover a shortfall in demand likely to last a long time. Here we find the reason why the stimulus packages the government assembled did not function well as a remedy for deflation.

Groping in the Dark on the Monetary Front

If there is a limit to what can be accomplished using fiscal policy, might not monetary policy offer a more effective way of curing deflation? We may view the policy responses of the Bank of Japan from the second half of the 1990s until today as a trial-and-error process aimed at fashioning a set of tools for this.

Traditional monetary policy employs a short-term interest rate—the policy interest rate—as a means of adjusting the funds circulating in the money market and influencing interest rates in general, and the BOJ has also relied on this orthodox tool, as mentioned earlier. Unfortunately, there are limits to what it can do when deflationary conditions take hold. With an economy caught in a liquidity trap and interest rates at rock bottom, making further cuts in interest rates is not possible. The BOJ found itself in a situation it had never encountered in the postwar period, one that not even the central banks of other countries had experience with. We should not be surprised that BOJ officials were perplexed about what should be done. At one point they lifted the policy interest rate overly hastily, hoping to break free of the zero interest-rate fetters, but the result was that the economy descended into an even more serious deflationary state.

In this context, some of those on the academic side began calling for a more radical monetary policy. They urged the BOJ to deliver a signal to the market containing a commitment to pursue a fixed policy course until Japanese prices were rising at a certain pace. The classic example of this kind of policy is inflation targeting. The central bank picks a number as an inflation target and informs the public that it will implement whatever policy measures are required to attain the target. This can have a major impact on the market's expectations of inflation. It is said that when one of the causes of falling prices is the widespread presence of a deflation mindset, such a policy stance can effectively reshape inflationary expectations.

The pros and cons of having the BOJ adopt inflation targeting are still being debated in Japan. Some economists have voiced negative opinions. Among them, some say that monetary management should not be aimed only at prices, while others point to a variety of problems that could occur if an inflation target were set while there were still questions about whether it would, in fact, engender an upward price trend. As a practical problem, however, the BOJ did not have the option of sticking to its conventional policy course. It had no choice but to experiment with unorthodox monetary tools, trying out methods it had never used before. One of them goes by the name of quantitative easing. Briefly stated, this is an attempt to stimulate financial markets by supplying them with extra liquidity even as interest rates remain in the vicinity of zero. The BOJ also began experimenting with statements clarifying the length of time it would follow its policy course, declaring that it would adhere to a stance of zero interest rates or quantitative easing until it had confirmed that prices were rising. This was a policy with a time limit, and in this sense it had an inflation-targeting nature.

The lessons the BOJ learned from the late 1990s on have influenced the way monetary authorities in leading countries responded to the global financial crisis triggered by the bankruptcy of Lehman Brothers in 2008. The US Federal Reserve, the European Central Bank, and other central banks boldly embarked on their own course of quantitative easing. Concerned that their countries, too, might descend into deflation, they aggressively bolstered their balance sheets. By then it had been recognized that the orthodox tool of adjusting interest rates to fine-tune liquidity in the money market was inadequate for resolving a major financial crisis and preventing a deflationary slide.

The importance of monetary policy has increased since World War II in the economic management of the leading countries. Once well-functioning financial markets are in place, they become closely linked through arbitrage among them. Central banks target their action mainly at the money market, but the adjustments made there spread speedily into other markets through a variety of channels. The linkages among financial markets support the effectiveness of monetary policy. They are apt to be severed, however, in the confusion of a big financial crisis like a bubble's collapse or the Lehman Shock. In that case the effects of the central bank's moves in the money market will not necessarily ripple quickly into the markets for commercial paper, government bonds, property-backed securities, foreign exchange, and so forth.

When the global financial crisis began, accordingly, it was recognized that central banks would have to do more than manipulate interest rates in the money market; they needed to intervene directly in, for instance, the markets for commercial paper and government bonds. In this way, the Japanese experience offers a way of interpreting the moves by central banks following the Lehman Shock. Central bankers in Japan, the United States, and other countries conducted operations in a number of markets, including those for commercial paper and property-backed securities. The BOJ had been actively buying Japanese government bonds ever since the late 1990s, and it stepped up these operations.

International Ramifications of Japan's Deflation Response

In the ongoing effort to contain deflation, Japan's policy of ultralow interest rates has been kept in place for longer than ten years. When the world's second-largest economy adheres to such an unusual course, naturally it has a major impact on the world economy. In financial markets, interest has focused in particular on what is called the yen carry trade. It involves raising funds in Japan, where interest rates are low, and investing them in countries where interest rates are higher. In the realm of economic theory, interest rates in all countries are supposed to move toward the same level when expectations of changes in exchange rates are taken into account, although some may have a risk premium attached, leaving them higher than others. In the real world, however, differences in nominal interest rates engender flows of funds across borders in many cases.

We should pay special attention to the yen carry trade in and after 2002, when the world economy was expanding briskly while Japanese interest rates remained close to zero. I do not know exactly how much carry trading was going on at the time, but clearly it was of a sufficient size to influence the yen's exchange rate. Carry trading works to weaken the currency borrowed, because carry traders sell the borrowed money after converting it into other currencies. The yen in 1995 was stronger than it had ever been before, but thereafter it lost value. When we measure it using the real effective exchange rate, we find that in 2005 it had fallen to a very low level, the weakest it had been in twenty years.

The weak yen gave Japanese exports an edge in overseas markets, notably those in the West. For the Japanese economy as a whole, the strong export performance was exceedingly good news, and it helped to trigger an upturn after the long demand slump dating from the bubble's collapse. While the speed of the economy's growth remained modest, the upturn became the longest uninterrupted expansion of the postwar period. From the American perspective, what could be seen was a one-way flow of imports arriving from Japan, steadily mounting deficits in the US current account, and reliance on funds brought in from Japan to finance the deficits. The lopsided relationship did not, in the end, become a politically explosive issue, since China was behaving in the same way as Japan, and on a larger scale. It is nonetheless clear, however, that there were close connections between Japan's economic situation and the United States' extraordinary overheating that led to the Lehman Shock.

To be sure, one must doubt that an economic expansion powered in this way was good for the Japanese economy. Even though the Lehman Shock did not trigger a financial crisis in Japan, the business climate turned colder than that in any other developed country when the world economy plunged into recession. That happened because the economy had been relying so heavily on exports to power the expansion. Over the years following the bubble's collapse, not enough had been done to rectify structural problems. Action to correct the pattern of excessive supply and energize the domestic market had been put off.

The downturn that followed in the wake of the global financial crisis has provided a valuable opportunity for rethinking the Japanese economy's structural problems from the bottom up. Whether this nation will be able to survive the difficult times and rebuild a dynamic economy will hinge on whether it can resolutely implement far-reaching reforms to remedy these problems. With the graying of society and the declining birth rate still in progress, work must also go forward on reforming the social security system and restoring health to public finance. For the Japanese economy, the next few years will be a crucial turning point.

English version originally published in *Discuss Japan—Japan Foreign Policy Forum,* no. 1 (Jun.–Jul. 2010).

Translated from an original article in Japanese written for Japan Echo Web (July 2010).

II-(3) The Reality of Financial Reform

The Burden of Bad Loans

Takenaka Heizō

The Structural Reforms of the Koizumi Cabinet, 2008

The problem of Japan's nonperforming loans

Japan's economy recorded a relatively high growth rate of 4.5 percent throughout the 1980s, but after that, from the end of the 1980s onwards, it experienced the so-called economic bubble. From 1985 to 1990, the growth rate was 27.3 percent, while the price of shares suddenly rose by 2.37 times.

However, the price of stocks and land, both considered indicators of favorable economic conditions, dropped drastically in the 1990s, and Japan underwent the collapse of the economic bubble and a resulting serious depression. Throughout the 1990s, the price of stocks dropped by 51 percent, and that of land dropped by 33 percent. During this period, despite the government's large-scale fiscal expenditures, the annual average growth rate of the economy was only 1 percent. This was the reality of the Japanese economy's "lost decade."

At the root of Japan's economic pathology was the "balance sheet" problem. This refers to a state in which the banking sector has a huge amount of bad debt and is unable to effectively perform financial intervention. Meanwhile, the borrower corporations have more loans than they can handle and are unable to pay them back, and are therefore stuck in a state of being unable to develop new business areas. Furthermore, since administration on the part of the financial supervisory authorities was not carried out adequately, the overall picture of the nonperforming debts never became clear. This worsened the lack of transparency in the market as a whole and aggravated anxiety about the direction of the economy, creating a negative cycle.

The opportunity to resolve this issue occurred several times during the 1990s. In 1995, when housing loan companies fell into management difficulties, the government injected ¥685 billion in public funds. However, because the explanation and style with which this was carried out lacked clarity, it resulted in strong criticism from the public, which saw it as an extreme way of rescuing unstable financial institutions. After that, in 1997, several major banks and securities companies collapsed, providing the opportunity for the streamlining of legal frameworks in order to obtain greater stability through the injection of public funds. The injection of public funds on the scale of ¥45 trillion was indeed carried out, and the closure of unprofitable financial institutions was implemented.

However, even after that, the uncertainty in the financial markets remained strong. Once the Financial Services Agency had implemented the injection of capital, it announced that this action had fixed the problem, and solidly maintained this stance. But the market did not see the problem as having been resolved at all, and as a result, there was a dramatic drop in bank shares, in spite of which the Financial Services Agency continued to make claims such as "the banks are sound" and "a financial crisis is impossible."

The Koizumi administration started in 2001. At the end of that year, major bank loans accounted for as much as 8.4 percent of overall nonperforming loans. Unless this problem was resolved, even if the government continued to implement a policy of expanded fiscal spending, Japan's economy had no chance of recovering. That was the view of conscientious experts. However, it was also obvious that, if the disposal of bad debts was continued, some companies would be forced into an untenable position. In this situation, proceeding with resolving the bad-debt issue was an extremely difficult political decision.

The date was February 2, 2002. Nine months had already passed since the inauguration of the Koizumi cabinet. In order to attend the annual meeting of the World Economic Forum, commonly known as the "Davos Conference," in which the world's economic leaders get together, I was staying at the Waldorf-Astoria Hotel in New York.

The participants from around the world, gathered at the Waldorf-Astoria conference hall, listened attentively to discussions about whether Japan would really change under its maverick leader, Prime Minister Koizumi. Undoubtedly, it was a matter of great concern as to whether the world's second-largest economic power would recover or whether it would continue to be a source of instability for the global economy.

In a speech during the forum attended by Paul Krugman and others as panelists, I spoke as follows: "Broadly speaking, there are two kinds of reform that Japan must grapple with. The first is a passive type of reform—'reactive'—and the second is a more aggressive one—'proactive.' The first kind aims at getting rid of the so-called negative legacy that was inherited without any choice. A typical example of that is dealing with the non-performing loans of banks. In contrast, the more active reforms are positive in nature, aiming at adapting to the new era. The postal privatization being advocated by Prime Minister Koizumi is symbolic of those."

When delivering speeches before audiences abroad, I use the expression "reactive" reforms for the passive types of reforms, and "proactive" reforms for the more aggressive ones. I also make the same kind of explanation to educated people who don't have a detailed knowledge of Japan's particular situation, and am able to get them to understand the broad outlines. Needless to say, both types of reform must be pursued simultaneously. Still, the reactive type of reform, above all, required urgent action, without any delay.

Throughout the 1990s, Japan spent more than ¥100 trillion on economic stimulus packages without the economy recovering. The reason for this "lost decade" is none other than the fact that the reactive reforms (i.e., disposing of the bad loans), which ought to have been undertaken first, were postponed. That is precisely why Prime Minister Koizumi, in his first address before the Japanese Diet, also put the problem of clearing up the bad loans at the top of the agenda.

However, in reality, no improvements were made to the bad-loan problem even after Prime Minister Koizumi took office, and newspapers and magazines at the time often mentioned the term "financial crisis" in their headlines. At the forum, as well, many tough questions concentrated on whether Japan, which had been unable to do anything for a whole decade, could really solve the problem: what measures would be taken that would enable the bad debts to be written off?

Unfortunately, as a member of the cabinet at that point, I was unable to confidently offer any counterargument. Despite having been in the cabinet for nine months, and having occasionally tried to raise the issue of dealing with the bad-debt problem during cabinet meetings, the Financial Services Agency (FSA), whose participation was critical, failed to demonstrate a forward-looking posture toward reform.

The supervising authorities held all the solutions to the banks' problems: in this case, the FSA. Only the FSA knew the true extent of the bad-loan situation, and whether the results of the inspections were good or bad. There was no way even for me, the minister of state for economic and fiscal policy, to learn the details of the inspection results. The FSA had absolute authority and control of the information, and not even a cabinet member had any way of laying a finger on it.

Something had to be done about the bad-loan problem, without which there was absolutely no way for the economy to recover. However, because of the nature of the problem, and without the ability to directly address the bad loans, time was simply being frittered away. Without my going inside the supervisory authority—the FSA—and crossing over the "wall of the authorities," I believed the solution of the bad-loan problem was despairingly difficult.

1. Entering the "Wall of the Authorities"

Debt overhang

I joined the cabinet as minister of state for economic and fiscal policy in April 2001. In the cabinet reshuffle of September 2002, I was also given the joint portfolio of minister of state for financial services. At that point, as the minister in charge of the fiscal supervisory authorities, I was finally able to grapple with bank reform, as the so-called point person responsible for the problem of bad loans. Already seventeen months had elapsed since the inauguration of the Koizumi cabinet.

In considering various economic policies as minister of state for economic and fiscal policy, I believed from the very outset that the resolution of the bad-loan problem was something that was absolutely unavoidable. That is why I had Prime Minister Koizumi, in his first general policy speech before the Diet, put the resolution of the bad-loan problem at the top of the agenda for reform.

Western economists often use the term "debt overhang" to signify a situation in which corporations bear excessive loans that can no longer be repaid, sending the whole economy into a state of terrible stagnation. The term especially began to be known among specialists after the appearance of the article "Corporate-Debt Overhang and Macroeconomic Expectations," published in 1995 by Owen Lamont in the *American Economic Review*, and the book *Firms, Contracts, and Financial Structure*, by Oliver Hart, published the same year by Clarendon Press, among others. Indeed, the term "debt overhang" aptly encapsulates the problems faced by the Japanese economy after the bursting of the bubble.

That Japan found itself in a dangerous situation approaching such a systemic risk could be confirmed through various economic indices and reports. Despite that, it was impossible to imagine that the central players in this story—the "main culprits" in the creation of the bad debts; namely, the banks—would take positive action to improve the situation. The 2001 Annual Report on the Japanese Economy and Public Finance contained an intriguing fact: those industrial sectors whose profit margins were increasingly squeezed after the bursting of the bubble—real estate, construction, wholesalers, and so forth—were being lent even more money by Japanese banks. The banks were pouring additional loans into precisely those sectors and corporations whose performance had worsened after the bubble burst, and in the end, increased the size of their bad debts. At the same time, moreover, those corporations and industries that had reformed and were returning to health could not get the funds they needed. The result was a clear vicious circle, affecting the whole economy.

Banks try to "shoot for the moon"

The actions taken by the banks—the central actors in Japan's bad-loan drama—could also be found in the United States in the 1980s during the savings and loan (S&L) crisis. Under normal circumstances, making additional loans to corporations that are already burdened with bad loans, and that lack the ability to repay them, would be considered counter to the commonsense maxim of "maximizing profit" on the part of banks. However, from the standpoint of the Japanese banks already extending such huge loans, if they did not lend extra money to the companies they had initially extended credit to, those companies would go under, only increasing the size of their unrecoverable loans and putting the banks themselves in a precarious position. For that reason, to avoid such a situation, there was a tendency for Japanese banks to take the option of "shooting for the moon"; that is, taking the gamble of making the additional loans and hoping for some "situation" to emerge that would improve things.

In the case of Japanese banks, it is especially difficult for shareholders to carry out due diligence (that is, shareholders of a bank should, under normal circumstances, be in a position to oppose unreasonable lending by that bank). The reason is that the shareholders of Japanese banks are often precisely those corporations to whom they have lent money. Also, the corporate governance of Japanese companies was never very strong in the first place. Accordingly, a situation arises in which not much can be expected from a mechanism allowing the main actors to solve the problem by themselves. The problem only becomes worse with time.

When I was given the responsibility of managing the country's economic and fiscal affairs in my cabinet post, I knew that the disposal of the bad-loan problem was an urgent issue whose resolution could by no means be postponed. Of course, it was not just the problem of the banking sector. It also meant, simultaneously, the need to clean up the balance sheets of those corporations and industries that could not pay back their loans. It was truly an issue that the entire cabinet had to contend with.

In that way, under circumstances in which the main actors involved—the banks—could not settle the bad-loan problem by themselves, it was absolutely necessary for the government as a whole to tackle it, for without the government's participation, there would be no way for the economy to recover. Moreover, I felt that this issue had to be the central obligation of the Koizumi cabinet. Nonetheless, the jurisdiction of the most important sector involved—the banks—fell under the "authorities" known as the Financial Services Agency (FSA). I was unable, in my position, to engage directly with them. For that reason, getting the authorities to move was a big task that I faced from the outset of my time in the Koizumi cabinet.

"Why not serve in two posts?"

As 2001 drew to a close and 2002 rolled around, the basic situation had not changed. The economy began to show some signs of improvement, but on the whole was getting worse. Amidst that, anti-deflationary measures began to gain importance as a focus of attention. Naturally, as one such measure, clearing up the bad-loan problem continued to be an important issue requiring resolution. Shortly after I returned to Japan after attending the 2002 Davos Conference, I visited Prime Minister Koizumi at his official residence, ostensibly to brief him on that trip. The date was February 6, 2002. There, I advised him once again that the most important anti-deflationary measure, still, was to dispose of the bad loans. The prime minister ordered me to write up a memo explaining the kinds of anti-deflationary measures that ought to be considered. The focus of the policy had now started to shift toward dealing with deflation. I got a sense at that time of the resolute determination of Prime Minister Koizumi, as the nation's top leader, to clear up the bad-loan problem. In order to resolve it, something had to be done to force the FSA to take action as the governmental authority in that area. The prime minister himself shared that view. I realized then that surely something could be accomplished as long it had the support of the prime minister.

Things progressed, and by June, a fierce battle was raging over the second "large-boned policy"[1] of the Koizumi cabinet ("Basic Policies for Economic Management and Structural Reform, 2002"). The Japanese economy seemed to have finally bottomed out shortly before then, in March, but there was still a deep sense of sluggishness, dragged down by worries about the banking system.

On June 7, 2002, something happened. At a meeting of the Council on Economic and Fiscal Policy (CEFP), Prime Minister Koizumi was to issue directives about the direction of tax policy, and the whole atmosphere in Kasumigaseki was tense. As a matter of fact, apart from that, I had received a personal call from the prime minister that morning. I was told to keep some time free that evening. He had reserved a table at a restaurant in the main building of the Akasaka Prince Hotel to have dinner with a few very close friends, and I was invited to join them.

Although it was an informal dinner, with just a few guests including myself, the focus of the conversation inevitably moved to the question of what could be done to promote structural reform further. At that time, the markets would not rely upon fiscal policy despite the difficult economic circumstances that prevailed. Moreover, there did not seem to be any anti-deflationary measure that would do the trick. Also, there was no visible progress in the discussion on the reform of the tax system, owing to the rigid stance of the Finance Ministry. As for myself, I believed that the grand premise to all reforms was the need to accelerate the disposal of bad loans.

In the middle of our dinner, one participant raised the banking problem. As a financial expert with detailed knowledge of the financial situation, his talk was permeated with a sense of crisis, as he said that the market had lost all faith, unfortunately, in the policies of the current FSA, and that was why the press was playing up the story of a "financial crisis" (the precarious situation in the financial industry). I had consulted this economist beforehand, back when I had received the directive from Prime Minister Koizumi to seek out appropriate personnel from the private sector.

In the midst of this conversation, the prime minister, who had been absorbed in thought, uttered these words: "Why not serve in two posts?"

At first, I couldn't readily tell what he meant. But then it struck me—maybe the prime minister was considering appointing me as the official in charge of fiscal matters. He surely does come up with some great ideas, I thought. While I could not be absolutely sure at that time, it was only later that I realized that it might have been then that he started to think of having me serve simultaneously as the state minister responsible for economic and fiscal policy and the state minister for financial services. While I had been the one who had been stamping his foot in frustration outside the walls of the FSA for so long, I felt a premonition welling up inside myself—although I was still only in a state of half-belief—that something quite serious might be about to happen to me.

In September 2002, speculation was rife that the prime minister would announce a cabinet reshuffle at the end of the month. Of course, he always kept everything about personnel matters to himself—that was the discernment of someone responsible for making appointments. As for myself, however, I felt that no matter what happened to my position, the Japanese economy would not stand any chance of recovery unless the upcoming cabinet reshuffle was taken as a renewed opportunity to build the framework necessary for the solution of the bad-loan problem. For that purpose, I was mentally prepared to go ahead with every imaginable sort of preparation.

Holding a retreat to develop strategy

In order to resolve the bad-loan problem, three things had to happen simultaneously.

First, the auditing of banks' assets had to be made more rigorous. In other words, it was absolutely necessary to get a grasp of the size of the bad loans, measuring them according to proper standards and without overlooking anything. Moreover, the results had to be publicly announced. Second, banks had to increase their capital adequacy. Banking, after all, is a risky business, and a certain level of equity capital is necessary. Even though that was a legal requirement, the market was awash with rumors that some banks had an insufficient capital adequacy, or that they were about to reach that point in the near future. In order to eliminate such market anxiety, the banks had to enhance their own equity capital ratio—or if that was impossible, get an injection of public funds to do so—or else credit insecurity would result. Third, the governance of the banks needed to be reinforced. After all, the fact that they had made the bad loans in the first place—along with the fact that their profitability was low—was indicative of the banks' poor management. In addition, if there was the slightest chance that inappropriate information disclosure was being made, that would also be impermissible. All of the above points thus focused on the need to tighten the governance of the banks.

The strategy retreat that I conducted with just a handful of my staff members, and the three points that we focused on there, toward a resolution of the bad-loan problem, consistently served as the backbone of the financial revitalization plan that unfolded thereafter.

"Serve concurrently as financial services minister!"

In the political world of September 2002, several developments were happening in relation to Prime Minister Koizumi's first cabinet reshuffle. This was true politics, with people trying to get their rights and interests reflected in public policy, while simultaneously trying to set up an advantageous situation for themselves in personnel terms.

September 30 was the day that the new cabinet would be announced. At 11:30 a.m., a cabinet meeting was held for the ministers to submit their resignations en masse. Then, at 2 p.m., the first new ministers started to be called in. Tango Yasutake, secretary to the prime minister, phoned the ministers' room. Similar to the last time, the entrance to the prime minister's residence was swarming with people. In the prime minister's executive office, witnessed by leaders of the ruling party (also something that had happened the previous time), I was given the double posting of financial affairs minister and state minister in charge of economy and fiscal policy. In contrast to the mixed feelings reflected uniformly in the expressions of the ruling party leaders, I felt that the prime minister was in a good mood throughout the proceedings.

The firm decision of Prime Minister Koizumi truly involved surprise appointments. Far from relieving me of my position, he had given me the additional assignment of putting me in charge of financial affairs. A few years later, I mentioned to him, "You certainly were able to pull off a bold personnel move," and he responded with laughter, saying only, "It was a come-from-behind notion."

After that, an economic leader close to the prime minister told me, "At that time, Prime Minister Koizumi was probably prepared to commit joint suicide with you, I think."

That day marked the turning point in Japan's banking reform. We would now rush into full battle after having made the first preliminary skirmishes.

2. Struggle for the Program for Financial Revival (1)

Finally getting inside the "authorities"

On September 30, 2002, I was officially given the additional post of financial affairs minister. I was now in a position responsible for problems related to the whole economy: the general economy, public finances, and the financial system. While I had foreseen to a certain degree how tense I would be beforehand, once I did take the post, I could see that I was really in for something huge. However, I had no time to waste. The market was in disarray, politics were highly charged, and I had to deliver a solution, whatever it took, under the full gaze of the mass media. Specifically, in line with the instructions from the prime minister, I had to come up with the fundamental policies for the disposal of bad loans in the short space of one month after assuming my post. The horrific one-month period in which I had to put together the "Program for Financial Revival " (the Takenaka Plan) had finally begun.

On the first day after the formation of the new cabinet—that is to say, the first day I visited the offices of the FSA as its minister—I summoned the leaders of the agency and gave them a directive. Namely, I instructed them to assemble experts to form a review team in order to draw up the fundamental policies for financial revitalization. I am sure there was some puzzlement on the part of the FSA office staff on account of the suddenness of my actions. However, I was immediately able to get them to accept these as the policies of the minister. As a matter of fact, the organization of the review team had already been decided upon a few weeks earlier at the "strategic retreat" I had had with my staff.

The bureaucrats belonging to the FSA are a group of financial administration professionals, and the organizational successors of the Banking Department and Securities Department of the old Ministry of Finance (before the FSA was split off in a reorganization). Nonetheless, this group of professionals was paralyzed by a sort of functional failure. They were prisoners of the idea of bureaucratic infallibility (the public demonstration of an attitude implying that all the policies adopted so far have been impeccable). But the true meaning of the word "reform" is to recognize problematical points as problems, and to rectify those things that are inappropriate in the status quo. The official position of the FSA at that time was that "the financial system is healthy," that "credit risk can be managed through proper auditing," and that "there is nothing wrong with the banks' capital adequacy."

Of course, as the person in charge of an administrative bureaucracy, I could not make any statement that would whip up a sense of crisis. However, if it were true that the financial system was healthy, then there would not have been any need to halt the deposit payoff system (the system of limiting the amount of guaranteed deposits at each financial institution) in the first place. Nonetheless, ever since June 1996, the FSA had put into place a measure to stop that system. Also, if it were true that credit risk management was sufficient, why was there mention of the endless string of corporations known as "zombie companies," whose finances were in doubt? And if the capital adequacy was sufficient, then why had the banks' stocks plunged to such depths? In the fifteen months from the inauguration of the first Koizumi administration at the end of April 2001 until right before I became financial services minister, the banks' stock prices had already been shorn of about 37 percent of their value.

It was absolutely necessary for there to be recognition of these problems—or, to put it bluntly, to force the proud bureaucrats of the FSA to accept their existence—before banking reform could start down the path of realization. In other words, the bureaucrats, who were supposed to be competent and brilliant, had to be released from the straitjacket of "infallibility." For that purpose, I felt I should approach the problem by assembling a group of experts, especially those who would argue their views vehemently, and have them carry out debates with the bureaucrats, after which I, as the minister, would render the final decision. (Actually, this approach was also applied in the resolution of the problems of the postal service privatization and regional/local financial reform).

On my very first day as minister in the FSA offices, I told the administrative staff that I would appoint one of my secretaries, Kishi Hiroyuki, who had supported me as an aide while I was minister of state for economic and fiscal policy, as my political affairs secretary attached to the FSA. As I will explain in greater detail, there is clearly a limit to what an individual minister can carry out. The minister often finds himself for hours at end in the Diet, or preoccupied with dealing with political parties, so he is forced to leave much of his work to be done by the administrative staff. There is, additionally, a large limit on the free time a minister can spare to gather outside information directly. That is when "active brains" are necessary—private staff members who support the minister in collecting information both at home and abroad. Many Diet members do not have any such staff members, so they end up saying they have to "use the bureaucrats." In the end, however, those parliamentarians are forced to become the bureaucrats' lapdogs. In the area of banking reform, it was absolutely necessary to enlist the services of strategists such as Kishi. So I built up a support framework together with Magara Akihiro, who would be responsible for political matters.

On my first day as financial services minister, time passed hurriedly amidst the tension.

The Takenaka Team takes off

On the next day, October 1, 2002, I summoned FSA commissioner Takagi Shōkichi to my ministerial office, right after a cabinet meeting. It had always been extremely difficult for me, from the very beginning, to get my relationship with the bureaucrats right. From the bureaucrats' vantage, I was a troublemaking type of minister who denied their infallibility; that is to say, I was someone who came in to make bold reforms based on the premise that problems did exist in the banking system. Yet it was also evident that no reforms could be accomplished without the cooperation of the bureaucrats. To that end, it was absolutely necessary for me to get the commissioner to see things from my vantage point, as well as to have all directives carried out systematically through him, and to elicit the cooperation of the administrative secretaries. Commissioner Takagi and FSA administrative secretary Inoue Hiroyuki always cooperated with me positively, despite frequently being placed in a difficult situation.

At our meeting, I gave the commissioner a list of the members of the review team, the establishment of which I had decided upon the day before. On normal occasions, the administrative staff would prepare the candidates list, showing it to the minister to get his opinion before deciding upon it themselves. However, I had already prepared a list a few weeks before—at the time of the strategy meeting—and put on it the names of the people whom I thought absolutely had to be on the special review team. Although it was a highly unusual and unilateral way of presentation, Commissioner Takagi accepted it as is. That, as far as I was concerned, was a bit unexpected, for I had anticipated a little more dissension on his part.

Taking time out from the briefing I got from my predecessor as financial services minister, Yanagisawa Hakuo, as well as deciding upon the appointment of Vice-Minister Itō Tatsuya, I started to get detailed explanations from the FSA administrative staff about the agency's policies. While the newspapers reported on the discord between Yanagisawa and myself daily with odd and amusing articles, the former minister painstakingly and carefully briefed me that day on the status quo of the FSA and the problems that existed, etc. He then patted me on the back, saying he sincerely hoped I could work out the difficult situation. Though our thoughts and positions differed, I had to take off my hat to Yanagisawa, who had done his job so far under strain as a person responsible for setting policy, for his approach. I then thought that, as long as I had assumed the heavy responsibility of financial services minister, espousing my own theories, I would have to go about my job with my head held high, and come up with results no matter what.

Though there was a pile of work ahead of me in order to get a detailed grasp of what was going on in the FSA, I quit the offices relatively early that night. That was because I had to meet the experts whose names were on the review team candidate list shown to the administrative staff earlier that day. I was going to try to make the case for the team before them in one fell swoop. Given the time constraints placed upon us, preparations had been made in advance to invite almost all of the experts together in one venue. Of course, I could not warn them beforehand about the true purpose of the meeting—namely, to ask them to become members of the team. So I had invited them to an "exchange of opinions on the banking problem." By 9 p.m., they had already assembled at the designated conference room in the ANA Intercontinental Hotel in Tokyo.

I kept my introductory words to them brief, telling them about my having assumed the ministership the day before. Soon after, however, I told them the real reason for my calling them there. I explained to them how the bad-loan problem had to be solved, and how the prime minister had directed me to come up with the basic direction of the plan in the short period of one month. I continued by telling them that I needed the cooperation of private-sector experts such as themselves. The members whose names I had included on the list were all, in my eyes, experts who were representative of Japan, and all, I was convinced, shared my awareness of the problem.

One of the participants told me, "I believe this is Japan's last chance to extricate the economy from the lost decade." Someone else said, "If you are able to responsibly change the FSA's existing attitude, Mr. Takenaka, then we will gladly cooperate with you."

However, one scholar blurted out: "Japan will never be able to solve its bad-loan problem. I am unable to be involved in such an impossible task as this!"

For a moment, I could hardly believe my ears. The chance for Japan to improve its economy had finally arrived. That was why I had pinned my expectations on these experts, who I had assumed knew the economy well, thinking they would surely cooperate—unlike politicians, who were only interested in gaining political advantage for themselves. But my expectations were neatly dashed.

I am unable to say even now whether that particular expert had really given up on resolving the bad-loan problem, or whether he was just averse to joining forces with the Koizumi-Takenaka political team. I often hear the criticism voiced that some politicians and bureaucrats have lost their will and don't want to take a risk. But I had to tell myself that even more than that, there were unavoidably also those in the private sector and the academic world who held different opinions.

After his outburst, the floor was silent for a while. Then, a leader-like figure among those present, Kōsai Yutaka, spoke in a quiet voice, as follows: "True, the resolution of the bad-loan problem will not be so easy, given the delayed response so far. Even so, Mr. Takenaka has devoted himself this much. Why don't we somehow try to work with him, too, and do our best?"

As they say, "He who ceases to be a friend never was a good one." While one other person failed to sign on to the project, there was also, fortunately, someone recommended by the prime minister who joined. In the end, the membership of the review team was settled upon. The team's goal was to discuss the highly important basic policies leading to the disposal of the bad loans. It included specialists on the economy as well as banking and accounting practitioners Kōsai Yutaka, Okuyama Akio, Kimura Takeshi, Nakahara Nobuyuki, and Yoshida Kazuo. Later on, the media came to call the group the "Takenaka Team." For about one month after that, the members were to draw much attention from many quarters. Looking back on it now, without their high-spiritedness and their advanced level of technical knowledge, the banking crisis would undoubtedly still be with us today. It was a truly an "epistemic community"; that is, a network of experts sharing like-minded interests and aspirations.

Postponing the lifting of the payoff suspension once more

It was October 2, 2002, the second day of my service as financial services minister. Already I had kicked into high gear on the job. Twice that day, I had to make consensus-building arrangements with the Liberal Democratic Party (LDP). With many in the party suspicious and jittery about "what Takenaka is up to," I had to maneuver behind the scenes with Chairman Asō Tarō of the Policy Research Council, telling him about the launch of the Takenaka Team and the makeup of its membership.

Frankly, most LDP members, in policy terms, were extremely negative toward the disposal of the bad loans. It was obvious that they were under strong pressure from related industries. In addition, politically speaking, there was clear displeasure toward the fact that the prime minister had refused to relieve me of my post despite the loud chorus for that to happen, and had instead pointedly gone ahead with my double appointment as financial services minister. Moreover, those feelings were being hurled at me point-blank.

That was why it wasn't easy to talk with the LDP. Besides, although "consensus-building" was supposed to be what I was doing, there was no intention on my part, from the very beginning, to listen to the wishes of the party and modify the contents or nature of the review group. It was plain to me that to do so would simply end up in an embrace of the status quo. Asō had called upon Aizawa Hideyuki, said to be the "boss" in the LDP on financial matters, to join the meeting, and the two men listened to my talk. While I endured some criticism, I was able to persist somehow, and the Takenaka Team could now get underway.

My second big task on that day was to make a quick decision to renew the extension of the deposit payoff system. The so-called payoff system had been suspended ever since 1996, on account of the heightened financial fears stemming from the bank problem. That suspension was to have been partially lifted in 2002 (for fixed-term deposits, etc.), and then in April 2003 for everything else, according to the basic direction of policy that was decided upon. However, given the delay by the banks in disposing of their bad loans, it was evident that the instability of the financial markets had yet to be dispelled. Furthermore, the fact that the full lifting of the suspension of the deposit payoff system was to happen in just half a year only served to fan fears about the financial system. As we were moving toward the disposal of the bad loans, it was absolutely necessary to avoid a destabilization of the markets through a full lifting of the payoff system suspension. As the financial services minister, I had to take care of this business right off the bat.

That day, I went by myself to visit Prime Minister Koizumi at his official residence in order to propose in a straightforward manner the extension of the payoff suspension. He gave his approval immediately. The problem, though, was how to explain it publicly. As the official in charge of the financial authorities, I was in no position to state, "We are extending the payoff suspension because of the instability of the markets." So the only thing I could do was to perform some rhetorical maneuvers. I was painstakingly careful to use this kind of language: "For the time being, we must concentrate on the disposal of bad loans. During that interval, therefore, we will postpone the date when the payoff system suspension is to be removed."

As symbolized by the payoff issue, I was facing a difficult problem as financial services minister for the time being. As I have reiterated many times already, reforms cannot kick into action unless it is made clear that problems exist with the status quo. Nonetheless, as the financial services minister, I could not risk upsetting the stability of the markets by stressing the existence of such problems too explicitly. Indeed, the critics of the government (including some among the LDP, along with the opposition) skillfully took advantage of the difficulties inherent in my need to maintain a fine balance among the bureaucrats, the markets, and the media. While we were burdened with a problem not easily solved, it was imperative for us to accelerate financial (banking) reform.

The "drastic medicine" duo of Takenaka and Kimura

On October 3, 2002, the first meeting of the Takenaka Team was held at last. It was the fourth day since I had assumed office as financial services minister. Now it was time for the issue of banking reforms to appear on the main stage. It goes without saying that the speed with which the review committee was launched would have been impossible under normal circumstances. It was only made possible because everything from the makeup of the membership to the items of business to be discussed had been worked out already, on the whole, in the strategy retreat. From the standpoint of someone familiar with the policy process, the speed involved—opening a new committee on one's fourth day of office—ought to have been greeted with surprise. However, the concerned parties did not react to the speed itself at all, but rather just spoke about how radical the Takenaka Team was. They described the policies being advocated as "hard-landing," saying we were trying to dispose of the bad loans in one fell swoop.

Although people in various positions described our policies as "hard-landing" in order to incite fear, I had no idea at all what such policies were supposed to be like. I decided to rebut their comments with the following explanation: "We are not aiming at a 'hard landing' but a 'good landing.' The policies taken so far have been 'never landing' [i.e., never arriving at a solution], and those would lead in the long run to a 'crash landing' for the economy."

Under such scrutiny, the first meeting of the Takenaka Team took place, and the participants laid forth their pointed arguments with flying colors. Every once in a while, the FSA's administrative staff would come up with a labored rebuttal, but the team members were able to swiftly vanquish them one after another. One of the goals behind the establishment of the review committee was to set the bureaucrats free from the confines of their sense of infallibility, and I felt that it got off to a good start in that respect.

In the first meeting, there was one item on the agenda that I had particularly wanted to have debated: namely, what sort of authority did the FSA actually have? A fundamentally important point when progressing with reforms is to know what needs to be done, and what authority has been granted toward that end. It was thus necessary to make a thorough consideration of the legal undergirding and the practical methods available. I believed that it was absolutely necessary to confirm that point, as someone who had "entered the authorities" for the very first time. I had learned, through debates and discussions, that the exercise of authority needs to be prescribed very rigorously, and accordingly, all the steps in the process need to be cleared in a painstaking manner, one by one.

Concurrently with the progress of the Takenaka Team, one segment of the media started to make attacks criticizing the enlistment of Kimura Takeshi on the team. An acute sense of alarm was spreading on account of Kimura's assertion that major borrowers needed a thorough accounting of their management.

As I wrote earlier, Kimura's arguments were extremely justifiable, for without doing what he proposed, there would be no solution to the bad-loan problem. However, all the large corporations that were burdened by problems had a strong influence within Japanese society. It was plain that they were organizing a grand campaign aimed at politicians and the mass media in an attempt to maintain the status quo. They ridiculed Kimura and me as the "drastic medicine" duo. On that day, the Tokyo Stock Exchange dipped below 9,000 points, and one person associated with the market commented, "It's because you put Kimura on the Takenaka Team that the stock prices are falling." In fact, that was practically the same as admitting that stock prices were dropping because the true state of affairs at the companies would be discovered if the commonsense policies advocated by Kimura were adopted.

On the following day, October 4, 2002, I issued an important directive in my capacity as state minister of economic and fiscal policy to the administrative staff of the Cabinet Office. The pursuit of banking reform had to be done in a unified fashion, linked with broader macroeconomic policies as a whole, in order to revitalize the entire economy and whip deflation. To that end, I instructed Kawade Eiji, administrative vice-minister of the Cabinet Office, to make preparations to discuss anti-deflationary measures at the upcoming October 7 meeting of the Council on Economic and Fiscal Policy (CEFP). Along with Kagomiya Nobuo, deputy director general for economic and fiscal management in the Cabinet Office, Kawade actively addressed my request. As a matter of fact, one of the important points that Prime Minister Koizumi anticipated I would carry out was precisely such a unified review of the economy, fiscal policy, and the banking system.

That evening, the prime minister invited me to dinner once again. Banking reform had already transcended the dimension of economic policy, and had begun to take on a tense immediacy that directly affected the political situation. Ever since the cabinet reshuffle, the coverage by the media had heated up to an excessive degree, with every move I made being analyzed and discussed. In that kind of environment, Prime Minister Koizumi showed special concern for my situation in a variety of ways. During our meal that night, he instructed me not to flinch as I made bold reforms, encompassing the economy, fiscal policy, and banking as a whole. Incidentally, the discussion at our meal was being photographed through the window from the next building by means of a telephoto lens. That's how overheated the media coverage had become.

Take the high road!

Between October 5 and 7, 2002, I had to be in Singapore to attend the East Asia Economic Summit of the World Economic Forum (WEF). The WEF, the foundation that runs the Davos Conference, holds the summit every summer (as an Asian version of Davos). Come to think of it, nine months after arguing for banking reform at the January Davos Conference, I was now attending a conference in the capacity of a "financial authority" myself.

At the summit, the politicians, business leaders, and experts from the various countries told me, as the newly appointed financial services minister, how they were looking forward to my realizing the previous arguments I had made about getting Japan to recover. That stood in sharp contrast to the debate on the topic as it was in Japan, which was at the height of confusion. My argument was also the standard assertion of experts worldwide.

After returning to Japan, I had an opportunity to talk with Yoshikuni Shinichi, Asian representative of the Bank of International Settlements (BIS). Although Yoshikuni started his career at the Bank of Japan (BOJ), he is now active on the larger international stage. As a matter of fact, I have been a friend of his since university days. Right before I became a government minister, I visited London as an academic, and had dinner there with Yoshikuni, who was then the BOJ's London representative. Over our meal, we talked about Japan's bad-loan problem. He encouraged me by saying that what I was trying to do was totally correct, and that I shouldn't be shaken by criticism but rather carry out my original intentions. Those words from my friend, active on the international scene, heartened me greatly.

However, on the next day, October 7, 2002, right after I returned to Japan, there was intense criticism awaiting me. A commentator on a commercial TV news show had this to say: "Takenaka was against the injection of public funds for the failing *jūsen* housing-loan companies. He lacks all principles by saying they are needed now!"

That was a through-and-through personal attack. The reason that public funds needed to be injected into the banking system at that time was that day-to-day payments are settled through people's bank accounts. In order to safeguard the social infrastructure that such a settlement system represents, public funds were necessary on an emergency basis. That function of public funds is recognized worldwide. However, the *jūsen* companies, whose failed management became a problem in 1995, were not institutions that handled deposits from ordinary citizens. In other words, they were not banks. Despite that, public funds were used to rescue them. That was because if they were to fail, their biggest lender, Nokyo (Japan Agricultural Cooperatives), would also see its management undermined. Nokyo is a kind of "bank" that constitutes a payment settlement system, taking in deposits. That meant that public funds should be injected into Nokyo if necessary, but only if blame was correspondingly placed on its management.

Even now, I believe that it was a mistake to use public funds for the *jūsen* institutions (which, I repeat, are not banks), as it was done for political reasons in order to cover up Nokyo's irresponsibility. Any expert understands that.

The next few days, the Takenaka Team worked somberly, without much fuss, on drawing up the basic policies for the disposal of the bad loans. While holding meetings in the FSA offices with the administrative staff, at the same time I continued to meet personally with the main members of the team late at night. It was always after midnight when I returned home. Anyone who becomes a government minister is not allowed to be sick. No matter how high a fever you are running, you still have to appear in the Diet or meet with the party if called in order to answer questions. That was why I did my best to return home before the middle of the night after becoming minister. But in this particular period, we had to put together an important policy package in a short time, no matter how much trouble it was. And all through this time, the stock market continued its downward slump.

On October 10, 2002, the Nikkei average was about to fall past the 8,100-point level. The press started to label this the "Takenaka shock," saying that the anxiety had spread ever since I had become financial services minister and tried to change the course of policy. But that was a ridiculous argument. All I was doing was to assert that the banks themselves had to get a clear, accurate grasp of the extent of their assets (lent funds) on the basis of the market price of those assets. Also, I said that the banking system would be secured, even if it meant using public funds if necessary. The decline in the stock market resulted from its adjustment to the insufficient disposal of the bad loans to date. I was positive that once the new policies started to take effect, the trend of the stock market was sure to reverse.

On that day, Prime Minister Koizumi called me to his residence and told me: "Don't let anything faze you. Take the high road!"

His comments at that time confirmed my feeling that no matter what resistance we faced, we could accomplish the disposal of Japan's bad loans under the leadership of this prime minister.

3. Struggle for the Program for Financial Revival (2)

Framework of the revitalization program (1): Tightening asset assessment

From the moment I became financial services minister, Takenaka-bashing started to swirl in political circles, and there was heated reporting in the mass media that I would serve as a catalyst for developments in the political situation. However, as far as I was concerned, the most pressing matter, of course, was to develop policies that would bring the bad-debt problem to an end. The important thing, then, was the nature of those policies. I seriously thought that this was the last chance for Japan's economy to recover. In the few spare moments I had in between being hounded by politicians and the media—that is to say, at night and on weekends—I had to proceed steadily forward with drawing up policy. Day after day, study meetings were continually held by the Takenaka Team both within and outside of the FSA.

As for the status of the Takenaka Team itself, its goal was to provide consistent intellectual input to me as the person in charge, having studied and deliberated policies that were deemed desirable. Typically, people in the world of politics are entirely against letting private-sector individuals who lack public office or qualifications get involved in the drawing-up of policy. So it was necessary to give the impression that the team's members were just freely engaging in debate as experts, and that the official policies of the FSA were being decided upon by the financial services minister as the person in charge; namely, me.

If I had attempted to give the review team, on the surface, a great amount of official authority, there was bound to be interference that would try to negate the existence of the team itself. In order to avoid that, I made it clear that everything was being done under my aegis (in my official capacity as minister). That also bore significance in the sense of co-opting the bureaucrats in advance, as they had to abide by my decisions as long as those decisions had been made in my capacity as minister. The bottom line is that the Takenaka Team produced no reports. I had to stress, from beginning to end, that the policies were being developed by me, as minister, drawing upon the opinions of influential individuals.

In the evening of Friday, October 11, 2002, a meeting was held secretly in a room at the Akasaka Prince Hotel in Tokyo with members of the Takenaka Team. There, I decided upon the broad outlines of the policies to be announced, in consultation with the other members. While the basic policies had to be drawn up within a month from the time of the cabinet reshuffle, it was necessary for us to settle upon the framework of the policies as early as possible, given the difficult process leading up to their announcement. That was precisely why I kicked into high gear right after assuming office, making it possible for me to decide upon the broad outlines at the early stage of the twelfth day. This was the result of the Herculean motivation and dedication of the team members, as well as the preliminary work that had been undertaken in a planned fashion since the time of the strategy retreat.

The framework of the package—later to be announced as the "Program for Financial Revival"—was by and large as follows. First, starting with a general point, the acceleration of the bad-debt disposal would concentrate on the banks (i.e., the major banks) for the interim. That was because it was essential, more than anything, to resolve the bad-debt problems of those banks if the financial markets were to be stabilized. Additionally, those major institutions had both the sufficient fiscal strength and the human resources to give them the potential power to solve their problems. In contrast, the situation at regional banks and at small and mid-sized financial institutions was quite different. It was important to obviate needless political backlash by removing them from the reform list for the time being. One can therefore say that it was an appropriate decision, judging matters practically, to focus efforts on disposing of the nonperforming loans of the big banks first.

In that regard, we set the bold numerical goal of halving the bad-debt ratio (the ratio of nonperforming loans to all loaned assets) of the big banks in a period of two and a half years from what at that time was a level of 8.4 percent. It is politically risky to state specific numbers, as one will obviously be called to account if they are not reached. That is why bureaucratic-led efforts go out of their way to avoid specifying numerical goals. But I believed that these explicit numerical goals were absolutely necessary, even if just to evince the government's indomitable resolve. If the numbers failed to be achieved, I could simply take responsibility.

Three basic points of recognition were important in attaining these goals: (1) tightening the asset assessment of the banks; (2) enhancing capital adequacy; and (3) reinforcing the banks' governance. I had pointed out these three items consistently ever since the strategy retreat. As for determining how to realize those goals, however, that was precisely the job of the Takenaka Team members in their discussions. In other words, it was their chance to "show their stuff"; that is, their brains.

The first of the three goals—namely, tightening the asset assessment of the banks—required clarification and tightening of the standards being applied, so as not to let the banks make lenient assessments that would lead to bad-debt coverups. While this is a point that is frequently misunderstood, the assessment of bank assets (namely, judging whether a loan is nonperforming or not, and deciding how much it is worth) is not the job of the FSA, but of the banks themselves. The FSA's role is to make an "ex post facto" evaluation of those assessments; that is, after the initial assessment. The financial administration by the government has now shifted to such ex post facto checks from the previous style of prior intervention found in the previous "convoy system" era (i.e., prior to 1998, when the larger banks had been regulated by the Ministry of Finance with greater efficiency in order to give the more poorly managed banks an equal footing in the system). The problem was whether the rules for asset assessment were properly set in order. Unfortunately, the extent of the market distrust suggested that the asset assessment rules themselves needed to be organized and reinforced further.

In that respect, various technical steps had to be taken to shore up the rules in conformance with the market, such as the adoption of the discounted cash flow (DCF) method, which discounts future cash flow in line with the current market price. Moreover, another concern was that different banks would make different assessments of their respective loans to the same corporation, which would mean that some banks were carrying out such assessments too leniently. To work around that, the assessments by various banks of their loans to the largest borrowers, at least, needed to be consolidated.

Another necessity was to develop a mechanism for applying healthy pressure on the banks, making them carry out proper assessments of their loaned assets in a responsible fashion. Specifically, if a huge gap emerged between the assessment of the assets carried out by a bank itself and the amount later determined by the FSA's own assessment, it was presumed that those results should be publicized and subject to public scrutiny. That was how important it was for the banks themselves to conduct the assessment of their assets.

Also, in connection with that, it was necessary for the auditing firms whose job it was to audit the banks to conduct rigorous assessments. We decided that we had to appeal once again to the morals of those companies so as to make the auditing process more rigorous.

Framework of the revitalization program (2): Enhancing capital adequacy

As for the second item on the list—enhancing capital adequacy—I decided to state expressly that public funds would be injected if the need arose. As a matter of fact, the existing statutes (the Deposit Insurance Law) clearly state that fact, meaning it would not normally be necessary to include it again in the program. However, the markets were dominated by the idea that the FSA was backward-looking in its policies. I therefore felt that I had to reiterate the message that the bad-debt problem would be resolved with resolute determination, following the letter of the law, and with administrative duties carried out without fuss. I knew that public opinion would start to make a big deal about "Takenaka wanting to inject funds." But I had to show the markets that the government was prepared to take resolute action responsibly, even if it meant taking that risk.

As far as public funds were concerned, moreover, there was another important fundamental problem: was the current framework sufficient? Under current law, public funds can be injected only in emergency fiscal situations, and even then, only when the banks in question have made an application for them. However, it is precisely to avoid such emergency situations that such funds are to be injected in the first place. Accordingly, it was thought worthwhile to discuss a new framework for public funds.

Regarding the issue of capital adequacy, there was one issue that was decisively important: the problem of deferred tax assets. This is a technical accounting term that most people had not yet heard of at that time. Even so, during that particular period, the term "deferred tax assets" was being bandied about by the mass media.

Deferred tax assets come into existence when a bank cannot write off a nonperforming asset for tax purposes until a subsequent accounting period, even though it has cleared its books of that asset. It is a form of prepaid tax, and is to be refunded to the bank at the stage when it finally charges the loss against its assets (to be more exact, the amount of its payable tax is reduced by the amount of the loss). In other words, the "un-repaid" tax represents an "asset" of sorts to the bank. Of course, such a concept is established only in an accounting sense. For that reason, when the capital adequacy ratios of Japanese banks are calculated, those deferred tax assets have traditionally been included among their total assets.

However, the problem is that such assets disputably may, in fact, never be paid back later "with certitude." To be more specific, if a bank cannot post a sufficient profit at a certain time, it will be unable to charge the amount of the loss against its taxes, no matter how much it wants to do so, as the amount of the loss would exceed the payable tax. It is because of its imprecise nature that, in the United States and other countries, the calculation of a bank's capital adequacy ratio does not permit the unrestricted inclusion of deferred tax assets in the total assets of that bank, but rather puts a certain "brake" on them (normally up to 10 percent of its core capital). However, there is no such restriction in Japan, meaning that such deferred tax assets had ended up accounting for a large share of banks' total equity (up to 49 percent). A big portion of the banks' capital adequacy ratio—low even without that fact—thus comprise such shaky assets.

It was accordingly a point of utmost importance to set some sort of maximum limit on deferred tax assets, as far as the calculation of capital adequacy was concerned.

Next, regarding the third point on the list—reinforcing the governance of the banks—the banks faced a fundamental problem that predated the bad-debt problem: poor management. However, the government's adoption of the so-called convoy system in administering the banks resulted, particularly, in what seemed to be a striking deficiency of governance. That is precisely why the bad-debt issue grew to be such a big problem for the economy. We focused on the fact that the major banks were already accepting public funds on account of the string of financial emergencies that had occurred since 1997. In return for the acceptance of funds (and, in turn, placing a burden on the country's citizens), the banks were obliged to present plans for restoring their health in the form of "management reconstruction plans." If, indeed, the management of the banks were unable to follow such a plan, the idea was that they were to be subject to the requisite administrative punishment. Seen dispassionately, it would seem natural that the acceptance of public funds ought to require such a measure. However, the former administrative authorities failed to hold the banks to account. Thus, as far as reinforcing the governance of the banks was concerned, we felt that it would be effective to apply such a measure.

The Program for Financial Revival was quite comprehensive in nature, containing many other pieces of wisdom besides the ones mentioned here. But I was able to boil down into six points those things that I felt deserved the greatest emphasis in the disposal of the nonperforming loans, as follows:

(1) thoroughly implementing market-price computation so as to make a more rigorous assessment of banks' assets (through the adoption of the discounted cash flow method, etc.);
(2) unifying the categorization of the assessment of large borrowers with loans at several different banks (the so-called horizontal skewering of something that was previously handled vertically);
(3) making banks' self-assessments sounder by publicizing any differences between them and those conducted by outside auditors;
(4) making it clear that public funds would be utilized, if necessary, and that new public funds would be considered;
(5) regulating deferred tax assets properly; and
(6) issuing operational improvement directives to those banks that failed to live up to their management reconstruction plans.

As I have shown above, on just my twelfth day as financial services minister, I had already determined the basic framework of the Program for Financial Revival with the main members of the Takenaka Team. The only important thing still to be carried out was the process of getting it established as official policy. Specifically, we had to carefully prepare simulations of the effects and influence those policies would have when put into effect. Having completed the stage of contemplating the policies that would lead to disposal of the nonperforming loans, we were now about to enter the stage of having to persuade the parties involved.

At any rate, the truth was that almost everyone around us was, at heart, opposed to the disposal of the nonperforming loans. The battle was now drawing to a head: amidst such fierce opposition, how could we push through the framework without compromising?

Mounting opposition

Starting on Monday, October 14, 2002, I had one week to complete the preparations before finally announcing the program. As I have said, its framework had already been determined, out of the public view. Now, however, we had to carry out the patient, steady work of completing the program while making specific checks, and at the same time, start the confusing process of getting the assent of the related parties.

First of all, I decided that I would make the final explanations to Prime Minister Koizumi early the following week. In addition, in connection with that, I began to send out feelers in three directions, little by little.

I first sent out feelers toward the banks. Ever since becoming financial services minister, I knew that people in the banking industry were trembling with fear in regard to the strengthening of policy. Nonetheless, I made the decision to refrain from contacting them directly. There ought to be a "constructive relationship of tension" between the FSA, which stands in the position of supervisor or overseer, and that of the banks, which are the supervised or overseen. Issues such as the disposal of nonperforming loans, furthermore, demanded such a "relationship of tension." Eventually, though, I decided to contact the top executives of the banks at this juncture. So, through paying courtesy calls on the banks, I began to test their reactions and get a sense of how they felt, bit by bit, while staying conscious of the framework of the Program for Financial Revival, which had already been worked out.

The second direction I sent feelers out to was other ministries and agencies within the government; that is, I had to make adjustments with them. Although it was unthinkable that they would move to directly oppose the disposal of the nonperforming loans, it was still absolutely necessary to get their cooperation. With the worsening economy, the bank reforms had to be carried out this time. That made it necessary to move forward with various other measures to revitalize the economy, as a set package. In parallel with the disposal of the nonperforming loans, moreover, those corporations that had borrowed excessively also needed to be reconstructed (nonperforming loans and excessive borrowing being two sides of the same coin). To that end, we had to get some sort of support from the Ministry of Finance (MOF) and the Ministry of Economy, Trade and Industry (METI). I placed a request with Chief Cabinet Secretary Fukuda to schedule a meeting with six related cabinet ministers on Wednesday, October 16, at which I sought broad cooperation.

The third direction in which I sent out feelers was to the ruling coalition, particularly the Liberal Democratic Party (LDP). This was the biggest annoyance of all, because, after all, both the banks and the largest corporate borrowers were opposed to the acceleration of the disposal of nonperforming loans. In their heart of hearts, they wanted to maintain the status quo. Moreover, those corporations and industries descended upon Nagatachō (the area in Tokyo where the LDP party headquarters is located) in droves. It was a huge Takenaka-bashing campaign, with the interests of the industry (i.e., the anti-reformers) linked up with the interests of (anti-Koizumi) politicians. I first sent out feelers to Chairman Asō Tarō of the Policy Research Council in the form of explanations of our current status. Whenever I was to meet him, though, he unfailingly asked if Aizawa Hideyuki, chairman of the LDP's special task force on anti-deflationary measures, could join us. Technical problems of a financial nature were mostly discussed with Aizawa.

At the meeting held in the middle of the week, I delivered my explanations while sensing that the general atmosphere of the party was not enthusiastic about the acceleration of the nonperforming loan disposal. I said, "I will be able to report the general outlines of the program next week."

As a matter of fact, in their negotiations with me, the LDP had "taken hostages" in the form of bills currently being debated. In the current session of the Diet, the FSA had presented several bills, the passage of which obviously needed the support of the ruling coalition. However, just in that week, when I was about to announce the Program for Financial Revival, the LDP Policy Research Council had turned down and sent back a bill proposed by the FSA to promote bank mergers. It was an expression of intense opposition, as if to say, "We won't easily let things go at Takenaka's pace."

I was fully aware that the banks, ministries/agencies, and ruling coalition were suspicious and distrustful of both me and my method of discussing things a little at a time without stating anything specific. During that process, something gradually came to light. Namely, the banks and the ruling coalition (who were obviously working hand in hand) overreacted much more than I had expected to the problem of deferred tax assets. If an upper limit were placed on the amount of deferred tax assets that could be declared, as in the United States, many banks would find themselves in a situation of insufficient capital adequacy, meaning they might have to receive capital injection. That, indeed, was the banks' Achilles' heel. To have such a weak financial foundation was in itself problematic, but they started to speak out against it using language that suggested that the Takenaka administration was out to arbitrarily drive them to failure. At the same time, though, this suggested that they had little interest in the other aspects of the program, that is, asset assessment and stepped-up governance. Unlike the problem of deferred tax assets, which would have an immediate impact, these other two aspects would only start to take effect in the medium range, slowly but steadily.

It was now Sunday, October 20, 2002. The week's work had been finished, and the weekend had rolled around. From the following day, Monday, I had to start moving rapidly toward the program's decision and announcement. I worked together with Vice-Minister Itō, my secretarial staff, and my friends from the Takenaka Team all day long and into the night to decide on the sequence of steps to be taken in the upcoming week. First, I was to deliver a prepared paper to the administrative staff of the FSA on Monday, in which I would reveal my ideas. Soon after that, I was to make a report to the prime minister about the contents of the report, getting his understanding, and then consult him on how to respond to the ruling party. As many counterarguments could be expected, we carefully girded ourselves with a list of potential questions and answers.

At last, on Monday, I was to show the Program for Financial Revival to the administrative staff of the FSA. That meant that, sooner or later, its contents would be leaked externally. As such, it would be only a matter of time before we could expect counterarguments to come roaring out of the ruling party and the press. So it was my intention to make all the possible preparations I could with that in mind. Needless to say, this was the last chance we had to dispose of the nonperforming loans, and we had done everything humanly possible in the way of working out the policy. So my state of mind was that everything was now in the hands of God.

"Takenaka throws a fastball. The LDP flinches!"

On Monday, October 21, 2002, I had to give the outlines of the Program for Financial Revival to the administrative staff of the FSA. Also, I was scheduled to appear in a question-and-answer session in the Diet that day.

In the afternoon, I formally explained the outlines of the Program for Financial Revival to Prime Minister Koizumi, and he agreed to it in principle. The point about which I had foreseen the greatest opposition from related parties was the treatment of deferred tax assets. Of the various proposals we had thought of, I explained to the prime minister that I was fundamentally thinking of the strictest version for the time being, and I won his understanding. That evening, I showed the entire draft of the program to the FSA administrative staff.

The FSA administrative staff had probably never experienced such a top-down style of policymaking before, and I am sure they were greatly dissatisfied. But I felt that the only way to draw up a solid policy framework in the face of such opposition and interference, as well as to effect such a fundamental change of direction, was to carry it out in a top-down fashion in one fell swoop. That night, I also had the opportunity to explain to several key media representatives the main drift and general direction of the program.

The next day, Tuesday, October 22, 2002, the FSA administrative staff presented me one item in the program proposal I had shown them the day before that they believed definitely had to be modified. As I had expected, it concerned the treatment of deferred tax assets. In the proposal I had shown them, the term was to be decided and an upper limit clearly set for the amount that could be declared. It was an extremely strict proposal, and I understood well that it could force many banks into a position of insufficient capital adequacy if it were followed to the letter. However, my strategy was to risk the presentation of a strict proposal on this point, as the related parties were excessively interested in it. And so I was able to confirm that my original plan for the program was to be promoted as is, including the point about the treatment of deferred tax assets.

On that day, Prime Minister Koizumi gave me a clear indication of how he wanted to progress from there. That evening, a meeting of the LDP executives was to be held in a conference room in the Diet building, and he told me to attend and to explain the Takenaka plan straight away. His directive took me aback at first, but then I sensed that it was a carefully worked-out strategy of his. Normally, making such a sudden explanation at the executive meeting would be unheard of. The standard way to do things was for the Policy Council to first debate the issue, after which the General Council would receive the proposal in the end. That was why I had originally planned to make my report to the Policy Council for the time being in the format of an "interim report." But the prime minister unexpectedly ordered me to go to the executive meeting and deliver my explanation there.

At the evening meeting, the party secretary general, the policy council chairman, and other big names from the LDP were all present. I was determined just to give a general outline of the Program for Financial Revival in a matter-of-fact way. A few technical questions were raised, most of which had to do with the deferred tax assets issue. After an exchange of views back and forth, Aoki Mikio, then the secretary general of the LDP's Upper House caucus, flatly stated, "There's no way we can win an election with this! Don't do something that will depress the stock market before the election."

With those few words, everything was decided. For practical purposes, the proposal had been sent back. The interim report that I had planned for the same day had to be shelved, too. At the same time, though, it was a warning to the top officials of the party to "get things in shape." With members of the press swarming outside the door, the meeting ended in a tumultuous mood.

The news of the meeting spread through the government like a flash. At the meeting of related cabinet ministers held later that night, some of the members criticized me, saying, "How come you didn't tell us anything earlier?"

Until that point, I had repeatedly made requests to the whole government to lend support to my drastic measures for the disposal of the nonperforming loans by developing a comprehensive package of measures. Despite that, many of the ministers now spoke as if it was no longer their affair. But the fact that the LDP had reached such a state meant that there was a lot of pressure on each ministry. Although I felt like responding to each of the criticisms, I instead decided to take them to mean that everything was all right with respect to promoting the policies.

Regarding this chaotic situation, much of the media reported, "The chaos resulted from the academician Minister Takenaka failing to do the proper behind-the-scenes maneuvering." However, it was not as simple as that. Rather, it was nothing less than shock therapy being administered by the prime minister. In the *Nihon Keizai Shimbun* the next day, a large headline read, "Takenaka Throws a Fastball. The LDP Flinches!" That was exactly the strategy that the prime minister had laid. Also, in the cabinet meeting held the following week, he made the following statement: "It may be hard for Minister Takenaka right now, but it is not merely a problem of the Financial Services Agency, but of the whole government. May all the ministers collaborate and work on the problem!"

The shock therapy administered by the prime minister was beginning to serve as a powerful impetus toward pulling everything together.

Backlash from the banking industry

While coordination needed to be carried out between the government and the ruling coalition, there was also a simultaneous necessity, in parallel with that, to deepen my contacts with the banking industry, one of the central players in the bad-debt problem. It was plain that the backlash from the LDP stemmed from its links with this powerful industry and its opposition to the program. On the morning of Wednesday, October 23, 2002, I had decided to assemble the presidents of all the major banks and give them an explanation of my basic ideas. The venue was the Mita Chamber of the Ministry of Finance (MOF). From early morning, many members of the press had gathered there. I arrived right on time, but the bank presidents were already there. Of course, the strained relations with the ruling coalition made it impossible to unveil the entire program at that stage. I instead told them why I had ended up making a drastic overhaul of the policies toward bad-debt disposal this time. I also stuck to a general explanation of the basic stance adopted; namely, that it covered tightening asset assessment, enhancing capital adequacy, and reinforcing governance.

The retort by the banks mainly comprised comments such as: "We have always followed the guidance of the FSA, and have made sufficient efforts." I told them only this: "Isn't there a gap between what you are all saying and how the markets evaluate it?" We argued on different planes, but I was all right with that.

On the next day, October 24, 2002, the morning edition of the *Nihon Keizai Shimbun* scooped what it called the "Takenaka proposal," our financial reform proposal. As we had made fine adjustments to the plan day in and day out, we could not ascertain exactly which version had been leaked, but one thing that could not be denied was that the policy proposal given to the [FSA] administrative staff had been leaked in some form or other. Grabbing the opportunity, opposition to the proposal grew ever fiercer, especially regarding the limits to be placed on the declaration of deferred tax assets. There are several theories about the source of the leak, but I think it was a retired bureaucrat from the FSA. The leak was probably planned so as to intensify sentiments against the Takenaka plan.

On October 25, 2002, I had another chance to hobnob with the banks, and the subject was not much different from the previous time. No matter how far this went, there was an inevitable gap between the banking industry, on the one hand, as the perpetrator of the problem and the subject of governmental scrutiny, and the government, on the other hand, which had to properly carry out oversight duties from the perspective of the national economy. That evening, the representatives of the banks held a joint press conference. They were naturally against the financial reforms this time, and what they had to say was distinctly anti-Takenaka.

When my staff members and I watched the proceedings of the press conference, we were struck with the clear realization that we could "win" this. The players who had created the non-performing loans in the first place, and who were now causing so much trouble for the Japanese people, were now seen in a position of opposing the reforms. Moreover, the sight of the bank presidents grouped together at the press conference like a bunch of incompetents, fully exposing their buddy-buddy group consciousness left over from the days of the old convoy system, was a graphic indication of the lack of governance at the current banks, as well as their lack of strategy. The public would never support such banks—I was convinced of that.

On the next day, October 26, 2002, the *Asahi Shimbun* came out with an editorial that offered a slightly different tone than those written before. Ever since I had become minister, several media entities had pointed out the slowness of the bad-debt disposal up to that time, but later, without any scruples, suddenly their tone criticizing me intensified. However, the editorial on the 26th argued in the following manner:

> **The Irresponsibility of Takenaka-Bashing**
>
> As soon as the contents of the bad-debt

disposal plan drawn up by Financial Services Minister Takenaka were reported, the executives of the Liberal Democratic Party (LDP), the heads of the banks, and others were quick to jump on the criticism bandwagon. What a poor sight they are—the very people who ought to have long ago solved this problem, which is an ulcer eating away at the Japanese economy. Without any responsible plan of their own, they seem to have no compunction at all about relocating any questions about their own blame to the back burner. (Excerpt from the *Asahi Shimbun*, October 26, 2002)

I decided to doggedly pursue the negotiations with the ruling coalition, as I felt I had to pull the Program for Financial Revival together in a week's time.

"Three generals, three policymakers" meeting in times of emergency

Although October 27, 2002, was a Sunday, I had scheduled a meeting on that day with the top officials of the FSA. We had to get the final agreement of the ruling coalition before the week was out, in order to reach the point where we could make an announcement of the plan. That was also something that the prime minister himself had publicly promised when reshuffling the cabinet. For that purpose, I had to give explanations to a broad segment of the ruling coalition' membership, and absolutely had to get the cooperation of the administrative staff in the FSA as well. On that same day, also, I visited several top party members to give my explanation. I also made the rounds by phone so as to get people to agree to the plan.

In the morning of Monday, October 28, 2002, a special meeting was held at the Akasaka Prince Hotel. This was called the "three generals, three policymakers" meeting because it involved the secretaries-general of the three ruling coalition parties—the LDP, the New Kōmeitō, and the New Conservative Party, respectively—and the policy council chairman from each. As a matter of fact, I did not know the phrase "three generals, three policymakers" at that time. In other words, this was an emergency procedure that skipped over normal party procedures, and meant that the Program for Financial Revival would be put together under the responsibility of the chief secretaries and policy council chairmen of the three ruling coalition parties. I still believe that such an extraordinary measure was taken because Prime Minister Koizumi made the request to Secretary-General Yamazaki, directing him to apply the full strength of his administration to put the program together.

At the "three generals, three policymakers" meeting, severely divergent opinions were raised against the Program for Financial Revival, and against the treatment of the deferred tax assets in particular. That was to be expected, but it illustrated the rocky road ahead.

However, Secretary-General Yamazaki whispered this to me as we left: "The fact that we are holding the 'three generals, three policymakers' meeting means that in the end the program will be put together, in any event." That meant that the bad-debt problem would not be allowed to fester any longer, and thus would not become a political situation. It was a declaration of intent by the leaders of the ruling coalition that they would take charge of putting it together. That, clearly, was good news. The stalled process of coordination had now started to move. But one could expect that, in such a case, rather tough negotiations would be required so as not to compromise on the program's contents.

At the end of the first "three generals, three policymakers" meeting, I got the sense that if only we could somehow overcome the problem of the deferred tax assets successfully, we might be able to quell objections to the rest of the items successfully as well, and reach an agreement. The objections to the other items, which were hidden in the shadow of the deferred tax assets problem, were for the time being smaller than expected. Obviously, many people were underestimating the effects of reform in asset assessment and governance. I wished that somehow the next few days would pass without any problems emerging in regard to the other items, and that everyone's attention would be focused on the issue of deferred tax assets. Those were my fervent prayers as I watched the proceedings moving along.

Meanwhile, on the same day another meeting was held, this time among the related ministers in the government. The chief cabinet secretary and six ministers attended. I felt that even those ministers who had not necessarily been positive to that point would now show a cooperative mood, as might be expected. In particular, the agreement to establish the Industrial Revitalization Corporation of Japan (IRCJ) at that day's meeting could be said to have been a big accomplishment. The IRCJ would clean up the situation of excessive corporate borrowing—the other side of the banks' bad-debt problem—and work to revitalize industries and corporations. The disposal of nonperforming loans and the revitalization of industries and corporations were two sides of the same coin; namely, to clean up the balance sheets of banks and corporations. The Takenaka Team also discussed such matters from the outset, but pessimistically believed that it would be impossible to go so far as to establish such an institution. However, probably on account of the effects of the shock therapy, an agreement was reached to establish the IRCJ as a national institution to clean up the balance sheets. At any rate, the Ministry of Finance (MOF) had unmistakably flexed its muscles here.

Over the two-day period of October 29 and 30, 2002, further meetings were held by the "three generals, three policymakers." Although a few twists and turns were experienced, the Program for Financial Revival was moving closer to agreement, including the final adjustments on the wording of the proposal. In the movement toward putting it together, I agreed to make modifications on just one point. Instead of our original plan to place a maximum cap on deferred tax assets, I agreed to let the Financial System Council debate the issue further. That meant that public funds would no longer have to be injected right away. Except for that, however, everything else in the program was just as the original framework stated. I was convinced that its contents were sufficient to someday produce the effect of accelerating the disposal of nonperforming loans.

Although various debates were held at the stage when the Program for Financial Revival was put together, my perceptions at the time were as follows:

The Program for Financial Revival was a comprehensive package carefully worked out by some of Japan's best experts. Its framework rested on these six pillars: (1) reinforced asset assessment (discounted cash flow, etc.); (2) unified auditing of assets (the horizontal "skewer," with loans by the same corporation at several financial institutions assessed using the same standards); (3) publicly announcing any discrepancies between self-auditing and audits done by outside auditors; (4) utilizing public funds; (5) responding to the issue of deferred tax assets; and (6) rigorously reviewing corporations' management reconstruction plans. Of those six, further discussions were still to be had on the treatment of deferred tax assets, but the five other items were just as they had appeared in the original plan. Despite massive opposition, our record was five wins and one tie. With that, we would be able to steadily pare down the number of nonperforming loans. I would venture to say, though, that it was difficult to make an exact prediction about how long it would take to resolve the bad-debt problem. If all went well, it might take six months to a year, but if they didn't, it might take even longer. In that case, I would probably have to accept the blame and resign. But I felt that even if that happened, it wouldn't matter, for that was my job. Be that as it may, I had complete confidence in the direction of the policies.

On October 31, 2002, after the announcement of the program, I spent the whole day at the Diet, and then visited Prime Minister Koizumi afterward. I expressed my gratitude for his leadership, then summarized the news reporting on that day, telling him, "The media are saying a lot of different things." He replied to me in his usual dry, casual fashion, "You'll find out in time. Don't let it get to you."

I thought then that it was only thanks to a prime minister like this that such a difficult policy could be put together. I had to come up with results no matter what. I then called together the top officials of the FSA and gave them directions about the next step to be taken.

4. The Path Leading to the Financial Crisis: Response Conference

Two tugs-of-war

The next important step that had to be taken was to draw up the progress schedule. There was indeed much work to be done in order to produce results. We had to draw up strict guidelines for the introduction of new methods, such as the DCF (discounted cash flow) method, to make asset assessment more rigorous. Otherwise they would get watered down. We had to determine when and in how much detail to make the announcement of the discrepancies between self-auditing and FSA audits. Here, too, we had to draw up a solid framework, or else it would get watered down, too. We had also decided that reviews would be made of management reconstruction plans and that administrative orders would be issued to improve them if necessary, but the question was how to go about that specifically. To tell the truth, the survival or death of the Program for Financial Revival depended on the results of the specific institutional design that still needed to be done. That was why I had set up the Task Force on Financial Issues, made up of experts. Still, I absolutely needed to get the cooperation of the administrative staff of the FSA.

I only realized this point after I had assumed the office of financial services minister, but governmental administration really is the accumulation of many minute legal actions. It is precisely because bureaucrats control each of those that they wield such great power. While I did ask for the cooperation of the administrative staff, I also made the effort to involve myself actively in the discussions of details. Most politicians and commentators almost never show any interest or understanding of that level of discussion.

In mid-November, Prime Minister Koizumi invited Vice-Minister Itō, FSA Administrator Takagi, and me to a meal, at which he gave us the highest encouragement. He was probably aware of the importance of carrying out the specific execution of the policy after its broad outlines had been decided upon. That was the reason he gave us such special consideration. The administrative staff at the FSA was likely to be keenly aware of the change in policy direction, and the prime minister's strong stance toward it, including the developments that had happened up until that point. They worked hard to draw up the progress schedule as well as making the necessary behind-the-scenes maneuvering.

There was another task I had to carry out in combination with that. Namely, I had to draw up a simulation of the bad-debt transition after the Takenaka Plan came into effect. The original goal had been to halve the ratio of nonperforming loans from the current 8.4 percent to 4.0–4.9 percent in two and a half years. Still, I had to finalize a scenario for its realization even further. I had to come up with several scenarios that showed how the bad-debt ratio would change at certain points in time, correlating macroeconomic variables such as economic growth with such microeconomic variables as the ratio of transition from normal debt to those lenders on the "watch list," and the ratio of transition from those on the "watch list" to the "management list." As I will describe later, the bad-debt ratio did steadily decrease, but that was only because there had been such extremely precise numerical corroboration in the background. Some people said that the number of bad loans decreased by accident, and not because of the Takenaka Plan, but that was not the way it was at all.

But the main interest of the public at large was not with such minutiae as progress schedules. The same could be said all the more about simulations and technical problems such as transition rate probability, which never figured in anyone's conversations. All people were concerned with was how much longer the chaotic situation of the economy and politics would persist.

Looking at just the economy, the focus of public opinion was on how much worse the economy would get under the Takenaka Plan, and how much lower the stock market would go. From the time I took my double posting as financial services minister until the announcement of the Takenaka Plan, the stock market had slumped another 10 percent or so in a one-month period.

I viewed this is as a kind of tug-of-war. It was clear to many related persons that the Program for Financial Revival, if implemented step by step, would produce improvements in the economic situation over the medium-range future. In time, the forces moving in a positive direction would inevitably come into play. On the other hand, however, it was also obvious that several adjustments would be necessary in the process of disposing of the nonperforming loans. Among those adjustments would be the liquidation of those companies that clearly could not be revived. So in the short term, there would be negative economic forces at work. But in the medium-range future, the positive forces would definitely win out. The problem was when the turning point would come. That was, to a certain extent, the tug-of-war in the market.

In the political world, in contrast, attention was focused on movements toward a reckoning of my responsibility for the worsening economy, etc. Takenaka-bashing no longer stopped at mere personal attacks on me—people were now attempting to shake the foundations of the whole Koizumi administration, using that as an excuse. Indeed, developments started to influence the political situation visibly. Quite literally, this was a political tug-of-war between the reformers and the reactionary forces. Of course, by "reactionary forces" I do not mean just the old guard of the ruling coalition, but also the opposition parties; above all, the Democratic Party of Japan (DPJ). However, while the old guard considered my plan to be too severe, the DPJ mainly criticized it for being too watered down. For a short period at the end of the 1990s, the DPJ had taken the leading role in support of fiscal normalization. Despite that, they went into full-bore attack mode against me once I started the full-scale process toward the realization of such policies. Rather than make judgments about the propriety of individual policies, they were adjusting their position depending on the way the wind was blowing. That, after all, is what politics is.

Anyway, I was somehow able to announce the progress schedule by the end of November 2002, and, without making any fuss, started the task of building the framework working toward the execution of the Takenaka Plan. I was convinced that if I kept up the pace and steadily implemented the reforms, the bad-debt problem could definitely be resolved. Nonetheless, the Takenaka-bashing only got worse. The market tug-of-war and the political tug-of-war both continued for more than six months, and ended only when the market turned around in May 2003 after public funds were injected into the banks.

It was now mid-November, with the year drawing to a close. As one of the duties of my other cabinet post as state minister of economic and fiscal policy, I was nearing the important stage of compiling the budget. Needless to say, the actual work of drawing up the budget is the task of the Bureau of Accounts at the Ministry of Finance (MOF). As the economic and fiscal policy minister, my position was to create an overall picture of the budget for the advisory council from the standpoint of the entire government, and to perform macroeconomic checks. But the world at large was more interested in placing greater emphasis on my words and actions as financial services minister.

Under those circumstances, I was able to steadily feel indications that the effects of the Program for Financial Revival were starting to percolate through the market.

A bad-faith trial estimate

While at the FSA, I existed in a completely different dimension from the bashing I was getting in the political world, and it was important to continue the reform process there, without a fuss, in line with the progress schedule. Without relying on the administrative staff, I myself carefully addressed each problem, one by one, while consulting experts such as Kimura Takeshi, Kubori Hideaki, and Nomura Shūya. I was convinced that without such a process, the bad-debt disposal policies could not be made effective.

Specifically, there were several points in the progress schedule that were extremely important.

The first was to discuss and debate the procedural theory underpinning the new techniques (such as DCF) that would make asset assessment more rigorous, as well as to clarify the schedule for reflecting that in the audit manuals. I decided to have special examinations carried out relating to asset appraisals. I re-examined the format of business reports, and decided also to introduce external audits of capital adequacy ratios.

In addition, I decided to set the official approach to the business improvement orders for those banks that failed to meet the goals of their own management reconstruction plans, as well as clearly articulating where the responsibility lay, along with the schedule.

It was our common awareness that "strategy lies in the details," and in the interludes between Diet deliberations, we patiently and consistently continued with our work.

I believe that it is precisely because we designed the system so strictly concerning the above points, and also managed them so strictly, that they were followed up later by solid results. Also, that was only possible because I was "within the gates" of the financial authorities.

However, the difficult tug-of-war with the market was still going on. Despite the steady advances we made in organizing the framework for bad-debt disposal, the forces that feared a negative impact in the short term went into action, pushing the stock market down even further. Several of these were preliminary forecasts, one of which was the existence of trial estimates showing how much unemployment would increase on account of the bad-debt disposal.

Long before I became financial services minister, in June 2001, I had utilized the Economic and Social Research Institute (ESRI) of the Cabinet Office, to which I was assigned as state minister of economic and fiscal policy, to perform such trial calculations regarding the measures in the Program for Financial Revival. I had enlisted the services of Professor Nishimura Kiyohiko of the University of Tokyo to do the work.

Professor Nishimura's trial estimate was the result of carefully accumulated calculations, such as how much debt would be forgiven and how many corporations would go under as a result. He also looked at how many bankruptcies were caused by liquidation and how many by reconstruction. When most people hear about a company's management failing, the first thing that comes to their minds is workers losing their jobs. However, the crucial thing here is that bankruptcy does come in two forms: liquidation and reconstruction.

In the case of bankruptcy by liquidation, the company is literally liquidated, with many staff members losing their jobs. However, a large fraction of bankruptcies are of the reconstruction type. Here, while management is naturally taken to task for its responsibility, etc., the company itself does remain, reviving itself and surviving by specializing into its most competitive divisions, allowing a major portion of the staff to continue working. It was in order to encourage this type of corporate reconstruction that the government decided to establish the Industrial Revitalization Corporation of Japan (IRCJ).

In the trial estimate by Professor Nishimura, the number of people predicted to lose their jobs ranged from 130,000 to 190,000, with the number of people leaving their jobs ranging from 390,000 to 600,000. Not so many bankruptcies are of the liquidation type at all, suggesting that the situation could be improved without much confusion, even using the most careful estimates.

However, another trial estimate of the number of jobless was also released that differed widely from Professor Nishimura's: the one calculated by the Japan Research Institute (JRI). According to their calculations, the number of people who would have to leave their jobs as a result of the Program for Financial Revival would reach somewhere between 780,000 and 1.65 million. That was two to three times the Nishimura estimate. It is all fine and good in a policy debate for differing figures to be presented. But that particular estimate, no matter how favorably interpreted, had a giant bias built into it. I doubted whether the people at JRI who performed the calculation could really withstand their pangs of compunction as economists.

The JRI estimate served as a boon to the Takenaka-bashers. It was cited in the Diet by members of the Japan Communist Party (JCP), who asked me some tough questions. When asked what I thought of the numbers, I responded defiantly, "The trial calculation is strongly biased, and cannot be trusted. I supposed it can't be helped, anyway, as it was done by a subsidiary of the banks, which resent the disposal of the nonperforming loans."

Incidentally, the actual number of jobless after the financial reforms took effect fell considerably below the Nishimura estimate. In fact, the overall number of unemployed actually dropped by 580,000 in the two-year period from when the program took effect in October 2002.

Bad-faith policies

While such a bad-faith debate was taking place, an even worse policy debate was spreading throughout the political world. It reflected the blatant attempt, by those industries and corporations that might feel the effects of the Takenaka Plan, to apply pressure on the "taboo" of revising accounting standards. The debate took place at various levels, but largely concerned efforts to postpone the adoption of fair-value accounting, as well as to put an end to the asset-impairment accounting methods currently being used. But all that was really putting the cart before the horse. The blame ought not to be put on the standards that were adopted, but on the underlying real situation.

Accounting standards, after all, are the aggregate of the accounting standards recognized by society as fair. Until that point in time, I had pushed forward with reforms, having decided upon a schedule to establish worldwide accounting standards in Japan. That is a process that is demanded of every country, not just Japan. However, in Japan, the fact that some companies would be inconvenienced led to debate about the postponement of the adoption of those standards. That is just the same as trying to switch to a different measuring stick because it would be embarrassing for people to find out that something had gotten shorter. That would just make things even worse, and would only amplify the distrust of the markets.

This kind of debate especially picked up pace in March 2003 or so, when the stock market fell even further. On March 11, 2003, the Nikkei 225 stock index dropped below 7,900. The five top LDP executives, in a meeting held that day, discussed whether to abolish fair-value accounting. Immediately after the FSA's administrative staff told me about that, I received a phone call from the prime minister while I was biding time in the Liaison Office in the Diet. Having heard that accounting standards were growing into a problem, he called me to confirm the news. It was a typical demonstration of consideration by Prime Minister Koizumi, who didn't insert himself in debates about petty things, but always paid close attention whenever he thought the central core of a policy might be hijacked. I answered him by saying that such a policy would be impossible.

However, the media responded even more touchily than before to the movements of stock prices in the market, and the "anything-goes" mood also grew stronger as far as policy was concerned. In the March 12, 2003, edition of the *Yomiuri Shimbun*, the following report was made, in harsh criticism of the government:

> **Lack of a Policy Has Invited the Crisis Situation**
> . . . The government and the Bank of Japan ought to immediately affirm a revision in their economic policy. Debate must begin about putting together a rather substantial supplementary budget. As far as the prime minister and Financial Services Minister Takenaka are concerned, the Program for Financial Revival, largely drawn up under the guidance of Takenaka, needs to come under review. (*Yomiuri Shimbun*, March 12, 2003)

That evening I had the opportunity, by chance, to speak at a seminar hosted by the previous cabinet chief secretary Abe Shinzō (who later became prime minister). I made the following explanation during that seminar: "The Japanese economy's relative performance, when seen in global terms, is not so bad at all. From now on, also, the beneficial effects of the Program for Financial Revival will definitely emerge. You should save today's newspaper, with its articles that all seem rushed and panicky, and look at it three years from now. I'm sure it will seem very funny then!"

The press was fomenting a political crisis, and in the world of politics, criticism of me began more and more to be coupled with a demand for changes in accounting standards, as if the two were a set. Some people even went so far as to say that companies would suffer terribly because I had danced to the tune of the United States in my attempt to incorporate accounting standards such as fair-value accounting, etc. Certain discussions confused fair-value accounting with asset-impairment accounting, while others confused accounting standards with BIS standards (for capital adequacy). Just as "overnight commentators" had appeared on the scene in the debate about deferred tax assets a short while back, there were similar kinds of commentators talking about the issue of accounting standards. Looking back on things dispassionately, there were obviously powerful forces at work at that time trying to create a political situation, and part of that was intentionally being fomented by the media.

On March 16, 2003, four days after the Abe seminar, LDP General Council chairman Horiuchi Mitsuo launched an attack on me personally, calling for "the scholar's dismissal." On the next day, the 17th, people had gathered for the monthly economic report, and several leaders of the ruling coalition resoundingly spoke out for calling off fair-value accounting and BIS standards. On the 23rd, a "three generals, three policymakers" meeting was held, and discussions about revising the accounting standards were held even between those in the highest echelons of the ruling coalition. In my spare moments, I met with LDP Policy Research Council chairman Asō Tarō and Aizawa Hideyuki, but that didn't do any good either.

When I first heard discussions of this type, I thought that people must have been joking. It was hard for me to believe that party executives at the nerve center of the government of Japan, which boasts a 500-trillion-yen economy, would even be thinking about such things. Any arbitrary alteration of accounting standards, in itself, would bring shame to all of Japan in the eyes of the world. I took the approach of not compromising on this point one bit. Still, these kinds of discussions only intensified within the ruling coalition. The old shape of the LDP was still there, with pressure being applied on the government by those representing the interests of certain groups of people, without any concern for how ugly their efforts might be. There was also a thinly veiled intention to push forward a supplementary budget and reshuffle the cabinet, while falling short of producing a political crisis.

On March 28, 2003, the budget for the 2003 fiscal year was passed. Amidst the political and economic confusion, and with the election for the LDP president looming in September, all eyes were focused on the prime minister's press conference that day. He said, "There won't be any supplementary budget or cabinet reshuffle. If you want to vote for me in September, that'll be fine, and if you want to make me quit, you can do that, too." It was a courageous, manly conference.

Stock market falls to post-bubble low

Honestly speaking, it was contrary to my expectations that bad-faith policies such as changing accounting standards should be openly debated to that extent. It had never occurred to me whatsoever that even the leaders in charge of policymaking in the ruling coalition could engage in such unprincipled discussions. As I wrote earlier, this was completely putting the cart before the horse. It was just like saying about a patient who once weighed sixty kilograms but had unexpectedly lost twenty, "Well, we don't want to cause worry for everyone, so let's change the calibrations on the weight scale to make it look like they weigh a little more," or "Let's make a rule from now on saying that it's OK to wear an overcoat when measuring their weight." No matter how hard one tried to patch things up on the surface, the market would soon catch on. Moreover, it would have the opposite effect of making things harder to be seen, creating more confusion.

Under such circumstances, the April 12, 2003 morning edition of the *Yomiuri Shimbun* printed an editorial saying that there was no choice but to accept the change in accounting standards:

> **Freeze Fair-Value Accounting—A Necessary Measure for an Emergency Escape**
>
> Japan's economy is now on the brink of crisis. If corporations are forced at this juncture to adopt accounting procedures that will strip them naked, there is a danger that many of them will be forced to go under. Especially of concern are the banks, whose equity capital is being worn away by the disposal of nonperforming loans. (*Yomiuri Shimbun*, April 12, 2003)

Naturally, any move like altering accounting standards was out of the question.

My feeling was that the emergence of such opinions resulted from the sudden acceleration of the adjustment of the balance sheets of the banks and their corporate borrowers after the Program for Financial Revival came into effect. I understood it to be a good sign, as it was evidence that the originally expected effects were finally starting to appear.

In this period, the criticisms directed toward the bank reforms (as well as the criticisms directed at me personally) were coming from two different directions. The first comprised a stance that treated the reforms being implemented as too radical, saying that they would only confuse and worsen the economy, and urged a switch to more moderate policies. On the other hand, however, quite a few people criticized the Takenaka reforms for not going far enough, saying that nothing could come out of them.

For example, an editorial in the *Nihon Keizai Shimbun* on May 1, 2003, dealt with the theme of procrastinating on the bad-debt problem as follows:

> **The Government and Banks Should Cast Off Their Procrastinating Nature**
> Last autumn, when the minister of state for economic and fiscal policy and financial services minister Takenaka Heizō took over the post of financial services minister from Yanagisawa Hakuo, keeping his old post as well, there was a burgeoning sense of anticipation that there would be a big movement toward the restoration of the financial [banking] system. . . . That is because Mr. Takenaka expressed his idea that the government had to make an active response if the problem was to be solved. Even so, the anxiety about the financial system has not waned in the half year or more since then. . . . The government, as ever, is not squarely addressing the problem of alleviating people's fears about the financial system. . . . Part of the problem is the fact that the Program for Financial Revival, which came out last October, was debated and presented without undergoing thoroughgoing preparation. (*Nihon Keizai Shimbun*, May 1, 2003)

In the morning of May 4, 2003, a Sunday, many of the discussion programs on television contained criticism after criticism of the bad-debt disposal policies as being too soft. Watanabe Shōtarō of Kao Corp. said, "The Takenaka Plan is not moving forward." Sakakibara Eiji of Keio University declared, "The Takenaka Plan is a failure without the injection of public funds." People who had once criticized the Takenaka Plan as "radical" insofar as the problem of declaring deferred tax assets was concerned, and who had resisted the early injection of public funds, now turned around and took the position that the plan was "soft."

A column in the *Mainichi Shimbun* on the same day encapsulated all of this:

> **No Use for a Saint Heizō**
> . . . When Takenaka Heizō appeared on the scene as financial services minister, aiming to completely cure the banks, we pinned expectations on him while accepting that some risks would be involved. For some reason, though, the man who had appeared to be the "Devil Heizō" now seems to be ending up as the tolerant Saint Heizō? . . . We have no use for someone who is nothing more than a lowly helper of the authorities. (*Mainichi Shimbun*, May 4, 2003)

While brushing off the "let a hundred schools of thought flourish" approach of the media, I sensed that the effects of the program were beginning to filter through. However, the market tug-of-war that I cited earlier was still continuing. Although the positive effects were supposed to reveal themselves in the medium-range future, the stock market continued to decline because of worries about the negative effects of balance-sheet adjustments in the short term.

With stock prices so low, it was anticipated that the debates following the Golden Week holidays would be even more chaotic. I had no inkling yet, at that time, that a monumental turning point was about to arrive after the Golden Week holidays—one that would shift the direction of the Japanese economy.

5. Resona Bank: The Injection of Public Funds

The Resona issue comes to the fore

The first news I got about it came from my private secretary for political affairs, Kishi Hiroyuki, in the late hours of May 6, 2003. A dinnertime conference of cabinet ministers had met earlier that day, and my briefing session with Kishi was insufficient. While I was at the dinner meeting, he was eagerly going around gathering information, as usual, and happened upon an astounding piece of news. Namely, he learned that a third-party audit of the recently merged Resona Bank, in its evaluation of the bank's deferred tax assets, held a grim opinion of the situation, and it appeared that the bank's capital adequacy might even fall below the required minimum (of 4 percent).

It goes without saying that if the bank could not restore its capital adequacy after dipping below 4 percent, public funds would have to be injected, according to Article 102 of the Deposit Insurance Law, the so-called "#1 Measure." We would have to wait for the figures of the prior fiscal year (which had ended March 31, 2003) to be released later that month to confirm it, but in that interval, this problem threatened to rise to the surface.

At that time, I told Kishi, "Act calm and collected, follow the rules, and don't let day-to-day stock price movements get to you. Let's proceed without hiding the problem." In fact, these words were also meant as advice to myself.

Previously, Kishi, who was also my political private secretary, had also gotten wind of many different pieces of information and had provided them to me. Although the information I got from the FSA administrative staff was obviously important, bureaucratic organizations always tend to be risk-averse, so they generally filter the information that they pass on to ministers. In order for me not to become wrapped around the bureaucrats' fingers, so to speak, by being given only the information they thought I should know, it was utterly important for me to have someone such as Secretary Kishi, who was handling political affairs without belonging to the administrative staff. It was from him that I received such important information.

The next day, I kept a close eye on the kind of information that the administrative staff was giving me. That morning, the auditing corporation sent information about Resona Bank. For the most part, it was the same as the information given to me the previous night by Kishi. In various proceedings before then, the administrative staff had been aware that I had information obtained through the political-affairs route. I told them that I would deal with the case in accordance with the three following principles: "Don't hide anything, don't bend the principles, and do everything by the rules."

In addition, I directed them to make arrangements in advance to deal with any contingencies. That was my way of telling them that, depending on the situation, funds might have to be injected based on Article 102 of the Deposit Insurance Law. One of the top FSA officials then said to me, "We have been telling ruling party officials that there won't be any banks this time whose capital adequacy will be found to be insufficient in the current round of financial statements." That was a comment that could easily be expected from a bureaucrat whose nature it was to be obsessed with his own infallibility. Reclaiming the issue as my own, I said, "Don't let it bother you. I will explain everything should the need arise."

That same evening, I visited the prime minister at his official residence to explain the state of the progress of the Program for Financial Revival. After finishing the explanation, I decided to give him only a rough outline of the Resona matter. Yet it was a problem that might come to require extremely important decisionmaking on the part of the cabinet. Having gotten the sense that the prime minister would probably hold a financial crisis-response meeting and agree to the injection of public funds, I left his residence.

On May 9, 2003, it was Secretary Kishi again who told me that he had received word that people within the FSA were working behind the scenes to try, somehow, to avoid a situation in which Resona's capital adequacy ratio would drop below 4 percent. The banks, bureaucrats, and auditing firms were likely thinking that if a new situation arose this time, they would no longer be able to justify their past actions. I believed that it was precisely those sorts of repeated actions that were the fundamental factor postponing the solution to this problem for a whole decade. I made a repeated directive to FSA commissioner Takagi to make sure that everyone in the FSA absolutely followed the three principles of "don't hide anything, don't bend the principles, and do everything by the rules."

Buckling under

On Sunday, May 11, 2003, another piece of information came to me via Secretary Kishi. Apparently, Resona's auditing firm had buckled under and estimated the declared deferred tax assets leniently, so that the bank's capital adequacy ratio now ended up just above the 4 percent line. Among the various auditing firms, there seemed to be a fierce clash between the forces that attempted to make evaluations properly and those who feared rocking the boat and wanted to pretend that nothing happened in the past. There seemed to be a similar game of cat and mouse in the banks as well. Perhaps the same kind of thing was happening in the FSA, too. As if symbolic of such intra-organizational conflict, a so-called "record of meetings" between the banks and auditors started to circulate a few days later. While there was no way to confirm the document's authenticity, the fact that it did circulate at all shows how great the internal confusion and conflict was.

On Wednesday, May 14, 2003, I visited the prime minister's residence again, this time accompanied by top staff members from the FSA. The purpose of our visit was to explain the financial statement situation at the banks as a whole, as the statements were scheduled to be released soon after. That kind of visit was made regularly by the financial authorities. Of course, we had to talk about the Resona problem this time, too. The provisional report of the financial statement that we had received from Resona, however, had shown the 4 percent capital adequacy ratio being maintained, meaning that it would not pose any particular problem. That was similar to the information that Kishi had given me three days earlier. The mood emanating from the administrative staff was that Resona's capital adequacy ratio would exceed 4 percent in this year's round of financial statement announcements.

After completing the series of explanations, I sent the administrative staff back to the FSA, and faced Prime Minister Koizumi alone, one on one. He, too, seemed to sense the prevailing mood. At that point, I ventured an explanation that went even further, telling him that there was a possibility that Resona's capital adequacy ratio had fallen below 4 percent, and that I, myself, believed the likelihood of that happening to be rather high. The prime minister then responded quietly, "What you're saying is that the explanations that I heard just now are all wrong, right?"

I went on to tell him about the first piece of news I had received about this issue, and then about the fierce clash that continued thereafter, ending up at the current stage, in which the provisional numbers showed the 4 percent level somehow being maintained. I followed up by explaining how we were proceeding somberly, not hiding anything, not bending the principles, and doing everything by the rules. Prime Minister Koizumi then said emphatically, "Do it just like that!"

The auditing firms were probably concerned about the fact that a great social problem would arise if the assessment discovered a situation of inadequate capital. It is a fact that there were many related parties who tried to capitalize on that, hoping for a result that would somehow maintain the 4 percent capital adequacy ratio for this fiscal period. However, whether or not there is insufficient capital adequacy is not the problem of the auditing firms, but something that the financial supervising authorities need to consider. I wanted the auditing firms to fulfill their social responsibility of conducting fair audits, keeping their confidence and pride as accountants. I expected that from them.

Be that as it may, there was no doubt that everything would come to a head that night for all parties concerned, including the banks, the auditors, and the FSA. On May 14th, a long night lay before us, exactly one week after I had first received word about the Resona problem.

Take action, but make no apologies

On Thursday, May 15, 2003, I received a message from the FSA while commuting by car to work. According to the message, it was highly likely that Resona's outside auditors were going to allow a declaration of only a certain portion (three years) of the deferred tax assets; that was probably going to be their final conclusion. That meant that the FSA department handling the case was surely aflutter at the moment. In other words, by limiting the amount of assets that could be declared, it was a sure thing that Resona's capital adequacy ratio would fall well below the 4 percent level. This meant that the only recourse that could now be taken was to inject public funds. Moreover, that had to be done expeditiously. The moment of truth had arrived for the auditing authorities—that is, the FSA.

There is a phrase often used by the Bank of England that goes something like, "Take action, but make no apologies." This means that it is important for banking authorities, who have to remain fully vigilant in preventing rumors, to first develop a responsible framework, as they must be ready to act quickly if some sort of problem arises, even before an explanation can be given. If a bank is facing financial difficulties, the authorities cannot merely announce it, but need to announce the fact only after they have effected a situation in which those difficulties can be eliminated.

The same thing naturally is also called for in the governmental administration of Japanese banks. In situations where capital levels fail to meet certain standards, it is impossible to leave the matter to the markets unattended for even the slightest moment. That is why the law (the Deposit Insurance Law) arranges for a financial crisis-response meeting to be called in such cases; there, the decision is made to inject public funds if necessary. After consulting with the top staff of the FSA, I unofficially decided to hold such a meeting on Saturday, May 17, 2003, and then went to the prime minister's residence to tell both the prime minister and the chief cabinet secretary my intention. However, I had just visited the prime minister's office the day before. So, from the position of "taking action but making no apologies," I had to keep the issue of the crisis-response meeting under wraps, no matter what it took, until the very day of the meeting itself. I thus went to the prime minister's residence ostensibly to give the chief cabinet secretary the same explanation about the banks' financial statements that I had given the day before. Actually, however, the prime minister's room is linked to the chief cabinet secretary's room by an inner corridor; I used this to visit the prime minister, as I did not want to be seen by reporters. There, I received swift approval for both the meeting itself and its date and time. The next task at hand was to marshal the strength of the whole FSA to attend to the matter.

That night, I got together with the top FSA staff in a full-fledged strategy meeting. There were a multitude of technical financial matters, minute legal procedures, and political considerations to be taken care of— for example, the order of business leading up to the crisis-response meeting, the decision on how much money to inject, and the behind-the-scenes consensus-building process—all of which were very different tasks from one another, and complex. I have only one word to describe the quality of the work performed by the FSA administrative staff at that time, from Commissioner Takagi on downward, and that is "spectacular." Under a truly airtight regime, they conducted a series of many elaborate, precise tasks. The staff would pull all-nighters two days in a row to get everything done.

On the night of March 15, 2003, I was about to leave the FSA to go home when I was confronted by a newspaper reporter in the corridor. He said, "I've caught wind somehow that Resona Bank and its auditors are at odds with each other. Any comment about that?" I responded, "Oh, really? I haven't heard anything, really. Well, you know, it's the financial statement season, so who knows what you might hear!"

I fervently hoped that no information would leak out in the two days leading up to the crisis-response meeting. It was the same feeling that I had had long before, when we were drawing up the Takenaka Plan. At that time, everyone was focused on the issue of deferred tax assets, and I had prayed that they would not pay attention to the other items in the plan. Now I remembered my state of mind back then.

The bulk of the preparations were completed by the night of Thursday, March 15, 2003. The most difficult task was deciding when and with whom to make the consensus-building moves behind the scenes, and how much to tell them. As with any other policy, in the parliamentary cabinet system of government, where the government and the ruling party or parties are one and the same, it is absolutely necessary to have advance consultation with the ruling coalition leaders. If that is not done, the legislative process and all that follows will get bogged down. On the other hand, if the task of consensus-building is done too carefully, information is likely to leak out. And this time, especially, it involved the extremely atypical case of a financial crisis-response meeting. In bureaucratic lingo, building up a consensus with influential individuals this way is called "critical passage" consensus-building. The bureaucrats in the Ministry of Finance (MOF) and related agencies are particularly adept at this, in terms of both techniques and experience. I had to get them to give full rein to their powers this time.

Another point that was important—this time only—was when and how to let the Bank of Japan (BOJ) know. In times of chaos and confusion, the BOJ must rely on emergency finance. The fact that the BOJ has such an emergency finance framework in itself serves to stabilize the market. However, I felt that the BOJ should be notified only at the very last moment. I had to consider the risk that information would leak to the outside from the Bank.

This is an interesting point, but the amount of distrust felt by the top officials of the FSA toward the BOJ was by no means small. Although the BOJ wields a great amount of authority, conversely it hardly ever has to take direct blame for its actions. In its dealings with the Diet and others, then, the burden of the BOJ is clearly much less onerous than that of the FSA. The FSA's top officials' bone of contention was that "in situations with sizable authority but little accountability, the management of information tends to be loose." They told me that similar situations had happened in the past. At any rate, it was important to spare no pains in managing information, including the BOJ problem.

The financial crisis-response meeting

Starting on May 16, 2003, Prime Minister Koizumi went down to Okinawa for two days, as he had already been scheduled to attend the Japan–Pacific Islands Forum (PIF) Summit Meeting then. So I made several calls to Okinawa on that day, informing him about how the preparatory work was going, and received the necessary directives from him. On May 17, he was to return to Tokyo's Haneda Airport shortly after five o'clock in the afternoon and go directly to his residence from there. The plan was to give him a briefing right off the bat, after which the financial crisis-response meeting would be held. The amount of funds to be injected was decided at around ¥2 trillion (around $16.7 billion at the prevailing exchange rate of $1=¥120), allowing the bank to have a level of capital adequacy equal to that of the top regional banks.

The very last task to be taken care of was to make contact with the "critical-passage" bigwigs, and to build consensus with them. On the night of May 16, 2003, it was finally determined that the financial crisis-response meeting would be held the next day. Starting that evening, the major FSA officials and I shut ourselves up in a conference room in the ANA Hotel in Akasaka (Tokyo) in order to hold the final strategy meeting. The following afternoon, we were to make an announcement saying that the crisis-response meeting would be held. We did so with the full awareness that the news would make the evening newspapers. The problem was trying to prevent the morning newspapers from scooping the news. Our only choice, in the end, was to go about the behind-the-scenes consensus-building with all the "critical-passage" top officials, starting the next morning, successively. To that end, we had to make painstaking preparations to find out where to contact those officials at what times, and to assign one staff person to serve as the contact point for each of them. In addition, we had to give careful consideration to the fact that banking is a global business. For that reason, we also had to set up a system to communicate with the bank-auditing authorities overseas as well. We finally completed all the necessary preparations at around 11:30 p.m. on May 16, 2003.

With this load off our shoulders, it was time for us to have some tea. However, just at that moment, the Nikkei Net (a Web magazine run by the *Nihon Keizai Shimbun*) ran the news that "a financial crisis-response meeting will be held tomorrow, with funds to be injected into Resona Bank." All our preparations for the "critical-passage" consensus building had now fallen through. How had the news leaked? Where did it leak from? All sorts of thoughts raced through our heads in the blink of an eye. But we had no time to dawdle here, not even a second.

We could no longer wait until the next day. Seeing that now the morning newspapers would print the news, we had to contact all the major "critical-passage" officials right away. So we shifted gears immediately and started making the rounds by phone at a ferocious pace. Because it was so sudden, and because it was a weekend (Friday night), we couldn't reach everyone very easily, but still, we struggled desperately to do so. We had divided up the responsibility among us of whom to call, and it was not until past 3 a.m. when I finally finished contacting all the officials I had been put in charge of calling directly. All of us were completely exhausted. Despite that, we still could not afford to slip up at tomorrow's conference. All of us were ready to fight.

Injecting public funds

The new day dawned: it was May 17, 2003, the day that the financial crisis-response meeting was to be held. I got to the FSA office with plenty of time to spare, arriving around noon. I had already been informed by the security detail that around fifty members of the press were packed in the office. The building in which the FSA is located has several entrances. I usually used the front entrance or the underground parking entrance, but the reporters were already posted there, so I went in through an entrance I had never used before, the one on the side of the Ministry of Foreign Affairs (MOFA). I was able to slip into my office quietly, escaping the attention of the reporters.

After I entered my office, I had to take care of several final details. I continued making a few phone calls to build consensus. After that, I phoned the prime minister down in Okinawa and made final confirmation of the arrangements. Article 102 of the Deposit Insurance Law provides for the capability to apply for the injection of public funds in cases where a bank's capital adequacy ratio dips below 4 percent and cannot recover. In that case, public funds will be injected if the FSA deems it necessary for the purpose of averting systemic risk. This system was a measure of last resort, just like using a family's heirloom sword; moreover, it was a sword that could not be pulled out. Be that as it may, the first financial crisis-response meeting was about to be held in the process of disposing of Japan's nonperforming loans, and the injection of public funds was to be decided upon.

As scheduled, Prime Minister Koizumi arrived back at his official residence shortly before six o'clock in the evening. He did not show any signs of having been worn out by the trip from Okinawa, and listened quietly as I briefed him about the details of the events leading up to the meeting. At 6:30 p.m., also very close to being on schedule, the first financial crisis-response meeting began. After thirty minutes of somber proceedings, the meeting came to an end. That was how the disposal of nonperforming loans—a key element of Prime Minister Koizumi's reforms—and the symbolic injection of public funds into Resona Bank was decided.

Obviously, it was going to be even more difficult for me now that the meeting had ended. The first thing I had to do was to explain the measure properly to the Japanese public. The first hurdle was the press conference held after the meeting. It started at 7:40 p.m.

I started out by explaining the events leading up to this point, and then explained three points concerning its significance. First, this was "not the failure, but the recovery" of Resona Bank. Second, the step was "not a crisis, but a step to prevent a crisis." Third, it was "not a nationalization of the bank, but public support." Those opposing the injection of public funds from a political standpoint tended to stress the negative images of failure, crisis, and nationalization. However, those were not correct explanations. Indeed, my explanations of "recovery, not failure," "crisis prevention, not a crisis," and "public support, not nationalization" accurately reflected the spirit of Article 102 of the Deposit Insurance Law.

Another focus of my comments in the press conference concerned so-called shareholder responsibility. According to the current legal framework, the injection of public funds cannot imply the usurpation by the national government of the stock value of existing shareholders. Before that, some used to venture the opinion that existing shareholders ought to be held accountable as long they received assistance in the form of national funds. But as a matter of fact, shareholders do suffer a diffusion of the valuation of their stock holdings through the effective capital increase (i.e., diffusion) generated by the infusion of capital in this way. Furthermore, because of the limits placed on the distribution of dividends by management reconstruction plans, the shareholders must answer for their responsibility to that extent as well. That is the current legal framework. If, in addition, some people call for the valuation of the holdings of existing shareholders to be reduced to zero, then that would clearly be an infringement of property rights as spelled out in the Constitution. If shareholders are to be held accountable to that extent, then the Deposit Insurance Law needs to be changed first, and for that to happen, the overarching premise provided by the Constitution would need to be amended also. That was the nature of the discussion.

The press posed many other questions at the conference, making it very long. The fervor of the reporters combined with the heat of the lights caused me to break out in a sweat. In order for the public to correctly understand the measure taken this time, I carefully and repeatedly explained the concepts underlying the law, namely, "recovery, not failure," "crisis prevention, not a crisis," and "public support, not nationalization." The press conference lasted for more than an hour.

And then, the turnaround

The reactions of the newspapers the next morning were mixed.

The headlines in the *Asahi Shimbun* symbolized this: "Decision to Inject Public Funds into Resona" and "A Split Judgment: 'Successful Outcome' and 'Failed Policy.'"

In any event, I had to continue explaining the injection of public funds from now on in various ways: to the ruling coalition, the Diet, the media, the public, and so forth. Besides that, at the same time as I accelerated efforts in that respect, Resona Bank's management system needed reorganization. Having anticipated the need for such an arrangement, we had already included detailed decisions in the Program for Financial Revival about how to go about the superintendence of a bank that had received an injection of public funds.

The first explanation I made was before the ruling coalition. Although consensus-building of sorts had been done right before the financial crisis-response meeting with the "critical-passage" officials, further explanation was now necessary. In the first place, it was more difficult than expected to get the politicians to correctly understand such things as how the Deposit Insurance Law was organized, what the real situation at Resona Bank was like, and what sort of standards had been used to make our judgment. Some segments of the mass media were already advancing laughable arguments far removed from those correct policy arguments, concerning themselves with such things as the "suffering" caused by the Koizumi reforms and Takenaka's "bullying" of the banks.

On May 18, 2003, the day following the crisis-response meeting, I lost no time in meeting with the three ruling coalition secretaries-general, giving them an explanation about the Resona issue. The meeting was realized thanks to the advice of Lower House member Yasuoka Okiharu, who proposed the meeting to LDP secretary-general Yamazaki Taku. In fact, ever since I had become financial services minister, Yasuoka had unfailingly phoned me with advice at all the critical junctures. He had also appealed for the importance of solving the bad-debt problem during the developments up to this point.

The most important issues now, having injected funds into Resona Bank, were how to formulate its management framework and precisely whom to put in the top positions of management. Injecting capital into the bank at the expense of the public treasury would only bear significance if a solid management system were set in place that could turn the bank around.

No later than one day after the crisis-response meeting did I start the job of choosing the bank's management. Getting insight from people in the business world, I intended to make a decision on the new CEO very swiftly. Simultaneously, I felt it was necessary to decisively make use of external board members for the purpose of creating a management framework with reinforced governance. On Monday, May 19, 2003, right after I arrived at the FSA offices, I instructed the administrative staff to consider making Resona Bank a company that had adopted a committee-management board structure. Incidentally, at that point in time, several major Japanese companies, including both Sony Corporation and Nomura Securities Co., Ltd., were transitioning to become such companies, but there were no major banks that had done so yet.

For Resona's new top executive, I thought I would ask Hosoya Eiji, who had just retired as executive vice president of the East Japan Railway Company (JR East), and started to make the necessary behind-the-scenes moves to build consensus. I was also actively proceeding with the selection of the external board members. On Friday, May 30, 2003, less than just two weeks after deciding to inject public funds, I reached the point that a public announcement of the new management team could be made. With that, the creation of the management framework was finished for the most part. The revival of Resona Bank from then on was completely in the hands of the new management, revolving around Hosoya and others.

During the period this was all going on, the Diet was the scene of heated debates about the Resona issue. The deliberations there were peppered with a series of comments that seemed clearly to have ulterior motives from our vantage point, including "The FSA must have applied pressure," or "There must have been some deception involved." Those comments were merely attempts by the opposition to make a public show of their political position. Worse still was the document presented in the Diet by the Democratic Party of Japan (DPJ) purporting to be evidence of whistleblowing inside Resona. They then followed up on that by saying, "The FSA applied pressure on Resona." Of course, there was no way for me to argue about a document with such dubious origins, whose authenticity could not be confirmed one way or the other. Much later (in 2006), a notorious incident occurred during the Livedoor hearings in the Diet when an e-mail produced by Diet member Nagata Hisayasu was found to be falsified. At this point (in 2003), however, documents of such dubious origins were still being brazenly bandied about by members of the Diet without any qualms.

I took this as a good opportunity to resolve to push forward with reforms within the FSA. The document that showed up in the Diet deliberations lacked any reliability whatsoever, to be sure, but it still behooved us, as the authorities, to set ourselves straight. Many corporations now attach great importance to compliance, and have set up sections devoted solely to that. However, come to think of it, there were no "compliance sections" in any of the ministries or agencies in Kasumigaseki. I thereupon decided to set up within the FSA the first-ever compliance office to appear in the government offices of Kasumigaseki. This experiment was later imitated in several other government offices.

Having undergone a variety of debates and discussions, the Japanese economy was at last ready to experience an important turning point. This was because two important changes were starting to be evident. First, the stock market started to rebound. In the market tug-of-war, the positive forces of the medium term were finally starting to win out over the negative forces of the short term. A little while after the financial crisis-response meeting, at the end of May, the stock market clearly shifted its direction upward. Three years after that (in 2006), the stock market had climbed 110 percent, and bank stocks 260 percent. It was clear that the injection of public funds had shifted the underlying sentiment of the market.

The second change was revealed in the financial statements gathered from the major banks at the end of May 2003, showing that the banks' bad-debt ratio was clearly starting to go down.

To accomplish the goal of halving the bad-debt ratio in two and half years from the 8.1 percent level seen in the half-year period ending in September 2002, there had to be a decline of approximately 0.8 points in the ratio every six months. The statements for the period ending in March 2003 showed a period-on-period decline of 0.9 points for the bad-debt ratio—a margin of decline that would enable the banks to meet the goal. Having reviewed the financial statements, I was convinced, without a doubt, that the Program for Financial Revival would succeed.

In May 2003, after the first ever financial crisis-response meeting, the gears of the Japanese economy were steadily starting to move toward normalization.

6. Further Financial Reform

Another cabinet reshuffle

In the morning of Tuesday, August 12, 2003, the GDP figures for the second quarter of 2003 were released. They were better than expected, showing an annualized growth rate of 2.3 percent. At that point in time, I thought that such figures served as renewed confirmation of the positive effects of the Program for Financial Revival. But the world of politics was still devoid of any discussion that the economy was improving. I believed that there was now a need to promote an additional set of financial reforms so as to make the economy's recovery conclusive.

On Sunday, September 8, 2003, the voting for the LDP president finally began. Besides Prime Minister Koizumi, the other candidates running for office included Fujii Takao, Kamei Shizuka, and Kōmura Masahiko. As with the previous election, the main argument was over the fundamental nature of macroeconomic policies. Specifically, the candidates other than the prime minister all supported an increase in public spending. In other words, they all supported traditional demand-expansion policies rather than structural reform. Moreover, they did that despite the fact that the underlying tendency of the economy was clearly moving toward recovery. This suggested that many people still believed at that point in time that economic recovery would be difficult without increased public spending. In addition, there was probably pressure from vested interests prior to the LDP presidential election.

The debate in the media was also confused. In different newspapers published on September 13, 2003, there were two diametrically opposite editorials printed, as follows:

> **Candidates Who Do Not Learn from the Past**
> Exactly what era are these political debates supposed to be from? We can hardly believe our ears. . . . The three candidates challenging Prime Minister Koizumi in the upcoming LDP presidential election all emphasized the need for increased public spending (pump-priming measures) in order to lift the economy. . . . That kind of thinking comes from a decade or so ago. (*Asahi Shimbun*, September 13, 2003)

> **Don't Relax the Hand of Policy toward a Full-Blown Recovery**
> . . . The government ought not to loosen the hand of policy until the recovery of the economy becomes full-blown. Any moves toward a recovery ought to be given a powerful boost. (*Yomiuri Shimbun*, September 13, 2003)

On September 20, 2003, the LDP presidential election finally took place, ending up with an overwhelming victory for Prime Minister Koizumi. Reportedly a lot of political horse-trading took place during this period. There is no way for me to know for sure, as I was neither a member of the Diet nor a member of the LDP.

In any event, to make Japan better, structural reform had to be continued, no matter what. Ever since the injection of funds into Resona, the fruits were finally beginning to emerge. The reforms now had to be accelerated, whatever the risk. Before that, though, there was an election to be won. That is, we had to win the power struggle. At that time, there were probably various different players around Koizumi who were making all sorts of deals. He taught me once again, I felt, just how difficult it is to maintain the prime ministership.

On Monday, September 22, 2003, the cabinet was going to be reshuffled. Amidst the media hoopla, my car was being tailed by press cars from the morning onward. At the FSA offices, before noon, the top officials gave me a toast under the supposition that I would resign as financial services minister. At one o'clock, I was called into the prime minister's residence. On the television in the reception room, NHK was reporting that the post of financial services minister had been taken from me, leaving me with only the post of state minister in charge of economic and fiscal policy. The network also broadcast another person's name as my successor. I was then called into the adjacent office of the prime minister, where I was handed my letter of appointment once again. It read, "Appointed as minister of state for economic and fiscal policy and financial services minister." The prime minister had kept me in both posts.

That night, on TV Tokyo's "World Business Satellite" (a business news program), my friend Robert Feldman (chief economist at Morgan Stanley Asset Management, Tokyo) posed an astute question to a political reporter who was sitting with him. He asked, "How come political reporters keep on making mistakes?"

7. The Endgame of the Lost Decade

The lessons of financial reform

With the cabinet reshuffle of September 27, 2004, I left the post of financial services minister. In the two years that I had grappled with the disposal of nonperforming loans as the financial services minister, as well as the periods both preceding and following it, I felt that I learned several valuable lessons about the process of determining policy and implementing it. Of course, there is no end to reform. On the financial side of things, there are still many problems remaining in terms of boosting profitability and disposing of the debts of small and medium-sized firms. Let me be so bold here, however, as to offer three lessons based on my experiences so far.

The first lesson, as I have reiterated several times, is that leaving all the details of policy to the bureaucrats without designing a system solidly will never produce any results. "Strategy lies in the details," after all. I believe that the Program for Financial Revival yielded positive effects precisely because of that.

The responses to Resona Bank became possible only because the details of the program had been worked out, down to the details of individual procedures, and because a meticulous work schedule had also been planned to implement it. The banks had become experts at using procrastinating techniques up until then, so we incorporated devices throughout the program that would not let them do that. Also, we even intentionally devoted an entire chapter of the program to the details of how a bank would be managed if public funds were used. That is precisely why we were able to enable bank governance without creating a management vacuum, and why we could avoid disruption during crisis periods. It also allowed us to get a good start on the revival process.

Those detailed items rarely came up for scrutiny, be it in the tough negotiations with the ruling coalition, the criticisms by the press, or the questions by the opposition in the Diet. Nevertheless, the strategy of the Takenaka Team lay in those details, though they were unnoticed by many.

The second lesson is how the bureaucratic mind, which clings to its own sense of infallibility, acts as such a solid wall of bedrock against reform. I have already written in detail about direct instances of resistance, but what I would like to emphasize is that the same mechanism also operates in the private sector and the media. For example, it is evident that independent auditors, who played an important role in evaluating capital adequacy, were conflicted on account of worries about consistency with previous audit results. Even private-sector professionals have the problem of their own sense of infallibility.

In addition, in the world of journalism, including newspapers, there are many striking cases of weasel-worded discussions resulting from people sticking with arguments they have made in the past. For instance, one person who was critical of the Program for Financial Revival at the time has this to say in a recent article: "The fact that the disposal of nonperforming loans proceeded is not so much because Takenaka made the correct diagnosis, but because of several fortunate circumstances." I don't deny at all that we were lucky. But if results only depended on whether one had good or bad luck, then there would be no need for government to go to any trouble at all.

Everyone is stuck with their own sense of infallibility. I can't help being reminded of these words in the *Analects* of Confucius: "Someone who makes a mistake and doesn't rectify it is making another mistake."

The third lesson is related to the second one, and that is that Japan has yet to fully make a reckoning with its past policies and administration. That, sad to say, is a problem that I was unable to overcome myself. I wrote about people's sense of their own infallibility and clinging to actions made in the past, but it goes without saying that the word "reform" means to reform things that need reforming. All the same, that does not mean that problems from the past ought to be left unexamined, without being held to account. The banks that had kept on shunting aside their problems got caught up in the rigorous checks made by the Takenaka Plan, and some of them ended up being subjected to harsh punishment. However, it also needs to be carefully examined whether the governmental bureaucracy itself took sufficient action during the time that the banks pushed aside their problems. In the two years that I served as financial services minister, my main focus was on changing the conditions in what might be called a time of emergency. However, I believe that at some time, somewhere in the future, the bureaucracy's past actions will also require review.

That examination should not be limited to a review of the governmental administration of banks alone. However, in today's Japan, such a review is rarely undertaken. After all, it ought to be proper to review why the bubble economy happened in the first place, and whether the government's policies and the bureaucracy's response were sufficient. Moreover, such a review should be undertaken by experts who are independent of the bureaucracy, and with a sufficient amount of authority vested in them. In the West, legislatures have been known to enlist the services of experts to make investigations, and Japan should definitely conduct the same kind of investigations, using those cases as reference material.

In the reporting period that ended immediately before the end of the Koizumi administration (namely, the April 2005 to March 2006 fiscal year), the bad-debt ratio of Japan's major banks had declined to 1.9 percent, or one-fourth of the peak level of 8.4 percent. The resolution of the bad-debt problem, the epitome of reactive reforms, served as an important breakthrough that enabled the implementation of the Koizumi reform program while also providing us with several important lessons.

Courtesy of author.

Originally published as chapter 2 of *The Structural Reforms of the Koizumi Cabinet: An Insider's Account of the Economic Revival of Japan* by Nihon Keizai Shimbun Shuppansha in 2008; abridged by about one-quarter.

Note

1. The phrase "large-boned policy" (*honebuto no hōshin*), where the adjectival noun *honebuto* or "large-boned" implies breadth, sturdiness, power, and decisiveness, was used by Koizumi to distinguish himself as a strong, decisive leader capable of restructuring an out-of-date socioeconomic system.—Ed.

Part III

Deflation and Monetary Policy

Part III addresses monetary issues in two areas. The first is deflation, with essays in this regard discussing the causes of deflation and monetary policies addressing it. The second comprises issues arising from the Big Bang and the financial crisis, essays on which consider the large-scale liberalization of the financial system in 1996 and Japan's financial crisis in 1997.

1. Deflation

Deflation occurs when the inflation rate dips below zero or remains extremely low. It was around the year 2000 that deflation became recognized as a major problem that the government should rectify. Prior to 2000, "price issues" referred to rising prices, and economic policy in relation to prices was designed to lower the inflation rate. As the economy continued to languish, however, deflation attracted growing attention as a cause of the slump on the grounds that when prices fall, real interest rates rise and real debt increases, exerting a negative effect on the economy. Intuitively, too, the economy does not grow much in nominal terms under deflationary conditions. In other words, both corporate sales and nominal wages tend to stall, placing the economy in a bleak light.

Responding to the expectation that monetary policy would play a major role in escaping deflation, the government opted for lower interest rates, zero interest, and quantitative easing so as to increase the amount of available money. From 2013, Abe's cabinet took a step into the unknown when it began experimenting with policies such as the introduction of inflation targeting, "monetary easing of a different dimension," negative interest rates, and yield curve control as part of its "Abenomics" program.

Yoshikawa Hiroshi's essay entitled "Do Expectations Raise Prices?" criticizes the monetary policy pursued under Abenomics. Abenomics' "monetary easing of a different dimension" sought to raise people's inflation expectations by instituting large-scale monetary easing so as to reach a 2 percent inflation target. The author rejects this mechanism, arguing that prices are decided by wages and by the cost of individual goods and services.

"Chronic Deflation in Japan," authored by Nishizaki Kenji, Sekine Toshitaka, and Ueno Yōichi, examines structural factors underpinning the many causes of Japan's chronic deflation, including the zero lower bound on the nominal interest rate, people's price expectations, and a decline in potential growth capacity.

In "Why Has Japan Failed to Escape from Deflation?" Watanabe Kōta and Watanabe Tsutomu conduct an international comparison of price changes, demonstrating that for companies in Japan, zero inflation has become the default.

Iwata Kikuo takes a pioneering reflationary approach in "Encouraging Moderate Inflation," arguing that Japan can free itself from deflation by setting inflation targets and increasing the monetary base.

The best way of gleaning official views on monetary policy in Japan at any given point in time is to look at lectures given by the governor of the Bank of Japan (BOJ) in his official capacity. Two such lectures were chosen for this volume—one by Shirakawa Masaaki, the BOJ governor prior to Abenomics, and the other by Kuroda Haruhiko, governor during Abenomics. "The Bank of Japan's Efforts toward Overcoming Deflation" is a speech given by Shirakawa in his last year as governor, while "Overcoming Deflation: The Bank of Japan's Challenge" was delivered by Kuroda in his first year in the post when "monetary easing of a different dimension" had just begun.

2. The Big Bang and the Financial Crisis

In addition to the battle with deflation, the Heisei years saw two other major monetary developments: Prime Minister Hashimoto Ryūtarō's 1996 financial sector reforms and the financial crisis that occurred in the fall of 1997. The former, dubbed the "Big Bang," comprised extensive financial deregulation. The latter was the result of the 1997 Asian currency crisis, which had a heavy impact on Japanese financial institutions with their many underlying problems, prompting the collapse of securities firms and banks and large-scale injections of public capital.

Iwata Kazumasa's "The Japanese Big Bang and the Financial Crisis" discusses the Big Bang and developments leading to the subsequent financial crisis.

Yanagisawa Hakuo is a politician who was responsible for monetary policy in a number of capacities between 1998 and 2002, including the role of minister of state for financial services. His essay "Financial Regulation in the Wake of the Banking Crisis" discusses responses to the financial crisis from the perspective of a monetary administrator.

In "The Financial Crisis and the Lost Decade," Fukao Mitsuhiro analyzes various issues from the time of the bubble through to the financial crisis in the context of Japan's monetary system.

Ikeo Kazuhito is the economist who first proposed the Big Bang. In "Following Up on Japan's Financial Big Bang," he reflects on the track record for the decade following the Big Bang.

III-(1.1) Do Expectations Raise Prices?

Yoshikawa Hiroshi

Discuss Japan—Japan Foreign Policy Forum, 2017

The "different dimension" of monetary easing that started in April 2013 has failed to achieve its target: a core CPI (all items except for fresh food) inflation rate of 2 percent in two years. The latest core CPI inflation rate was negative 0.4 percent. This rate is lower than the level toward the end of the term of office of former BOJ governor Shirakawa Masaaki.

At its monetary policy meeting held on November 1, 2016, the Bank of Japan postponed the timing for achieving the 2 percent price target from "during FY 2017" to "around FY 2018." The target date was postponed for the fifth time in the past three and a half years (see figure 1). The Bank of Japan has admitted that it will not achieve this target during the term of office of BOJ governor Kuroda Haruhiko, which will end in April 2018, or within five years.

Why have prices not risen after the Bank of Japan bought ¥250 trillion worth of government bonds and expanded its current account to ¥300 trillion? In this paper, I will focus on expectations, which are claimed to play an important role in quantitative easing in a zero interest-rate environment. On August 27, in the United States, BOJ governor Kuroda delivered a lecture titled "Re-anchoring inflation expectations via quantitative and qualitative monetary easing with a negative interest rate." Inflation expectations, or expectations of price hikes, are discussed as a key point in monetary policy.

* * *

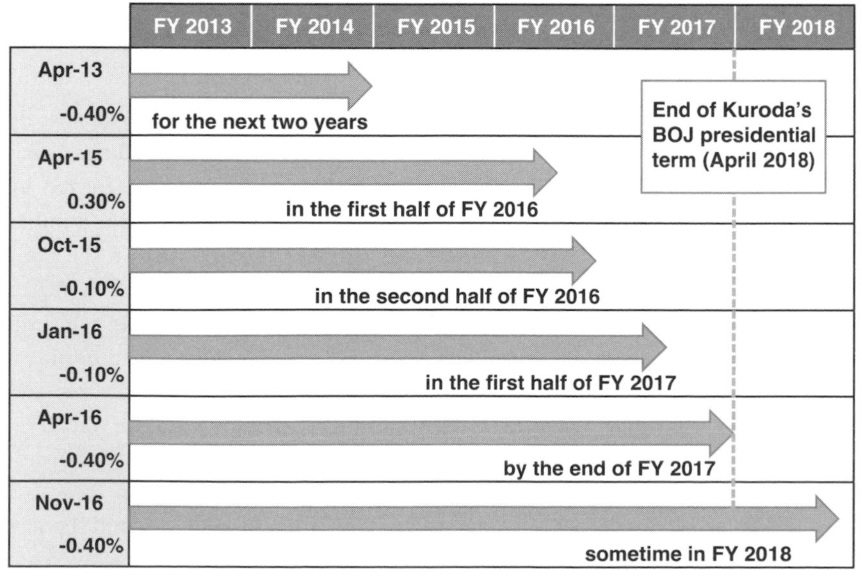

Figure 1. The accomplishment period for the CPI inflation target of 2 percent was revised five times

Note: The figures show the growth rate of consumer prices after the BOJ monetary policy meeting as compared to the same month of the previous year. Fresh foods are excluded, and the figures account for the increase in the consumption tax.

In normal economic conditions, monetary policy is interest-rate policy. How is monetary policy effective in a zero interest-rate environment? The nominal interest rate may have a zero lower bound. However, it is the real interest rate that affects the economic behavior of companies and households. The Bank of Japan's official position is that BOJ governor Kuroda's monetary easing aims to push real interest rates down. The real interest rate is the nominal interest rate less the expected inflation rate. Even if the nominal interest rate does not fall, the real interest rate falls if the expected inflation rate rises.

The expected inflation rate indicates expectations of changes in prices. Naturally, the way prices are determined is the biggest question. Reflationary policy, which assumes that an increase in the quantity of money raises prices, is based on the quantity theory of money. Deflation (a decline in prices) occurs because of an insufficient supply of money. According to the quantity theory of money, increasing the quantity of money is the only way to stop deflation.

The logic of the quantity theory of money is stronger than advocates of reflationary theory say it is. The "comprehensive assessment" of policy announced by the Bank of Japan on September 21 states that one of the reasons that prices had not risen as initially expected (in April 2013) was falling oil prices from the summer of 2014. US economist Milton Friedman, who was a champion of the modern quantity theory of money, emphasized that the trends of general prices are not affected by oil prices, but are determined by the quantity of money.

As the economy has been stagnant for a long time and the potential growth rate has declined, monetary policy is hardly effective. As a result, prices are not rising. The quantity theory of money says that this is not correct, because the theory says that prices are determined not by the real growth rate, but by the quantity of money.

According to the classical quantity theory of money, the relationship between the quantity of money and prices is in a black box, and expectations do not play any particular role. "Expectations" has become a key word in the field of macroeconomics, which has changed significantly in the past thirty years. According to the new macroeconomic theory on which the theory of reflation is based, if the central bank expands the money stock (money supply) significantly, the expected rate of inflation will climb and prices will also rise. This is the global standard of macroeconomics.

The question is whether or not this macroeconomic model is an appropriate model of the real situation of the economy. In a theoretical model, there is only one representative consumer who believes in the quantity theory of money. I do not think that the mainstream macroeconomic model is a macro model that describes the real situation correctly.

Some point out that the expected inflation rate has climbed since the "different dimension" of easing was introduced in April 2013. The Bank of Japan has often mentioned expected inflation statistics. However, these statistics do not describe meaningful expected inflation. What is in question in relation to the goal of monetary policy is individual companies' and households' expectations of percentage changes in prices.

The difference between the returns on inflation-indexed bonds and straight government bonds (premium) is a measure of expected inflation. However, these are only expectations on which participants in the financial market of inflation indexed bonds have agreed. This is the result of a "Keynesian beauty contest."

***

When we think about prices, we need to start by distinguishing the prices of commodities, such as crude oil, which are significantly affected by market conditions, from the prices of a number of goods and services that constitute the consumer price index. The former prices, or prices of primary commodities, including agricultural products and crude oil, are determined on international markets in accordance with supply and demand. A number of commodities are traded on futures markets, and expectations play a considerable role.

The prices of manufactured goods and services are determined in a completely different way from the way the prices of primary commodities are determined. The prices of manufactured goods and services are determined by producers, who place the greatest importance on production costs.

The producer needs to set prices that companies and individuals—the potential buyers—are expected to agree on. Bakeries that raise the price of bread without careful consideration will lose customers if the price is not considered fair. Production costs should be able to be observed by both sellers and buyers, and should make sense to them. The quantity theory of money is useless for this pricing process at a micro level. No seller will raise the price of coffee or steel sheets merely because prices are expected to rise.

The production cost is determined by the labor cost and raw materials expenses (the expenses for energy and finished goods include the costs of raw materials). The prices in yen of imported raw materials change due to the international prices of primary commodities (in dollars) and exchange rates. Domestic prices fall (or rise) when crude oil prices fall (or rise) or the yen appreciates (or weakens).

A fall in the oil price would certainly lower commodity prices, but advanced economies other than Japan's have not fallen into deflation. I pay particular attention to trends in nominal wages, which have a significant impact on production costs, as a variable that is the key to deflation in Japan. Advanced economies did not experience deflation after the war because nominal wages did not fall after the war as they did before the war. The downward rigidity of nominal wages blocked deflation. In Japan, however, the downward rigidity ceased to exist from around the end of the 1990s to the first decade of the 2000s.

Expectations do not play a major role in the pricing process at a micro level. Expectations mean expectations of future events, such as price hikes. Two entities, such as the seller and the buyer, or the company and the labor union, cannot agree on the future. When both parties determine prices and wages, it is the past and present that play the key role. In this respect, the pricing process is fundamentally different from financial and asset markets, which are constantly looking to the future.

***

The experiment that ran for three and half years from April 2013 has revealed that deflation is not a monetary phenomenon. Some say that the "different dimension" of easing succeeded in the first year, but I doubt that. Looking at the individual items of the consumer price index, we find that utility charges and a number of services, as well as energy, reflected the effect of rises in utility costs.

The main factor that has caused prices to change is not the quantity of money, but oil prices. During the period, expectations have not played a role in determining prices. Expectations will not play a significant role in determining consumer prices.

English version originally published in *Discuss Japan—Japan Foreign Policy Forum*, no. 38 (Apr. 2017).

Translated by Japan Journal, Ltd. First appeared in the interview column on page 26 of the *Nikkei Shimbun* on November 29, 2016, under the title "Kitai de bukka wa agerareru ka" (Do Expectations Raise Prices?). (Courtesy of author)

III-(1.2) Chronic Deflation in Japan

Nishizaki Kenji, Sekine Toshitaka, and Ueno Yōichi[1]

Asian Economic Policy Review, 2014

Japan has suffered from long-lasting but mild deflation since the latter half of the 1990s. Estimates of a standard Phillips curve indicate that a decline in inflation expectations, the negative output gap, and other factors such as a decline in import prices and a higher exchange rate all account for some of this development. These factors, in turn, reflect various underlying structural features of the Japanese economy. This paper examines a long list of these structural features that may explain Japan's chronic deflation, including the zero lower bound on the nominal interest rate, public attitudes toward the price level, central bank communication, weaker growth expectations coupled with declining potential growth or the lower natural rate of interest, risk-averse banking behavior, deregulation, and the rise of emerging economies.

1. Introduction

Why have price developments in Japan been so weak for such a long time? What can leading-edge economic theory and research tell us about the possible causes behind these developments? Despite the obvious policy importance of these questions, there is no consensus among practitioners or in academia. This paper is an attempt to shed some light on these issues by relying on recent works on the subject in the literature.

The paper proceeds as follows. Section 2 presents some stylized facts regarding deflation in Japan. It shows that Japan has indeed experienced long-lasting but mild deflation, and that its weak price developments are not attributable to any specific item—this is the case not only in a breakdown of time-series data, but also in cross-country comparison. The section also looks into the correlation of inflation with the output gap, the unemployment rate, and money. Section 3 then explores the causes of prolonged deflation in Japan based on the now-standard New Keynesian Phillips curve, examining each of the explanatory variables—namely inflation expectations, the output gap, and other factors—in turn. In doing so, we not only describe developments in these variables, but also discuss what the driving forces underlying them are in order to discover the more fundamental reasons for the chronic deflation. Section 4 concludes the paper. Two appendices document chronologies of the Bank of Japan's (BOJ's) communications on price stability, as well as government and media reports that reveal public attitudes toward the price level.

2. Stylized Facts

2.1 Price developments

Japan has suffered from long-lasting but mild deflation since the latter half of the 1990s (table 1). After reaching 11.6 percent in the first half of the 1970s, annual average consumer price index (CPI) inflation rates declined, becoming around zero or slightly negative from the middle of the 1990s. A similar trend can be observed for inflation rates calculated using the gross domestic product (GDP) deflator, although they tend to be somewhat weaker than CPI inflation. The weakness of these prices from the mid-1990s onward becomes more evident once the hike of oil prices and the depreciation of the yen against the US dollar are taken into account.

A breakdown of CPI inflation into its major components suggests that most of the components contributed to the slowdown in CPI inflation from the mid-1990s onward. For instance,

Table 1. Price developments (annual average, percent)

	1971–1975	1976–1985	1981–1985	1986–1990	1991–1995	1996–2000	2001–2005	2006–2009
CPI (excluding fresh food)	11.6	6.5	2.5	1.2	1.3	0.0	-0.4	0.0
GDP deflator	10.4	5.5	1.5	1.2	0.7	-0.9	-1.3	-0.9
Oil price	53.7	26.7	-4.3	2.6	-4.1	14.5	16.4	7.2
Yen/USD	-3.4	-5.5	0.6	-7.6	-7.3	3.3	0.8	-4.7
Contribution to CPI (excluding fresh food)								
Energy	0.9	0.7	0.0	-0.2	0.0	0.0	0.1	0.1
Durable goods	0.3	0.1	0.0	-0.1	-0.1	-0.2	-0.2	-0.2
Other goods	6.3	2.3	1.3	0.5	0.4	-0.1	-0.2	0.2
Services	4.3	3.4	1.3	1.0	1.0	0.3	0.0	0.0

Sources: Bank of Japan, Cabinet Office, and Ministry of Internal Affairs and Communications.
Notes: The CPI is adjusted so as to exclude the effects of changes in consumption tax rates and subsidies for high school tuition. This applies when the CPI is quoted in later tables and figures.
CPI, consumer price index; GDP, gross domestic product.

durable goods prices, which had pushed down inflation already since the mid-1980s, fell more rapidly in the 2000s. Price changes in other goods and services, which used to raise inflation, became almost flat or turned negative in the 1990s. On the other hand, the energy component raised inflation from 2000 onward, reflecting developments in commodity markets.

2.2 Cross-country comparison

Japan's CPI inflation rates have been consistently lower than those of the US and the Euro area (figure 1, top left-hand panel). For instance, the difference between CPI inflation rates in Japan and the US (based on five-year backward-moving averages) amounted to about -2 percentage points in the 1990s (second panel on the right-hand side). The difference widened to around -3 percentage points for the 2000s before narrowing somewhat, following the Lehman shock.

Japan's inflation is lower with regard to prices of both goods and services. The gap in goods-price inflation shows some volatility, presumably due to the effects of the exchange rate and commodity prices (figure 1, top right-hand panel). Meanwhile, the gap in service-price inflation has been more stable, even in the latter half of the 2000s (second panel on the left-hand side).

The comparatively low CPI inflation in Japan does not seem to be attributable to any specific item. While it is true that the inflation gap between Japan on the one hand and the US and the Euro area on the other is particularly pronounced in durable goods prices (figure 1, third panel on the left-hand side)—probably because of the greater weights attached to information technology-related devices (e.g., PCs and flat-panel TVs), the greater competition among retailers of these products, and the difference in the method of quality adjustment in the CPI compilation—durable goods are not the only component where there is a notable gap (third panel on the right-hand side). For instance, when stripping out the effects of housing rents, the measurement of which differs considerably from country to country, service-price inflation is notably weaker in Japan (bottom right-hand panel).

The weakness in nominal variables in Japan can also be observed in unit labor costs and long-term bond yields, which are rough proxies for the cost of labor and capital for producing goods and services.[2]

2.3 Correlation with other variables

There exists a clear positive correlation between inflation and the output gap (indicated by the thick regression line at the top left-hand panel of figure 2).[3] However, that positive correlation appears to have weakened—as indicated by the flatter regression line for the post-2000 sample—and shifted downward as inflation slowed from the 1980s to the 1990s and then the 2000s.

Similarly, a clear correlation can be observed between nominal wage increases and the

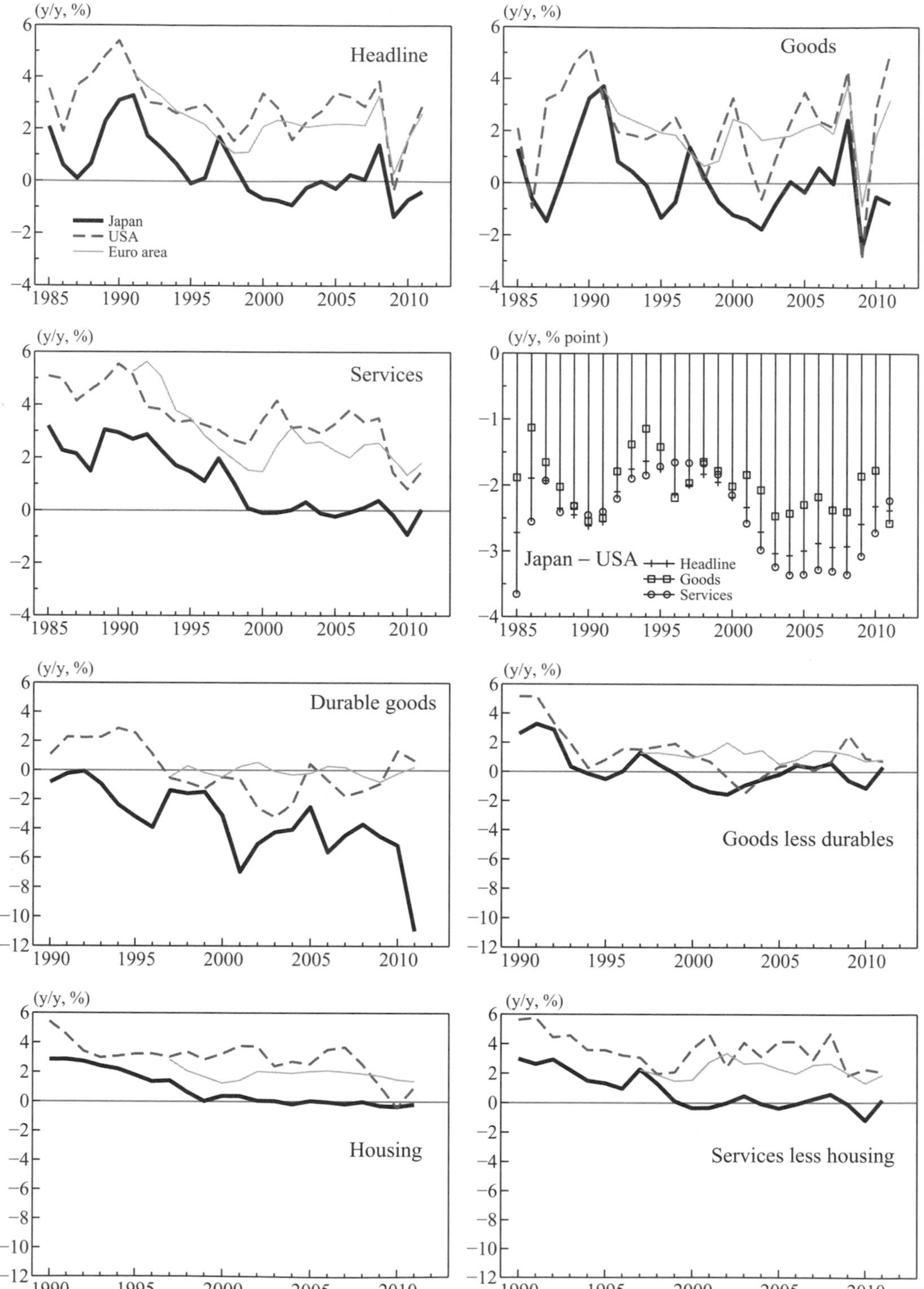

Figure 1. Cross-country comparison (consumer price index)

Sources: Ministry of Internal Affairs and Communications, US Bureau of Labor Statistics, Eurostat.
Notes: The index lines in the second panel on the right-hand side show the difference in headline inflation rates and those of goods and services (the inflation rate in Japan minus the rate in the USA). Five-year backward-moving averages are taken to smooth out cyclical fluctuations.

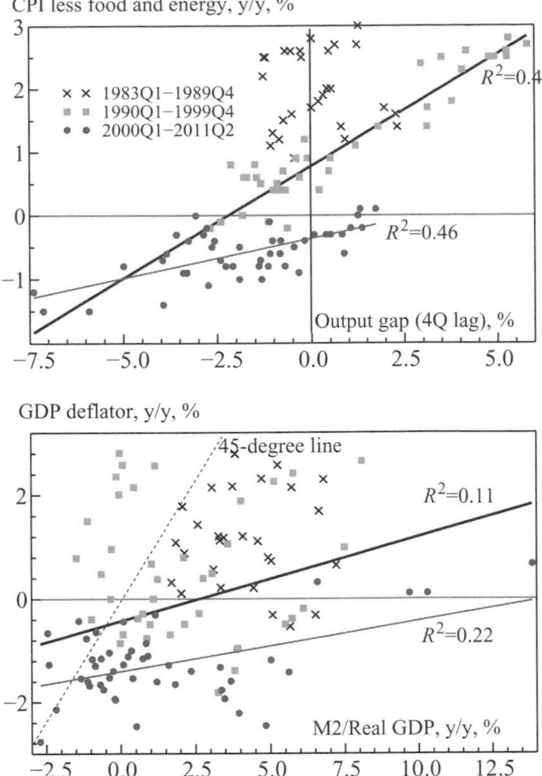

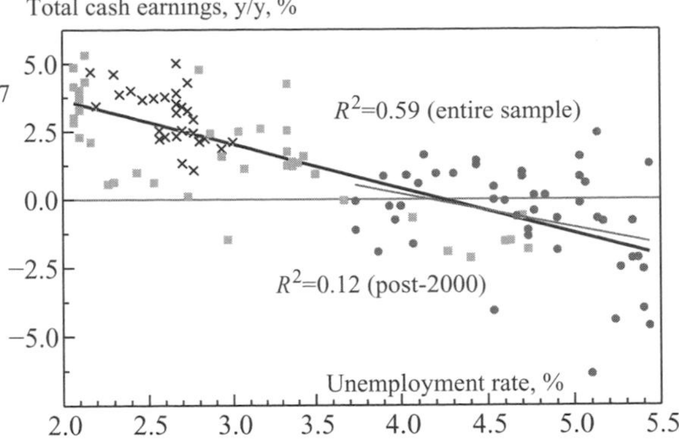

Figure 2. Correlation with other variables.
CPI, consumer price index; GDP, gross domestic product

Sources: Bank of Japan, Cabinet Office, Ministry of Internal Affairs and Communications, and Ministry of Health, Labour and Welfare.

Notes: In each figure, regression lines are calculated for the entire observation period (thick line) and the post-2000 period (thin line). The R^2 values are for the corresponding regression lines.

unemployment rate (right-hand panel of figure 2). However, that correlation becomes weak if the sample is limited to the period after 2000—the coefficient of determination (R^2) drops to 0.12 from 0.59 for the entire sample.

In contrast, no clear correlation emerges between inflation and money. If money velocity v is stable, cross-plots of inflation rates Δp and changes in money over real GDP $\Delta m - \Delta y$ should scatter around the 45-degree line (lower left-hand panel of figure 2).[4] However, there is no strong correlation between these two variables, and the slopes of the regression lines are far from the 45-degree line.[5] This may be taken as an indication that money velocity is not sufficiently stable in Japan.[6]

3. Pathology

In order to examine the causes for this long-lasting deflation, we couch our investigation in terms of the now-standard New Keynesian Phillips curve, which explains inflation π_t by inflation expectations $E_t\pi_{t+1}$, the output gap $Gap_t = y_t - y_t^n$, and other factors u_t, such that:

$$\pi_t = \beta E_t \pi_{t+1} + \alpha Gap_t + u_t. \quad (1)$$

Whether the long-lasting deflation beyond a business-cycle frequency can be explained by the Phillips curve is debatable, but we think that it is attributable to persistency in explanatory variables, as discussed below. Following Cogley and Sbordone (2008), we first estimate equation (1) by introducing time-varying trend inflation $\bar{\pi}_t$. In addition, inflation inertia and time-varying coefficients are taken into account (see appendix I of Nishizaki et al. 2012, for details of the estimation):

$$(\pi_t - \bar{\pi}_t) = \rho_t(\pi_{t-1} - \bar{\pi}_t) + b_t E_t(\pi_{t+1} - \bar{\pi}_t) + a_t Gap_t + u_t. \quad (2)$$

Here, trend inflation $\bar{\pi}_t$ corresponds to long-run inflation expectations, to which inflation converges in the absence of additional shocks.

Table 2. Inflation contribution of Phillips curve variables (annual average, percent)

	1987–1990	1990–1995	1996–2000	2001–2005	2006–2009
CPI (excluding fresh food)	1.4	1.3	0.0	-0.4	0.0
Contribution to CPI:					
Own lag	0.5	0.4	0.0	-0.1	0.0
Trend inflation	1.5	1.2	0.7	0.6	0.9
Output gap	0.6	0.1	-0.3	-0.4	-0.3
Others	-1.2	-0.4	-0.4	-0.6	-0.6

CPI, consumer price index.

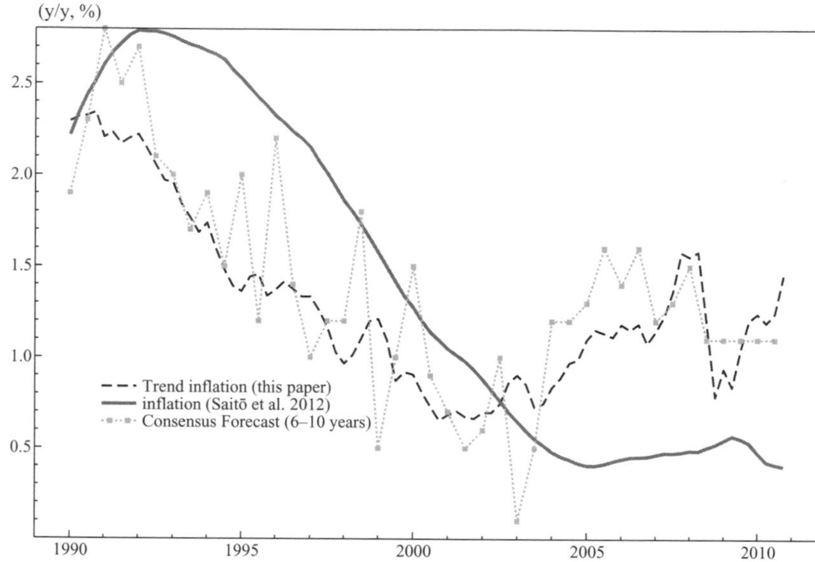

Figure 3. Expected inflation

Sources: Ministry of Internal Affairs and Communications, Consensus Economics Inc., and Bloomberg.

Table 2 shows the contributions of $\bar{\pi}_{t-1}$, $\bar{\pi}_t$, Gap_t, and u_t to the actual rate of CPI inflation. As can be seen, each of the four components contributes to the weakness in price developments. For example, the positive contribution of trend inflation diminished from the mid-1990s, while the contribution of the output gap turned negative. Moreover, the negative contribution of others increased somewhat during the 2000s.

In the remainder of this section, we will examine developments in each of the explanatory variables and consider what the driving forces underlying these developments are.

3.1 Inflation expectations

There is a wide range of evidence suggesting that inflation expectations in Japan have declined. For instance, in contrast with the US, Fuhrer et al. (2012) find that inflation expectations in their estimated Phillips curves in Japan have not been firmly anchored to stable long-run inflation expectations. However, questions remain regarding how far and why those inflation expectations have declined. We will address these questions one by one.

How far have inflation expectations declined?

Figure 3 shows various measures of expected inflation. All of them suggest that expected inflation has declined to a greater or lesser extent over the past two decades or so. For instance, a survey of professional forecasters (the Consensus Forecast) shows that their forecast of inflation for a horizon of six to ten years declined from 3 percent in the early 1990s to almost zero in the first half of the 2000s. Inflation expectations then recovered somewhat and have recently been stable around 1 percent. Trend inflation, as estimated in the manner described earlier, tracks Consensus Forecast inflation, partly because it utilizes information from the Consensus Forecast survey to detect trend inflation (see Nishizaki et al. 2012). Furthermore, a broadly similar inflation trend is obtained by Saitō et al. (2012), who estimate trend inflation in their dynamic stochastic general equilibrium (DSGE) model by imposing a standard set of theoretical restrictions without relying on survey data.

Particular importance is placed on the question of whether or not expected inflation has fallen into negative territory (Watanabe 2012). The reason is that, as argued by Benhabib et al. (2001) and Bullard (2010), if expected inflation was indeed negative, then Japan may have found itself in a liquidity-trap equilibrium, in which the central bank was prevented from escaping from such a trap by cutting its policy interest rate due to the zero lower bound on the nominal interest rate. Heuristically, the Fisher equation, $i = r^n + \pi^e$, where i is the short-term nominal interest rate, r^n is the natural rate of interest, and π^e is expected inflation, suggests that the zero lower bound on i becomes binding only when π^e becomes negative as long as r^n remains positive. We will discuss the possibility of a negative r^n later.

Although no consensus has yet emerged, it is quite likely that expected inflation has remained positive. Most surveys conducted either among professional forecasters or households suggest that long-run expected inflation has declined, but has not turned negative. Such surveys include, for example, the previously mentioned Consensus Forecast as well as original household surveys conducted by Watanabe (2012). Of course, the reliability of these surveys may be questioned—for instance, households do not necessarily take quality adjustments into account, and underlying inflation expectations therefore may be lower than what the survey responses suggest. However, as seen above, these survey results seem to be consistent with the model-based inflation expectations estimated by Saitō et al. (2012).

Why have inflation expectations declined?

Turning to the question of why expected inflation has declined over the past two decades or so, from a theoretical perspective, the reason may be that (i) the central bank has lowered its target rate for inflation; (ii) monetary policy has not been effectively employed, so that the public perception of the targeted inflation rate has been dampened;[7] or (iii) the public has become more suspicious about the achievability of the target rate once the nominal interest rate has reached the zero floor. Related to (i), some observers argue that the BOJ in fact may have targeted near-zero inflation rate at once. For instance, Ueda (2013) documents that one group of the BOJ's Policy Board members preferred a 0 percent inflation target in late year 2000. Itō (2004) observes that around that time, many Policy Board members strongly argued that a decline in prices was desirable because it was due to supply-side factors, such as technological innovation and cheap imports—see the argument of "norm" below.

The central bank's communication strategy may also have mattered. Appendix I summarizes how the BOJ has communicated its thinking on price stability. This summary reveals that (i) the BOJ has continuously defined price stability as a situation of neither inflation nor deflation; (ii) the BOJ openly acknowledged as early as in 1997 the possibility of a measurement bias, a year after the publication of the Boskin Commission Report (Boskin et al. 1996); and (iii) the BOJ has improved its style of communication; for example, by putting a numerical figure for the price stability understanding/goal/target, which was raised to 2 percent in January 2013.

As argued by Tobin (1972), Okun (1981), and Akerlof and Shiller (2009), public attitudes (or "norm") toward the price level may also have mattered in forming inflation expectations. On that score, it is important to note that, in the 1990s, coupled with a very strong yen, the public seems to have felt that prices in Japan were too high compared with prices in other industrial countries—at least, that was what the tone of the government and the media at the time, which tended to report that Japanese prices should be slashed, suggested (appendix II). In fact, that perception was warranted, as seen in the wide difference between domestic and foreign prices during the 1990s (see figure 6). It was only after the turn of the millennium that the media began to pay more attention to the hazardous effects of deflation. The number of newspaper articles on deflation jumped in 2001, which may indicate that public attitudes toward the price level changed discontinuously at that time (figure 8 of Nishizaki et al. 2012). The press coverage seems to have been affected by the government's "declaration of deflation" in 2001 and 2009, when its Monthly Economic Report used the term "deflation," as indicated in appendix II.

3.2 The output gap

There is a consensus among researchers that the output gap has remained negative for almost the entire period since the mid-1990s. Figure 4 shows various measures of the output gap. Regardless of whether a production function approach (BOJ) or a survey measure (Tankan) is employed, the results suggest that the output gap has remained negative since the early 1990s, except for short intervals in the latter halves of the 1990s and the 2000s. Saitō et al.'s (2012) model-based measure points to a broadly similar trend.

However, no consensus has emerged regarding why the output gap has remained negative for such a long duration. As discussed below, there are various attempts to explain the phenomenon. As these explanations are not mutually exclusive, it may well be the case that the mechanisms they describe have worked simultaneously.

Why has the output gap remained negative for a long time?

The simplest answer to the question of why the output gap has remained negative for a long time could be mere bad luck. That is, it is just a matter of bad fortune that Japan has been hit by a series of large negative demand shocks. These include the demand shock resulting from the collapse of the asset-price bubble in the early 1990s, the Japanese financial crisis and the Asian

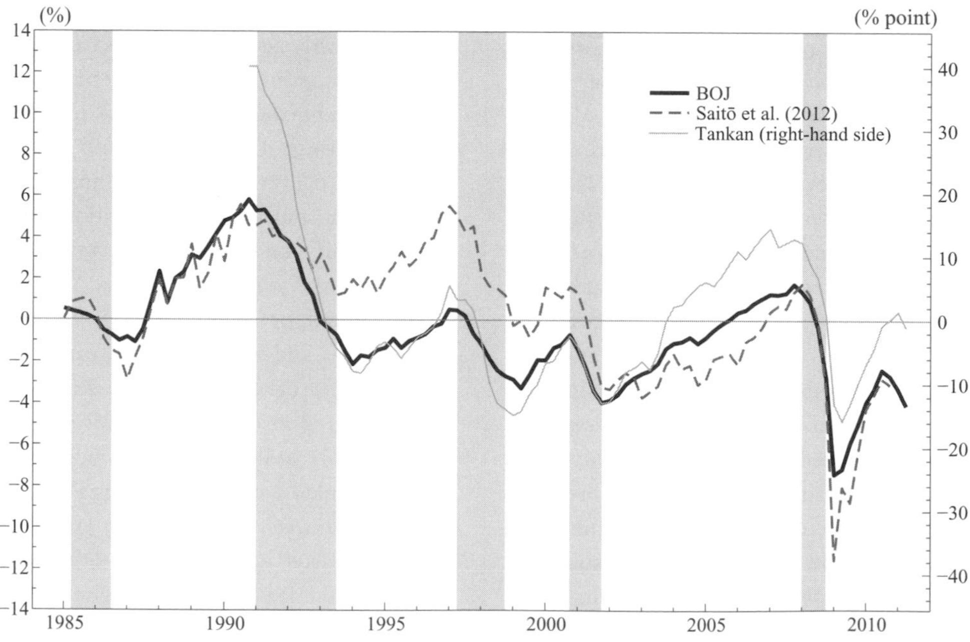

Figure 4. Output gaps

Notes: DSGE, dynamic stochastic general equilibrium; GDP, gross domestic product. "BOJ" refers to the output gap estimated by the Research and Statistics Department, Bank of Japan (Hara et al. 2006), while "Tankan" refers to the weighted averages of the production capacity DI and employment conditions DI in the Short-Term Economic Survey of Enterprises in Japan, or Tankan. The FY 1990–2010 averages of capital and labor shares in the National Accounts are used as weights. Finally, "Saitō et al. (2012)" is the output gap estimated based on Saitō et al.'s (2012) DSGE model, where the output gap is defined as the deviation of real GDP from its potential level (Fueki et al. 2010). The shaded bars indicate periods of recession.

currency crisis in the latter half of the 1990s, the collapse of the US dot-com bubble in the early 2000s, and the global financial crisis in the latter half of the 2000s. Instead of sighing over these "unlucky" events, however, researchers are trying to understand the forces underlying them. Since the deterioration of the output gap has been accompanied by a decline in the potential growth rate, researchers have been trying to explain the link between the two.

One strand of explanations of the negative output gap suggests that it is caused by a decline in the natural rate of interest and the zero lower bound on the nominal interest rate. For instance, following the approach of Laubach and Williams (2003), Watanabe (2012) shows that, along with the potential growth rate, the natural interest rate in Japan has declined to an extent that it has fallen into negative territory. In that case, once the central bank faced the zero floor, it was no longer able to lower the policy rate in tandem with the decline in the natural interest rate. This may have produced a negative output gap, since the policy rate was too restrictive compared with the natural rate. Couching his argument in terms of the Fisher equation, $i = r^n + \pi^e$, Watanabe (2012) suggests that instead of negative inflation expectations π^e, the reason why the economy has fallen into a liquidity trap is the negative natural interest rate r^n. Essentially, this line of argument is the same as Krugman's (1998).

However, just as in the case of inflation expectations, whether the natural rate of interest, which is unobservable, has become negative is a matter of debate. Figure 5 shows various measures of potential growth that are assumed to be linked with the natural interest rate. All of the measures of potential growth—be they based on a production function approach (BOJ), estimates from a model (Saitō et al. 2012), a corporate survey (Corporate), or the forecasts of economists (Consensus Forecast)—point to a decline in the potential growth rate, but none of them show a negative potential growth rate except for a short

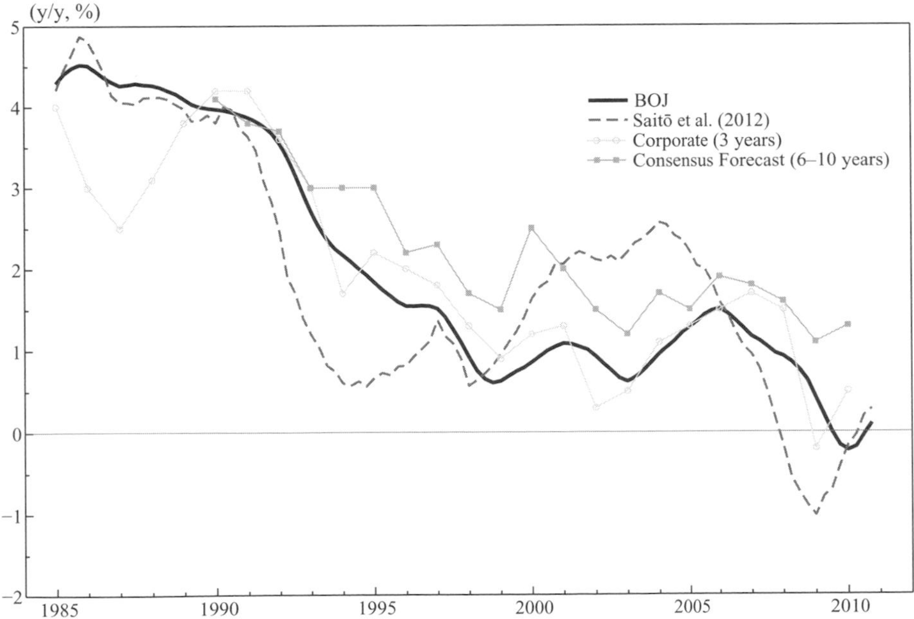

Figure 5. Potential growth

Notes: DSGE, dynamic stochastic general equilibrium; GDP, gross domestic product. "BOJ" refers to the potential growth rate estimated by the Research and Statistics Department, Bank of Japan (Hara et al. 2006), while "Saitō et al. (2012)" refers to the potential growth rate estimated based on Saitō et al.'s (2012) DSGE model. "Corporate (3 years)" refers to the outlook for the three-year forecast real demand growth rate for industry in the Annual Survey of Corporate Behavior (Cabinet Office). Finally, "Consensus Forecast (6–10 years)" refers to the Consensus Forecast for the average real GDP growth rate for the next six to ten years.

interval around the Lehman shock. Furthermore, in their analysis of historical breakdowns of the inflation rate, Saitō et al. (2012) show that the effects of the zero lower bound of the nominal interest rate on inflation are rather small, as long as these effects are captured by negative monetary policy shocks.[8]

Another strand of explanations sees a link between lower (but not necessarily negative) potential growth and the deterioration in the output gap via growth expectations. Saitō et al. (2012) argue that weaker growth expectations have squeezed demand more than supply. The key question is whether permanent or transitory negative shocks on productivity have lowered potential growth. In the case of permanent shocks, a "preemptive" reaction of the demand side to a future decline in supply potential may reduce demand heavily, and thus lead to deterioration in the output gap. On the other hand, in the case of transitory shocks, consumption smoothing may lead to a limited reaction on the demand side, and thus improve the output gap. The impulse response analysis of Saitō et al. (2012) shows that, in line with this reasoning, a permanent negative shock to productivity drags down inflation, while a transitory shock lifts inflation.

Moreover, Saitō et al. also explore the theoretical possibility that prices will become weaker if, for some reason (e.g., a lack of innovative entrepreneurs or government regulation), the supply side of the economy cannot fully respond to a change in the demand structure. For instance, it is widely assumed that population aging leads to changes in the demand structure, such as a greater demand for health care and a lower demand for, say, automobiles. If the quantity and price of health-care services are heavily regulated and cannot accommodate the growing demand of the elderly, then general prices may decline, as the elderly may save their money instead of purchasing automobiles in the expectation that health-care services will be provided in the future. Another study that examines the impacts of population aging on inflation through changes in the demand structure is that of Katagiri (2012), who uses a multi-sector DSGE model with search friction. Meanwhile, Kimura et al. (2010), while not treating the output gap explicitly, argue that a decline in the natural rate of interest may reduce private expenditures because of an increase in the present discounted value of government debt.

Yet another strand of explanations focuses on the financial side. Given that Japan's growing government debt has been financed by banks, which have increased their purchases of Japanese government bonds (JGBs), the question naturally arises whether there is any relationship between the behavior of banks and the output gap. Aoki and Sudō (2012) construct another DSGE model, in which the value-at-risk (VaR) constraint leads banks to accumulate large amount of JGBs instead of financing private investment (a crowding-out-like phenomenon). They show that this worsens the output gap and thus puts downward pressures on prices. They also demonstrate that a decline in the potential growth rate due to a negative permanent productivity shock tightens the VaR constraint, and thus puts downward pressure on inflation.

Related issues

If, as suggested above, a lower natural rate of interest or lower potential growth is responsible for the prolonged negative output gap, the next question that arises is why Japan's growth potential has declined. Including Hayashi and Prescott's (2002) seminal study of Japan's "lost decade," there is extensive literature on this issue, which is beyond the scope of this paper to examine. Shirakawa (2012) and Watanabe (2012) suggest that the malfunction of financial intermediaries after the collapse of the asset-price bubble, as well as the demographic trends of population aging and decline, may have played a role. Recently, Nishimura (2011) has highlighted the link between these two factors using an overlapping generations model in which demographic aging and decline trigger a drop in asset prices, and thus lead to a distortion in financial intermediation. On the other hand, Ikeda and Saitō (2012) have constructed a DSGE model in which a decline in the working-age population lowers the real interest rate, and that effect is amplified by a fall in land prices in the presence of collateral constraints.

Another, separate issue is why the slope of the Phillips curve has become flatter, as seen in figure 2.[9] Again, extensive literature has developed in the context of the Great Moderation. Potential explanations of the flattening of the Phillips curve include the following: that the impact of the global output gap on Japan's inflation has increased as a result of globalization (Borio and Filardo 2007); that the strategic complementarity in firms' price-setting behavior plays a role (Watanabe 2012); and that the downward rigidity of nominal wages matters (Fuhrer et al. 2012). However, the last is contradicted by evidence of symmetric wage changes presented by Kuroda and Yamamoto (2014).

3.3 Other factors

In an open-economy setting, external factors are added to a Phillips curve, such as the one represented by equation (1). For instance, since Japan heavily relies on imports of natural resources, commodity prices are frequently added to the equation. However, given the developments in the energy components shown in table 1, developments in commodity prices, including energy, cannot explain the chronic deflation in Japan. Import prices, which largely reflect developments in commodity prices, have shown a number of ups and downs, which is in contrast with the prolonged and steady decline in consumer prices. For this reason, in what follows, we will focus on other external factors, namely the exchange rate and domestic–foreign price differences.

Does the appreciation of the yen matter?

Over the past few decades, the yen's nominal effective exchange rate has appreciated as a trend. At the same time, although the evidence is still mixed, the pass-through of changes in the exchange rate may have declined, as, for example, Otani et al. (2003) suggest.[10] If this is indeed the case, then at least superficially it might seem rather difficult to argue that the appreciation of the yen has played a significant role in the deflation in Japan. However, if the equilibrium markup diminished along with the declining pass-through, this would lead to lower prices domestically.

There are other arguments that suggest that the appreciation of the yen matters. For instance, Watanabe (2012) demonstrates theoretically that, as argued by McKinnon and Ōno (2001), once expectations of a yen appreciation are firmly embedded among the public, Japan may fall into a liquidity trap in the presence of the zero lower bound on the nominal interest rate. Heuristically, if uncovered interest rate parity holds—that is, $i = i^* + \Delta d$, where i^* is the short-term nominal interest rate in a foreign country and Δd is the expected rate of depreciation—i may be subject to the zero lower bound and the economy may hence fall into a liquidity trap, when $\Delta d < 0$ (i.e., when the yen appreciates). Furthermore, as will be discussed later, Iwasaki et al. (2012) show that the less-flexible exchange-rate regime of the Chinese renminbi (yuan) has the effect of amplifying the downward pressure of Chinese productivity shocks on Japanese inflation.

Do domestic–foreign price differences matter?

As seen in appendix II, in the 1990s, wide differences between domestic and foreign prices were a matter of concern for both policymakers and the public. The 1990s were indeed a period in which prices in Japan were considerably higher than those in other major advanced economies (figure 6). However, the difference declined substantially in the 2000s.

Japan deregulated in a wide range of areas during the late 1990s and early 2000s, including zoning laws for large retailers, which may have contributed to slashing domestic–foreign price differences by reducing margins and/or improving productivity in the distribution chain.[11]

Supply shocks in emerging economies may also matter. Although supply shocks, as Sekine (2009) suggests, have affected inflation not only in Japan, but also in other industrial economies, the impact may have been more pronounced in Japan as a result of the close trade links with the dynamic emerging economies of Asia, particularly China. Using industrial panel data, Iwasaki et al. (2012), for instance, find that the impact of a higher share of imports from emerging economies, which can be regarded as a proxy of productivity shocks in these economies, is greater in Japan than in the US and Europe. Furthermore, Iwasaki et al.

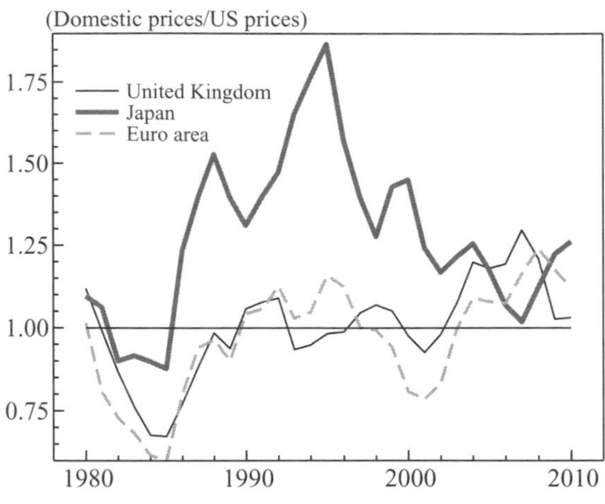

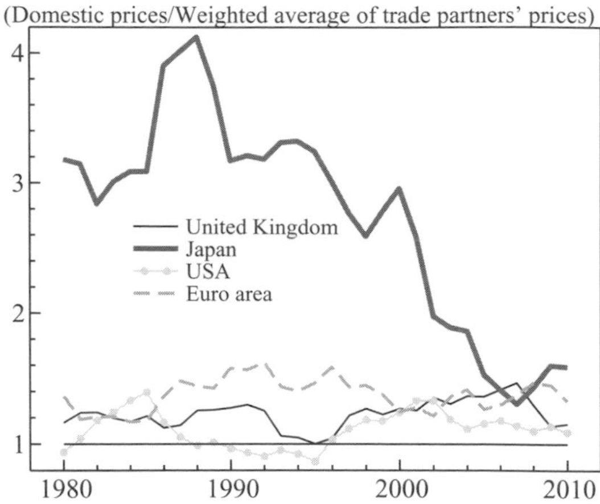

Figure 6. Deviation from purchasing power parity (PPP). NEER, nominal effective exchange rate

Sources: Bank for International Settlements (BIS), International Monetary Fund (IMF), and Bloomberg.
Notes: Domestic–foreign price differences are calculated as *P/P* e*, where *P* is the domestic price, *P** is the foreign price, and *e* is the market exchange rate. In the left-hand-side figure, *P** is US prices and *e* is the bilateral exchange rate against the US dollar, whereas in the right-hand-side figure *P** is prices for major trade partners and *e* is the nominal effective exchange rates. In the figure on the left, *P/P** is obtained from the PPP exchange rate in the IMF World Economic Outlook database and *e* is obtained from Bloomberg. In the figure on the right, *e* is obtained from the BIS nominal effective exchange rates (a narrow base comprising twenty-seven economies) and *P/P** is calculated by the authors using the above bilateral PPP exchange rate and the weights of the BIS NEERs.

(2012) construct a three-sector, three-country DSGE model (consisting of a tradable final goods sector, a tradable intermediate goods sector, and a non-tradable goods sector, with the countries corresponding to Japan, China, and the US) that incorporates the features that (i) Japan heavily exports intermediate goods to China in exchange for final goods; (ii) Japan–China trade links are stronger than Japan–US and US–China trade links; (iii) intermediate goods are less substitutable than final goods; and (iv) the Chinese renminbi is fixed to the US dollar.

Iwasaki et al.'s (2012) impulse response analysis of a rise in Chinese productivity in the tradable final goods sector shows that Japanese inflation falls more than US inflation. This is because, given the strong trade links, Japan imports more low-cost final goods from China than the US. Despite an increase in imports from China, Japan's trade balance deteriorates less than that of the US, since more final-goods production in China leads to a higher demand for Japanese intermediate goods. The model suggests that this results in an appreciation of the yen vis-à-vis the US dollar, which puts additional downward pressure on Japanese inflation. This deflationary impact could be mitigated if China were to adopt a more flexible exchange-rate regime.

4. Conclusion

This paper examines a long list of structural features that may explain Japan's chronic deflation. At this stage of our investigation, it is still difficult to single out one specific or dominant explanation for Japan's prolonged period of deflation, and it may well be the case that it is the result of a combination of factors. We hope that further research will shed more light on the issue.

The long list of hypotheses aside, an issue arises whether or not monetary policy can overcome these deflationary forces. Shortly after his appointment as the BOJ governor, Kuroda (2013) stated: "There are many factors—both at home and abroad—exerting downward pressure on prices in Japan: an increase in cheap imports from overseas, increased distribution efficiency mainly due to deregulation, and the consequent low-price strategies of firms as well as an increased preference among households for low prices. Notwithstanding these factors, it is the Bank's mandate as the central bank to achieve price stability by addressing them. Indeed, no other country in the world is undergoing such a prolonged period of deflation."

On April 4, 2013, the BOJ introduced a new operational framework for its quantitative and qualitative monetary easing to lift inflation to 2 percent over a time horizon of about two years. The new framework is thought to affect all three variables examined in section 3. First, by the BOJ's clear and simple commitment to achieve a 2 percent target, inflation expectations are aimed to rise and be anchored to that level. Second, the output gap is expected to improve through a decline in funding costs. Third, although this is a byproduct of monetary easing, import prices are likely to rise for the time being, reflecting developments in the foreign-exchange market. There are some indications that the economy is moving in the right direction. However, since the transmission lag of monetary policy is long and variable, it is too early to tell its full effects at the time of writing this paper. One thing that we can say for certain is that we economists will learn a lot from this ambitious monetary policy framework.

Courtesy of Japan Center for Economic Research (JCER).

Originally published in *Asian Economic Policy Review* 9, no. 1 (Jan. 2014): 20–39.

Notes

1. We would like to thank Ueda Kazuo, Andrew Levin, Maeda Eiji, Shioji Etsurō, Kitaura Nobutoshi, David Weinstein, Neil Ericsson, Ichiue Hibiki, the editors of the *Asian Economic Policy Review* (*AEPR*), and the participants in the AEPR Conference, the BOJ-CARF Joint Conference, and the BIS Research Workshop, as well as those in seminars at Columbia University, the Federal Reserve Board, and the Federal Reserve Bank of New York, for useful comments and discussions. We are solely responsible for any remaining errors in the paper. The views expressed in this paper do not necessarily reflect those of the Bank of Japan.
2. See figure 4 of Nishizaki et al. (2012). Recently, Yoshikawa (2013) argues that it is a change in Japanese labor markets that has caused deflation in Japan through a decline in nominal wages. However, based on industry-level data, Kuroda and Yamamoto (2014) conclude that wage deflation does not seem to be a primary factor of Japan's prolonged deflation.
3. The output gap is lagged by four quarters to maximize its correlation with inflation.
4. This is because $\Delta p = \Delta m - \Delta y + \Delta v$ (or $MV = PY$).
5. Kimura et al. (2010) point out that in recent years, the correlation has become less certain not only in Japan, but also in other major industrial countries.
6. See Sudō (2011) for a discussion of recent developments in money velocity in Japan.
7. This point was raised by a discussant. Suboptimal monetary policymaking may have affected not only inflation expectations, but also the output gap, discussed later.
8. Saitō et al.'s (2012) DSGE model does not explicitly model the zero lower bound, and thus estimated monetary policy shocks are assumed to capture the effects of the zero lower bound.
9. In fact, in our unreported estimates of the Phillips curve, the coefficient on the output gap a_t in equation (2) does not change much over time. This may suggest that a bivariate relationship like figure 2 may be disguised due to the existence of an omitted third factor. To put this another way, our estimates may suggest that deflation has remained mild despite the large negative output gap, not because the responsiveness to the output gap has declined, but because inflation expectations have been firmly anchored around the level of 1 percent.
10. See also Shioji (2014).
11. An effect of narrower margins can be captured by a markup shock in the New Keynesian Phillips curve estimated by Saito et al. (2012). It might be possible to obtain more direct evidence for a change in margins using firm-level data, as demonstrated by Ariga et al. (1999). Unfortunately, there are no studies that have pursued this avenue of research in recent years.

References

Akerlof, George A., and Robert J. Shiller. 2009. *Animal Spirits: How Human Psychology Drives the Economy, and Why It Matters for Global Capitalism*. Princeton: Princeton University Press.

Aoki Kōsuke, and Sudō Nao. 2012. "Asset Portfolio Choice of Banks and Inflation Dynamics." Bank of Japan Working Paper Series, no. 12-E-5, Bank of Japan.

Ariga Ken, Ōkusa Yasushi, and Nishimura Kiyohiko G. 1999. "Determinants of Individual-Firm Markup in Japan: Market Concentration, Market Share, and FTC Regulations." *Journal of the Japanese and International Economies* 13 (4): 424–450.

Benhabib, Jess, Stephanie Schmitt-Grohé, and Martin Uribe. 2001. "The Perils of Taylor Rules." *Journal of Economic Theory* 96 (1–2): 40-69.

Borio, Claudio, and Andrew Filardo. 2007. "Globalisation and Inflation: New Cross-Country Evidence on the Global Determinants of Domestic Inflation." BIS Working Papers, no. 227, Bank for International Settlements.

Boskin, Michael J., Ellen R. Dulberger, Robert J. Gordon, Zvi Griliches, and Dale Jorgenson. 1996. "Toward a More Accurate Measure of the Cost of Living: Final Report to the Senate Finance Committee from the Advisory Commission to Study the Consumer Price Index." Accessed December 9, 2013. http://www.ssa.gov/history/reports/boskinrpt.html.

Bullard, James. 2010. "Seven Faces of 'The Peril.'" *Federal Reserve Bank of St. Louis Review of Economic Dynamics* 92 (5): 339–352.

Cogley, Timothy, and Argia M. Sbordone. 2008. "Trend Inflation, Indexation, and Inflation Persistence in the New Keynesian Phillips Curve." *American Economic Review* 98 (5): 2101–2126.

Fueki Takuji, Fukunaga Ichirō, Ichiue Hibiki, and Shirota Toshitaka. 2010. "Measuring Potential Growth with an Estimated DSGE Model of Japan's Economy." Bank of Japan Working Paper Series, no. 10-E-13, Bank of Japan.

Fuhrer, Jeff C., Giovanni P. Olivei, and Geoffrey M. B. Tootell. 2012. "Inflation Dynamics When Inflation Is Near Zero." *Journal of Money, Credit and Banking* 44:83–122.

Hara Naoko, Hirakata Naohisa, Inomata Yūsuke, Itō Satoshi, Kawamoto Takuji, Kurozumi Takushi, Minegishi Makoto, and Takagawa Izumi. 2006. "The New Estimates of Output Gap and Potential Growth Rate." Bank of Japan Review Series, 2006-E-3.

Hayashi Fumio, and Edward C. Prescott. 2002. "The 1990s in Japan: A Lost Decade." *Review of Economic Dynamics* 5 (1): 206–235.

Ikeda Daisuke, and Saitō Masashi. 2012. "The Effects of Demographic Changes on the Real Interest Rate in Japan." Bank of Japan Working Paper Series, no. 12-E-3, Bank of Japan.

Itō Takatoshi. 2004. "Inflation Targeting and Japan: Why Has the Bank of Japan Not Adopted Inflation Targeting?" In *The Future of Inflation Targeting*, edited by Christopher Kent and Simon Guttmann, 220–267. Sydney: Reserve Bank of Australia.

Iwasaki Yūto, Kawai Masahiro, and Hirakata Naohisa. 2012. "Shinkōkoku ni okeru kyōkyū shokku no kokusai hakyū: Sankakoku DSGE moderu ni yoru infurēshon no bunseki" [Monetary Policy, Exchange Rate Regimes and Three-Way Trade]. Bank of Japan Working Paper Series, no. 12-J-7, Bank of Japan.

Katagiri Mitsuru. 2012. "Economic Consequences of Population Aging in Japan: Effects through Changes in Demand Structure." IMES Discussion Paper Series, no. 12-E-03, Institute for Monetary and Economic Studies, Bank of Japan.

Kimura Takeshi, Shimatani Takeshi, Sakura Kenichi, and Nishida Tomoaki. 2010. "The Role of Money and Growth Expectations in Price Determination Mechanism." Bank of Japan Working Paper Series, no. 2010-E-11, Bank of Japan.

Krugman, Paul R. 1998. "It's Baaack: Japan's Slump and the Return of the Liquidity Trap." *Brookings Papers on Economic Activity* 29 (2): 137–205.

Kuroda Sachiko and Yamamoto Isamu. 2014. "Is Downward Wage Flexibility the Primary Factor of Japan's Prolonged Deflation?" *Asian Economic Policy Review* 9 (1): 143–158.

Kuroda Haruhiko. 2013. "The Bank's Semiannual Report on Currency and Monetary Control." Statement before the Committee on Financial Affairs, House of Representatives, 26 March 2013.

Laubach, Thomas, and John C. Williams. 2003. "Measuring the Natural Rate of Interest." *Review of Economics and Statistics* 85 (4): 1063–1070.

McKinnon, Ronald, and Ōno Kenichi. 2001. "The Foreign Exchange Origins of Japan's Economic Slump and Low Interest Liquidity Trap." *World Economy* 24 (3): 279–315.

Nishimura Kiyohiko G. 2011. "Population Ageing, Macroeconomic Crisis and Policy Challenges." Speech at the 75th Anniversary Conference of Keynes' General Theory, University of Cambridge.

Nishizaki Kenji, Sekine Toshitaka, and Ueno Yōichi. 2012. "Chronic Deflation in Japan." Bank of Japan Working Paper Series, no. 12-E-6, Bank of Japan.

Okun, Arthur M. 1981. *Prices and Quantities: A Macroeconomic Analysis*. Oxford: Blackwell.

Ōtani Akira, Shiratsuka Shigenori, and Shirota Toyoichirō. 2003. "The Decline in the Exchange Rate Pass-Through: Evidence from Japanese Import Prices." *Monetary and Economic Studies* 21 (3): 53–81.

Saitō M., Fueki T., Fukunaga I. and Yoneyama S. 2012. "Nihon no kōzō mondai to bukka hendō: Nyūkeinjian riron ni motozuku gainen seiri to makuro moderu ni yoru bunseki" [Structural Problems and Price Dynamics in Japan: Conceptual Consolidation and Macro-Model Analysis Based on New Keynesian Theory]. Bank of Japan Working Paper Series, no. 12-1-2, Bank of Japan.

Sekine Toshitaka. 2009. "Another Look at Global Disinflation." *Journal of the Japanese and International Economies* 23 (3): 220–239.

Shioji Etsurō. 2014. "A Pass-Through Revival." *Asian Economic Policy Review* 9 (1): 120–138.

Shirakawa Masaaki. 2012. "Deleveraging and Growth: Is the Developed World Following

Japan's Long and Winding Road?" Lecture at the London School of Economics and Political Science (co-hosted by the Asia Research Centre and STICERD, LSE).

Sudō Nao. 2011. "Accounting for the Decline in the Velocity of Money in the Japanese Economy." IMES Discussion Paper Series, no. 11-E-16, Institute for Monetary and Economic Studies, Bank of Japan.

Tobin, James. 1972. "Inflation and Unemployment." *American Economic Review* 62 (1): 1–18.

Ueda Kazuo. 2013. "Response of Asset Prices to Monetary Policy under Abenomics." *Asian Economic Policy Review* 8 (2): 252–269.

Watanabe Tsutomu. 2012. "Zero-kinrika no chōki defure" [Long-Lasting Deflation under the Zero Interest-Rate Environment]. Bank of Japan Working Paper Series, no. 12-J-3, Bank of Japan.

Yoshikawa Hiroshi. 2013. *Defurēshon: "Nihon no manseibyō" no zenbō o kaimei suru* [Deflation: Unravelling the Full Extent of the "Japanese Disease"]. Tokyo: Nihon Keizai Shimbunsha.

Appendix I

Bank of Japan's Communication on Price Stability (chronology)

Note: Most of the quotes that follow have been translated by the authors.

April 27, 1994: *Principles for the Conduct and the Goal of Monetary Policy* (speech made by BOJ governor Mieno)

> One of the main goals of monetary policy is delivering "sustainable growth without inflation" in the medium-to-long run. . . . The question is often posed as to which price indicator, the Consumer Price Index or the Wholesale Price Index, the definition of price stability should be based on. However, it is inappropriate to single out a price indicator, as the goal of monetary policy is the stability of prices, not the stability of a price index.

October 11, 1996: Financial Innovation, Financial Market Globalization, and Monetary Policy Management (speech made by BOJ governor Matsushita)

> The Bank of Japan . . . intends to manage monetary policy appropriately with the aim of maintaining price stability, preventing inflation or deflation of domestic prices.

June 27, 1997: A New Framework of Monetary Policy under the New Bank of Japan Law (speech made by BOJ governor Matsushita)

> It is, however, not easy to define price stability. There are diverse types of price indicators: for example, the consumer price index, wholesale price indexes, and the GDP deflator. Each of these has its limitations, such as the range of items covered or the timing of release. Further, many studies have been conducted more recently on the possibility that these indicators offer a substantially biased measurement of prices.

October 13, 2000: On Price Stability

> [I]t is not deemed appropriate to define price stability by numerical values. . . . Price stability, a situation neither inflationary nor deflationary, can be conceptually defined as an environment where economic agents including households and firms can make decisions regarding such economic activities as consumption and investment without being concerned about the fluctuation of the general price level.

March 9, 2006: The Introduction of a New Framework for the Conduct of Monetary Policy

> Price stability is a state where various economic agents including households and firms may make decisions regarding such economic activities as consumption and investments without being concerned about the fluctuations in the general price level. . . . Price stability is, conceptually, a state where the change in the price index without measurement bias is zero percent.

March 9, 2006: An Understanding of Medium-to-Long-Term Price Stability

> It was agreed that, by making use of the rate of year-on-year change in the consumer price index to describe the understanding, an approximate range between zero and 2 percent was generally consistent with the distribution of each Board member's understanding of medium-to-long-term price stability. Most Board members' median figures fell on both sides of 1 percent.

May 27, 2007: Outlook for Economic Activity and Prices

> The "understanding" expressed in terms of the year-on-year rate of change in the CPI takes the form of a range approximately between 0 and 2 percent, with most Policy Board members' median figures falling on one side or the other of 1 percent.

December 18, 2009: Clarification of the "Understanding of Medium-to-Long-Term Price Stability"

> In a positive range of 2 percent or lower, the midpoints of most Policy Board members' understanding are around 1 percent."

February 14, 2012: The Price Stability Goal in the Medium to Long Term

> The Bank judges that "the price stability goal in the medium to long term" is in a positive range of 2 percent or lower in terms of the year-on-year rate of change in the consumer price index (CPI) and, more specifically, set a goal at 1 percent for the time being.

January 22, 2013: The "Price Stability Target" under the Framework for the Conduct of Monetary Policy

> The newly introduced "price stability target" is the inflation rate that the Bank judges to be consis-

tent with price stability on a sustainable basis . . . [T]he Bank sets the price stability target at 2 percent in terms of the year-on-year rate of change in the consumer price index (CPI)—a main price index.

Appendix II

Government and media reports on price level

Government reports

July 1993: Annual Report on Japan's Economy (FY 1993)

> While Japanese income per capita converted to US dollars is one of the highest in the world, living standards in reality as such are not. This is mainly because of the gap between internal and external prices. . . . Consumers would be better off if prices in Japan declined, narrowing this domestic–foreign price difference.

June 1999: Report of the Committee on Price Problems under Zero Inflation

> Deflation is a situation where sub-par growth and a fall in prices take place simultaneously. . . . A fall in prices does not necessarily incur recession. . . . It would be appropriate for the authorities to aim at zero inflation. However, some margin needs to be taken into account, given the positive measurement bias in the consumer price index.

March 2001: Monthly Economic Report

> The Japanese economy is in a mild deflationary phase, if deflation is defined as "a continuing decline in prices."

December 2001: Annual Report on Japan's Economy and Public Finances (2000–2001)

> [U]nder the current situation of the Japanese economy, even mild deflation is believed to have adverse effects on the economy.

November 2009: Monthly Economic Report

> Recent price developments show that the Japanese economy is in a mild deflationary phase.

Op-ed articles in major newspapers

October 10, 1994: Can We Self-Praise Price Stability? (*Nikkei Shimbun*)

> A 10 percent appreciation of the yen would increase households' real purchasing power by 30 to 40 thousand yen on average. The Price Report for FY 1994, which the Economic Planning Agency published last week, stressed price stability amid the appreciation of the yen by presenting the above estimation. The CPI increased by 1.2 percent in FY 1993. . . . However, the Report appears to sing its own praises too much on price stability. In fact, consumer prices in Japan should have been lowered.

July 27, 1998: Is Inflation Adjustment Really a Good Deal? (*Asahi Shimbun*)

> Some commentators in the market as well as in academia have turned to inflation in order to lift the economy. They claim that deliberately created inflation would sort out the problems of Japan's economy, where sales have declined and prices have fallen. This is so-called inflation adjustment. . . . The costs of pursuing such a policy are much too large. It is difficult to imagine that this is a worthwhile policy.

March 17, 2001: Conquer Deflation, Once Admitted (*Nikkei Shimbun*)

> Among major advanced economies, Japan is the only country where prices have continued to decline. The government and the Bank of Japan should quickly come up with specific policies to conquer this deflation.

November 16, 2003: Don't Forget the Homework of Conquering Deflation (*Asahi Shimbun*)

> Deflation places a greater burden on firms and individuals who borrow money, as the amount they have to pay back does not fall even when prices fall. This is the problem of deflation.

Ⅲ-(1.3) Comment on "Chronic Deflation in Japan"

Ueda Kazuo

Asian Economic Policy Review, 2014

Nishizaki et al. (2014) provide a useful summary of stylized facts and existing studies about Japan's deflation. Put simply, inflation may be written as π = F(Z, MP), where π is the inflation rate, MP represents monetary policy measures, and Z is all the other variables affecting inflation. Deflation may ensue if (i) MP is not effectively used; (ii) the power of MP to affect inflation is low due, say, to the zero lower bound on interest rates (ZLB); or (iii) significant negative shocks, Z, hit the economy. Most of Nishizaki et al.'s discussion is devoted to Z, but in addition, interactions between Z (a decline in the natural rate of interest/inflation expectations) and ZLB, and those between MP (central bank communication) and Z (inflation expectations), are also discussed. In the following, I would like to point out some factors that might have affected inflation developments in Japan which are not quite addressed by Nishizaki et al.

Let me first mention the possibility that Nishizaki et al. only briefly discuss; that is, deflation may have been caused by an inappropriate use of MP, or for that matter, by the Bank of Japan's (BOJ) implicit policy of targeting a near-zero inflation rate. The case in point is the two exits—one in 2000 and the other in 2006—from a forward guidance strategy despite a negative core consumer price index (CPI) inflation rate. As Ueda (2013) points out, the BOJ internally discussed what the appropriate inflation target was at the end of the year 2000, but was unable to choose between slightly positive inflation and zero inflation. Such developments may have affected the public's or the market's perception of the BOJ's resolve to fight deflation, despite efforts aimed at improving communication, as discussed in Nishizaki et al. Although the two exits and/or the doubts about the BOJ's intention to target a positive inflation rate were probably not a direct cause of deflation, they may have undermined the power of subsequent easing measures to stimulate the economy.

Nishizaki et al. point out, as do other recent discussions of Japan's Phillips curve, that the curve has become flatter since the late 1990s. Thus, inflation did not rise much in the mid-2000s despite a fairly strong recovery. Going forward, inflation may not go up to the current 2 percent inflation target easily. On the other hand, the flattening of the curve has meant that deflation did not accelerate during the last fifteen years. Thus, inflation has been rigid downward as well. This is puzzling because of the large and persistent gross domestic product gap that is discussed by Nishizaki et al. It is even more puzzling because wages have not been as rigid downward as has the CPI. One wonders if there has been a dynamic that has exerted a significant effect on the relative price between the CPI and wages. One candidate is the share of wages in national income; firms hired too many workers and paid wages that were too high in the late 1980s and early 1990s in anticipation of a serious labor shortage. The bursting of the asset-price bubble and the subsequent economic stagnation necessitated an adjustment process of a rising output price relative to wages.

A flatter Phillips curve has been found elsewhere as well. For example, Fuhrer et al. (2012) report that a Japan-style Phillips curve, although slightly different from that estimated by Nishizaki et al., fits the US data well. Fuhrer et al. then use their estimated equation to produce out-of-sample forecasts of inflation, which turn out to be negative for 2011–2020. Obviously, their predictions have not come out correctly. However, an examination of why the predictions were incorrect and/or a closer comparison of the two countries' experience based on such an analysis would shed more light on the chronic nature of Japan's deflation.

No discussion of Japan's stagnation is complete without a discussion of the negative feedback loop comprising asset price deflation, financial instability, and economic stagnation. In fact, the deflation measured using the CPI seems to have been a sideshow compared to that of asset prices. Nishizaki et al. devote considerable space to their discussion of the possibility that the real interest rate was higher than the natural rate as a result of ZLB and either a negative natural rate or a negative expected inflation. The component of aggregate demand that fell most significantly during the last two decades, however, was investment in structures. For this component, what mattered must have been the expectation of a large and consistent fall in property prices rather than a near-zero deflation as measured by the CPI. Or one could say that the natural rate was negative because of this dependence of investment on asset prices.

Courtesy of Japan Center for Economic Research (JCER).

Originally published in *Asian Economic Policy Review* 9, no. 1 (Jan. 2014): 40–41.

References

Fuhrer, Jeff C., Giovanni P. Olivei, and Geoffrey M. B. Tootell. 2012. "Inflation Dynamics When Inflation Is Near Zero." *Journal of Money, Credit and Banking* 44:83–122.

Nishizaki Kenji, Sekine Toshitaka, and Ueno Yōichi. 2014. "Chronic Deflation in Japan." *Asian Economic Policy Review* 9 (1): 20–39.

Ueda Kazuo. 2013. "Response of Asset Prices to Monetary Policy under Abenomics." *Asian Economic Policy Review* 8 (2): 252–269.

III-(1.4) Why Has Japan Failed to Escape from Deflation?

Watanabe Kōta and Watanabe Tsutomu[1]

Asian Economic Policy Review, 2018

Japan has failed to escape from deflation despite an extraordinary monetary-easing policy over the past four years. Monetary easing undoubtedly stimulated aggregate demand, leading to an improvement in the output gap. However, since the Phillips curve was almost flat, prices have hardly reacted at all. Against this background, the key question is why prices were so sticky. To examine this, we take sectoral price data for Japan and seven other countries including the US, and use these data to compare the shape of the price change distribution across the eight countries. Our main finding is that Japan differs significantly from the other countries in that the mode of the distribution is very close to zero for Japan, while it is near 2 percent for other countries. This suggests that while in the US and other countries the "default" is for firms to raise prices by about 2 percent each year, in Japan the default is that, as a result of prolonged deflation, firms keep their prices unchanged.

1. Introduction

From the second half of the 1990s, Japan has suffered a period of prolonged deflation, in which the consumer price index (CPI) has declined on a trend. During this period, both the government and the Bank of Japan (BOJ) have tried various policies to escape from deflation. For instance, from 1999 to 2000, the BOJ adopted a zero interest-rate policy in which it lowered the policy interest rate to zero. This was followed by quantitative easing from 2001 until 2006. More recently, in January 2013, the BOJ adopted a price stability target with the aim of raising the annual rate of increase of the CPI to 2 percent. In April 2013, the BOJ announced that it was aiming to achieve the 2 percent inflation target within two years; in order to achieve this objective, the BOJ introduced quantitative and qualitative monetary easing (QQE), which sought to double the amount of base money within two years. Furthermore, in February 2016, the BOJ introduced a negative interest-rate policy, in which the BOJ applies a negative interest rate of minus 0.1 percent to current account deposits held by private banks at the BOJ. This was followed in September 2016 by the introduction of "yield curve control," in which the BOJ conducts operations using Japanese government bonds (JGB) so as to keep the ten-year JGB yield at 0 percent. Table 1 contains an overview of recent policy decisions made by the BOJ between 2013 and 2016.

However, these efforts by the BOJ to escape from deflation have not been successful. That is, while the annual rate of change in the CPI (excluding fresh food) did initially turn positive, price developments have subsequently weakened again. Specifically, after leaving negative territory and returning to zero in May 2013, the annual rate of change in the CPI turned positive in June 2013 and rose to 1.5 percent by April 2014 (excluding the effects of the consumption tax hike in April 2014). This was a direct consequence of the depreciation of the yen in 2012–2015, when the yen depreciated about 40 percent vis-à-vis the US dollar (from 78 yen/dollar in 2012 to 125 yen/dollar in 2015), a depreciation which was induced by the BOJ's monetary easing. However, since then, inflation has gradually slowed as consumption demand declined. If the effect of the consumption tax hike is excluded, inflation has fallen to under 1 percent since October 2014.

Table 1. Monetary policy decisions made by the Bank of Japan in 2013–2016

January 22, 2013	Joint statement by the government and the BOJ on overcoming deflation and achieving sustainable economic growth was released. BOJ set an inflation target of 2 percent
April 4, 2013	BOJ introduced Quantitative and Qualitative Monetary Easing (QQE) BOJ decided to double the monetary base to achieve the 2 percent inflation target with a time horizon of about two years
October 31, 2014	BOJ expanded QQE by increasing its annual net purchases of JGB from ¥50 trillion to ¥80 trillion
January 29, 2016	BOJ decided to apply a negative interest rate of minus 0.1 percent to part of BOJ current account balances
September 21, 2016	BOJ decided to use yield curve control with the target level of ten-year JGB yields set to zero

BOJ, Bank of Japan; JGB, Japanese government bonds.

Given this, it looks unlikely that the BOJ's 2 percent target will be achieved in the foreseeable future.

The present paper investigates why it has been so difficult for Japan to escape from deflation. To do so, we focus on the fact that Japan's deflation since the mid-1990s has consisted of an extremely mild decline in prices. The largest annual decline of the CPI for any month during this period was only around 2 percent, and for the period as a whole the average annual decline was slightly less than 1 percent. Therefore, even though it was deflation, it was very mild and did not turn into the kind of severe deflation one might associate with the term. The deflation certainly did not turn into the kind of deflationary spiral many policymakers had feared. Of course, the fact that it was possible to avoid severe deflation itself is a good thing. However, from the perspective of escaping from deflation, it is possible that because the decline in prices was "neither here nor there," the market forces to turn the price decline into an increase were also weak. To put this differently, the fact that prices did not decline much even during the period of weak aggregate demand means that the Phillips curve was almost flat. It is this flattening of the Phillips curve that has made it more difficult to escape from deflation. Given that the flattening of the Phillips curve was at least partially caused by an increase in price stickiness, the key question is why prices became so sticky in the 1990s. Against this background, the aim of this present paper is to measure to what extent price stickiness increased over the last two decades and examine why this happened.

The analysis in the present paper makes extensive use of sectoral price data. Japan's CPI is constructed from items such as margarine and shampoo, and the total number of items used in computing the CPI is 588. For each of these items, about 570 prices are collected by price collectors of the Statistics Bureau of Japan every month. Therefore, the total number of prices collected each month reaches about 250,000. Roughly speaking, the headline CPI announced each month is the average of this large number of prices, and averages such as this certainly are an important statistical indicator. However, the average is not the only useful indicator. Other statistical indicators—e.g., higher-order movements as well as the mode of the distribution of price changes for individual items—also can provide a wealth of information on developments in price movements. The present paper seeks to take advantage of such information by looking at what kind of shape the distribution of price changes takes and how this distribution evolves over time. We supplement this analysis by comparing the shape of the item-level price change distribution for Japan with those for seven other countries, including the US, to determine whether and why prices are stickier in Japan than the other countries.

The rest of the present paper is organized as follows. Section 2 provides a description of the salient features of Japan's deflation; in particular, the mildness of the price decline and the flattening of the Phillips curve. Section 3 then examines the shape of the distribution of price changes of individual items in the consumer price statistics and how this shape changed over time. Section 4 examines the relationship between the share of items for which the rate of change is close to zero and the overall CPI inflation rate. Section 5 then conducts a cross-country comparison of the price change distribution in order to identify causes behind the prolonged deflation in Japan, while section 6 provides a summary and discusses some policy implications.

2. Characteristics of Japan's Deflation since the Mid-1990s

Japan's deflation has two important characteristics. First, deflation has lasted for a long time. Prices declined for two decades from the mid-1990s, so that it has clearly been prolonged. Second, however, in terms of the pace of deflation, even when prices were falling relatively fast, they never fell at a rate beyond 2 percent, and the average for the period is only 1 percent. In this sense, deflation was mild.

These two characteristics become even clearer when Japan's deflation experience is compared with deflation in the US during the Great Depression. The deflation during the Great Depression was severe, with prices falling at an annual rate of more than 8 percent. However, this deflation ended in about three years, so its duration was short. The reasons for these differences in the deflation rate and the duration are not easy to identify because the two deflationary episodes concern not only different countries, but also different eras. That being said, these differences may stem, at least partially, from differences in the price-setting behavior of producers and distributors in the two countries.

As pointed out by Gordon (1981), during the Great Depression in the US, firms quickly adjusted prices in response to changes in demand and supply. That is, prices were flexible. However, in Japan, price flexibility has fallen in recent years, so that even when demand and supply conditions change, there has been a strong tendency for firms not to change prices immediately. For example, based on a survey of Japanese manufacturers, Abe et al. (2008) report that more than 90 percent of firms responded that they "do not immediately change prices even if demand and supply conditions change." Moreover, in a survey published by the Cabinet Office (2013), only 21 percent of firms answered that they fully passed on increases in marginal costs to consumers, while the majority indicated that they could not fully pass on such cost increases.[2]

A possible reason that Japan's deflation since the mid-1990s was mild is that firms did not see a need to lower prices at a quick pace. For example, it is possible that firms did not experience any change in marginal costs, so that they did not have to change prices. However, it is very likely that firms did experience a substantial change in marginal costs. This can be seen by looking at the evolution of the Phillips curve for Japan over the period 1971–2016 that is displayed in figure 1. In the 1970s and 1980s, when unemployment decreased, inflation increased; that is, an increase in demand would lead to an increase in production and a fall in unemployment. This, in turn, increased marginal production costs, pushing up inflation. However, from the 1990s onward, this relationship between unemployment and inflation rapidly weakened. The slope of the Phillips curve became much shallower, and for the period since 2000 has been close to zero; that is, changes in the

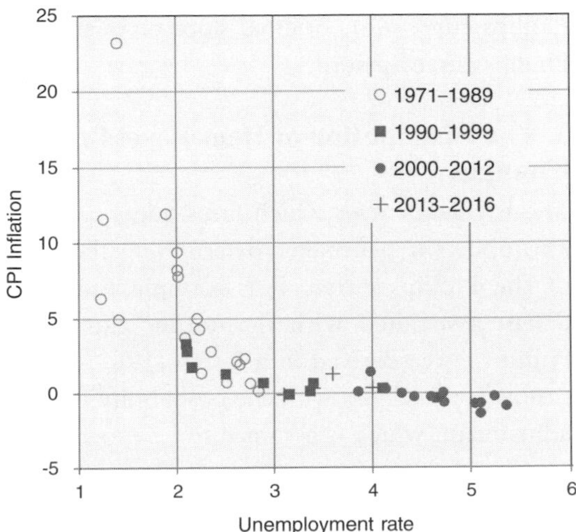

Figure 1. Phillips curve, 1971–2016

unemployment rate are not reflected by changes in the inflation rate. If we look at the period since 2000 in more detail, we find that even though the unemployment rate fluctuated within the range of 3.9–5.4 percent, the rate of change in the CPI hovered in a narrow range between -1.4 percent (in 2009) and 1.4 percent (in 2008), and in many years remained close to zero. Even during the global financial crisis (GFC), which resulted in a sharp rise in the unemployment rate, the CPI did not fall much.

The flattening of the Phillips curve has some important implications with regard to overcoming deflation. Spurring demand through QQE and fiscal stimulus measures should help to reduce unemployment and lead to an improvement in the output gap. Yet, if the Phillips curve is more or less flat, a reduction in the unemployment rate or improvement in the output gap is less likely to result in price increases, making it more difficult to overcome deflation. Watanabe (2013) shows, through a numerical exercise based on the estimated slope of the Phillips curve, that the output gap would have to increase by 5.3 percentage points each year in order to achieve the 2 percent inflation target in two years. This means, assuming that Japan's potential gross domestic product (GDP) growth rate is 1 percent, it would require real GDP to grow at a rate of 6.3 percent per year, which is clearly unrealistic. In other words, overcoming deflation only by stimulating demand is impossible. Instead, it is vital to return the Phillips curve to its original slope or to shift the Phillips curve upward.

3. The Distribution of Item-Level Price Changes

The frequency with which firms adjust prices is an important parameter determining the slope of the Phillips curve. For example, the coefficient associated with the output gap in the Phillips curve derived in a Calvo (1983) setting is positively related with the probability of price adjustment, which is assumed to be exogenously given and constant over time. If the probability of price adjustment is low, changes in economic conditions (as represented by changes in the unemployment rate) will not be factored into prices quickly, so that the slope of the Phillips curve will be shallow.

This suggests that the change in the slope of the Phillips curve in Japan may have been caused by a decline in the frequency of price adjustments. This raises a host of questions, such as: Did the frequency of price adjustments actually decline? If it did decline, for which items was this the case? What were the causes of this decline in the frequency of price adjustments? Has the adjustment frequency started to increase again since April 2013, when QQE began? In order to find answers to these questions, this section looks at price developments in the individual items making up the CPI. Specifically, the shape of the distribution of price changes of individual items and the evolution of that distribution over time are examined.

3.1 The shape of and changes in the item-level price-change distribution

Figure 2 shows the distribution of price changes (monthly annual changes) for each of the 588 items making up the CPI. The vertical axis shows the sum of the CPI weights of the items included in each bin on the horizontal axis. The dotted line shows the distribution for March 2014, when the inflation rate was relatively high (+1.3 percent) due to monetary easing, while the solid line shows the distribution just before the start of the BOJ's policies to overcome deflation when the inflation rate was -0.2 percent (December 2012). Looking at the dotted line, the density is highest in the bins from -0.75 percent to -0.25 percent and from -0.25 percent to +0.25 percent, and these two bins alone make up about 50 percent of the total CPI weight.

The rate of change of the CPI (excluding fresh food) for March 2014 was +1.3 percent, and the figure clearly shows that this increase does not reflect a uniform increase in prices of 1.3 percent; rather, there is substantial heterogeneity in the rates of price change. Comparing the distribution for March 2014 with that for December 2012 shows that the former has a fatter upper tail (for items whose prices increased) and a thinner lower tail (for items whose prices decreased) than the latter, and it is this that is responsible for the

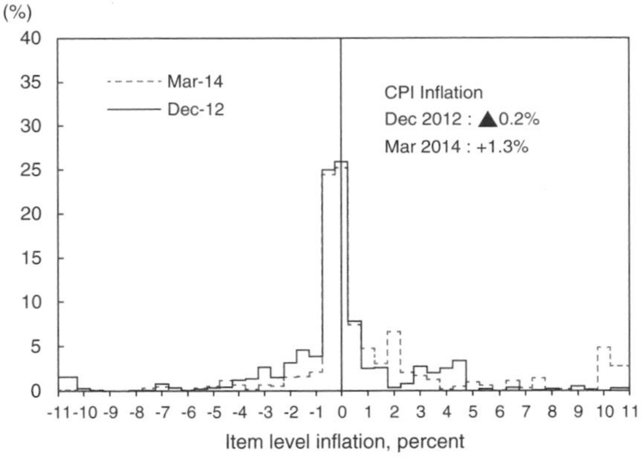

Figure 2. Distribution of price changes across items

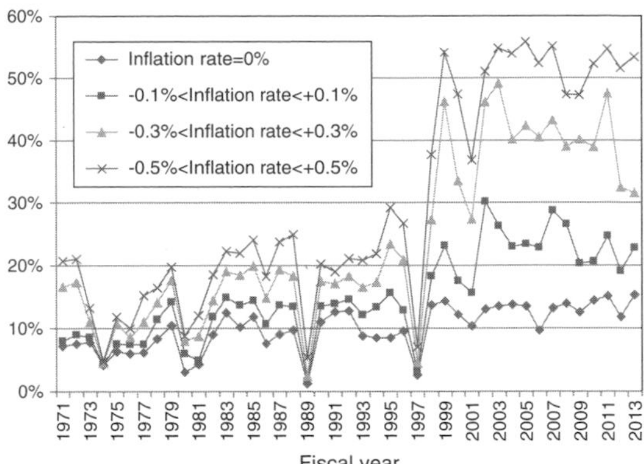

Figure 3. Fraction of items with a near-zero inflation rate

rise in the CPI inflation rate from -0.2 percent in December 2012 to +1.3 percent in March 2014. However, the shapes of the central part of the distribution (representing items whose prices remained unchanged) are almost identical.

In order to examine when the distribution started to take this shape with the peak in the vicinity of zero, figure 3 plots time-series data on the share of items for which the rate of price change was "close to zero." Four different definitions of "close to zero" are used: ±0.5 percent, ±0.3 percent, ±0.1 percent, and ±0 percent. Then, for each year, items for which the rate of change was close to zero are identified and the CPI weights of those items are summed up; it is this value which is shown on the vertical axis in figure 3. Starting with the case in which "close to zero" is defined as ±0.5 percent, the share of items whose rate of price change was close to zero was only 10 to 20 percent during the period of high inflation in the 1970s. This indicates that during this inflationary period, almost all items registered price changes every year and only for a limited number of items was the rate of change close to zero, presumably due to circumstances specific to those items. During the 1980s, as overall CPI inflation decelerated, the share of such items increased to a level of about 20 to 25 percent. Note that the sharp drop in 1989 seen in figure 3 reflects the effect of the introduction of the consumption tax, as a result of which prices inclusive of tax increased. Similarly, in 1997, the increase in the consumption tax rate resulted in another sharp drop in the share.

However, it is from 1995 that the most conspicuous change in the share of such items can be observed: with the exception of 1997, the share rose rapidly until 1999. In 1999, the share of items whose rate of price change was close to zero reached 55 percent, and it has remained at that high level, with some fluctuations, ever since.

3.2 Item-level price change distributions before and after QQE

Next, let us examine whether and how items whose price remained unchanged contributed to inflation under the BOJ's monetary easing since spring 2013. Table 2 shows simple estimates of the transition probabilities of being in a particular inflation state in March 2014, given that the good was in a particular inflation status in December 2012. Items are divided into those whose price in December 2012 had risen on an annual basis, those whose price had remained unchanged, and those whose price had fallen, with similar categories for March 2014. Examining the topmost row of table 2 as an example, the table is read as follows: among items whose price had fallen in December 2012, 23 percent also registered a price decline in March 2014, while for 30 percent of these items, prices in 2014 remained unchanged, and 48 percent of items that had registered a fall in 2012 actually saw a price increase in 2014. Note that for the construction of this transition matrix, price changes between -0.75 percent and +0.75 percent are defined as "zero" price changes, while anything below is defined as a price decrease and anything above as a price increase.

The results in table 2 show that an extremely high share—79 percent—of items that registered no price change in 2012 remained in that category in 2014. However, the share of items that transitioned from no price change in 2012 to an increase in 2014 is only 16 percent. In other words, items that registered no price change in 2012 made hardly any contribution to the increase in CPI inflation, suggesting that the BOJ's inflation targeting policy and QQE had very little effect on these items. However, among the items that registered a price increase in 2012, 64 percent also registered an increase in 2014 and contributed to raising the inflation rate. Moreover, among the items that registered a price decrease in 2012, 48 percent saw a price increase instead, and this also contributed to pushing up inflation. Thus, items with flexible prices contributed to raising the inflation rate, while items with sticky prices tended to register no price change and were the major obstacle to increases in the CPI inflation rate.

4. Why Have Prices Become Stickier?

4.1 Exogenous versus endogenous changes in price stickiness

There are two possible reasons why prices in Japan have become stickier since the mid-1990s. The first is a structural change in the economy, such as a change in the competitive environment that firms operate in, leading firms to change their price-setting behavior and resulting in an increase in price stickiness. Previous studies point to a variety of factors that may have resulted in structural changes in the competitive environment; for example, the second half of the 1990s is a period when the rise of new firms in emerging economies such as China gathered pace, intensifying global competition. This may have created a situation in which firms were unable to pass on any increases in marginal costs to customers.

An alternative explanation is that the increase in price stickiness since the mid-1990s may have been caused endogenously rather than exogenously. Based on a menu-cost model, Ball and Mankiw (1994) argue that price stickiness can change endogenously depending on the level of trend inflation. That is, when trend inflation is high, the profits foregone by a firm that does not adjust prices will be considerable. Such a firm would fall behind if it alone does not raise prices while its rivals do. As the profits foregone due to not adjusting prices are large, firms will choose to adjust prices despite incurring menu costs. As a result, prices are flexible and the Phillips curve is steeper. In contrast, when trend inflation is close to zero, as has been the case in Japan since the mid-1990s, the profit foregone due to not adjusting prices is smaller than the menu costs, so that firms will put off adjusting prices. Prices are stickier and the slope of the Phillips curve is smaller. In this way, changes in trend inflation lead to endogenous changes in price stickiness. See Levin and Yun (2007) and Bakhshi et al. (2007) for more on this issue.

Note that whether the increase in price stickiness arose exogenously or endogenously has quite different implications. If the increase in price stickiness is due to exogenous structural changes, prices should continue to be stickier, and it seems unlikely that the slope of the Phillips curve will return to its previous level. In contrast, if the

Table 2. Transition probability matrix from December 2012 to March 2014

		Item level inflation in March 2014 (%)		
		Negative	Zero	Positive
Item level inflation in December 2012 (%)	Negative	23	30	48
	Zero	4	79	16
	Positive	16	20	64
Unconditional probability (%)		11	57	32

Note: "Zero" here is defined as a price change between ±0.75 percent.

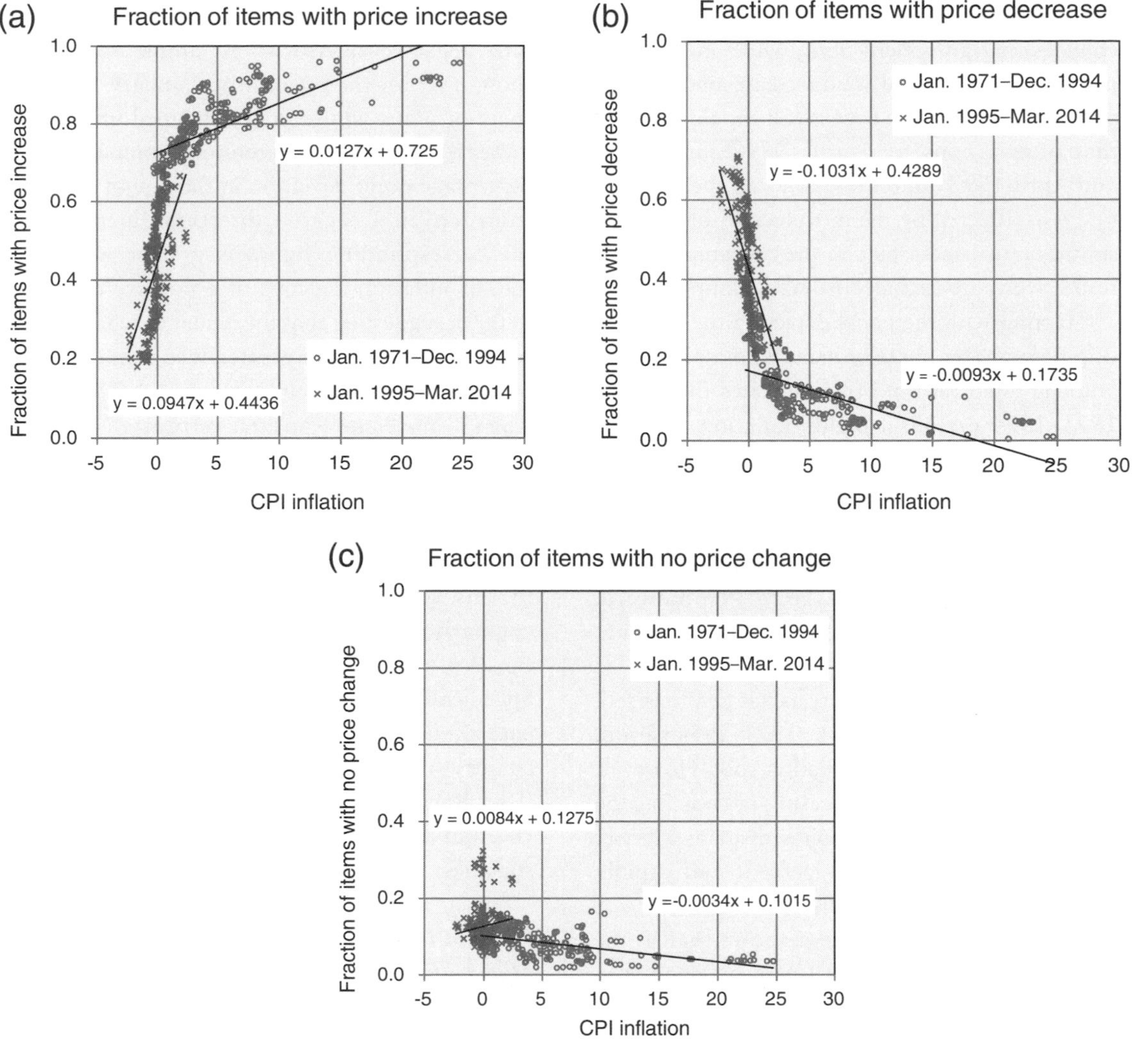

Figure 4. Fraction of items with (a) price increase, (b) price decrease, and (c) no price change

increase in price stickiness emerges endogenously with a decline in trend inflation, then price stickiness should decline and the slope of the Phillips curve should return to where it was once trend inflation picks up.

4.2 The relationship between the fraction of items with no price changes and the rate of inflation

To determine whether the increase in price stickiness occurred exogenously or endogenously, this subsection examines the relationship between price stickiness and trend inflation. Specifically, we check whether the share of items whose prices are not adjusted is inversely correlated to the rate of inflation.

To examine whether this is the case, the shares of items whose prices increased, fell, or remained unchanged are calculated for each month from January 1971 to March 2014. In the panels of figure 4, these shares are depicted on the vertical axis and the inflation rate is depicted on the horizontal axis. Each circle or cross represents an observation for one month; the former relate to January 1971 to December 1994, and the latter relate to January 1995 to March 2014. It should be noted that "unchanged prices" here are defined as price changes that are strictly zero, while any positive price change is defined as an increase and any negative price change as a decrease. It should be noted that observations for April 1989–March 1990 and April 1997–March 1998, when the inflation rate was affected by the introduction of the consumption tax and a hike in the consumption tax, respectively, are excluded from the sample.

Starting with the panel depicting the relationship between the share of items whose prices rose and the inflation rate, this indicates that in the 1971–1994 period, a higher inflation rate was associated with a higher share of items whose prices increased. The same relationship can be observed for the 1995–2014 period, but there is a distinct break in the relationship somewhere around 3 percent inflation. From 1995 onward, the share of items with increased prices declines more quickly with the rate of inflation.

Turning to the share of items whose prices fell, the figure indicates that in the 1971–1994 period, this tended to fall when inflation rose. However, similar to the share of increasing price items, the share of decreasing price items displays a break in the neighborhood of 3 percent and rapidly increases when inflation falls to zero.

A simple linear regression shows that in the 1971–1994 period, a fall of 1 percentage point in the inflation rate led to a decline of 1.3 percentage points in the share of items whose price increased, and a rise of 0.9 percentage points in the share of items whose price fell, indicating that the decline in the former was greater than the increase in the latter. Consequently, a decline of 1 percentage point in the inflation rate raised the share of items whose price remained unchanged by 0.4 percentage points. The fact that the fitted regression line of the circles in figure 4c is downward sloping provides a graphic representation of this relationship. In other words, price stickiness as measured by the share of unchanged items increases as the inflation rate declines from a positive value to zero. This finding suggests that the observed increase in price stickiness is, at least partially, due to the endogenous mechanism described by Ball and Mankiw (1994).[3]

Figure 4c also shows that price stickiness decreases as the inflation rate falls from zero into negative territory.[4] A simple regression shows that for the period from January 1995 the share of items whose price remained unchanged increases by 0.008 percentage points for a 1 percentage point deviation in the rate of inflation from zero in a negative direction. Interestingly, the corresponding figure is greater when the rate of inflation deviates in a positive direction (0.003), suggesting that the extent to which prices become less sticky is greater when the inflation rate moves from zero into negative territory than when it moves into positive territory. Note that this is the opposite of downward price rigidity.

5. Cross-Country Comparison of Price-Change Distributions

In this section, we conduct a cross-country comparison to investigate in further depth the causes of the increase in price stickiness in Japan. Specifically, we compare the item-level price-change distributions for eight major industrial countries: Canada (CA), France (FR), Germany (DE), Italy (IT), Japan (JP), Switzerland (CH), the UK, and the US, with a particular focus on price stickiness in Japan and the US.

5.1 Item-level price-change distributions as of March 2014

Figure 5 compares the item-level price-change distribution for Japan as of March 2014 with those for Canada, the UK, and the US. Starting with the US, the peak of the distribution lies between 2 percent and 3 percent. Although there is also a small peak around zero, the peak around 2 to 3 percent is much higher. The shape of the distribution is quite different from that for Japan. It seems that in the US, price increases of around 2 to 3 percent are the default, meaning that unless there are special circumstances, US firms raise their prices every year in the range of 2 to 3 percent. However, in Japan the default is to leave prices unchanged, and this likely gives rise to the difference in the distributions.

Looking at the results for the other two countries, the peaks of the distributions for both Canada and the UK are in the range of 1 to 2 percent. In other words, for all three countries—the

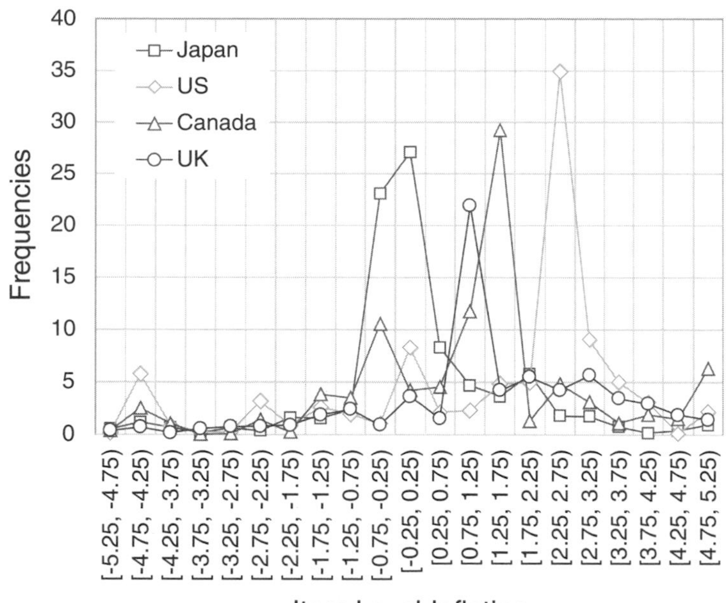

Figure 5. Price-change distributions for Japan, the US, Canada, and the UK, March 2014

US, Canada, and the UK—the peak of the distribution is in the vicinity of 2 percent. These countries have an inflation target of 2 percent, and the peak of the distribution and the level of the inflation target more or less coincide with each other. We will come back to this issue later.

5.2 The fraction of items with a near-zero price change conditional on the mean of the item-level price-change distribution

As we saw in the previous section, the shape of the item-level price-change distribution differs depending on the level of trend inflation. Therefore, a simple comparison of price-change distributions in different countries at a particular point in time may be misleading, since the rate of inflation in different countries differs at any particular point in time. In what follows, we instead focus on the distribution of item-level price changes in period t conditional on the mean of the distribution in the same period (i.e., the rate of inflation in period t). We compare such "conditional" distributions for the eight industrial countries.[5]

The first thing we do is to calculate, for each country, the fraction of items with a near-zero price change for a given overall inflation rate. A "near-zero" price change here is defined as a price change within ±0.25 percent. The results are displayed in figure 6. The vertical axis in figure 6 measures the fraction of items with a near-zero price change, and the horizontal axis measures the inflation. As can be seen, a common feature across countries is that the fraction of items with near-zero inflation tends to decrease with the rate of inflation. In other words, prices tend to be stickier the closer the rate of inflation is to zero.

However, a number of important differences across countries can be observed. First, the fraction of items with near-zero inflation is significantly higher in Japan than in the other countries, irrespective of the rate of inflation shown on the horizontal axis. In other words, the difference in price stickiness between Japan and the other countries cannot be accounted for by differences in trend inflation. Note that this result may be due to differences in terms of data granularity. The number of items in the Japanese item-level price data is 588, which is comparable to the number of items in the data for Germany and the UK, but much larger than for the other countries (see footnote 4 for the number of items in the other countries). The granularity of the Japanese data is finer in this sense, so that it is possible that there are more zeros in the Japanese data. To check whether this is the reason for the higher fraction

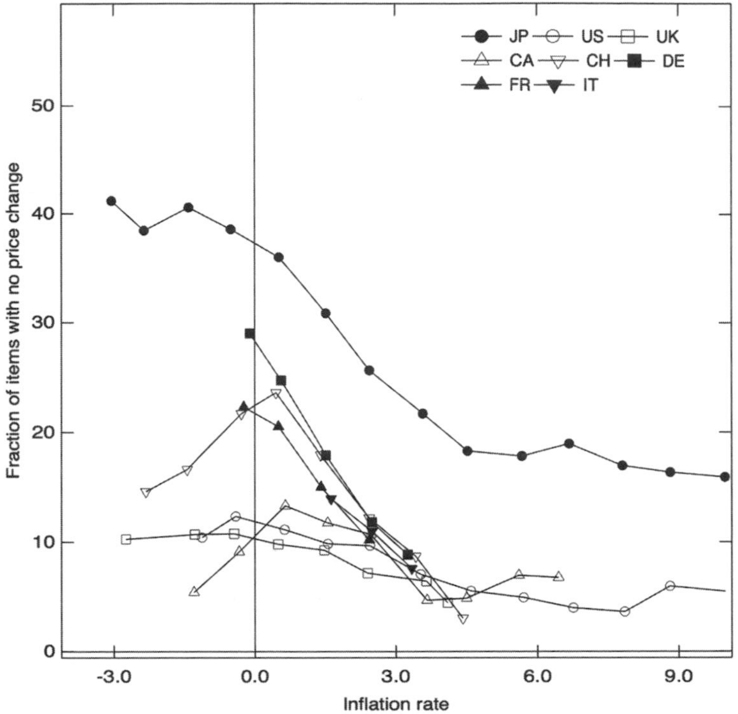

Figure 6. Fraction of items with no price change conditional on the inflation rate

Note: JP, Japan; US, United States; UK, United Kingdom; CA, Canada; CH, Switzerland; DE, Germany; FR, France; IT, Italy.

of items with near-zero inflation, we constructed a new dataset in which we reduced the number of items from 588 to about 300 through aggregation and repeated the same exercise as in figure 6. However, we found no significant difference in the result.

Second, the fraction of items with near-zero inflation for Japan takes the highest value when the inflation rate is somewhere around -2 percent and tends to become smaller as the rate of inflation goes deeper into negative territory, which is again consistent with the prediction by Ball and Mankiw (1994). The same tendency can be seen for the other countries, but the location of the peak is different from that of Japan. For the US and the UK, the peak occurs for a negative value, but it is not that far from zero. For Canada and Switzerland, the peak is located in positive territory. Meanwhile, for the other three countries (Germany, France, and Italy), no peak is observed, since there are not many observations with a negative inflation rate. However, looking at the curves for these countries, it appears that any peak likely would *not* be located in positive territory, at least for Germany and France.

Note that if the mode of the conditional distribution is located somewhere around zero irrespective of the rate of inflation, we would expect the fraction of items with zero inflation to monotonically increase as the rate of inflation comes down from positive to zero, reaching its maximum when the inflation rate is zero. However, the fact that this does not happen in some countries suggests that the mode of conditional distribution in those countries deviates from zero depending on the inflation rate.

5.3 The mode of the item-level price-change distribution conditional on the mean of the distribution

As we saw in figure 5, the mode of the item-level price-change distribution as of March 2014 was in the vicinity of zero for Japan, while it was above zero for the US, Canada, and the UK. To investigate this in more detail, we now show in figure 7 the mode of the *conditional* distribution for each of the eight countries.[6] We see that for Japan the mode is much lower than for the other countries, irrespective of the rate of inflation. For example, when the inflation rate, which is shown

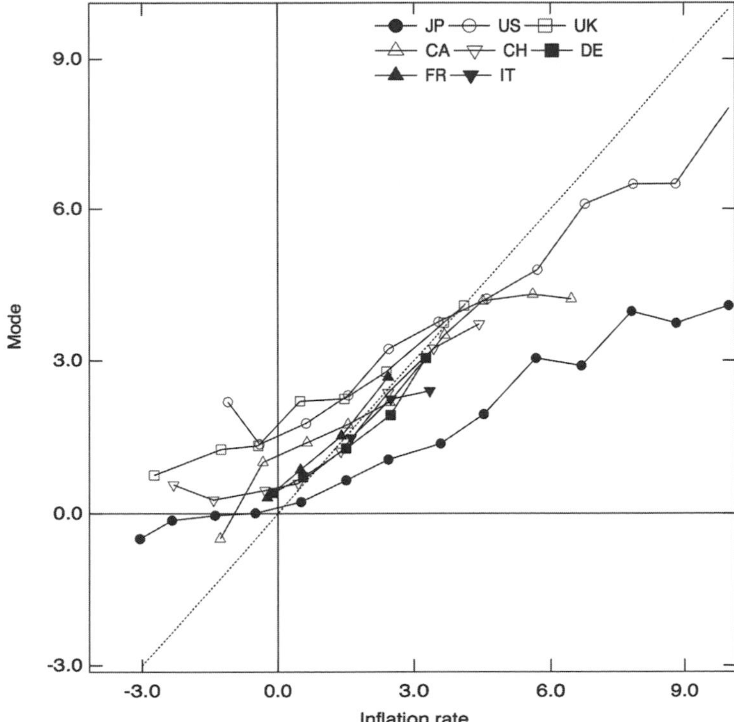

Figure 7. The mode of the price-change distribution conditional on the inflation rate

on the horizontal axis, is 3 percent, the mode is about 1 percent for Japan, while it is around 3 percent for the US.

A feature that is common to all countries is that the mode and the mean of the item-level price-change distribution do not necessarily coincide. Specifically, the mean tends to be greater than the mode when the mean is high, indicating that the distribution is skewed to the right. Such positive skewness arises when prices rise for a particular set of sectors (for example, due to an energy price hike or a currency depreciation), but remain unchanged for the other sectors, thereby resulting in relative price changes. In contrast, when the mean is low, the mean tends to be smaller than the mode, indicating that the distribution is skewed to the left. The presence of such a positive correlation between the mean and the skewness of the cross-sectional price change distribution has been discussed by Ball and Mankiw (1995) and others.[7]

It is important to note that, for Japan, the mean and the mode coincide when the inflation rate is in the vicinity of zero, indicating that the threshold associated with symmetry/asymmetry of the distribution is somewhere around zero. However, this is not true for the other countries. For example, the threshold is slightly above 3 percent for the US, which is much higher than for Japan. This means that the inflation rate can reach 3 percent in the US without any changes in relative prices across sectors. However, for Japan, 3 percent inflation can be achieved only with a positive supply shock. To the extent that supply shocks are inherently short-lived, this implies that 3 percent inflation would not be sustainable for Japan. It may be the case that inflation expectations are well anchored somewhere near 2 to 3 percent for countries like the US, but they are anchored at 0 percent for Japan, so that Japan has to rely on positive supply shocks, such as yen depreciation, to achieve positive inflation.

5.4 The dispersion of the item-level price-change distribution conditional on the mean of the distribution

Finally, we examine how the dispersion of the distribution, which is referred to as relative price variability (RPV), is related to the rate of inflation. Previous studies on RPV empirically show

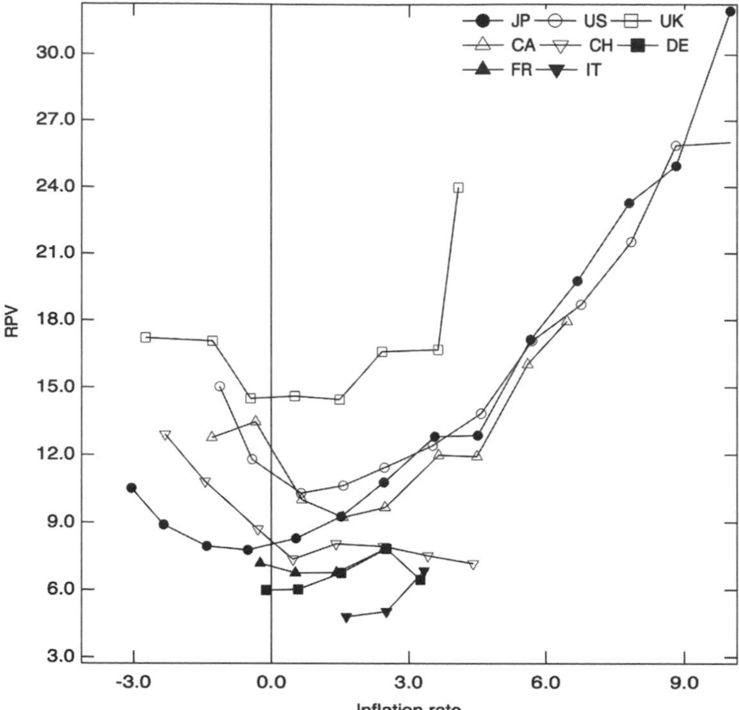

Figure 8. Relative price variability conditional on the inflation rate

that RPV tends to increase with the rate of inflation. Sheshinski and Weiss (1977) and Weiss (1993) provide an explanation of these empirical results based on menu cost models. Specifically, Weiss (1993) argues that, at moderate inflation rates, an increase in inflation raises the relative size of each price increase; in addition, the degree of synchronization in firms' price adjustments is rather low, so that RPV rises with inflation. However, Weiss (1993) also argues that, at very high rates of inflation, most firms raise prices within the same period (so that price adjustments are synchronized) and at similar rates, so that RPV declines as the rate of inflation increases.

Figure 8 shows the relationship between RPV, which is measured as the difference between the tenth and ninetieth percentiles of a distribution, and the inflation rate for the eight countries. We find the presence of a U-shaped relationship in all countries except Italy and Germany, for which the number of observations with negative inflation rates is quite limited.[8] More interestingly, the bottom of the U shape differs across countries. It is slightly below zero for Japan, but positive for the other countries. For example, the bottom is located at 1 percent for the US, 1.5 percent for Canada, 0.5 percent for Switzerland, 1.5 percent for France, and 1.5 percent for the UK.

Weiss' (1993) theoretical argument implies that RPV takes a minimum value when price changes are synchronized to the utmost extent. Suppose, for example, that price indexation is adopted in an economy and the rate of indexation is exogenously fixed at $\bar{\pi}$. In this case, price adjustments are synchronized across almost all firms, and RPV is minimized when the inflation rate is equal to $\bar{\pi}$.[9] This suggests that the observed difference in the bottom of the U shape between Japan and the other countries stems from the difference in $\bar{\pi}$ across countries. Note that the literal definition of $\bar{\pi}$ is the rate of price change associated with price indexation. However, a more realistic interpretation is that there is an implicit understanding among sellers and buyers that prices will be revised each year at a fixed rate, which is given by $\bar{\pi}$. In this sense, $\bar{\pi}$ may be interpreted as the reference level of inflation shared by firms.[10] Figure 8 indicates that this reference inflation level is somewhere around 1 to 2 percent in all countries other than Japan, where it is in the vicinity of zero.

6. Summary and Policy Implications

The main findings of this present paper can be summarized as follows. First, for the majority of the 588 items constituting the Japanese CPI, and for those which constitute about 50 percent of the CPI in terms of weight, the annual rate of price change was close to zero. In this sense, price stickiness was high. This situation started during the onset of deflation in the second half of the 1990s and continued even after the rate of inflation turned positive in 2013 and 2014 due to monetary easing by the BOJ.

Second, we show that the fraction of items with a near-zero price change increased as the overall inflation rate fell and approached zero, which is consistent with the argument that as inflation approaches zero, prices become stickier due to menu costs.

Third, the cross-country comparison of item-level price-change distributions showed that Japan differs significantly from other countries in that the mode of the distribution is very close to zero for Japan, while it is near 2 percent for the other countries examined, including the US. Importantly, this result remains unchanged even if we control for differences in trend inflation across countries, implying that the observed increase in price stickiness in Japan since the second half of the 1990s cannot be by fully accounted for by the menu cost-type argument.

Our empirical results indicate that inflation expectations are anchored somewhere near 2 percent for the US and the other countries, but they are anchored at 0 percent for Japan. Put differently, whereas in the US and the other countries the default is for firms to raise prices by about 2 percent each year, in Japan the default is that, as a result of prolonged deflation, firms keep prices unchanged. Such pricing behavior in Japan has contributed significantly to the flattening of the Phillips curve, thereby making it difficult to escape from deflation. One of the most important lessons to be learned from the Japanese experience during the Abenomics period is that it is extremely difficult to eliminate the deflationary mindset and the pricing behavior based on this mindset once it has become deeply ingrained in society.

Courtesy of Japan Center for Economic Research (JCER).

Originally published in *Asian Economic Policy Review* 13, no. 1 (Jan. 2018): 23–41.

Notes

1. We would like to thank Aoki Kōsuke, Christian Broda, Fujiwara Ippei, Hayakawa Hideo, Monma Kazuo, Roberto Rigobon, Shiratsuka Shigenori, Ueda Kazuo, Yamaguchi Hirohide, Yoshikawa Hiroshi, and David Weinstein for valuable comments on earlier versions of this present paper, and Murase Takuto for preparing part of the dataset used in the present paper. This research forms part of the project on "Understanding Persistent Deflation in Japan" funded by a JSPS Grant-in-Aid for Scientific Research (no. 24223003).
2. According to the survey by the Cabinet Office (2013), 23 percent of firms answered that they passed on about half the increase in marginal costs, 12 percent answered that they passed on less than half, and 26 percent answered that they could not pass on any cost increases at all.
3. Similar results have been reported for other countries; for example, Gagnon (2009).
4. Note that all of the studies to date using micro-price data deal with periods of positive inflation, and there are no examples of studies on the relationship between the inflation rate and price rigidity when this is zero. Gagnon (2009) also mainly focuses on a period of positive inflation, although in 2001 and 2002 the prices of fresh vegetables and fruits in Mexico fell due to weather factors, and the annual change in the CPI for goods became negative. It appears that during this period, symmetry held in that price stickiness tended to decrease the more the inflation rate in terms of the CPI for goods fell below zero (see figure 4 in Gagnon 2009). However, this bout of deflation lasted only for a few months, so it is not possible to tell whether this is a robust tendency.
5. The number of items and the observation period for each country are as follows: for Japan, the number of items is 588 and the observation period is 1970 to 2016; for the USA, the number of items is 182 and the observation period is 1970 to 2015; for Canada, the number of items is 170 and the observation period is 1985 to 2016; for Germany, the number of items is 577 and the observation period is 1991 to 2016; for France, the number of

items is 262 and the observation period is 1990 to 2016; for Switzerland, the number of items is 268 and the observation period is 1982 to 2016; for Italy, the number of items is 215 and the observation period is 1996 to 2010; and finally, for the UK, the number of items is 687 and the observation period is 1997 to 2016. The number of items for each country may not be the same throughout the observation period. Note that the analysis in this and later subsections is based on unweighted data (e.g., the unweighted rather than the weighted mean of the item-level price-change distribution).

6. See Watanabe and Watanabe (2017) for details on the estimation method of the mode of the item-level price-change distribution. See Cavallo and Rigobon (2011) for more on the estimation of the mode of a price-change distribution.
7. Ball and Mankiw (1994) argue that if the distribution of sector-specific shocks, such as oil price hikes, is skewed to the right, firms in a particular sector that experiences a large shock have an incentive to raise their prices, while firms in a sector that experiences only a very small shock do not want to change their prices, since this would incur menu costs. Therefore, even if the mean of the sector shock distribution is zero, the mean of the inflation rates in individual sectors could be positive, creating a positive correlation between the mean and skewness. More recently, Choi (2010) has argued that the degree of price stickiness differs across sectors, so that even common shocks (i.e., shocks common to all sectors) may have different impacts on prices across sectors, thereby creating skewness in sectoral price change distributions.
8. Choi (2010) finds similar a U-shaped relationship between inflation and RPV for the USA and Japan.
9. See Watanabe and Watanabe (2017) for a more detailed discussion of this issue.
10. Okun (1981) and Schultze (1981), among others, argue that firms have implicit contracts with their customers, which constitute social norms. An interpretation of our result is that inflation norms differ between Japan and the other countries, possibly reflecting the experience of prolonged deflation in Japan.

References

Abe Naohito, Tonogi Akiyuki, and Watanabe Tsutomu. 2008. "Kigyō shukka kakaku no nenchakusei: Ankēto to POS dēta ni motozuku bunseki" [Who Adjusts Prices: Manufacturers or Retailers?]. *Economic Review* 59 (4): 305–316.

Bakhshi, Hasan, Hashmat Khan, and Barbara Rudolf. 2007. "The Phillips Curve under State-Dependent Pricing." *Journal of Monetary Economics* 54 (8): 2321–2345.

Ball, Laurence, and N. Gregory Mankiw. 1994. "Asymmetric Price Adjustment and Economic Fluctuations." *Economic Journal* 104 (423): 247–261.

———. 1995. "Relative-Price Changes as Aggregate Supply Shocks." *Quarterly Journal of Economics* 110 (1): 161–193.

Cabinet Office (Japan). 2013. Annual Report on the Japanese Economy and Public Finance 2013: Summary. Accessed 3 August 2017. http://www5.cao.go.jp/keizai3/2013/0723wp-keizai/summary.html.

Calvo, Guillermo A. 1983. "Staggered Prices in a Utility-Maximizing Framework." *Journal of Monetary Economics* 12 (3): 383–398.

Cavallo, Alberto, and Roberto Rigobon. 2011. "The Distribution of the Size of Price Changes." NBER Working Paper Series, no. 16760, National Bureau for Economic Research (NBER).

Choi Chi-young. 2010. "Reconsidering the Relationship between Inflation and Relative Price Variability." *Journal of Money, Credit and Banking* 42 (5): 769–798.

Gagnon, Etienne. 2009. "Price Setting During Low and High Inflation: Evidence from Mexico." *Quarterly Journal of Economics* 124 (3): 1221–1263.

Gordon, Robert J. 1981. "Output Fluctuations and Gradual Price Adjustment." *Journal of Economic Literature* 19 (2): 493–530.

Levin, Andrew, and Yun Tack. 2007. "Reconsidering the Natural Rate Hypothesis in a New Keynesian Framework." *Journal of Monetary Economics* 54 (5): 1344–1365.

Okun, Arthur M. 1981. *Prices and Quantities: A Macroeconomic Analysis*. Washington: Brookings Institution.

Schultze, Charles L. 1981. "Some Macro Foundations for Micro Theory." *Brookings Papers on Economic Activity*, no. 2, 521–592.

Sheshinski, Eytan, and Yoram Weiss. 1977. "Inflation and Costs of Price Adjustment." *Review of Economic Studies* 44 (2): 287–303.

Watanabe Tsutomu. 2013. "What's Required to Stop Deflation?" *Japan Spotlight*, May/June 2013, Japan Economic Foundation, 30–35.

Watanabe Kōta, and Watanabe Tsutomu. 2017. "Price Rigidity at Near-Zero Inflation Rates: Evidence from Japan." Working Paper Series, no. CARF-F-408, Center for Advanced Research in Finance (CARF).

Weiss, Yoram. 1993. "Inflation and Price Adjustment: A Survey of Findings from Micro-Data." In *Optimal Pricing, Inflation, and the Cost of Price Adjustment*, edited by Eytan Sheshinski and Yoram Weiss, 3–17. Cambridge, MA: MIT Press.

III-(1.5) Encouraging Moderate Inflation

Iwata Kikuo

Japan Echo, 2001

According to the preliminary figures on gross domestic product (GDP) for October–December 2000 that were released on March 12, 2001, real GDP showed an annualized growth rate of 3.2 percent, exceeding earlier projections. That same day, however, the Nikkei average of 225 select shares on the Tokyo Stock Exchange fell a massive 456 points, indicating that the market expects deflation to continue. Between September 1995, when the official discount rate was cut to 0.5 percent, and December 2000, domestic wholesale prices (all prices adjusted for the April 1997 hike in the consumption tax) and consumer prices (excluding perishables) saw average annual drops of 1.2 percent and 0.02 percent, respectively.

Meanwhile, the Nikkei has slipped to its lowest level in the post-bubble era. Land prices in the nation's six largest cities have tumbled as well. As of September 2000, the value of commercially zoned land was just 18 percent of its September 1990 peak, the same level as in 1981. Residentially zoned land was down to 1986 levels, worth only 42 percent of its 1990 peak. These falling prices have pushed up the real value of debt in the economy. Real debt is determined by dividing the nominal value of debt by the price index. With interest rates and nominal values fixed, the decline in prices has increased the burden that borrowers have been saddled with. For example, in the third quarter of 1999, the real value of debt incurred in 1993 was 21 percent higher than it would have been if the GDP deflator had remained at an average of 1.7 percent, the level it was between 1980 and 1991, from 1992 on. Because the price of the stocks and real estate held by borrowers has fallen much more than prices generally, the real value of their assets (the nominal value divided by the price index) has plunged. As real debt increases while real assets decline, households and businesses have seen a substantial diminution of their real net assets (real assets minus real debt).

This change for the worse is especially pronounced in the balance sheets of nonmanufacturing companies, particularly small and medium-sized firms. In FY 1999 (April 1999–March 2000), the value of land held as assets by companies in nonmanufacturing industries was listed on their books as ¥133.4 trillion. But the market value of that land is estimated by Kokusai Securities to be barely half that figure, only ¥69.6 trillion.

While deflation continues, it is hard for companies to reduce their debts, which are fixed at nominal rates, because the nominal sales needed to repay the debts do not grow. Smaller nonmanufacturing companies, in particular, still bear scars from the collapse of the bubble economy. Their net outstanding debt (debt minus credit) has remained high since the 1990s. In addition, because falling land prices have left these firms without surplus collateral, they are unable to borrow funds and are thus incapable of undertaking structural reforms even if they wish to do so. This is why investment in information technology has not spread nearly as far in nonmanufacturing industries as it has in their manufacturing counterparts.

Moreover, because many companies used land as collateral when borrowing money, the drop in land prices has burdened banks with an increasing load of bad loans. Wiping these nonperforming assets off their books will lower banks' capital adequacy ratios. Moreover, if the Nikkei average remains at around the 12,000 mark, banks will be burdened with latent losses, and their capital adequacy ratios will fall even further. In order to shore up their ratios, banks will cut back even further on lending, causing investments in plant and equipment to contract.

A drop in the stock market will not only lead to less capital spending but also produce a reverse wealth effect from deflated asset values, leading consumers to clamp down on spending.

Aiming for 3 Percent Inflation

When formulating monetary policy, it is necessary to consider the risk of Japan's economy falling into a deflationary trap. Because the economy remains under the two deflationary pressures of plummeting prices and asset values, the zero-interest policy has only served to give the economy a temporary reprieve from that trap, and a slowdown in the US economy could deal it a damaging body blow.

However, many members of the Bank of Japan's Policy Board feel that falling prices resulting from marked advances in technology and distribution are "good price declines" that are beneficial to the economy and should not be labeled as deflation. They feel that these "good" declines should be distinguished from "bad price declines" brought on by weak demand. Proponents of the "good price declines" theory have confused drops in prices brought on by such companies as clothing retailer Uniqlo, which offer comparatively low prices, with falling average prices over a wide range of goods and services. Competitive pricing occurs in both inflationary and deflationary economies. The United States offers the best example of this. Even while experiencing mild inflation (an average of 2.6 percent per year between 1992 and 1999), America experienced long-term prosperity as the IT revolution made prices comparatively lower.

In a hypothetical situation where nominal interest rates and wages move up or down according to supply and demand, and where everyone can foresee these changes, it would not matter whether there was inflation or deflation. In the real economy, however, nominal interest rates will never fall below 0 percent. In addition, even if unemployment rises, nominal wages will not drop correspondingly. Because of this, continually falling prices will keep real interest and wages high, squeezing corporate profits. Employment and capital investment will both diminish.

Furthermore, when corporate and household balance sheets deteriorate dramatically, as was the case in Japan following the collapse of the bubble economy, banks become unable to properly fulfill their intermediary function in the economy. The cost of transferring resources (labor, capital, and land) from unproductive sectors of the economy into productive ones rises considerably, and the economic well-being of the people declines—the opposite of what the "good price declines" theorists stress.

The above clearly demonstrates that the path to Japan's economic revival lies in pursuing technological advances and undertaking structural reforms in an economy that is mildly inflationary, as the United States and other industrial countries have done. The first thing Japan must do is to discard the "good price declines" theory and escape deflation. As for the monetary policy necessary to accomplish this, I would propose stepping up open-market purchases of long-term government bonds (for the present, about two to three times the current level of ¥400 billion per month) to achieve targeted inflation rates. Based on the experiences of other countries, an appropriate target would be between 1 percent and 3 percent, but in order to offset the cumulative effects of deflation since the bubble's collapse, the target should be set high at 3 percent for the time being.

Good for Fiscal Discipline, Too

A number of arguments have been made against inducing inflation, but they have generally been unconvincing. The first argument is that it will not make any difference. People who make this argument have concluded that it is not going to work before it has even been tried. This is the same as simply not wanting to implement this policy. Those who are opposed should make clear the mechanism that would cause the policy to negatively affect the economy.

There are also those who argue that targeting inflation through a quantitative expansion of the money supply will not work because

Japan already has excess liquidity. Although the Marshallian *k* (ratio of the quantity of money to nominal GDP) is higher than in the past, whether or not this represents excess liquidity should be judged by analyzing the relationship between the money supply, price, and bubbles in the property market. Excess liquidity cannot be said to exist while commodity and asset prices are experiencing deflation.

A third type of argument goes like this: Printing money to cover the national deficit will sap fiscal discipline. As confidence in government bonds wanes and the outlook for inflation becomes more uncertain, interest rates will actually rise. This argument is also faulty. If the government establishes a target for inflation and sets an upper limit, uncertainty regarding future inflation will in fact recede. What is more, if a clear prospect of an end to deflation emerges, the fiscal burden of stimulating economic activity will lessen. This would actually make it possible for the government to regain fiscal discipline.

Some people contend that a policy of sparking inflation will set back the cause of structural reform. Since the 1980s, countries like Britain, New Zealand, Sweden, and the United States have escaped from financial crises much the same as the one Japan is in now by undertaking financial reforms and deregulation. But no country has ever realized the fruits of structural reform while in the midst of deflation. Deflation itself delays structural reforms by raising the costs of transferring resources from inefficient sectors of the economy to more efficient ones.

The remaining argument made against this financial policy is that it is not a silver bullet. I agree, but this is not grounds for opposition. What I am proposing here is establishing the proper macroeconomic environment, one that is indispensable if structural reforms are to be achieved.

Courtesy of Japan Echo.

English version originally published in *Japan Echo* 28, no. 3 (Jun. 2001): 42–43.

Translated from "Yuruyaka na infure mezase" (Aim for Moderate Inflation) on page 27 of the *Nihon Keizai Shimbun*, March 13, 2001. (Courtesy of Nihon Keizai Shimbunsha)

III-(1.6) The Bank of Japan's Efforts toward Overcoming Deflation

Shirakawa Masaaki
Speech at the Japan National Press Club, 2012

Introduction

It is a great honor for me to have the opportunity to speak to you today at the prestigious Japan National Press Club. This is my third time speaking here, having initially done so in May 2008—my first public speech after becoming governor of the Bank of Japan—and then again in May 2010, around the time when the European debt problem triggered by the crisis in Greece started to overshadow the global financial markets. Given that today happens to be just a few days after the Bank implemented measures to further enhance monetary easing, this is my first opportunity to provide a thorough explanation of this latest policy decision. The previous two speaking events before the club were valuable opportunities for me, because they resulted in my being presented with many thought-provoking opinions and questions and provided the chance to put my own thoughts in order. With that in mind, I really look forward to exchanging views with you after delivering my speech.

As I have just mentioned, the Bank decided the following three measures this week, at the Monetary Policy Meeting on [February] 14th, with a view toward clarifying its monetary policy stance and to further enhance monetary easing in order to overcome deflation and achieve sustainable growth with price stability (chart 1). First, the Bank introduced a numerical expression of price stability in the form of the price stability goal in the medium to long term. Second, as for its conduct of monetary policy for the time being, the Bank stated that it will "continue pursuing powerful monetary easing with the aim of achieving the goal of 1 percent in terms of the year-on-year rate of increase in the consumer price index (CPI) until it judges that the 1 percent goal is in sight." And third, the Bank increased the total size of the Asset Purchase Program introduced in the fall of 2010, from about ¥55 trillion to about ¥65 trillion, by adding another ¥10 trillion earmarked for the purchase of Japanese government bonds (JGBs).

Today, I will first explain the aim of and thinking behind these decisions. In the second half of my speech, I will focus on the challenge of overcoming deflation, which is the goal of the aforementioned measures, and discuss the causes of deflation as well as our thinking on necessary policy actions. After short-term interest rates in major economies, including Japan, declined to virtually zero, the scope of the operational tools of monetary policy has expanded from traditional ways of raising and cutting interest rates to the area of unconventional policy tools such as the purchase of various financial assets. Therefore, please forgive me if some parts of my speech inevitably become somewhat technical.

1. The Price Stability Goal in the Medium to Long Term

Numerical expression of price stability

I will begin with the price stability goal in the medium to long term. This is the inflation rate that the Bank judges to be consistent with price stability sustainable in the medium to long term. The Bank judges it to be "in a positive range of 2 percent or lower in terms of the year-on-year rate of change in the CPI" and, more specifically, has set a goal of 1 percent for the time being.

The Bank conducts monetary policy based on the Principle of Currency and Monetary Control as clearly stipulated in the Bank of Japan Act;

namely, that the policy shall be aimed at "achieving price stability, thereby contributing to the sound development of the national economy." In doing so, the price stability must be of the sort that is sustainable in the medium to long term. Then what kind of state does this "price stability" refer to? Conceptually, we can express it as "a state where economic agents such as households and firms may make decisions regarding economic activities without being concerned about fluctuations in the general price level." In the conduct of monetary policy, price stability needs to be expressed in numerical terms. Individual central banks express price stability in numerical terms within the context of each country's situation and name the expression differently. Examples of such numerical expressions include the Bank of England's "target," the "definition of price stability" adopted by the European Central Bank and the Swiss National Bank, and the US Federal Reserve's previously adopted "longer-run projection," as well as the "longer-run goal" it introduced recently.

"Understanding," "goal," and "target"

Six years ago, in March 2006, the Bank introduced its own framework under which it expressed price stability in numerical terms, named "an understanding of medium- to long-term price stability." After undergoing a series of changes in expression, the Bank's recent "understanding" was "a positive range of 2 percent or lower, centering around 1 percent" on the basis of a year-on-year rate of change in the CPI.

The word "understanding" was chosen for a definite reason. Back then, the Bank was approaching the exit from its quantitative easing policy, which had lasted for the five years since 2001, and the Policy Board members had a wide range of views with regard to price stability in the coming new phase. At the same time, all the members recognized the need to publish, as the Policy Board, the basic idea of price stability in numerical terms. As a result, the decision was made to ask individual Policy Board members to present their own understanding of price stability in specific inflation rates and issue numerical expressions in the form of a range covering the presented rates, and this was published as the "understanding."[1]

Over time, however, a growing number of voices began to be heard, pointing to the difficulties in understanding the Bank's judgment from a collection of individual views held by each member. Others expressed the view that connotations of "understanding" did not allow for smooth interpretations of the Bank's policy stance in its efforts toward achieving price stability, and in overcoming deflation in light of the current situation. The Bank's decision to introduce "the price stability goal in the medium to long term" also took into account such various views. Let me summarize the differences between the "goal" and the former "understanding." First, the goal introduced represented a judgment by the Bank, not the views of individual Policy Board members. Second, while judging that the goal was "in a positive range of 2 percent or lower in terms of the year-on-year rate of change in the CPI," the Bank clarified this by setting it at a more specific 1 percent for the time being (chart 2). And third, in order to strengthen the so-called policy duration effects, the goal is more clearly linked to the Bank's policy commitment on the duration of powerful monetary easing, including the virtually zero interest-rate policy, which I will explain in more detail later.

Based on my explanation up to this point, the question of why the Bank did not choose alternatives such as "target" might arise. The basic idea of the "goal" introduced is largely in line with the basic thinking held by some central banks abroad with regard to using the word "target," in that it expresses the inflation rate the Bank judges to be consistent with the mission of a central bank, and is one that the Bank aims to achieve in the medium to long term. In Japan, however, it is still often the case that "inflation targeting" is mistakenly considered equivalent to conducting monetary policy in an automatic manner in pursuit of a certain inflation rate. In reality, in many countries, including those adopting inflation targeting, monetary policy is conducted not in such an automatic manner but with an emphasis on price and economic stability in the medium to long term, as I will explain in more detail later.

The Bank judged that the Japanese wording of "the price stability goal in the medium to long term" would be the most appropriate name for the actual conduct of monetary policy.

In the case of Japan, while inflation rates have remained low over a protracted period, the sustainable levels of such rates could rise gradually in the future if efforts to strengthen the economy's growth potential bear fruit.[2] In view of the high uncertainty surrounding future developments, including possible structural changes in Japan's economy and the global economic environment, the Bank judged it appropriate to attach the term "goal" to the inflation rate that the Bank aims to achieve in the medium to long term, instead of the expression "target," which gives a rigid impression, and to review it once a year in principle.

2. Strengthening of Policy Duration Effects

Clarification of determination to pursue monetary easing

Next, I would like to explain the second step taken at the latest Monetary Policy Meeting—the strengthening of policy duration effects. In order to generate policy duration effects, central banks make a commitment to the future course of monetary policy based on certain conditions. When short-term interest rates almost hit zero, leaving little room for further decline, there is a need to introduce measures that influence the entire yield curve, including the longer end, in place of the traditional operation of controlling short-term interest rates. Long-term interest rates are formulated based on the expected future path of short-term interest rates and risk premiums. Therefore, if market participants believe that a central bank's commitment to monetary easing will continue for a long period of time, and that a short-term interest rate that is a policy rate will stay low for an extended period, then this will exert a downward force on long-term interest rates.

The Bank has made the best use of policy duration effects while engaging in maintaining the zero interest-rate policy since 1999 and quantitative easing policy since 2001. More recently, based on the understanding of medium- to long-term price stability that I explained, the Bank made it clear that it would "continue the virtually zero interest-rate policy until it judges that price stability is in sight." Although this commitment had played a certain role in encouraging the stable formation of long-term interest rates, the Bank made two changes this time, with the aim of further clarifying its policy stance toward overcoming deflation. First, the condition for policy duration is now more clearly specified based on the 1 percent inflation rate that is set as a price stability goal for the time being. Second, the Bank judged that it was more appropriate to express the policy stance on the conduct of monetary policy in a more active manner; that is, not only acknowledging the continuation of the virtually zero interest-rate policy but also pointing to other policy measures that have actually been taken. For this reason, it introduced a new policy commitment, which says, "For the time being, the Bank will continue pursuing powerful monetary easing by conducting its virtually zero interest-rate policy and by implementing the Asset Purchase Program mainly through the purchase of financial assets, with the aim of achieving the goal of 1 percent in terms of the year-on-year rate of increase in the CPI until the goal is in sight." At the same time, based on the experiences of the forming and bursting of a bubble in Japan and the global financial crisis following bubbles in recent years, a condition to the above commitment was set that, even when price stability was maintained, the Bank would check to see whether any significant risk was materializing, including the accumulation of financial imbalances, from the viewpoint of ensuring sustainable economic growth (chart 2).[3]

Commitment of timing and commitment of conditions

This kind of policy commitment aimed at generating policy duration effects is also adopted by central banks abroad. One way of doing this is to refer to a specific duration or timing of an exit, just like the US Federal Reserve does. According to its statement, the US Federal Reserve currently anticipates that economic conditions are likely to warrant an exceptionally low level of its policy rate "at least through late 2014," but holds significant reservations with regard to such anticipation being subject to change depending on economic and price outlooks. On the other hand, the Bank of Japan makes its commitment on a condition based on the CPI inflation rate, instead of the specific timing of an exit from monetary easing. The Bank judged it better to present a condition in terms of an inflation goal, rather than specifying the timing of an exit from monetary easing to gain greater credibility of commitment, and consequently more effectiveness of monetary policy, given the high uncertainty surrounding the economic and price outlooks in Japan at this juncture. As long as economic and price outlooks entail high uncertainty, it is impossible to specify the exact timing of an exit from monetary easing, but there is no uncertainty with regard to the Bank's policy stance to pursue monetary easing until it sees the exit. Given the current state of Japan's economy, the Bank believes that this type of policy commitment is more effective in showing its strong determination to pursue a policy aiming at overcoming deflation.

Relation to inflation targeting

I have explained that the Bank recently introduced the combination of "the price stability goal in the medium to long term" and "strong policy commitment based on the CPI inflation rate." How is this related to the so-called inflation targeting?

I would like to note at the outset that, after going through a bubble in Japan and experiencing the recent financial crises, monetary authorities around the world have made efforts to improve their frameworks for the conduct of monetary policy by learning from each other's lessons in the wake of those crises, and consequently have converged to share the following three elements in such frameworks.

First, they published specific inflation rates considered to be consistent with their responsibility. As I have already explained, although the wording differs, such as between the Bank of England's "target," the "definition" used by the European Central Bank and the Swiss National Bank, the US Federal Reserve's "goal," and the Bank's *medo* (in English, "goal"), their characteristics are basically the same.

Second, and more importantly, they have placed increasing emphasis on economic and price stability in the medium to long term, instead of the short term, when using the numerical expression of price stability in their conduct of monetary policy. In many cases, bubbles are formed when the economy enjoys price stability, and their bursting results in significant fluctuations in economic activity and prices later. Even if the authorities try to control the effect of supply shocks such as volatility in crude oil prices in the short run, economic activity suffers a significant burden, and price stability ultimately is endangered in the long run. All these kinds of experiences in recent years underscore the importance of pursuing price stability that is sustainable in the medium to long term. Even in the United Kingdom, where the monetary policy framework is called inflation targeting, the actual conduct of monetary policy is increasingly aimed at achieving the inflation target in the medium to long term while paying attention to economic and financial stability, instead of achieving the target at all costs in the short term.

Third, and related to the second element, major central banks have come to publish their economic and price outlooks covering a longer period. Having said that, the longer the period of forecasts, the greater their inevitable decline in terms of reliability. Therefore, these central banks increasingly emphasize medium- to long-term perspectives in showing their basic thinking on the mechanism behind the outlook and assessing risks, instead of focusing too much on highlighting the forecast numbers themselves.

Given that the monetary policy frameworks of major central banks have converged as described, I think it no longer important to play with the taxonomy of which one is inflation targeting or not. In fact, while Chairman Bernanke made it clear that the newly introduced longer-run goal does not mean the introduction of inflation targeting, some nevertheless do call it inflation targeting. If the new monetary policy framework adopted by the US Federal Reserve can be called inflation targeting, a similar view could be taken in the case of the Bank's new framework.

3. Expansion of the Asset Purchase Program

A ¥10 trillion increase in the purchase of JGBs

Now I would like to touch upon the third step taken at the latest Monetary Policy Meeting. That is, the expansion of the Asset Purchase Program (chart 3).

As part of the comprehensive monetary easing introduced in October 2010, the Bank has purchased various types of financial assets through this program. Using the newly established segregated fund on its balance sheet, which is also used for funds-supplying operations over the longer term, the Bank has purchased JGBs—both short-term and long-term—and, in an exceptionally unusual practice for a central bank, risk assets including commercial paper, corporate bonds, exchange-trade funds (ETFs), and Japan real estate investment trusts (J-REITs). The purpose of this operation is to encourage a decline in longer-term market interest rates and a reduction in various risk premiums so that financial conditions surrounding the ultimate borrowers of funds, such as firms and households, will become more accommodative. In the process of enhancing monetary easing, the total size of the program had been increased repeatedly, from the initial ¥35 trillion in October 2010 to ¥55 trillion, and the Bank made a decision to further increase it to ¥65 trillion by earmarking another ¥10 trillion for the purchase of JGBs at the latest Monetary Policy Meeting. The cumulative increase in the total size of the program is about ¥30 trillion.

In addition to this program, the Bank regularly purchases JGBs at the pace of ¥1.8 trillion per month, or ¥21.6 trillion per year, for the purpose of meeting the stable long-term demand for funds. Adding up the purchases through such operations and those through the program, the Bank is going to purchase a large quantity of JGBs until the end of this year at the pace of ¥3.3 trillion per month, or about ¥40 trillion per year. At the end of last year, the amount of JGBs held by the Bank was ¥66.1 trillion, representing 14.2 percent of nominal GDP. Although you may have the impression that the US Federal Reserve has aggressively purchased government bonds, its holdings at the end of last year were 10.8 percent of nominal GDP. The holdings by the European Central Bank, which started making such purchases in 2010, represented 2.2 percent of nominal GDP.

Such a significant scale of government bond purchases entails risk, to which more attention needs to be paid. More specifically, once the purchase of government bonds by a central bank is perceived as financing government debt and not conducted for the purpose of monetary policy, this could instead invite a hike in long-term interest rates and lead to financial market instability. The Bank has repeatedly cautioned about this risk, and rigidly maintains its policy of not conducting purchases of JGBs for the purpose of financing government debt.

Ensuring accomodative financial conditions

As a result of the comprehensive monetary easing consisting of the aggressive purchase of financial assets and the virtually zero interest-rate policy, financial conditions in Japan have become extremely accommodative (chart 4). More specifically, interest rates—including longer-term ones—in short-term money markets where financial institutions lend and borrow funds have stayed at very low levels, and credit spreads have been stable at low levels in corporate bond and commercial paper markets. Bank lending rates have already reached significantly low levels, but continue to decline gradually. According to various surveys, firms see their financial position and financial institutions' lending attitudes as being on a clear improving trend.

On the other hand, in the period after the Lehman Shock, the increase in quantitative indicators such as the size of the Bank's balance sheet and the monetary base—money provided by a central bank—has been moderate compared to that in the United States and in Europe, sometimes inviting the misunderstanding that the Bank's monetary easing is insufficient. When interest rates decline to extremely low levels, people tend to hang on to money. This situation is called a "liquidity trap." Once caught in this, it is no longer possible to measure the degree of monetary easing by simply looking at quantitative financial indicators. In fact, when we ask business managers about confronting challenges, few complain about a shortage of on-hand liquidity, and many point to a lack of demand or business. In any case, in such a situation, what is more important is the easiness of financial conditions in a broad sense, such as developments in short-term and long-term funding rates for firms and risk premiums, as well as funding conditions of firms and households. In the case of the United States and Europe, a significant expansion of the central bank balance sheet was indispensable to restoring stability in financial markets that had suffered significant damage to their functioning after the Lehman Shock. Once provided to financial markets, the funds remained stacked up in deposits with central banks because of negligible opportunity costs amid extremely low interest rate levels. On the other hand, in the case of Japan, damage to the functioning of financial markets was relatively limited, and financial system stability was maintained, even at the time of the Lehman Shock. Therefore, without having quantitative expansion on the scale seen in the United States and Europe, the Bank could realize more accommodative financial conditions. Although tensions in global financial markets heightened again last year due to the European debt problem, the Bank has managed to firmly maintain accommodative financial conditions in Japan. It is expected that the recent determined increase in the Asset Purchase Program earmarked for JGBs will further strengthen the easing effects by affecting the entire yield curve, including the longer end.

4. Our Thinking on Deflation and Needed Actions

Cause of deflation

So far, I have explained the Bank's new policy steps, which aim at overcoming deflation and bringing the economy back to a sustainable growth path with price stability. Conducting monetary policy in this way, how significant an effect can be expected in terms of achieving the goal of overcoming deflation? Put differently, what kinds of measures are needed for Japan's economy as a whole to ensure that this goal will be achieved? Using the time left for today's remarks, I would like to share with you our thinking on deflation. A good starting point is to have an accurate understanding of the fundamental cause of deflation in Japan.

The various causes of deflation in Japan have been provided and discussed for years. For example, for some time, downward pressures on prices came from deregulation and the streamlining of distribution systems, which were pursued under policy initiatives to reduce international price differentials. In Japan, both employers and employees tend to make wage adjustments for the sake of securing employment. As a result, even under severe economic conditions, the unemployment rate in Japan did not rise compared to that in the United States and in Europe, while the declining trend for wages became more evident. Such a declining trend in wages is one of the factors explaining deflation in Japan.

In the meantime, there is an argument that deflation has continued because of an insufficient amount of money—in other words, insufficient monetary easing by the Bank. However, such an argument needs to be properly fact-checked (chart 5). Let's take the typical example of money stocks, which are cash and deposits held by firms and households. The Marshallian *k* is the ratio of money stocks to nominal GDP that is used to measure the size of money stocks in relation to economic activity. In Japan, the ratio had been about 1.1 until the mid-1990s, which means that money stocks and nominal GDP were almost same. Since then, the ratio has continued to rise against the background of prolonged monetary easing and is now about 1.7—in other words, the amount of money stocks is about ¥805 trillion, while nominal GDP is about ¥467 trillion. This ratio of 1.7 is the highest among major economies. Conducting a similar exercise with the monetary base and the size of the central bank balance sheets results in the same conclusion: the ratio of Japan is the highest among major economies.

As I have stated, the Bank has managed to maintain accommodative financial conditions despite the rising tensions in global financial markets against the background of the European debt problem. Viewed in this way, it appears that the problem of Japan's economy is not a lack of money, but rather a lack of business chances and growth opportunities to make the best use of money.

Ultimately, deflation is a decline in the general price level, and therefore must be caused by a deterioration in the supply and demand balance of the macro economy—i.e., a shortage of demand against supply. An output gap—an indicator for supply and demand balance estimated on the basis of certain assumptions—has continued to indicate a shortage of demand since 2000, with the exception of a very short time period.

Looking back at real GDP growth rates in Japan from a relatively long viewpoint, the rates have gradually declined from 4.4 percent in the 1980s to 1.5 percent in the 1990s and to 0.6 percent in the 2000s (chart 6). There are several reasons for this decline. First, the negative legacy of the bubble bursting had continued to weigh on the economy since the beginning of the 1990s. To be more specific, while firms and financial institutions were tackling the challenge of balance-sheet repair, Japan's economy as a whole failed to adjust to a changing environment, such as increasing globalization and the rapid aging of the population. In particular, the effects of the population aging at a much greater speed in Japan than in the rest of the world have become more evident since entering the 2000s. The aforementioned widening of the output gap certainly means a shortage of demand against supply capacity, but in the current conjuncture it is specifically a shortage of demand against the supply capacity of existing goods and services. Rather, it might be interpreted as a widening mismatch of demand and supply in a sense that the supply side fails to sufficiently meet new demand in the new environment, such as demand from seniors.

In any case, when growth rates trend down in this way, households increasingly grow concerned about future income; this results in stagnant consumption, and the corporate sector restricts investment in future business. If these events occur, this will lead to a vicious cycle in which contraction of expenditures by firms and households drags down actual growth rates and growth expectations.

The relationship between economic activity and prices could be compared to that between fundamental physical strength and body temperature. In order to raise the body temperature to a normal level, it is necessary to improve fundamental physical strength. Likewise, we need to face the reality that, in order to raise prices appropriately, it is indispensable to strengthen Japan's growth potential and growth expectations, and deflation cannot be overcome without such efforts. Of course, there are some cases where an increase in prices takes place without changes in growth. The two oil shocks in the 1970s and the 1980s are typical examples. However, it also should be noted that a temporary increase in prices will not improve the performance of firms or quality of people's lives, as you can easily see in the case where crude-oil price hikes are transmitted to general prices, and we certainly do not wish to see such a situation materialize. The bottom line is that it is important to realize desirable inflation rates in proper sequencing so that improvement in economic activity leads to a rise in prices in a natural manner.

Efforts toward strengthening growth potential

Strengthening growth potential is an extremely difficult challenge for Japan, especially given the constraint it faces; namely, the rapid aging of the population. Let me provide you with a rough calculation. The economic growth rate consists of two components: the rate of growth in the number of workers and the GDP per worker; that is, the rate of growth in productivity (chart 6).[4] Of these two components, the rate of growth in the number of workers started to decline in the 2000s and decreased at an annual rate of 0.3 percent on average during that decade. Based on long-term projections of demographic trends recently released by the National Institute of Population and Social Security Research, the rate of decline in the number of workers will increase further to 0.7 percent in the 2010s, 0.8 percent in the 2020s, and 1.2 percent in the 2030s. Meanwhile, although the rate of growth in productivity has fluctuated due to the effects of the Lehman Shock, the recent trend is 1 percent on average in the past twenty years and about 1.5 percent on average for the period in the 2000s before the Lehman Shock. The rate of growth in productivity in Japan itself is comparable to those of other G-7 economies and was highest in the period in the 2000s before the Lehman shock. However, adding this rate of growth in productivity to the rate of decline in the number of workers leaves us with a grim outlook; that is, not only will the annual rate of economic growth in the 2010s remain around 0.5 percent, but it may decline further in the longer run.

How can we strengthen the economy's growth potential? First, while it is difficult to induce a dramatic increase in the number of workers, it is still possible to slow the pace of decline in the number by making it easier for elderly people and women to participate in the workforce. Nevertheless, the key to strengthening growth potential lies in efforts to raise productivity growth. In doing so, firms' efforts to capture global demand and cultivate new diversifying domestic demand become necessary. On the policy front, it is important to take measures such as deregulation in order to create an environment that encourages firms to take on these challenges. Financial institutions' expertise in identifying good business opportunities and providing risk money also becomes important with regard to providing financial support to firms in the course of making such efforts. Above all, it will be vital for society as a whole to realize the harsh reality and critical issues facing Japan's economy and share a sense of values, which should include acceptance of change as well as the need to improve the [nation's] economic metabolism.

The most significant contribution that a central bank could make in terms of strengthening growth potential is to maintain accommodative financial conditions and support firms from the financial side by creating an environment that makes it easier for them to explore new growth strategies. The Bank will continue to pursue powerful monetary easing, taking full account of the price stability goal in the medium to long term that I have discussed today. It is also an essential role of the Bank to make efforts to minimize the effects on the financial market and the financial system in Japan, and to do its utmost to ensure stability even in the event that some kind of destabilizing factor arises overseas amid the high uncertainty surrounding global financial developments, including the European debt problem. Furthermore, in an extraordinary measure for a central bank, the Bank has been proceeding with a new fund-provisioning measure to provide support for strengthening the foundations for economic growth. This is aimed at encouraging firms to explore new growth strategies by taking advantage of financial institutions' expertise in identifying good business opportunities.

In any event, there is no magical wand that can be used to strengthen growth potential. It is important for business firms, financial institutions, the government, and the central bank to continue making efforts in their respective roles as they face changes in the environment surrounding Japan's economy, such as globalization and the aging of the population. The goal of overcoming deflation will be achieved through such efforts to strengthen growth potential and support from the financial side.

5. Economic and Price Developments and Outlooks

Lastly, let me brief you on recent economic and price developments as well as the outlook for Japan's economy, in order to show how much progress has been made in terms of overcoming deflation.

Japan's economic activity experienced a sharp rebound from the plunge caused by the earthquake disaster* in the second half of last year. Recently, economic activity has been more or less flat, reflecting downward forces deriving from the effects of a slowdown in overseas economies and the appreciation of the yen as well as upward forces stemming from firm domestic demand, such as in terms of private consumption. Although this state of the economy is expected to continue for the time being—beyond early spring—the economy is expected to return to a moderate recovery path as the pace of recovery in overseas economies picks up, led by emerging and commodity-exporting economies, and as reconstruction-related demand after the earthquake

* This refers to the Great East Japan Earthquake, which took place on March 11, 2011.—Ed.

disaster gradually strengthens. The year-on-year rate of change in the CPI is expected to remain at around 0 percent for the time being but should gradually increase to around 0.5 percent in the next two years or so. According to the Bank's projections released last month of the economic and price outlooks through fiscal 2013, the real GDP growth rate is expected to be -0.4 percent in fiscal 2011, 2 percent in fiscal 2012, and 1.6 percent in fiscal 2013. As for the CPI, the year-on-year rate of increase is expected to gradually rise, from -0.1 percent in fiscal 2011, to 0.1 percent in fiscal 2012, and 0.5 percent in fiscal 2013 (chart 7).

Looking back, the rate of decrease in the CPI (all items exclusive of fresh food) marked a low of -2.4 percent in mid-2009, recording the largest decline in recent years. Thereafter, amid the economic recovery trend, albeit a moderate one, and the narrowing of the negative output gap, the rate of decrease in the CPI has been slowing and finally reached almost zero percent on a year-on-year basis. In this sense, we have been making progress in our steps toward overcoming deflation. We admit, however, that the inflation rate still has a long way to go before it reaches the 1 percent goal that the Bank has set for the time being, as indicated by "the price stability goal in the medium to long term."

In addition, the environment surrounding Japan's economy is attended by various uncertainties. We cannot rule out the possibility that future developments in the European debt problem will spill over to Japan's economy through strains in the global financial market. In terms of domestic factors, there are still many uncertainties regarding the supply and demand balance of electricity and the effects of the yen's appreciation, as well as the pace of strengthening in reconstruction-related demand. At the same time, however, we must not overlook the fact that positive signs have recently begun to appear among developments at home and abroad. Tensions in global financial markets regarding the European debt problem have abated somewhat since around the end of 2011. Some improvement has recently been observed in the US economy, mainly in the employment situation, despite the burdens of balance-sheet repair. Shifting our focus to Japan's economy, reconstruction-related demand has begun to materialize in both public works and private demand, and private consumption has recently been firm due in part to a recovery in demand that had been temporarily slowed after the earthquake disaster last year.

The Bank has decided to further enhance monetary easing, through the measures I have discussed, with the aim of supporting the recent positive developments from the financial side. The Bank will continue making its utmost efforts to overcome deflation and achieve sustainable growth with price stability. At the same time, I would like to repeat that, in order to strengthen the foundation of Japan's growth potential, there is a need to concentrate all the efforts made by concerned parties. Firms and financial institutions need to make efforts in an aggressive manner to make the best use of accommodative financial conditions, and government measures to support such initiatives in the private sector are required. In doing so, given that our economy is facing the frontline challenge of a rapidly aging population, our responses in tackling this challenge must be at the cutting edge. We need to determinedly pave the way by ourselves, recognizing that it is not possible to find case studies for solutions and best practices in other countries. If we succeed in overcoming this challenge by ourselves, our country can provide the rest of the world with a new type of economic and social norm for the first time since we presented the high-growth economic model. I would like to finish my remarks by stressing the importance of solving problems through using our own wisdom and will.

Thank you.

Speech was originally given at the Japan National Press Club in Tokyo, February 17, 2012, and subsequently published online by the Bank of Japan.

Notes

1. For more details, please refer to "The Bank's Thinking on Price Stability" (March 10, 2006) and Minutes of the Monetary Policy Meeting on March 8 and 9, 2006.
2. In the "Economic and Fiscal Projections for Medium to Long Term Analysis" released by the Cabinet Office in January 2012, the following two figures are provided as estimates of the rate of increase in the CPI for the medium to long term: (1) around 1 percent (an average of 1.1 percent for the period until FY 2020) under the assumption that economic developments at home and abroad require vigilance; and (2) around 2 percent (an average of 1.7 percent for the period until FY 2020) if measures proposed in the "Basic Strategy for Revitalizing Japan" are steadily implemented amid robust economic developments at home and abroad and the average growth rates for the period until FY 2020 rise to about 2 percent.
3. During the bubble period in Japan, the rate of increase in the CPI (all items excluding fresh food, after adjusting for the effect of a consumption tax hike) was 0.4 percent in fiscal 1987, 0.6 percent in FY 1988, and 1.6 percent in FY 1989.
4. As for various measures for the rate of growth in productivity, see chart 13 of Shirakawa Masaaki, "Deleveraging and Growth: Is the Developed World Following Japan's Long and Winding Road?" Lecture at the London School of Economics and Political Science (co-hosted by the Asia Research Centre and STICERD, LSE), January 10, 2012. http://www.boj.or.jp/en/announcements/press/koen_2012/data/ko120111a1.pdf

Chart 1. Decisions at the Monetary Policy Meeting (Feb. 14, 2012)

- The Bank decided to clarify its monetary policy stance and to further enhance monetary easing at the latest Monetary Monetary Policy Meeting in order to overcome deflation and achieve sustainable growth with price stability.

1. Introduction of "the Price Stability Goal in the Medium to Long Term"

✓ The inflation rate consistent with price stability sustainable in the medium to long term.

✓ A positive range of 2 percent or lower in terms of the year-on-year rate of change in the consumer price index (CPI). A goal of 1 percent is set for the time being.

2. Clarification of the Bank's Determination to Pursue Monetary Easing

✓ Aiming at achieving the goal of 1 percent in terms of the year-on-year rate of increase in the CPI.

✓ Pursuing powerful monetary easing by conducting the Bank's virtually zero-interest-rate policy and by implementing the Asset Purchase Program mainly through the purchase of financial assets until the Bank judges that the 1 percent goal is in sight.

⇒ On the condition that the Bank does not identify any significant risk, including the accumulation of financial imbalances, from the viewpoint of ensuring sustainable economic growth.

3. Increase in the Asset Purchase Program

✓ About 55 trillion yen → about 65 trillion yen. (The total size of the Program is increased by about 10 trillion yen, with the increase earmarked for the purchase of Japanese government bonds.)

⇒ In addition to purchases under the Program, the Bank regularly purchases Japanese government bonds at the pace of 21.6 trillion yen per year.

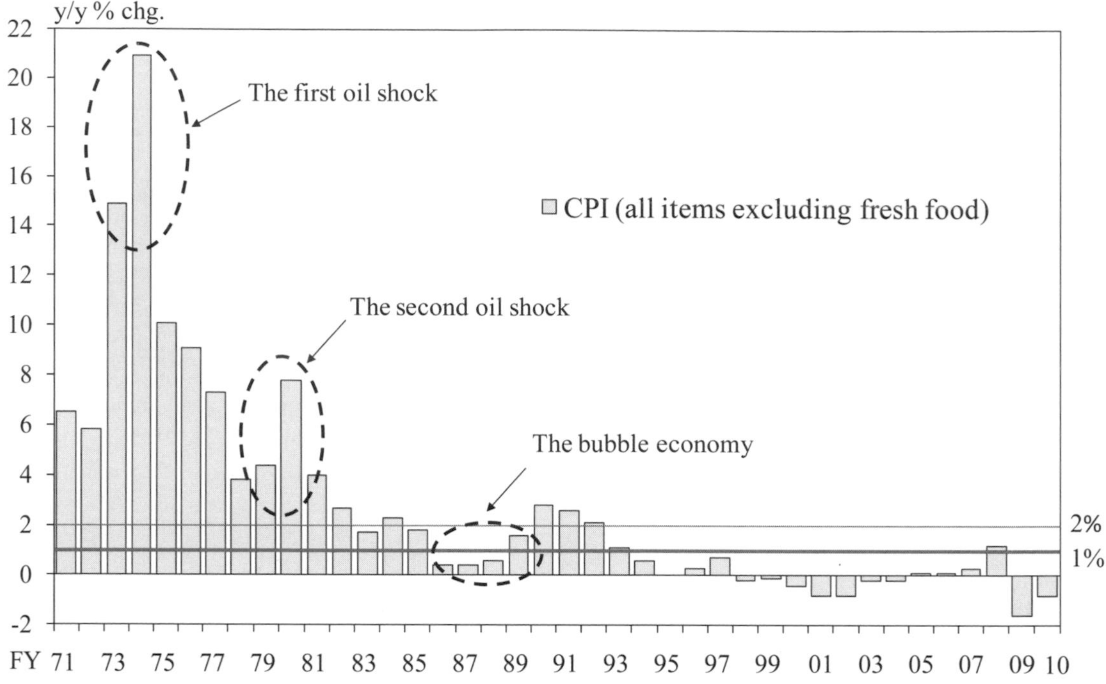

Chart 2. Changes in Japan's CPI

Source: Ministry of Internal Affairs and Communications.
Note: Figures are adjusted to exclude the effect of changes in the consumption tax rate.

Chart 3. Increase in the Asset Purchase Program

The program has had four increases, expanding to about ¥65 trillion from the initial size of about ¥35 trillion (the latest increase was decided on Feb. 14).

tril. yen	Started in Oct. 2010	Mar. 2011	Aug. 2011	Oct. 2011	Feb. 2012	Amount outstanding as of Feb. 10, 2012
Total size	About 35	About 40	About 50	About 55	About 65	43.1
JGBs	1.5	2.0	4.0	9.0	19.0	3.8
T-Bills	2.0	3.0	4.5	4.5	4.5	2.4
CP	0.5	2.0	2.1	2.1	2.1	1.5
Corporate bonds	0.5	2.0	2.9	2.9	2.9	1.7
ETFs	0.45	0.9	1.4	1.4	1.4	0.8
J-REITs	0.05	0.1	0.11	0.11	0.11	0.07
Fixed-rate operation	30.0	30.0	35.0	35.0	35.0	32.8
Intended time of completion	Around end-Dec. 2011	Around end-June 2012	Around end-Dec. 2012	Around end-Dec. 2012	Around end-Dec. 2012	

Note: In addition to purchases under the program, the Bank regularly purchases JGBs at the pace of ¥21.6 trillion per year.

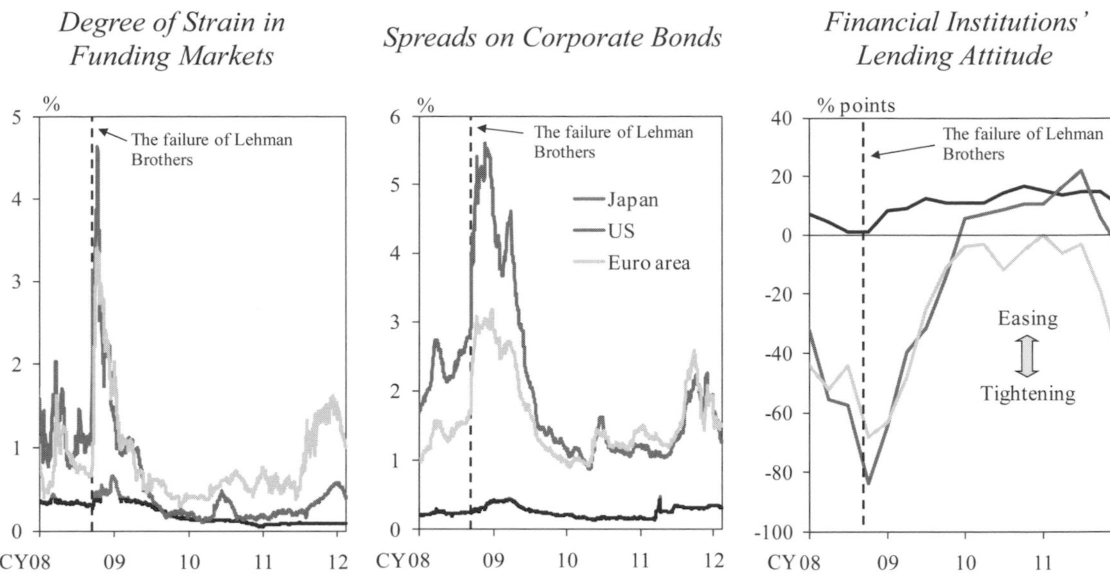

Chart 4. Financial Condition of Major Economies

Sources: Bloomberg; Japan Securities Dealers Association; Bank of Japan; FRB; ECB.
Notes: 1. The degree of strain in money markets is three-month Libor minus three-month T-Bill rates. Data for German government bonds are used for the Euro area.
2. The spreads on corporate bonds (rated AA) are corporate bond yields minus government bond yields.
3. Financial institutions' lending attitude is the average of the DIs for large, medium-sized, and small firms for Japan, large and medium-sized firms for the United States, and large firms for the Euro area.

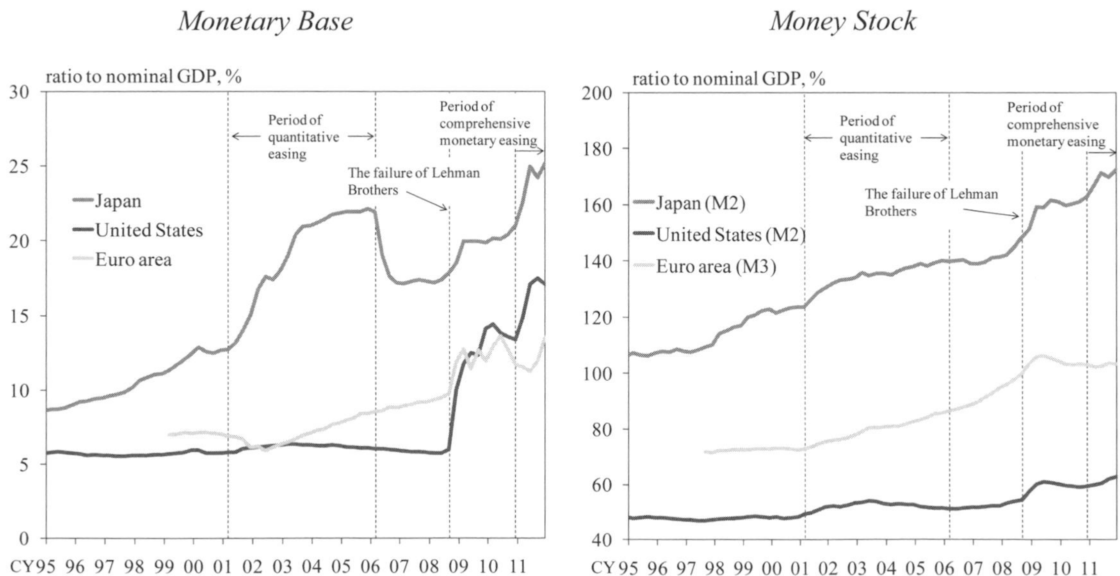

Chart 5. Money Supply of Major Economies

Sources: Cabinet Office; Bank of Japan; FRB; BEA; ECB; Eurostat.
Note: Monetary base is the sum of banknotes in circulation, coins in circulation, and current account deposits at a central bank.

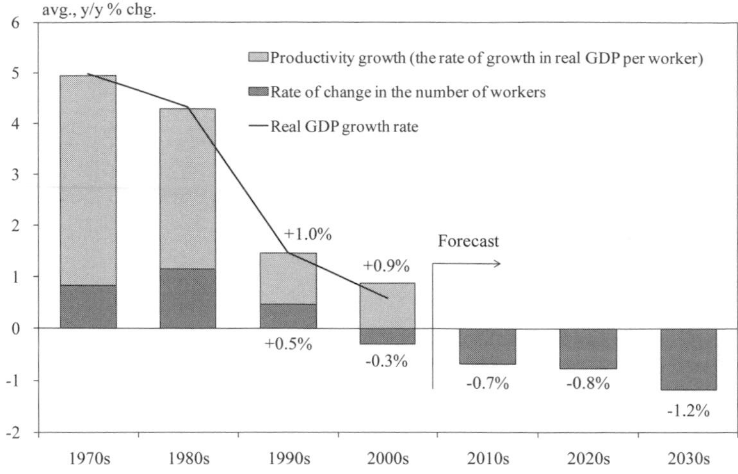

Chart 6. Decline of Real GDP Growth in Japan

Sources: Cabinet Office; Ministry of Internal Affairs and Communications; National Institute of Population and Social Security Research.

Notes: 1. Data are on a fiscal-year basis.

2. The rates of change in the number of workers from FY 2011 onward is calculated using the projected future population (medium variant) and the projected labor-force participation rates (assuming that the labor-force participation rates in each age/sex group remain the same as those in 2010).

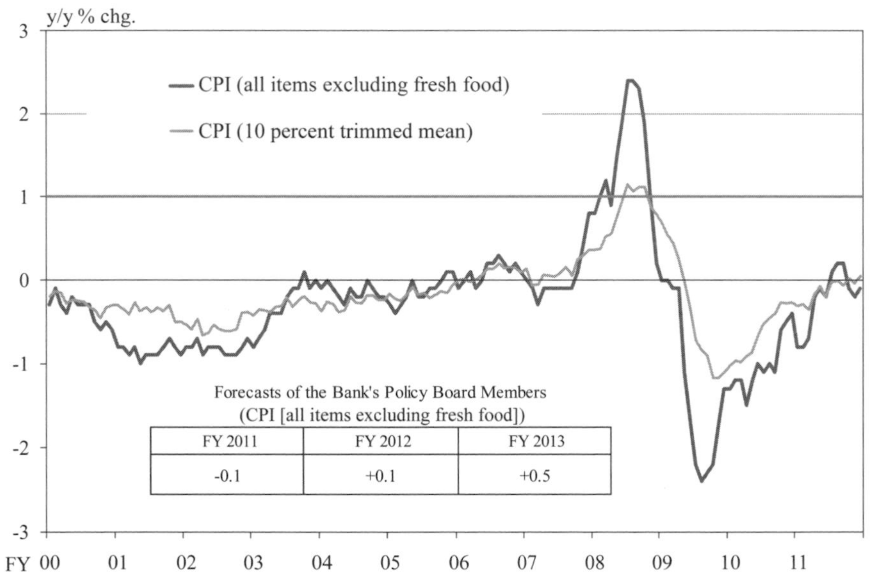

Chart 7. Underlying Trend of Japan's CPI

Source: Ministry of Internal Affairs and Communications.

Note: Figures for the 10 percent trimmed mean are weighted averages of items; these items are obtained by rearranging year-on-year rates of price change in ascending order and then excluding items in both the upper and lower 10 percent tails by weight.

III-(1.7) Overcoming Deflation

The Bank of Japan's Challenge

Kuroda Haruhiko

Speech at the Council on Foreign Relations in New York, 2013

Introduction

Good morning. I am honored to be given an opportunity to speak this morning at the long-established Council on Foreign Relations.

Today, I will talk about what Japan's deflation is all about and what challenges Japan is faced with, followed by how the Bank of Japan is trying to overcome deflation.

1. Deflation that Japan Has Been Experiencing

Japan has been mired in deflation for the past fifteen years. Let me bring up some figures. In Tokyo, the minimum fare for the subways of ¥160, or $1.60, has not changed since 1995. During the same period, the fare in New York increased from $1.50 to $2.50. As fees for public services are not likely to be reduced as a rule, the minimum fare for the subways in Tokyo has not declined, but prices as a whole have declined moderately for a long period in Japan.

The feature of Japan's deflation is that it is moderate but persistent. This is a phenomenon quite different from the deflation seen in the days of the Great Depression. In the period of deflation that occurred in the United States during the Great Depression, prices plunged in a short period. Prices declined significantly in the two years of 1931 and 1932, by almost 10 percent annually, but deflation continued for only four years. In contrast, Japan's consumer prices have fallen 4.1 percent in the past fifteen years from FY 1998 to FY 2012. That is merely a 0.3 percent decline on an annual average basis. However, the deflation in Japan has been extremely persistent. Young Japanese people have been born into a life of carrying the recognition that prices either will be constant or decline.

The continuation of price declines, albeit moderate ones, for a protracted period has deprived Japan's economy of vitality. In a state of deflation, the holding of cash or deposits will become a relatively better investment. In fact, cash and deposits held by Japanese firms have reached ¥230 trillion, close to 50 percent of nominal GDP. Persistent deflation has created an environment in which the status quo is better than making investments in new initiatives, and has brought a sense of stagnation to Japan. In an economy with few new challenges and investments, growth potential will decline gradually. Therefore, it is necessary to overcome deflation this time around and enhance people's willingness to take on new challenges.

There have been economic cycles during the past fifteen years. However, even when the economy recovered, prices did not increase in a sustainable fashion. The major reason for this is that, due to prolonged deflation, persistent deflationary expectations—that is, the recognition that it is natural for prices not to increase—have become entrenched among people, and they took actions based on such expectations. In such a situation, firms, households, and even labor unions will act on the assumption that prices will not increase, and thus it has become intrinsically difficult to increase prices.

In the past, the Bank of Japan (BOJ) took a variety of initiatives, including the adoption of unconventional measures ahead of other central banks, such as a zero interest-rate policy, quantitative easing, and—in the latest wording—forward guidance. Nevertheless, while those policies were effective in terms of stimulating economic activity, they could not change people's persistent deflationary expectations. The greatest challenge in overcoming deflation this time is to raise people's inflation expectations.

2. Introduction of Quantitative and Qualitative Monetary Easing

The BOJ introduced quantitative and qualitative monetary easing (QQE) in April. The new policy aimed at working directly on inflation expectations, with the goal of increasing inflation to the global standard of 2 percent. The question is: how?

The conclusion we reached was, first, to show our clear commitment to achieving the 2 percent price stability target in a stable manner as soon as possible; and, second, to underpin this determination by launching massive monetary easing that clearly differed from the past policies. Specifically, we declared that there would be a doubling in two years of the monetary base the BOJ provides. With this QQE, Japan's monetary base two years from now will become ¥270 trillion, or $2.78 trillion, reaching 56 percent of nominal GDP. For reference, the current monetary base in the United States is ¥329 trillion, or $3.39 trillion, which is 20 percent of nominal GDP.

To build the monetary base, on the asset side of the BOJ's balance sheet, the holdings of Japanese government bonds (JGBs) would be doubled. An associated massive purchase of JGBs would alter supply and demand conditions in the JGB market and put strong downward pressure on long-term interest rates.

However, there was a problem. The ten-year government bond yield in Japan was less than 1 percent. How could we make additional room for monetary easing? The point was the real interest rate, which is the nominal interest rate minus the expected inflation rate. In this regard, the situation facing Japan, in which expected inflation rates were stagnant, fortunately provided a breakthrough to this question. By raising inflation expectations while containing a rise in nominal interest rates, we would be able to lower real interest rates, which affect decision-making with respect to business fixed investment and private consumption.

Let me elaborate on this. In the United States and Europe, amid stagnant growth, observed inflation rates have been hovering around central banks' targeted inflation rate of 2 percent, and firms' and households' medium- to long-term expected inflation rates have also been stable at around 2 percent. In other words, expected inflation rates are anchored close to targeted inflation rates. In such cases, central banks cannot afford to raise expected inflation rates further. Therefore, to lower real interest rates, nominal interest rates need to be lowered. When long-term interest rates fall to the historic low level of less than 2 percent, room to further lower real interest rates becomes limited, as there is not much room to further lower nominal interest rates.

By contrast, in Japan, expected inflation rates have been anchored at too low a level compared with the 2 percent price stability target, and thus there is sufficient room to raise them. If a rise in nominal interest rates can be contained to a lesser extent than an increase in inflation expectations, then real interest rates can be lowered by that extent. With such a decline in real interest rates, business fixed investment and private consumption are expected to be stimulated, thereby elevating economic activity. Observed prices are also expected to increase gradually. In addition, a rise in observed inflation will lead to an increase in inflation expectations.

There is little time today to explain all the transmission channels of the QQE, but I have covered the core part. Through its effects, it is our aim to stimulate the economy, improve the output gap, and, above all, shift inflation expectations upward, and achieve the 2 percent price stability target as soon as possible.

3. Achievements under QQE and Perspective on Overcoming Deflation

Now that six months have passed since the QQE was introduced, is it working? As it turns out, there have been improvements in financial markets, economic activity and prices, and people's expectations, and the QQE has been exerting its effects powerfully. Let me point out some examples.

In the financial markets, stock prices have risen by more than 30 percent since the beginning of the year. This substantially exceeds the rate of increase not only in Europe, which is around 13 percent, but also in the United States, which is around 16 percent.

On the real economy front, real GDP has marked high growth since the turn of the year: around an annualized 4 percent for two consecutive quarters. The unemployment rate has recently declined to the levels seen prior to the Lehman Shock, around 4 percent.

People's expectations have also changed. Consumer confidence indicators clearly have tilted upward since around the end of last year. Looking at business confidence indicators, according to the BOJ's business survey called the Tankan survey, the diffusion index (DI) for business conditions bottomed at minus 9 percentage points in the last December survey; it has improved to plus 2 percentage points in the latest September survey—the same level as that in December 2007, prior to the Lehman crisis.

Turning to price developments, expected inflation rates have increased as a whole, according to market indicators and various surveys. The break-even inflation rate (BEI) has increased to close to 1.7 percent, from around 0.70 a year ago. In the opinion survey on the general public's views and behavior conducted by the BOJ, in which consumers are asked their views on the inflation rate one year from now, the proportion of consumers who answered that prices would increase was just over 50 percent in the last December survey, but increased to above 80 percent in the September survey. In addition, the DI for selling prices in the Tankan survey, which is calculated based on a question asked of firms regarding developments in selling prices of their own products and services, have improved for large firms from minus 15 percentage points in the last December survey to zero in the September survey.

Looking at the observed inflation rates, the CPI inflation rate turned positive in June for the first time in 14 months, and accelerated to 0.8 percent in August.

As explained, stock prices have been rising and the real economy has been improving steadily. The inflation rate has turned positive and inflation expectations have risen. Such improvements in economic activity, prices, and people's expectations could be factors in increasing interest rates. Nevertheless, thanks to strong downward pressure stemming from the BOJ's JGB purchases, Japan's long-term interest rates have been slightly lower than those of a year ago, with ten-year JGB yields hovering at less than 0.7 percent. In addition, while long-term interest rates have been rising since May in the United States and other overseas economies, those in Japan have been more or less flat or slightly declining. Commercial banks' lending rates on new loans—an average of loans to firms and individuals—have declined to a historic low of below 1 percent.

Meanwhile, as people's inflation expectations have been increasing gradually on the whole, real interest rates have been declining. Thus, the situation we have aimed for has been generated. This decline in real interest rates is likely to stimulate business fixed investment, housing investment, and private consumption, thereby bolstering the economy. In addition, the QQE and various measures by the government seem to have been gradually improving people's sentiments, making them proactive and igniting their spirits. In fact, there are signs that firms' funding is becoming active. The year-on-year rate of increase in bank lending, which declined to below 0.5 percent in the first half of FY 2012, has since been moderately expanding to slightly over 2 percent. The amount of corporate bonds issued in the April–June quarter reached a high level for the first time since the July–September quarter of 1998, which was coincidentally the quarter in which deflation began. Initial public offerings by firms have also become active recently.

So far, the QQE has been exerting its intended effects, which is quite encouraging. By continuing to pursue the QQE with a strong determination to achieve the 2 percent price stability target, we are convinced that we will definitely overcome deflation.

Concluding Remarks

Japan has a solid growth base. It has first-class technology and human resources. What has been lacking is positive sentiment—both the confidence in our ability to succeed and in our spirits—which were lost amid the sense of stagnation under persistent deflation. The overcoming of deflation will progress in line with a dispelling of this sense of stagnation. I am a firm believer that Japan will regain confidence and grow with vigor again.

There is another tailwind for Japan. The recent decision to hold the 2020 Olympics in Tokyo is boosting the level of people's sentiments. At the time of the Olympics, seven years from now, we will welcome you to a Japan that has regained its brightness. However, I am afraid that you may not be able to ride the subways in Tokyo for a minimum fare of 160 yen at that time.

Thank you for your attention.

Speech originally given at the Council on Foreign Relations in New York, October 10, 2013, and subsequently published online by the Bank of Japan.

III-(2.1) The Japanese Big Bang and the Financial Crisis

Iwata Kazumasa

Japan Review of International Affairs, 1999

The Japanese "Big Bang" began in April 1998 with the implementation of a revised Foreign Exchange and Foreign Trade Law. This program of financial deregulation got underway twenty-one years later than in the United States and eleven years later than in Britain. It has already begun to have a major impact on the asset-handling behavior of Japan's investors, businesses, and households. Businesses are preparing to start "multilateral netting" of their financial transactions with overseas counterparts without the intermediation of banks, and families fed up with the low yields offered by domestic financial institutions are placing increasing amounts of their assets in foreign-currency deposits with non-Japanese institutions and in mutual funds (known in Japan as investment trusts) marketed by foreign securities companies.

Meanwhile, Japan's financial institutions, especially banks, are suffering from the effects of their tardiness in cleaning up the bad loans resulting from the collapse of the "bubble economy," the existence of rules and practices left over from the convoy-style system of regulation that was applied until the 1980s, and the discretionary application of regulatory authority in a way that discourages financial innovation. The financial services industry, with its lagging position in the innovative fields of derivatives and securitization, along with its inadequate systems of risk management, shows clear signs of being in decline.

Fallout from the Big Bang

Foreign financial institutions gain power

In their response to the Big Bang and the failure of domestic institutions to deal with it adequately, non-Japanese institutions can be grouped into two major categories: those that are skeptical of the Japanese reform program, such as hedge funds, and those that see the reforms as offering a good chance to expand their presence in the Japanese market, to which access was limited; the latter group are taking advantage of this chance to extend the scope of their activities greatly through alliances with and acquisitions of Japanese institutions, entry into the securitization business, and other moves. They have increased their presence in Japan through such moves as Bankers Trust's establishment of a joint venture with the Nippon Credit Bank, GE Capital's de facto acquisition of Toho Mutual Life Insurance, and Merrill Lynch's taking on of branches and employees from Yamaichi Securities (table 1). In addition, non-Japanese players have been steadily increasing their presence in the Japanese market. They have been doing this mainly through sales of mutual fund shares as long-term assets and the acceptance of foreign-currency deposits, and also through entry into the securitization business.

Foreign institutions have now in fact taken over the leading role in the Japanese Big Bang, overshadowing their local counterparts. The so-called Wimbledon phenomenon—the dominance of foreign players in Britain's financial markets after that country's Big Bang—is becoming evident in Japan as well. Of course, the original objective of Japan's Big Bang was not to strengthen the financial services industry, but rather to enhance economic welfare through the qualitative and quantitative improvement of financial services for domestic and foreign users. The reconstruction of the financial system for this purpose must of course make it open to the outside, and it is important to render the Tokyo

Table 1. Alliances between Japanese and Foreign Financial Institutions

Japanese	Foreign	Type of alliance
Long-Term Credit Bank of Japan	Swiss Bank	Multilateral alliance (not realized)
Nippon Credit Bank	Bankers Trust	Alliances between Japanese and foreign financial institutions
Yasuda Trust	Goldman Sachs	Multilateral joint venture
Sakura Trust	Chase Manhattan Bank	Real-estate intermediary
Sumitomo Trust	Citibank	Custodian
Mitsui Trust	Société Générale	Sales of mutual funds
Yamaichi Securities	Merrill Lynch	Sales of investment management and mutual funds
Nikko Securities	Salomon Smith Barney	Assumption of branches and employees
GE Edison Life (Toho Life)	GE Capital	Joint venture for mutual fund evaluation
Meiji Life	Dresdner Bank	Joint venture for life insurance
Daihyaku Life	Westdeutsche Landesbank	Acquisition of investment management business
Nippon Life	Putnam Investments	Capital injection
Dai-ichi Life	Capital Group	Alliance in products and human development
Yasuda Fire & Marine	TCW	Alliance in development and sales of mutual funds

market fair, highly transparent, and efficient so as to attract money from around the world.

Changes in the Assets of Japanese Families

It is predicted that the asset holdings of Japanese households will change significantly in the period to come. Up until now, the household sector has tended to hold the bulk of their assets in bank or postal savings deposits or in life-insurance policies. The share of assets held in savings has been on a high level, like that of Germany. In the United States over the past twenty years (1975–1995), the share of assets in savings deposits fell 16.6 percentage points, while the shares of mutual funds and insurance rose 5.7 points and 9.7 points, respectively. And holdings of securities were up 7.5 points, of which 3.8 points consisted of increases in direct ownership of stocks.

If Japanese households were to exhibit the same pattern of change over the twenty years from 1995 to 2015, the share of savings deposits would drop from 55.2 percent to 30.6 percent, while that of mutual funds would jump from 2.7 percent to 15.1 percent. Holdings of securities would go from 19.5 percent to 32.0 percent, with a rise in the share of directly owned stocks from 7.0 percent to 8.9 percent (table 2).[1] Despite the fact that the past performance of Japanese mutual funds has not been stellar at all, a sizable increase in their share can be expected, the reason being a major shift in the public-sector flow of funds.

Table 2. Projected Shift in Personal Asset Portfolio Composition, Japan (percent)

	1995	2015
Demand deposits	10.0	8.1
Time deposits	45.2	22.5
Insurance	25.4	37.5
Securities	19.5	32.0
Stocks	7.0	8.9
Bonds	3.1	3.5
Mutual funds	2.7	15.1
Trusts	6.6	4.6
Total	100.0	100.0

As of the end of FY 1996 (March 1997), public and private (corporate) pension funds in Japan totaled ¥126 trillion and ¥64 trillion, respectively. Until now, postal savings and public pension funds have been managed by the Trust Fund Bureau of the Ministry of Finance as part of the government's Fiscal Investment and Loan Program. But given the rising levels of mandatory contributions and direct budget appropriations for the public pension system, and also in light of the equity of intergenerational income transfers, it is now seen as desirable for the earnings-related benefit scheme of pensions to be shifted to private-sector management (while leaving the basic pension scheme within the public sector).[2]

In the area of corporate pensions, given the issue of portability and the problem of increasing future liabilities under the existing plans, it is desirable that Japan adopt a system of contribution-based plans like the United States' 401(k) plans, which are invested directly by the individual participant; this can be expected to lead to increased use of mutual funds. The assets currently accumulated under the public pension system are for the earnings-related benefit scheme. If these are switched to private-sector management and corporate plans are switched to contribution-based ones, pension assets on the order of ¥190 trillion will become available for investment through private funds.

The postal savings system is also likely to be made independent of the Trust Fund Bureau because of the reform of the Fiscal Investment and Loan Program. My personal view is that the postal savings system should be reborn in the form of a core bank or collateralized banking arrangement. With collateralized banking, it will not be necessary to provide deposit insurance or government guarantees of principal. The safety of the deposits will be guaranteed by the safety of the assets held by the system. The assets in which the postal deposits are to be invested must of course be safe, such as government bonds, but it is also important that investments reflect the preferences of depositors. Otherwise, the system is liable to be a "pocket bank" for politicians and bureaucrats, just as the Fiscal Investment and Loan Program has been up to now (Iwata and Fukao 1998). In simple terms, the asset holdings of Japanese households can be expected to shift from savings deposits to investment funds. But we should note that the shift to investment funds (i.e., the development of parallel banking) for family savings will lead to hitherto unseen risks.[3]

Concerns about Financial Stability

The rise of systemic risk

Concerns about the stability of the Japanese financial system were greatly heightened in November 1997 by the bankruptcy of Hokkaido Takushoku Bank and the self-liquidation of Yamaichi Securities. The bankruptcy of Hokkaido Takushoku was viewed favorably by international financial markets as representing the removal from the scene of an insolvent institution, and stock prices rose on the news. But it also meant that the Ministry of Finance had failed to keep its previously expressed commitment not to let any of Japan's twenty big commercial banks—the so-called city banks among them—go under. MOF disclaimed any responsibility for Yamaichi's going out of business, but doubts did arise as to whether, for example, there had really been no possibility for the institution, one of Japan's four largest brokerages, to stay in operation, or whether the decision to have it go out of business "voluntarily" rather than go bankrupt was aimed at rescuing regional financial institutions that had entrusted some of their holdings of government bonds to Yamaichi.

When major institutions like Hokkaido Takushoku and Yamaichi fail, it is necessary to isolate the risks and crises of individual institutions from the market as a whole so as to prevent the spread of financial panic and systemic risk. In particular, when Sanyo Securities went bankrupt (also in November 1997), the result was the defaulting of obligations on the money market, since under Japanese bankruptcy law it is not possible to leave loans in force. In addition, the excess liabilities of the banks that failed turned out to be larger than originally reported, and mutual mistrust grew up among participants in the money market. This interfered with the smooth functioning of the market. For example, Hokkaido Takushoku had been declared to have ¥300 billion in net worth before its bankruptcy, but it became clear after the fact that it actually had excess liabilities of ¥1.1 trillion. The malfunctioning of the money market was a surprise to the financial regulatory authorities, and it was an event that had the potential to set off a financial panic.

The regulators' failure to ensure that the money market continued to operate smoothly was not the only problem. With the emergence of revelations of deep-seated corruption within the financial regulatory system, public trust in both the regulators and the financial system rapidly waned, and people started shifting their money to the safe haven of the postal savings system. In the period of November–December 1997, Japan was actually on the verge of setting off a global financial meltdown. Some Americans even began calling for the Japanese financial system to be placed under quarantine so as to isolate it from the rest of the world.

Going back to the old regime

To deal with the crisis, the National Diet in February 1998 amended the Deposit Insurance Law and enacted the Emergency Measures Law for Stabilization of Financial Functions. These measures set aside a total of ¥30 trillion in public funds, including ¥17 trillion for protection of depositors and ¥13 trillion to improve the capital adequacy of financial institutions and thereby alleviate the crunch in lending to businesses. That same month, public funds totaling ¥2.1 trillion were used for the purchase of preferred shares and subordinated debt issued by banks. A peculiar feature of the plan was that these capital injections were available only for healthy banks. This was despite the fact that the target of government support should obviously not have been either insolvent banks or healthy banks with capital adequacy ratios of 8 percent or more, but rather banks whose capital was becoming inadequate and yet that could still be made viable through management efforts, restructuring, or mergers.

As of 1997 the regulatory authorities were planning to implement a system of "prompt corrective action" in April 1998; the objective was to secure the smooth closure of banks whose liabilities had come to exceed their assets. This represented a major shift from the established approach, which had been one of "forbearance." The United States had instituted just such a system of corrective measures in 1991 in connection with an overhaul of its federal deposit insurance scheme. The reason for this shift was the lesson of past experience that by holding to the doctrines of "too big to fail" (meaning that large banks must be kept afloat) and of "essentiality" (meaning that even regional banks should be rescued if their failure would gravely damage local economies), problems were merely deferred, resulting in a greater burden on taxpayers.

In Japan's case, however, the failures of Hokkaido Takushoku and Yamaichi produced fears about both the financial system and the employment situation, leading to the reemergence of the "too big to fail" and "essentiality" doctrines. In the wake of the November 1997 failures, former prime minister Miyazawa Kiichi spoke up in the Diet to assert the need for infusions of public funds in order to calm financial fears, presenting an argument based fundamentally on the tenets of essentiality. Former chief cabinet secretary Kajiyama Seiroku also made a similar case, drafting a plan for the floating of ¥10 trillion in government bonds, a scheme that ultimately formed the basis of the ¥30 trillion package (Kajiyama 1997, 1998). As a logical requirement of the government's policy shift, the implementation of prompt corrective action was postponed.

In effect, what happened was a shift from an approach modeled on that adopted by the United States, when the problem of bad loans was dealt with through a combination of corrective action and securitization through the Resolution Trust Corp., to the approach taken by Japan's federal government during the 1930s, when troubled banks were rescued by the Reconstruction Finance Corp. The shift settled the financial jitters somewhat for the time being, but it did not bring about a solution to the problem. Because of the ongoing slump in the economy, the volume of nonperforming assets continued to grow.

The growing mountain of bad loans

In connection with their acceptance of public funds in September 1998, banks unveiled a new set of statistics on their bad loans, conducted by self-assessment under new rules. The total was ¥73 trillion, an amount far in excess of the ¥27 trillion figure that had been announced as of September 1997, while about ¥50 trillion was written off directly or indirectly. Banks had been listing the solvency of their borrowers in five categories: sound, requiring attention, in danger of bankruptcy, effectively bankrupt, and bankrupt.

For the new self-assessment of problem assets, they split their credit exposures into four classes: (1) normal, (2) requiring case-by-case attention, (3) subject to major concern, and (4) uncollectible. According to this classification, they found they had ¥66 trillion of credits in category 2, ¥7 trillion in category 3, and ¥86 billion in category 4.

A problem here is that the distinction between categories 2 and 3 is not all that clear, and some banks appear to have included some category 3 credits under category 2. Also, the Asian financial crisis that hit in the latter part of 1997 caused some category 1 credits to slip into the third or even fourth category, although an earlier self-assessment that was conducted as of March 1998 was based on the status quo in the April–September period of 1997, and so it did not include Asian credits gone bad. Furthermore, the first category also included lending to, for example, major construction companies, some of which had in fact soured.

The proposal made by Kajiyama (1998) called for mandatory bad-loan provisions amounting to 20 percent of the category 2 credits. In practice, Japanese banks have set aside reserves of only 2 percent to 5 percent against losses on loans in this category, but a study of past data indicates that about 15 percent is required. In addition, though the provisions against credits in categories 3 and 4 should be around 90 percent, as of the end of FY 1997 (March 1998) the actual figure for domestic banks in total was only 58.1 percent, showing the clear inadequacy of bad-loan reserves (indirect write-offs). And banks are even further behind in terms of direct write-offs of nonperforming credits.[4]

If mandatory provisions of 20 percent for category 2 credits were enforced, the market judged that six of Japan's nineteen major banks (down from twenty, because Hokkaido Takushoku failed) were strongly likely to fall into insolvency, and so those banks with lower capital adequacy ratios began to come under attack. The main target was the Long-Term Credit Bank of Japan, which had been one of the recipients of public funding in March based on an assessment of its soundness at that stage, even though it had a capital-adequacy ratio of 10.8 percent.

The bridge-bank concept

With the LTCB having come under attack starting in June 1998, an emergency package of nine financial laws, including provisions for the establishment of "bridge banks" to take over the operations of failed institutions, was finally passed by the Diet in October after extended debate between the ruling Liberal Democratic Party (hereafter referred to as LDP) and opposition groups. The problem with the bridge-bank proposal, originally floated by the LDP, was that it was vague in its provisions concerning when a bank would be considered to have failed and when the borrowers could be considered still "sound," that is to say, eligible for the continued extension of credit. Also, it allowed for bridge banks to remain in existence for five years, and it was thus feared that the plan would merely put off problems. Furthermore, unlike a similar plan that had been implemented in the United States for dealing with bank insolvencies, the LDP plan's purpose was not to reduce injections of public funds; rather, it took such injections for granted.

In a highly unusual move, the LDP accepted virtually the entire set of revisions proposed by the biggest opposition party, the Democratic Party of Japan (hereafter referred to as DPJ), for the draft of the Law Concerning Emergency Measures for the Reconstruction of the Functions of the Financial System (Financial Reconstruction Law), under which the bridge-bank plan was introduced. The DPJ's draft provided for the option of nationalization of banks (or, as it was put in the law, placing them under "special public administration") and for the establishment of a financial resuscitation committee independent of the Ministry of Finance to supervise the process of dealing with the financial crisis.

The idea of separating financial regulatory authority from the fiscal authority held by MOF was ultimately not implemented in a clear fashion, but thanks to the introduction of the bridge-bank scheme, an arrangement was put in place to prevent the occurrence of systemic risk by dividing insolvent banks into "good" and "bad" parts and protecting sound borrowers by having the "good" banks acquired by other banks.

"Bad" banks, meanwhile, were to have their operations liquidated and could have their unrecoverable loans taken over by the Resolution and Collection Corporation (formed by combining the Housing Loan Administration Corporation and the Resolution and Collection Bank). In addition, a set of rules similar to those of the "prompt corrective action" program was adopted to serve as the basis for determining, mainly in line with banks' capital-adequacy ratios, when it is necessary to issue directives for the improvement of banks' operations and when banks should be judged to have failed.

The bridge-bank plan was one that distinguished between the "good" and "bad" parts of failed banks. What is more important for the revival of the banking business in Japan is for healthy and viable banks to make this sort of distinction on their own initiative, and for the government to provide infusions of public funds for the "bad" banks. We should recall Japan's experience immediately after World War II, when emergency legislation allowed banks to set up separate accounts for their old and new business.

The Core of the Crisis and the Use of Public Funds

As a result of the poorly timed adoption of a fiscal austerity program by the administration of former prime minister Hashimoto Ryūtarō, the economy continued to decline while he was in office, and the volume of bad loans increased. While the bridge-bank plan was being debated between the LDP and its opponents in the Diet, the market started targeting those banks that would become insolvent if the ratio of mandatory provisions for category 2 credits were raised from 20 percent to 40 percent. The view in the marketplace was that if the ratio were set at 40 percent, only four banks would escape insolvency, and only one would be left with a capital adequacy ratio above 2 percent.

The LDP reached an agreement with two opposition parties, the Liberal Party and the Heiwa Kaikaku, a new political group, on a bill for promptly putting financial institutions back on their feet, under which public funds could be provided not just to deal with failed banks, but also to beef up healthy ones. The opposition DPJ and Liberal Party had come out against laxness in extending public funds to banks, particularly as had been done under the emergency package enacted in May. But in the final stages of putting together the legislation on bridge banks, the DPJ made an about face, deciding to support the injection of public funds to the tune not of ¥30 trillion but of ¥60 trillion (consisting of ¥25 trillion for healthy banks with capital-adequacy ratios of 8 percent or above, ¥18 trillion for dealing with nationalized banks, and ¥17 trillion to protect depositors). It remains unclear what sort of process took place within the party to cause this policy switch, but it seems likely that the Democrats came under heavy pressure from their supporters in labor unions (specifically Rengo, the Japanese Trade Union Confederation), who were fearful of further deterioration in the employment situation. Quite likely the DPJ also began to feel a real sense of crisis that if matters were allowed to continue on their current course with no corrective action, the entire banking sector might collapse.

The Long-Term Credit Bank of Japan, which had been under attack by the market since June 1998, eventually had to be placed under special public administration—in other words, temporarily nationalized. It now appears virtually beyond doubt that the LTCB was actually already insolvent already in March, but neither MOF nor the Financial Supervisory Agency has admitted to this misjudgment.

Expansion and contraction of the credit supply

At the root of the bad-debt problem is the fact that banks overextended their lending during the speculative years of the 1980s. Banks have some ¥166 trillion in real-estate loans outstanding; furthermore, the total volume of their lending, expressed as a percentage of gross domestic product, has hardly declined at all, despite the fact that the value of the real estate and other assets serving as collateral for the loans has plunged ¥670 trillion from its peak level, and stock values have dropped ¥310 trillion. By comparison with the ratio to nominal GDP that prevailed in the first half of the 1980s, the volume of loans outstanding at all banks as of 1997 was up by ¥114 trillion. Even if we only consider the nineteen

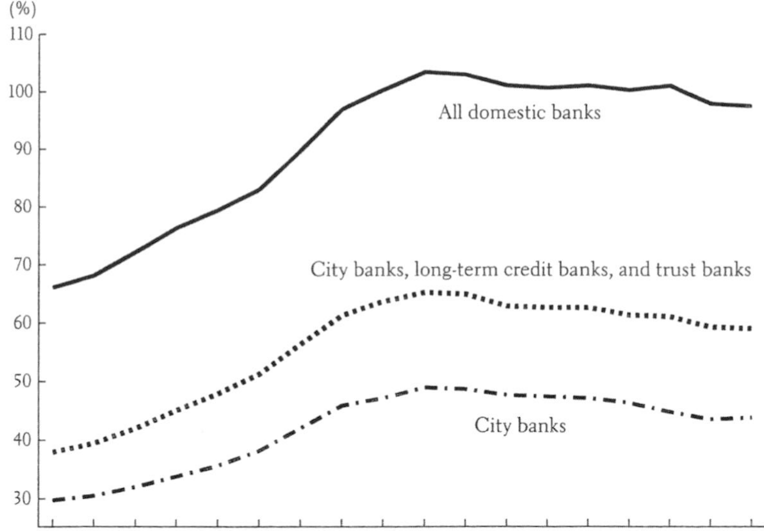

Figure 1. Ratio of Loans Outstanding to Nominal GDP

Sources: *Keizai tōkei geppō* (Economic Statistics Monthly), Bank of Japan; *Kokumin keizai keisan nenpō* (Annual Report on National Accounts), Economic Planning Agency.

major banks (city banks, trust banks, and long-term credit banks), the excess comes to more than ¥70 trillion (see figure 1). By contrast, the total amount of equity capital (defined as tier 1 primary capital and 45 percent of unrealized capital gains on stock portfolios) was only ¥33.5 trillion for all domestic banks and ¥14.5 trillion for the nineteen major banks. This means that the credit crunch produced by capital-starved banks' reluctance to lend cannot be alleviated without injections of public funds on quite a large scale.

Problems with injections of public funds

Despite the extreme graveness of the situation, with the economy continuing to deteriorate and prices of stocks and land remaining depressed, the nineteen big banks initially hesitated to apply for injections of public funds, fearing that they might be called to account for past management decisions. The reason it was decided to base the injections on requests by banks rather than to make them mandatory was that regulatory authorities feared that managers would become the target of civil suits by shareholders. But in the end, fifteen of the banks applied for funds totaling about ¥7.5 trillion. These applications came only after the government announced that, for the time being, it would not call banks to account for past mistakes.

Paul Krugman has argued that the reason Japanese banks with about 30 percent of their assets tied up in bad loans have been reluctant to apply for public funds is that the introduction of the money will dilute the remaining value of their institutions to shareholders (Krugman 1998). But his argument overlooks the fact that if the infusions are of a certain scale (totaling in excess of ¥50 trillion for all domestic banks), the residual value for shareholders will in fact increase.[5]

Such infusions of public funds ultimately place a burden on taxpayers. Already more than ¥4 trillion in government money has been extended through the deposit insurance system. The Resolution and Collection Bank's average rate of collection of bad credits in the past comes to only 22 percent. If it is possible to recover that amount with respect to the remaining ¥30 trillion in bad credits, that will leave ¥23.4 trillion to be paid for with public funds, which comes out to ¥213,000 per person. If the total of the bad-loan mountain actually comes to ¥100–150 trillion instead of ¥73 trillion, as estimated by Moody's and others, the burden may be twice as much. In order to eliminate the excessive volume of nonperforming assets as quickly and cheaply as possible, it is necessary to provide incentives to the banks directly involved to strive for their own survival ("open bank assistance") and to extract as much value as possible out of the bad loans.[6] The provision of public funds to viable banks should take the form of the purchase of stocks of the "bad" banks that have been separated from the "good" banks on their balance sheets. That is because using public funds in this manner provides a high degree of transparency. The discretionary provision of public funds to particular banks leads not only to moral hazard, but also to possible problems conflicting with the Anti-Monopoly Act, as seen in the case of France's Crédit Lyonnais.

Disclosure and Reform of the Regulatory System

In March 1998, when injections of public funds were first made available, all the city banks applied for roughly the same amount, about ¥100 billion. But there was no disclosure at this point of the size of the banks' bad-debt portfolios, particularly of the volume of category 2 credits at the individual banks. At this stage there was no change in the traditional convoy-style uniformity of speed and direction among Japanese banks. And in November 1998, fifteen major banks again applied for public funds, coming under an officially monitored program of operational improvement just one step short of nationalization. This turn of events represented quite the opposite of the Big Bang's principle; namely, that institutions should take responsibility for their own affairs.

The financial authorities have also been unenthusiastic about disclosure. When it came time to close the books for the year ending March 1998, they allowed banks a choice of valuation methods for their stock portfolios, either valuing them their lowest prices or at their cost at the time of acquisition. This represented an abandonment of the move toward adopting the internationally accepted accounting principle of valuing stocks at current market prices, and it meant an official approval of the concealment of unrealized losses on stock portfolios. The authorities have in fact repeatedly tinkered with accounting standards to obtain better results at the end of reporting periods. Accounting standards are the bedrock of market discipline, and meddling with them in this way undermines the conditions required for the operation of a market economy by thickening the veil of concealment around enterprises.

In order to build a fair and highly transparent financial system, it is best for holdings of stocks to be marked to market. One might argue for valuation at acquisition cost for stocks that are owned under cross-shareholding arrangements with other corporations and are therefore not meant to be sold, but in view of the fact that even these stocks are now being sold off, consistent application of the market-value principle is best. It would also be preferable in terms of transparency to value holdings of land at their market prices, but when prices are declining, to use a market-value appraisal just once means concealing future unrealized losses. It seems desirable to use "fresh-start accounting" so as to take into account the value of hidden assets and goodwill, eliminating carried-over losses by charging them against shareholders' capital, but the Commercial Code does not allow for this quasi-reorganization procedure.

Inflation and corporate veils

In a famous speech he delivered at Berlin University in 1926 titled "The End of Laissez-Faire," John Maynard Keynes declared that to destroy the capitalist system it was not necessary to have a revolution, but merely to remove money supply control and trigger rampant inflation. In the same speech, he stated that thickening the corporate veil would also destroy the capitalist system. The greatest failing of Japan's (and Asia's) market economies is the lack of transparency in business management, public regulation, and the relationship between businesses and regulators. The concealment of losses through changes in accounting standards proves that neither the financial authorities nor the institutions they regulate have any understanding of why there is a "Japan premium" charged to Japanese institutional borrowers in the international money market.

The disclosure of banking information in Japan is woefully inadequate. This has made it extremely difficult to achieve political consensus on injections of public funds, and it has resulted in problems being put off. Sweden experienced a bubble economy similar to Japan's, accompanied by excessive bank lending, and public funds amounting to 4 percent of nominal GDP were used to rescue the financial system. But thanks to the speediness with which a political agreement was reached and the smoothness of the subsequent economic recovery, the final cost to taxpayers was only about 2 percent of nominal GDP.

In the securities industry, meanwhile, scandals involving the corporate racketeers known as *sokaiya* led to revelations that brokerage firms have shifted profits between their own accounts and those of clients, and in the aftermath of Yamaichi's failure it came out that the regulatory authorities had tacitly approved the shifting of bad credits to overseas subsidiaries for window-dressing purposes. It is doubtful that Japanese securities companies have been performing their fiduciary duties adequately.

Measures to protect investors

A fund has now been established to protect investors in case securities companies fail. But foreign securities firms, skeptical of the quality of disclosure among their Japanese counterparts, are insisting on setting up a separate fund of their own. In the insurance industry, meanwhile, a system aimed at protecting policyholders has been instituted, but its design is inadequate, with no means of dealing with the shortfall of funds that would result from a chain reaction of insurance company bankruptcies.[7] In fact, when Nissan Mutual Life Insurance failed, policyholders ended up having to bear the burden of losses that could not be covered by the funds available in the existing protection fund. It is also unclear whether policyholders were fully protected in the merger between Toho Mutual Life Insurance and GE Capital. The new system of policyholder protection that will go into effect in 1999 (requiring ¥700 billion in funds) still leaves individuals subject to a burden that is excessive by comparison with the protection offered bank depositors and brokerage clients. In order to detonate the Big Bang successfully, a financial services law should be enacted to provide for a uniform set of rules for investors across all sectors of the financial services industry, but no progress is being made toward the creation of this essential legislation (Iwata 1998).

In order to prevent a deepening of the financial crisis and build a new financial system, banks' risk management must be reinforced, and the regulatory systems of the financial authorities must be improved. The first requirement is to re-establish the reliability of disclosed information. For this purpose, auditors and accountants who knowingly approve mistaken business accounting reports should be subject to legal penalties. When major accounting irregularities are discovered, they must be reported directly to the regulatory authorities. It would be helpful to establish auditing committees consisting mainly of outside auditors within banks.

In the area of banks' risk management, the inadequacy of internal systems—in particular the ongoing lack of sufficient firewalls between front-office and back-office operations and the underdeveloped state of the legal departments in the latter—are sapping Japanese banks' international competitiveness. The entry into the Japanese scene of foreign financial institutions will mean the remaking of financial markets along Anglo-Saxon market-economy lines, and it will also transform the traditional employment patterns at financial institutions. American manufacturers made a comeback by imitating the good practices of Japanese-style management and by emulating their Japanese rivals. Japanese financial institutions need to adopt a similar strategy of surviving by imitating the good practices of the Anglo-Saxon model and emulating their international counterparts. Finally, the system of financial regulation needs to be made to cover the full range of financial services—not just banking, but also such fields as insurance, securities, and consumer credit. For this purpose, we hope that a financial services law will be enacted promptly, and that, under this law, the Bank Supervision Department of the Bank of Japan and MOF's local finance bureaus will be integrated into a new financial supervisory organ.

Courtesy of Japan Institute of International Affairs.

Originally published in *Japan Review of International Affairs* 13, no. 1 (1999): 55–73.

Notes

1. This prediction was contained in a report submitted in March 1998 by the Financial Services Group (chaired by the author) in the Economic and Social Prospects Subcommittee of the government's Economic Council.

2. In a 1997 report on reform of the pension system, the Ministry of Health and Welfare offers five options. While privatization of the earnings-related benefit scheme would result in the problem of placing a double burden on the transitional generation, the ministry calculates that such a move would reduce benefit payments from the Employees' Pension System by about 40 percent and allow premium rates to be held to 20 percent.

3. In the United States, starting in the 1970s, the traditional banking business declined, but financial intermediation continued in other forms, coming to be conducted not through banks but through mutual funds and finance companies. This sort of non-bank intermediation of funds between households and business corporations is called "parallel banking." Mutual funds and pension funds are now functioning as forces holding up stock prices in the United States. In Japan's case, investors are confronted with the "open-end fund puzzle" where yields on mutual funds are lower even than interest on time deposits. In the United States, meanwhile, investors face a different closed-end fund puzzle; namely, that the market prices of mutual funds diverge widely from the value of their net assets. Meanwhile, the financial crisis that has spread from Asia to Russia and Latin America has highlighted the inadequacy of disclosure by hedge funds and risk management by banks. It appears likely that the causes of this sort of twenty-first-century-style financial crisis lie in the gap, both in industrial countries and in the developing world, between the progress of financial globalization and the lack of adequate risk-management systems.

4. In September 1998, a special purpose company was introduced for the securitization of real-estate collateral and bad loans. To date, however, there has only been one application, the reasons being that there are limits on borrowing and equity issues, that initial investment items cannot be replaced with different ones, and that the tax incentives are inadequate.

5. Krugman uses a set of calculations to show that the remaining value to bank stockholders will be reduced due to the dilution of value if public funds are injected (though deposit insurance will protect their customers in case of bank failure). Yet it is easy to show that the value to stockholders can increase if injections of public funds exceed ¥50 trillion. This is approximately double the ¥25 trillion planned injection of funds into healthy banks. Hisamatsu suggested to me that Krugman's "simple arithmetic" overlooked the scale of the public funds being injected (see Hisamatsu 1998).

6. In May 1998, Columbia University associate professor Charles W. Calmoris presented a proposal for the government to purchase either low-coupon subordinated debt or low-dividend preferred shares, with the principal to be returned after a certain period (such as five years) through the issuance of common shares. The injection of public funds that was implemented in November used a scheme resembling this proposal.

7. In a report issued in October 1996 by the Financial Working Group of the Action Program Committee of the Economic Council (consisting of Ikeo Kazuhito, Yanagishima Yukichi, and the author), it was argued that a time delay should be allowed before banks could directly undertake insurance operations because the system of protection for insurance policyholders was inadequate. This report served as the fuse for the announcement of the Big Bang program in the autumn of 1996.

References

Hisamatsu Yoshiaki. 1998. "Komento" [Comment]. *Memorandamu*. October 19.

Iwata Kazumasa and Fukao Mitsuhiro. 1998. *Zaisei tōyūshi no keizai bunseki* [Economic Analysis of the Fiscal Investment and Loan Program]. Vol. 15 of *Shirīzu gendai keizai kenkyu* [Modern Economics Research Series]. Tokyo: Nihon Keizai Shimbun Shuppansha.

———. 1998. "Furyō ginkō wa tsubushinasai: Kin'yū sābisuhō naki kin'yū kantoku taisei de iinoka" [Close Bad Banks: Is a Financial Regulatory System without a Financial Services Law Good Enough?]. *Ronsō Tōyō Keizai*, no.15 (September): 58-65.

Kajiyama Seiroku. 1997. "Waga Nihon keizai no saisei no shinario" [Scenario for a Japanese Revival]. *Shūkan Bunshun*, December 4.

———. 1998. "Nihon kōkokuron" (An Alternative Agenda from a Senior Liberal Democrat). *Bungei Shunjū* 76, no. 6 (June): 94–102. [Editor's note: An abridged English version of this article appeared in the *Japan Echo* 25 (5), October 1998, pp. 16–22.]

Keynes, John Maynard. 1926. "The End of Laissez-Faire." Reprinted in *Essays in Persuasion*, vol. 9 of *The Collected Writings of John Maynard Keynes*, edited by the Royal Economic Society. Cambridge: Cambridge University Press, 1971–89.

Krugman, Paul. 1998. "Japan's Bank Bailout: Some Simple Arithmetic." Massachusetts Institute of Technology (MIT), October 17. Accessed January 5, 1999. http://web.mit.edu/krugman/www/bailout.html.

III-(2.2) Financial Regulation in the Wake of the Banking Crisis

Yanagisawa Hakuo

Japan Echo, 1999

The session of the National Diet that started at the end of July last year focused largely on the critical situation in Japan's financial sector. After months of intense debate between the ruling Liberal Democratic Party and the opposition, two new laws were enacted in October concerning my field of responsibility as chairman of the Financial Reconstruction Commission: the Financial Reconstruction Law and the Financial Strengthening Law.*

The two new laws, which our commission is now implementing, have tremendous power. In my view, they have set up a virtually impeccable system. If anything, they are so nearly perfect as to give rise to the concern that the public will come to rely excessively on the government to back up the financial sector. The safety net that has been put in place is so attractive that people may decide that they would like it to be kept in place indefinitely.

The Financial Reconstruction Law provides for the rescue of failed banks. If it were just a matter of protecting depositors, the Deposit Insurance Law would be enough. Under this law, deposits are insured up to a maximum of ¥10 million in principle, but this maximum has been temporarily waived. In other words, bank deposits are currently guaranteed in full.

During the Diet deliberations on the financial crisis, however, it was argued that just protecting depositors is not enough. As the failure of Hokkaido Takushoku Bank demonstrated, when a bank goes under, the businesses that have relied on it for loans also suffer, and may even be driven to bankruptcy themselves. The legislators thus decided that steps should be taken to protect borrowers as well as depositors.

Let us look at it from the corporate borrower's point of view. The company has gone to considerable effort to explain its business to the bank, and as a result it has been able to borrow funds and keep its business running. But then suddenly the bank vanishes. What is the company to do? "Borrow from another bank," one might say. That, however, is no easy matter. In practice, relationships like those between borrowers and lenders take considerable time to build. This is especially true of the relationship between a company and its main bank. The people at the main bank learn everything about the company. They may even know more about it than its own chief executive. Because the relationship is so intimate, if the main bank vanishes, the blow to the corporate borrower is serious indeed. It cannot just go out and casually find a replacement.

This was the line of thought that caused the legislators to decide that sound borrowers, as well as depositors, should be protected against bank failures. And this led to enactment of the Financial Reconstruction Law in its present form. I might add that this law has the effect of protecting the bank's full range of creditors, not just those whose claims on it are in the form of ordinary deposits. The only parties to suffer are the shareholders. (It is only reasonable that they should lose, of course, inasmuch as the bank whose shares they own has failed.) All other concerned parties are virtually unaffected. The

* The full names of the two new laws are the Law Concerning Emergency Measures for the Reconstruction of the Functions of the Financial System and the Financial Function Early Strengthening Law.—Ed.

operations of the failed bank may be taken over by another institution in one of a variety of ways, such as in the form of a subsidiary or through absorption into the other institution's operations, but in any case, the takeover includes the full set of existing obligations and relationships.

We have applied this law to the Long-Term Credit Bank of Japan and the Nippon Credit Bank; we also applied it recently to Kokumin Bank, a smaller regional institution.

Beefing Up Banks' Capital

The same Diet session last year also enacted the Financial Strengthening Law, the object of which is to supply increased capital for financial institutions so as to raise the level of confidence in the Japanese financial sector—even though it means using public funds for the purpose.

When an institution's assets deteriorate—for example, when loans that it has made become uncollectible—the only buffer against the resulting losses is its equity capital. How much capital should a bank have to cover against such losses? Toward the end of the 1980s a consensus emerged within the United States that a bank should have capital equal to around 8 percent of its total assets. This 8 percent capital adequacy requirement was adopted by the Bank for International Settlements as the standard for banks operating internationally.

Major banks in Europe and North America generally have capital ratios of about 10 percent, and some have figures as high as 12 percent. This inspires a high level of confidence in them, and it enables them to win high credit ratings—an important factor in minimizing the interest rates they have to pay on borrowed funds.

It was against this backdrop that we decided we should aim to raise the capital adequacy ratio of Japan's internationally active banks to at least 10 percent. We used this as the basis for calculating the amount of additional capital required. (In the end, ¥7.5 trillion in public funds was provided for fifteen banks, one of which was a regional institution.)

The first aim of providing injections of public funds to beef up banks' capital was to allow them to complete the process of writing off their nonperforming assets, including hidden losses in their securities portfolios. Second, we wanted to stop the credit crunch that resulted from banks' reluctance to lend. Banks that are short of capital cannot afford to take on credit risks, and so they inevitably tighten their lending policy. Another concern was of course the prospect of recovering the public funds later. These three points formed the basis of our decisions earlier this year on the injection of public funds into the banking sector.

I have consciously refrained from declaring publicly that the problem of banks' bad debts and other nonperforming assets has ended. But what I have said at press conferences and elsewhere is that "the long-delayed process of making provisions for nonperforming assets has been completed."

One basis for this statement is the assessment that we have conducted of banks' assets. Assessing the soundness of loans and other assets properly is a fundamental requirement, but Japanese banks have tended to be lax in this area. As recent newspaper reports suggest, Kokumin Bank offers one example. There and elsewhere, credits that were in fact irrecoverable were listed on balance sheets as assets. This has done serious damage to confidence in banks. So we have taken a very strict approach to assessment. I will not go into the details here, but we have used a variety of techniques to classify assets by their degree of soundness.

The second basis for my statement is the size of the reserves that have been set aside to cover losses. If a bank has a loan to a particular client listed as part of its assets, but business conditions suggest that it will not be possible to recover the full amount—if it is judged, for example, that a loss of 15 percent should be anticipated on this loan—then an amount equal to that expected loss should be set aside as a reserve. Provisions of this sort are required to cover prospective losses on assets that have gone partially bad; they need to match the level of deterioration in the quality of such assets. The process of setting aside these necessary reserves has been completely finished.

Self-Reliance First

Many observers have suggested that we have

not been strict enough in demanding that banks restructure their operations in return for the infusions of public funds. The Financial Strengthening Law is actually quite well crafted in this respect. Under it, I have directed banks to address the issue of restructuring, along with the issue of executive responsibility for losses that have been incurred, as part of the plans for restoring sound management that they are required to submit when receiving the capital infusions. We had to be very careful in our handling of this aspect, because if we made the initial requirements too stringent, even banks that needed and were eligible for more capital would have refrained from applying for it.

It is up to each bank to design and implement its own restructuring program. We have not set any sort of uniform targets. What we have required is that the banks provide plans showing how they will come up with the increased profits necessary to buy back the investment certificates the government has acquired. Overall, the plans call for about 30 percent of the additional profits to come from cost cutting and for the remaining 70 percent to come from the restructuring of operations, including selective pruning and concentration on more profitable areas.

Our final objective in beefing up Japan's financial sector is to enable Japanese institutions to compete successfully in international markets. This is an issue that goes beyond the immediate scope of the rehabilitation plans that the banks have been required to submit.

As is widely known, Japan's pool of savings is immense, and domestic and foreign financial institutions are now engaged in fierce competition with each other for these funds. What we do not want to see is the "Wimbledonization" of this market; that is, a situation where all of the competitors are foreign. And in order to prevent this from happening, I believe that a regrouping within the financial sector will be necessary, involving mergers and alliances among existing institutions.

Another concern I have relates to smaller regional institutions like the recently failed Kokumin Bank. Though it is not a problem at larger institutions, I am afraid that just possibly the management of some of these smaller banks may decide that, because the government has set up a strong safety net, they will take advantage of it to give up on their own banking operations, having found them unprofitable. In other words, now that this sturdy safety net is in place, eliminating fears of the consequences of a fall, how do we stop people from taking a plunge deliberately? I am not saying that this is what happened in the case of Kokumin Bank, but I do think it is a possibility that we need to recognize.

If a bank is short of capital, it is only natural to expect its executives to turn everywhere possible for additional equity investments. And if it is having cash-flow difficulties, its executives should naturally do their utmost to drum up additional deposits. They should not rely on the safety net until they have done everything in their own power to save their own institutions. In other words, banks must rely first on themselves, striving to find the necessary funds as if their own lives were at stake.

English version originally published in *Japan Echo* 26, no. 4 (Aug. 1999): 35–37.

Translated from "Kōteki shikin chūnyūgo no kin'yū gyōsei" [Financial Administration after the Injection of Public Funds], in *Ajia Jihō* (May 1999): 4–22; shortened to about one fourth. This article is based on a lecture delivered on April 13, 1999. (Courtesy of Asian Affairs Research Council)

III-(2.3) The Financial Crisis and the Lost Decade

Fukao Mitsuhiro[1]

Asian Economic Policy Review, 2007

Japanese banks incurred heavy losses in the early 1990s due to the bursting of the bubble economy of the 1980s. Japanese regulators allowed undercapitalized banks to operate under a very lenient application of capital requirement rules. At first, the regulators did not have strong institutional mechanisms and budgetary funds to take care of weakened banks. Even after obtaining strong power and money in 1988 to tackle the banking problem, the regulators would not nationalize a large number of banks because they could not manage nationalized banks themselves. The recent recovery of the Japanese economy gives the Financial Services Agency a chance to make up for the lost decade of regulatory discipline.

1. Introduction

Japanese banks incurred heavy losses in the early 1990s due to the bursting of the bubble economy of the 1980s. By 1997, even some large banks started to run out of capital base due to the rapidly accumulating loan losses with a very low nominal economic growth rate. Banks could not obtain sufficient profit margins on their commercial lending activities because borrowers faced fairly high real borrowing costs due to deflation. As a result, the capital injections into banks by the government in 1998 and 1999 could not revitalize the banking sector.

In the second half of the 1990s, the primary supervisor of banks was reorganized twice; its aegis also changed from the Ministry of Finance to the Financial Supervisory Agency, and then the Financial Services Agency (FSA). Generally speaking, these supervisors have allowed banks to understate the amount of their bad loans. They also allowed undercapitalized banks to operate under a regime with a very lenient application of capital requirement rules. The only exception was the period between 1998 and 1999 when the Financial Reconstruction Commission supervised the regulators. In my opinion, this forbearance policy was induced by the following factors. First, the regulator did not have sufficiently strong institutional mechanisms and budgetary funds to take care of weakened financial institutions until 1998. Second, a strict application of the standard would have meant an effective nationalization of a large part of the banking sector, given that many large banks were undercapitalized. Since it was almost impossible for the regulator to manage a number of banks directly, they allowed weak banks to operate until the economy recovered. Third, the regulator did not want to sentence to death the weak banks that had followed all the instructions from the regulator himself, including requests to save even weaker banks than themselves.

As the Japanese financial system gradually deteriorated in the late 1990s, the government expanded the financial safety net to avoid systemic crisis and to protect various types of creditors. As the government expanded the safety net to protect virtually all the stakeholders of banks, the financial market gradually lost its disciplining forces on individual banks. Certainly, the safety net always generates some form of moral hazard among the creditors of banks. Especially when there is an element of systemic risk in the banking sector, it would be necessary to use very strong medicine, even though it has severe side effects. According to many observers of the Tokyo Stock Exchange, the recovery of stock prices since May 2003 is due to the increasing confidence in the eventual bailout of bank shareholders by the

Japanese government. Many analysts call this recovery a "moral-hazard rally." The protection of equity holders spread to industrial companies and to life-insurance companies. Banks sometimes wrote off a part of the debt of insolvent borrowers without wiping out shareholders' equity.

As recently as March 2003, the Nikkei 225 index was below the 8,000 mark, and many large Japanese banks and insurance companies were not sure whether they could survive through the end of the financial year. However, thanks to the very low exchange rate and strong expansion of Japan's exports, the Japanese manufacturing sector recovered very strongly after 2003. As the Japanese economy recovered from the long, deep stagnation after the bursting of the asset-price bubble, Japanese financial institutions could also restore their profitability. Three factors contributed to this rapid recovery of Japan's financial institutions. First, a strong recovery of the economy reduced the number of newly defaulting companies. Second, a significant reduction of excessive debt in the corporate sector was achieved by the massive write-off of bad loans by banks and the repayment of loans by borrowing firms. Third, Japan's banks and insurance companies could enjoy the strong recovery of stock prices from the spring of 2003 to early 2006.

In the face of the recovery of the health of Japan's financial institutions, the FSA is trying to tighten its regulatory standards on banks and insurance companies. The FSA has announced a reduction in the allowable amount of deferred tax assets for the calculation of a bank's regulatory capital. It is also trying to tighten the definition of solvency margin requirements on insurance companies by modifying the risk parameters. If Japan can continue this recovery for a few more years, Japan's financial institutions will be able to achieve a reasonable level of soundness relative to those in other major countries.

2. The Bubble and Japan's Financial System

2.1 The origin of the bubble economy in the 1980s

In order to examine the origin of Japan's financial problems, we briefly review the magnitude of the Japanese asset-price bubble in the 1980s. The asset-price bubble was created by the following three factors: loose monetary policy, tax distortions, and financial deregulation.[2] In the following, we only discuss the third factor.

The financial system in Japan was liberalized very gradually. The driving forces behind this liberalization process were the massive issuance of government bonds in the late 1970s and the increasing internationalization of financial markets. Ceilings on bank-deposit interest rates were liberalized gradually from large-denomination to smaller denomination deposits from 1985 to 1994. Restrictions on the issuance of corporate bonds were gradually liberalized during the 1980s. As a result, large listed companies, which are the traditional customers of Japanese banks, gradually shifted their funding from banks to the capital market. Banks faced the prospect of a profit squeeze due to rising funding costs and a declining customer base.

In view of the declining rents from the traditional business of retail deposit-taking and commercial lending to large firms, banks tried to increase their middle-market business. Most banks started to increase real-estate lending. In expanding such lending, banks exclusively relied on collateral and paid little attention to the cash flow of the underlying business. This was because nominal land prices in Japan had been on a rising trend since the end of World War II, and the pace of land-price inflation was higher than the government bond interest rate on average. This land-price performance created a general perception among bankers that they could always avoid loan losses so long as loans were secured by real estate. This was certainly true until the collapse of the bubble in the 1990s. Many banks solicited loans to customers by providing information on real-estate investment opportunities. During the bubble period, even an ordinary salaried worker living in Tokyo could easily borrow up to 100 million yen for any purpose at the long-term prime rate if his or her house was used as collateral. Thus, financial liberalization created a perfect environment for an asset-price bubble where firms and households could easily acquire real estate with borrowed money in the 1980s.

The financial intermediation by banks

expanded significantly in the 1980s. The bank lending–gross domestic product (GDP) ratio rose from 70 percent of GDP in the late 1970s to 108 percent by 1990. The composition of the loan portfolio of Japanese banks also changed dramatically. The share of the manufacturing sector in the loan portfolio declined from 25 percent in 1977 to less than 15 percent by the end of the 1980s. On the other hand, the share of loans to real-estate and financing companies rose sharply in the same period. Since lending to financing companies such as *jūsen* (housing loan companies) is often on-lent for real-estate investments, the involvement of banks in real-estate-related lending was very large in the 1980s.

2.2 A slow-moving financial crisis: 1991–1996[3]

Reflecting a successive tightening of monetary policy from May 1989 to February 1991, stocks and real-estate prices started to decline rapidly. The ratio of the land-price index to the nominal GDP index has declined twice in the past thirty years. In the early 1970s when the ratio declined, the nominal land price did not decline much; that fall was induced by a sharp inflation of prices for goods and services. However, in the 1990s, the fall in this ratio was induced by a fall in nominal land prices. These differences are important in evaluating the fallout from the collapse of the bubble. In the first episode, investors who bought land with borrowed money could repay their debt. On the other hand, in the second episode, real-estate investors could not honor their debt obligations.

At first, bankers and bank supervisors thought that the fall in land prices would be temporary. They expected that by waiting for an economic recovery, banks could eventually recover most of their bad loans. However, the wait-and-see strategy did not work this time, and real-estate prices continued to fall. The understatement of bad-loan problems by some banks rapidly became a falsification of financial statements. Since a falsification of the financial statements of listed companies carries a stiff criminal penalty, the management of banks with large bad loans faced a difficult choice: covering up the extent of their problem to keep their bank open, or facing the bank run that would follow the disclosure of the real situation. Bank management chose the first option. Apparently, bank supervisors actively supported this choice by the banks until early 1997.

Table 1 shows the historical data of the problem loans of Japanese banks. Since the disclosure of the bad-loan situation improved gradually, the data are not consistent over the years (row B). For example, the definition of bad loans outstanding has been broadened twice; as a result, the disclosed figures jumped up due to these discontinuities. Until FY 1995, only major banks disclosed loan-loss figures. Japanese banks lost ¥96.8 trillion due to bad loans from March 1992 to March 2006 (cumulative amount of row A) amounting to 19 percent of GDP in 2006.

Despite the massive write-offs and reserving, the disclosed bad loans increased until March 2002. In my opinion, the disclosed bad-loan figures understated the real situation during the late 1990s and early 2000s. Banks tried to show a higher capital ratio than the true picture by understating the loan losses incurred.

Reflecting the increasing loan losses and declining stock prices, the credit ratings of Japanese banks declined rapidly. Financial deregulation and asset-price deflation completely changed the relative creditworthiness position of Japanese banks.

Against this dire picture, both the Ministry of Finance and the Bank of Japan denied the severity of the bad-loan problem and collaborated to postpone the costly resolution of insolvent financial institutions. There are several reasons for the slow response by policymakers. First, a number of large financial institutions were either insolvent or severely undercapitalized. Second, in order to resolve the crisis, the use of public money was necessary. However, using taxpayers' money was not popular. Third, top officials in the Banking Bureau of the Ministry of Finance rotate every few years. As a result, there is a strong incentive for them to postpone the resolution of politically difficult problems.

One important factor in this context was the mismanagement of the *jūsen* crisis. *Jūsen* companies are nonbank financial institutions created as subsidiaries of banking groups. *Jūsen* started

Table 1. Disclosed loan losses of Japanese banks (all commercial banks) (trillion yen)

Financial year (March)	1993	1994	1995	1996	1997	1998	1999	2000	2001	2002	2003	2004	2005	2006
Loss from bad loans (A)	1.6	3.9	5.2	13.4	7.8	13.3	13.6	6.9	6.1	9.7	6.7	5.4	2.8	0.4
Specific reserves	0.9	1.1	1.4	7.1	3.4	8.4	8.1	2.5	2.7	5.2	3.1	1.6	0.1	-0.4
Write-off and loan sales losses	0.4	2.1	2.8	6.0	4.3	4.0	4.7	3.9	3.1	4.0	3.5	3.7	2.8	0.7
Cumulative amount of (A)	1.6	5.5	10.7	24.1	31.9	45.1	58.8	65.7	71.8	81.5	88.2	93.6	96.4	96.8
Bad loans outstanding (B)	12.8	13.6	12.5	28.5	21.8	29.8	29.6	30.4	32.5	42.0	34.8	26.2	17.5	13.1
	←→ Only for major banks			←→		←→								
Definition of B	Defaulted loans and loans in arrears for more than six months			Defaulted loans, loans in arrears for more than six months and loans with concessional interest rates below the official discount rate		Defaulted loans, loans in arrears for more than ninety days and loans with concessionary terms (similar to the US Securities and Exchange Commission rule)								

Source: Financial Services Agency and the Bank of Japan.

their business as housing-loan companies, but their business was limited by two factors. The Japan Housing Loan Corporation, a government loan company, provided subsidized loans with prime collateral. Parent banks also started to provide housing loans in the late 1970s. As a result, the *jūsen* companies were gradually marginalized in the housing-loan market. In the 1980s, *jūsen* companies started to shift their business to more risky real-estate loans. *Jūsen* companies often took second-rate collateral to make high-risk loans.

After the collapse of the bubble, *jūsen* companies quickly became insolvent. This became obvious for related parties by 1992–1993 period, but the parent banks and Ministry of Finance officials decided to wait for a recovery of real-estate prices. By 1995, it became a serious political problem. Since *jūsen* companies financed their real-estate loans with money borrowed from small agricultural credit unions, the failure of *jūsen* companies would induce the failure of a number of such unions. Since agricultural credit unions had a strong lobby in the Diet, Japan's national parliament, politicians put strong pressure on the Ministry of Finance to resolve the *jūsen* crisis without inducing the failure of agricultural credit unions. As a result, ¥680 billion of public money was used to cover part of the losses of the credit unions without bankruptcy procedures and without asking the managers to take responsibility. Seven of the eight *jūsen* companies were liquidated, and most of the losses were borne by their parent banks. Public opinion was extremely critical of this rather skewed loss-sharing scheme of *jūsen* resolution devised by the Ministry of Finance and politicians, making it politically impossible to discuss the further use of public money to resolve the financial crisis. As a result, any resolution was postponed further.

Market participants were well aware of Japan's problem. As the asset-price deflation continued, the funding costs of Japanese banks started to increase relative to European and American banks due to the rising credit risk of Japanese banks. Even the soundest Japanese banks had to pay a risk premium (the so-called Japan premium) for their interbank dollar borrowings. However, a risk premium did not surface in the Japanese interbank market, because the Bank of Japan provided funds to borrowing banks directly without charging a risk premium.[4]

2.3 Causes of the deteriorating capital of Japanese banks

The fundamental cause of the deterioration of bank capital was the high rate of loan losses. Table 2 shows the profit-loss accounts of all commercial banks. During the stagnant decade from 1993 to 2002, banks made around ¥9 to 10 trillion each year as a lending margin (row A, defined as interest and dividends earned minus interest paid). Revenue from such sources as bond and currency dealings and service charges were about ¥3 trillion in that decade (row B). This includes all other revenue except capital gains realized on stocks and real estate. Revenues from the banks' principal operations therefore amounted to

Table 2. Profitability of the Japanese banking sector (trillion yen)

Financial Year	1990	1991	1992	1993	1994	1995	1996	1997	1998	1999	2000	2001	2002	2003	2004	2005
Lending margin (A)	7.1	8.9	9.8	9.2	9.7	10.8	10.7	10.0	9.6	9.7	9.4	9.8	9.4	9.0	8.7	8.7
Other revenue (B)	2.6	2.2	2.5	2.8	2.1	3.3	3.7	3.6	3.1	2.5	3.0	3.1	3.6	4.3	4.6	5.2
Operating costs (C)	7.1	7.5	7.7	7.7	7.8	7.8	8.0	8.0	7.5	7.3	7.1	7.0	7.0	6.7	6.4	6.5
Salaries and wages	3.7	3.9	4.0	4.0	4.0	4.0	4.0	4.0	3.6	3.5	3.4	3.2	2.8	3.1	2.8	2.8
Gross profit (D) = (A) + (B) – (C)	2.6	3.5	4.5	4.3	4.0	6.3	6.4	5.6	5.2	4.9	5.3	5.9	6.0	6.6	6.9	7.4
Loan losses (E)	0.8	1.0	2.0	4.6	6.2	13.3	7.3	13.5	13.5	6.3	6.6	9.4	7.0	6.1	4.2	2.0
Net operating profit (F) = (D) – (E)	1.8	2.5	2.5	-0.4	-2.2	-7.0	-1.0	-7.9	-8.3	-1.4	-1.3	-3.5	-1.0	0.5	2.7	5.4
Realized capital gains (G)	2.0	0.7	0.0	2.0	3.2	4.4	1.2	3.6	1.4	3.8	1.4	-2.4	-4.1	0.6	-0.1	0.5
Net profit (F) + (G)	3.8	3.3	2.5	1.7	1.0	-2.6	0.2	-4.2	-6.9	2.3	0.1	-5.9	-5.1	1.1	2.6	5.9
Asset	927.6	914.4	859.5	849.8	845.0	848.2	856.0	848.0	759.7	737.2	804.3	772.0	739.0	750.0	748.0	757.0
Outstanding loans	522.0	537.0	542.0	539.0	539.0	554.0	563.0	536.0	492.0	476.0	474.0	465.0	435.0	423.0	414.0	428.0

Source: Japan Center for Economic Research (2006).
Note: Financial statements of all commercial banks. Other revenue (B) includes all other profits, such as dealing profits and fees, but excludes realized capital gains on stocks and real estates. Realized capital gains (G) includes gains on stocks and real estates.

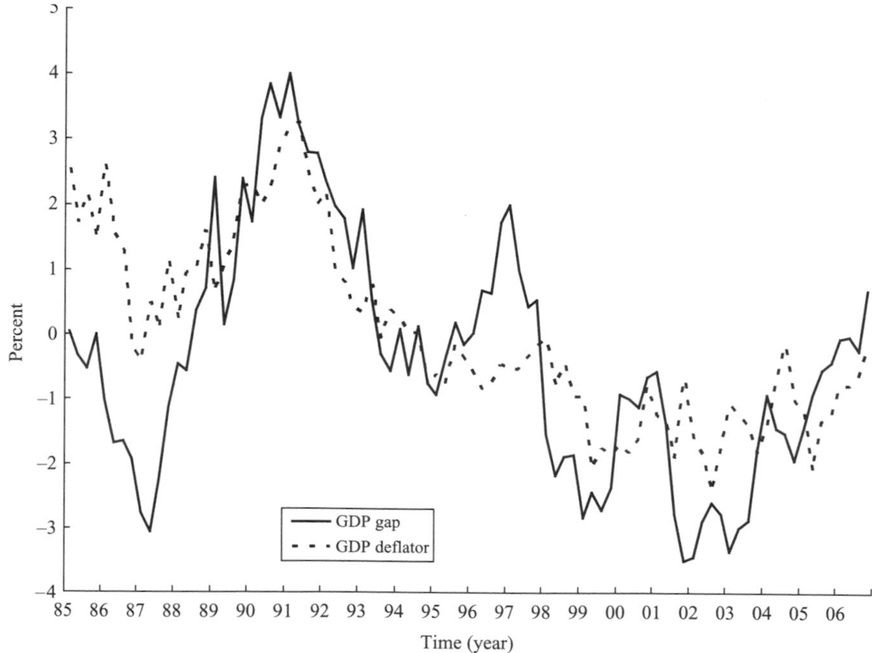

Figure 1. Gross domestic product (GDP) gap and GDP deflator inflation rate

Source: Estimated by the Japan Center for Economic Research in 2007.
Note: The GDP deflator inflation rate is the annualized rate of the quarterly inflation rate after a three-quarter moving average. The effects of changes in the consumption tax are removed from the inflation rate.

roughly ¥12 to 13 trillion a year (row A + row B). On the other hand, total costs—including personnel and other operating expenses—were over ¥7 trillion (row C).

Banks have suffered over ¥6 trillion in loan losses each year since FY 1994, and more than ¥13 trillion yen in FY 1995, 1997, and 1998 (row E). As a result, banks have not reported a positive net operating profit in the decade from 1993 to 2002 (row F). However, because of the occasional realization of capital gains on stocks and real estate (row G), banks could show a positive bottom line in some of these years (row F + row G).

Clearly, the profit margins of Japanese banks were too small to cover the increased default risk after the bursting of the bubble. Banks have not succeeded in increasing their lending margins under the strong competitive pressure from government-backed financial institutions and the weakened position of borrowers in the deflationary economy. Moreover, under the terms and conditions of the government capital injection in March 1999, banks are legally required to maintain and increase loans to small- and medium-sized firms. Shinsei Bank, which reduced its loans to small- and medium-sized firms, was ordered by the FSA to increase these loans. Because of this situation, banks often disregarded the internal-model-based required lending margin when making new loans to small companies.

3. The Role of Financial Supervision in the Crisis

3.1 Financial crises in 1997 and 1998

In November 1997, the failure of Sanyo Securities, Hokkaido Takushoku Bank, and Yamaichi Securities sharply increased financial instability. These events generated a severe credit crunch in the Japanese financial market, inducing an extremely serious recession. Figure 1 shows the GDP gap estimated by the Japan Center for Economic Research and the annualized inflation rate computed using the GDP deflator. The GPD deflator started to fall in the 1994–1995 period when the yen exchange rate rose to an extremely high level of more than ¥80 per US dollar. This deflation was aggravated sharply by the sharp recession induced by the financial crisis of 1997–1998.

Then what caused this enormous problem for Japan? In my opinion, there were two factors behind this financial crisis.[5] One was the crash of the stock and real-estate market bubble in the 1990s. The second was the loss of confidence in the accounting and auditing system in Japan. We note that the actual amount of bad loans discovered at failed financial institutions has been far larger than the amount published prior to their failure. The Hokkaido Takushoku Bank was forced into failure even though it posted profits and paid dividends for the year to March 1997. Financial statements for that year reported ¥0.3 trillion in capital; inspections after the failure found a negative equity of ¥1.2 trillion as of March 31, 1998. This indicates window-dressing of almost ¥1.5 trillion.

Likewise, Yamaichi Securities was hiding ¥260 billion of losses on securities investments—worth more than one-half of its equity capital—which neither Ministry of Finance inspections nor Bank of Japan examinations were reportedly able to uncover.

Depositors and investors who held bank debentures issued by the long-term credit banks imposed some market discipline. Deposits flew out of banks with low credit ratings because depositors feared that they would not be able to withdraw their deposits quickly if these banks were closed. The Long-Term Credit Bank of Japan (LTCB) and Nippon Credit Bank faced a rapid early redemption of their debentures in 1997 because their debentures were not explicitly covered by the deposit insurance system. The stock prices of weaker banks fell sharply and triggered mild bank runs.

These financial-institution failures exacerbated suspicions both at home and abroad regarding the financial statements and supervision of Japanese financial institutions. It was this mistrust of financial statements that widened the "Japan premium" charged in overseas markets, clogged the domestic call market (which is used for short-term interbank loans), and multiplied the number of cash-pressed financial institutions turning to the Bank of Japan for loans. Japanese financial markets clearly experienced a kind of credit crunch because of a rash of failures, declining asset prices, and growing mistrust of financial statements and regulators.

Figure 2 shows the Bank of Japan survey of industrial companies on the lending attitudes of their banks. The shaded portions show the periods when the Bank of Japan raised short-term interest rates to impose tighter monetary policy. From the end of 1997 until early 1999, the lending attitudes of banks were very tight despite the fact that the Bank of Japan was trying to ease monetary policy.

This credit crunch in turn cut into corporate investment and hiring, increased bankruptcy rates, and reduced consumption and housing investments because workers feared losing their jobs. That resulted in a further contraction of credit in what became a vicious cycle. In other words, unreliable financial statements proved to be a serious impediment to the functioning of a market economy.

The contraction was somewhat abated by the emergency economic package announced by the Liberal Democratic Party and the Ministry of Finance at the end of 1997. The government prepared ¥13 trillion for the capital injection to solvent banks, and ¥17 trillion for the protection of the depositors of failed banks. The Ministry of Finance should have used the fund effectively: by forcing banks to write off all the bad loans, the financial institutions and the financial oversight by the government could have regained the public confidence. However, most of the money was left unused. Only ¥1.8 trillion of the ¥13 trillion was thinly injected into twenty-one large banks at the end of March 1998 without any complete examination or comprehensive cleanup of the bank balance sheets.

The failure of the capital injection became

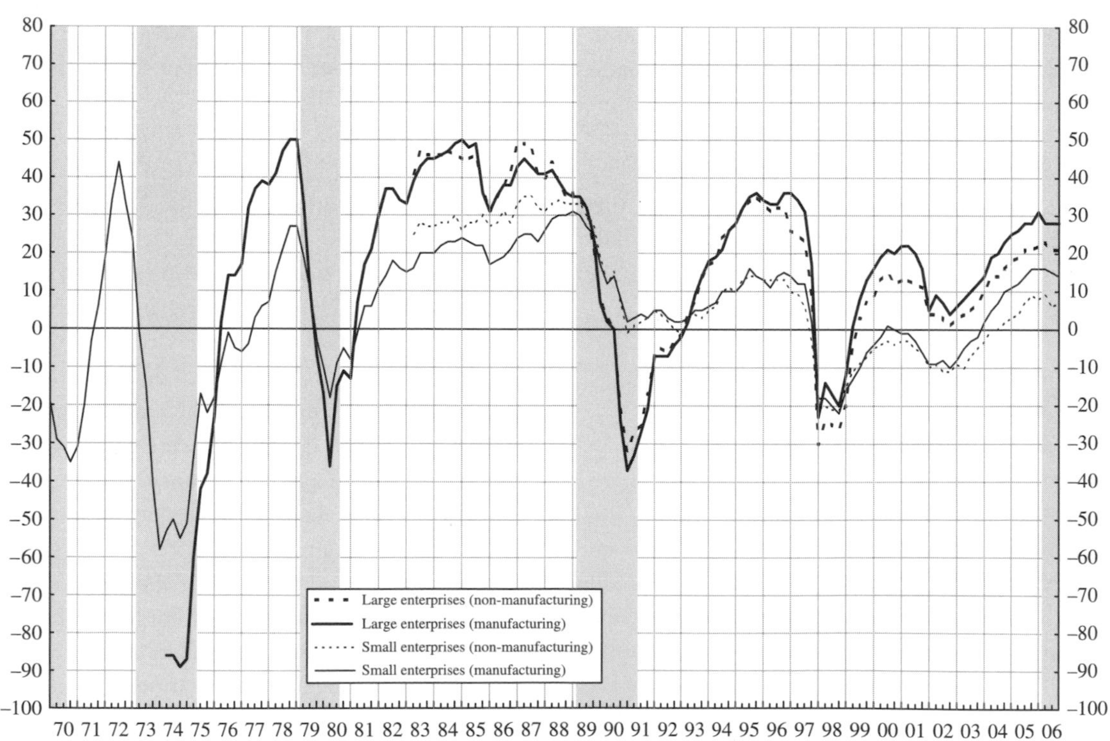

Figure 2. Diffusion index of lending attitude of financial institutions, based on the short-term economic survey of all enterprises in Japan ("Accommodative" – "Severe"; percentage points)

Source: Bank of Japan CD-ROM, updated by the author.
Note: There is a major break in the data series in the fourth quarter of 2003. Shaded areas indicate the periods when the Bank of Japan raised its policy rate.

apparent only a few months later. In the summer of 1998, the stock price of the LTCB fell sharply when Sumitomo Trust and Banking effectively refused a merger with the LTCB. The LTCB was a big bank with ¥26.2 trillion of assets at the end of March 1998. In October 1998, just before the LTCB went bankrupt, the Financial Revitalization Act and the Bank Recapitalization Act were enacted in a disorderly atmosphere. This time, the government prepared ¥60 trillion, about 12 percent of GDP. This ¥60 trillion was made up of ¥25 trillion for capital injections into solvent banks under the Bank Recapitalization Act; ¥18 trillion for the resolution of failing banks under the Financial Revitalization Act by capital injections into banks rescuing other banks, bridge banks, and the disposition of bad loans; and ¥17 trillion for the protection of depositors by the Deposit Insurance Corporation (DIC).

Under the Financial Revitalization Act, the LTCB and Nippon Credit Bank were nationalized in October and December 1998. Under the Bank Recapitalization Act, ¥7.5 trillion of capital was injected into fifteen major banks at the end of March 1999. Unlike the previous attempt, this program was much better designed, and succeeded in eliminating the persistent Japan premium that started in late 1997. The gradual recovery of the Japanese economy and the announcements of big mergers among major banks also contributed to calming the public concern over the financial system until 2002.

3.2 The evolving Japanese depositor protection system

In this section, we review the evolution of the Japanese deposit-insurance system and other schemes to protect the creditors of banks.[6]

The Deposit Insurance Law established the DIC in 1971. The initial role of the DIC was to protect depositors of failed financial institutions up to ¥1 million per person by the direct payout of insured deposits. The limit of coverage was increased twice to ¥10 million by 1986, and the DIC obtained a new power to assist in the mergers of failed institutions and sound institutions to protect depositors.

The DIC fund had never been used until 1992, when the DIC assisted the Iyo Bank in rescuing Toho-Sogo Bank. It was relatively easy to find a willing buyer when bank branches carried a regulatory rent. Until the early 1990s, deposit interest rates were controlled below market rates. Moreover, the establishment of new branches was also controlled by the Ministry of Finance. As a result, when there was a weak bank, it was relatively easy to find a rescuer who wanted to obtain a new subsidiary or new branches with negative equity. This allowed the Ministry of Finance to continue the so-called convoy system without using any public money. However, in the early 1990s, the ceiling on deposit interest rates was phased out, and regulations on branching was considerably loosened. This change made the job of bank regulators much more difficult, but their mindset did not change until 1998.

After a few failures of small financial institutions in 1994 and 1995, the Deposit Insurance Law was amended in 1996 to allow the DIC to fully protect depositors beyond the normal ¥10 million as a temporary emergency measure until March 2001 (table 3). At the same time, the "general" deposit insurance premium was raised from 1.2 to 4.8 basis points (1 basis point = 0.01 percent) to cover the cost of protection up to ¥10 million. In addition, a special deposit-insurance premium of 3.6 basis points was introduced to cover the cost of deposit protection beyond the ¥10 million limit (table 4). At the end of 1997, the DIC obtained the power to purchase bad loans from failing financial institutions when they collectively created a new bank.[7] The borrowing limit of the DIC from the Bank of Japan and private financial institutions was also raised from ¥1 trillion to ¥10 trillion.

Despite the full protection of all the deposits beyond the limit of normal coverage, public concern over the soundness of the financial system became extremely intense after the successive failures of Sanyo Securities, Hokkaido Takushoku Bank, and Yamaichi Securities in late 1997. Depositors were not sure that the DIC had enough money to honor the commitment of the government to protect all deposits.

In October 1998, just before the LTCB went bankrupt, the Financial Revitalization Act and

Table 3. Development of deposit insurance coverage

Type of Deposit	All domestic yen deposits
1971/4	Up to ¥1 million of principal amount per person is protected. Interest is not protected.
1974/6	Up to ¥3 million of principal amount per person is protected. Interest is not protected.
1986/7	Up to ¥10 million of principal amount per person is protected. Interest is not protected.
1995/7/3	**Ministry of Finance announces that DIC will protect all deposits for five years.**
1996/6	**Deposit Insurance Law is amended to allow DIC to protect all deposits and other liabilities of banks until March 2001.**

Type of Deposit	Domestic yen Current deposits	Domestic yen Ordinary Deposits & Specified Deposits	Domestic yen Time Deposits	Payment accounts under Processing
1996–2002/3/31	**Fully protected**	**Fully protected**	**Fully protected**	Effectively fully protected
2002/4/1–2003/3/31	**Fully protected**	**Fully protected**	¥10 million	Effectively fully protected
2003/4/1–2005/3/31	**Fully protected**	**Fully protected**	¥10 million	**Fully protected**
2005/4/1	**Fully protected**	**Zero-interest accounts with payment services are fully protected**	Other payment deposits and time deposits are protected up to ¥10 million per person	

Notes: Prepared by the author based on Deposit Insurance Corporation of Japan (2003) and other publications. Words in bold indicate unlimited protection by the DIC. Foreign currency deposits and negotiable certificates of deposit (NCDs) are not protected by the DIC. In May of 2000, the introduction of limited protection was postponed for one year from March 2001 to March 2002. In April of 2001, in addition to the ¥10 million of principal, interest was now protected as well.

Table 4. Deposit insurance premiums (percentage)

Fiscal year	Ordinary premium		Surcharge premium	Total premium
	General deposits	Specified deposits		
1971–	0.006			0.006
1982–	0.008			0.008
1986–	0.012			0.012
1996–	0.048		0.036	0.084
2001	0.048	0.048	0.036	0.084
				Weighted average premium
2002	0.080	0.094		0.084
2003–	0.080	0.090		0.084
2005	0.083	0.115		0.084
2006–	0.080	0.110		0.084

Source: Deposit Insurance Corporation of Japan (2005).
Notes: Fiscal year starts on April 1 of the indicated year. Specified deposits are fully guaranteed deposits without any upper limit per person. Until 2004, specified deposits include current deposits, ordinary saving deposits, and specific deposits. Specific deposits are payment accounts under processing. From 2005, specified deposits include only zero interest-rate payment deposits. The surcharge premium was applied from FY 1996 to 2001.

the Bank Recapitalization Act were enacted in a disorderly atmosphere. The purposes of these two laws can be summarized as follows. The Financial Revitalization Act is a special law regarding the resolution of insolvent deposit financial institutions, while the Bank Recapitalization Act, on the other hand, is concerned with capital injections into financial institutions that are solvent, but that are losing the confidence of investors and depositors, so that they are facing difficulties in raising capital in the market on their own.[8]

Where the regulatory authority judges that a

financial institution has negative equity, or is likely to stop repaying its deposits in the near future, the Financial Revitalization Act is to be applied. By putting the institution under national receivership, the law tries to protect their customers, including both depositors and borrowers. After the effective nationalization, however, this act attempts to privatize the institution promptly by making the management efficient, by providing additional capital, and by disposing of its bad loans. Public funds will be used to protect depositors and to replenish its damaged capital base. On the other hand, where a financial institution is solvent, but undercapitalized, the Bank Recapitalization Act is to be applied. Public funds can be injected into its capital base. By doing this, it will be possible to stabilize the performance of the financial institution and restore their credibility.

What are the reasons behind the enactment of these laws? In relation to the Financial Revitalization Act, it could be argued that bankruptcy code and reorganization order, which nearly corresponds to chapter 10 of the former US Bankruptcy Act of 1898, were not designed to deal with the insolvency of financial institutions. Under these laws, often applied to the resolution of insolvent industrial companies, procedures are taken to suspend the repayment of the debts that existed before a failure. These actions are necessary to treat all the creditors of the insolvent company equally. But for a large-sized financial institution, which holds an enormous number of clearing accounts for depositors, and has financial transactions with both domestic and overseas clients, to suspend payments for only a few days would have tremendous adverse effects on the financial market. Depositors would not be able to make their daily payments, and those clients who could no longer borrow from the bank would face the risk of chain-reaction bankruptcies. So as to avoid such a broad range of negative effects, the disposal of insolvent banks should not be accompanied by a general suspension of payments.

The Financial Revitalization Act is designed for financial institutions that have a large influence on the stability of the financial system, or have an important role in a particular region. When those banks face financial difficulties, the act fully protects their creditors by using public funds. At the same time, the act penalizes both the shareholders and the management of the banks. Although the Financial Revitalization Act was legislation with a sunset clause that provided a time limit of March 2001, it was necessary, even after its expiration, to maintain the act as a permanent law so as to deal with insolvent financial institutions. As a result, the Deposit Insurance Law incorporated this law as an emergency measure in its May 2000 revision.

The Financial Revitalization Act was applied to the LTCB in October 1998 and to the Nippon Credit Bank in December 1998, and both banks were put under national control. The outstanding shares were wiped out, and they were nationalized without any compensation to the existing shareholders.

There was an argument that by putting those banks under national control, an enormous number of settlements over transactions on financial derivatives would come up simultaneously and this would create disorder within the world financial market. Nonetheless, thanks to the cooperation of the financial regulatory authorities, nationalization did not bring about any turmoil in the market. In addition, all the depositors were protected, and chain-reaction bankruptcies were avoided. One of the purposes of the act—namely, to protect the clients of the bank—was thus achieved. On the other hand, the relevant authorities must work harder to privatize banks in national receivership, or to lead them to make a fresh start by transferring their business to a third party.

With regard to Bank Recapitalization Act, it is not necessary to have such legislation unless there is a sense of financial disorder. The capital of private enterprises should be raised through voluntary market transactions. Looking at this from an economic point of view, shares can be issued in the market so long as the business conditions are disclosed sufficiently and investors can expect a reasonable return on the investment corresponding to the risk involved. The expected return on stock, which investors require the company to earn explicitly or implicitly, is called the cost of

Table 5. Measures against financial crisis

Article 102 of the Deposit Insurance Law The prime minister may take the following measures to the concerned financial institution when such measures are necessary to avoid very serious disruptions to the stability of the financial system of the country or the region where the institution operates. The decision has to be taken after a deliberation of a council for financial crises that consists of the prime minister, the chief cabinet secretary, the minister for financial stability, the commissioner of the Financial Services Agency, the minister of finance and the governor of the Bank of Japan.	
Type 1 Measure	
If the financial institution is solvent and has not failed:	The DIC underwrites shares of the financial institution. The government can impose a reduction of stated capital.
Type 2 Measure	
If the financial institution is insolvent or has failed:	The DIC provides aid beyond the minimum cost of resolution to protect creditors of the financial institution. The institution will be controlled by the financial receiver.
Type 3 Measure	
If the financial institution has failed and is insolvent and if Type 2 measure is insufficient to achieve stability:	Nationalization of the financial institution without compensation to existing shareholders.

Source: Prepared by the author.
Note: A failed institution is one that that has stopped the payment of deposits or is highly likely to do so. DIC, Deposit Insurance Corporation.

shareholders' equity; that is, the total amount of both dividends and capital gains.

However, when confidence in the financial system is seriously eroded, it is extremely difficult for financial institutions with large loan portfolios to disclose the details of their business conditions to such an extent that investors will be satisfied. Therefore, even for banks which have positive going concern values, it would be almost impossible to raise a large sum of capital to stabilize their business conditions, since investors would require an extremely high cost of shareholders' equity. Where the risk of market failure caused by the incomplete transmission of information is larger than the risk of government failure, it would be possible to justify the capital injection of public funds into financial institutions.

At the time of the enactment of these two acts, the Deposit Insurance Law was also amended. As a result, a principle for the resolution of failed financial institutions was established and a new mechanism for rehabilitating solvent but under-capitalized ones was introduced. The DIC took on the following temporary roles in this process: to act as an administrator of failing institutions; to establish bridge banks to keep failed institutions running; to own stocks of temporarily nationalized institutions and choose directors for them; to purchase bad loans from financial institutions; and to purchase shares of under-capitalized institutions so as to bolster their capital positions.

In May 2000, the Deposit Insurance Law was further amended so as to prepare a permanent resolution scheme for failing banks, because the Financial Revitalization Act and the Bank Recapitalization Act were scheduled to expire at the end of March 2001. In this amendment, procedures of systemic exception from the minimum-cost principle became a permanent feature of the system.

Table 5 summarizes Article 102 of the Deposit Insurance Law of May 2000 that stipulates the measures that can be taken in a financial crisis. A Type I measure corresponds to the Bank Recapitalization Act, and Type 2 and Type 3 measures correspond to the Financial Revitalization Act. The prime minister can protect all the creditors of a bank if he thinks that such a measure is necessary to avoid serious disruptions in the financial market.

The termination of the full protection of deposits was postponed for one year from the end of March 2001. In March 2002, while the full protection of time deposits was removed, the government postponed the removal of the full protection of payment deposits once again. Another ¥10 trillion yen was added to the ¥17 trillion fund for the protection of depositors. A permanent protection of all zero-interest deposits with payment services was also introduced in April 2005 (see table 3). Since no deposit-taking financial institutions have been allowed to fail without the full protection of all deposits, we do not know if this partial protection system will function well in the Japanese financial market.

Type 2 and Type 3 measures of Article 102 should be applied to financial institutions in the same way that the normal bankruptcy procedures are applied, although public funds are used to protect their creditors. Where the going-concern value of a financial institution exceeds its liquidation value, reorganization would be desirable. But where the going-concern value is less than the liquidation value, an orderly and gradual liquidation would be desirable. In both cases, shareholders' capital will be cancelled and board members will have to resign.

The following problems arising from Type 2 and Type 3 measures of Article 102 should be pointed out. First, when a financial institution is put under national control, the nationalized bank has to honor its existing employment contracts, since the status of the juridical person of the bank is maintained. As a result, unlike the case of the bankruptcy of an ordinary corporation where most employees are dismissed, the employees of a failed financial institution are well protected, even though their compensation can be cut by 25 percent at most. Moreover, all the liabilities to workers will be protected in the same manner as other liabilities. Therefore, even a very generous retirement allowance will be protected with public funds. Second, in the resolution of an insolvent financial institution under the Financial Revitalization Act, the predecessor of the Type 2 and Type 3 measures of Article 102, all of its subordinated debts were protected. The subordination clauses of these debts were triggered only when the issuing financial institutions applied to the court for protection under the bankruptcy code or a reorganization order. Since this resolution procedure was not counted as a formal bankruptcy procedure, all the subordinated debts of Japanese financial institutions were treated as ordinary debt and protected by public funds. In this regard, the primary problem lies in the past financial supervisory policy that allowed banks to count such "subordinated debts" as their Bank for International Settlements (BIS) capital.

In the resolution procedure of the LTCB and Hokkaido Takushoku Bank, for example, their subordinated debt did not work as capital. Therefore, it is necessary to reexamine the contracts of subordinated debts. Those debts to which subordination clauses are not applicable within the framework of Type 2 and Type 3 measures of Article 102 for the resolution of insolvent financial institutions should be excluded from the BIS capital with a short transition period.

One major problem in applying the Type 1 measure—a capital injection into a solvent bank—or Type 2 and 3 measures—bankruptcy procedures—is the choice of measure for a particular financial institution. The government can underwrite the capital increase of a particular bank with a Type 1 measure only when the bank has positive equity capital. In addition, the stocks or preferred shares bought by the government must be marketable. Thus, in order for the government to recapitalize a particular bank, the business condition of the bank needs to become stable through the capital increase, and also there must be an expectation of a reasonable return on the injected public funds. In the case of Type 2 and Type 3 measures, on the other hand, a financial institution can be put under national control (outright nationalization in a Type 3 measure) or under national receivership with an assignment of financial receivers (Type 2 measure). To put a bank under effective national control so as to protect their depositors and borrowers, one of the following conditions needs to be satisfied: the bank must have negative equity capital; the bank must have stopped repaying its deposits; or there must be a strong possibility of suspending deposit repayment.

Whether the financial institution has negative equity or whether there is a possibility of suspending repayment of deposits determines whether the measures will be applied. In practice, however, the category in which the bank is going to be classified depends upon the judgment of the authorities. Between a well-capitalized bank and an insolvent bank, there are numerous financial institutions that are more or less marginally capitalized. Whether a particular bank can survive or not depends not only upon the management, but also on the macroeconomic conditions at home and abroad.

3.3 Protection of shareholders in the Resona Bank rescue of 2003

The first application of Article 102 of the Deposit Insurance Law was the case of the Resona Bank rescue in 2003. Resona Bank is the biggest bank under Resona Holdings, a bank holding company with assets of more than ¥30 trillion. The Resona Group was formed by the integration of Daiwa Bank in Osaka and Asahi Bank in Tokyo, and it was the fifth-largest group just after the four so-called megabank groups.

Resona group banks supplemented their capital with massive deferred tax assets (DTA). Banks usually generate DTA with the following two factors: First, Japanese tax rules allow losses to be carried forward for five years, but no loss can be carried backward.[9] When combined, the tax rate of national and local corporate taxes is about 40 percent. As a result, when banks accumulate losses in taxable income, they can show a DTA of up to 40 percent of the estimated taxable income in the coming five years. This DTA will be unwound when the bank earns taxable income. Second, the tax rules for the writing-off of bad loans are stricter than the relevant accounting rules. As a result, sometimes a bank can recognize loan losses in their financial statements, but cannot recognize the losses in their statements for tax purposes. The overpaid tax on loan losses can be carried as a DTA. The DTA will be unwound when the bank can recognize loan losses under tax rules.

In short, DTA are the net present value of a future tax shelter due to accumulated loan losses. DTA have real value only when a bank can generate taxable income in the near future. DTA have no liquidation value because the tax authority will not reimburse the DTA in the case of a bankruptcy of the bank. Therefore, the quality of a DTA as an asset is low unless the bank becomes very profitable.

Resona Bank had more than ¥401 billion of DTA, which was greater than its shareholders' equity of ¥366 billion. Moreover, Resona Bank reported losses in the three years to the end of March 2003. In order to realize ¥400 billion of DTA in the coming five years, the bank would have to earn ¥200 billion of taxable income every year, and the after-tax ROE would have to be as high as 32 percent:

> Taxable income (¥200 billion) × tax rate (40 percent) × 5 years = ¥400 billion
> After-tax income (¥120 billion) / equity (¥366 billion) = 32.7 percent

This is clearly an unrealistic scenario. In fact, Asahi & Co., which had been auditing Asahi Bank, refused to allow Resona Bank to show any DTA on their financial statement for March 2003. However, Shin Nihon & Co., which had been auditing Daiwa Bank, allowed Resona Bank to keep ¥400 billion of DTA. Resona management took the more lenient opinion of Shin Nihon & Co. and terminated their auditing contract with Asahi & Co. The FSA apparently agreed with Shin Nihon & Co. and Resona management, and treated Resona Bank as a solvent financial institution.

When the Resona Bank problem surfaced, the FSA effectively allowed banks to keep an almost unlimited amount of DTA on their balance sheet. This put tremendous pressure on accountants who had to set a limit on DTA for their clients. In the final days of Resona Bank, Mr. Hirata Satoshi, a certified public accountant for Asahi & Co., apparently killed himself. For a long period of time, he had been auditing Asahi Bank, which became a part of the Resona Group as a result of a merger. When Asahi & Co. management took a strict stance against Resona Bank's DTA, he was caught between Resona Bank and Asahi & Co. The accounting rules on DTA were clearly too ambiguous to be used for BIS capital rules. The FSA should have limited the use of DTA as the core capital of banks.

Even with a lenient audit, Resona Bank could not satisfy BIS capital rules, and the bank asked the FSA to provide a capital injection of about ¥2 trillion under the Type 1 measure of Article 102 of the Deposit Insurance Law. The FSA invoked prompt corrective action on May 17, and it also convened a council for financial crises on the same day. The prime minister decided to provide Resona Bank with ¥1.96 trillion of capital through the DIC. The DIC exchanged the stock of Resona Bank with that of Resona Holdings, a listed company. The DIC obtained ¥296 billion of common stock and ¥1,664 billion of preferred stock. In this exchange, the government effectively bought common stocks of Resona Holdings at ¥52 per share, the prevailing stock price of Resona Holdings just before the announcement of public assistance.

This injection of public money into the Resona Group started a strong rally on the Tokyo Stock Exchange. The share prices of major banks recovered sharply. In my opinion, this rally was the reaction to the big surprise in the market regarding the Resona rescue. While the existing shares of the LTCB and Nippon Credit Bank had been wiped out, the shareholders of Resona Bank were protected by public money. This was certainly a perverse but effective way to support bank stock prices.

After this injection of public money, the newly appointed Resona management undertook a reexamination of their books. On October 10, the management revised the projected current profit of the Resona Group for the midterm ending September 2003 from a profit of ¥22 billion to a loss of ¥1,760 billion yen. The downward revision was huge: ¥1,788 billion in just four months, amounting to 93 percent of the injected capital. The downward revision of Resona Bank alone included ¥435 billion in additional loan loss reserves and ¥330 billion in resolution costs for related companies.

The government rescue of the Resona Group indicates that the FSA protected the shareholders of banks in addition to the depositors. Banks are also increasingly accepting a partial reduction of the outstanding debts of weakened borrowers without eliminating shareholders' equity. As a result, the Japanese stock market has partially lost its most important role in this period of a rallying stock market: pricing corporate performance and allocating funds to the most efficient companies.

The safety net always generates some form of moral hazard among market participants. When there is an element of systemic risk in the banking sector, however, it is necessary to use very strong medicine even though it has severe side effects. According to many observers of the Tokyo Stock Exchange, the recovery of stock prices since May 2003 is due to the increasing confidence in the eventual bailout of bank shareholders by the Japanese government. This strong medicine could stabilize the fragile expectations of market participants at this critical period.

3.4 The malfunctioning of prompt corrective action and BIS rules

As the financial system gradually deteriorated, the government expanded its protection from depositors to owners of subordinated debts and bank shares. As a result, market forces were removed one after another. In such conditions, the disciplinary forces of bank supervisors would become much more important. However, this force was not working, either.

Capital requirements on banks are a very important regulatory instrument to provide corrective incentives to bank management and to protect deposit insurance system funds. However, the FSA did not use capital requirements and prompt corrective action as stipulated by the law.

Figure 3 shows the degree of insolvency of all the failed deposit-taking financial institutions from the introduction of prompt corrective action in April 1998 to September 2002. Altogether, out of the 976 DIC-protected financial institutions that existed at the end of March 1998, 132 institutions have failed. The degree of insolvency is defined as follows:

> Degree of insolvency = DIC grants to protect all depositors / Total disclosed debt just before the failure.

The average degree of insolvency was 25.1 percent. The DIC-protected financial institutions

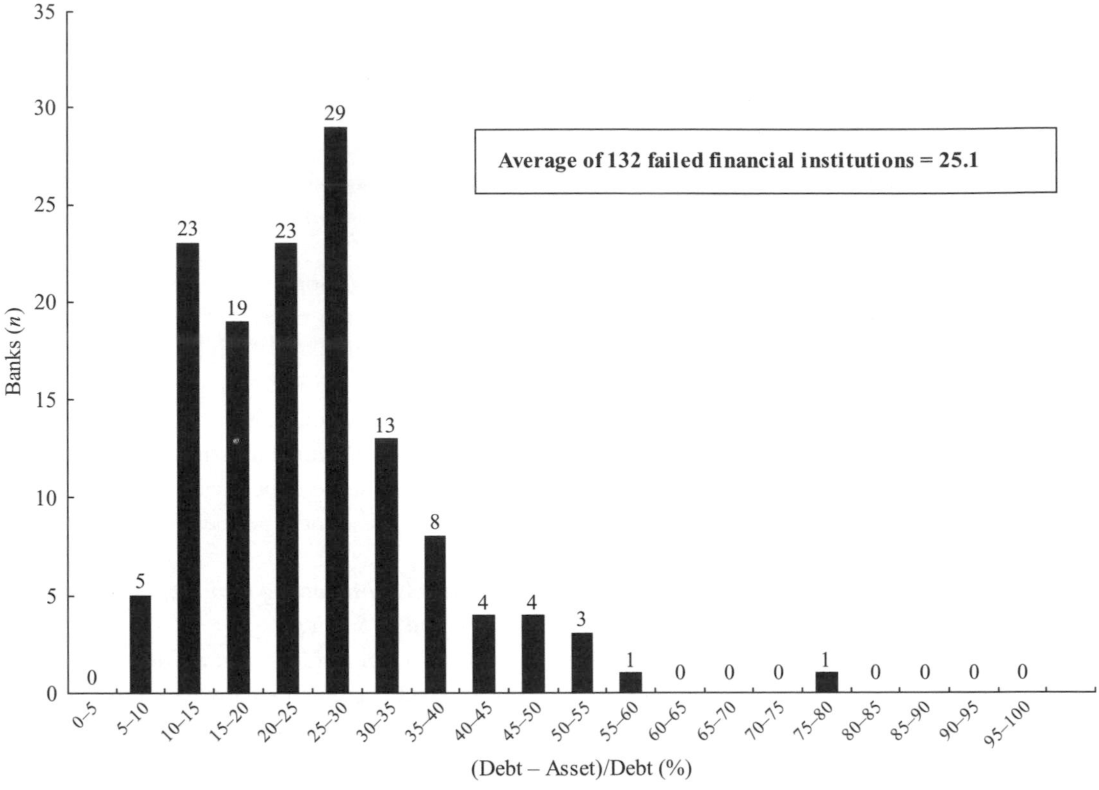

Figure 3. Degree of insolvency of failed deposit-taking financial institutions from April 1998 to September 2002
Note: Estimated by Japan Center for Economic Research.

include commercial banks, *shinkin* cooperative banks, credit unions, and labor banks (*rōkin*). The average degree of insolvency of failed institutions is about the same among different groups and the size of the institutions. Even large banks showed a relatively large degree of insolvency: Hokkaido Takushoku Bank, 18.8 percent; LTCB, 11.6 percent; and Nippon Credit Bank, 29.3 percent.

Table 6 shows the weak capital structure of Japanese banks. On the surface, the core capital of all commercial banks was ¥24.8 trillion at the end of March 2003 when the Nikkei 225 index hit the trough. However, this figure includes ¥10.6 trillion of DTAS that have no liquidation value. In addition, there is sizable underreserving for bad loans. Our estimates are in table 6. If we subtract ¥5.4 trillion of underreserving for March 2003 and ¥10.6 trillion for DTA from their core capital, Japanese banks had only 8.8 trillion yen of capital. The government provided ¥7.3 trillion of this capital. Thus, their net private capital was only ¥1.5 trillion. Against this capital, the banks had a stock portfolio of ¥23.2 trillion. Clearly, the banks did not have enough capital to support this huge stock investment.

Table 7 shows the distribution of the core capital ratios (leverage ratios) of the major Japanese banks. By adjusting for underreserving and DTAs, four banks had negative equity at the end of March 2003. The weighted average capital ratio declined from 3.21 percent in March 2000 to 0.36 percent in March 2003. Only two banks maintained leverage ratios of more than 6 percent. One was Shinsei Bank, which is the former LTCB (nationalized in October 1998 and privatized in March 2000). The other was Aozora Bank, which is the former Nippon Credit Bank (nationalized in December 1998 and privatized in December 2000).

Despite the declining net assets of banks, all

Table 6. Stock portfolios and capital in the banking sector (trillion yen)

Year (March)	Market value of shares held by banks A	Book value of shares held by banks B	Capital account (core capital) C	Deferred tax asset D	Estimated underreserving E	Equity capital held by the government F	Private net capital account C + (A – B) × 0.6 – D – E – F	Nikkei 225 index
1991	77.7	33.1	30.2	0.0	n/a	0.0	57.0	26,292
1992	56.4	34.5	31.3	0.0	n/a	0.0	44.4	19,346
1993	56.4	34.5	31.8	0.0	n/a	0.0	44.9	18,591
1994	61.9	36.5	32.3	0.0	n/a	0.0	47.5	19,112
1995	52.0	39.8	32.3	0.0	n/a	0.0	39.6	15,140
1996	64.3	43.0	27.9	0.0	n/a	0.0	40.7	21,407
1997	54.1	42.9	28.5	0.0	15.0	0.0	20.2	18,003
1998	50.8	45.7	24.3	0.0	4.9	0.3	22.2	16,527
1999	47.1	42.7	33.7	8.4	4.0	6.3	17.7	15,837
2000	54.5	44.4	35.6	8.2	5.8	6.9	20.8	20,337
2001	44.5	44.3	37.6	7.1	7.5	7.1	16.0	13,000
2002	34.4	34.4	30.2	10.6	6.8	7.2	5.6	11,025
2003	23.2	23.2	24.8	10.6	5.4	7.3	1.5	7,973
2004	28.5	28.5	29.0	7.2	5.7	8.9	7.2	11,715
2005	27.7	27.7	31.4	5.7	6.9	8.1	10.7	11,688
2006	33.2	33.2	37.3	2.3	8.3	5.2	21.5	17,059

Source: Federation of Bankers Associations of Japan, "Analysis of Bank Financial Statements," various issues.
Note: Table represents the banking accounts of all banks in Japan. Estimated required loan loss reserves is defined as follows: 1 percent of category I loan + 20 percent of category II loan + 70 percent of category III + 100 percent of category IV loan.
Since the Financial Services Agency stopped disclosing classified loan figures from March 2003, the classified loan figures and the required loan-loss reserves were estimated from the disclosed bad loan figures.

Table 7. Distribution of adjusted capital/asset ratio of major Japanese banks

Year (March)	Number of banks (percent) Total	Less than -2	-2–0	0–2	2–4	4–6	More than 6 percent	Weighted average (percent)	Nikkei 225 index
2000	18	0	0	1	16	0	1	3.21	20 337
2001	18	0	0	10	6	0	2	1.91	13 000
2002	15	0	2	10	1	0	2	0.80	11 025
2003	14	1	3	8	0	0	2	0.36	7 973
2004	15	0	1	6	5	0	3	1.63	11 715
2005	17	0	0	5	6	1	5	2.06	11 688
2006	13	0	0	3	5	0	5	3.15	17 059

Source: Estimated by Japan Center for Economic Research.
Notes: Major banks include city banks, long-term credit banks, and major trust banks. We excluded three new but small trust banks: Nomura Trust, Mitsui Asset Trust, and Resona Trust.
Two privatized long-term credit banks after nationalization maintain "More than 6 percent" capital.
Adjusted Capital = Core Capital + Unrealized Capital Gains and Losses + Loan Loss Reserves – Estimated Required Loan Loss Reserves – Deferred Tax Asset.
Estimated Required Loan Loss Reserves = 100 percent of defaulted loans + 70 percent of risk loans + 20 percent of doubtful loans + 1 percent of normal loans.
Adjusted Capital/Asset Ratio = Adjusted Capital/Gross Assets.

Table 8. Ratio of deferred tax assets in the core capital of major Japanese banks

	March 2003		
	Core capital (A) (billion yen)	Net DTA (B) (billion yen)	Ratio (B/A) (percent)
Mitsubishi Tokyo Financial Group	3,338	1,303	39.0
UFJ Holdings	2,665	1,522	57.1
Resona Holdings	635	522	82.2
Resona Bank	366	401	109.6
Saitama Resona Bank	155	44	28.4
Sumitomo Mitsui Financial Group	3,168	1,842	58.1
Mizuho Financial Group	4,322	2,105	48.7
Mitsui Trust Holding	341	346	101.5

Source: Disclosure materials of individual banks.
Notes: Net deferred tax asset (DTA) means deferred tax assets minus deferred tax liabilities.

the banks had been complying with BIS capital requirements. Under the Japanese accounting rules on banks and lenient application by the regulators, BIS capital ratios were manipulated in many ways. First, banks underreserved against bad loans, as explained earlier. This tends to increase bank capital by the same amount. Second, banks kept large amounts of DTA despite the fact that most of them had been losing money for the past ten years. Table 8 shows the share of DTA in the core capital of major Japanese financial groups as of March 2003. The DTA of the Resona Bank and Mitsui Trust Holdings is larger than their core capital. The DTA of the other banking groups are also very large compared with their core capital: more than half each for UFJ and the Sumitomo Mitsui Financial Group. If we apply the US capital-requirement rule that sets a maximum limit of DTA of 10 percent of core capital, most major Japanese banks cannot comply with BIS capital requirements. Third, friendly life-insurance companies held stocks and subordinated loans of banks. At the end of March 2003, the ten major life-insurance companies held ¥1.1 trillion of bank shares and ¥4.4 trillion of subordinated loans. Banks, in turn, held ¥1.0 trillion of surplus notes and ¥0.9 trillion in subordinated loans of life-insurance companies.[10] In addition, life-insurance companies hold part of the preferred capital notes of banks that are issued through their special-purpose entities in tax-haven countries. This practice is so-called double gearing, and the cross-held quasi-capital should not be treated as the genuine capital of banks or life-insurance companies.[11]

In 2003, a strict application of the standard would have meant the effective nationalization of a large part of the banking sector, given that too many big banks were undercapitalized. Since it was almost impossible for the regulator to manage that number of banks directly, they allowed weak banks to operate until the economy recovered. However, as the health of the banking sector recovers, the excessively lenient treatments should be removed; the FSA has started to rectify this in recent years.

4. Concluding Note: The Recovering Japanese Economy and Financial System

While financial institutions and the FSA tried to muddle through the crisis with the window dressing of financial statements and the very lenient application of capital requirements, the Japanese economy started to recover strongly through export-led growth in 2003. The booming of China and the US, together with a very low yen exchange rate, pulled Japan out of deep stagnation. As the deflationary GDP gap shrank, the rate of deflation improved slowly (figure 1). These favorable changes reduced the bad loans.

Banks also improved their profit margin by reducing costs and by increasing income from fees and commissions (table 2). The prolonged banking crisis was largely over by 2006, and the remaining problems are confined to some regional financial institutions.

The government also helped bank profits by reducing the presence of government-sponsored financial institutions, although it is difficult to quantify the magnitude. Under the strong initiative of former prime minister Koizumi Junichirō, the government decided to remove the competitive advantages of the postal saving system and postal life insurance by privatizing them in 2006. The government also decided to reduce the size of government-sponsored financial institutions by privatizing some of them, and by reducing their lending activities that directly compete with private financial institutions.

The FSA is also trying to improve regulatory discipline by redefining the capital requirements on banks and insurance companies. A new 40 percent ceiling on the maximum allowable DTA in the BIS core capital was introduced in March 2006; it will be reduced to 20 percent by March 2008.

These reforms are improving the regulatory discipline in Japan's financial sector. However, the FSA has to strive much harder to upgrade Japan's regulatory standards to the level of other developed countries. The FSA should restrict double-gearing among banks, life-insurance companies, and bank customers. It should also pay careful attention to the capital structures of big financial groups rather than superficial BIS ratios. The dysfunctional solvency margin requirement on insurance companies should be tightened considerably. At the very least, the FSA should remove deferred taxes from the definition of solvency, prohibit double-gearing among financial institutions, and raise the risk parameters on stock portfolios. Given the improving health of financial institutions, this is the golden opportunity for the FSA to make up for the lost decade of regulatory discipline.

Courtesy of Japan Center for Economic Research (JCER).

Originally published in *Asian Economic Policy Review* 2, no. 2 (Dec. 2007): 273–297.

Notes

1. In preparing this paper, I have relied on my earlier papers on Japan's financial regulation, including Fukao (2000, 2003, 2004, 2005). I would like to thank the staff of the financial research team at the Japan Center for Economic Research for their excellent research assistance.
2. See Shigemi (1995) and BIS (1993) on the causes of asset price inflation in major countries. Barthold and Itō (1992) discuss some aspects of tax distortions.
3. See Nakaso (2001) for a very detailed discussion of Japan's financial crisis until 2000.
4. See section 3.2.2 of Nakaso (2001).
5. Fukao (1998) documented the progression of the financial crisis in 1997.
6. See Deposit Insurance Corporation of Japan (2002, 2003).
7. Since this measure was likely to preserve weak financial institutions as new banks under a largely unchanged management structure, this method of assistance was abolished in March 1999 after the assisted merger of Fukutoku Bank and Naniwa Bank was carried out in October 1998.
8. See Fukao (2000) on the details of these acts.
9. By the amendment of the corporate tax law of fiscal year 2004, this five-year limit was extended for seven years. However, this rule is applicable to losses incurred after FY 2001 and cannot be applied to the losses incurred earlier.
10. Surplus notes are issued by mutual insurance companies, and are similar to preferred shares without voting rights. They are counted as a part of capital in calculating the solvency margin requirements for insurance companies.
11. See Fukao (2005) on the details of this practice among banks and life-insurance companies.

References

Bank for International Settlements. 1993. "63rd Annual Report." Basel: BIS.

Barthold, Thomas A., and Itō Takatoshi. 1992. "Bequest Taxes and Accumulation of Household Wealth: US-Japan Comparison." In *Political Economy of Tax Reform*, edited by Itō Takatoshi and Anne O. Krueger, 235–292. Chicago: University of Chicago Press.

Deposit Insurance Corporation of Japan. 2002. "The New Deposit Insurance System." Tokyo: Deposit Insurance Corporation of Japan.

———. 2003. "Annual Report 2003." Tokyo: Deposit Insurance Corporation of Japan.

———. 2005. "Annual Report 2005." Tokyo: Deposit Insurance Corporation of Japan.

Federation of Bankers Associations of Japan. *Analysis of Financial Statements of All Banks*. Various issues.

Fukao Mitsuhiro. 1998. "Japanese Financial Instability and Weaknesses in the Corporate Governance Structure." *Seoul Journal of Economics* 11 (4): 381–422.

———. 2000. "Recapitalizing Japan's Banks: The Functions and Problems of Financial Revitalization Act and Bank Recapitalization Act." *Keio Business Review* 38:1–16.

———. 2003. "Japan's Lost Decade and Weaknesses in Its Corporate Governance Structure." In *Japan's Economic Recovery*, edited by Robert M. Stern, 289–327. Northampton: Edward Elgar.

———. 2004. "Weakening Market and Regulatory Discipline in the Japanese Financial System." In *Market Discipline across Countries and Industries*, edited by Claudio Borio, William C. Hunter, George G. Kaufman, and Kostas Tsatsaronis, 119–133. Cambridge, MA: MIT Press.

———. 2005. "Fixing Japanese Life-Insurance Companies." In *Reviving Japan's Economy*, edited by Itō Takatoshi, Hugh T. Patrick, and David E. Weinstein, 241–272. Cambridge, MA: MIT Press.

Goldman Sachs Group Inc. 2003. FORM 8-K, January 15.

International Monetary Fund. 2003. *Japan: Financial System Stability Assessment and Supplementary Information*. IMF Country Reports, no. 3/287, September, Washington, DC: IMF.

Nakaso Hiroshi. 2001. *The Financial Crisis in Japan during the 1990s: How the Bank of Japan Responded and the Lessons Learnt*. BIS Papers, no. 6, October, Basel: Bank for International Settlements.

Shigemi Yūsuke. 1995. "Asset Inflation in Selected Countries." *Bank of Japan Monetary and Economic Studies* 13 (2): 89–130.

III-(2.4) Following Up on Japan's Financial Big Bang

Ikeo Kazuhito
Japan Echo, 2007

The year 2006 marked the tenth anniversary of the Japanese Big Bang, a comprehensive program of financial deregulation that was proclaimed with great fanfare in the autumn of 1996 (taking its name from the deregulation of the capital market in Britain in 1986 under Prime Minister Margaret Thatcher). The anniversary attracted very little attention; however since the start of 2007, financial market reform has once again emerged as a priority policy issue, and the *Economic and Fiscal Reform 2007 (Basic Policies 2007)* document approved by the cabinet on June 19 declares that the Financial Services Agency will come up with a plan for enhancing the competitiveness of Japan's financial markets, which the entire government will move to execute.

The prospects for financial market reform have become cloudier since the ruling coalition's defeat in the July 29 upper house election and the subsequent upheaval on the political front, including the sudden decision by Prime Minister Abe Shinzō to step down. We cannot yet be sure what sort of policy initiatives his successor, Fukuda Yasuo, will undertake. Be that as it may, the task of making Japan's financial markets more competitive is one that must be addressed in order to ensure the future of the Japanese economy.

Many people focus on the strength of Japanese manufacturing, the export sector in particular, placing their hopes in it as the locomotive for the economy as a whole. The manufacturing sector, however, accounts for less than 20 percent of Japan's total employment. Furthermore, in order to maintain their competitive edge, domestic manufacturers have been moving their operations offshore to an increasing degree. The overall trend over the long run is a decline in jobs in domestic manufacturing, although some companies recently shifted the research and development division back to Japan. The competitive strength of Japanese manufacturers and the health of the Japanese labor market are separate matters. So we need to look beyond manufacturing for employment security.

This means that services and other nonmanufacturing industries have a major role to play as sources of new jobs (and tax revenues). Raising the productivity of these industries is an urgent agenda. And a prime target for attention in this respect is the financial services industry. Improved competitiveness and growth in this industry will contribute to the desired enhancement of Japan's industrial structure and to the raising of overall economic productivity. In order to achieve this, individual financial institutions will need to make appropriate efforts, but we must also move to strengthen the competitive position of the Tokyo market, the "mother market" in which these institutions operate.

A goal of the Japanese Big Bang was to turn the Tokyo market into a competitive international financial center. However, the 1996 reforms were not sufficient to accomplish this. Here I would like to review Japan's Big Bang, assessing its significance and its limitations, and consider the issues that we should address next.

A Changed Economic Environment

The need for a reform of Japan's financial system actually emerged more than a decade before the 1996 Big Bang. The cause was the major metamorphosis of the Japanese economy that occurred in the late 1970s. By the start of the 1980s, after experiencing oil shocks twice, Japan found itself facing an economic situation very different from before. The period of high-speed growth was over: The potential growth rate had fallen to 2–3 percent, and the pace of corporate investment had also slowed down. However, the process of population aging had yet to begin in earnest, and so the household sector increased its savings rate.

The result was a large surplus of savings over investments—in other words, an overflow of funds. This was an unprecedented development in modern Japanese history. Since embarking on its modernization and industrialization drive in the late nineteenth century, Japan had, with only a few temporary exceptions, always had an investment rate exceeding the savings rate, meaning a shortage of funds. The 1980s brought the opposite situation.

The current Japanese financial system had been built and developed to match the requirements of an economy with an under-accumulation of capital. Its architecture evolved to collect the maximum amount of savings possible. The financial institutions had no problem finding productive uses for the funds that they managed to gather. Particularly in the period after World War II, when the chronic shortage of capital was especially severe, the authorities' imposition of artificially low interest rates resulted in an extremely large amount of demand for investment funds, and financial institutions could make profits by merely allocating this scarce resource.

The metamorphosis of the economy caused this financial architecture to cease to be appropriate. A system whose main focus was on collecting savings from the public could not be expected to cope well with a situation where people spoke openly of a "money glut." It was at this juncture that the need arose for a reform of Japan's financial system to match the new conditions. The focus had to be shifted from the gathering of savings to the finding of suitable investment targets. However, the inertia of the long-established system was serious, and the pressure to adopt a new architecture was defied. The discussion of reform that started in the mid-1980s should have addressed the need for a total overhaul of the financial architecture, but instead it concentrated on the trivial issue of the wall between banking and the securities industry, generating extended but fruitless debate.

Because of this failure, the mismatch between the current financial system and the new economic environment became even greater. And this led to what may be called a "runaway expansion of credit." During the latter half of the 1980s, under the overwhelming pressure of surging money, Japan's financial institutions madly expanded their lending and other investment activities without conducting the necessary reforms and revamping of their organizational setups. This produced what we now call the "bubble economy."

The 1996 Big Bang

The speculative bubbles of the late 1980s burst early in the 1990s, leaving Japan's financial institutions laboring under a heavy load of bad loans, but amid the efforts to clear up this mess, the more fundamental issue of the mismatch between the current financial system and the real economy remained unaddressed. With all their energy taken up by the struggle to clear away their nonperforming loans, those who were working in the financial sector were less than enthusiastic about tackling systemic reform, whereas their customers—particularly the major corporations that also had access to overseas financial centers like London and New York—became increasingly dissatisfied with the financial services on offer in Tokyo.

The upshot of this dissatisfaction on the users' side, distilled through the complex political process of the time, was the financial Big Bang of 1996. In the autumn of that year, the administration of Prime Minister Hashimoto Ryūtarō proclaimed the goal of bringing the Tokyo market up to the level of London and New York by 2001 and announced reforms to create a "free, fair, and global" financial system. Unlike earlier reforms, which were implemented gradually, the idea was that this overhaul needed to be carried out in a single stroke; hence the "Big Bang" label.

In practice, the changes were made to a certain extent in stages rather than all at once. Even so, the process moved with considerably more urgency than the earlier reforms. The effects went a long way to deal with the issues that had been brushed aside during the 1980s. That is why I argue that Japan's Big Bang may be seen as a "consolation match" for the financial reforms of the previous decade.

The mid-1990s were a time of considerable unsteadiness in the Japanese financial sector, and so the call for a sweeping overhaul generated much concern and opposition. Some even seriously asserted that the Big Bang was a plot by the American financiers to assert hegemony over the Japanese. Support for maintenance of the existing setup was deep-rooted. However, looking back from our present vantage point, we can see that the decision to override the resistance and implement the reforms was probably what made it possible for Japanese finance to retain at least a toehold in the global market. One can imagine that Japan's financial institutions would have dropped completely out of the global scene if the Big Bang had been averted and deregulation had been further delayed. It was indeed a difficult time for banks and other institutions as they tried to clear away their bad loans, but the execution of the reforms in this "consolation match" was a highly significant development, marking the start of the Japanese financial sector's revitalization.

Winning a consolation match, however, does not gain one a gold or silver medal; at best it results in a bronze. The financial Big Bang alone was not enough to make the Tokyo market catch up with rivals like London and New York. Even now, more than a decade later, Tokyo has not established a solid position as an international financial center. Nonetheless, some notable changes have taken place. For example, approximately thirty commercial banks have been consolidated into six or eight groups. This notwithstanding, much also remains unchanged.

The Advantages of Market-Oriented Finance

Given Japan's current stage of economic development, its financial system needs to strengthen its capacity to find and support investment opportunities. It is not funds, but rather investment opportunities that are scarce, and so promising ones should not be ignored. However, the question of which ones are promising cannot be answered using any single yardstick; in many cases, the value of an investment cannot be determined until after it is made.

Under these circumstances, we need a setup that will allow multiple investors with different backgrounds and criteria to assess opportunities from their various perspectives. This is precisely what the capital market provides. In the past, when Japan was still at the stage of catching up with advanced countries, it was possible to assess investment opportunities by looking at the precedents that these advanced countries offered. This was something that experienced bank employees could do. Now, however, relying just on bankers is liable to cause many good prospects to be overlooked. We need to make more use of the market and bring a variety of actors into the process of judging potential investments.

Another consideration is the increased need to transfer and disperse risk in order to support investment projects that have been judged promising. This requires use of the capital market. Banks can only take on a limited volume of risk. They are subject to the capital adequacy requirements of the Bank for International Settlements, and on a more immediate level, the depositors on whom they rely for the bulk of their funds do not want their money to be jeopardized by excessive risk-taking on the part of the banks holding their deposits.

For these reasons, it is necessary to shift the architecture of Japan's financial system toward greater use of market-oriented finance. Just because this shift is necessary, though, does not mean it will spontaneously occur. Although it has been talked about for quite a while, the desired progress in this direction has not been made. Why is this process taking so long?

The fundamental reason is that market-oriented finance is only possible where the appropriate institutional infrastructure has been put in place—something that has yet to be accomplished in Japan. The lag relates to the point I cited above about the inertia of a long-established system: Change has been slow to come because the Japanese financial system is so highly developed on the bank-centered basis. In other words, because the current Japanese financial system has a long history, the creation of a market-oriented system means destroying or casting aside the existing setup—which is well crafted in its own way.

Moves to scrap an existing set of arrangements tend to generate deep-seated opposition. It is harder to build a market-oriented financial system at the cost of scrapping an existing, well-developed system centered on banks than it is to create a market-oriented system from scratch. Since this is the challenge Japan faces, the process is bound to be time-consuming, and we are still only part of the way toward completing it.

The Need for Systemic Improvements

Financial instruments represent promises to pay income to the holder in the future in accordance with conditions set in advance; they have no intrinsic material value. In order for people to be able to confidently conduct transactions involving these instruments, they must be able to determine in advance how reliable the promises are, and they must also be virtually certain that the agreed transactions will be implemented at the designated times. In Japan's financial system, this information gathering and certainty about implementation have generally been provided through the construction of long-term relationships.

To establish a system of market-oriented finance, by contrast, it is essential to have a system of disclosure supporting the gathering of information in advance and a system of corporate governance assuring the implementation of the agreed transactions in the future. In addition, there must be a regulatory system capable of preventing unfair transactions. Japan's financial Big Bang achieved considerable results in the areas of liberalization and deregulation, but it did not complete the task of establishing these systems.

The mission of doing so was not forgotten, however, and recent years have brought substantial progress in this respect. Since around 2000, we have seen developments including the comprehensive revision of accounting standards, revision of bankruptcy laws, enactment of a new Companies Act, and enactment of the Financial Instruments and Exchange Act based on a major overhaul of the previous Securities and Exchange Act. Thanks to these and other moves, Japan has finally reached the point at which the conditions are in place for the expansion of market-oriented finance.

That said, the "financial instruments" covered by the Financial Instruments and Exchange Act do not include the bulk of bank deposits and insurance policies, which are covered by the preexisting Banking Act and Insurance Business Act, respectively. This is an example of the difficulties that arise because Japan is not building a market-oriented financial system from scratch. Given these circumstances—"historical path dependence" in economic terminology—the most realistic approach is probably to move ahead with the systemic shift through further expansion of the channels for market-oriented indirect finance.

In traditional indirect finance, banks intermediate between borrowers (users of funds) and investors (providers of funds). In market-oriented indirect finance, by contrast, the intermediation is performed through the market; it therefore involves both the linking of borrowers to the market and the linking of the market to investors. The typical technique used to link borrowers to the market is securitization. And the most common way of linking the market to investors is through investment trusts (mutual funds), pension funds, and other forms of institutionalized funds. If both types of links are present, they create a market-oriented channel of indirect finance between borrowers and investors.

In Japan's case, the most practical way to change the existing financial architecture is by developing this market-oriented channel of indirect finance as a complement to the traditional channel of indirect finance, thereby making two separate channels available. In the case of market-oriented indirect finance, on the one hand, direct participation in the market is limited mainly to financial institutions. This can be expected to lighten the burden of creating systems to protect investors in the capital market. On the other hand, since market-oriented indirect finance relies on increasingly multilayered agency relationships, the risk of agency-related problems may become more serious. Here the burden of creating systems to avert such risk may become heavier than in the case of direct finance. For example, it is necessary to ensure that fund managers act honestly and do not betray the trust of the individual investors whose money they are investing. Explicit rules concerning fiduciary responsibility are required for this purpose, along with arrangements to make sure that the rules are enforced.

A Better Regulatory Environment

The expansion of Japan's market-oriented indirect finance will require an ongoing process of quiet, steady improvement of the relevant systems as described above; there is no shortcut. But if we hope to raise the status of the Tokyo market as an international financial center, we must also work at improving the regulatory environment and securing qualified human resources. The regulatory environment and human resources are considered to be the two most important factors, whereas the elements that determine the international competitive position of financial markets extend across a very broad range.

A financial market must be trusted, and the presence of strict regulators who can be relied on to guard vigilantly against unfair dealings is essential in order to provide the ultimate guarantee of market trustworthiness. Financial markets cannot achieve proper development if their regulators are too loose and fail to protect investors adequately. Investors will not place their funds in a market where they fear losses due to unfair practices.

At the same time, however, the regulatory setup for financial markets must have the flexibility to cope with constantly changing market and technological progress. The regulators must not act as a hindrance to free activity by financial market participants; on the contrary, they need to act as a positive force encouraging innovation in the market. A regulatory approach that makes it unnecessarily difficult to do business will stunt the development of financial markets.

This means that the regulators must have both a restrictive side, firmly preventing unfair dealing, and a pro-business side, supporting the creative ingenuity of market participants. These two sides are liable to conflict with each other and the upholding of both sides might be easier said than done. The quality of the regulatory environment is determined by the adeptness of regulators at balancing these two aspects.

A related challenge is to achieve both "freedom" and "fairness" in accordance with the Big Bang goal of making the Japanese financial system "free, fair, and global." If all the attention goes to making the market free, unfair dealing is liable to run rampant. A financial market must not be a dog-eat-dog world where participants can do anything at all as long as they do not violate the written rules—or one where it is fine to make profits through shady activities as long as you do not get caught. Conversely, if a market is fair but not free, innovative activities will be stifled, and over the long run it will lose its competitiveness and fall into decline.

To be frank, Japan still falls quite short in terms of providing a well-balanced, high-quality regulatory environment for financial markets. Another problem in terms of international competitiveness is the qualitative and quantitative shortage of specialized personnel. Tokyo is seen as an extremely difficult place to secure skilled persons who are well versed in financial business. And under such conditions, there is no hope for the Tokyo market to develop a concentration of advanced financial services.

This means that we must also earnestly tackle the challenge of deepening the pool of superior human resources with knowledge of finance. It is not enough to raise specialists in financial engineering; we must also work to cultivate the financial literacy of personnel in general. To achieve this, we will need to improve both our educational system and corporate personnel systems.

Courtesy of Japan Echo.

English version originally published in *Japan Echo* 34, no. 6 (Dec. 2007): 19–22; adapted with permission and guidance from the author's spouse, Ikeo Aiko.

Translated from an original article in Japanese also written for *Japan Echo*.

Koizumi's Reforms

Part IV Overview

When Koizumi Junichirō came to power in April 2001, he vowed to "destroy" the ruling Liberal Democratic Party (LDP). This was an expression of his intention to bring about major change in the traditional direction of politics and policies. As promised, the Koizumi cabinet had many features that set it apart from its predecessors, one of which was the pursuit of "small government"—a very unusual move for a Japanese administration. Prime Minister Koizumi pursued structural reform based on the principle that all that could be done by the private sector should be left in private-sector hands. Moreover, where policymaking had previously strongly reflected LDP wishes, Koizumi used the Council on Economic and Fiscal Policy—an advisory institution comprising the prime minister, other key ministers, and several private-sector experts—to reflect his own thinking directly in policy.

Originally an economist, Takenaka Heizō supported Koizumi's operation of the new administration as minister of state for economic and fiscal policy. Takenaka's "Koizumi's Miracle Cabinet" is adapted from a chapter of his book *Kōzō kaikaku no shinjitsu* (The Structural Reforms of the Koizumi Cabinet; see also II-(3)), in which he reflects on the Koizumi reforms based on his own experiences as a cabinet minister. This particular chapter deals with events around the time of the cabinet's inauguration.

Of the various structural reforms undertaken by the Koizumi cabinet, the reform on which Koizumi himself placed the greatest priority, and the one over which he fought most with anti-reform factions within the LDP, was the privatization of postal services. As a Koizumi advisor, economist Matsubara Satoru was one leader in the postal-service privatization debate. In his "Privatize the Postal Services," he notes the difficulties faced by the postal services prior to privatization and makes specific proposals toward privatization.

IV-(1) Koizumi's Miracle Cabinet

Takenaka Heizō

The Structural Reforms of the Koizumi Cabinet, 2008

The tale begins a little more than a decade ago.

Not long after the collapse of the bubble economy, a certain executive friend of mine organized a series of study sessions with a politician named Koizumi Junichirō—breakfast meetings generally held at venues like the Royal Park Hotel in Tokyo's Ningyōchō neighborhood. Participating in these meetings and their wide-ranging discussions gave me the chance to get to know this most unconventional politician. I had met Koizumi previously, but it was these study sessions that provided my first opportunity to discuss policy issues with him at length.

At the time, the impact of the bubble's collapse was manifesting itself in a variety of ways and policy debate was in a muddle. As an economist, I commented that the easy answer offered by the policy mainstream—fiscal expansion—had no hope of bringing about a solution. I remember advocating efforts to invigorate the economy and achieve fiscal health by quickly dealing with the nonperforming loan problem and implementing structural reforms such as deregulation aimed at reducing the size of government.

I was profoundly struck then by how Koizumi never took notes during these sessions, but remained perfectly still, sometimes with his eyes closed, listening intently to what others had to say. Later I would learn that this was a style he maintained consistently even after being appointed prime minister. In short, he would carve through all the extraneous details and keep only what really rang true.

The courage to discard details to avoid making big-picture mistakes is a quality demanded of top leaders—to take home only what really rings true. This is why Prime Minister Koizumi's convictions, in a fundamental sense, never wavered. And when he did speak, his words came with an intensity and freshness that reached the listener at a truly deep level.

After the collapse of the bubble, there was a rush to implement a variety of reforms in Japan. Nonetheless, because policy decisions were driven by the bureaucracy and by *zoku giin* (Diet members who act in the interest of certain government ministries and the industries they regulate), the necessary reforms were all postponed to another day. The public felt powerless. Overseas observers, too, began to voice concern about Japan. An article on the Japanese economy in the February 16–22, 2001 issue of *The Economist* exemplified the period's gloomy outlook for the Japanese economy, forcefully warning that the Japanese banking problem was the greatest financial threat to the world economy, and even raising the possibility of a global financial panic starting in Japan.

It was perfectly clear that revitalizing Japan would require forging ahead with the necessary reforms under a strong political leader; a leader who would hold the proper course without wavering, a leader of uncompromising principle. I felt it would be a miracle for such an unorthodox person to assume the office of prime minister in Japan. In typical Japanese politics, which are concerned with influence-peddling and scornful of top-down decision-making, such a person would not normally rise to the top.

Nevertheless, Koizumi assumed office on April 26, 2001 amid a national frenzy, ushering in the "Miracle Cabinet."

1. The Arrival of an Unfettered Leader

The people wanted Koizumi

How is it that a maverick like Koizumi Junichirō was selected to be prime minister when his rise to the highest political office in the land should have been unthinkable given the conventional wisdom about Japanese politics? And how did he manage to sustain such high approval ratings for five and a half years? The answer lies in the context of Japan's "lost decade" of economic stagnation. These ten years were more than just a time of economic deterioration: the refusal of politics and the broader social system to change drove the nation as a whole into a period of conspicuous functional decline.

To put this in more concrete economic terms, a long-range perspective was needed to strengthen socioeconomic fundamentals. The situation required not only short-term demand-driven policies but also broad structural reforms to strengthen the supply side as a whole.

Economist Clement Juglar, considered the father of business cycle theory, offered the profound observation that "the only cause of depression is prosperity." What Juglar points out is that an economy necessarily cycles through periods of prosperity and decline. Governments and central banks use policy in an attempt to minimize the magnitude of the swings, but regardless of the efforts made, the cycle itself cannot be completely controlled. Temporary booms and busts are unavoidable.

Conversely, Juglar's observation also suggests something else: that although the cycle may be unavoidable, the median point around which the cycle fluctuates is important. You have to ask fundamental questions like, "Does the economy, though sometimes better and sometimes worse, have a core growth rate of 1 percent, or does the cycle center on 3 percent growth?"

After the collapse of the bubble, Japan was resigned to a low level of economic growth, and in fact the economy fluctuated with an average of about 1 percent growth. Compared to the mid-4-percent growth experienced during the preceding decade of the 1980s, this was a drastic decline. As Juglar noted, economies swing better and they swing worse, yet in the case of the Japanese economy, the situation remained negative for an awfully long time. Root causes in fundamental aspects of the economy needed to be addressed.

Nevertheless, during this period the government sought economic recovery entirely through the expansion of government spending. In a recession caused by a temporary shortfall of demand, there may well be a role for a policy of reining in the magnitude of a cycle through increased public spending (though, as Buchanan and Wagner note, there is no guarantee). Yet it was evident that such an extended period of low growth was due not to a temporary shortfall of demand but to the very makeup of the economy—to a supply-side pathology. Although strengthening it would require a variety of structural reforms, the central economic policy of the Japanese government during the 1990s was to stimulate demand through fiscal expansion.

Actually, the importance of structural reform was already being officially discussed within the government during the time of the Obuchi administration, in a report by the Economic Strategy Council, a body that was chaired by Higuchi Hirotarō (then president of Asahi Breweries) and on which I served with, among others, Professor Nakatani Iwao (currently president of Tama University). The council argued that the changing economic climate should be addressed by promoting deregulation and privatization—by increasing the potential for growth by tapping into the freewheeling thinking of the private sector. The end of the Cold War and the expansion of market economies around the world had brought a sharp rise in global competition. At the same time, dramatic technological progress created demand for the development of a socioeconomic framework suited for the "digital revolution." In other words, Japan found itself right in the middle of a massive shift in the global competitive environment as new frontiers were emerging in both markets and technology.

Nevertheless, the economic policy implemented by the government consisted only of fiscal expansion through increased public works. Additional economic measures through supplemental budgets and the like in the 1990s reached a cumulative total of ¥130 trillion. Government fixed-capital formation, which had been 6.4 percent of GDP at the end of the 1980s, rose to 8.4 percent by FY 1995.

This inclination to rely exclusively on the expansion of public works throughout the 1990s was not simply a matter of issuing the wrong prescription for the economy. Clearly, the policy of expanding public works also has a political dimension.

The construction industry is known to have strong ties to the party in power. The industry supports the party through political contributions and electoral cooperation, while the party supports the industry by expanding public works. The bureaucratic machine maintains enormous influence by meditating the relationship between the two. Numerous scholars have analyzed this "iron triangle" linking industry, politicians (specifically, *zoku giin*, or politicians with a vested interest in a given policy field), and bureaucrats.

No matter how much one tries to expand demand though financial policy, the effectiveness will be short-lived unless deregulation and the disposal of nonperforming loans are also given sufficient attention. This is why, despite the ¥130 billion in additional economic measures implemented in the 1990s, the average growth rate remained no better than about 1 percent. Ultimately, the economy stagnated during this period rather than improved; the only steady growth was in the budget deficit. After being momentarily eliminated in 1990, budget deficits grew during the next decade; in the sense that things were unsustainable as they were, they looked a lot like effective bankruptcy.

Revitalizing the economy and putting the lost decade behind us required fundamental changes in economic policy—nothing less than structural reform. It was essential to undertake a drastic overhaul that touched on the central issue of the interdependence of politics and industry. Accomplishing this required the installation of a miracle prime minister. A strong leader like Koizumi, who talked of "smashing the Liberal Democratic Party" and, later, how he was "willing to face death" for the sake of postal privatization, enjoyed phenomenal popular support.

Reform demands an oddball

Prime Minister Koizumi is frequently described using the term *henjin*, following the appellation employed by Tanaka Makiko (foreign minister in the first Koizumi cabinet) during the 1998 campaign for president of the Liberal Democratic Party. In a controversial wisecrack, she described the contest between Obuchi Keizō, Kajiyama Seiroku, and Koizumi Junichirō as a fight among a *bonjin* (mediocre man), a *gunjin* (soldier), and a *henjin* (oddball). Leaving aside the issue of whether it is appropriate to describe candidates for prime minister in such terms, I think describing Koizumi as an oddball actually has positive connotations and brilliantly captures something essential about him.

As I mentioned above, in addition to the economic aspects, the structural problems facing Japan are integrated with the political interests that support them. The nature of such problems is that an ordinary politician bound by political constraints—even one who has risen to a powerful position such as that of prime minister—simply cannot effect change. Reform is only possible under a leader free of vested interests and unaffiliated with people or groups bound by such interests. Under Japanese politics as usual, it would be all but inconceivable for such a person to assume the role of prime minister, at the pinnacle of both party and government.

Before being elected prime minister, Koizumi had previously campaigned for the position both in 1995, when Hashimoto Ryūtarō soundly beat him, and in 1998, when he faced Obuchi and Kajiyama and was forced to settle for third place. Japanese politics dealt harshly with a candidate who rejected ties to special interests and championed reform.

Nevertheless, amid the stagnation of the lost decade, the public finally came to seek a maverick leader like Koizumi. Candidates in the 2001 Liberal Democratic Party presidential campaign appealed to voters from April 11 through voting day on April 24. Polls at the midpoint of the campaign, however, began to show Koizumi, who had at first seemed no more likely to prevail than in his previous campaigns, with a commanding lead.

Just after these interim polls, I met Koizumi at a restaurant in Akasaka, joining my friend the executive who facilitated the study groups I mentioned earlier. During dinner, Koizumi, with his usual jauntiness, talked about how things were beginning to go his way. I sensed that we might really see the birth of a great leader and couldn't help noticing myself tensing up.

I was invited to attend the spring imperial garden party a few days later on April 17 and there had the opportunity to speak with Diet member Abe Shinzō (who later became prime minister). At the time, Abe was working hard as a young representative of the Mori faction in support of the Koizumi campaign. Abe presented his own analysis of the election, speaking excitedly about how clear the shift was to Koizumi's advantage. The countdown to the emergence of Koizumi as prime minister had begun.

A clean break with vested interests

Numerous anecdotes illustrate Prime Minister Koizumi's uniqueness, but I think it would be somewhat off-target to brand him an oddball as a result. The important thing is Koizumi's extraordinary ability to focus—his tenacious will. It is something I felt keenly and constantly after beginning my work as a cabinet member.

After the formation of his cabinet, Koizumi celebrated his sixtieth birthday. One cabinet member sent him a bouquet of flowers, but Koizumi went out of his way to have it returned, explaining that it was his practice never to accept gifts from people. On another occasion, a cabinet member who had returned from business overseas presented Koizumi with a necktie bought during the trip. This, too, Koizumi refused to accept for the same reason.

These are both minor examples, but they demonstrate Koizumi's strong desire to prevent such attachments from interfering with his political activities. Some might call Koizumi an oddball for not accepting birthday presents from close friends, but such is the Koizumi way. Eliminating such ties and taking a principled stance enabled him to embark, without wavering, on a path of thorough reform. I think it was the people's visceral understanding of this attitude that led them to hold such high expectations of Koizumi.

This posture of Koizumi's would also be on full display in many aspects of the reform discussed later. In a Japanese political culture that values personal relationships above all, where an accounting is made of past debts, it is amazing that someone like Koizumi managed to keep being elected for so many years. That he would assume the top leadership position of prime minister is unprecedented. When Koizumi won the party presidency and I was asked to serve as minister, I knew instinctively that Japan was sure to change.

Actually, I had once received a similar request during the formation of an earlier cabinet. Naturally, I thought it was an honor that a scholar like myself should be asked, but I had lived my life planning to be an academic and was quite satisfied with my life as a researcher. I certainly couldn't imagine working in the unfamiliar world of politics, and declined on the spot.

When Koizumi approached me, however, I was overcome by a completely different reaction. This was the miracle prime minister—a man who was dedicating himself to the fight to change Japan. I felt that if there were something I could do, I owed it to myself not to run away but to rally to the cause. As I look back now, I can see that this may have been the naïve and reckless decision of a political outsider. Still, there was something substantial about Prime Minister Koizumi that inspired such thoughts. It wasn't anything as simple as Koizumi's personal charisma, or our personal relationship until that point. Nor, as some have suggested, was it merely that I saw an opportunity to put my own ideas as a specialist into practice. It was something bigger; I had a vision of Koizumi speaking for the Japan of today and standing up to fight the good fight.

2. The Launch of the Koizumi Cabinet

The Koizumi study group

Nudged along by the executive previously mentioned, a series of special study sessions were begun shortly before Koizumi officially declared his candidacy for the party presidency. The idea was to help develop a concrete management framework in preparation for when it came time to really administer the government. We met a total of five or six times to engage in focused policy debate related to the specifics of managing an administration. It was my job to select the speakers.

I identified experts from various fields, people I could trust whom I had come to know through my work as a researcher, and asked them to give lectures. Not only were they all talented scholars working at the forefront of their fields, they also aspired to making Japan better. All of them responded positively when they heard the project was for Koizumi. Despite his busy schedule in readying himself for the presidential election, Koizumi made the time to attend, and the sessions resulted in active discussions.

These discussions were of enormous benefit in getting the Koizumi administration off to the running start that I discuss later. One of the things that left the deepest impression on me personally was a comment by Professor Kitaoka Shinichi, a political scientist from the University of Tokyo who would later serve as deputy permanent representative of Japan to the United Nations:

> Until now, the Liberal Democratic Party has distributed cabinet posts sequentially based on the number of times people have been elected, while also maintaining equilibrium among party factions. Furthermore, to ensure that posts are distributed to nearly everyone who has a minimum number of electoral victories, cabinets have been frequently reshuffled. However, this prevents even a strong politician from continuing as minister and executing policy responsibly. This results in policies that can only retreat to the safe ground of dependence on the bureaucracy, which led us to the critical situation we find ourselves in today. That's why, if you really want to pursue effective policy, you must choose the best people to be your ministers and plan to stick with them for a stable cabinet.

Kitaoka made a convincing case. For Koizumi, who was trying to transcend faction-based politics and dependence on the bureaucracy, I think this notion of a stable cabinet must have struck a chord. In fact, Prime Minister Koizumi would form five cabinets. In doing so, however, he never chose people based on their rank in terms of past electoral victories, and he remained committed to a policy of targeting individuals rather than working through factions. In this sense, he stuck fast to the spirit of choosing the right people for the right jobs and maintaining a stable cabinet.

Other topics that were discussed were the need to move quickly in disposing of nonperforming loans; to seek, as other countries were, to restore the primary balance as a first step toward achieving fiscal health; and to move slowly but deliberately to ensure steady progress. The importance of being strategic in providing information about government policy was also discussed.

As I discuss later, in Koizumi's first general policy speech, immediately after launching his cabinet he introduced a number of key phrases, such as "no growth without reform" and "town meeting," that indicated his drive for reform and helped get the administration off to a running start. The discussions at the study group played an important role in suggesting a direction for the concrete reform policies that came later.

The first cabinet

On April 26, 2001, the Japanese Diet named a new prime minister. Under today's parliamentary cabinet system, where the ruling party or parties form the government, the head of the ruling coalition's leading party is chosen to be prime minister. Accordingly, Koizumi Junichirō became Japan's eighty-seventh prime minister. This marked the birth of the Koizumi cabinet, which would enjoy strong popular support, and support of an unconventional prime minister. Mass media coverage was nothing short of frenzied.

Needless to say, the biggest challenge in forming a cabinet was personnel—deciding whom to pick. The first Koizumi cabinet was distinguished by the fact that it completely ignored the existence of factions; the prime minister himself selected his cabinet by targeting specific individuals. Although it is perfectly natural from an organizational management perspective for a chief executive to exercise personal authority and responsibility in appointing his own executives, this had not happened before in Japanese politics. This bold execution of so ordinary an act had enormous political repercussions. Normally, each party faction would recommend candidates for cabinet posts, which would then be chosen to maintain factional balance. By interviewing each faction, reporters were for the most part able to predict candidates in advance. This time, however, was completely different.

Also remarkable was Koizumi's selection for cabinet posts of five women and three people drawn from the private sector rather than from the ranks of National Diet members—a bold selection that pointedly ignored the traditional tacit agreement that ministerial posts were awarded to those who had accumulated enough election victories. Koizumi formed a cabinet that transcended factional and tenure balance. In doing so he acted decisively and alone, without consulting anyone else.

I received the call that day around 3:30 in the afternoon. I can remember being met, having made my way to the prime minister's official residence, with a bewildering cacophony of flashing cameras and noise. I was directed to the cabinet waiting room on the second floor, where I briefly greeted the other new members of the cabinet. Takebe Tsutomu, who had been appointed minister of agriculture, forestry, and fisheries, and would later serve as secretary general of the Liberal Democratic Party, smiled at me and said, "Ah, Professor Takenaka! This cabinet will be implementing reforms that are important for Japan. I look forward to working with you." Not having yet gotten my bearings, I was most grateful for his words. Later, when the BSE issue broke, Takebe would contribute to reform at the Ministry of Agriculture, Forestry and Fisheries by conducting a thorough investigation. Nevertheless, some would take the twisted tack of questioning Takebe's own responsibility for the very ills of the past that he was trying to reform. The constant fight against such pressures was one of the prices of reform.

The mass media provided extensive coverage for days, focusing in particular on individualistic cabinet members such as Foreign Minister Tanaka Makiko and Finance Minister Shiokawa Masajūrō. Still, the content and approach of such reporting plainly indicated that the media at the time was having fun with Koizumi's "cabinet theatrics." Most observers tended to look with amusement on his selection of a cabinet composed of individuals irrespective of factional allegiance. Many members of this first Koizumi cabinet, myself included, would never have become ministers had it been formed under the customary rules of faction and tenure.

The coverage of Foreign Minister Tanaka, who was known for her outspoken, pull-no-punches style, was particularly intense. Rather than being favorable, it unreservedly treated her as a curiosity. It was evident that the media would toss about various stories and then turn to the attack. I personally tried to avoid being provoked by such coverage, but it was no easy task.

Shortly after the cabinet was formed, I had the opportunity to have dinner with Fujinami Takao, who served as chief cabinet secretary under Prime Minister Nakasone. I had been introduced to Fujinami by a senior colleague from my days at the Japan Development Bank (now the Development Bank of Japan), and had discussed policy matters with him occasionally in the past. Concerned about my unexpected decision to accept a ministerial post, he spoke with the voice of experience in offering the following advice: "You're probably going to face a lot of obstacles. Politicians have a rough time of it. Even if you're up against another politician, there's common ground to work things out, but there's just no fighting the media. Don't waste your breath. Do your best, but please be careful." The media had fiercely attacked Fujinami over the Recruit scandal. To tell the truth, I do not think I fully understood his advice at the time. Still, observing the extraordinary coverage of Tanaka Makiko made me aware in my own way of how hard it would be to work as a minister at the center of government.

And so it was that the first Koizumi cabinet was launched amid an unusual clamor of media attention and popular interest.

The general policy speech that got things rolling

With the entire country watching, Koizumi gave his general policy speech to the full session of the

Diet on May 7, the twelfth day after the launch of the cabinet.

Speeches presented by the prime minister to the Diet include the administrative policy speeches given at the start of the ordinary Diet session at the beginning of the year, and the general policy speeches given at the start of extraordinary sessions and sessions that follow the launch of a new cabinet. In general, while administrative policy speeches are somewhat lengthy affairs that cover policy broadly, the nature of a general policy speech, which tends to be shorter and more targeted, is to give a clear accounting of the prime minister's priorities. In both cases, however, the prime minister is addressing the Diet, and the speech is extremely important to the management of his administration. At the same time, opposition parties look to these speeches as a source of material to attack.

A prime minister's speeches before the Diet have special significance in setting the direction of policy. Governmental policy is normally determined through a long and difficult process. First, the policy direction is set by coordinating the interests of the various ministries and agencies within the government. Then a concrete plan must be worked out. And then things get really difficult. Under the parliamentary system, the fundamental principle that the ruling party forms the government means that setting government policy requires passing through the party process. Specifically, this means deliberation by the Policy Affairs Research Council and ultimately the approval of the supreme decision-making body, the Executive Council.

Speeches by the prime minister, however, are subject to none of this tedious process. What to weave into the draft of the speech, therefore, can be a decisive factor for a prime minister who wants to take the lead in establishing a policy direction. Prime Minister Koizumi took particular care in focusing his energies on drafting his first general policy speech. I, too, did my best to contribute some good ideas.

Drafts of speeches before the Diet are normally prepared by the prime minister's office, specifically the Cabinet Affairs Office. Well aware of the importance of speeches before the Diet, the bureaucrats at each ministry work desperately to have phrasing beneficial to their own ministry included in the text. The prime minister's office, therefore, always finds itself waging a battle for the control of information as it tries to draft a text whose content is driven by the prime minister.

Koizumi was fully aware of the situation and made the special gesture of instructing the Cabinet Affairs Office to pay attention to what I had to say. I was sincerely grateful for these instructions, as they helped ensure that structural reform got off to a running start.

Over five and a half years, incidentally, the Cabinet Affairs Office, having received similar instructions from Prime Minister Koizumi, always consulted me in advance when preparing a speech before the Diet. And each time I was able to circumvent the complicated party process in aiming for an in-depth speech that would promote further reform led by the prime minister.

Prime Minister Koizumi's general policy speech before the 151st session of the Diet on May 7, 2001 was watched attentively by all quarters. Cheers rose from the ruling party seats, and even representatives from the opposition leaned forward expectantly to hear this special speech by the prime minister. The speech brimmed with enthusiasm for reform, and, looking back today, I think it clearly signaled the starting point for Koizumi's structural reforms.

In the speech, Koizumi first declared that his cabinet would carry out reform based on the belief that there could be no growth without it, and then committed himself to taking an approach unbound by past experience, one of "no fear, no hesitation, and no constraints." Broadly speaking, he presented an economic policy menu with three main goals. First was the final disposal of nonperforming loans within a period of two to three years. The Koizumi reforms would not have been possible without success in disposing of nonperforming loans. Second was the creation of a competitive economic system for the twenty-first century. Needless to say, although the wording was still abstract at this point, here one finds a hint of the postal privatization and other deregulation and administrative reforms to come. Third was fiscal structural reform. Here he announced a clear change of course from the policies of the past, including a reduction in public works spending, and presented the goal of "not relying on new borrowing for expenditures other than interest payments on past loans." Needless to say, this is the goal of ensuring a surplus in the primary balance.

In addition, so that these reforms could be accomplished through dialogue with the public, Koizumi also used his speech before the Diet to announce plans for a series of town meetings and the launch of an email newsletter.

As should be clear, the foundation for this framework was laid in the deliberations held during sessions of the Koizumi study group. The idea of town meetings and an email newsletter, by the way, came from a student in one of my seminars when I was teaching at Keio University. Personally, I found myself greatly excited by such ideas that sprang from young people. Email newsletters are commonplace today, but at the time people were only maybe thinking of setting up websites, and it was a real innovation for the administration to communicate directly with the public (those who signed up, that is) through such means. I conveyed to the prime minister my desire to see this vision realized, and it was incorporated into the speech.

There was one area, however, where my expectations were off the mark: when Koizumi announced the short-term goal of capping new government bond issues at no more than ¥30 trillion for the following fiscal year. The value of government bond issues, after all, is the difference between annual expenditures and tax revenues. Naturally, when both are in flux, their difference (the value of government bond issues) can fluctuate greatly. Although establishing a short-term target had the advantage of being easy to understand, it was also risky. I suspect a bureaucrat with the Ministry of Finance probably planted the idea, but this ¥30 trillion target was a commitment Koizumi had made during his campaign for party president, and it found its way into his speech before the Diet. As is widely known, the Taxation Bureau's later failure in estimating tax revenue generated controversy by making it impossible to achieve this target in the first year. To this day I feel the Ministry of Finance bears a heavy responsibility on this point.

A masterful response to questions at the Diet

Koizumi's first speech before the Diet was certainly not a long one, but it clearly established basic policies, such as leaving to the private sector what the private sector does best and delegating to local governments what local governments are capable of. It also generated numerous key phrases, such as the "spirit of one hundred sacks of rice," referring to an anecdote about how the Nagaoka clan, having received a sizable food donation during hard times, sold it and invested the proceeds in a school rather than consuming it immediately, thereby putting up with hardship today to create a better tomorrow.

The masterstroke, though, was the way the prime minister handled questions concerning the speech from each party's representatives. As demonstrated then, Koizumi's style from the outset was to move to the attack with an aggressive challenge as a forceful driver of policy. For this he would always command the attention of both the people and the mass media.

Two days after the speech before the Diet, during the House of Representatives plenary session, Edano Yukio of the Democratic Party of Japan stood to ask Koizumi about his basic position on postal privatization, a pet issue of Koizumi's for many years. The prime minister, rather than reading his prepared remarks, responded boldly with raised voice, ". . . the nonsensical reasoning of the former Ministry of Posts and Communication won't hold water with the Koizumi administration . . ."

As a general rule, questions before the plenary session, particularly when the prime minister is responding, are answered with a solemn recitation of texts prepared by the bureaucracy. Concerned about consistency with past policy, it is difficult to bluntly criticize present conditions. Yet the Koizumi style was completely different from the moment he took office. Unconstrained by the prepared answers, he responded to questions directly, based on his own way of thinking. And, rather than limit himself to lukewarm criticism of the status quo, he mercilessly and completely rejected the bad for what it was. I imagine that the bureaucrats from the former Ministry of Posts and Communications (now the Ministry of Internal Affairs and Communications) must have felt bowled over with shock as they listened to the exchange. Personally, I remember listening from the raised tier of seats for ministers and feeling quite giddy.

And so the Koizumi administration overturned various Japanese political conventions and got underway with a flurry of exceptions. This was, of course, only the start. But in leading the way for the unprecedented structural reform still to come, it was unmistakably a good start. The public had its expectations for powerful leadership raised by this unconventional prime minister. The first public opinion survey NHK conducted after the launch of the cabinet on April 26, 2001, showed a very high level of support—the highest on record—for the administration, at 81 percent. Seen against the 7 percent approval rating of the Mori administration that immediately preceded it, this was a historical upturn, indeed.

Courtesy of author.

Originally published as chapter 1 in *The Structural Reforms of the Koizumi Cabinet: An Insider's Account of the Economic Revival of Japan*, published by Nihon Keizai Shimbun Shuppansha in 2008; slightly abridged.

IV-(2) Privatize the Postal Services

Matsubara Satoru

Japan Echo, 2004

Throughout much of the history of administrative reform in Japan, the very idea of privatizing the postal services (mail, savings, and insurance) was considered taboo. Even the second Ad Hoc Commission on Administrative Reform of the early 1980s, whose bold recommendations led to the privatization of the Japanese National Railways Public Corporation, the Tobacco and Salt Public Corporation, and the Nippon Telegraph and Telephone Public Corporation, was unable to consider postal service privatization. Subsequent blue-ribbon panels on the promotion of administrative and fiscal reform have similarly refrained from referring to privatization of the postal services in their official reports; at most they have touched on the issue of achieving greater efficiency in postal service operations as part of minor sections discussing state-operated enterprises.

Meanwhile, the assets of the postal savings system have ballooned to an amount in excess of ¥250 trillion, interfering greatly with the operation of the private-sector financial system. On top of this, the postal life-insurance system has assets amounting to ¥110 trillion; together with the postal savings funds, these form a huge pool of assets managed by the government, leading some to suggest only half-jokingly that Japan operates under a regime of "financial socialism." The fact that this huge pool of funds exists apart from the market, flowing into inefficient government-affiliated "special corporations" and the like, has undeniably acted as one of the elements sapping the vitality of the Japanese economy.

The Hashimoto Council Backs Down

One major factor that long hindered reform of the three postal services was the fact that they were operated as part of the government proper rather than as a separate set of public corporations. In addition, the idea of reform was blocked by the great political power of groups with a vested interest in the status quo, such as the National Association of Commissioned Postmasters and the Japan Postal Workers' Union.

The situation seemed to change under the administrative reform drive launched by the administration of Prime Minister Hashimoto Ryūtarō in 1996, which set the goal of halving the number of central government ministries and agencies. Since this reform initiative concerned itself with the organization of the government itself, it also considered the possible reform of the postal services. Furthermore, this reform program aimed not merely to halve the number of ministries and agencies, but also to cut back on their actual functions. The principle proposed by the Administrative Reform Council that Hashimoto himself chaired was to distinguish between planning and implementation, with the government to limit its functions to the former. Needless to say, the postal services are on the implementation side, and so the discussions of the council led in the direction of moving these services outside the government—in other words, privatizing them.

In September 1997 the Administrative Reform Council came up with its interim report, which included a call for the postal services to be split up into their three major constituent operations and partially privatized. More specifically, the recommendation was for privatization of the postal life-insurance system, "preparation for privatization" of the postal savings system, and continued government operation of the mail service.

This proposal was consistent with the trends in postal reform seen in other countries, and I believe it was right on target. But the release of the interim report produced an outpouring of opposition from the entire camp of vested-interest groups, including the Ministry of Posts and Telecommunications, the National Association of Commissioned Postmasters, and the Japan Postal Workers' Union. And in the final report that it released just three months later, the council backed down from its privatization proposal, calling instead for the three postal services to be left together and turned into a single new government-operated public corporation. This was the basis for the postal service reform plan that was actually adopted, according to which a postal services agency (Japan Post) was to be established in 2003.

A Peculiar Plan

To those of us who are experts on privatization and deregulation, the term *government-operated public corporation* itself has a very peculiar ring. The whole idea of having a public corporation is for its operations to be separate from the government, as was the case with the Japanese National Railways, the Tobacco and Salt Public Corporation, and Nippon Telegraph and Telephone. The plan for this new state-run public corporation involves a number of logical contradictions, the biggest of which is that its employees are to be civil servants. This was not the case with any of the three former public corporations, nor has it been the case with any of the various other organizations set up as special corporations under government auspices.

Obviously, there is a limit on what can be accomplished in terms of approaching private-sector-style management in a public corporation whose employees are civil servants. If post offices were privatized, they could sell stationery, for example. And in some other countries where they have already been privatized, they even sell souvenirs. But civil servants could never be allowed to sell souvenirs.

Each of the three postal services competes with the private sector to a large degree: The postal savings system competes with banks, the postal life-insurance system with life-insurance companies, and the parcel post service with parcel delivery companies. A government-run corporation providing these services is bound to have its freedom of movement severely curtailed in practice, and sooner or later it will inevitably find itself running into operational difficulties.

A further problem with the plan for a government-run public corporation is the existence of the 19,000 "special post offices" that account for more than 70 percent of the 25,000 post offices around the country. The system operates by designating private individuals to be post office directors, a job that carries national civil service status, and reforming their homes or other private edifices to serve as post offices. The common pattern is for the post office to be on the ground level and the director's family quarters to be upstairs.

Incidentally, special post office directors become civil servants without having to pass any of the regular national civil service examinations. That is why I refer to this system as a back door into the civil service.

Under this system, even the smallest rural post office has a director earning a substantial salary. And in addition to its director, each of the special post offices generally has several civil servants working as postal employees (though, unlike the director, these employees are required to have passed a civil service exam).

In addition, the mail service has a system of "postal agencies," under which post office operations are contracted out to private-sector individuals or organizations. Virtually all of the post offices one sees in places like department stores and train-station buildings are in this category. They handle not only mail services but also postal savings and insurance transactions. In fact, just about the only service available at special post offices that postal agencies do not offer is content-certified mail.

Changing all the special post offices into postal agencies would reduce costs substantially. A single special post-office director could, for example, run ten postal agencies. That would make it possible to cut the number of directors from the present 19,000 to 1,900. Furthermore, if the postal services were privatized, the special post offices could double as convenience stores—or conversely, existing convenience stores could set up postal service counters.

Difficult Conditions for the Postal Services Corporation

In deciding to turn the postal services into a state-operated public corporation, the authorities have given up the option of exercising this sort of flexibility. Not only that, but in return for securing government-operated status, the postal services have been required to accept two conditions; namely, the elimination of investment of funds through the Fiscal Investment and Loan Program and the entry of private-sector enterprises into the mail business, both of which will severely impact the finances of the new public corporation.

With its assets of ¥250 trillion, the postal savings system is the biggest financial institution in the world. Traditionally the system had little need to concern itself with the investment of these funds, because for the most part they were handled by the Trust Fund Bureau of the Ministry of Finance, which invested them through the government's Fiscal Investment and Loan Program. The postal savings authority handled the investment of only a fraction of the total. But starting in April 2001, the system became responsible for the investment of all of its own funds.

For years the postal savings system sought to gain control over the investment of its own assets. Its wish has been granted, but when it is turned into a public corporation, it is bound to find itself subject to severe limitations on its investment freedom. Financial institutions ordinarily manage their portfolios by mixing stocks and other relatively high-risk assets with government bonds and other lower-risk assets. But the new public corporation will presumably be forbidden to make risky investments and required to hold the bulk of its funds in the form of government bonds and other low-risk assets. This will be particularly true if, as is likely, depositors' principal and interest continue to be guaranteed by the government. It will not be acceptable for the public corporation to incur losses on its investments that will have to be covered out of the government's regular tax revenues. And, needless to say, low-risk investments will be low-return investments. So with the choice to become part of a government-operated public corporation, the postal savings system has abandoned the option of developing truly attractive financial products.

The entry of private-sector enterprises into the mail business is also a source of concern. The mail service has been running a deficit for the past three years. Postage for an ordinary letter is now ¥80. If you include the price of the envelope and writing paper, the cost per letter probably comes to about ¥100. Meanwhile, there is now a new phone service that lets you make a three-minute call anywhere in the country for ¥20. So for ¥100 you can talk for fifteen minutes. And of course, if you use email, the cost per message is infinitesimal.

The mail service still makes a lot of money by delivering bills, but this business is now being challenged by the spread of electronic billing systems. NTT DoCoMo, the leading mobile phone service, has started providing a ¥100 monthly discount for users who opt to receive their bills by email. If other utilities like electric and gas companies switch to email billing, the mail service's revenue base will be severely eroded.

And on top of this, it is expected that private businesses will be allowed to enter the field of providing regular mail service when the new public corporation is set up. If the corporation has to cut prices to compete with these new entrants, its already bleak earnings picture will become even bleaker. Ordinarily the prescription to deal with such a situation would be to grant the corporation a large degree of freedom, permitting it to get into businesses like home moving, for example, as the parcel delivery companies in the private sector already have. But there is no chance that civil servants will be allowed to work as movers. So the corporation will have to try to match its competitors' price cuts as best it can while its earnings picture continues to deteriorate and while its freedom to maneuver continues to be limited. There is a danger that it will follow the same path of financial decline as the national railway system did in the past.

Another surprising feature of the government's plans for the new public corporation is that a separate management organ, the Postal Services Policy and Planning Bureau, has been set up within the Ministry of Public Management, Home Affairs, Posts and Telecommunications. Since Japan Post will surely be topped with its own management structure, this organ seems like a redundant superstructure. But there is a good explanation for its creation: The ministry wants to hold on to regulatory authority over the postal services. As we have noted above, the three services (mail, savings, and insurance) are all in competition with private-sector businesses. But even after the new public corporation is launched, they are to be subject to a different set of regulatory laws from their private-sector counterparts. For example, the postal savings system will be subject to supervision by this bureau under the Postal Savings Act, unlike banks, which are regulated by the Financial Services Agency. Similarly, the mail service will be supervised by this bureau, unlike private-sector parcel delivery companies, which are overseen by the Ministry of Land, Infrastructure, Transport and Tourism.

Surely organizations operating the same sorts of businesses in the same market should be subject to the same regulatory laws and supervisory agencies. The Postal Services Policy and Planning Bureau should be abolished, and the regulatory legislation should be revised so that each of the postal services will be covered by the same law and supervised by the same agency as its private-sector counterparts.

A Concrete Proposal for Privatization

The plans for the government-operated public corporation are full of contradictions, and to make matters worse, a law now prohibits its operations from being reviewed after it is established. This prohibition shows the power of the postal interests lobby. Other recent laws introducing major organizational changes, such as the law splitting up Nippon Telegraph and Telephone and the law establishing the public system of long-term care insurance, have included provisions mandating review within a certain period following their implementation. But the new public corporation must never be reviewed. It is supposed to be maintained forever, contradictions notwithstanding.

However, the situation has changed somewhat since Koizumi Junichirō became prime minister this April. Regardless of the review ban, early in June Koizumi launched a panel to consider the future operation of the postal services following the establishment of the new public corporation. It is headed by Tanaka Naoki (president of the 21st Century Public Policy Institute) and has nine other members, including Kasai Yoshiyuki, president of the Central Japan Railway Co. (one of the companies resulting from the breakup and privatization of the Japanese National Railways). I am also on this panel. The majority of the members, including Tanaka and me, are privatization advocates.

This group is not so much an advisory council to the prime minister as an organ reporting directly to him. It can be expected to take major strides in proposing policies aimed at privatization of the postal services. The actual content of the proposals is subject to the panel's deliberations, but one approach that has already been put forward is the one drawn up by the nonpartisan legislators' study group on postal services privatization chaired by Koizumi, with Matsuzawa Shigefumi (Democratic Party of Japan) acting as managing secretary; I served as expert advisor for the group. The proposal it made calls for the postal services to be split into their three main constituents under a holding company and then to be privatized. (The proposal is presented in a book coedited by Koizumi and Matsuzawa titled *Yūsei min'eika ron* [The Case for Postal Service Privatization], published by PHP Institute in 1999.)

One attractive feature of this proposal is that it would make it possible for a variety of reform initiatives to be undertaken in the privatized companies after the breakup in line with their specific operating conditions. This is an approach that has worked well in the case of the Japanese National Railways. In 1987 the national railways were split up into a number of operating companies, mainly on regional lines. Each was set up as an unlisted government-owned stock company. Three of the companies—East Japan Railway Co., Central Japan Railway Co., and West Japan Railway Co.—subsequently did well enough for their shares to be listed on the stock market, and in June this year it was decided that they would be completely privatized. Meanwhile, though, other companies in the Japan Railways group, such as the Hokkaido Railway Co., have yet to be listed and continue to receive tax breaks from the government.

When some people hear the word *privatization*, they assume it means complete privatization in a single stroke, but as the example of the JR companies shows, it is possible for the process to be conducted over an extended period of, say, ten or fifteen years, taking into account the trends in the operations of the individual companies involved. This is an advantage of using the establishment of government-owned stock companies as the first step.

Needless Fears of Gaps in the Network

Back when Prime Minister Hashimoto's Administrative Reform Council released its initial report suggesting the postal services be split up and partially privatized, the former Ministry of Posts and Telecommunications conducted a campaign based on the claim that privatization would make it impossible for the network of local post offices to be maintained. This claim ignores the reality of how such networks function.

The parcel delivery company Yamato Transport has set up a network that covers all of Japan, though there is no law requiring it to do so. NTT DoCoMo already provides its mobile phone services to regions encompassing 99.9 percent of the nation (in population terms) and is continuing to extend its coverage. In network-service industries, having a comprehensive network is a powerful business weapon.

Consider this comment: "Having a nationwide network that covers even depopulated and remote locations is one of our major strengths. Contrary to what the postal administration says, I believe that maintaining such a nationwide network is strategically crucial. To put it another way, if privatization were to produce a withdrawal of mail service from remote locations, we would be delighted. This would give us an unrivaled hold on the business in these locations" (from the above-cited *Yūsei min'eika ron*, pp. 150–51).

The author of these words is Koshijima Kuniyuki, a senior executive of Yamato Transport. In view of what he says, I believe that there is no need to worry about privatization causing gaps in the mail service network. But if people continued to be concerned about this possibility, it would be all right to enact some sort of legislation mandating the maintenance of post offices in remote locations and the continuation of universal mail delivery. Even now, for example, subsidies are being provided to the operators of bus routes in remote districts.

The postal services together represent a ¥4.2 trillion business and employ some 300,000 people. The post office network extends to 25,000 locations. The postal savings system, with more than ¥250 trillion in assets, is the world's largest financial institution. The services are closely linked to the everyday lives of people around the country. Privatization is the way to free this mammoth organization from the constraints of being a government-operated public corporation. The issues are how to avoid the emergence of gaps in the nationwide service network and how to keep the privatized organizations from overwhelming their existing rivals in the private sector.

In the panel that the prime minister has set up, we will be discussing such issues carefully over the coming year. The panel's deliberations are also likely to have a major impact on the design of the systems of the postal public corporation due to be launched in 2003. The government's handling of this matter will serve as a key test of its commitment to the structural reform program that Koizumi has proclaimed. We should recognize that privatization of the postal services is the trump card for revitalization of Japan's economy and society.

Courtesy of Japan Echo.

English version originally published in *Japan Echo* 31, no. 5 (Oct. 2004): 24–27.

Translated from "Yūsei min'eika: Nihon o saikasseika saseru kirifuda" [Postal Privatization: A Trump Card to Revive Japan], in *Voice* (August 2001): 64–71. (Courtesy of PHP Institute)

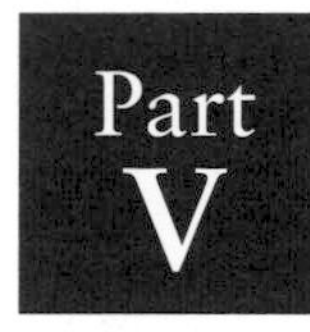

Part V

Abenomics

Abe Shinzō became Japan's prime minister for the second time in December 2012, and remained in power right through to September 2020. "Abenomics" was the name for the programs of economic policies spearheaded by his cabinet. Abenomics centered around the "three arrows" advocated by Abe immediately after his appointment. The first arrow was aggressive monetary policy; the second, flexible fiscal policy; and the third, a growth strategy to stimulate private-sector investment.

Komine Takao identifies achievements and issues with Abenomics approximately four years into the program in "Abenomics at a Watershed: Proper Approach to Monetary Policy," suggesting that the program might now need to change course.

In "Quantitative and Qualitative Monetary Easing Effects and Associate Risks," Iwata Kazumasa and Fueda-Samikawa Ikuko evaluate the effects and risks of quantitative and qualitative monetary easing in the second year of "monetary easing of a different dimension."

Murata Keiko addresses the limits of the government's series of growth strategies in "What Do Growth Strategies Need?: Sweeping Away Anxiety Regarding the Future" Noting that the growth strategies failed to boost corporate and household expectations, she points to the importance of work-style reforms in increasing expected lifetime income.

Okina Kunio is an economist who has consistently criticized the monetary policy of Abenomics. In his essay "Agenda for the BOJ Governor in His Second Term," he delineates the challenges facing BOJ governor Kuroda Haruhiko in his second term, which began in 2018.

V-(1) Abenomics at a Watershed

Proper Approach to Monetary Policy

Komine Takao

Discuss Japan—Japan Foreign Policy Forum, 2016

One of the main topics people have discussed since the start of Prime Minister Abe's second term in December 2012 is the government's economic policy, which is commonly referred to as Abenomics. Nearly three and half years have passed since then, and now it seems that the initial form of Abenomics has been driven to take a major change in direction. In this paper, I will discuss Abenomics, focusing primarily on its monetary policy. This particular area has been forced to take a different turn because the limitations of the policy's stance in the past are now apparent.

Abenomics is Beginning to Lose Touch with its Goals

It is easier to assess Abenomics by dividing it into two periods. The first period runs from the inauguration of the first cabinet of Prime Minister Abe to March 2014, a period during which the economy remained relatively steady. The second period runs from April 2014, a time at which the economy came to a temporary standstill.

First, I will use certain economic indicators to confirm a few things about these periods. There are three major economic goals that Abenomics aims to achieve: a 2 percent rate of increase in consumer prices, a 3 percent nominal growth rate, and a 2 percent real growth rate. The 2 percent rate of increase in consumer prices and other goals were clearly specified in the joint statement the government and the Bank of Japan (BOJ) jointly announced in January 2013 immediately after the inauguration of the Abe cabinet. The targets of the 3 percent nominal growth rate and the 2 percent real growth rate were presented in the growth strategy laid out in June 2013 (the official name is "Japan Revitalization Strategy: Japan is Back"), which stated that Japan aimed to secure an average annual economic growth rate of around a nominal 3 percent or a real 2 percent over the next ten years.

Last year three new "arrows" were launched, and the administration stated that the Japanese economy aims to increase nominal GDP to ¥600 trillion by FY 2020. However, this is nearly the same as the 3 percent nominal growth, because, according to the "economic recovery scenario" in the projections released by the Cabinet Office in July 2016 ("Economic and Fiscal Projections for Medium to Long Term Analysis"), the nominal GDP will rise to nearly ¥600 trillion (more precisely ¥583 trillion) by FY 2020 if the economy continues to grow at an annual rate of about 3 percent in the upcoming years. The first item (1) in figure 1 provides a comparison between changes in the rate of increase in consumer prices and the 2 percent target. Although consumer prices moved out of negative territory and leveled off at the 2 percent mark by the first half of 2014, in the second half of the year they began to deviate from the target and head toward the lower side. As of the time of writing, they have nearly returned to the level they were at when Abenomics began.

Items (2) and (3) provide a comparison between the expected value of GDP and the actual GDP in the event that the economy grows at a nominal rate of 3 percent and a real rate of 2 percent. Although GDP moved close to the target value up until early 2014 in both cases, over time it also began to deviate from the target and head toward the lower side.

The economic policy of Abenomics largely delivered its intended results in the first period,

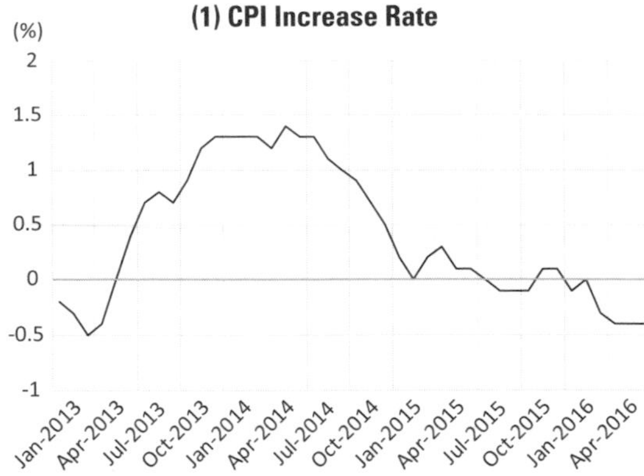

Source: Consumer Price Index (all items, excluding fresh food), Ministry of Internal Affairs and Communications.
Note: Data of FY 2014 (April 2014–March 2015) is reduced 2% as the impact of the consumption tax increase

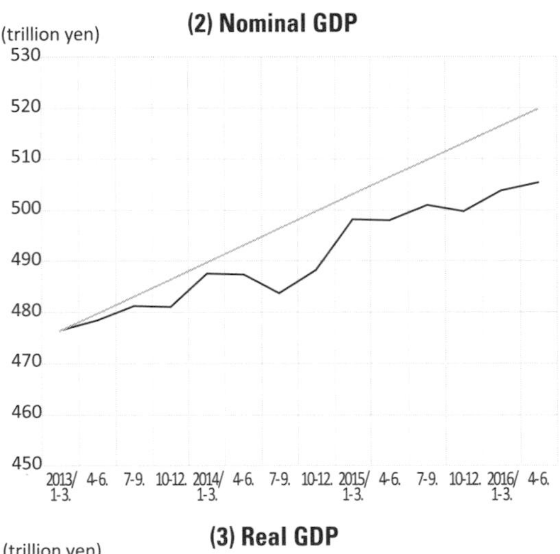

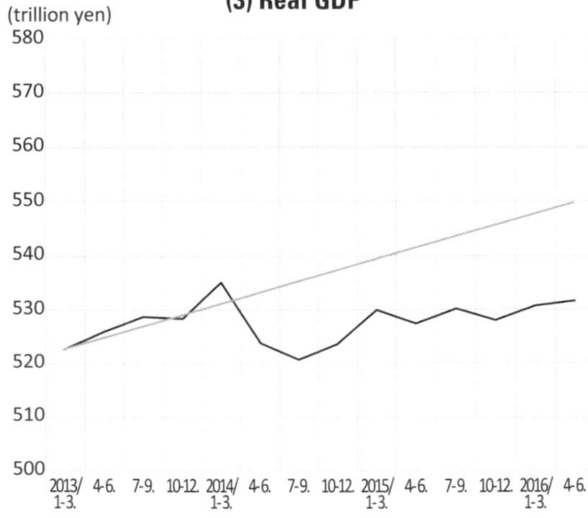

Figure 1. Targets of Abenomics and Actual Statistics

Note: The gray line represents the target; the black line plots the actual statistics.

but the actual economy began to deviate from the target in the second period, suggesting that the limitations of Abenomics had come to the surface.

Emerging Limitations and Adverse Effects of the So-Called Monetary Easing of a Different Dimension

Why has such a difference emerged between the first period and the second? In my opinion, it is because the economic effects that emerged in the first period represent an essentially short-term phenomenon that has not only disappeared, but has even had an adverse effect on the second period. This was particularly noticeable in Japan's monetary policy.

Monetary policy in Abenomics has generally proceeded along the following course. First, as mentioned previously, an inflation target calling for a 2 percent increase in consumer prices was clearly specified in the joint statement in January 2013 immediately after the inauguration of the first Abe cabinet. Next, the so-called monetary easing of a different dimension was launched under the auspices of Kuroda Haruhiko, the new governor of the BOJ, in April that year. Under this form of monetary easing, the BOJ intended to implement a monetary policy of a different dimension both quantitatively and qualitatively by (1) doubling the monetary base and the amount of the long-term government bonds and exchange-traded fund (ETF) holdings of the BOJ in two years, and (2) extending the average remaining life of long-term government bonds to be purchased by the bank by more than double to (3) achieve the 2 percent consumer price target as soon as possible in a roughly two-year period.

Given that it became difficult to achieve the 2 percent target, the BOJ implemented additional monetary easing measures, such as increasing the purchase amount of bonds to about ¥8 to 12 trillion every month in October 2014. Because consumer prices failed to reach 2 percent even with these measures, at the end of January 2016 the BOJ began adopting the so-called negative interest-rate policy of imposing a negative interest rate on some of the current accounts of banks at the BOJ.

As described earlier, this monetary policy produced great results during the first period of Abenomics. Unfortunately, these positive effects faded away in the second period, and ultimately resulted in a counteraction. The reasons for this development are as follows.

First, the limitations of the BOJ's surprise method of moving the market by announcing an unexpected and bold policy came to the surface. The initial impact of Abenomics came from an announcement. When the second Abe administration began in December 2012, the yen exchange rate fell and stock prices rose, even though the cabinet had yet to announce any policies. The market expected that once Prime Minister Abe came to power, the monetary policy would be eased significantly and a growth-oriented economic policy would be adopted.

This trend of a weaker yen and rising stock prices gained additional momentum following the implementation of strong "monetary easing of a different dimension" by the newly appointed BOJ governor Kuroda. Because this monetary policy was larger than many market players expected, it took the market by surprise and led it to drastically change its conventional views. This appeared to add extra momentum to the trend of the weaker yen and rising stock prices. Likewise, because additional large-scale monetary easing was implemented in October 2014 at a time the market did not expect, it once again reacted to this surprise, causing the value of the yen to fall. For this surprise policy method to succeed, the BOJ needs to send out an ongoing series of surprises that are highly praised by the market. However, while the negative interest-rate policy launched in January 2016 surprised the market, it failed to earn its favor, and in contrast, appears to have strengthened the market's deflationary mindset.

What stuck out in my mind at that time was a comment about negative interest rates made in the Economy Watchers' Survey (February 2016) conducted by the Cabinet Office. One general retailer said, "Elderly customers keep a tight hold on their wallets because they heard something on TV or in the newspaper about the adverse effect of negative interest rates. Many customers think that the idea of negative interest rates means that the money they have will decrease without them even realizing. I feel it's quite possible that we'll see an atmosphere in which people are trying to spend as little as possible." As this comment reveals, negative interest rates do seem to have heightened people's anxiety about the future, because many believe that negative interest rates will cause their savings to shrink. It also shows that people feel that if Japan's economic situation is so bad that it requires a policy they've never heard of, then that policy is not worth implementing.

Secondly, the method of emphasizing the strong motivation of the authorities by making a strong commitment has also reached its limit. With the "monetary easing of a different dimension" implemented in April 2013, the BOJ made a firm commitment about the period for achieving the target. At the monetary policy meeting, the central bank set the goal of "achieving the 2 percent target for consumer prices as soon as possible within a roughly two-year period." Speaking at a press conference held around that time, Governor Kuroda said that the BOJ would not hesitate to make adjustments if they were needed, taking into account the given situation, because the economy and finance are living creatures.

This commitment of "2 percent in two years" and "not hesitating to make adjustments when necessary" gave the impression that the BOJ was really prepared, and was extremely effective in producing the announcement effect described earlier. This commitment was continuously reiterated and became a kind of policy mantra of the BOJ. While it is not uncommon for a central bank to set an inflation target, it is unusual to specify a precise time period for achieving that target. In addition, a statement such as "not hesitating to make adjustments when necessary" is basically the same as making a promise to take additional easing measures if achieving the 2 percent target in two years proves difficult. There is no problem with making this pledge as long as the economy is working well, but if the economy fails to move as intended, it could end up holding the BOJ back.

After that, the rate of increase in prices partially deviated from this 2 percent target because of the effects of unexpected circumstances, such as falling oil prices. The additional monetary easing in October 2014 also failed to produce the expected results, and in the end the BOJ was unable to achieve its target of 2 percent in two years. However, because the BOJ did not abandon its target of achieving 2 percent as soon as possible and implementing additional monetary easing without hesitation, the market came to expect an ongoing series of new easing steps. It can be argued that the negative interest-rate policy adopted in January 2016 was a measure made up by the BOJ. It knew this policy was incredibly reckless, and realized that it was tied down by the framework the bank had set up on its own.

Thirdly, while the weaker yen initially generated a favorable turn of the economy, the limitations of this approach gradually became evident.

Here I will provide a brief summary of what the weaker yen brought about in the first period of Abenomics. Looking at each fiscal year, the yen-to-dollar exchange rate fell about 17 percent from ¥83 in FY 2012 to ¥100 in FY 2013. Import prices in yen rose substantially by 14 percent. This rise in import prices pushed up prices, and the rate of increase in consumer prices (general, excluding fresh food) turned positive, from negative 0.2 percent in FY 2012 to 0.8 percent in FY 2013.

As for export prices, Japanese companies were faced with two options: increase the export volume by lowering sales prices in foreign currencies, or increase the sales amount in yen (raise export prices in yen) by keeping sales prices in foreign currencies the same. Japanese companies selected the latter. This choice was reflected by the fact that export prices in contract currency terms declined only 1 percent in FY 2013, while export prices in yen rose by 10 percent. As a result, the revenues of companies in the manufacturing industry increased significantly (ordinary income in the manufacturing industry increased 38 percent in FY 2013 according to the Financial Statements Statistics of Corporations by Industry from the Ministry of Finance). These higher prices and improved corporate earnings also had an impact on stock prices, which in turn rose.

The depreciation of the yen caused economic performance to improve dramatically during the first period of Abenomics. However, after the second period it gradually became apparent that the effects of the weaker yen would not lead to sustainable growth for the following two reasons.

First, the rise in prices and improvement in corporate earnings as a result of the weaker yen only come to the surface when the yen depreciates. To sustain this effect, the value of the yen must continue to fall, but this is impossible. The positive impact the weaker yen has on economic performance is essentially a short-term phenomenon.

Second, companies did not use these higher earnings to expand the scale of their businesses, which in turn cut short the mechanism for economic expansion. In the second period of Abenomics, one thing that has been frequently pointed out is that, although the value of the yen fell, capital expenditures did not increase; wages failed to rise while corporate earnings expanded, and the volume of exports ultimately failed to increase. The export volume increased only 1 percent in FY 2013, but this was because companies did not lower sales prices. Companies were also aware that the improvement in corporate earnings did not stem from their own raw potential, but rather that it was a short-term phenomenon. In addition, the reason companies did not try to boost the export volume by lowering sales prices was that they recognized that it was not the time to export products by manufacturing them in Japan, but rather the time to increase local production close to areas where products are consumed. Thus, even though their earnings increased, they did not boost their capacity in Japan or raise wages.

Change in Direction Required for Abenomics

I have discussed the limitations of Abenomics mainly from the standpoint of its financial policy. While there is not enough space for sufficient discussion in this article, the same things could be said about its fiscal policy. Abenomics had a positive impact in the first period, but in the end ran out of steam and failed to strengthen the basis for growth in the second period.

During the first period of Abenomics, public fixed-capital formation (which is largely the same as public investment) increased 10.3 percent in

FY 2013, and the direct effect of this alone drove up the real GDP growth rate in FY 2013 by 0.5 percent. However, public fixed-capital formation declined 2.6 percent in FY 2014 and then 2.7 percent in FY 2015, effectively dragging down growth. Public investment has a positive impact on growth only when it is increasing. In other words, the government must continue to increase public investment every year so that it can drive up the growth rate. This is something that is completely impossible for Japan given the strained state of its public finances.

In short, the effects of both the monetary and fiscal policies of conventional Abenomics have largely disappeared. However, Prime Minister Abe indicated that he intended to "accelerate the pace of Abenomics" after his ruling coalition scored a major victory in the Upper House elections in July 2016. If this means that he intends to further promote his present monetary and fiscal policies, that would be risky for the following reasons. We will take a look at these reasons, using the monetary policy once again as a point of reference.

The first reason is that if the government tries to continue moving the monetary policy forward while maintaining a strong commitment as described earlier, it will have no choice but to implement extraordinary policies that are rather far-fetched. The unconventional policy of negative interest rates has already been implemented, and even "helicopter money" is now being discussed. There are several definitions of helicopter money, but the main point here is that the BOJ would underwrite government bonds issued by the government. As a result, the government would not be liable for its debts.

Many financial experts have a positive view of negative interest rates, seeing them as a potent tool for monetary easing. On the other hand, there seem to be a few experts who actively support helicopter money because of concerns about an increase in the national burden due to factors such as the decrease in BOJ payments and hyperinflation, etc.

To me, both negative interest rates and helicopter money are extremely unnatural policies because they run counter to what we call the "providence of the economy"—that is, they are economically speaking counterintuitive. When we take a straightforward look at negative interest rates, the idea essentially implies that if we deposit money, that money will decrease, while if we borrow, the money we have will increase. If this kind of negative interest rate truly occurs, it will bring about an inconceivable economy in which people no longer deposit money in banks but instead go on borrowing money that will never be used. Also, if government spending can be covered by helicopter money without any form of obligation, the government will no longer need to levy taxes. If such a sweet deal existed, every

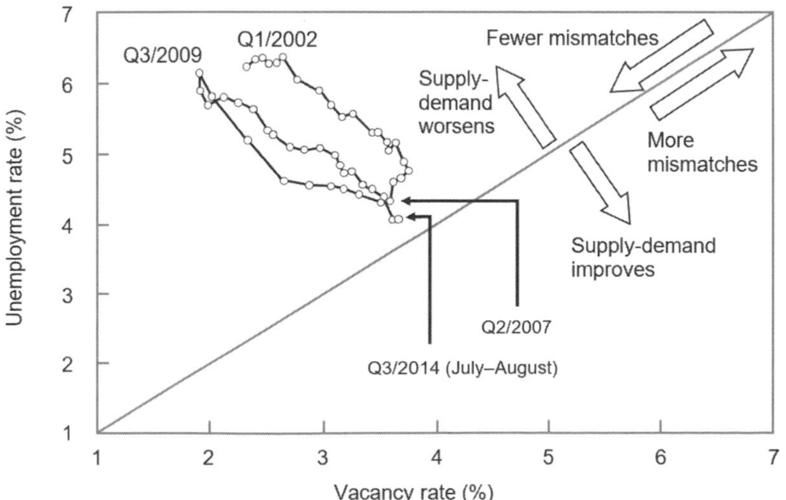

Figure 2. Recent Trends in the UV Curve

Sources: MIC, Statistics Bureau, Labor Force Survey and MHLW, Report on Employment Service.
Notes: 1. Unemployment rate = Number of people completely unemployed / (Number of people employed + Number of people completely unemployed)
2. Vacancy rate = (Number of active job openings − Number of placements) / (Number of active job openings − Number of placements + Number of people completely employed)
3. Data are seasonally adjusted.

country in the world would have already implemented it by now.

The reason the Japanese government is pursuing such far-fetched policies is that it feels bound to honor its commitment of achieving the 2 percent target as soon as possible and not hesitating to implement additional monetary easing. The government should allow itself greater flexibility in this commitment. Because the economy is influenced by many factors, such as conditions overseas and technological innovations, it is not possible to realize the ideal economy through government policies alone. In regard to prices, the government needs to avoid commitments that specify a time frame, such as "two-year period" and "as soon as possible." It should view target prices as a kind of a guide, and position them as the desirable level the government should aim to achieve over the long term.

Second, the government should change its stance of policy approach from a short-term emergency response to a long-term structural reform. The extraordinary fiscal and monetary policies implemented by Abenomics can only be rationalized in the case of an emergency that cannot be addressed by ordinary policies.

If someone were to ask me if I felt we faced an emergency now, I would say, "No." Take the employment situation, for example. Figure 2 shows a chart called the UV-curve, which plots the actual figures for the unemployment rate on the vertical axis and the job vacancy rate on the horizontal axis. The labor demand matches up with the labor supply on the 45-degree line in this chart, and unemployment that exists at that time can be regarded as structural due to the mismatch of demand and supply, instead of the result of the lack of demand.

As you can see in figure 2, the curve went above the 45-degree line at the beginning of 2016. This means that even if the economy is stimulated further, it will still be difficult to improve the employment situation. In other words, we are now at a level that is close to full employment. Looking at this, it is difficult to say that the current Japanese economy faces a crisis that requires the government to implement extraordinary policies.

The decision was made in July 2016 to implement additional monetary easing measures. However, what is needed now is not forcibly stimulating the economy by boosting demand, but instead strengthening growth potential from the long-term perspective. Going forward, I believe that the government should work on structural issues such as deregulation, reforms in the ways people work, and social security reform to raise the productivity of the Japanese economy as a whole and develop its basic growth potential.

English version originally published in *Discuss Japan—Japan Foreign Policy Forum*, no. 35 (Oct. 2016).

Translated from "Tokushū: Hakuhyō no sekai keizai / tenki no Abenomikusu—Tadashii kin'yū seisaku no arikata" [Special Feature: World Economy Walking on Thin Ice / Abenomics at a Watershed—Proper Approach to Monetary Policy], *Chūō Kōron* (September 2016): 90–97. (Courtesy of Chūōkōron Shinsha)

V-(2)

Quantitative and Qualitative Monetary Easing Effects and Associated Risks

Iwata Kazumasa and Fueda-Samikawa Ikuko

JCER Financial Research Report, 2013

1. Introduction

It will shortly be one year since the second Abe cabinet took office and the policy package known as Abenomics—consisting of bold monetary policy, flexible fiscal policy, and growth strategy to encourage private investment—was revealed. Monetary policy, the first of the "three arrows" released by the Abe administration, entered a new phase in April of this year, referred to as quantitative and qualitative monetary easing (QQE).

The FY 2013 JCER Financial Research Team examined the effects that this QQE will have on financial markets and fund flows in Japan and abroad, comparing the latest policy with three unconventional monetary policies introduced by the BOJ in the past—the zero interest-rate policy pursued from February 1999 to August 2000, the quantitative easing policy pursued from March 2001 to March 2006, and the comprehensive easing policy pursued from October 2010 to March 2013. The group particularly focused on management policy related to Japanese government bonds (JGBs) as, in Japan, with its growing mountain of government debt, the effectiveness of monetary policy needs to be seen in relation to fiscal management. Also, with the BOJ's balance sheet expanding dramatically due to the introduction of QQE, the group also studied the kinds of potential risks that lie beyond the time horizon of two years indicated by BOJ governor Kuroda. This is because given that, under Abenomics, which makes ending more than fifteen years of deflation and tepid growth its top priority, QQE is a "new phase" of "bold" monetary easing, the group considered it meaningful to deepen understanding of the risks and side effects that QQE may cause and to prepare for them in advance. This report outlines the effects and side effects of QQE.

2. Verification: What Occurred in the New Phase of Monetary Easing?

2.1 What was the "new phase of monetary easing"?—The BOJ expanded its balance sheet 1.3-fold in half a year

QQE is "quantitative easing" in the sense that it consists of (1) changing the main operating target for money market operations from the uncollateralized overnight call rate to the monetary base; (2) conducting money market operations so that the monetary base will increase at an annual pace of about ¥60–70 trillion; and (3) doubling the monetary base and holdings of long-term JGBs, commercial paper (CP), corporate bonds, exchange-traded funds (ETFs), and real-estate investment funds (J-REITS) in two years. It is also "qualitative easing" in the sense that it consists in making JGBs of all maturities—including forty-year bonds—eligible for purchase, and more than doubling the average remaining maturity of JGB purchases to seven years, which is equivalent to the average maturity of the amount outstanding of JGBs issued.

The outstanding amounts of the BOJ's long-term JGBs and the monetary base expanded dramatically due to the introduction of QQE, hitting new all-time highs (see figure 2-1). Compared with the end of March, long-term JGBs increased 38 percent from ¥91 trillion to ¥126 trillion, and the monetary base jumped 27 percent, from ¥146 trillion to ¥186 trillion. Also, due to purchases of other assets such as CP and corporate bonds, the BOJ's total assets rose to ¥208 trillion at the end of September, and its balance sheet ballooned

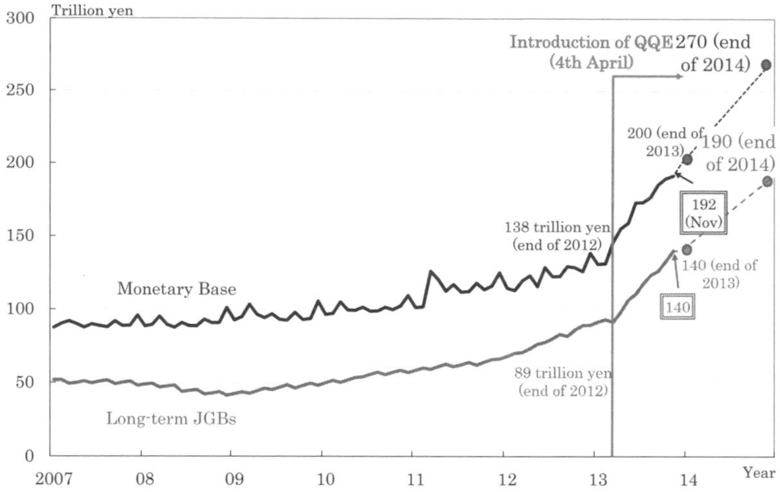

Figure 2-1. The BOJ expands its monetary base and outstanding JGBs to hit new all-time highs

Source: "Monetary Base and the Bank of Japan's Transactions," and "Bank of Japan Accounts," Bank of Japan.

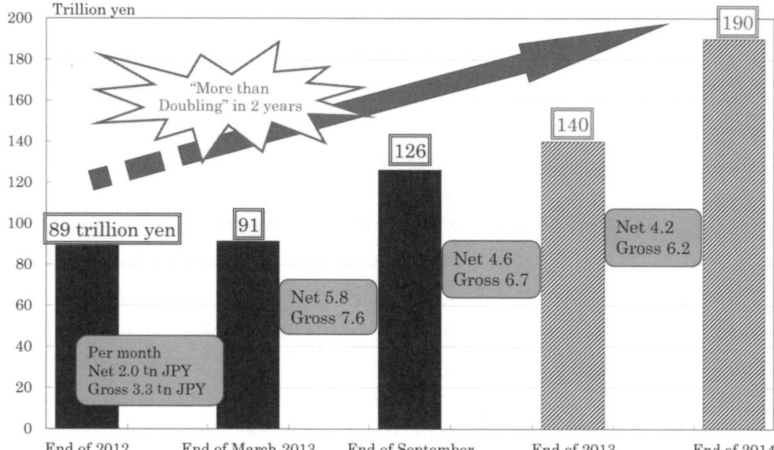

Figure 2-2. BOJ bought around ¥7.6 trillion in JGBs per month in the half year to September 2013

Source: "Japanese Government Bonds held by the Bank of Japan," "Bank of Japan Accounts (Every Ten Days)," Bank of Japan.
Note: The solid bars are actual purchases and the diagonal-hatched bars are BOJ's forecasts.

almost 1.3-fold in half a year. While the size of the balance sheet expanded 1.3-fold in five years under quantitative easing, and 1.4-fold in one and a half years under comprehensive easing, the rate of expansion has increased further.[1]

According to the BOJ, at the end of 2014 the monetary base is expected to reach ¥270 trillion, which is equivalent to double the monetary base at the end of 2012 (¥138 trillion), and long-term JGBs are also expected to more than double from ¥89 trillion to ¥190 trillion at the end of 2014. In the half year from April to the end of September, the BOJ bought ¥7.6 trillion worth of JGBs per month from the market on a gross basis (see figure 2-2). Calculating back from the forecast outstanding amount of JGBs at the end of 2013 of 140 trillion yen, the BOJ is expected to buy around ¥6.7 trillion in JGBs per month until the end of 2013 and around ¥6.2 trillion in JGBs per month in 2014 in order to reach its target.

The BOJ, which has been buying as much as ¥7 trillion worth of JGBs per month, has been the biggest player in the bond market since April. According to the Flow of Funds Accounts statistics, in the June quarter, while the BOJ was a net buyer of ¥19 trillion in long-term JGBs,[2] domestic banks (bank accounts of city banks, long-term credit banks, and trust banks) were a net seller of almost ¥17 trillion in long-term JGBs (see figure 2-3). This appears to be because, under QQE, domestic banks actively put in bids in the BOJ's purchasing operations and sold their long-term JGB holdings.

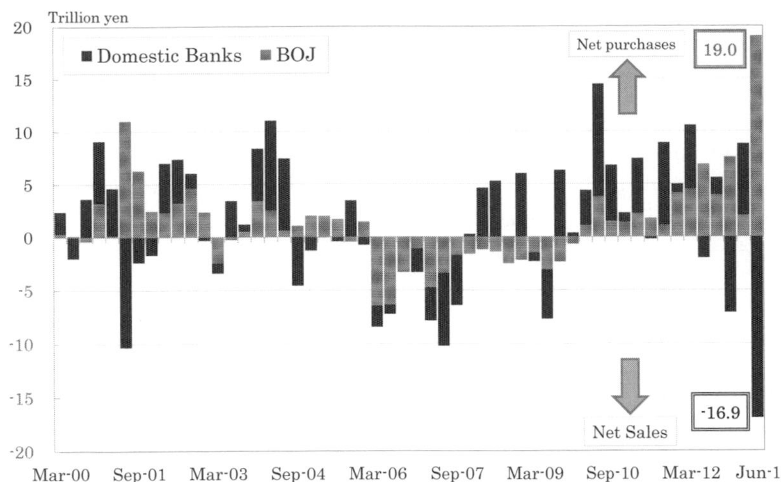

Figure 2-3. The value of BOJ's net long-term JGB purchases hit a new all-time high

Source: Flow of Funds Accounts, Bank of Japan.

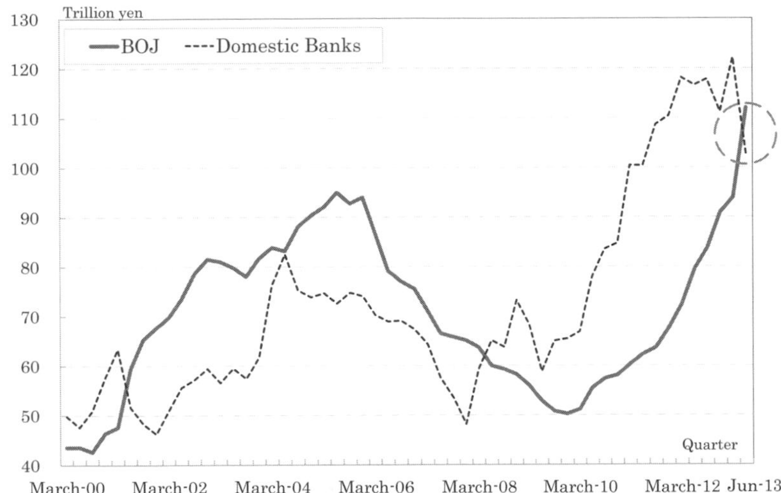

Figure 2-4. BOJ's long-term JGB holdings topped those of domestic banks for first time in five years

Source: Flow of Funds Accounts, Bank of Japan.

A similar trend was also seen in the June quarter of 2001, directly after the BOJ introduced the quantitative easing (QE) policy (see figure 2-3). Back then as well, the BOJ was a net buyer of ¥11 trillion in long-term JGBs, while domestic banks were a net seller of more than ¥10 trillion in JGBs. On this occasion, both the value of net purchases by the BOJ and the value of net sales by domestic banks are double what they were back then.[3]

In the United States, Carpenter, Demiralp, Ihrig, and Klee (2013a) have confirmed from the flow-of-funds accounts statistics that it was the household sector, including hedge funds, that sold large amounts of long-term treasury securities and mortgage-backed securities to the US Federal Reserve Board (FRB) under the asset-purchase program initiated in 2008, and that, after the sale of treasury securities, it switched to corporate bonds, CP, and local government bonds.[4] Some of the empirical studies point to "preferred habitat" models in which investors do not have the same objectives, and therefore prefer to hold different types and maturities of securities, and indicate that a portfolio rebalance effect came into play as a result of the FRB's asset purchases.

The presence of the BOJ in the bond market has also increased dramatically in terms of the outstanding amount of its long-term JGB holdings. At the end of June this year, the BOJ's long-term JGB holdings (¥112 trillion) topped those of domestic banks (¥102 trillion) for the first time in five years (see figure 2-4). If the BOJ's presence increases on both the flow and stock fronts of bond market, as captured by the expression "the whale in the pond,"[5] this will increase the risk that bond prices will fluctuate dramatically as a result of the BOJ's bond-buying operations[6] and the risk that long-term interest rates will rise (bond prices will fall sharply) at the mere suggestion of the sale of long-term JGBs by the BOJ.

2.2 Both quantitative forward guidance and interest-rate forward guidance are necessary

According to the expectancy theory concerning the term structure of interest rates, in the case of bonds with the same creditworthiness as short-term JGBs and long-term JGBs, long-term interest rates will equal expected short-term interest rates plus a term premium. A term premium can be thought of as "a premium reflecting consideration for the risk associated with uncertainty and the preferences of market participants" (Shiratsuka and Fujiki 2001). For example, if interest rates rise unexpectedly, long-term bond prices will fall, and when an unforeseen situation arises and funds are urgently required, cash conversion costs may arise. The return on long-term bonds needs to be higher than the return on short-term bonds to cover such interest-rate risks and liquidity risks.[7]

Monetary policy aims to have an impact on longer-term interest rates by working on both expected short-term interest rates and the term premium. More specifically, forward guidance affects expected short-term interest rates, and quantitative expansion has an impact on the term premium (Stein 2012). According to Kiley (2012), decline in expected short-term interest rates has a greater impact on the real economy than quantitative expansion. In contrast, a decline in the term premium works to push up asset prices (Iwata 2013).

Utsunomiya, Iwata, and Fueda-Samikawa (2013) have verified the effects of unconventional monetary policies to date, including QQE. More specifically, they have grasped from news analysis whether or not the impact of unconventional monetary policies was seen in long-term interest rates and asset prices in Japan, and confirm that QQE has to some degree had the effect of lowering not only short-term interest rates but also long-term interest rates and the effect of pushing up asset prices (stock prices and foreign-exchange rates).[8] They have also concluded that similar effects were not seen with the unconventional monetary policies pursued in the past.

Under the current QQE policy, forward guidance that is both state contingent[9] and calendar based, expressed in the statement, "Our goal is to achieve 2 percent inflation as soon as possible with a two-year timeline as a reference point," was revealed.[10] However, while quantitative forward guidance of doubling the monetary base was revealed, interest-rate forward guidance was not made clear. As Iwata (2013) has also pointed out, "introducing clear and trustworthy forward guidance on interest rates" has become an unavoidable issue for the BOJ, since if it wants to have an impact on the investment behavior of the non-financial sector, it will have to work on expected future short-term interest rates.

2.3 BOJ extended the maturity of its long-term JGB holdings for the first time

Under QQE, JGBs with all maturities, including super long-term forty-year bonds, were made eligible for purchase. With respect to its monthly purchases of long-term JGBs, the BOJ explained that the bank had decided to extend the average remaining maturity of the bank's JGB purchases from slightly less than three years to about seven years, which is roughly equivalent to the average maturity of the amount outstanding of JGBs issued.[11] The flow of purchases based on the amount outstanding of the bank's issue-by-issue holdings of JGBs at the end of each month and adjusted for redemption and buyback and retirement by the Government Debt Consolidation Fund shows that, since April, the BOJ has bought large quantities of medium-term and long-term JGBs with four to fifteen years remaining to maturity (see figure 2-5).

Also, the BOJ began buying thirty- and forty-year bonds, which it hardly ever bought before. As a result, the average remaining maturity of long-term JGBs bought from the market suddenly lengthened from 3.1 years before QQE implementation (from October 2012 to March this year) to an average of 7.2 years after implementation

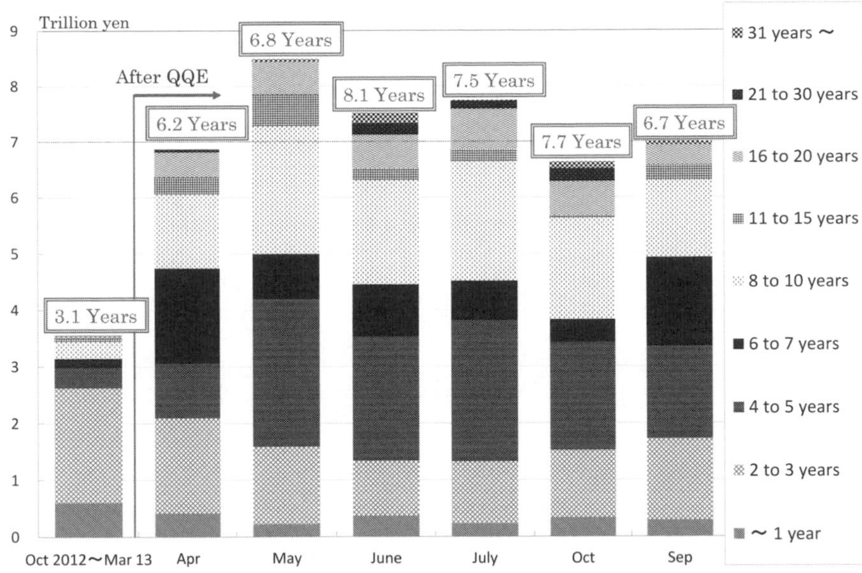

Figure 2-5. JGBs of all maturities, including forty-year bonds, were made eligible for BOJ's purchase

Source: Trial calculations of authors based on the Bank of Japan's Issue-by-Issue Holdings of JGBs by Amount Outstanding published by the BOJ and Auction Results for JGBs and Buyback Auction Results published by the Ministry of Finance.
Note 1: The increase in the outstanding amount from the end of the previous month was calculated for each JGB issue and this was taken as the flow of purchases. However, since adjustment for reduction in the outstanding amount as a result of redemption, and buyback/retirement is made, the purchase amounts are on a gross basis.
Note 2: Oct. 2012 to Mar. 2013 data are averaged for the period from October 2012 through March this year. This includes JGBs purchased through the asset purchase fund.
Note 3: The box above the bar chart is the average remaining maturity of long-term JGBs bought per month by the BOJ.

(see the red box in figure 2-5). Since the long-term JGBs on the BOJ's balance sheet are JGBs excluding treasury discount bills, it needs to be considered that, in the case of a bond issued as ten-year interest-bearing JGB, for example, even if the remaining period to maturity is less than one year, it will still be classified as a long-term JGB.

The BOJ has bought longer-term JGBs from the market; as a result, the average remaining maturity of long-term JGBs both in terms of flow (value of purchases per month) and in terms of stock (outstanding value of JGB holdings) has also lengthened dramatically. The line in figure 2-6 shows the average remaining maturity of the BOJ's JGB holdings calculated by matching the Bank of Japan's Issue-by-Issue Holdings of JGBs by Amount Outstanding published monthly by the BOJ and JGB-related data published by the Ministry of Finance.[12] According to the trial calculations of the authors of this report, remaining maturity increased from 3.9 years at the end of March this year to 4.9 years at the end of September; that is, the average remaining maturity of long-term JGBs grew as much as one year in the space of half a year after the introduction of QQE. If the current rate of purchases continues, the average remaining maturity of JGBs held by the BOJ is expected to exceed seven years by the end of 2014.

Likewise, in the days of quantitative easing and comprehensive easing, the amount outstanding of the BOJ's long-term JGB holdings expanded due to the increase in value of long-term JGB buying operations, but if anything, the average remaining maturity based on the amount outstanding became shorter. In contrast, after the introduction of QQE, alongside an increase in the amount outstanding of long-term JGBs, the remaining maturity has also grown longer. As shown by the line in figure 2-6, the remaining maturity grew

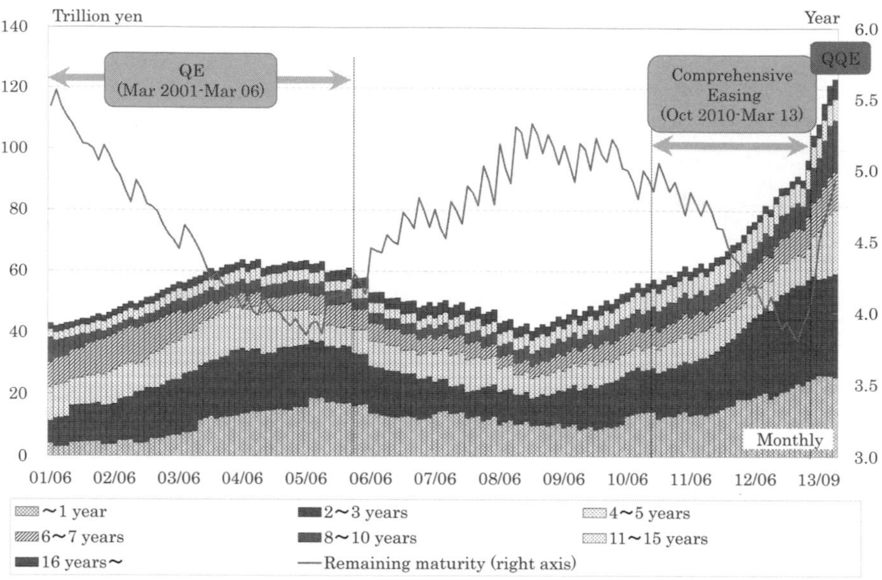

Figure 2-6. The remaining maturity of the BOJ's long-term JGBs grew shorter in past easing phases

Source: Trial calculations of authors based on the Bank of Japan's Issue-by-Issue Holdings of JGBs by Amount Outstanding published by the BOJ and Auction Results for JGBs and Buyback Auction Results published by the Ministry of Finance.
Note 1: Face-value basis. Includes JGBs purchased through the asset purchase fund.
Note 2: Long-term JGBs are JGBs excluding treasury discount bills, and there is no distinction in terms of time period left to reach maturity (remaining maturity).

shorter by around one year under comprehensive easing, but recouped this in the space of just half a year after the introduction of QQE. Compared with the past two phases of quantitative easing, this is a change in the opposite direction, and it is precisely herein that the "new phase" lies.

Under the quantitative easing policy pursued from March 2001 to March 2006, the BOJ gradually raised the target amount of the outstanding balance of current accounts at the bank from ¥5 trillion to ¥30–35 trillion. In step with this, the BOJ also repeatedly increased purchases of long-term JGBs per month from ¥400 billion at the outset to ¥1.2 trillion (October 2002). However, since the JGBs which the BOJ bought from the market during this time were mainly JGBs with three years or less remaining to maturity, the average remaining maturity of JGBs held by the BOJ shrank from 5.4 years in June 2001, for which public data exists, to 3.8 years temporarily in September 2005. As explained later, the fact that the BOJ made medium-term bonds (two to six years) eligible for purchase in its bond-buying operations from June 2001 may have had an impact on the shrinking of the remaining maturity.

As shown in figure 2-7, the BOJ continued to buy more than ¥14 trillion of long-term JGBs per year after the end of quantitative easing. The reason the amount outstanding of long-term JGB holdings decreased at this time in spite of such purchases may be that the shorter-term JGBs bought under the quantitative easing policy successively matured and disappeared from the BOJ's balance sheet. As a result, the remaining maturity of the BOJ's long-term JGB holdings gradually grew longer from around half a year before quantitative easing was ended through to September 2008, when the Lehman Shock occurred. If the BOJ had expected quantitative easing to have the effect of encouraging declines in long-term interest rates, it should have examined operations that would lengthen the remaining maturity of its long-term JGB holdings.[13]

Under the comprehensive easing policy pursued from October 2010 to March of this

Trillion yen

	Fiscal Year	Amount of long-term JGB purchases
Zero Interest-rate Policy (February 1999 to August 2000)	1999	5.4
	2000	5.3
	2001	7.9
Quantitative Easing Policy (March 2001 to March 2006)	2002	13.4
	2003	14.8
	2004	14.6
	2005	14.5
	2006	14.4
	2007	14.5
	2008	15.5
	2009	22.0
Comprehensive Easing Policy (October 2010 to March 2013)	2010	22.9
	2011	27.5
	2012	44.9
QQE (April 2013 to present)	2013	45.6

Figure 2-7. The BOJ continued to buy more than ¥14 trillion worth of long-term JGBs per year after the QE

Source: "Sources of Changes in Current Account Balances at the Bank of Japan and Market Operations," Bank of Japan.
Note: The figures for the year of 2013 represent the total from April to September.

year, (1) purchases of long-term JGBs by newly created asset-purchase funds and (2) previously conducted purchases to boost the money supply and ensure the stable supply of funds to markets consistent with the upward trend in bank-note demand associated with economic growth (¥21.6 trillion per year, so-called *rinban* operations) were handled as completely separate operations in terms of purpose and type of holdings.[14] Figure 2-6 above shows the amount outstanding and remaining maturity for the two operations combined, and it is clear that, even including *rinban* operation purchases of JGBs with relatively longer terms, the remaining maturity of the BOJ's JGB holdings shrank once again under comprehensive easing. This appears to be because, at the time, the BOJ limited long-term JGBs bought from the market via asset purchase funds to those with maturities of 1 or 2 years. The term of long-term JGBs eligible for purchase was extended in April 2012 "from the viewpoint of effectively influencing longer term interest rates,"[15] but even so, it was still one to three years. In the two and a half years from October 2010, when the comprehensive easing policy was introduced, to March of this year, the remaining maturity of long-term JGBs on the BOJ's balance sheet shrank from 4.9 years to 3.9 years.

2.4 The remaining maturity of the Fed's holdings of treasury securities also grew

Under QQE, the remaining maturity of the BOJ's JGB holdings has grown. Likewise, in the United States, the average remaining maturity of the Federal Reserve's holdings of Treasury securities grew as a result of Operation Twist, which was implemented by the FRB in the fall of 2011. According to Bernanke, Reinhart, and Sack (2004), in the United States for at least the past fifty years, the average remaining maturity of the System Open Market Account's (SOMA) treasury holdings has been between one year and four years, but, all of a sudden, this grew by more than three years from 7.0 years at the end of 2011 to 10.4 years at the end of 2012 (FRB 2013). The average remaining maturity grew threefold compared to before the Lehman Shock. This is because the FRB sold short-term treasury securities with a remaining maturity of less than three years, while at the same time buying long-term treasury securities from the markets to curb longer-term interest rates. At the end of 2012, treasury securities with six years or more remaining accounted for around 60 percent of total treasury securities held in the SOMA portfolio, and the remaining share was treasury securities with a duration of three to five years (treasury securities with a remaining duration of less than three years virtually disappeared). Under the credit easing policy pursued by the FRB in the wake of the Lehman Shock,[16] both the average remaining maturity and duration, which give the weighted-average maturity of a treasury security's cash flows, were comparatively stable, but from the introduction of Operation Twist onward both lengthened. On the balance sheets of both the BOJ and the FRB, the mismatch between the terms of assets and liabilities has increased (meaning that the weight of long-term assets increases on the assets side and the weight of short-term liabilities increases on the liabilities side).

2.5 Due to the removal of the bank-note rule, the BOJ needs to ensure confidence in its monetary policy

The BOJ instituted the so-called bank-note rule in March 2011, when it embarked on quantitative easing. This rule limits the BOJ's long-term JGB buying to the value of bank notes in circulation. This rule is intended to maintain balance in the maturity structure of the BOJ's assets and liabilities. Also, for the BOJ, which had embarked on an unconventional monetary policy, the bank-note rule can also be construed as "the central bank's final indication of discipline" (Saitō and Sudō 2009) against political pressure, to prevent any misunderstanding that the purchases of long-term JGBs were for the purpose of fiscal financing, as the underwriting of government bonds by the BOJ is prohibited under Article 5 of the Finance Act.

With the introduction of the comprehensive easing policy in October 2010, the BOJ decided to apply the bank-note rule only to so-called *rinban* operations; that is, purchases of long-term JGBs in response to the upward trend in bank notes associated with economic growth. At the time, the rule was not applied to purchases of long-term JGBs through asset-purchase funds, which were positioned as extraordinary temporary measures. The scale of *rinban* operations was gradually increased from the introduction of quantitative easing onward, reaching ¥1.8 trillion per month in March 2009 (¥21.6 trillion per year; see figure 2-8). Meanwhile, in recent years, year-on-year growth in the circulation of bank notes has remained stable at around 3 percent, except for around April 2002, when the payoff suspension was partially lifted. It is clear from the data for *rinban* operations alone (purchases of ¥1.8 trillion of JGBs per month) that it was only a matter of time before long-term JGBs, which continuously showed year-on year double-digit growth, would break through the ceiling of the bank notes in circulation.

Date of Decision		Amount per Month (100 million yen)	Amount per Year (trillion yen)
—		4,000	4.8
2001	Mar 19	Introduction of the bank-note rule	
	Aug 14	6,000	7.2
	Dec 19	8,000	9.6
2002	Feb 28	10,000	12.0
	Oct 30	12,000	14.4
2008	Dec 19	14,000	16.8
2009	Mar 18	18,000	21.6
2013	Apr 4	Temporary removal of the bank-note rule	

Figure 2-8. The bank-note rule and the value of long-term JGB purchases by the BOJ

Source: Generated from the executive summary of BOJ Monetary Policy Meeting, and other sources.

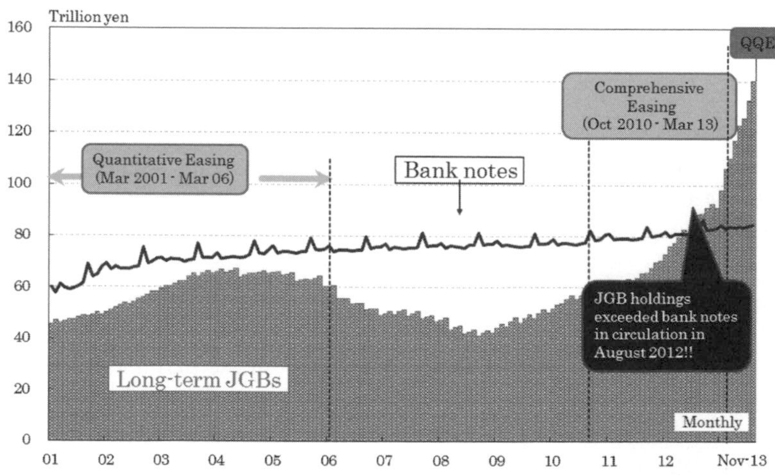

Figure 2-9. BOJ long-term JGB holdings total 1.5 times the bank notes in circulation

Source: "Bank of Japan Accounts," Bank of Japan.
Note: Including JGB from the Asset Purchase Program

With the introduction of QQE, the BOJ decided to temporarily drop the bank-note rule. As of the end of September 2013, the BOJ held long-term JGBs (¥126.1 trillion) equivalent to 1.5 times the bank notes in circulation (¥83.6 trillion) (see figure 2-9). The minutes of the BOJ Monetary Policy Meeting held in April record the comments of one member who said, "The bank could facilitate communication to the public in a clear and intelligible manner if the JGB purchases to be introduced at this meeting were interpreted as simultaneously pursuing the objective of *rinban* operations—to supply currency consistent with the underlying steady development of the economy—and that of the program—to overcome deflation." However, as also pointed out by Okina (2013), if long-term JGBs expand in a way that is not consistent with the "continuous snow cover" of bank notes and the BOJ's current account deposits, it will become more difficult for the central bank to make monetary adjustments flexibly in line with fluctuations in the excess or shortage of funds. Now that the bank-note rule is no longer being applied, albeit temporarily, the BOJ must make clear that the purpose of purchases of long-term JGBs is not to prop up JGB prices or to monetize government debt, and it must continue to ensure confidence in monetary policy.

2.6 The BOJ abolished the JGB purchase rule and began buying new issues in its operations

To coincide with the start of bond-buying operations in 1967, the BOJ established the JGB purchase rule,[17] which prohibits it from purchasing bonds issued within the past year in its bond-buying operations (the so-called one-year rule). Later, in response to the zero interest-rate policy introduced in February 1999, the BOJ relaxed the JGB purchase rule and extended the scope of its buying operations from twenty issues from among ten- and twenty-year bonds to all issues of ten- and twenty-year bonds (see figure 2-10). Also, in response to the quantitative easing policy introduced in March 2001, in May 2001 the BOJ made medium-term bonds—which includes two-year bonds, four-year bonds, five-year bonds, and six-year bonds—eligible for purchase. Further, in January 2002, the BOJ abolished the one-year rule and made all fixed-rate JGBs with all maturities, except for the most recent two issues, eligible for purchase. Then, in April of this year, with the introduction of QQE, the BOJ abolished the JGB purchase rule completely.

Because the BOJ made newly issued JGBs eligible for purchase in its bond-buying operations, the bond market started to see "BOJ trades," in which the bank that was the primary dealer sold newly issued bonds to the BOJ shortly after their issue as part of bond-buying operations. The rationale was, "Though the profit margin is small, the bonds are sure to sell straight away for a profit."[18] Due to the increase in BOJ trades, in the case of the 329th ten-year JGB issue, for example, two trading days after the issue, the

Figure 2-10. JGB purchase rule from inception to its complete abolition

January 1967	JGBs are eligible for purchase once one year has elapsed since issue.
—	Twenty issues of ten-year bonds and twenty-year bonds are eligible for purchase.
March 25, 1999	All issues of ten-year bonds and twenty-year bonds are eligible for purchase, in principle.
May 18, 2001	Medium-term bonds (two-year bonds, four-year bonds, five-year bonds and six-year bonds) are made eligible for purchase.
January 16, 2002	The "one-year rule" is abolished. All fixed-rate JGBs with all maturities, except for the most recent two issues, are made eligible for purchase.
December 19, 2008	Thirty-year bonds, floating-rate bonds, and inflation-indexed bonds are made eligible for purchase.
April 4, 2013	The JGB purchase rule is completely abolished. All long-term JGBs, including forty-year bonds and new issues (excluding the most recent two issues) are made eligible for purchase.

Source: Generated from the "History" section of the BOJ's website, the BOJ Financial Markets Department (2004), and the executive summary of the BOJ Monetary Policy Meeting.

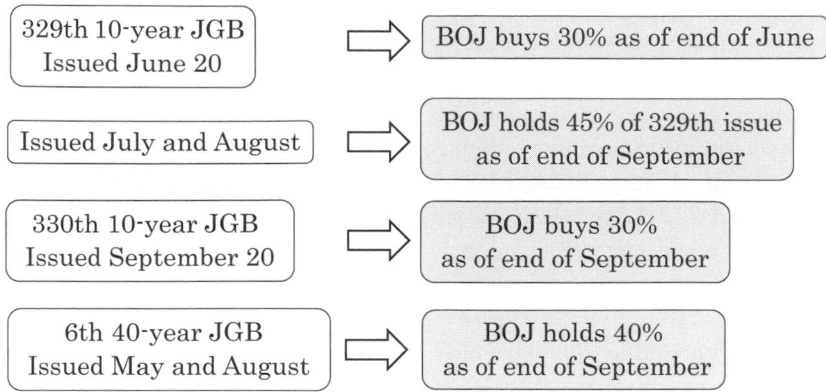

Figure 2-11. BOJ Trades: in some cases the BOJ holds more than 40 percent of new JGB issues

Source: Generated from "Japanese Government Bonds held by the Bank of Japan" and "Market Operations" of the BOJ; and JGB Auction Results, published by the MOF.

BOJ had bought 30 percent of the issue value (see figure 2-11). Under QQE, it was revealed that the BOJ planned to buy long-term JGBs equivalent to 70 percent of the new issues per month, but, in addition to purchases on the scale of ¥7 trillion in JGBs per month, also in terms of the concentration of issues bought, the impact on the liquidity of JGBs was likely to be considerable. While financial institutions judge for themselves which issues to sell in operations, if a situation in which the BOJ sucks up almost half the JGBs from the market within just a few months of their issue occurs frequently, this may give the market the idea that JGBs are being underwritten by the BOJ, which is prohibited by the Finance Act. In this sense, too, the BOJ needs to send out a clear message to the markets and the Japanese people that monetization is not the purpose of its JGB purchases.

3. To Escape Deflation, Consistency between Monetary Policy and JGB Management Policy is Required.

3.1. An increase in JGB issues and lengthening of redemption periods weakened monetary policy effects

As shown in figure 2-6, under QQE, the average remaining maturity of the BOJ's long-term JGB holdings has grown dramatically. In the meantime, the redemption period of JGBs issued each year has also increased (see figure 3-1). The average redemption period grew three years, from four years and ten months in FY 1999 to seven years and eleven months in FY 2013, based on the initial projection. This is because, wanting to reduce the burden of interest payments caused by mounting government debt, Japan attempted to issue longer-dated JGBs while interest rates were low to prepare for future rate increases (see figure 3-2).

Fujikawa, Iwata, and Fueda-Samikawa (2013) have attempted an analysis focusing on the possibility that the effects of past quantitative easing policies were offset by a supply-side factor other than the increase in the amount of JGB issuance; that is, the lengthening of the redemption period. Chadha, Turner, and Zampolli (2013) have shown empirical results to the effect that when the average remaining maturity of US Treasury securities in financial markets becomes shorter because the FRB bought long-term securities from the market, this strengthens downward pressure on their long-term interest rate. The FRB gradually raised the target interest rate from June 2004, but this did not lead to a rise in long-term interest rates, which former Federal Reserve chairman Alan Greenspan at the time described as a "conundrum." The prevailing view was that the savings of emerging economies had accumulated in the safe assets of advanced economies in the form of foreign reserves, but the shortening trend of the remaining maturity of treasury securities

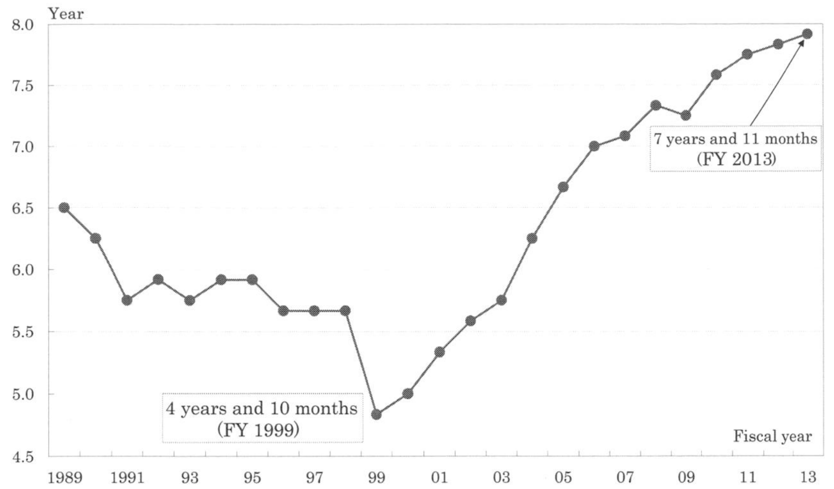

Figure 3-1. Redemption periods of JGBs also grew dramatically (based on annual JGB issuance)

Source: Debt Management Report, Ministry of Finance.
Note 1: Includes short-term JGBs (six-month and one-year Treasury Bills).
Note 2: FY 2013 figure is based on initial projections.

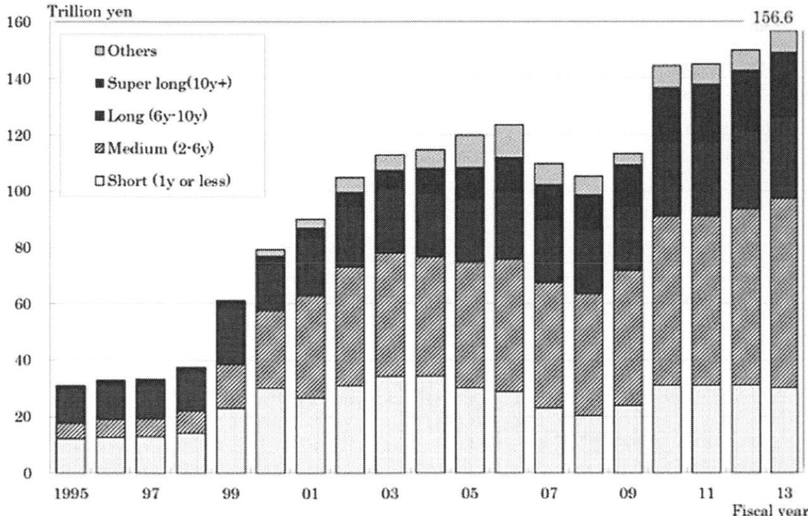

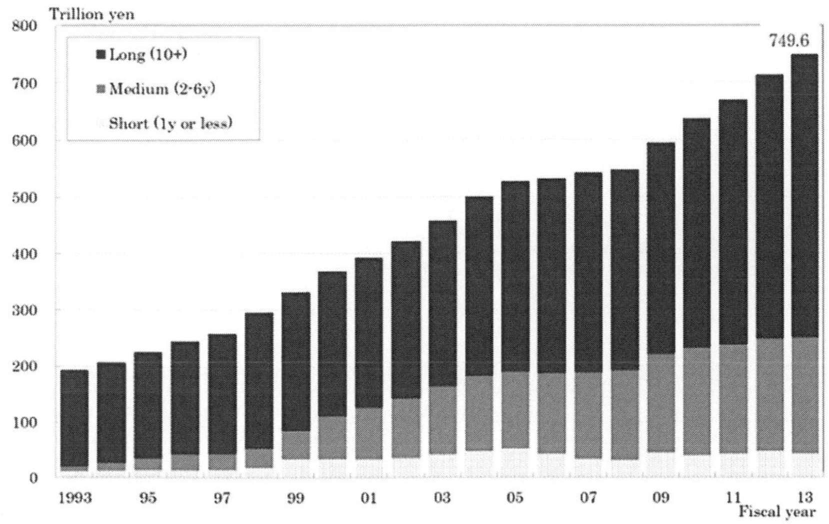

Figure 3-2. BOJ will shift to buying long-term bonds in phases of issuance of JGBs and low interest rates

Source: JGB Issuance Plan for 2013 published by the MOF.
Note 1: The upper figure shows flow (JGB issuance); lower figure shows stock (outstanding JGBs).
Note 2: FY 2013 figures are based on initial projections.

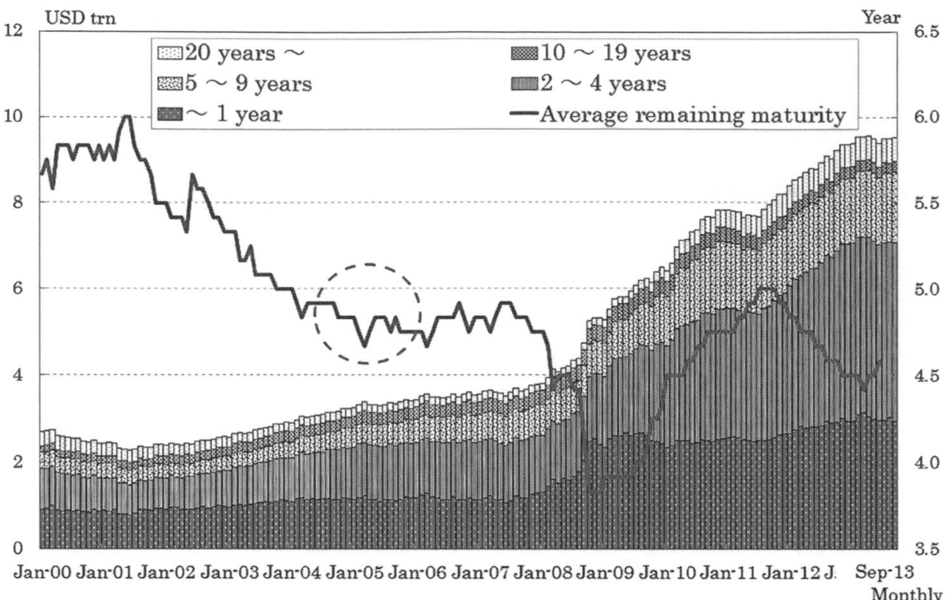

Figure 3-3. In the United States, privately held treasury securities continued to shorten after the rate hikes in 2004, and the rise in long-term interest rates was curbed

Source: US Department of the Treasury, "Treasury Bulletin."
Note: The bar graph shows the private sector's holdings of US Treasury bonds (by term); the line on the chart shows the average remaining maturity.

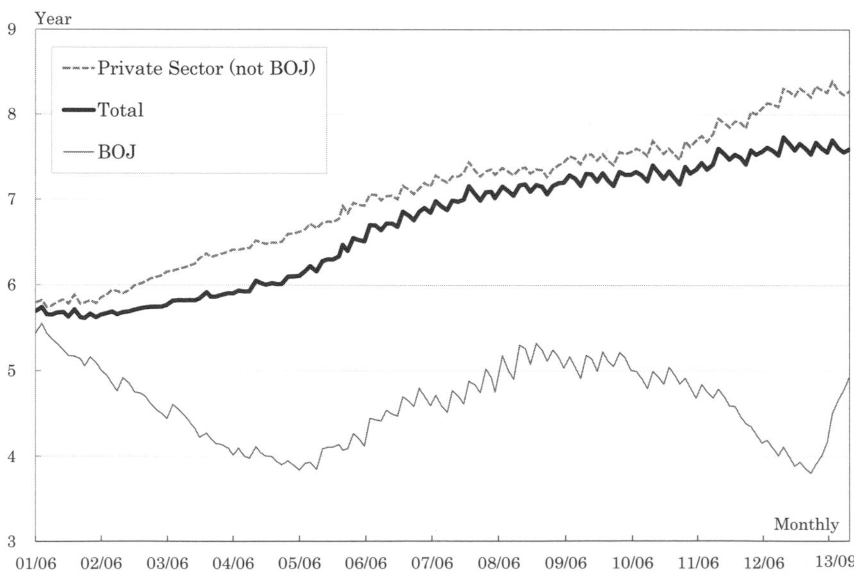

Figure 3-4. Average remaining maturity held by non-BOJ sectors has extended for a long time

Source: Trial calculations of authors based on the Bank of Japan's Issue-by-Issue Holdings of JGBs by Amount Outstanding, published by the BOJ; and JGB Auction Results, published by the MOF.

held by the US private sector may also have had an impact (see figure 3-3).

In Japan, with the introduction of QQE, the BOJ started to buy large amounts of long-term bonds but, in the meantime, on the issue side, the average redemption period of JGBs has grown longer, and so the average remaining maturity of the long-term JGBs held by the private sector (that is, not the BOJ) has increased under the impact from the issue side (see figure 3-4). At the end of September 2013, whereas the average remaining maturity of the BOJ's long-term JGB holdings was 4.9 years, the average remaining maturity of JGBs held by the private sector was much longer than this, at 8.3 years.[19]

Fujikawa, Iwata, and Fueda-Samikawa (2013) have confirmed through empirical analysis that the effect of past monetary-easing policies of curbing longer-term interest rates was weakened as a result of the lengthening of redemption periods of JGBs. From 2001, when the quantitative easing policy was implemented, the lengthening of the redemption periods pushed long-term interest rates up almost 0.5–0.9 percentage points. This result suggests that JGB management policy offset the quantitative easing effect. While it is rational behavior for Japan to issue long-dated JGBs in a low-interest-rate environment, under Abenomics, which makes escape from deflation its top priority, JGB management policy must be consistent with monetary policy that attempts to curb interest rates across the yield curve.[20]

3.2 Arrangement between the Bank of England and the HM Treasury

In March 2009, the Bank of England, which is the central bank of the United Kingdom, established the Asset Purchase Facility as part of its financial stability measures, and embarked on quantitative easing. In response to this, Alistair Darling, who was chancellor of the exchequer at the time, sent an open letter[21] to Bank of England governor Mervyn King, saying, "I recognize the importance of ensuring that debt management policy is consistent with the aims of monetary policy. I am today confirming that the Government's debt management policy remains to minimize, over the long term, the costs of meeting the Government's financing needs, taking into consideration account risk, whilst ensuring that debt management policy is consistent with the aims of monetary policy. . . . However, the Government will not alter its issuance strategy as a result of the asset transactions undertaken by the Bank of England for monetary policy purposes." To further enhance the effects of QQE, a cooperative arrangement between the Japanese government and the BOJ is required.[22]

4. The BOJ's Financial Health Needs to Be Ensured through a Loss-Coverage Provision

4.1 The BOJ's balance sheet risk is on the liabilities side

As seen above, on the BOJ's balance sheet, the maturity mismatch between assets and liabilities is expanding. The lengthening of the average remaining maturity of long-term JGBs on the assets side is directly linked to the lengthening of duration. The lengthening of duration means there is a higher risk of bond prices falling if interest rates rise, but since, in FY 2004, the BOJ changed the long-term JGB valuation method from lower of cost or market to the amortized cost method,[23] "even if the market value of JGB holdings falls due to a rate rise, there is no valuation loss" (Bank of Japan, Planning Office 2004). The amortized cost method is a valuation method applied to held-to-maturity debt securities under corporate accounting standards; the BOJ records the face value of long-term JGBs on the assets side of the balance sheet and amortizes the difference between the acquisition cost and the face value equally every period until maturity.

If anything, the BOJ's risk of impairment of its balance sheet as a result of rising rates is on the liabilities side. This is because, under the supplemental reserve facility,[24] the BOJ pays 0.1 percent interest on the balance of current account deposits at the bank exceeding legal reserve requirements of around ¥8 trillion (so-called excess reserves). The risk may materialize when the 2 percent CPI price stability target has been reached and the BOJ has raised the rate of interest on these excess reserves. Under QQE, the balance of current account deposits at the BOJ is expected to rise to ¥175 trillion at the end of 2014. When the time comes for the BOJ to raise the interest rate on excess reserves after the tapering of easing, the BOJ's interest payments will increase and may squeeze its current account surplus. If the BOJ's surplus declines, this may also lead to expansion of the public burden through a decline in remittances to the treasury.

4.2 In the United States, it is feared that the FRB's interest payments and losses on sales of securities will balloon due to rate hikes after the tapering of easing

The FRB also has similar concerns concerning the decline in remittances to the treasury. Carpenter, Ihrig, Klee, Quinn, and Boote (2013) estimate the impact on financial statements should the FRB continue its current asset-purchase program (purchases of $45 billion in US treasury securities per month and purchases of $40 billion of MBS per month) until the end of 2013.[25] According to their estimates, if the FRB purchases $1 trillion in assets in 2013,[26] by the end of 2013, the FRB's assets[27] will expand to $3.75 trillion and the outstanding balance of current-account deposits will expand to $2.7 trillion. Also, assuming that the FRB raises the benchmark interest rate half a year after it stops asset purchases, starts selling MBS another half a year after that, and spends three to four years reducing the amount outstanding of MBS to zero, due to expansion of interest payments and losses, remittances to the treasury would have to stop for four years.[28] During this time, the FRB would record deferred tax assets. If interest rates were 1 percentage point higher than the baseline scenario, the period during which remittances to the treasury would stop would increase to six and a half years.

Carpenter et al. (2013) conclude that the more the central bank's balance sheet expands due to asset purchases and the more long-term interest rates rise, the greater the burden of interest payments on excess reserves and losses on sales of MBS will be, and so the period during which the FRB's profits are squeezed, preventing remittances to the treasury, will become longer. Given this situation, Federal Reserve chairman Ben Bernanke said in his testimony to Congress on February 26 of this year that "remittances to the Treasury could be quite low for a time in some scenarios, particularly if interest rates were to rise quickly."[29]

4.3 Side effects of QQE: The possibility that remittances to the treasury will be halted in an exit

In light of Carpenter et al. (2013), Inagaki, Fueda-Samikawa, and Iwata (2013) have analyzed the risks Japan will face when it starts to exit QQE. Under QQE, the BOJ will continue to purchase around ¥7 trillion of long-term JGBs per month until March 2015, and if it can achieve its target of 2 percent inflation in two years as forecast, the BOJ will have to make its next move and start to taper easing. Here, the first phase of the exit strategy is considered to be the reduction of purchases: the BOJ will reduce the amount of long-term JGB purchases per month by ¥380 billion every month over a period of one and a half years. It is assumed, however, that bond-buying operations to boost the money supply will continue after the tapering of easing. Next, as the second phase, let us assume that, from April 2017, half a year after it stops reducing its purchases, the BOJ gradually raises the rate of interest on excess reserves from its current level of 1 percent to 2.5 percent.[30] At this time, interest payments per year will increase to a peak of around ¥2.6 trillion.[31] Meanwhile, many of the long-term JGBs on the asset side are low-interest long-dated bonds, and even if interest rates start to rise, interest income will not increase significantly. The increase in interest payments will squeeze the BOJ's profits, and, unless provisions are reversed, the current account surplus will turn negative for around three years from FY 2019 (see figure 4-1). Since this will also prevent the payment of dividends even if legal reserves are set aside, the BOJ may be unable to make remittances to the treasury[32] for around three years.

If the benchmark interest rate is raised from 0.1 percent to 3 percent, interest payments will peak over ¥3 trillion, and remittances to the treasury will be halted for around four years. Also, if achievement of the inflation rate target is delayed and purchases of ¥7 trillion in JGBs are extended for half a year, the current account deficit will persist for around five years, and during this time, remittances to the treasury will stop. It was ascertained from the results of the analysis that, in an exit from QQE, the more interest rates rise and the more the BOJ's balance sheet expands, the greater the decline in the current account surplus will be. As for higher-than-expected interest rates and extension of the period of purchases, the size of the deficit will be greater in the case of

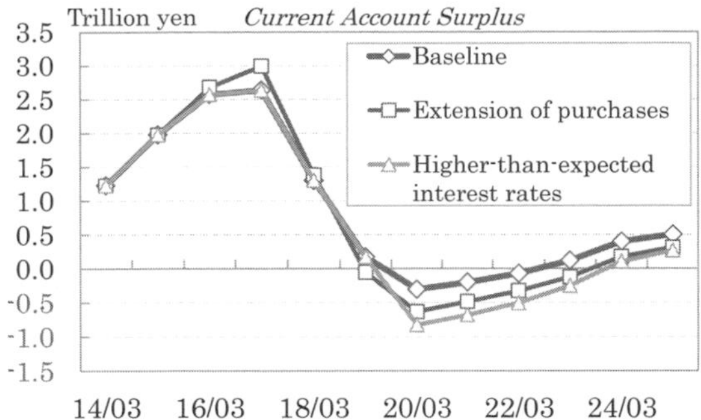

Figure 4-1. BOJ's remittance could be reduced to zero in the phase of exit from QQE

Note: Extraordinary profit or loss arising from foreign exchange factors, the disposal of fixed assets, etc., which fluctuate considerably every year, are not taken into consideration.

the former and the period of suspension of remittances to the treasury will be longer in the case of the latter.

This analysis has not taken into consideration extraordinary income or loss arising from foreign-exchange loss or gain or the disposal of fixed assets, etc., which are factors that fluctuate dramatically every year, but, for example, if the yen value of foreign debt securities declines due to a stronger yen and a loss on disposal of fixed assets occurs, profits will be pushed down further. As envisaged by Carpenter et al. (2013), if the FRB embarks on the sale of its asset holdings (in the case of the BOJ, its long-term JGBs) in a rising interest-rate environment, a loss on the sale of debt securities will arise. The BOJ needs to explain to the Japanese people in advance and ask them to understand that if remittances to the treasury are dragged down to zero by such a combination of factors, this will increase the public burden.

4.4 Escape from deflation is the priority, and the BOJ's financial health should be ensured by the government

Under the new Bank of Japan Act enacted in 1998, the independence of the BOJ was ensured, and the loss-coverage provision in the supplementary provisions of the old Bank of Japan Act was eliminated. Under the old act, if the BOJ's current account surplus turned negative (despite the reversal of reserves, etc.), the government had to supply an amount equal to the shortfall, but under the new act, this provision disappeared, and the BOJ is responsible for its own financial health.

However, in a rising interest environment in the future, the BOJ's ordinary income may turn negative. While it depends on the size and duration of the deficit, when the reversal of provisions and reserves is not enough to cover the shortfall, the current account surplus will turn negative and remittances to the treasury can no longer be made, and if the BOJ is tied up with maintaining its financial health, monetary tightening may be delayed. This is because, as also pointed out by Ueda (2003), if the BOJ attempts to overcome the excess of debt with its own operations, it will need to earn a large amount of "seigniorage" (i.e., profits from printing money) and this will necessitate a high money-supply rate and inflation. The BOJ's accounting regulations stipulate that the BOJ must operate so that its own capital adequacy ratio is within the range of 2 percentage points above or below 10 percent (Furuichi and Mori 2005), but the BOJ's capital adequacy ratio has been around the 7 percent mark since FY 2002 (7.5 percent in FY 2012). Also, in view of the fact that the capital adequacy ratio is already below the lower bound of the guideline level, the more importance the BOJ attaches to its financial health at the exit, the more likely the scenario of unwanted inflation and difficulties managing monetary policy becomes.[33]

To begin with, under the new Bank of Japan Act, revenues from purchases of long-term JGBs undertaken by the BOJ as part of its monetary policy are paid to the national treasury, but the BOJ must assume its responsibility for disposing of any losses. On this point, Okina (1999) says that "from the point of view of clarification of responsibility, it is only natural that the cost of the central bank's actions should bounce back to the central bank," but there are limitations when it comes to the BOJ assuming the responsibility for disposing of the losses arising from a "new phase" of measures like the current phase.[34] The gains arising as a result of the irregular monetary policy and subsequent losses must be seen comprehensively, and the Japanese government and the BOJ must also come to some prior arrangement concerning their allocation.

4.5 There is also the risk of increased uncertainty in the inflation and interest rate outlook

As explained above, the BOJ needs to continue explaining to the market that the purchases of long-term JGBs are not for the purpose of monetization. Let us examine the type of factors that cause changes in the current account balances at the BOJ according to BOJ statistics (see figure 4-2). According to the BOJ's definitions, banknotes (A) and treasury funds and others (B) give rise to a surplus/shortage of funds (C), which are subject to BOJ loans and market operations (D). The amount remaining after market operations (the sum of the surplus/shortage of funds [C] and market operations [D]) will be the change in current account balances at the BOJ. Examination based on the period from FY 2000, when unconventional monetary policies were implemented, shows that the BOJ bought long-term JGBs and treasury discount bills from the market mainly to cover the shortage of funds arising from "treasury funds and others" originating from net JGB issuance (redemptions – issuance).

Also, the long-term JGBs and the treasury discount bills bought by the BOJ in its market operations are now reaching maturity, and since redemption payments which were supposed to have been made by the government to private financial institutions (current account balances at the BOJ) are now being paid to the BOJ, the shortage of funds due to treasury funds and others appears to be expanding (Bank of Japan, Financial Markets Department 2013).

If the level of JGB issuances continues to increase in the future and redemption periods lengthen, the difference between the value of long-term JGB issuances and the value of redemptions shown in figure 4-2 will expand further and may cause further expansion in the shortage of funds (parts shaded blue in Figure 4-2). If a situation develops where the BOJ buys long-term JGBs to ensure financial sustainability, this could be seen

Figure 4-2. BOJ buys JGBs to cover the shortage of funds caused by fiscal factors, etc.

Trillion yen

Fiscal Year	2000	2001	2002	2003	2004	2005	2006	2007	2008	2009	2010	2011	2012
Banknotes (A)	-1.6	-9.2	-3.2	-0.3	-3.3	-0.3	-0.9	-0.6	-0.4	-0.5	-3.6	0.1	-2.5
Treasury funds and others (B)	-33.2	-35.7	-63.5	-35.7	-65.0	-38.4	-38.8	-39.0	-36.9	-35.8	-34.3	-25.4	-38.7
L-T JGBs issued	-98.6	-116.5	-125.3	-151.0	-171.0	-158.3	-153.7	-126.8	-107.9	-112.6	-121.6	-126.0	-128.8
L-T JGBs redeemed	53.1	47.2	36.7	63.9	69.5	81.2	88.3	69.4	75.8	75.6	60.9	81.7	71.7
	-45.5	-69.3	-88.6	-87.1	-101.5	-77.1	-65.4	-57.4	-32.1	-37.0	-60.6	-44.3	-57.1
Treasury discount bills issued	-179.6	-181.3	-169.3	-212.8	-269.1	-221.3	-234.9	-259.7	-298.3	-388.3	-347.9	-373.6	-395.5
Treasury discount bills redeemed	169.1	156.3	133.6	176.6	244.8	216.7	218.7	238.5	267.2	338.8	338.7	347.1	381.9
	-10.5	-24.9	-35.7	-36.2	-24.3	-4.6	-16.1	-21.2	-31.1	-49.4	-9.2	-26.4	-13.7
General coordinating budget/ foreign exchange/others	22.8	58.4	60.8	87.6	60.7	43.2	42.8	39.5	26.3	50.7	35.5	45.4	32.1
Surplus/shortage of funds (C)=(A)+(B)	-34.8	-44.9	-66.7	-36.1	-68.3	-38.7	-39.7	-39.6	-37.4	-36.2	-37.9	-25.3	-41.2
Market operations (D)	22.2	66.7	70.0	41.5	67.7	34.2	20.2	42.1	45.3	37.5	55.2	19.0	64.9
Outright purchase of L-T JGBs (E)	5.3	7.9	13.4	14.8	14.6	14.5	14.4	14.5	15.5	22.0	22.9	27.5	44.9
Outright purchase of treasury discount bills (F)	1.2	69.9	56.7	38.4	42.3	19.2	19.3	17.9	20.5	20.8	15.7	5.5	32.2
Others (G)	15.7	-11.1	-0.1	-111.7	10.8	0.5	-13.4	9.7	9.3	-5.3	16.5	-13.9	-12.2
Net change in current deposit (H)=(C)+(D)	-12.5	21.8	3.3	5.4	-0.6	-4.6	-19.5	2.6	7.9	1.3	17.3	-6.3	23.7

Source: Sources of Changes in Current Account Balances at the Bank of Japan and Market Operations (Final Figures).
Note: Issuance of JGBs is indicated as a negative figure, as it takes money out of the market; redemption of JGBs is indicated as a positive figure, as it returns money to the market.

as fiscal financing and might also lead to instability in financial markets. As also shown in results of analysis by the BOJ (2013), an asymmetric relationship exists between long-term interest rates and volatility such that, at times of rising interest rates (falling prices), sales to avoid losses are more likely to occur and volatility increases. Due to this asymmetry, in rising interest rate environments, the risk of the destabilization of financial markets also tends to increase. It may also be necessary to envisage in advance the risk of increased uncertainty in the inflation and interest rate outlook.

5. Tapering of Easing in the United States and Japan May Also Cause a Reversal of Money Flows from Asia

If the United States undertakes monetary tightening at the same time Japan starts to look for an exit, this may have an impact on money flows around the world, especially in Asian emerging economies. When FRB chairman Ben Bernanke commented on June 19 of this year that the United States was likely to start tapering the third round of quantitative easing (QE3) by the end of the year, bonds and shares of Asian countries were sold and money flowed out of these countries.

According to the empirical results of Tōji, Iwata, and Fueda-Samikawa (2013), as a result of the comments by Ben Bernanke in June, rising long-term interest rates and falling stock prices were confirmed in South Korea, the Philippines, and Singapore; rising long-term interest rates were observed in Malaysia; and falling stock prices were observed in Indonesia. In the meantime, money flows appear to have reversed into the US from emerging Asian economies. Later, in September, when the Federal Open Market Committee decided to postpone the tapering of QE3, long-term interest rates fell in Thailand and Hong Kong, and the local currencies of Malaysia and Indonesia strengthened against the dollar. As a result of validation, in all cases, a statistically significant relationship with the postponement of QE3 tapering was observed. The first round of quantitative easing (QE1), pursued by the FRB from November 2008 to March 2009, was also confirmed to have brought about a flow of funds into Asian countries, lowered long-term interest rates in Asia, and strengthened Asian currencies. Meanwhile, Japan's QQE caused the currencies of Malaysia, the Philippines, Singapore, and Thailand to rise against the Japanese yen.

In Asian countries, generally speaking, foreign-currency–denominated assets account for a larger share of the central bank's total assets than in Japan, the United States, and Europe. This is because in many countries in Asia, the central bank engages in exchange intervention on its own account,[35] and since domestic financial markets are underdeveloped, the central bank has no choice but to carry out market operations in the foreign-exchange market (Nishihara 2005). Meanwhile, on the liabilities side, locally denominated debt such as banknotes accounts for the majority of debt, and due to the currency mismatch of assets and liabilities, these countries have a relatively high level of interest-rate risk exposure. Given that, especially since the Lehman Shock, local currencies have grown stronger as a result of inflows of funds from advanced economies, Asian economies have increased their foreign currency reserves. Part 4 pointed out that the mismatch in the maturities of assets and liabilities on the BOJ's balance sheet has grown, and this has increased the risk of impairment of the balance sheet, but Asian central banks face the risk of impairment of their balance sheet due to the "currency mismatch" of assets and liabilities.[36] Problems with central banks' balance sheets are also occurring in Asia.

When tapering of quantitative easing starts in earnest in the United States and Japan in the future, there is the risk that the bonds and shares of Asian countries will be sold, triggering sudden fund outflows from Asia. In this event, if Asian central banks start to protect their currencies, absorbing the local currency through exchange intervention, there is also the risk that bank lending to domestic corporations and households will be reduced and Asian economies will cool down. The spillover effects that the monetary policies of advanced economies have on the management of monetary policy and the real economy in Asian countries also need to be monitored carefully.

6. Conclusion

This report has examined the impact that the policy of quantitative and qualitative easing, the first "arrow" of Abenomics, has had on financial variables in Japan and abroad. In contrast to the numerous unconventional monetary policies introduced in the past, QQE, launched in April of this year, had a certain effect on long-term interest rates, exchange rates, and stock prices. However, to make the policy effects extend to real investment, the BOJ needs to lower the term premium through quantitative easing and issue clear and trustworthy forward guidance on interest rates.

The BOJ expected QQE to have the effect of lowering the share of long-term JGBs held by the private sector and curbing rises in interest rates. Since, in the meantime, the government issued long-term JGBs and attempted to curb interest payment expenses, the remaining maturity of the long-term JGBs held by the private sector increased around two years in a period of ten years. In light of confirmation of the possibility that the JGB management policy of lengthening redemption periods weakened monetary policy effects, consistency between monetary policy and government-bond management policy will be required in the future. The arrangement made between the Bank of England and HM Treasury in March 2009 might serve as a reference.

One of the risks associated with QQE is the BOJ's balance sheet problem. Since the BOJ is increasing its long-term JGB holdings during its QQE program, the interest income earned from them is expanding, pushing up profits (current account surplus). However, when, in an exit, the BOJ raises interest rates on excess reserves, there is the risk that the BOJ's remittances to the treasury will stop for at least three years, increasing the public burden. The greater the extent to which achievement of the inflation target is delayed and the BOJ's balance sheet expands, and the greater the extent to which inflation exceeds expectations and short-term interest rates rise, the more the amount of interest payments on excess reserves will swell, and the more the BOJ's profits (current account surplus) will be squeezed. If the BOJ is tied up with maintaining its own financial health when this happens, monetary tightening may be delayed. The BOJ and the government ought to come to a prior arrangement on the allocation of risks or gains arising at the end of the irregular monetary policy.

In a rising interest-rate environment, the risk that financial markets will become unstable tends to increase. It is also necessary to anticipate that any change in monetary policy in the United States and Japan will increase the volatility of Asian financial markets and cause a change in global money flows.

If a situation develops where the BOJ purchases long-term JGBs to ensure financial stability, this could be seen as fiscal financing and lead to instability in financial markets. The critical question is how to strike a balance between price stability in the medium to long term (monetary policy) and fiscal sustainability (fiscal policy, including JGB management), while fully considering the risk of increased uncertainty in the inflation and rate outlook.

Courtesy of Japan Center for Economic Research (JCER).

Originally published by the Japan Center for Economic Research (JCER) in FY 2013 JCER Financial Research Report: General Remarks.

Notes

1. In FY 1988, at the peak of the Japanese bubble a quarter of a century ago, the total assets of all banks expanded 25 percent in the space of a year. At the time of writing, the BOJ's balance sheet is expanding at twice that rate.
2. According to the Guide to Flow of Funds Accounts Statistics provided by the Research and Statistics Department of the BOJ, JGBs excluding treasury discount bills, and financing bills issued by the Special Account for Fiscal Investment and Loan Program, are included in long-term JGBs. Also, since financing bills (FBs) and treasury bills (TBs) were integrated and issued as "Treasury Discount Bills" in February 2009, TBs are included in "JGBs and financing bonds."
3. Under the comprehensive easing policy pursued from October 2010 to March of this year, both the BOJ and domestic banks were net buyers of long-term JGBs.

4. According to Carpenter et al. (2013a), sellers of long-term JGBs were households, brokers and dealers, and insurance companies.
5. The *Nikkei* (*Nihon Keizai Shimbun*), article on the fifth page of the morning edition titled "Erratic fluctuations in stock market show no signs of abating."
6. In this regard, the BOJ is devising ways to soften the shock to the bond market by, for example, making the value of purchases per operation smaller and increasing the frequency of operations.
7. According to Okina (2013a), in the case of bonds with different creditworthiness, such as government bonds and corporate bonds, a premium added to interest rates according to the credit risk of the borrower (credit risk premium) is also taken into consideration.
8. Ueda (2013), published during the work of this analysis, explains that "QQE has not worked as theoretically expected, and the structure is fragile in that the weak yen and stock prices are underpinned by speculative investors with a short-term perspective."
9. Woodford (2012) explains that non-state-contingent guidance is unwise.
10. Forms of forward guidance are based on Shirai (2013). Shirai comments that "forward guidance expressions may change as time passes."
11. Release dated April 4, 2014, titled "Introduction of the Quantitative and Qualitative Monetary Easing."
12. Nakazawa and Furukawa (2011) and Saito and Sudo (2009) are used as references for the approach to maturities.
13. Ueda (2013) mentions that purchases of long-term JGBs through asset-purchase funds under comprehensive easing were restricted to JGBs with remaining maturities not exceeding three years, and that these were, for all intents and purposes, assets close to the monetary base. Ueda also states that "in some respects, the BOJ conducted operations selecting JGBs which in themselves would have little effect."
14. Statement of BOJ Monetary Policy Meeting showing the size of the increase in the value of purchases by asset purchase funds, etc. clearly stated in notes, "In addition to purchases under the Asset Purchase Program, the bank regularly purchases Japanese government bonds at the pace of ¥21.6 trillion per year."
15. Release dated April 27, 2012, titled "Enhancement of Monetary Easing."
16. Whereas the BOJ's quantitative easing policy was a policy that focused on the liabilities side of the balance sheet—that is, deposits in BOJ current accounts—the FRB's credit-easing policy focused on the assets side of the balance sheet.
17. According to the release dated January 16, 2001, titled "(Reference) Points of Recent Decision," the official name of the JGB purchase rule is the "Rule for Selection of Issues Eligible for Purchase in JGB Buying Operations."
18. *Nikkei Veritas*, article on page 2 of the October 6, 2013, edition, titled "All quiet on the JGB front: the dangerous sense of confidence created by BOJ trades."
19. In the United States, the duration of treasury securities held by the private sector (i.e., not the FRB) is more than double that of the SOMA's holdings of treasury securities (FRB 2013). This is a bigger gap than in Japan (1.7 times).
20. On this point, Komiya (2002) says, "If changing the maturity structure of privately held debt securities is expected to have some kind of desirable effect in relation to macro-economic policy, then this should be done through government bond management policy by the financial authorities. Especially as things are in Japan, judging from the size of the amounts of issuance, redemptions, and sales and purchases of medium-term and long-term bonds, the influence of the BOJ is but slight compared with that of the MOF."
21. http://webarchive.nationalarchives.gov.uk/+/http://www.hm-treasury.gov.uk/d/chxletter_boe050309.pdf
22. Iwata (2010) mentions, with respect to foreign exchange intervention, that "consistency between monetary policy management and intervention policy not only enhances the effects of intervention policy but also enhances the effects of monetary policy."
23. The difference between the acquisition cost and face value is recorded as the "JGB interest payment" in the profit and loss statement.
24. The BOJ has paid 0.1 percent interest on the current account deposits held by financial institutions at the bank that exceed legal reserve requirements since October 2008, following the Lehman Shock.
25. Bernanke (2012) has said that one possible exit strategy, besides selling asset holdings, is to exert upward pressure on short-term interest rates by raising the interest paid on deposits (reserves).
26. At the time of writing (November 2013), most analysts expect that the timing of the tapering of easing will be postponed until 2014.
27. Strictly speaking, this is the outstanding amount of assets in SOMA (the System Open Market Account).
28. With respect to the FRB's halting of MBS purchases and their sale, Krishnamurthy and Vissing-Jorgensen (2013) say that selling MBS, which are

scarce, has a greater impact on the private sector than selling JGBs, which mainly affects the government's financing costs.

29. http://www.federalreserve.gov/newsevents/testimony/bernanke20130226a.htm
30. Monetary tightening through long-term JGB selling operations was not included in the scope of this analysis, on the grounds that it was unrealistic in view of the shock to the bond market, but Carpenter et al. (2013) have analyzed the extent to which losses on the sale of MBS would squeeze the FRB's profits. Also, here, fund absorption through the sale of bills is regarded as synonymous with raising the rate of interest on excess reserves in the sense that the BOJ incurs interest payments.
31. The BOJ's "other ordinary expenses" (including interest payments on excess reserves) were ¥43.2 billion in FY 2012.
32. Remittances to the treasury are the current account surplus after payment of corporate, inhabitant, and enterprise taxes less the transfer to the statutory reserve (5 percent of the current account surplus) and dividends (¥5 million per year, 5 percent of the amount of paid-in investment). Remittances to the treasury are tax-deductible.
33. Okina also argues for the revival of the loss-coverage provision from the same perspective.
34. The BOJ could also raise the cash-deposit ratio to reduce the burden of interest payments on excess reserves. However, in this case, since private banks would essentially be subject to taxation by being forcibly made to hold reserve deposits with super low-interest rates (Fukao 2013), this could have an impact on the corporate sector and the household sector in the form of a premium added to lending interest rates.
35. In Japan, since the government holds the majority of foreign currency reserves, the risk of impairment of the BOJ's balance sheet due to currency mismatch is not as high as for Asian central banks.
36. On the assets side of the balance sheet, relatively low-interest United States Treasury securities have increased, while on the liabilities side, liabilities denominated in the local currency have expanded, and, on the basis of the interest rate differential alone, there is a strong possibility that central banks face a negative spread.

References

Bernanke, Ben S. 2012. "Monetary Policy since the Onset of the Crisis." Speech at the Federal Reserve Bank of Kansas City Economic Symposium, August 31, Jackson Hole, Wyoming.

Bernanke, Ben S., Vincent R. Reinhart, and Brian P. Sack. 2004. "Monetary Policy Alternatives at the Zero Bound: An Empirical Assessment." *Brookings Papers on Economic Activity*, no. 2, 1–100.

Carpenter, Seth B., Selva Demiralp, Jane E. Ihrig, and Elizabeth C. Klee. 2013a. "Analyzing Federal Reserve Asset Purchases: From Whom Does the Fed Buy?" Finance and Economics Discussion Series, no. 2013-32, Board of Governors of the Federal Reserve System (US).

Carpenter, Seth B., Jane E. Ihrig, Elizabeth C. Klee, Daniel W. Quinn, and Alexander H. Boote. 2013b. "The Federal Reserve's Balance Sheet and Earnings: A Primer and Projections." Finance and Economics Discussion Series, no. 2013-56, Board of Governors of the Federal Reserve System (US).

Chadha, Jagjit S., Philip Turner, and Fabrizio Zampolli. 2013. "The Interest Rate Effects of Government Debt Maturity." BIS Working Paper Series, no. 415, Bank for International Settlements.

Cúrdia, Vasco, and Michael Woodford. 2011. "The Central-Bank Balance Sheet as an Instrument of Monetary Policy." *Journal of Monetary Economics* 58 (1): 54–79.

Federal Reserve Bank of New York, Markets Group. 2013. *Domestic Open Market Operations during 2012*. April. https://www.newyorkfed.org/medialibrary/media/markets/omo/omo2012-pdf.pdf.

Kiley, Michael T. 2012. "The Aggregate Demand Effects of Short- and Long-Term Interest Rates." Finance and Economics Discussion Series, no. 2012-54, Board of Governors of the Federal Reserve System (US).

Krishnamurthy, Arvind, and Annette Vissing-Jorgensen. 2013. "The Ins and Outs of LSAPs." Paper presented at Jackson Hole Economic Policy Symposium, August 23, Federal Reserve Bank of Kansas City.

Stein, Jeremy C. 2012. "Evaluating Large-Scale Asset Purchases." Speech at the Brooking Institution, Washington, DC, October 11.

Ueda Kazuo. 2013. "The Response of Asset Prices to Abenomics: Is It a Case of Self-Fulfilling Expectations?" CIRJE Discussion Paper Series, no. CIRJE-F-885, Faculty of Economics, University of Tokyo.

Woodford, Michael. 2012. "Methods of Policy Accommodation at the Interest-Rate Lower Bound." Paper presented at the Jackson Hole Economic Policy Symposium, August 31, Federal Reserve Bank of Kansas City.

References originally in Japanese

Bank of Japan. 2013. *Kin'yū shisutemu repōto* [Financial System Report]. BOJ Reports and Research Papers, October 2013.

Bank of Japan, Financial Market Bureau. 2004. *Kokusai shijō to Nippon Ginkō* [Government Bond Market and the Bank of Japan]. BOJ Reports and Research Papers, April 2004.

———. 2013. *2012-nendo no kin'yū shijō chōsetsu* [Financial Market Control in FY 2012]. BOJ Reports and Research Papers, May 2013.

Bank of Japan, Planning Office. 2004. *Nippon Ginkō no seisaku: Gyōmu to baransu shīto* [BOJ's Policy & Operations and Balance Sheet]. BOJ Reports and Research Papers, June 2004.

Inagaki Yasuhide, Fueda-Samikawa Ikuko, and Iwata Kazumasa. 2013. "Ijigen kanwa no deguchi de hassei suru kosuto" [Cost to Be Incurred at the Exit from Different Dimension Easing]. Financial Research Report 2013-4, Japan Center for Economic Research (November 2013).

Iwata Kazumasa. 2010. *Defure tono tatakai: Nichigin fukusōsai no 1800-nichi* [Battle with Deflation: 1,800 Days of BOJ Deputy Governor]. Tokyo: Nihon Keizai Shimbun Shuppansha.

———. 2013. "Abenomikusu to Keinzu no kōkai shokan" [Abenomics and Keynes' Open Letter]. *Iwata Kazumasa no banri ikkū* (column), Japan Center for Economic Research. October 29, 2013.

Japan Center for Economic Research, and Komiya Ryūtarō, eds. 2002. *Kin'yū seisaku rongi no sōten: Nichigin hihan to sono hanron* [Main Issues of Monetary Policy Debates: Criticism for the BOJ and Objection]. Tokyo: Nihon Keizai Shimbun Shuppansha.

Nakazawa Masahiko, and Yoshikawa Hiroshi. 2011. *Defureka no kin'yū seisaku: Ryōteki kanwa seisaku no kenshō* [Monetary Policy under Deflation: Verification of Quantitative Easing Policy]. PRI Discussion Paper Series 11A-03, Ministry of Finance, Policy Research Institute, March 2011.

Nishihara Rie. 2005. "EMEAP chūgin no baransu shīto to shijō risuku kanri" [The Balance Sheet of EMEAP Central Banks and Market Risk Management]. BOJ Reports and Research Papers, January 2005.

Okina Kunio. 1999. "Zero infureka no kin'yū seisaku ni tsuite: Kin'yū seisaku e no gimon, hihan ni dō kotaeruka" [Monetary Policy under Zero Inflation: How to Respond to the Questions and Criticism about Monetary Policy]. *Kin'yū kenkyū* (Institute for Monetary and Economic Studies, Bank of Japan) 18 (3): 121–154.

———. 2011. *Posuto-manetarizumu no kin'yū seisaku* [Monetary Policy of Post-Monetarism]. Tokyo: Nihon Keizai Shimbun Shuppansha.

———. 2013a. *Kin'yū seisaku no furontia: Kokusaiteki chōryū to hi-dentōteki seisaku* [Monetary Policy's Frontier: Global Trends and Untraditional Policies]. Tokyo: Nihon Hyōronsha.

———. 2013b. *Nippon Ginkō* [The Bank of Japan]. Tokyo: Chikuma Shobō.

Okina Kunio and Shiratsuka Shigenori. 2003. "Komittomento ga kitaikeisei ni ataeru kōka: Jikanjiku kōka no jisshōteki kentō" [Commitment's Effects on the Formation of Expectation: Empirical Study of Time Axis Effects]. IMES Discussion Paper Series, Institute for Monetary and Economic Studies, Bank of Japan, June 2003.

Saitō Yoshihiko, and Sudō Tokihito. 2009. *Kokusai ruiseki jidai no kin'yū seisaku* [Monetary Policy of the Era of Accumulated Government Bonds]. Tokyo: Nihon Keizai Hyōronsha.

Shirai Sayuri. 2013. *Waga kuni no kin'yū seisaku to fōwādo gaidansu: Kin'yū seisaku un'ei ni tsuite no komyunikēshon seisaku* [Japan's Monetary Policy and Forward Guidance: Communication Policy on the Management of Monetary Policy]. Speeches at the International Monetary Fund (19 September) and the Board of Governors of the Federal Reserve System, Washington, DC (20 September), Bank of Japan, September 2013. Originally in English as "Monetary Policy and Forward Guidance in Japan."

Shiratsuka Shigenori, Teranishi Yuki, and Nakajima Jōchi. 2010. "Kin'yū seisaku komittomento no kōka: Waga kuni no keiken" [Effects of Monetary Policy Commitment: Experiences in Japan]. *Kin'yū kenkyū* (Institute for Monetary and Economic Studies, Bank of Japan) 29 (3): 239–266.

Shiratsuka Shigenori, and Fujiki Hiroshi. 2001. "Zero kinri seisakuka ni okeru jikanjiku kōka: 1999–2000-nen no tanki kin'yū shijō dēta ni yoru kenshō" [Time Axis Effects under the Zero Interest Rate Policy: Verification with Short-Term Market Data in 1999–2000]. *Kin'yū kenkyū* (Institute for Monetary and Economic Studies, Bank of Japan) 20 (4): 137–170.

Tōji Takayuki, Iwata Kazumasa, and Fueda-Samikawa Ikuko. 2013. "Ryōteki kin'yū kanwa ni honrō sareru Ajia: Ryōteki kanwa shukushō de manē wa Ajia kara Beikoku ni gyakuryū suru ka?" [Asia at the Mercy of Quantitative Easing: Will Money Flow back from Asia to the US as Quantitative Easing Is Reduced?]. Financial Research Report 2013-5, Japan Center for Economic Research, November 2013.

Ueda Kazuo. 2005. *Zero kinri to no tatakai: Nichigin no kin'yū seisaku o sōkatsu suru* [Fighting against Zero Interest Rates: Reviewing the BOJ's Monetary Policy]. Tokyo: Nihon Keizai Shimbun Shuppansha.

———. 2012. "Hi-dentōteki kin'yū seisaku no yūkōsei: Nippon Ginkō no keiken" [The Effectiveness of Non-Traditional Monetary Policy: The Case of the Bank of Japan]. CARF Working Paper Series CARF-J-079, Center for Advanced Research in

Finance, University of Tokyo, January 2012. Originally in English as CARF Working Paper Series CARF-F-252 (August 2011).

———. 2013. "Ijigen no kin'yū kanwa: Chūkan hyōka" [Different Dimension Monetary Easing: Interim Assessment]. CARF Working Paper Series CARF-J-099, Center for Advanced Research in Finance, University of Tokyo, September 2013.

Utsunomiya Hideo, Iwata Kazumasa and Fueda-Samikawa Ikuko. 2013. "Ijigen kanwa ga chōki kinri to shisan kakaku ni oyoboshita eikyō: Kinri no fowādo gaidansu dōnyū ga kadai ni" [Influence of Different Dimension Easing on Long-Term Interest Rates and Asset Prices: On the Introduction of Forward Guidance on Interest Rates]. Financial Research Report 2013-2, Japan Center for Economic Research, November 2013.

V-(3) What Do Growth Strategies Need?

Sweeping Away Anxiety Regarding the Future

Murata Keiko

Discuss Japan—Japan Foreign Policy Forum, 2018

The Abe cabinet has approved the Japanese government's growth strategies (Future Investment Strategy 2018) and the Basic Policy for Economic and Fiscal Management and Reform (known as the *honebuto no hōshin*, or big-boned policy outline).

Growth strategies for this year aim to realize "Society 5.0," with projects such as driverless automatic driving, next-generation healthcare systems, and e-government as priority areas, and aim to increase the potential growth rate through technological innovation. The strategies also incorporate various other measures for growth, such as human-resource development, work-style reforms, regulatory reforms, and economic partnerships, as stated in the big-boned policy outline, which is a growth strategy in a broad sense.

* * *

This is the sixth year under the growth strategies adopted by the Abe cabinet. The first growth strategy, which was formulated six months after the inauguration of the second Abe administration in June 2013 (the Japan Revitalization Strategy), was positioned as the third of the "three arrows" of Abenomics' economic policies.

In the Japan Revitalization Strategy, the Abe cabinet considered people's inability to have confidence and hope for the future as a result of economic stagnation to be a serious problem, and took the view that the first "arrow" of Abenomics (monetary policies) and the second "arrow" (fiscal policies) lit a lamp of expectation for the future of the Japanese economy. The role of the growth strategy was to transform the expectations of corporate managers and individuals into actions, and the strategy was to draw out the full potential of the private sector as a route to growth.

In the period that followed, the Abe cabinet formulated growth strategies every year. Unfortunately, however, there is no indication that the Japanese economy has increased its growth potential. The economic growth rate has remained steady, averaging around 1.3 percent, but has not reached the government's target of 2 percent real growth. Since the economic growth potential should be assessed from a medium- to long-term perspective, a further grace period may be needed until the growth strategy delivers results in terms of productivity and potential growth rate.

One thing I can say, though, is that the expectations and confidence of companies and individuals for Japan's economy, which were stressed in the first growth strategy, subsequently ran out of steam. According to the Cabinet Office's Annual Survey of Corporate Behavior, the real growth rate for the Japanese economy in the next five years as predicted by corporations rose slightly from 1.3 percent in the previous year to 1.5 percent immediately after the inauguration of the second Abe administration. However, the same rate sank to a level of between 1.0 percent and 1.1 percent in the last three years. The growth strategies adopted by the Japanese government are not leading to improved corporate expectations for long- and medium-term growth rates.

In the meantime, household expectations for the Japanese economy showed a noticeable improvement immediately after the implementation of Abenomics. In a survey that asked households about the Japanese economy's long-term

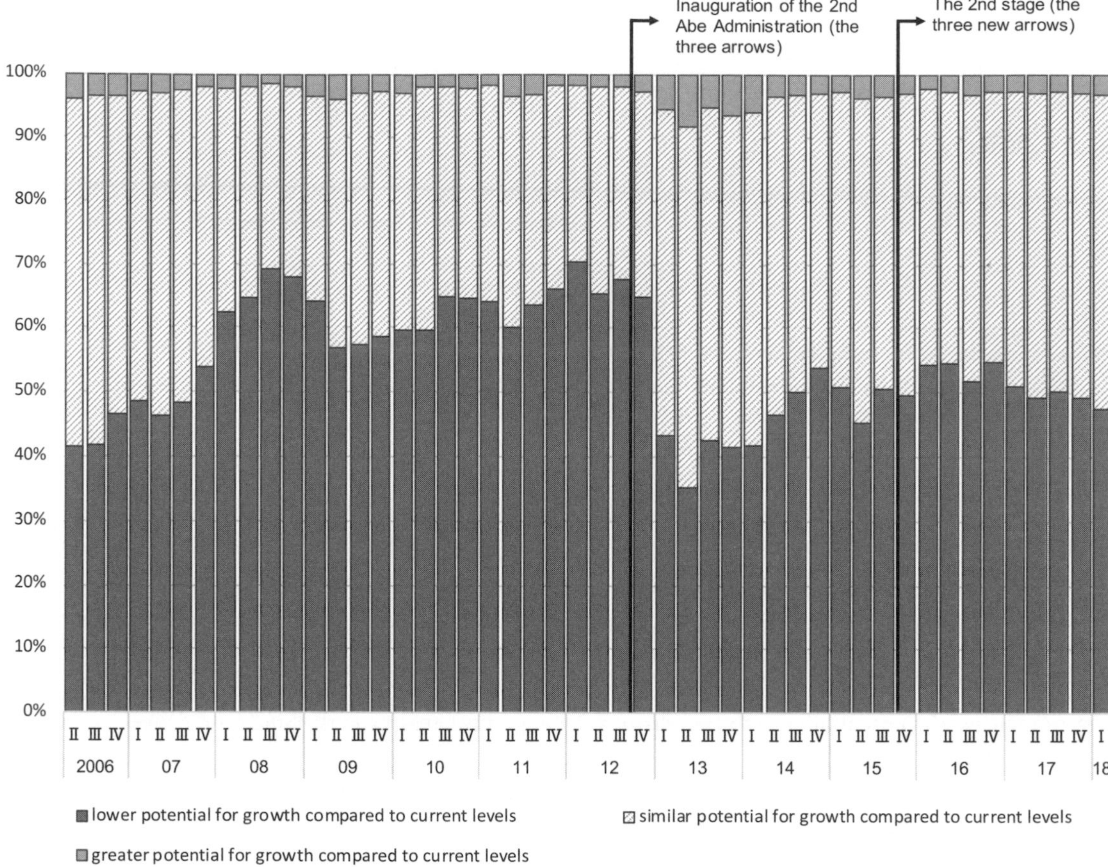

Perception of the Japanese economy's long-term growth potential (household)

Source: Created by author from data in the BOJ's Opinion Survey on the General Public's Views and Behavior.

growth potential, the pessimistic response of "lower potential for growth compared to current levels," which had previously accounted for more than half of the responses, decreased by around 30 percent in early 2013 (see figure above).

However, the number of people who took a pessimistic view grew again after the summer of 2013 when the third "arrow" was shot. The situation did not improve in the fall of 2015 when Abenomics moved to its second stage (known as the "three new arrows"). Growth strategies adopted by the Japanese government are not leading to an improvement in household expectations for the future of the Japanese economy, either.

* * *

For these reasons, I would like to consider growth strategies from the perspective of households, which are my field of study, in the following section as a point that has not been discussed very extensively.

Looking at the medium- and long-term trends in household expenditures, which account for 60 percent of Japan's gross domestic product (GDP), average real expenditures increased at the low rate of 1 percent from FY 2001 to FY 2010 and 0.7 percent in the period from FY 2011. Average real disposable income rose 0.6 percent from FY 2001 to FY 2010 and 0.5 percent from FY 2011 to FY 2016. In particular, growth of this income slowed to 0.4 percent in the period from FY 2013 to FY 2016.

Looking at the contribution of (real) compensation growth for employees to disposable income, the contribution rose 0.1 percent from FY 2001 to FY 2010 and 0.6 percent from FY 2011 to FY 2016. The contribution showed particular improvement in the period from FY 2013 to FY 2016, rising 0.8 percent. However, taxes and social insurance premiums (including the portions covered by companies) are deducted from the disposable income that actually reaches households. Increases in wage income are not leading to disposable income growth due to causes that include higher tax and social insurance premium burdens.

However, household expenditures gradually decline in level after the head of household peaks in her or his fifties. For that reason, we must keep in mind the impact of aging on consumption from a macroeconomic viewpoint.

Accordingly, I examined medium- and long-term household expenditure trends by householder age group based on data from the Family Income and Expenditure Survey by the Statistics Bureau of the Ministry of Internal Affairs and Communications (real data with imputed rent adjusted through equivalent exchanges).

To begin with, income dropped gradually among all age groups in the working generation (wage-earner households) in the period from 2000. Consumption remained relatively steady (in other words, the average propensity to consume stayed almost unchanged) among households headed by workers in their fifties. On the other hand, households headed by workers in their forties and thirties experienced a greater decline in expenditures, leading to a decrease in their propensity to consume.

We can explain this situation by taking the view that expected lifetime income is decreasing more among young people based on the standard life-cycle-permanent-income hypothesis. Households do not attempt to lower their expenditure level when they judge a continuing income decline to be a temporary phenomenon and predict that lifetime income will remain unchanged despite the situation. Under these circumstances, consumption propensity should rise as a result. This view is also in accordance with the slowing of a seniority-based wage curve from the medium- and long-term viewpoints.

Consumption propensity has declined substantially among households headed by workers in their thirties, albeit under the observed condition of income hitting bottom in the last few years. There is a possibility that these households are perceiving their income improvement as a temporary phenomenon.

In the meantime, looking at elderly households, income fell among households headed by people sixty years old or older (the sum of wage-earner households and households without an occupation) in the period from 2000. Their propensity to consume rose for both households in their sixties and those in their seventies and older, contrary to the younger households.

In the period from 2011, too, consumption propensity showed a gradual increase among households headed by people seventy years old and older. However, a downtrend in consumption propensity was observed in the same period among households headed by people in their sixties. The former positive trend resulted from a decrease in income among people in their seventies due to smaller pension benefits, larger tax burdens, and other causes. The latter downward trend was due to an increase in income: more heads of households in their sixties were working compared to earlier, which pushed up their income of households whose heads were in their sixties as a whole.

Positive effects on anticipated personal lifetime income arise when households become able to expect a high growth potential in the Japanese economy. Such a change is anticipated to increase consumption.

According to an analysis by Professor Ogawa Kazuo of Kansai Gaidai University (published in the *Keizai kyōshitsu* column of the *Nikkei Shimbun* on December 22, 2017), the consumption growth rate affects corporate growth expectations in Japan. If households' expectations of Japan's economic growth improve as a result of the government's growth strategy and the rate of increase in consumption rises, companies will be more willing to invest in plants and equipment, and this should lead to an increase in productivity and growth.

* * *

So what should be done about it? First, we should be more aware that the growth strategy has not improved the outlook for the Japanese economy for both firms and households. The details of growth strategies are important as a matter of course. Whether or not the confidence of the public can be won is equally important. Presenting a package of policies and future prospects for the Japanese economy that can be easily understood by the public as a whole is indispensable in that respect.

For example, it is necessary to present the fiscal and social security outlook and prospects, even if their content is harsh, in a straightforward manner to dispel the uncertainty of individuals. By increasing the credibility of policies, confidence in the growth strategy will increase, which is expected to lead to increased consumption and capital investment. The public's uncertainty about the future will gradually be alleviated as these steps are actually taken.

It is also essential to advance work-style reforms at the same time to raise the expected lifetime income of households so that they can increase their consumption with a sense of security. That is the second thing we can do.

The labor market should be changed to a neutral, more flexible labor market where people can work at any stage of their life, regardless of age or sex, at the appropriate market value without concern, and where changing jobs is not disadvantageous. This is a desirable course from the perspective of facilitating the movement of labor from low-productivity to high-productivity sectors of the Japanese economy, which continues to face a labor shortages, and therefore from the perspective of increasing productivity.

English version originally published in *Discuss Japan—Japan Foreign Policy Forum*, no. 50 (Oct.–Nov. 2018).

Translated by the Japan Journal, Ltd. The article first appeared in the *Keizai kyōshitsu* column of the *Nikkei Shimbun* on June 28, 2018, under the title, "Seichō senryaku ni nani ga hitsuyō ka (I): Kokumin no sakiyuki fuan fusshoku o" (What Do Growth Strategies Need? (I): Sweeping Away Anxiety Regarding the Future). (Courtesy of author)

V-(4) Agenda for the BOJ Governor in His Second Term*

Okina Kunio

Discuss Japan—Japan Foreign Policy Forum, 2018

The Bank of Japan (BOJ) has demonstrated its unwavering dedication to the achievement of a 2 percent inflation target over the last five years.

In his inaugural news conference held five years ago, BOJ governor Kuroda Haruhiko referred to the Joint Statement of the Government and the Bank of Japan on Overcoming Deflation and Achieving Sustainable Economic Growth, which was announced in January 2013, saying, "It can be summed up as we will do whatever it takes to achieve 2 percent inflation at the earliest date possible." Deputy Governor Iwata Kikuo also expressed his strong commitment to achieving the price stability target no matter what the situation would be, saying, "We should not make excuses by saying that it wasn't our responsibility if we fail to achieve the inflation target."

After five years of this policy, in January of this year consumer prices (excluding fresh food) rose 0.9 percent year on year, while those prices excluding energy as well (core CPI) rose only 0.4 percent. Meanwhile, the unemployment rate for the latest month has fallen to some 2 percent amid the strong recovery of the global economy.

Given that the pledged target has significantly remained unachieved to date, should the BOJ continue to pursue its current policy of placing the 2 percent price stability target above everything else? There has been no change in Governor Kuroda's stance to date. Newly appointed deputy governor Wakatabe Masazumi is known as a "reflationist," or a vocal advocate of aggressive easing, like Iwata. Unlike his predecessor, Wakatabe appears to be keen on ramping up stimulus by using fiscal policy in order to achieve the target. It seems obvious to me that the appointment of Wakatabe as deputy governor reflects the preference of the Abe administration.

On the other hand, it seems quite likely that further easing to achieve the price stability target when the economy is at full employment will destabilize the financial system. In this regard, the Japanese economy in the late 1980s is a case in point. During this period, Japan's wholesale prices dropped significantly, with a limited increase in consumer prices of less than 1 percent. (Please refer to the figure above.) These price conditions were the main reason why the BOJ had great difficulty in correcting its loose monetary policy despite the pronounced growth of an asset-price bubble.

The bubble subsequently burst, and the Japanese economy began suffering a prolonged recession for a number of years to come. By going through this difficult period, the BOJ became painfully aware that it must carefully monitor not only prices, but also the economy as a whole, including financial imbalances in particular.

Almost concurrently with the period of the post-bubble years in Japan, many central banks in industrialized economies were still in the process of beating excessively high rates of inflation with inflation targeting, which came into the spotlight as a tool for overcoming inflation. A formidable number of related research papers were produced by academia. Consequently, most of the central banks adopted an inflation target of something like 2 percent. The limitations inherent in this monetary policy experienced in Japan were not clearly understood by the central banks in Europe and the United States until after the

* This is the second of two articles written by the author on this topic.—Ed.

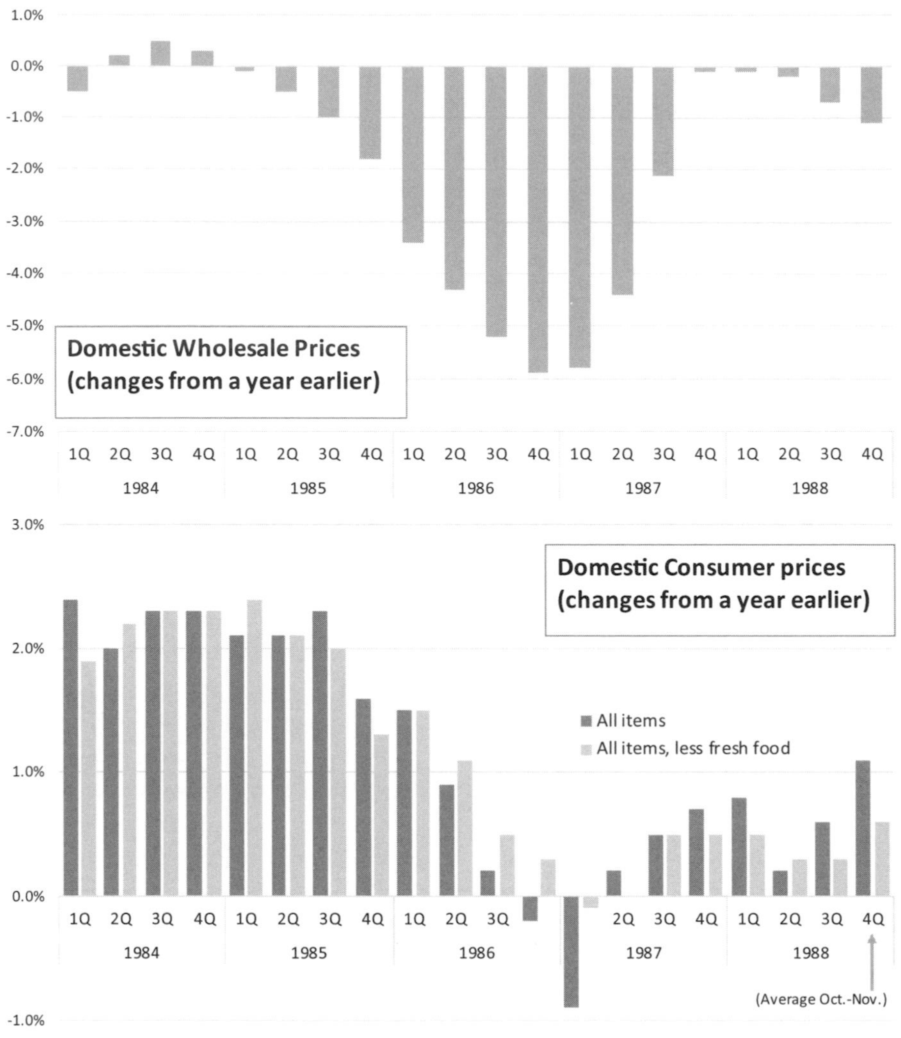

Consumer Prices in a Bubble Economy

Source: Bank of Japan *Jōsei handan shiryō* (Quarterly Economic Outlook), winter 1989.

global financial crisis of 2008, when the policy had already been implemented by many of them.

Looking back on half a century, seemingly legitimate reasons on different occasions (e.g., the battle against the revaluation of the yen, international cooperation aimed at weakening the dollar, growth driven by domestic demand) have, along with the persistent fears of the yen's appreciation, made the monetary policy inflexible. In light of a key lesson from past experience, I believe that further commitment to realizing 2 percent inflation in the near future by monetary policy alone would entail a significant risk.

As examined above, Japan's monetary policy has been in line with what Governor Kuroda has said and the expectations of the Abe administration, while involving a significant associated risk. What, then, should the BOJ's policy framework be for the next five years?

It should be the most realistic approach for the new leadership to return to the principles of the joint statement announced by the government and the BOJ that I discussed earlier in this article, given that Governor Kuroda has often stated that the joint statement is still in effect, and Prime Minister Abe Shinzō made it clear that he has no intention of revising the joint statement at the House of Councilors budgetary committee meeting on March 2, 2018.

Here, I would like to examine what the joint statement was like. In his inaugural news conference five years ago, Governor Kuroda said, "It can be summed up as we will do whatever it takes to achieve 2 percent inflation at the earliest date possible." Indeed, in the accord, the BOJ established its price stability target in terms of consumer prices increasing 2 percent over the previous year, emphasizing the early achievement of the target.

The joint statement, however, also calls for the BOJ to "ascertain whether there is any significant risk to the sustainability of economic growth, including from the accumulation of financial imbalances."

In a speech explaining the joint statement three days after its release, Shirakawa Masaaki (the BOJ's former governor) stated that overseas central banks have not set dates for achieving price stability irrespective of the adoption of inflation targeting. He also said that the BOJ's view on aiming for sustainable price stability is based on a similar understanding, and that it will bear in mind the risk of financial imbalances, while not confining itself to a specific date for achieving the inflation target.

Currently, the BOJ's yield curve control (maneuvering both short- and long-term interest rates) has led to the loss of fiscal discipline by the government, with bank profits being squeezed by a vanishing lending spread. This policy has also invited the significant decline of the functioning of the long-term government bond market, distorting price formation in the stock market through the BOJ's massive purchases of exchange-traded funds (ETFs). The joint statement does not give higher priority to the achievement of the inflation target over maintaining financial stability.

In the statement, the government pledged that, in strengthening its coordination with the BOJ, it would "steadily promote measures aimed at establishing a sustainable fiscal structure." While pursuing further monetary easing on a large scale would run the risk of making fiscal discipline weak, it does not seem realistically possible for the BOJ to directly disagree with the government taking advantage of low interest rates in government financing. The joint statement between the government and the BOJ must have been an important framework in order to call for the establishment of a sustainable fiscal structure to be used as a condition for further commitment to monetary easing.

It is likely that the government and the BOJ will pursue the price stability target further without conducting a comprehensive reassessment of the principles of the joint statement. What would then happen to the fiscal management?

In the event of a negative shock to the economy, the BOJ would come to a deadlock without any effective monetary policy. In this scenario, the central bank's monetary policy will be coordinated more closely with the government's fiscal policy without being debated under the banner of monetary easing aimed at a 2 percent inflation target, making it possible for the government to obscure monetization and its influence on monetary policy by emphasizing that the BOJ manages monetary policy alone with independent criteria.

Meanwhile, it will become far more necessary for the BOJ to revise its monetary policy as long as the economy remains at full employment, even if the price stability target fails to be achieved. In the event of this scenario, it is possible that the BOJ will deliberately leave unchanged the disparity between the apparent priority on achieving price stability and its real intention. In fact, the BOJ has clearly changed its policy instrument target from the quantity of monetary base to interest rates. The BOJ significantly reduced the amount of asset purchases while officially advocating the need for JGB purchases of ¥80 trillion per year. It seems to me that the BOJ's leadership team maintains a practical approach with the rather philosophical view that it will be OK as long as the players in the market understand the BOJ's real intentions, despite certain inconsistencies.

However, this type of approach lacks accountability and poses a significant risk. Market players usually try to interpret the BOJ's real intentions every time bank executives refer to the issues related to price stability efforts. The BOJ's messaging is interpreted as a signal to, say, induce the yen's depreciation, to support the stock market, and to lay the groundwork for exit strategies. Should there be any noticeable gap between the market estimations and the BOJ's real intentions, the market will be destabilized.

This offers certain points for discussion when it comes to talking about the exit strategy for the negative interest-rate policy. It is likely that the financial imbalances that have been obscured by the negative interest-rate policy will become evident when exiting from the ultra-loose monetary policy.

It will therefore be necessary for the BOJ to secure greater leeway for its monetary policy by hammering out specific measures designed to minimize the shock to the financial market as well as the losses being forced on financial institutions, while restoring the sustainability of government finances in advance when it comes to taking steps toward the exit. In order to do so, the government and the BOJ should exchange views, including a number of proposals that have already been offered, in an open manner with private-sector experts as well.

The BOJ, however, continues to reject any discussion of exit strategies because the prospect of achieving the inflation target remains out of view. Given this situation, concerns might start looming rapidly that the government and the BOJ will pass the impairment of the BOJ's balance sheet on to financial institutions by adopting measures that include a significant increase in the reserve requirement ratio for financial institutions when moving toward an exit.

In January 2016, the BOJ unexpectedly introduced a negative interest-rate policy, of which it had denied any possibility until its announcement. The BOJ may have made the surprise move because it was concerned that the move would invite strong criticism from financial institutions that would see their profits being squeezed, and the policy adoption would eventually be deadlocked if the introduction were announced in advance. Paradoxically, this surprise move by the BOJ has led to a more persistent deflationary mindset and made banks into the BOJ's enemies. Many market players have painful experience with Governor Kuroda's tactful announcements, which are often intended to produce a market surprise.

As Governor Kuroda attempts to reject discussions of exit strategies more forcefully, his stance will make market players even more concerned about the exit program, leaving them to speculate about any news. This will further restrict the BOJ's dialogue opportunities with the market, creating a vicious cycle. The BOJ must improve its dialogue with the market and assume accountability without creating a "Taper Tantrum."

English version originally published in *Discuss Japan—Japan Foreign Policy Forum*, no. 47 (May–June 2018).

Translated by The Japan Journal, Ltd. The article first appeared in the *Keizai kyōshitsu* column of *Nikkei Shimbun* on 14 March 2018 under the title, "Nichigin shintaisei no kadai II: Bukka-mokuhyō no hitori aruki kiken—'Kyōdō seimei' no zentai saikakunin o" (Agenda for BOJ Governor in Second Term II: Further Commitment to Maintaining the Price Stability Target Entails a Risk—It Is Important to Return to the Principles of the "Joint Statement"). (Courtesy of author)

Part VI

The International Economy

A central challenge for trade policy during the Heisei era was the Trans-Pacific Partnership (TPP) agreement. The TPP was launched in 2006 with a limited number of countries participating. Subsequently, thanks to the United States coming on board, it became a large-scale economic partnership agreement. Views at home were divided as to whether Japan, too, should participate. In 2011, Prime Minister Kan Naoto from the DPJ announced that Japan would participate, but he failed to garner consensus. The greatest cause of concern in relation to TPP participation was the potential impact on domestic agricultural products. In 2013, Prime Minister Abe announced that Japan would join the TPP, and in 2015 agreement was reached among the various interested parties. When Donald Trump became US president in January 2017, however, the United States left the TPP, and the agreement promptly fell apart. Japan played a leading role in rebuilding the TPP, which was established by eleven countries—absent the United States—as TPP-11.

As an agricultural expert, Yamashita Kazuhito has continued to stress the need to liberalize agricultural products. In "Japan Should Move Quickly to Participate in the TPP Negotiations," he discusses the pros and cons of TPP participation as of 2012, looking at the significance of TPP accession.

Mireya Solís and Urata Shūjirō review the Abe administration's trade policy in "Abenomics and Japan's Trade Policy in a New Era." They note that the government's bringing together of the TPP-11 in particular was a major achievement given the opposition faced at home from agricultural groups, and, internationally, the exit from the TPP of the United States under President Trump.

The essay "Is US-Japan Trade Friction Avoidable?: Blaming Trade Partners for Deficits Is Pointless" by Kiyota Kōzō discusses in economic terms the friction between the two countries caused by President Trump, noting that protecting industries with tariffs has a negative impact for the country as a whole and that imposing high tariffs on imports invites retalitation and shrinks world trade.

In "Challenges after the TPP-11 Agreement: A Guide toward Establishing Global Rules," Kimura Fukunari lauds the TPP-11 as a major achievement and discusses expectations of Japan as a free-trade leader.

VI-(1) Japan Should Move Quickly to Participate in the TPP Negotiations

Yamashita Kazuhito

Discuss Japan—Japan Foreign Policy Forum, 2012

Disciplining Big Powers' Actions in Line with International Economic Rules

China has emerged in the East Asia region, with its GDP now exceeding Japan's. It has also attempted to use its military to protect its maritime interests, stirring conflict with neighboring countries.

This situation raises concerns that China could implement measures that threaten both Japanese and global economic activities, such as banning exports of rare earth and other natural resources, imposing restrictions on investment, and resorting to other means backed by its tremendous national strength. In the same way the World Trade Organization (WTO) dispute-settlement procedures nullified one-sided measures such as Section 301 of the United States Trade Act, a framework is needed for disciplining China for its actions pursuant to the rules to which numerous countries have agreed.

These reasons suggest why it would be effective for Japan to participate in the Trans-Pacific Partnership (TPP) negotiations along with other developed countries of the Asia-Pacific region, including the United States, Australia, New Zealand, and Singapore, take the initiative in establishing advanced rules on regional trade and investment, and present those rules to China and other countries. If TPP participants expanded to include most of the countries and areas of the Asia-Pacific region, it is likely that Chinese companies would see it as in their best interest to comply with the rules. In other words, it is desirable to first establish the TPP among countries capable of complying with high-level rules, and then to incorporate China in order to establish a Free Trade Area of the Asia-Pacific (FTAAP) for the dual purposes of economic development and political stability in the overall region. This is necessary not only for controlling China's actions, but also those of the United States, where the benefits of certain industries can easily influence national trade policies.

Having Japan's Interests Reflected in the Global Rules through the TPP

Attempts are being made in the TPP negotiations to promote market liberalization to a level above that promised by WTO member countries, by means such as eliminating tariffs on goods and greater liberalization of service trade. Efforts are also being made to establish new rules and disciplines in areas the WTO has failed to control, such as investment, competition, trade and the environment, and trade and labor.

In the General Agreement on Tariffs and Trade (GATT) Uruguay Round negotiations, Japan was a member of the "core four" group (the United States, the European Union, Japan, and Canada), but these days Japan has barely secured its position following the United States, the European Union, China, India, and Brazil. Japan's position in the WTO has declined, rendering it less likely that its claims will be accommodated. In TPP negotiations, however, Japan could be influential alongside the United States, considering its economic size.

The TPP is an open and expansive economic partnership, and the rules agreed to within it are expected to serve as trade and investment rules governing wide regions, such as Asia-Pacific Economic Cooperation (APEC) countries. Also notable is that countries like Australia, New Zealand, and Singapore, which have exercised influence in the WTO beyond their respective economic capabilities due to their English proficiency and higher level of education, are TPP member countries, in addition to the United States, which has led WTO negotiations so far. The TPP is becoming an important convention in terms of both quantity and quality. Therefore, if the TPP establishes so-called WTO+ rules which encompass areas not yet under WTO scope, or further deepens existing WTO rules, the TPP rules are certain to be used as a reference when the WTO tries to establish them.

If TPP rules are brought into the WTO, Japan can reflect its interests in worldwide disciplines and rules by participating in the TPP talks and having its interests reflected there. This is why Japan needs to take part in the TPP negotiations promptly. It can only gain limited benefits if it participates just before negotiations conclude. Though opposition to the TPP on the grounds it would destroy the Japanese economy is poorly founded, if it is in fact valid, then Japan should take active part, since these negotiations are expected to establish trade and investment rules for the Asia-Pacific region, and for the world, and so Japan should strive to eliminate rules problematic for the Japanese economy.

Japan has made a top priority of maintaining many agricultural products as exempt from tariff elimination, not only in WTO negotiations but also in the bilateral economic partnerships it has concluded. Since Japan has consistently stuck with a defensive stance in negotiations on agricultural products, it has become difficult for it to elicit the compromises from other countries that it deserves in other areas. By shifting from protecting agricultural products via tariffs and prices to protecting them through fiscal policy, as in the United States and the European Union, and demonstrating through the TPP that Japan is capable of concluding high-quality agreements for eliminating all product tariffs, it could improve its diplomatic abilities in trade issues.

Some argue that it would be sufficient to leave rice as an exception in the TPP, just as in the GATT Uruguay Round negotiations Japan adopted a position of saving only rice, which has a great number of producers and wields strong political power. This led to an addition to the minimum access tariff-rate quota as compensation (minimum access, which was 5 percent of consumption if a non-tariff barrier was transformed into a tariff [this is called tariffication] in 1995, was increased to 8 percent by resorting to special treatment of tariffication), which was one of the factors that led to a decline in the rice production industry. In 1999, Japan inevitably shifted to tariffication due to the high minimum access level. (The minimum access has been 7.2 percent as a penalty for Japan delaying tariffication.) If Japan did not change its stance in negotiations, it would have no choice but to pay for compensation in the TPP negotiations as well. This would apply first to rice, if Japan wishes to treat it as an exception, and to other agricultural products if this is not sufficient, and even further to areas other than agriculture, as seen in lowered food-safety standards regarding BSE (bovine spongiform encephalopathy) and other concerns, and deregulation of service trade.

Importance as a Growth Strategy

There is a concern that Japan's smaller working-age population and aging society will seriously affect its economic productivity. If companies globalize through trade and investment, the technologies and energy of other countries can be imported to revitalize the innovation necessary for economic growth. Analyses have shown that corporate productivity rises by 2 percent by exporting products, 2 percent by making direct overseas investments, and 3 percent by conducting research and development overseas. Other analyses have demonstrated that investment in research and development in Japan by overseas companies has enhanced the related industry productivity by 4 percent.

Economic partnership with Asian countries is certainly important. However, from the above viewpoint, Japan's participation in the TPP negotiations, which include advanced countries in the Asia-Pacific region such as the United States, Australia, New Zealand, and Singapore, is more effective for revitalizing national innovation. Eliminating tariffs is not enough on its own for expanding overseas production and technological networks. It is more effective, through the TPP and other economic partnerships, to make trade rules more transparent, simplify trade procedures, build harmony with international standards, promote smoother migration of engineers and businesspeople over national boundaries for facilitating smoother trade, and encourage investment and prohibit unnecessary restrictions relating to investment. Significant results are expected, for instance, if measures for facilitating trade are incorporated into the TPP, such as electronic certificates, unification of contact points at trade-related organizations, and having products made in the same region distributed without tariffs as a rule.

Considerations for Those Affected by the Great East Japan Earthquake

Many people's incomes have fallen following the Great East Japan Earthquake and in the wake of the global economic recession triggered by the 2008 financial crisis. High prices for domestic agricultural products have placed a heavy burden on low-income consumers.

Talk of trade liberalization emphasizes profits from production enjoyed by exporting industries and damage suffered by affected industries competing with imported products. Opposition to the TPP commonly espouses the attitude of protecting vested interests, asserting that industries such as agriculture and medical treatment, which have been protected by regulations, are affected. However, we should never forget that consumers receive significant benefits from trade liberalization.

Protection of agriculture amounting to ¥4 trillion (OECD estimate), which has forced consumers to pay prices for agricultural products in excess of international prices, is equivalent to an additional 1.6 percent consumption tax. In other words, Japanese citizens have unknowingly borne a consumption tax amount of 6.6 percent (1.6 percent above 5.0 percent). This is an unclear and regressive burden.

Customers have borne this ¥4 trillion burden for domestic agricultural products alone. Duties and charges are also levied on overseas agricultural products, making their prices balance with those of domestic agricultural products. As such, consumers are made to pay the difference between these prices. The actual amount borne by consumers exceeds ¥4 trillion. Taking wheat as an example, consumers have assumed the same burden for domestic wheat, which accounts for only 14 percent of all wheat consumed, as for foreign-made wheat, which accounts for 86 percent of all wheat consumed. Replacing the amount borne by consumers with respect to domestic agricultural products with direct payment by fiscal burden would remove the duties and charges for foreign-made agricultural products without need for further fiscal burden. A Japanese shift to political measures based on a fiscal burden will decrease the amount borne by the general public.

If the TTP is realized and food prices decline, consumers may benefit from both price cuts and increased consumption, which would be good news for those who lost their jobs and incomes due to the Lehman Brothers collapse or the Great East Japan Earthquake.

Some argue that if it is certain that food prices will decline in the future, consumers will refrain from their purchasing, and this will aggravate deflation. However, unlike durable goods such as cars and televisions, consumers will not restrict purchases of food, which is a daily necessity.

Agriculture Is the Area that Needs the TPP More

Since agriculture is conducted on a smaller scale in Japan compared to the United States and Australia, some assert that it is expensive and less competitive. In terms of farm area per farming family, if Japan is 1, then the EU is 9; the United States is 100; and Australia is 1,902.

It is true that costs decrease as production size grows, but size is not the only important factor. If the above assertion proved true, the United States, which is the world's largest agricultural exporter, would be unable to compete with Australia because its scale is one-nineteenth that of Australia. This assertion does not consider the differences in crops being produced. The United States mainly produces wheat, soybeans, and corn, while Australia mainly produces livestock fed with pasture grass. Japan cannot appropriately

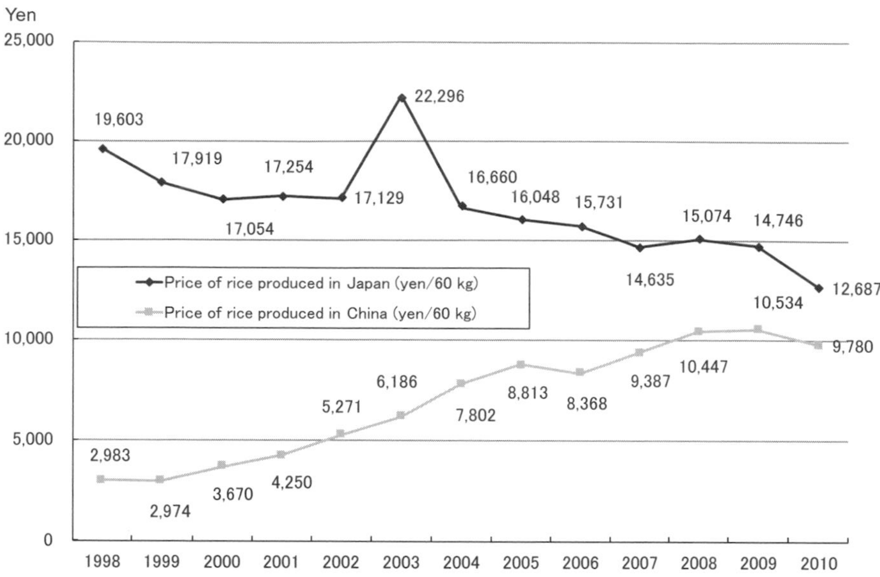

Change in Prices of Rice Produced in Japan and China (per 60 kg)

Source: The graph was adapted from Yamashita Kazuhito, *The Economics of the Agricultural Big Bang,* p. 278; raw data from MAFF.

be compared with these countries, since it mainly produces rice. Threats regarding Japanese rice production mainly come from China, but the number of farming families in China is only one-third that of Japan. Also notable is that, even for the same crop, great differences are found in yield per area and quality. Since the yield of wheat in France is triple that in the United States, a farming family owning 100 hectares of farmland in France is more efficient than one in the United States with 200 hectares.

There are japonica and indica varieties of rice, and huge differences in quality are present just in the japonica variety. Within Japan also, prices vary by 1.7–1.8 times even for the Koshihikari cultivar grown in the Uonuma region of Niigata Prefecture and other production areas. In the international markets as well, rice produced in Japan is highly regarded. Today in Hong Kong, the wholesale price (per kilogram) when purchased from a trading company of Japanese Koshihikari rice is ¥380, while the same cultivar produced in California is ¥240 and in China is ¥150, and the general japonica variety produced in China is ¥100. Comparing low-quality rice produced in other countries with rice produced in Japan is like comparing a light vehicle to a luxury Mercedes.

As shown in the figure below, the difference in the price of rice produced in Japan and that of similar quality produced in China (imported by imposing the minimum access) has dropped significantly in the past decade. Today, the price difference between domestic and imported rice produced in China has fallen to less than 30 percent. Since the price of rice produced in Japan at around ¥13,000 per 60 kilograms was realized by limiting the supply through the policy of reducing rice production, the price would fall to ¥9,000 if the policy were abolished; the prices of rice produced in Japan and China would reverse their positions.

It has been asserted that the TPP would greatly damage agriculture in Japan, yet even if prices of agricultural products declined, producers would not be harmed if subsidies were paid directly to agricultural producers for maintaining production, as is done in the United States and the EU. This allows maintenance of agriculture's multi-faceted functions other than agricultural production, including cultivation of water resources and prevention of floods. If prices drop unexpectedly, the amount paid directly can be increased. If an unexpected increase in imported products affects domestic industries, safeguard measures can be incorporated in the TPP conventions.

Regarding rice production, farming families engaged in additional professions would start leasing their farmland if rice prices went down due to abolishing the policy for reducing rice production. If subsidies were directly paid only to farming families exclusively engaged in rice production, their ability to rent land would rise, causing farmland to accumulate in these families and their scale of production to rise. If the yield rose when total consumption was constant, the area of rice paddies needed for rice production would decrease, which would expand the area of paddies where rice was not produced, causing the amount of subsidies for paddies set aside for rice production to increase. This was disliked by the Ministry of Finance. Efforts to improve cultivation for enhancing yield would no longer be made. If the yield of rice in Japan came close to that in California, the rice production cost of ¥6,000 per 60 kilograms by large-scale farming families would fall to ¥4,300, which is close to the price of rice produced in Thailand. If expanding the farming scale and increasing the yield further reduced costs, Japan's rice industry could be converted to an export industry. While the domestic agricultural market shrinks in the age of population decline, agriculture in Japan can only decline unless exports are promoted by eliminating tariffs and non-tariff barriers of trading-partner countries. Negotiations for trade liberalization are indispensable for Japanese agriculture as well.

English version originally published in *Discuss Japan—Japan Foreign Policy Forum*, no. 9 (Dec. 2011–Jan. 2012).

Translated from "TPP kōshō ni sōki ni sanka subeshi" [Japan Should Promptly Participate in Trans-Pacific Partnership Agreement Negotiation], *Gaikō* [Diplomacy] 9 (September 2011): 122–127. (Courtesy of Toshi Shuppan)

VI-(2) Abenomics and Japan's Trade Policy in a New Era

Mireya Solís and Urata Shūjirō[1]
Asian Economic Policy Review, 2018

1. Introduction

Japanese prime minister Abe Shinzō must have been disappointed with the decision of the newly inaugurated US president Donald Trump to withdraw the US from the Trans-Pacific Partnership (TPP).[2] Nevertheless, Prime Minister Abe is still hopeful for the return of the US, since the TPP, a high level and comprehensive free trade agreement (FTA) that involves twelve Asia-Pacific countries, has been central to his administration's economic and foreign policy strategies.

The central aim of Abenomics is to recover the Japanese economy from a long recession, and among trade policy instruments, FTAs are expected to play an important role. Under this strategy, the total share of trade covered by FTAs is targeted to increase to 70 percent by 2018 from 19 percent in 2013. The TPP was given special attention for its potential to become a new rules framework for the Asia-Pacific region. The 2016 Japan Revitalization Strategy heralded the historically significant signing of the TPP agreement in February 2016 (Prime Minister's Office [Japan] 2016).

The TPP was also an important foreign policy to strengthen Japan's alliance with the US. One of the important challenges for Abe, after returning to the prime ministership in 2012, was to rebuild a good relationship with the US, since it had worsened under the Democratic Party of Japan (DPJ) government. The importance of this goal increased as Japan's relationship with China became more problematic.

In light of these developments, the present paper evaluates Japan's trade policy under Abenomics, focusing on both the outcomes of the TPP negotiations and the set of alternative trade policies, now that the original TPP is not likely to be enacted. Section 2 reviews Japan's recent trade policy, and section 3 offers an overview of the outcomes of the TPP's negotiations. Section 4 discusses the potential direction of US trade policy under President Trump, as it has brought into question the viability of the TPP project, while section 5 makes suggestions for Japan's trade policy in light of the emerging trade environment. Section 6 concludes with an evaluation of Japan's trade policy under Abenomics.

2. Japan's New Trade Policy: FTAs

Japan became interested in FTAs in the late 1990s, as it was approached by several countries, including Mexico, Singapore, and Korea.[3] Previously, Japan had deemed that discriminatory FTAs would undermine the multilateral trade system, which is built upon the basic principle of nondiscrimination that had benefited Japan substantially. But FTAs have become the most important trade policy for many countries as multilateral trade negotiations under the World Trade Organization (WTO) have been in a stalemate. Japan changed its view toward FTAs as an increasingly large number of countries concluded FTAs, resulting in discrimination against Japan.

Japan began to establish FTAs actively in the early 2000s. As of the end of June 2017, Japan had fifteen FTAs (fourteen bilateral FTAs and one regional FTA with the Association of Southeast Asian Nations [ASEAN]). Japan is involved with three mega-FTAs: the TPP; the Regional Comprehensive Economic Partnership (RCEP), which involves sixteen East Asian countries, including Japan and China; and the Japan–European Union (EU) Economic Partnership

Agreement (EPA). The RCEP and the Japan–EU EPA are currently under negotiation. For Japan, the TPP is the most important initiative because of its high quality and comprehensive coverage, and its geopolitical implications.

3. The TPP: The Most Important Trade Initiative for Abenomics

Japan joined the TPP negotiations in July 2013, three years and four months after the negotiations began. Japanese leaders showed interest much earlier, but strong opposition, mainly from the agricultural sector, prevented the Japanese government from joining. The negotiations had to overcome a number of difficult issues, but a deal was struck on October 5, 2015. This section reviews Japan's involvement in the negotiations and examines possible impacts of the TPP on the Japanese economy.

3.1 Entering the TPP negotiations

DPJ prime minister Kan Naoto first expressed interest in Japan joining the TPP in October 2010. Faced with the long recession and lagging internationalization, Kan argued for the need to open the Japanese economy and society in order to regain vitality and dynamism (Prime Minister's Office [Japan] 2010). Kan also thought the TPP might help restore Japan's relations with the US, which had deteriorated under the previous DPJ prime minister, Hatoyama Yukio. Hatoyama had called for the establishment of an East Asian community excluding the US and had complicated the issue of US base relocation in Okinawa.

Despite his keen interest, Kan could not make a bid for TPP membership because of strong opposition, and he only made an announcement at the Asia-Pacific Economic Cooperation meetings in Yokohama in November 2010 that his government would start collecting necessary information and engage in pre-negotiation consultations with TPP countries. There was no progress on the TPP front until the DPJ's Noda Yoshihiko became prime minister in September 2011, because the Kan government was occupied with the Great East Japan Earthquake, which hit the northeastern part of Japan on March 11, 2011, and its aftermath. Prime Minister Noda decided to begin pre-negotiation consultations with TPP members in November 2011. But his initiative failed to prosper due to strong opposition within the DPJ fueled by resistance primarily from the agricultural sector, but also from the medical services and insurance services sectors.

The Liberal Democratic Party's (LDP) Abe Shinzō became prime minister for the second time in December 2012 after the LDP won the Lower House general election. Abe was very interested in joining the TPP negotiations to enable Japan to participate in making the economic rules for the Asia-Pacific, and to find a path back to economic growth. Despite his very strong interest, Abe could not decide to join the negotiations right away because there was very strong opposition from LDP members. The LDP had made a pledge during the Lower House election campaign to oppose joining the TPP negotiations as long as "tariff elimination without exception" was a precondition. The LDP also included additional conditions for joining the TPP negotiations in their election campaign: rejection of numerical export targets for manufactured products such as automobiles; defense of the national health insurance system; protection of food-safety standards; rejection of an investor-state dispute settlement (ISDS) that would damage sovereign rights; and consideration of Japan's special characteristics in negotiating government procurement and financial services.

Abe wanted to make sure that the US understood the LDP's position on the TPP during his first meeting with President Obama in February 2013. Abe felt reassured that the elimination of tariffs on all products was not a requirement for joining the TPP negotiations by referring to the joint statement: "Recognizing that both countries have bilateral trade sensitivities, such as certain agricultural products for Japan and certain manufactured products for the US, the two Governments confirm that, as the final outcome will be determined during the negotiations, it is not required to make a prior commitment to unilaterally eliminate all tariffs upon joining the TPP negotiations" (Ministry of Foreign Affairs [Japan] 2013).

Japan and the US agreed to hold bilateral

negotiations in parallel to the TPP talks to address the issues concerning non-tariff measures in nine areas, including insurance, investment, and competition policies. The two countries confirmed that they would continue to negotiate on issues related to distribution of automobiles and auto safety in Japan, while the US would maintain tariffs on imported automobiles from Japan and the tariffs would be eliminated gradually within the longest period permitted under the TPP.

3.2 TPP negotiations

The TPP negotiations were complex and time consuming due to both broad issue coverage and a high level of liberalization, as well as the very different levels of economic development among the negotiating members.[4] Despite the difficult odds, TPP countries successfully reached a conclusion due to the strong political commitment of the leaders of the negotiating countries, which was revealed by the intensity of the negotiations: there were nineteen formal negotiations and a series of additional meetings involving chief negotiators, ministers, and leaders.

Overall, the most difficult issues included market access in goods, particularly in agricultural products between Japan and the US, and intellectual property rights (IPRs), specifically the period of data protection for biologic drugs. The US (anticipating benefits for its competitive pharmaceutical industry) argued for twelve years, while Australia, New Zealand, and several other countries representing the users of drugs advocated for five years. A compromise between the two sides was reached with a protection period of eight years. Other difficult issues that persisted until the end of the negotiations included state-owned enterprises (SOEs), and investor-state dispute settlements (ISDS).

Market access in agricultural goods was a challenging negotiation for Japan and the US. Among Japan's five "sacred" agricultural products, market-access issues for rice, wheat, and dairy products were resolved, as Japan provided special and preferential treatment for the imports from the US by increasing import quotas. But negotiations remained stalled until the end on beef and pork.

The US was in a disadvantageous situation vis-à-vis Australia concerning beef and pork exports to Japan due to the tariff preferences awarded through the Australia–Japan FTA. It should be noted that the successful conclusion of the Australia–Japan FTA under the Abe administration contributed to the successful conclusion of the TPP negotiations, because it put pressure on the US to reach an agreement without a delay. Under the Australia–Japan FTA, the tariff rate on Japan's beef imports from Australia will decline from 38.5 percent (ad valorem equivalent of the specific tariff) to 19.5 percent (frozen beef in eighteen years) and 23.5 percent (chilled beef in fifteen years). The US demanded a larger reduction in tariff rates on beef imports. After intense negotiations, Japan agreed to lower the tariff to 9 percent after sixteen years.

Turning to pork imports, the US demanded the abolishment of the gate price system. Under this price system, the Japanese government sets a standard import price and collects a levy, which is equivalent to the difference between the standard import price and the cost, insurance, and freight import price when the cost, insurance, and freight import price is lower than the standard import price. The gate price system practically keeps the pork price in the Japanese market at least as high as the standard import price, making it a very effective protective system for Japanese pork producers. The negotiations resulted in an agreement that maintained the gate price system, but reduced the tariff rate. It should be noted that it was agreed that a special safeguard system would be introduced for both beef and pork imports in order to moderate the negative impact that may result from increased imports.

These compromises reflect Abe's strong political commitment to the success of the TPP. The Abe administration established the TPP Headquarters in the Cabinet Secretariat and appointed Amari Akira as minister in charge of TPP negotiations. The TPP Policy Unit, which is staffed by approximately 100 officials, is composed of two teams; one is in charge of TPP negotiations and the other deals with domestic issues. Before the TPP, FTA negotiations were conducted by government officials from four ministries: the Ministry of

Foreign Affairs (MOFA); the Ministry of Finance; the Ministry of Economy, Trade and Industry; and the Ministry of Agriculture, Forestry and Fisheries. Although the chief negotiator came from MOFA, a unified Japanese government position was not achieved due to the different positions of the ministries. The designation of a TPP minister who enjoyed strong support from Prime Minister Abe enabled the Japanese government to achieve a unified position in the TPP negotiations, so that it could overcome the fierce opposition from the agricultural sector.

3.3 The TPP agreement

The TPP aims to be a twenty-first century model agreement with comprehensive coverage and a high level of liberalization. It has thirty chapters, and it contains a number of new issues and greater depth of coverage compared to other FTAs. These include labor, the environment, SOEs, regulatory coherence, transparency, and anti-corruption. These issues have been recognized as barriers to free and fair business activities, but they were difficult to incorporate into FTAs because of opposition, mainly from developing countries. In the following, we examine some of the important achievements of the TPP.

3.4 Market access

Achieving a free and open business environment was an important objective.[5] However, as has been discussed earlier, market access talks were challenging. Table 1 shows the current level of tariff protection for the TPP 12 countries and their commitments on market access in goods, or tariff reduction/elimination. The figures under the headings "Final Bound" and "Most Favored Nation (MFN) Applied" indicate the shares of products with zero tariffs in the total number of products (tariff lines) registered under the WTO. In table 1, MFN Applied indicates the actual practice, while Final Bound indicates each country's formal pledges, which cannot be increased. For example, for Singapore's agricultural products, 99.8 percent of the tariff line products have zero tariffs in practice, but Singapore can raise tariffs on 95.9 percent of tariff lines without violating WTO commitments because only 4.1 percent of tariff lines are bound to zero. All TPP 12 members, with the exception of Japan, committed to eliminate tariffs on virtually all products with or without transition periods in the TPP. Considering the limited commitment on tariff elimination under the WTO, the commitment made by the TPP members to realize an open market is remarkable. Having discussed high levels of

Table 1. Tariff elimination rate under Trans-Pacific Partnership (TPP) (percent)

	Actual figures (2015)				TPP commitments				
	Agricultural products		Manufactured products		Total	Agricultural products		Manufactured products	
	Final bound	MFN applied	Final bound	MFN applied	Eventual elimination	Immediate elimination	Eventual elimination	Immediate elimination	Eventual elimination
Australia	31.3	77.0	18.8	45.9	100	99.5	100.0	91.8	99.8
Brunei	0.0	98.5	0.0	78.5	100	98.6	100.0	70.2	96.4
Canada	46.0	59.6	25.8	78.5	99	86.2	94.1	96.9	100.0
Chile	0.0	0.0	0.0	0.3	100	96.3	99.5	94.7	100.0
Japan	34.1	36.5	55.9	55.7	95	51.3	81.0	95.3	100.0
Malaysia	12.9	75.0	5.0	64.1	100	96.7	99.6	78.8	100.0
Mexico	0.4	19.6	0.3	55.2	99	74.1	96.4	77.0	99.6
New Zealand	54.8	72.4	46.4	62.5	100	97.7	100.0	93.9	100.0
Peru	0.0	52.6	2.2	70.0	99	82.1	96.0	80.2	100.0
Singapore	4.1	99.8	17.0	100.0	100	100.0	100.0	100.0	100.0
US	30.2	30.8	47.4	48.4	100	55.5	98.8	90.9	100.0
Vietnam	8.7	15.5	15.0	38.8	100	42.6	99.4	70.2	100.0

Source: WTO Tariff Profiles; Japanese Government, Cabinet Secretariat, TPP Section.

trade liberalization under the TPP, it should be noted that as much as 19 percent of agricultural products will remain protected for Japan. This outcome may be a victory for the negotiators, but it will certainly not bring about the agricultural reform sought by the Abe administration.[6]

The adoption of cumulative rules of origin in the TPP facilitates the construction and use of production networks/supply chains in TPP member countries, as intermediate goods/parts and components sourced in TPP member countries are treated as TPP products, and thus can be traded tariff-free.

The agreement on government procurement enables foreign suppliers to bid for central government procurement contracts in TPP member countries. These markets are open to WTO members that are parties to the Agreement on Government Procurement (GPA). Among the TPP members, only Japan, New Zealand, Singapore, and the US are GPA members. Hence, the TPP opened the government procurement markets of the remaining eight countries.

3.5 Services and investment

The TPP ensures national treatment to foreign service providers and foreign investors. In other words, foreign firms are not discriminated against vis-à-vis local firms in TPP member countries. However, sensitive areas such as the defense sector are excluded from this treatment based on the negative list approach, which allows for a more liberalized outcome by explicitly designating excluded sectors (a positive list approach only opens sectors explicitly listed). It is noteworthy that the TPP prohibits the application of a number of restrictions by the government on the behavior of foreign firms. These include the prohibition of performance requirements such as technology transfer requirements and restrictions on transfer of funds.

Special treatment of SOEs that would create an unfair competitive advantage is not permitted in the TPP. Leveling the playing field with SOEs enables foreign firms to expand their business in Malaysia and Vietnam, where SOEs dominate in their respective markets. The agreement on IPRs and the adoption of ISDS aims to encourage foreign direct investment flows with protection of intellectual assets and enforcement of obligations on the part of host country governments.

This examination of the TPP's features indicates that the agreement, if enacted, is likely to result in an expansion of trade in goods and services and investment by Japanese firms, contributing to the recovery of the Japanese economy, as envisaged by Prime Minister Abe.

3.6 Impact of the TPP on the Japanese economy

Several studies have examined the possible impact of the TPP on the Japanese economy by using a computable general equilibrium model (CGE), which mimics the system and functioning of actual economic activities involving consumers, producers, and the government. These studies assume the elimination of tariffs on goods. Some studies include other policies such as the elimination of non-tariff measures and liberalization of trade in services and investment.

The Japanese government analyzed the possible impact of the TPP on the Japanese economy by using a Global Trade Analysis Project model that takes into account tariff reductions/elimination, trade facilitation, and the elimination of non-tariff barriers (Cabinet Secretariat 2015). This study showed that the TPP would increase Japan's gross domestic product (GDP) by 2.59 percent (¥13.6 trillion) and employment by 1.25 percent (795,000 workers). For the agricultural sector, a decline in production of ¥130–210 billion is projected. The simulation assumed the following growth mechanism. First, tariff reductions/elimination, trade facilitation, and the elimination of non-tariff barriers would result in an expansion of trade, which in turn increases labor productivity. Second, an increase in labor productivity would increase wages, which in turn increases the labor supply. Third, increases in wages and labor supply would result in an increase in income, and thus higher savings. An increase in savings would augment capital stock, which in turn expands production capacity. The Cabinet Office study justifies these assumptions by providing supportive evidence from previous studies. However, the realization of some of these assumptions requires domestic policy reforms, and it may take time for the effects to be fully worked out. Indeed, the simulation results of the impact of tariff elimination alone showed a 0.66 percent increase in GDP (Prime Minister's Office [Japan] 2013).

Other simulation studies also show the TPP having positive effects on the Japanese economy, but the size of the increase varies widely among them, depending on the assumptions and the mechanisms of the models used in the analyses. Petri and Plummer (2016) show Japan's real income rising by 2.5 percent by applying a CGE model that incorporates heterogeneous firm behavior, which is one of the most remarkable recent developments in the area of theoretical and empirical economics. Their model introduces a mechanism under which increased competition resulting from globalization improves the productivity of the country by weeding out noncompetitive firms. Indeed, this is the mechanism that yields the largest impact. Kawasaki (2014a) and Gilbert et al. (2016) obtain estimates of the increase in real income of 1.6 percent and 0.31 percent, respectively. Kawasaki includes reductions/elimination of both tariff and non-tariff measures, while Gilbert et al. only consider reduction/elimination of tariffs. One of Kawasaki's most important findings is that a large contribution from FTAs to economic growth comes from the opening of the home market, while the opening of the FTA partners' markets provides only a relatively small contribution, indicating the importance of domestic policy reform.

Abe's decision to prioritize the TPP negotiations above all other trade initiatives suffered a significant setback when President Trump withdrew the US from the trade agreement. American trade politics, therefore, has emerged as a critical factor influencing the success of Japanese trade policy under Abenomics, and will continue to loom large as Japan adjusts its trade strategy to cope with the new direction in US trade policy.

4. A Pivot in US Trade Policy?

The growing divisiveness in US trade politics and the onset of the Trump administration embracing a swift departure toward an "America First" trade policy have profound consequences for Japan's trade policy goals under Abenomics. This section addresses some of the main factors contributing to the trade backlash in the American political debate and the main tenets of the Trump trade philosophy. The new American administration has already followed through on one major policy decision—withdrawal from the TPP—but there is greater uncertainty regarding the implementation of other campaign pledges on the trade front. Hence, Japanese trade policy must adapt to a new trade environment in which the US is no longer championing multilateral economic diplomacy, and where the disruptive impact of protectionist policies looms larger.

Since the enactment of the North American Free Trade Agreement (NAFTA) in 1994, the consensus on the merits of free-trade policies has increasingly eroded. The reasons for trade skeptics to object to the deep integration agenda are varied; they include concern over the loss of regulations to protect the environment and consumers, the legal arbitration recourse made available to foreign investors, complaints about the lack of negotiation transparency, and worries about asymmetrical bargaining outcomes in North–South FTAs. But no issue has galvanized the US political debate on trade as much as the impact of trade agreements on wages and employment.

The notion that the American worker has been a casualty of globalization began to gain traction during the NAFTA period, when opponents predicted major job losses due to unfair competition with cheap Mexican labor. The evidence proved otherwise. In the first years of NAFTA's implementation, the US unemployment rate decreased, and there was a gain in manufacturing jobs. More recently, it has been China's insertion into the world economy—as it gained WTO membership in 2001—that has animated skepticism on the merits of trade. Import competition from China had a significant impact on specific US manufacturing sectors such as apparel and furniture, and overall Autor et al. (2016) estimate that it was responsible for up to one sixth of the 5.8 million jobs lost in manufacturing from 1999 to 2011. But it is the other finding of the "China trade shock" which provides the most insight in understanding the fraying consensus on trade: displaced workers have faced a much more difficult and prolonged transition than previously reckoned—with long spells of unemployment, wage losses, and the lack of opportunities in depressed communities. Moreover, of the social programs available to laid-off workers, trade-adjustment assistance has played a marginal role (Autor et al. 2016).

The traditional case for trade—highlighting broad aggregate gains in economic welfare, while acknowledging concentrated costs—fails to resonate in a context of increased inequality, stagnation in middle-class income, falling rates of labor market participation, and lessened geographical and social mobility (Solís 2017a).[7] These adverse socioeconomic trends have created fertile ground for scapegoating trade with the consequent misdiagnosis of the root problems and ineffective policy responses. The vast majority of manufacturing job losses (87 percent) were caused by technological change (e.g., automation), but both trade and technology have helped spur efficiency, innovation, and productivity (Hicks and Devaraj 2015). Rather than attempting to block economic change, it would be more effective to address the growing skill deficits in the workforce and to encourage genuine labor mobility to enable workers to acquire new skills, enter new fields and occupations, and tap into the economic opportunity that comes with geographical mobility.[8]

Repairing the nation's safety net did not headline the 2016 presidential election. Instead, a critical view of the impact of trade agreements prevailed, with candidates from both parties reneging on the TPP. But it was Trump's protectionist message—calling for renegotiation or exit from existing FTAs and threatening punitive tariffs on main trade partners such as China or Mexico—which gained the most traction in the swath of Rust Belt states that hold a large share of Electoral College votes (Hendrix 2016).[9]

The findings on the electoral traction of a protectionist platform are important because it lowers the prospects for a future course correction in the Trump administration toward the conventional parameters of postwar US foreign policy; for instance, endorsing free trade as a source of economic prosperity and American influence abroad. In this case, electoral politics reinforce nationalistic views on trade policy long held by the new president and many of his trade advisors. Listed below is a highlight of the main threads in the Trump trade doctrine, as can be gleaned from public speeches, position papers, media interviews, and social media commentary (tweets).

- Trade is zero-sum and the US is losing the race. The losers (drained by import competition and the overseas relocation of industry) suffer de-industrialization and the extinction of job opportunities. In his inaugural presidential address, Trump talked about the carnage suffered by American workers because of international trade and offshoring, and asserted that protection can lead to prosperity (White House 2017).
- Reducing/eliminating the trade deficit is the end goal of trade policy. Asserting that GDP expansion is driven by the growth in consumption, investment, government spending, and net exports, Trump's trade advisors (Navarro and Ross 2016) conclude that when a country imports more than it exports, it lowers its economic growth.[10]
- A shift in priorities/resources from governance to enforcement, from rules to results. The American trade deficit reflects both flawed trade agreements and rampant cheating by US trade partners. Therefore, enforcement of trade disciplines will be pursued with renewed vigor. Signaling a potential return to a results-oriented trade policy, Trump's trade advisors hinted at "automatic triggers" to reopen trade agreements if the bilateral trade deficit expands (Mufson 2017).
- A preference for bilateral negotiations over multilateral deals. The preference for one-on-one negotiations comes from the notion that bilateral talks enhance the American bargaining advantage as the largest consumer market. It also underscores that rulemaking is not at the heart of the trade strategy, since multiparty deals are much better suited for dissemination of standards.
- The renationalization of manufacturing is a desirable/achievable goal. The goal is not only

to revive industries in decline (such as coal and steel), but also to return advanced manufacturing that currently operates across the global supply chain to the homeland (Donnan 2017).

- The comeback of unilateralism. In Trump's trade circles, there is deep skepticism toward the value of the WTO to advance US interests. During the presidential campaign, Trump alluded to the possible withdrawal from the multilateral trading body. Trump's trade advisors have complained that the one country, one vote rule violates US sovereignty because it gives equal weight to nations of disproportionate economic power (Navarro and Ross 2016, 12). The first trade policy report from the Office of the US Trade Representative to Congress under the Trump administration admonishes that the US may not abide by a negative finding from a WTO dispute settlement panel if it considers it runs counter to its sovereignty. And it goes on to emphasize the value of US trade laws, including section 301 (permitting the unilateral imposition of sanctions on countries deemed to engage in unfair trading practices), to aggressively "encourage true market competition" (Office of the United States Trade Representative, 2017, 4).

Importantly, the list above is a composite of the Trump administration trade *rhetoric*, which has yet to be operationalized into policy. The extent to which these precepts infuse actual trade initiatives will hinge on a number of factors: the buy-in or pushback from Congress, the mobilization of the private sector, and the responses from trading partners (Dadush 2017). But one major decision has already been implemented—withdrawal from the TPP—which directly impinges on the core initiative of Abenomics' trade policy.

5. Reassessing Japan's Trade Choices for the Future

The recalibration of Japan's trade strategy must factor in significant trends in the new environment: the abdication of US leadership in advocating multilateral trade frameworks, the slowdown of international trade (with the added headwind of policy uncertainty), and the potential escalation of protectionism.[11] This would mark a shift from the existing trend among G20 countries of relying on WTO legal restrictive measures (e.g., antidumping) to the cascading effects of retaliation to a large country's overtly discriminatory policies, such as punitive tariffs, extensive buy-national clauses, border taxes imposed on companies that outsource production, or import restrictions on products such as steel and aluminum on national security grounds.

Japan's best response in this difficult climate is to reinvigorate its multiparty trade negotiations advocating for high-quality liberalization. One immediate priority is to finalize the Japan–EU EPA after both parties reached an agreement in principle on July 6, 2017. The deal reflects compromises on government procurement (Japan agreeing to eliminate the "operational safety clause" hindering bids in rail transportation), dairy (e.g., Japan providing expanded access for cheese and wine) and automobiles (with the EU slated to eliminate tariffs on cars in seven years). The importance of the Japan–EU EPA goes beyond its expected economic gains (covering almost 10 percent of Japanese trade, it is estimated to generate income gains of 0.8 percent of GDP) (Kawasaki 2014b; Solís 2017b). The negotiation milestone was delivered on the eve of the G20 summit in Hamburg, to offer a reaffirmation from major economies of the benefits of trade liberalization, and drew a stark contrast with the Trump administration's approach to trade policy. However, significant challenges still loom ahead in bringing this mega trade agreement to fruition. For one, both parties have yet to agree on key issues: data flows and investment protection (Japan endorses ISDS, while the EU has adopted an investment court system which Japan has not incorporated in any of its FTAs). The hurdles to ratification are high in the aftermath of the European Court ruling that trade agreements that incorporate portfolio investment and investor protection disciplines must also be approved by national and regional parliaments.

A second vector in Japan's relaunched trade policy should be to salvage the TPP project. The US withdrawal from the TPP means that Japan can no longer use this trade agreement to fulfill the geopolitical goals of deepening the US alliance by overcoming divisive market-access issues and jointly supplying governance to the Asia Pacific region at a time of rising Chinese influence. It also means that preferential access to the US market through the TPP is off the table. Far from being meaningless, a TPP 11 (a TPP agreement without the US) serves Japan's economic and geopolitical interests well. A recent simulation study by Kawasaki (2017) shows that in a TPP 11, Japan's income gains through tariff reductions would fall from 0.24 percent to 0.07 percent of GDP; but the largest payoff for Japan has always centered on reducing non-tariff barriers, and in this area, the reduction in benefits is much smaller (from 1.13 percent to 1.04 percent of GDP). Overall, the decrease in expected income gains from losing the US market is not marked: from 1.37 percent to 1.11 percent of GDP. This result reflects two fundamental facts. First, the terms of access to the American market (not just its overall size) are crucially important. The US has low average most-favored-nation tariffs, and in the TPP it played hardcore defense in areas of competitive interest for Japan (autos and trucks, with liberalization pushed back decades). Second, the competitiveness gains for Japan mostly derive from its own domestic reforms tied to liberalization (e.g., services) and the adoption of behind-the-border rules (investment and IPR) that enhance the operation of its global supply chains.

Geopolitically, a relaunched TPP (TPP 11) helps Japan position itself vis-à-vis the other great trading powers in the region: it prevents China from becoming the single focal point of integration and preserves an economic rulebook that helps deter Chinese mercantilist practices. But it also discourages a US inward turn by raising the costs of American marginalization from mega trade deals, while keeping open the option of a future US return to the TPP. At the aggregate level, the trade diversion effects of a TPP 11 on the American economy will not be large, but the costs of exclusion will be significant for specific economic sectors. For example, without the TPP, American beef producers will face a much higher tariff in the Japanese market than Australian producers. These trade diversion costs will increase as other trade agreements materialize. For example, a study by the Council of Economic Advisors (2016) found that in the absence of the TPP, a modest outcome in RCEP would still disadvantage American firms in thirty-five industrial sectors with annual goods exports of $5.3 billion to Japan because of trade diversion effects. These cumulative disadvantages may help mobilize the American private sector and Congress to come back to the TPP. Delivering a TPP 11 will require political will and creative diplomacy. It will likely involve one or more of the following steps: amending the ratification clause so that US participation is no longer required to achieve a critical mass, engaging in surgical renegotiation to encourage developing Southeast Asian members to remain in a TPP 11, and encouraging the admission of new members across the Asia-Pacific (Urata 2017; Solís 2017c).[12]

Securing ambitious trade agreements in East Asia is also a high priority for Japan. The RCEP—comprising a third of global GDP—has the potential to deliver significant gains from trade liberalization. With sixteen members from the Indo-Pacific region, the RCEP differs from the TPP in terms of membership, scope, and modalities of negotiation. Based on the principle of ASEAN centrality, the RCEP aims to build from the network of ASEAN+1 FTAs to achieve further liberalization that is WTO-consistent. But the launch of RCEP was also enabled by a fundamental understanding between China and Japan—which had been pushing different blueprints for region-wide integration—spurred by Japan's interest in the TPP (Solís and Katada 2015). Reflecting the wide diversity in levels of development, RCEP embraces the notion of special and differential treatment and flexibility in implementation, and has a narrower scope (e.g., no provisions on government procurement, environment and labor, or SOEs).

A leadership deficit has resulted in protracted negotiations and has clouded the prospects for ambitious outcomes. India has made very conservative offers on tariff elimination, creating the prospect of a lowest-common-denominator effect. ASEAN has opted for a two-track process, first caucusing among its members before discussing topics with the rest of RCEP members, which encumbers negotiations (Elms 2016b). China did not play a leadership role in the ASEAN-centric initiative, opting instead to push for signature initiatives such as the Asian Infrastructure Investment Bank and One Belt, One Road (Ye 2015). Japan attached utmost priority to the TPP talks, as can be discerned from the creation of a TPP headquarters to pool elite bureaucrats with access to the Prime Minister's Office, but made no equivalent effort for RCEP talks. The uncertain fate of the TPP and a potential American turn inward create an opportunity for RCEP members to reinvest in achieving a significant liberalization outcome. Japan and other like-minded countries like Australia, New Zealand, Singapore, and possibly South Korea have an incentive to rebalance priorities and push for ambitious outcomes for an RCEP that could be the sole standard-bearer for the region. Their efforts could find a more receptive ASEAN as it seeks to attract investment at a time of rising protectionist threats to the global supply chain, as well as a more responsive China eager to deliver on RCEP to buttress its credentials as champion of economic multilateralism. A reinvigorated RCEP should also aim to establish clear accession protocols to expand its reach beyond the region and possibly include members of the Pacific Alliance, which have recently expressed interest (e.g., Chile and Peru).

Japan's trade strategy for the new era must also fashion a response to a likely entreaty by the Trump administration to negotiate a bilateral FTA. Vice President Mike Pence already alluded to the desirability of such a bilateral deal during the first meeting of the High Level Economic Dialogue in April 2017. But his Japanese counterpart—Deputy Prime Minister Asō Tarō—stressed instead the merits of drafting rules for the Asia-Pacific through the TPP. How the US and Japan will address this disconnect on the trade agenda will be of key importance.

Given the depth of trade and investment links between both countries (Japan is the second-largest foreign investor in the US and its fourth-largest trading partner, and the US is the largest foreign investor in Japan and its second-largest trading partner), a bilateral agreement could be a good option now that the US has ruled out participation in the TPP. However, such a trade deal would only offer a positive opportunity provided it builds on the standards of the TPP and provides further opportunities for mutual liberalization on sensitive issues (e.g., agriculture for Japan and autos for the US). At this juncture, the prospects for steady progress toward that end are far from certain. Japanese officials have consistently signaled that no further concessions on market access in agriculture are possible. Negotiations over market opening for automobiles may prove contentious given the Trump administration's fixation on trade deficits, and the fact that auto imports are by far the largest component of the bilateral trade deficit vis-à-vis Japan.

Therefore, a wait-and-see response is advisable until the Trump administration operationalizes its America First trade policy. Binding rules on currency manipulation, further tightening of rules of origin, one-sided demands for Japanese market opening without reciprocal concessions, and the adoption of automatic triggers to correct bilateral trade deficits would severely limit the benefits for Japan and could present insurmountable negotiation challenges. Under such a scenario, Japan could still engage in productive bilateral dialogue on the broader economic complementarities with the US (e.g., infrastructure and energy). In the long term, Tokyo should deploy a trade strategy that creates an incentive structure for the US to reengage in multilateral economic diplomacy by delivering on its own mega trade deals.

6. Conclusions

The Abe administration has deemed the TPP and other FTAs to be essential components of its growth strategy. As the TPP received top priority in Abenomics' trade policy, the US withdrawal from the agreement means it is no longer possible to meet the Abenomics target of 70 percent FTA coverage by 2018, and more broadly, it negates the political gains of deepening US-Japan relations through an Asia-Pacific trade deal. This major reversal notwithstanding, trade policy under Abenomics has achieved important milestones. The trade deal concluded with Australia in 2014, the TPP agreement finalized in 2015, and the agreement in principle with the EU reached in 2017 showcased a Japan now capable of concluding trade deals with large agricultural exporters that slash more agricultural tariffs than ever before, pool larger markets for trade and investment, and codify behind-the-border rules that streamline the operation of Japanese supply chains. Yet, the most significant weakness of trade policy under Abenomics is also evident in all these trade initiatives: the insufficient push for domestic reform due to the political decision of the Abe government to play defense in agricultural liberalization/modernization in order to protect the core interests of the agricultural lobby.

In this new and more uncertain era, the Abe government should capitalize on its stronger credibility to negotiate ambitious trade agreements to bring to life other mega FTAs, including a TPP 11, the RCEP, and the finalization of the Japan–EU EPA. These trade initiatives are important in their own right, but they will also be helpful in creating an incentive structure for the US to return to multilateral trade deals as the costs of exclusion begin to pile up. But it is also equally important for the Abe government to display greater zeal in carrying out necessary domestic policy reforms, since such reforms yield the largest economic gains and provide the groundwork for Japan to successfully negotiate high-quality FTAs.

Courtesy of Japan Center for Economic Research (JCER).
Originally published in *Asian Economic Policy Review* 13, no. 1 (Jan. 2018): 106–123.

Notes

1. The authors are grateful to Jennifer Mason for her capable research assistance.
2. The twelve countries that signed the TPP agreement are Australia, Brunei, Canada, Chile, Japan, Malaysia, Mexico, New Zealand, Peru, Singapore, the United States, and Vietnam.
3. See Solís and Urata (2007) on Japan's FTA policy.
4. Elms (2016a) provides a good account of the TPP negotiations.
5. Cimino-Isaacs and Schott (2016) provides a useful assessment of the TPP.
6. Honma and George Mulgan (2018) give a similar evaluation.
7. According to OECD data, the Gini coefficient in the United States increased from 0.34 in 1985 to 0.389 in 2012. The rate of labor-force participation among prime-aged males fell from 98 percent in 1954 to 88 percent in 2015 (Executive Office of the President 2016). Due to growing inequality, absolute mobility has declined sharply in the United States: 90 percent of children born in 1940 were better off than their parents, but only 50 percent of those born in 1980 were better off (Chetty et al. 2016).
8. For a more detailed discussion of these challenges and their influence on trade politics, see Solís (2017b).
9. Although trade bashing resonates strongly with Trump's base, the views of the general public on trade are more benign. A 2016 Pew survey showed that 51 percent (39 percent) of respondents had positive (negative) views of trade (Stokes 2016).
10. As Ikenson (2016) points out, the fundamental problems with this assertion are that it mistakes a national income identity with a growth equation, fails to consider that trade deficits reflect broad macroeconomic forces (low national savings), and that greater reliance on imports is correlated with higher growth and lower unemployment.
11. For a recent analysis of the deleterious effect of policy uncertainty on trade growth, see Constantinescu et al. (2017).
12. Vietnam and Malaysia have been more skeptical of a TPP without the United States because they made concessions in the TPP that were deeply sensitive domestically (for example, Vietnam made concessions on independent enterprise unions) in exchange for obtaining preferential access to the American market for the first time. Their willingness to remain in the TPP may hinge on rebalancing the package of concessions, but the attendant risk of unraveling the agreement through a renegotiation should not be neglected.

References

Autor, David H., David Dorn, and Gordon H. Hanson. 2016. "The China Shock: Learning from Labor Market Adjustment to Large Changes in Trade." NBER Working Papers, no. 21906, National Bureau for Economic Research (NBER), January 2016. https://www.nber.org/papers/w21906.

Cabinet Secretariat. 2015. "TPP kyōtei no keizai kōka bunseki ni tsuite" [On the Analysis of the Economic Impact of the TPP Agreement]. December 24, 2015. https://www.cas.go.jp/jp/tpp/tppinfo/2015/pdf/151224_tpp_keizaikoukabunnseki01.pdf.

Chetty, Raj, David Grusky, Maximilian Hell, Nathaniel Hendren, Robert Manduca, and Jimmy Narang. 2016. "The Fading American Dream: Trends in Absolute Income Mobility since 1940." NBER Working Papers, no. 22910, National Bureau for Economic Research (NBER), December 2016. http://www.equality-of-opportunity.org/papers/abs_mobility_paper.pdf.

Cimino-Isaacs, Cathleen, and Jeffrey J. Schott, eds. 2016. *Trans-Pacific Partnership: An Assessment*. Washington: Peterson Institute for International Economics.

Constantinescu, Cristina, Aaditya Mattoo, and Michele Ruta. 2017. *Trade Developments in 2016: Policy Uncertainty Weighs on World Trade*. Washington: World Bank.

Council of Economic Advisers. 2016. "Industries and Jobs at Risk if the Trans-Pacific Partnership Does Not Pass." Council of Economic Advisers, Reports and Issue Briefs, November 2016. https://obamawhitehouse.archives.gov/sites/default/files/page/files/201611_cost_of_tpp_delay_issue_brief.pdf.

Dadush, Uri. 2017. "Will America Trigger a Global Trade War?" Policy Brief PB-17/05, OCP Policy Center, February 2017. https://www.policycenter.ma/sites/default/files/2021-01/OCPPC-PB1705.pdf.

Donnan, Shawn. 2017. "US Trade Chief Seeks to Reshore Supply Chain." *Financial Times*, January 31, 2017. https://www.ft.com/content/8dc63502-e7c7-11e6-893c-082c54a7f539?mhq5j=e1.

Elms, Deborah. 2016a. "The Origins and Evolution of the Trans-Pacific Partnership Trade Negotiations." *Asian Survey* 56 (6): 1017–1039.

———. 2016b. "RCEP: Looking Ahead to 2017." Talking Trade, Asian Trade Centre, December 14, 2016. https://asiantradecentre.org/talkingtrade//rcep-looking-ahead-to-2017

Executive Office of the President of the United States. 2016. *The Long-Term Decline in Prime-Age Male Labor Force Participation*. Council of Economic Advisers, June 2016. https://obamawhitehouse.archives.gov/sites/default/files/page/files/20160620_cea_primeage_male_lfp.pdf

Gilbert, John, Furusawa Taiji, and Robert Scollay. 2016. "The Economic Impact of Trans-Pacific Partnership: What Have We Learned from CGE Simulation?" ARTNeT Working Papers, no. 157, Asia-Pacific Research and Training Network on Trade (ARTNeT). https://repository.unescap.org/bitstream/handle/20.500.12870/1385/ESCAP-2016-WP-The-economic-impact-of-Trans-Pacific-partnership.pdf.

Hendrix, Cullen S. 2016. "Protectionism in the 2016 Election: Causes and Consequences, Truths and Fictions." Policy Brief PB 16-20, Peterson Institute for International Economics, November 2016. https://piie.com/publications/policy-briefs/protectionism-2016-election-causes-and-consequences-truths-and-fictions.

Hicks, Michael J., and Srikant Devaraj. 2015. "The Myth and the Reality of Manufacturing in America." Center for Business and Economic Research, Ball State University, June 2015. https://conexus.cberdata.org/files/MfgReality.pdf.

Honma Masayoshi, and Aurelia George Mulgan. 2018. "Political Economy of Agricultural Reform in Japan under Abe's Administration." *Asian Economic Policy Review* 13 (1): 128–144.

Ikenson, Dan. 2016. "Navarro's Trade Views 'Misguided,' 'Dangerous.'" *The Hill*, December 23, 2016. https://thehill.com/blogs/pundits-blog/international-affairs/311683-navarros-trade-views-misguided-dangerous.

Kawasaki Kenichi. 2014a. "The Relative Significance of EPAs in Asia-Pacific." RIETI Discussion Paper Series 14-E-009, Research Institute of Economy, Trade and Industry (RIETI), January 2014. https://www.rieti.go.jp/jp/publications/dp/14e009.pdf.

———. 2014b. "Rise of the Mega EPAs: A Comparison of Economic Effects." FY 2013 column, Research Institute of Economy, Trade and Industry (RIETI), March 4, 2014. https://www.rieti.go.jp/en/columns/a01_0390.html.

———. 2017. "Emergent Uncertainty in Regional Integration: Economic Impacts of Alternative RTA Scenarios." GRIPS Discussion Papers, no. 16-28, National Graduate Institute for Policy Studies (GRIPS), January 2017.

Ministry of Foreign Affairs (Japan) 2013. Joint Statement by the United States and Japan. Japan-US Summit Meeting, February 22, 2013. https://www.mofa.go.jp/region/n-america/us/pmv_1302/pdfs/20130222_01.pdf.

Mufson, Steven. 2017. "Meet Mr. 'Death by China,' Trump's Inside Man on Trade." *Washington Post*, February 17, 2017. https://www.washingtonpost.com/business/economy/meet-mr-death-by-china-trumps-inside-man-on-trade/2017/02/17/164d7458-ea25-11e6-80c2-30e57e57e05d_story.html.

Navarro, Peter, and Wilbur Ross. 2016. "Scoring the Trump Economic Plan: Trade, Regulatory and Energy Policy Impacts." September 29, 2016.

Office of the United States Trade Representative. 2017. 2017 Trade Policy Agenda and 2016 Annual Report of the President of the United States on the Trade Agreements Program. March 2017. https://ustr.gov/sites/default/files/files/reports/2017/AnnualReport/AnnualReport2017.pdf.

Petri, Peter A., and Michael G. Plummer. 2016. "The Economic Effects of the Trans-Pacific Partnership: New Estimates." PIIE Working Paper Series, no. 16-2, Peterson Institute for International

Economics (PIIE). https://www.piie.com/sites/default/files/documents/wp16-2_0.pdf.

Prime Minister's Office (Japan). 2010. "APEC CEO samitto ni okeru sōri aisatsu" [Prime Minister's Speech at the APEC CEO Summit]. Speech at APEC CEO Summit, Yokohama, November 13, 2010. https://www.kantei.go.jp/jp/kan/statement/201011/13ceosummit.html.

———. 2013. "Nihon saikō senryaku" [Japan Revitalization Strategy]. June 14, 2013. https://www.kantei.go.jp/jp/singi/keizaisaisei/pdf/saikou_jpn.pdf.

———. 2016. "Nihon saikō senryaku 2016" [Japan Revitalization Strategy 2016]. June 2, 2016. https://www.kantei.go.jp/jp/singi/keizaisaisei/pdf/2016_zentaihombun.pdf.

Solís, Mireya. 2017a. "The Case for Trade and the Trans-Pacific Partnership." In *Brookings Big Ideas for America*, edited by Michael E. O'Hanlon, 138–146. Washington: Brookings Institution Press.

———. 2017b. *Dilemmas of a Trading Nation: Japan and the United States in the Evolving Asia-Pacific Order*. Washington: Brookings Institution Press.

———. 2017c. "A New Meaning for TPP: Restrain Trump-Era Protectionism." *Nikkei Asian Review*, January 28, 2017. https://asia.nikkei.com/Viewpoints/Mireya-Solis/A-new-meaning-for-TPP-Restrain-Trump-era-protectionism.

Solís, Mireya, and Katada Saori N. 2015. "Unlikely Pivotal States in Competitive Free Trade Agreement Diffusion: The Effect of Japan's Trans-Pacific Partnership Participation on Asia-Pacific Regional Integration." *New Political Economy* 20 (2): 155–177.

Solís, Mireya, and Urata Shūjirō. 2007. "Japan's New Foreign Economic Policy: A Shift toward a Strategic and Activist Model?" *Asian Economic Policy Review* 2 (2): 227–245.

Stokes, Bruce. 2016. "Republicans, Especially Trump Supporters, See Trade Agreements as Bad for the U.S." Pew Research Center, March 31, 2016. https://www.pewresearch.org/fact-tank/2016/03/31/republicans-especially-trump-supporters-see-free-trade-deals-as-bad-for-u-s/.

Urata Shūjirō. 2017. "Trump and the Perils of Protectionism: Averting an Economic Disaster." *Nippon.com*, January 16, 2017. https://www.nippon.com/en/in-depth/a05301/.

White House. 2017. "The Inaugural Address: Remarks of President Donald J. Trump—As Prepared for Delivery." January 20, 2017. https://trumpwhitehouse.archives.gov/briefings-statements/the-inaugural-address/.

Ye Min. 2015. "China and Competing Cooperation in Asia-Pacific: TPP, RCEP, and the New Silk Road." *Asian Security* 11 (3): 206–224.

VI-(3) Is US-Japan Trade Friction Avoidable?

Blaming Trade Partners for Deficits Is Pointless

Kiyota Kōzō

Discuss Japan—Japan Foreign Policy Forum, 2018

The new US administration inaugurated in January 2017 is moving to restrict international trade by pursuing a protectionist trade policy. Upon taking office, President Donald Trump declared his intention for the United States to withdraw from the Trans-Pacific Partnership (TPP) agreement and renegotiate the North American Free Trade Agreement (NAFTA). Furthermore, media reports show that the administration is moving to raise tariffs to correct bilateral trade deficits with certain trade partners, as the new administration considers the phenomenon to be quite problematic.

The intent behind the sequence of moves is to protect US producers from their foreign competitors. Many warn that such a protectionist tilt could plunge the world economy into chaos.

In the first place, why does a country's attempt to protect domestic producers from foreign competitors pose the risk of chaos? In this article, I would like to explain how protectionist trade policies could affect the economic perspective.

***

As a thought experiment, suppose that a country is shifting from a free-trade regime to a protectionist regime in which the government restricts trade by means of tariffs. Theoretically, this policy shift will have the following three effects.

The first effect is to maintain domestic production. The imposition of import tariffs enables domestic producers to avoid fierce competition from their foreign producers. Thus, such measures have a positive impact on domestic producers.

The second effect is to enable the government to collect tariff revenue. Until its shift to a protectionist regime, the country had been imposing no tariffs on imports, thus collecting no tariff revenue. However, the imposition of tariffs will bring revenue to the government insofar as the country continues to import goods. Thus, the country benefits from restricting trade in the form of tariff revenue.

The third effect is to push up prices of products subject to tariff protection. The driving force behind the first effect of maintaining domestic production is higher prices resulting from tariffs, and consumers of such products will be the ones to face higher prices. As such, the imposition of tariffs has a negative impact on consumers.

In general, this negative impact on consumers more than offsets the combined positive impact of the first two effects on domestic producers and government revenue. Consider the case of the Japanese automotive industry as an example. It is a huge industry, and, when those working in related industries are included, an extremely large number of Japanese people are involved in the production and/or sales of automobiles. However, Japan has an even greater number of car users. If the government were to impose tariffs on automobiles in an attempt to protect the domestic automotive industry, the amount in losses suffered by consumers in the form of higher prices would greatly exceed the combined amount in benefits gained by the domestic automotive industry and those derived in the form of tariff revenue. Thus, even if these benefits were to be entirely passed onto consumers, the net impact on Japan would be negative.

Furthermore, as companies expand their global value chains, one country's imports often include those exported by foreign subsidiaries of domestic companies, as exemplified by Japan's imports from China, which include various items manufactured by Japanese companies' subsidiaries in China. In such cases, when a country imposes tariffs to restrict imports, it is also restricting the procurement of parts and finished products from the foreign subsidiaries of domestic companies and may end up having a negative impact on domestic producers.

This holds true not only for tariffs, but also for other trade-distorting measures such as import quotas and export subsidies. For those reasons, protectionist trade policies are considered problematic.

Now, if the combined positive impact—i.e., benefits to domestic producers and tariff revenue—outweighs the negative impact on consumers, would this indicate that protectionist trade policy ceases to be problematic?

What we must not forget here is that when a country engages in international trade, there always is another country on the other side of the trade which may retaliate. When one country imposes high tariffs on imports from the other country and the latter retaliates by imposing high tariffs, prices of imported goods increase in both countries, and trade will shrink. If they continue to raise tariffs, trade will shrink further.

Indeed, we all remember how trade friction developed into a devastating war in the past. At the advent of the Great Depression in 1929, the United States took a hard-line policy of raising tariffs significantly to protect competing domestic producers. As other countries followed suit, global trade contracted sharply and the global economic slump deepened further. The contraction of trade led to the fragmentation of the world economy into blocs, and a tariff war among the blocs eventually evolved into World War II.

There is a growing fear that the current trends toward protectionism may lead to the aggravation of international trade friction. This is one factor behind the ongoing confusion.

***

Another important aspect of trade is that a country's trade deficit is not a trade issue. To simplify this, assume here that the trade balance is the same as the current account balance of payments. The balance of trade is the value of exports net of the value of imports. Meanwhile, from the expenditure side, gross domestic product (GDP) can be described with the following equation: GDP = Consumption + Investment + Government expenditures + Exports – Imports.

Now, if we focus on the fact that the income of an economy excluding taxes (i.e., disposable income) either is spent on consumption or saved, we can also describe GDP as: *GDP = Consumption + Savings + Taxes*. From these two equations, we can derive the following equation: *Consumption + Investment + Government expenditures + Exports – Imports = Consumption + Savings + Taxes*. This equation can be rewritten as: *Exports – Imports = (Savings – Investment) + (Taxes – Government expenditures)*.

This means that a country running a budget deficit with the government's expenditures exceeding its tax revenue, as has been the case for the United States in recent years, inevitably runs a trade deficit unless it has a savings surplus in an amount exceeding that of the budget deficit. Furthermore, since trade policy does not affect domestic savings and investment, it does not have any impact on trade balance, either. Accordingly, on a national level, a trade deficit is not a trade issue, but is a problem of savings-investment imbalance, including the government sector.

Likewise, even if one country continues to run a trade deficit with another country, such a persistent bilateral trade deficit is also not a trade issue. As noted in the *Daiki shoki* column in the January 21, 2017 issue of the *Nihon Keizai Shimbun*, it is only natural for one country to run a deficit or a surplus with the other in bilateral trade between a given pair of countries that differ in industrial structure and availability of natural resources.

The figure below shows Japan's balance of trade by country/region. We can see that Japan is running huge deficits with oil-producing countries in the Middle East. Being poor in natural resources, Japan has been importing natural resources and exporting manufactured products. Because of this pattern of trade, Japan tends

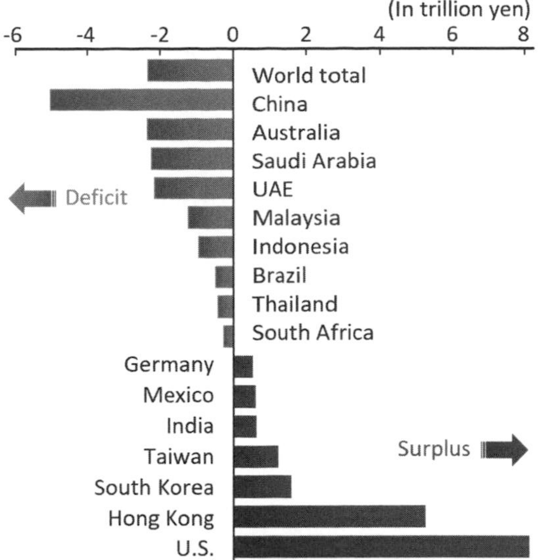

Japan's Trade Deficit by Country/Region (2015)

Source: Ministry of Finance, "Balance of Payments (Regional Balance of Payments)."
Note: The balance of trade includes the balance of trade in services.

to run deficits in its trade with resource-rich countries.

Simply because of this fact, do we find Japan's trade with those resource-rich countries unfair? Are we going to demand that oil-producing countries import more products from Japan or restrict oil imports? The answer is no. Seen from this perspective, it is obvious that a bilateral trade imbalance is not a trade issue.

***

This year marks the two hundredth year since David Ricardo, a British economist, proposed the concept of comparative advantage; i.e., since the birth of the idea of comparative advantage. What would Ricardo say if he were to see the current trade-restrictive trends? People often say that history repeats itself, but there are certain parts of history that must not be repeated.

Careful discussion must take place on the question of how we should redistribute benefits obtained from trade, as well as on the adjustment costs associated with trade liberalization. However, we need to go back to the basic principle and renew our understanding that trade is not a zero-sum game, but rather is a positive-sum game.

English version originally published in *Discuss Japan—Japan Foreign Policy Forum*, no. 38 (Apr. 2018).

Translated by the Research Institute of Economy, Trade and Industry (RIETI). The article first appeared in the *Keizai kyōshitsu* column of *Nikkei Shimbun* on March 7, 2017, under the title, "Nichi-Bei bōeki masatsu kaihi dekiru ka (2): Akaji aite-koku no hihan futekisetsu" (Blaming Trade Partners for Deficits Is Pointless). (Courtesy of author)

VI-(4) Challenges after the TPP-11 Agreement

A Guide toward Establishing Global Rules

Kimura Fukunari

Discuss Japan—Japan Foreign Policy Forum, 2018

In November, a new broad agreement based on the Trans-Pacific Partnership (TPP) was reached between eleven countries, excluding the US, in Da Nang, Vietnam. The Comprehensive and Progressive Agreement for Trans-Pacific Partnership (CPTPP, or TPP-11) represents a major step toward putting the TPP into practice. Four points were listed as requiring further negotiation, which are related to state-owned enterprises (Malaysia), services and investment in the coal industry (Brunei), dispute settlement (Vietnam), and cultural exceptions (Canada). Once these points have been agreed to and signed off on, however, the agreement will be ratified by at least six countries, irrespective of their economic scale.

* * *

With the US currently distancing itself from the TPP under the Trump administration, some have claimed that this will drastically reduce the economic effects of the TPP. The value of TPP-11, however, is that it sets out the direction in which the Asia-Pacific region should be heading, in terms of high-level liberalization of trade and establishing international rules. If the US were to put domestic politics aside and think things through rationally, they would probably realize that returning to the TPP would be more efficient than going to the trouble of setting up bilateral free trade agreements (FTAs).

Once the agreement comes into effect, other Asia-Pacific countries will no doubt get on board, even without waiting for the US to return to the table. There are plenty of countries that would be interested in a valuable agreement such as this.

Suspension of the Application of Certain Provisions	Items
Chapter 5 (Customs Administration and Trade Facilitation)	1
Chapter 9 (Investment)	1
Chapter 10 (Cross-Border Trade in Services)	1
Chapter 11 (Financial Services)	1
Chapter 13 (Telecommunications)	1
Chapter 15 (Government Procurement)	2
Chapter 18 (Intellectual Property)	11
Chapter 20 (Environment)	1
Chapter 26 (Transparency and Anti-Corruption)	1

The precursor to the TPP was the P4 (Pacific 4) agreed between Brunei, Chile, New Zealand, and Singapore. Comparatively speaking, the TPP-11 is an excellent middle ground because it will involve at least six countries.

Japan took the initiative ahead of the recent negotiations by submitting an early bill that would facilitate procedures to ratify the TPP and by resolving a number of outstanding domestic issues. Along with the economic partnership agreement (EPA) that Japan has almost finished negotiating with the European Union (EU), the broad agreement on the TPP-11 is a tremendous achievement that heralds the dawn of a new era in Japanese economic diplomacy.

Twenty items covered by the agreement have been "frozen" until the US comes back to the table. The frozen items are listed according to each section in the table above, with details specified in the text under individual items. There are no frozen items relating to areas such as customs or rules of origin. Eleven of the frozen items—more than half—are under the section on intellectual property, reflecting serious concerns from the US. These include matters such as biological data protection and copyright periods. The other key point is in the section on investment, where a partial freeze has been imposed on the scope of investor–state dispute settlements (ISDS). On the whole, these are relatively narrow items that will not detract significantly from the quality of the agreement.

As well as abolishing a high percentage of tariffs, the TPP-11 sets out a level of service and investment deregulation that has been beyond most of the existing FTAs in East Asia, and includes stipulations such as the principle of non-discrimination with regard to government procurement. It is also set to have a considerable impact on other FTA negotiations, including the East Asia Regional Comprehensive Economic Partnership (RCEP). On top of all this, the TPP-11 is attracting attention as a guide toward establishing global trade rules, particularly on e-commerce and state-owned enterprises.

* * *

The section on state-owned enterprises and designated monopolies is aimed at standardizing competitive conditions, so that goods and services will be sold or purchased by state-owned enterprises on the same footing as private companies. Provisions include requiring state-owned enterprises to act in line with commercial practices, ensuring that non-commercial assistance granted to state-owned enterprises does not have a negative impact on the interests of other signatory countries, and requiring countries to provide information on state-owned enterprises.

Many state-owned enterprises receive subsidies from the relevant government, whether directly or indirectly. This may give them an unfair advantage when it comes to competing with private companies. Some policy discipline needs to be imposed to avoid this sort of market distortion. In recent years, there have also been more and more state-owned enterprises branching out overseas. Under the principle of non-discrimination increasingly imposed in relation to investments based on FTA or bilateral investment treaties (BIT), however, it is increasingly important to ensure fair competition. In the future, readjustments will probably need to be made in relation to development assistance and investment as well.

Now that emerging countries with different economic systems are establishing a stronger presence—not least China—the need for international rules to ensure fair competition is greater than ever before. Aside from World Trade Organization (WTO) regulations on countervailing duties against subsidies, however, there are virtually no rules being implemented globally. Even in this section of the TPP, there were numerous exceptions in both the main text and appendices. It will be necessary to keep a close eye on things after the agreement comes into effect in order to determine the extent to which rules are effective. This is nonetheless a significant first step toward establishing important international rules.

* * *

The section on e-commerce stipulates (1) free flow of data; (2) prohibition of data localization requirements; and (3) prohibition of forced disclosure of source codes. The first two of these provisions include disclaimers stating that countries shall not be prevented from taking and continuing noncompliant actions if they are for the purpose of legitimately implementing public policy. It is therefore unclear whether these provisions will be rigorously enforced. This section is nonetheless crucial, because it sets out broader principles.

Attitudes toward e-commerce vary significantly between the US and the EU. In May 2018, the EU will be bringing the General Data Protection Regulation (GDPR) into effect in order to protect the privacy of individuals living in the EU. This will involve strict data localization, meaning that restrictions will be placed on removing data from the EU. In fact, the prohibition of data localization requirements is one of the areas in which EPA negotiations between Japan and the EU have failed to reach an agreement. While it is unclear how far major countries will go to align their systems in the future, at the very least, economic activity involving the EU will be subject to a number of restrictions.

According to estimates published by the McKinsey Global Institute in the US, the flow of data across international borders increased forty-five-fold during the decade from 2005 onward. This reflects ongoing qualitative changes in the international socioeconomic environment. There are countless issues that need to be addressed, including consumer protection, ensuring privacy, clamping down on market domination and tax avoidance by platform companies, and defending against cyberattacks. There is nonetheless a deep chasm between the US, which believes in the principle of freedom, and the EU, which is approaching these issues from a defensive point of view. China, meanwhile, intends to bring in a cybersecurity law in June as part of an ongoing drive toward strict data localization.

While emerging and developing countries may adopt policies aimed at restricting the flow of data in the interests of nurturing companies in their own country, the cost involved in doing so is considerable. Whereas China has undoubtedly restricted outsiders' market entry in order to nurture the Alibaba Group and Tencent, among others, countries that are smaller in scale might struggle to protect budding industries in the same way. Platform companies also have very similar business models, which can be imitated with relative ease in some cases.

Although there are definitely economies of scale to be gained from the network effect, it is getting a lot harder to achieve the prolonged market dominance enjoyed by large capital stock industries in the past. Even if emerging and developing countries are unable to develop platform companies right away, it would be wise for them to open up real gateways toward worldwide innovation, and to draw on current applications to create more jobs.

Bringing the TPP-11 into effect is also important from the point of view of pushing back against the current worldwide trend toward protectionism. Japan needs to continue playing an active role in establishing a new international economic order in the future.

English version originally published in *Discuss Japan—Japan Foreign Policy Forum*, no. 45 (Mar. 2018).

Translated by The Japan Journal, Ltd. The article first appeared in the *Keizai kyōshitsu* column of *Nikkei Shimbun* on December 14, 2017, under the title, "TPP11 gōi go no kadai (I): Sekai rūru kōchiku no shishin ni" (Challenges after the TPP-11 Agreement [Part 1]: A Guide toward Establishing Global Rules). (Courtesy of author)

Other Policy Issues

Part VII comprises essays on other issues in the Japanese economy during the Heisei era.

1. Inequality and Poverty in Japan

The inequality issue in Japan started to attract attention in the late 1990s with the publication of Tachibanaki Toshiaki's *Nihon no keizai kakusa* (Economic Inequality in Japan; 1998). Tachibanaki noted that the inequality of Japan's income distribution had become so great that it now topped the developed world. Japan had previously been called "a country of middle-class citizens" and was regarded as a relatively equal society, so Tachibanaki's observation came as a great shock to many people. Subsequently, when the Koizumi cabinet that emerged in 2001 pursued deregulation from the perspective of strengthening market forces, opponents claimed that giving priority to market mechanisms was creating inequality. That criticism may well have been one of the reasons for the subsequent shift of power into the hands of the DPJ. Academics, on the other hand, noted that the degree of inequality in Japan appeared higher because of the greater ratio of elderly people, among whom income inequality was greater than in younger age groups.

In "The Rising Tide of Poverty in Japan," Tachibanaki argues that Japan is already a land of inequality, raising issues such as poverty among single mothers.

2. Labor-Market Reform

Japan's postwar labor market had many typically Japanese features, including lifelong employment (long-term employment at the same company), the seniority wage system (wages increasing according to the number of years worked), and on-the-job training (employees building their capacity through the experience of various different job types). Once, this Japanese-style employment system was regarded as a strength of the Japanese economy, but as economic stagnation dragged on, it came to be perceived instead as the main obstruction to the growth of the Japanese economy, and reform efforts continue today.

Yashiro Naohiro began identifying problems in the Japanese labor market from as early as the late 1990s, and has remained a passionate reform advocate. In "Reforming Japanese Labor Markets," he discusses the directionality of Japan's labor-market reforms, introducing the reforms that are underway while noting the need for further efforts, including rectifying long working hours.

Tsuru Kōtarō draws on the latest debates in "A Farewell to Japanese Employment Practices: Why Is Reform of the Regular Employment System Necessary?" Citing "labor mobility" as a key term, he identifies issues in Japanese-style employment practices and directions for change.

3. Fiscal Reconstruction

Japan's fiscal deficit continued to grow throughout the Heisei era. While everyone understood that fiscal reconstruction was a major issue, progress was in fact extremely slow due to the succession of economic measures taken to pull Japan out of recession, the burgeoning social security bill accompanying the graying of Japanese society, and increased spending by the DPJ administration (2009–2012) to realize its rosy manifesto. Spending was slashed under the earlier administrations of Hashimoto Ryūtarō (1996–1998) and Koizumi Junichirō (2001–2006) so as to reduce the deficit, but neither administration completed the task.

Written by Jinno Naohiko during the DPJ years, the essay "Promoting Growth and Restoring Fiscal Health Simultaneously" suggests that the administration pursue both growth and fiscal consolidation. Jinno observes that along with fiscal consolidation, the government also needs to seek a new industrial structure.

Speaking as a public finance expert in "Stalled Fiscal Consolidation: Government Must Act Soon on Policy Normalization," Ihori Toshihiro calls on the government to abandon emergency policies as soon as possible and instead work on fiscal consolidation.

In "The Nation Needs to Conduct Fiscal Policy Reforms that Correct the Inequity between the Generations," Oguro Kazumasa discusses public finance from the perspective of redressing intergenerational inequality. He uses generational accounting to expose the extent of the burden that will be borne by future generations and proposes pension, medical care, and nursing care reforms.

4. Rural Japan

Amid nationwide population decline, rural Japan in particular is under threat. A private research group headed by former government minister and former governor of Iwate Prefecture Masuda Hiroya warned of the possibility of "local extinction." The group noted that if nothing was done, many municipalities were in danger of disappearance due to depopulation; it went on to specify the threatened municipalities by name. The profound shock of this revelation prompted the government to create a new organization to promote regional revitalization. Masuda Hiroya explains the essence of his local extinction theory in "The Death of Regional Cities: A Horrendous Simulation."

5. Population

Japan's population has been declining since 2008. To address this trend, the government has gradually begun to channel resources into measures to deal with falling birthrates. At this stage, however, birthrates have continued to drop, remaining a major socioeconomic issue for Japan.

Kōsai Yutaka, Saitō Jun, and Yashiro Naohiro discuss the relationship between population and economic growth as early as 1998 in "Declining Population and Sustained Economic Growth: Can They Coexist?" This paper was published in a major US economic journal.

Finally, Komine Takao and Kabe Shigesaburō look at how Japan's experiences might inform policymaking for other Asian countries in the future. In their essay "Long-Term Forecast for the Demographic Transition in Japan and Asia" they examine changes in the demographics of Asia as a whole. Based on their results, the authors signal that East Asia overall will experience the same population changes as Japan in future years, which will adversely affect economic growth and have a major impact on voting structures, savings rates, and social security systems.

VII-(1.1) The Rising Tide of Poverty in Japan

Tachibanaki Toshiaki
Japan Echo, 2005

People in Japan seem to have become generally conscious of the rising level of inequality within this country's society. One indication of this is the way the terms *kachigumi* (winners) and *makegumi* (losers) have become part of everyday conversation. Inequality can of course be considered on different levels. The simplest way of viewing it is in terms of inequality of outcomes, as typified by disparities in income. Equality of opportunity is also an important concept. This has to do with whether everyone is given an equal chance, without bias, in terms of receiving an education, looking for a job, getting promoted, and taking on various challenges. As I see it, both types of inequality are on the rise in Japan today. But this process is occurring largely under the surface, and we hear little discussion of the specifics.

In the following I would like to present some concrete and up-to-date information about the inequality of outcomes in Japan—that is, the gap between rich and poor—using data that have recently become available. I will look at both the change in Japan's status relative to other countries and the situation within Japan for those who find themselves living in poverty.

Already a Land of Inequality

At the end of 2004, the Organisation for Economic Co-operation and Development published the results of a survey of income distribution in its member countries. In table 1, I present some of the results, showing the degree of inequality in income distribution in twenty of the surveyed countries as measured by the Gini coefficient. The Gini coefficient is an index in which 0 represents perfect equality and 1 perfect inequality; in other words, the larger the number, the greater the inequality in income distribution, which is to say, the wider the gap between rich and poor. The results were calculated on the basis of household disposable income and adjusted for household size, after deducting taxes and adding transfer payments such as pensions.

For our purposes, the most striking thing about table 1 is the fact that Japan can be found among the nations with a relatively high degree of inequality in income distribution. If we divided the countries listed into three groups, with group 1 representing nations with a high degree of equality, group 2 those with an intermediate degree of equality, and group 3 those with a high degree of inequality, Japan would clearly fall into group 3. In other words, it has already joined the ranks of nations characterized by a large gap between rich and poor, alongside the United States, Portugal, Italy, New Zealand, and Britain.

In an earlier work, I pointed out the growing inequality in Japan's income distribution during the 1980s and the first half of the 1990s.[1] At the time, a number of criticisms were raised in response to this analysis, among them the assertion that, although inequality may indeed be progressing in Japan, it gives little cause for concern because, among the world's industrialized countries, Japan still ranks only a bit above the middle in terms of income inequality. Table 1 shows that this criticism is no longer valid.

There are a number of factors contributing to the increasing inequality, including the aging of the population, the shift in compensation systems toward merit-based and performance-based pay, the increase in the number of unemployed and low-paid employees as a result of prolonged economic stagnation, and the impact of the government's tax and social welfare policies. But the most important underlying factor is this country's embrace of American-style economic liberalism.

The same OECD survey also compared the poverty rates of member countries. Table 2 presents the results for all twenty-seven member countries using the most recent figures available. Measuring the poverty rate is not always easy, and international comparisons are particularly difficult. For one thing, the definition of poverty differs from one country to the next. In addition, one must find ways of compensating for differences in household size and overall national living standards. This OECD analysis defines the poverty level in each country as less than half the median income, with income adjusted for differences in household size.

Of course, this definition is adopted expressly for purposes of international comparison and is by no means ideal. Nonetheless, the shocking fact, as seen in table 2, is that Japan has the fifth-highest poverty rate of all the OECD nations, with a figure of 15.3 percent, ranking after Mexico, the United States, Turkey, and Ireland.

Of the top five countries, however, Turkey and Mexico should probably be excluded from any comparison with Japan, since they are still in the early industrializing phase of development. If we limit the comparison to highly developed countries, then Japan comes in third, after the United States and Ireland. It is also pertinent to note that Japan's poverty rate, which stood at 8.1 percent in 1994, nearly doubled in less than a decade.

The dramatic rise in poverty in Japan is manifested also in an increase in the number of people receiving "livelihood protection" assistance. Livelihood protection is a system under which the government uses public funds to help cover the living expenses of people who have very little or no income and are thus unable to support themselves. It is the last resort in terms of poverty relief.

The attached graph shows the dramatic rise in the number of households and individuals receiving livelihood protection assistance over the past decade. The number of households receiving assistance has soared in the last several years in particular, and now exceeds 1 million. This is a stunning development, considering that the number stood at only 600,000 households in 1995. And in terms of individuals receiving assistance, the figure has topped 1.4 million. This rapid increase in the number of people unable to support themselves is a clear indication that the problem of poverty in Japan is growing ever more serious.

One thing that needs to be emphasized here is that the number of people in poverty is nowhere near the same as the number of people receiving livelihood protection. Whereas people living in poverty are defined as those whose income falls below a certain level, people on livelihood protection are those who are in fact receiving public assistance. Simply put, not everyone in poverty is receiving livelihood protection, and in fact, the number of people in poverty is much larger than the number receiving livelihood protection. (Using the OECD's poverty rate of 15.3 percent and Japan's estimated population as of 2004 [127.69 million], we get a figure of 19.5 million Japanese living in poverty.)

Inasmuch as everyone living in poverty is by definition enduring economic hardship, it might be suggested that all such people should receive some form of assistance. However, the cost of providing livelihood assistance to all of them would place an enormous burden on public finances. In fact, well under a tenth of Japan's poor are receiving such assistance. Though the figures are somewhat old, a 1993 estimate found that the "catch rate"—the percentage of poor people getting livelihood protection benefits—was just 6 percent.

However, if we define poverty as a situation in which people lack the resources to maintain a minimum standard of living, it is difficult to know whether this figure is too low without first ascertaining the actual economic circumstances, state of health, and so forth of those who are not receiving aid. In fact, no country provides assistance to 100 percent of its poor; in the West, the catch rates range between 20 percent and 60 percent. Be that as it may, given the rapid rise in the number of people living in poverty in Japan, it is clear that finding some way of assisting the poor economically is becoming an important issue.

Table 1. Income inequality in 20 industrially advanced countries

	(Gini coefficient)
United States	0.357
Portugal	0.356
Italy	0.347
New Zealand	0.337
Britain	0.326
Japan	0.314
Australia	0.305
Ireland	0.304
Spain	0.303
Canada	0.301
Germany	0.277
France	0.273
Belgium	0.272
Switzerland	0.267
Norway	0.261
Finland	0.261
Austria	0.252
Netherlands	0.251
Sweden	0.243
Denmark	0.225

Source: Michael Förster and Marco Mira d'Ercole, *Income Distribution and Poverty in OECD Countries in the Second Half of the 1990s*, OECD, 2004 (available online at OECD iLibrary).

Polarization of Youth

We have seen that Japan has a very large number of people living in poverty. The next question is who these needy people are. To answer it, let us begin by examining the poverty rate by age group.

Table 3 presents data on the poverty rate by age group and also indicates what share of the poor each group comprises. The most striking thing about these data is the high rate of poverty among the elderly. Among people aged sixty-six to seventy-five, the poverty rate is 19.5 percent, and among those seventy-six and older it is nearly 24 percent. This state of affairs is underscored by the fact that the elderly account for a full 47 percent of those receiving livelihood protection assistance. In fact, it would be fair to say that the face of poverty in Japan is represented by the elderly. Poverty is especially common among elderly people living alone.

It might be supposed that poverty is uncommon among the elderly, since they are not expected to be able to work and are therefore eligible for pensions and long-term care insurance benefits. In fact, however, a large number of elderly people either do not qualify for pensions or receive very low benefits. Some did not enroll in a public pension plan for whatever reason; others enrolled but paid only a small amount in contributions.

If we look at other highly developed countries, there is little evidence that the aging of society has given rise to a swelling population of poor people. The difference is a well-developed

Table 2. Poverty rates of OECD countries

	(percent)
Mexico	20.3
United States	17.1
Turkey	15.9
Ireland	15.4
Japan	15.4
Portugal	13.7
Greece	13.5
Italy	12.9
Spain	11.5
Britain	11.4
Australia	11.2
New Zealand	10.4
Canada	10.3
Poland	9.8
Austria	9.3
Germany	8.9
Hungary	8.1
Belgium	7.8
France	7.0
Switzerland	6.7
Finland	6.4
Norway	6.3
Netherlands	6.0
Luxembourg	5.5
Sweden	5.3
Czech Republic	4.3
Denmark	4.3
OECD 24	10.4

Source: Same as table 1.
Note: "OECD 24" excludes Belgium, Spain, and Switzerland.

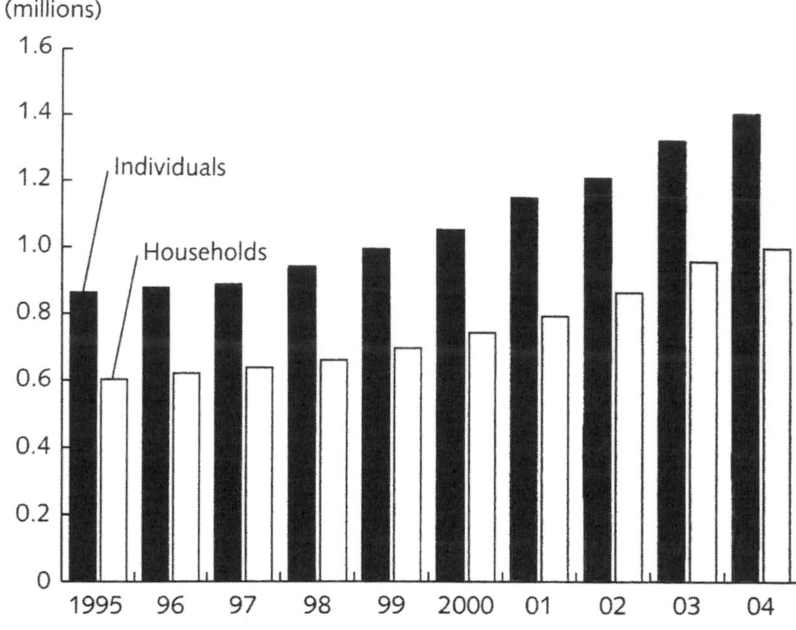

Recipients of Livelihood Protection Assistance

Source: Ministry of Health, Labour and Welfare, Survey of Trends in Livelihood Protection.
Note: Figures for 1995–2003 are averages for fiscal years (April–March); those for 2004 are preliminary data for October.

pension system. In Japan, the aging of society has increased the number of poor people, and has unquestionably contributed to the unequal distribution of income.

Another significant feature of the statistics shown in table 3 is the high poverty rate among the young: 14.3 percent among children seventeen or younger and 16.6 percent-second only to the elderly—among young adults eighteen to twenty-five years of age. Since young people only rarely have to worry about health problems, the factors underlying their poverty must be assumed to be completely different from those that account for poverty among the elderly. The cause, in a word, is high unemployment stemming from Japan's long economic stagnation. For several years now, unemployment among young people has topped 10 percent. In addition to those who are out of work, moreover, there are now somewhere between 2 million and 4 million so-called freeters, people without permanent employment, who move from one temporary job to another. The average yearly income of these workers is around ¥1.4 million, and even among them, the situation is polarized, with one large group making less than ¥1.1 million and another making between ¥2 million and ¥2.5 million annually. Those in the former group can clearly be said to be living in poverty. Even young people with regular employment rarely earn a high salary, since seniority pay is still the rule, but they can be certain of a steady income. Thus, a characteristic feature of Japanese society today is a growing economic gap within this younger age group, between low-income freeters and the perennially unemployed on the one hand and the permanently employed on the other.

Table 3. Poverty in Japan by age group

(percent)

Age group	Poverty rate	Share of total population in poverty
0–17	14.3	17.4
18–25	16.6	8.9
26–40	12.4	14.9
41–50	11.7	10.3
51–65	14.4	19.4
66–75	19.5	16.4
76 and over	23.8	12.7

Source: Same as table 1.

The Plight of Single Mothers

There are two other categories of people on public assistance. The first, consisting of the injured and disabled, accounts for 35.1 percent of the total, second after the elderly. The people in this category are naturally eligible for livelihood protection, being unable to work. With regard to the disabled, the ideal solution would be to provide work and a way to achieve independence, but the feasibility of this depends very much on the individual case.

The second category is that of single mothers, who account for 8.8 percent of the total. These are women raising children on their own as a result of divorce or the death of their husbands, and, less commonly, single women with children and no acknowledged father.

It is easy to explain why single-mother households are another typical face of poverty in Japan. To begin with, women generally have a harder time finding a job than men in Japan, and women who do work make less than men. This is because Japan has not developed women workers as a resource in the way that it has men. In addition, in many cases the children in these households are still very young, making it difficult for the mother to work outside the home. Moreover, a woman who suddenly decides to work after spending years as a full-time homemaker is unlikely to find a job that pays decent wages.

In fact, single-mother households are representative of the poor in all highly developed countries. This is particularly true in countries with higher divorce rates. And even Japan's divorce rate is rising, albeit belatedly. In most Western countries, however, various policies have been put in place to make it easier for single mothers to work. Many countries provide income tax breaks, generous child allowances, or preferential treatment with regard to the use of public child-care facilities on the condition that the mother work outside the home. Indeed, in some countries, assistance to single-parent households has become the centerpiece of welfare policy.

In Japan, assistance to single-mother households remains inadequate. There is a deeply entrenched belief that the divorced husband should provide for the mother and child through alimony and child-support payments. And neither government nor business has invested substantially in measures aimed at training single mothers and helping them find work.

Given Japan's deep-rooted traditional attitudes toward gender roles, it may be inevitable that policies have evolved in this way. As the notion of equal employment opportunity takes hold, Japan can probably be expected to improve its policies toward single-mother households by implementing tax breaks, child allowances, and child-care assistance as in the West. However, this kind of policy can also impose harsh demands on women, who may be forced to work in order to receive assistance.

Together with the elderly, the young, the injured, and the disabled, single-parent households are among the most vulnerable members of society. As these weak members of society slide into poverty, Japanese society is becoming increasingly unequal and its economic disparities ever more extreme. The time has come for a serious review of poverty policy in Japan.

Courtesy of Japan Echo.

English version originally published in *Japan Echo* 32, no. 5 (Oct. 2005): 47–50.

Translated from "Jakusha no hinkonka ga kakusa o jochō shiteiru," *Ronza* (June 2005): 102–7. (Courtesy of Asahi Shimbun)

Note

1. *Nihon no keizai kakusa* [Japan's Economic Disparities] (Tokyo: Iwanami Shoten, 1998).

VII-(2.1) Reforming Japanese Labor Markets

Yashiro Naohiro
AJISS-Commentary, 2016

Equal pay for equal work is a universal concept, but Japan is an exception. Japanese labor markets and labor unions are based not on occupations but on firms, so that the pay for equal work differs across companies. The average wage of non-regular workers in 2015 was on average 60 percent that of regular workers inside the firm. This has become a serious social issue with the growing number of non-regular workers, who make up nearly 40 percent of all workers. It is closely related to Japan's male–female wage gap, the second largest in the OECD next to South Korea, as women are more often non-regular workers. Prime Minister Abe Shinzō promised before the Upper House elections in August 2016 to eliminate the large wage gap by establishing a law on equal pay for equal work.

Nobody disagrees with the prime minister, but how to achieve this aim is a different matter. A major factor in the wage gap is the seniority-based wages of regular workers versus the market-based flat wages of non-regular workers. The wage disparities could not be eliminated without revising the seniority-based wages of regular workers, but this would not be welcomed by labor unions, which consist mainly of regular workers. The employers also consider seniority-based wages necessary for keeping skilled workers in the firm and profit-sharing to be a basis for harmonious labor relations. In this sense, unlike in other countries, there are no serious conflicts of interests between capital and labor in the company-based labor markets in Japan. However, there are various conflicts of interests between workers, such as regular and non-regular employees, those in large firms and small firms, and male and female workers. The principle of equal pay for equal work could only be achieved by partly sacrificing the vested interests of regular workers, in particular middle-aged males, who are the largest beneficiaries of seniority-based wages.

Regular workers also pay for their advantageous position. They do not have the right to choose their own jobs. It is in a sense a "blank-check employment contract" in which their jobs and work locations are not predetermined. Most workers are employed right after graduating from college or high school, and are trained in the firm through frequent job rotations. As the types of jobs differ, wages are not directly related to one's current job, but are basically determined by one's length of work at the same firm.

This employment practice used to be quite efficient with the high rates of economic growth in the past. With continuous expansion of firms and the introduction of new technologies, narrowly defined occupations easily become obsolete. Employment guarantees and seniority-based wages are less costly with high rates of economic growth and a pyramid-like age composition in the population. They are also effective measures for penalizing workers who voluntarily quit the firm.

However, the merits of these Japanese employment practices turned into disadvantages with changing economic circumstances. Prolonged sluggishness in GDP growth since the early 1990s has increased the cost to firms of hoarding excess workers during recessions. Seniority-based wages have become costly with an increasing share of middle-aged workers. Nevertheless, major Japanese firms have maintained their traditional employment practices by increasing the share of non-regular workers who can be easily dismissed during recessions to protect the regular workers. This is neither efficient nor equitable, but Japanese firms are the victims of their memories of past success.

The following are some appropriate policy measures. First, seniority-based wages are no longer fair, as they transfer the firm's limited funds for wages from the younger to the older generation, just as with public pensions. In addition, the scheme of increasing wages with age is closely related to mandatory retirement, which is considered age discrimination in developed countries other than Japan. In this sense, equal pay for equal work is important for improving the current distortions in Japanese labor markets.

An effective way of implementing the policy of equal pay for equal work would be to shift to firms the burden of proof that they are not discriminating against workers, replacing the current practice under which workers have to prove that they are the victims of discrimination. For example, Japanese firms might explain that regular workers have to move to local offices at the direction of their supervisors, while non-regular workers do not. However, the actual wage gap is likely to be much higher than that explained by the sacrifices of regular workers. Enforcing laws mandating equal pay for equal work would also be effective in reducing the unexplained wage differences among regular employees, in particular between male and female and old and young workers. Firms might complain about the additional cost of individual evaluations, but they would eventually be rewarded by better human-resource management.

Another issue is reducing working hours in Japan, which are consistently long by international standards. There are three explanations for this. First, it is a necessary shock absorber for avoiding layoffs of regular workers during recessions, as there is plenty of room for cutting overtime hours worked. Second, the intensive on-the-job training practiced at Japanese firms is a time-consuming process, as junior workers have to work together with senior workers in skill transfers. This is one reason that the workers in Japan on average only take about 50 percent of the paid holidays granted them. Third, overtime hours worked at higher wages are an important source of income for employees. Current labor law limits the extent of overtime hours worked without the consent of labor unions, but in most cases, they accept working longer hours. This is why the government is now considering setting a compulsory upper limit on working hours with no loopholes.

In sum, a major feature of Japanese labor markets is the conflict of interest between regular and non-regular workers, as well as that between traditional families with a full-time homemaker and families with two earners who prefer shorter working hours to additional wages. These conflicts cannot be settled in the government's labor councils that formulate labor laws, as they consist of representatives of employers and labor unions who mainly belong to large firms. This is why strong leadership by the prime minister is necessary for labor-market reform in Japan.

Courtesy of Japan Institute of International Affairs.

Originally published in *AJISS-Commentary*, no. 236 (Sept. 2016).

VII-(2.2) A Farewell to Japanese Employment Practices

Why Is Reform of the Regular Employment* System Necessary?

Tsuru Kōtarō

Discuss Japan—Japan Foreign Policy Forum, 2014

This June, the government's Council on Regulatory Reforms submitted a report on regulatory reforms to Prime Minister Abe Shinzō. The report discusses areas such as deregulation policies on employment, highlighting "reform of the regular employment system" as one of the three approaches to be taken to reforming Japan's employment system. Having served as a chairman of the working group on employment for compiling the report (see table, p. 301), I would like to give my perspective on the background, objectives, and specific policies regarding reform of the regular employment system.

"Labor Mobility" Is the Key Term

The Abe administration launched an economic growth package featuring a growth-generating structural reform strategy as an issue of top priority. This means that structural reform was the first item called for in order to produce economic growth.

There are three possible approaches we can take in order for the labor/employment system to contribute to economic growth. First is to increase labor-force participation rates for women and seniors while the labor population is in a long-term downward trend amid the challenges posed by population decline. Second is to improve individual workers' productivity by boosting human power through education and capacity development. Third is to raise economic productivity as a whole with implementation of labor-force reallocation by promoting labor-force transfer from low-productivity to high-productivity business areas.

The commonality among these three approaches is labor mobility. An example of labor mobility can be found in the non-labor-force population of women who are not actively looking for work but want to return to employment in the labor market.

Meanwhile, non-regular employment has been on the rise, reaching nearly 40 percent of the total labor force and posing a serious concern from a human-capital standpoint. Notably, definite-term contract workers in Japan currently represent 28 percent of the total labor force, a figure that is one of the highest among OECD member nations. Non-regular employees are typically provided fewer job-training opportunities by their employers as compared to regular employees, and an excessive ratio of non-regular employees can potentially diminish the overall quality of the labor force.

For that reason, transforming involuntary non-regular employees who wish for regular employee status into regular employees is quite important. This effort will promote labor mobility. Moreover, labor being shifted from mature sectors/industries to growing sectors/industries should also typically represent labor mobility.

An obstacle to promoting labor mobility is posed by the systems and institutions surrounding regular employment. A regular employee is generally characterized by a distinct status, including: (1) an indefinite contract; (2) full-time employment; and (3) direct employment (under

* Though there is no legal definition of "regular employment," it commonly indicates an open-ended period of employment, directly with the employer, and for scheduled hours. Any form of employment that does not meet these conditions is considered "non-regular."—Ed.

the employer's direction or orders). Compared with the United States and Europe, unlimited regular employment—which does not specify the scope of work, work locations, or hours of overtime work—is clearly more commonly practiced in Japan.

Unlimited regular employees have no choice but to accept job relocation and long work hours, whether they desire them or not. This kind of work practice has placed women and seniors, in particular, at a disadvantage because it impairs the balance between work and family/personal life. Accompanying that, companies tend to be overly careful in hiring regular employees because of the generous employment security and other fringe benefits provided. This has increased the number of definite contract workers, making it difficult to convert non-regular employees to regular employees.

Moreover, indefinite employment, unlimited regular employment, and employment dismissal regulations, each of which serve as an inter-compensatory factor, have formed a so-called iron triangle, and this has established Japan's membership-type employment system wherein being a member of a certain company or organization based on the premise of long-term employment carries a great deal of weight. It could be inferred from the above that this membership-type system has constrained Japan's labor mobility or reallocation in line with a change in its economic mechanism.

Regular Employment System Reform Is Not Tantamount to Easing Restrictions on Dismissals

Japan's regular employment system has, in a broad sense, tended to hamper labor mobility. So where should we insert the surgical knife of reform in the three factors forming this iron triangle that has long hampered regular employment reform? One option that has actually been commonly practiced is to convert indefinite-term employees to definite-term employees, but this has created such problems as employment instability and irrational income gaps.

Meanwhile, arguments for revising or deregulating dismissal rules are often used in the same context as reforming the regular employment system. However, I cannot help but feel strange about using such arguments as a threshold for discussions on reforming the regular employment system, because Japan's employment protection legislation is less rigorous than the average OECD nation's; in fact, dismissals are more common among small- and medium-sized companies than they are among large corporations.

Regulations on dismissals allow employers to release employees only when they have a rational and logical reason, as well as appropriateness in general societal terms, to do so (Article 16 of the Labor Contract Act). This in itself poses no particular problem.

While some observers seek clarification of more specific rules on dismissal in Japan, it is common practice even in Europe to let the law stipulate the basics and leave legal judgment on dismissal to the settlement of each individual dispute.

Legal principles for dismissal for the purpose of business reorganization (including four dismissal criteria), which are used as a basis when dismissing employees for economic reasons, have tended to be subject to serious consideration recently regarding each of the criteria. In response to changing times, operation of the law has become flexible to some extent in that procedural aspects are more greatly emphasized, ensuring that the necessary steps have really been taken before ultimately resorting to dismissing an employee.

This notwithstanding, some executives of large enterprises evidently feel the current dismissal rule is too strict. I assume such a perception, if it really exists, has something to do with the history of employment dismissal regulations having developed as a rule used when dismissing unlimited regular employees. The employer's duty to undertake efforts to avoid dismissal, which is one of the four criteria for dismissal for economic reasons, may substantiate my assumption.

In other words, I mean to what extent the company tried its best to reassign or redeploy the employee to another office or department, or solicit voluntary retirement before resorting to dismissal. The law obligates employers to protect employment at the cost of reassigning the employee's work location or duties. This thinking is merely based on the premise that the employee is hired as an unlimited regular employee.

In Japan, employment dismissal regulations could be applied even to an employee who has just undergone a certain probationary period, thus making it hard for the company to let the employee be subject to certain circumstances. This would be understandable if one was to interpret the rule to mean that the company cannot fire employees for their inability to handle a certain assignment because they were hired as unlimited regular employees.

In general, when dismissing an unlimited regular employee for poor performance or lack of ability, the employer will often even have to show proof that there are no other alternative job opportunities available for the employee within the organization, according to judicial precedents.

Conversely, there are a few other judicial precedents indicating that the employment dismissal regulations would provide no compassionate protection to unlimited regular employees if they violated the implied rule.

For example, the court ruled that punitive dismissal for refusing to accept job relocation or overtime work was valid in the "Toa Paint Case" (judgment of the Supreme Court of Japan, 2nd Petty Bench, December 19, 1969) and the "Hitachi Musashino Plant Case" (judgment of the Supreme Court of Japan, 1st Petty Bench, November 28, 1991). The validity of those court rulings appears debatable, but they are understandable from the standpoint of the employment dismissal regulations being designed to rigorously protect the unlimited regular employment system.

Everything Is Based on Assumptions Underlying the Unlimited Employment System

Unlimited attributes pertaining to regular employees—which can be paraphrased as an employer having considerable discretion over personnel matters, with employees obligated to accept future changes in work location and contents, as well as overtime—is closely related to many of the problems surrounding Japanese work styles.

For example, in a society assuming the majority of workers are unlimited regular employees, it is taken for granted that wives are mostly categorized as housewives who spend most of the time supporting their families, and they find it difficult to continue working as regular employees due to the heavy burden of parenting or of providing nursing care for elderly parents. One can argue that such a traditional peculiarity of Japanese society has doubly hindered women's participation in the labor market. Slow progress on work-life balance with empty slogans is also attributed to the assumption of the unlimited regular employment system.

Successful introduction of a white-collar exemption system (accommodating flexible work schedules for qualified white-collar employees by exempting them from labor-hour restrictions) would solely depend on whether or not working styles focusing on individual workers' autonomy are widely accepted. Yet there will be little chance for this to happen as long as the Japanese labor market assumes unlimited regular employment to be its underlying system. Moreover, with employers' discretionary power becoming overly strong in issues of human resources, the "unlimited" attribute of the proposed work style runs the risk of eventually being replaced by an "unrestrained" approach, which may lead to death from overwork, harassment, and exploitation, as happens at a "black corporation" (*burakku kigyō*).

Japan's company labor unions also have traditionally played a countervailing role to employers' overly strong discretionary powers that can potentially be wielded. In this sense, I believe the company union system is also based on unlimited regular employment.

Why We Need an Unlimited Regular Employee System

As discussed above, reform of the regular employment system aiming to promote labor mobility is badly needed in order to promote employment-system reforms for economic growth. To that end, reforming the unlimited regular employment system has been chosen as a priority to be used as a dawn of the labor "big bang." Therefore, while unlimited attributes in regular employment pose a challenge to be addressed, we must strive further to work on relevant employment rules for the introduction of a limited regular employee system, which will hire workers to full-time positions in limited areas, limited job categories, or with specified work hours.

Readers are advised to refer to the "Regulatory Reform Council's Working Group Report on Employment"[1] for approaches to new employment rules relevant to limited regular employment systems. Here I would like to respond to some of the criticisms leveled at the limited regular employment system.

The first criticism is that the limited regular employment system is a de facto system widely adopted by companies, with no particular regulations against its introduction. There is no need for the government, and the panel, to intervene by promoting the system through legislative measures.

According to a survey of nearly 2,000 large corporations by the Ministry of Health, Labour and Welfare, around half have already introduced a limited employment system. This fact notwithstanding, definite-term contract workers' percentage share of the total labor force in Japan is quite high among industrialized nations, as discussed earlier. Some research analysis has pointed out Japan's slow conversion from definite- to indefinite-term employment (around 25 percent in five years). In contrast, OECD nations have realized a 40 to 60 percent conversion within three years, representing a large variance with Japan (OECD, Employment Outlook 2006).

In view of the current situation where it is difficult to convert definite contract workers into unlimited regular employees, the limited regular employment system should play a pivotal role in absorbing definite contract workers who wish to become regular employees. To begin with, we should aim to convert 10 percent of the total labor force represented by definite contract workers into limited regular employees. The revised Labor Contract Act, which went into effect this April, allows limited-term contract workers to request a change of their contract to unlimited when the limited-term contract is renewed several times and the total employment period exceeds five years. This legislative attempt is designed to systematically create limited regular employees.

Regulatory Reform Items and Time Schedule

Item	Regulatory Reforms	Implementation Time Schedule
Employment rules for limited regular employees	Map out points for attention in employment management such as clarifying employment terms in order to promote diversified work styles for regular employees focusing on work duties	Discussions to begin in FY 2013, to be launched in FY 2014
Legislative revisions for discretionary work schedule, flexible work time, etc.	Working-hour legislation will be comprehensively reviewed in the Labor Policy Council from the standpoint of work-life balance and boosting labor productivity	Research to begin in first half of FY 2013; discussions to begin in fall of FY 2013; to be launched upon reaching conclusion within one year
Deregulation of job-placement agency business	Intends to expand job-search business that earns commissions from job seekers and shares a common awareness of an ideal user-oriented system from the standpoint of improving job-matching capabilities by utilizing private-sector job-placement businesses	Discussions to begin in FY 2013, to reach conclusion in early FY 2014
Revision of dispatch labor system	Intends to review contract terms for temporary workers, measures to develop temporary workers' careers, and non-discriminatory treatment of temporary workers	To be discussed in Labor Policy Council from fall of FY 2013; to be launched upon reaching a conclusion

Source: Excerpts from the "Regulatory Reform Council's Working Group Report on Employment."

In view of these new movements emerging, there is an urgent need to build an environment in which companies can promote the expansion of the limited regular employment system.

Clarify the Distinction in Employment Rules

What serves as a major challenge to the prevalence of the limited regular employment system is the lack of sufficient explanations about the distinction in the way limited and unlimited regular employees are treated through pre-employment documents such as employment rules and labor contracts, as well as termination documents. The Working Group's report prioritizes efforts to clarify the distinction between the two systems and to improve the predictability of issues arising from the difference.

The third criticism is that a limited regular employee's contract could be automatically terminated if that worker's workplace or position is eliminated. The panel is looking to ease employment dismissal regulations while expanding the category of regular employees who are easily dismissed. However, as in the judicial precedents thus far, principles of dismissal regulations should be applied to limited regular employees just as they are to traditional unlimited regular employees, and limited regular employees should be provided with an opportunity that carefully tests and confirms the dismissal's objective rationality in societal terms. Judicial precedents indicate that factors such as limited workplaces and designated work duties are fully considered, and limited regular employees are often treated differently than unlimited regular employees.

For example, in trials regarding an employer's attempt to undertake duties to avoid dismissal of a limited regular employee on economic grounds, the court often tends to assume that the employer has performed duties to avoid dismissal (or simply makes a judgment regardless of whether the employer has performed the duties) because chances for reassignment are limited within the designated workplace and limited scope of job duties. With respect to the criteria for selecting employees subject to dismissal—one of the four requirements for dismissal—dismissing all relevant workers following the closure of workplaces or positions is typically deemed rational (or rationality is not an issue).

In contrast, other requirements, such as the need to cut labor and the employer's reasonable explanation that is acceptable to the labor union and relevant workers, must also be an issue when dismissing limited regular employees. To avoid unnecessary disputes, the employer is required to specify a contract category in advance for limited regular employees in the employment contract, to effectively explain the specifics of the job category to the relevant workers, and to have them fully understand those specifics.

Are Limited Regular Employees More Advantageous?

As already discussed, limited and unlimited regular employees may well be treated differently even if the same dismissal rules are applied. It is important that basic principles and facts based on judicial precedent are shared and fully understood among everyone in Japan. With this taking root as a consensus between labor, management, and the judicial community, the rule may change. Conversely, it would undoubtedly be premature to legislate the rule without establishing a national consensus. I believe the Regulatory Reform Council is responsible for taking a leadership role in promoting the formation of a national consensus and developing a doctrine of precedent, and should not wait irresponsibly for the matter to take its own course.

The point to keep in mind when promoting a limited regular employment system is the way unlimited regular employees being converted to limited regular employees within the same organization should be treated. Employers must not push the conversion as if it were a "stab in the back" without providing the employee with sufficient information about limited regular employment systems.

Suffice it to say, the employment terms must first be agreed to, and any changes will need to be clarified in writing. The employee's intention still comes first when converting employment status within the same company. When an agreement is made for an unlimited regular employee to change to a limited position for a certain period of time for the purpose of parenting or academic study, returning to an unlimited position later, the rationale and sensibility in dismissing a limited regular employee should be applied to that employee. The situation needs to be handled carefully in this manner.

An employee with a limited framework may be seen as inferior to a regular full-time employee. Unlimited employees are in fact usually provided better treatment in return for accepting future job relocation, reassignment, and overtime. But full-time regular workers with limited duties, who account for the majority of limited regular employees, will be provided with opportunities to enjoy benefits with different facets. We should not forget this point.

Employment with limited duties means working in line with one's own career-development goals, while taking advantage of and recognizing one's own strengths and value. This type of approach explores external frontiers of new job opportunities, which is expected to provide the employee with leverage in pay and other benefit negotiations.

This goes with the panel's policy philosophy promoting labor mobility, as formulated in its report, which reads: "Those who work actively with hopes in accordance with their willingness will be provided support." This poses two choices: Are you going to stay with the current comfortable stability while working as a "jack-of-all-trades" employee, sticking to a company or an organization? Or are you going to develop your own work style, exploring new frontiers and opportunities, while believing in your professional abilities despite challenges, and maintaining a good balance with your family and private life? Reform of the regular employment system would present the latter as a viable option.

English version originally published in *Discuss Japan—Japan Foreign Policy Forum*, no. 18 (Jan.–Feb. 2014).

Translated from "Saraba 'Nihon-gata koyō': Naze seishain kaikaku ga hitsuyō na no ka—Nihon o sukū kisei kaikaku kaigi no teian" [A Farewell to Japanese Employment Practices: Why Is Regular Employment System Reform Necessary?—Proposals Made by the Regulatory Reform Council], *Shūkan Ekonomisuto* [Weekly Economist] (October 14, 2013): 64–67. (Courtesy of Mainichi Shimbunsha)

Note

1. Available in Japanese at https://www8.cao.go.jp/kisei-kaikaku/kaigi/publication/130605/item4.pdf.

VII-(3.1) Promoting Growth and Restoring Fiscal Health Simultaneously

Jinno Naohiko

Discuss Japan—Japan Foreign Policy Forum, 2010

These days people are talking about how Japan's public finances are in danger of going bankrupt, but I frankly do not understand what they consider to be a state of bankruptcy. Certainly the government has gone heavily into debt, but for the most part, the outstanding government obligations are domestic in nature. That is, they are bonds held by Japanese parties, not by overseas investors. In effect, the Japanese are in debt with each other. It is like a family in which the husband has borrowed money from the wife, rather than from some loan shark. Under the circumstances, no problem will arise as long as inflation does not set in and interest rates do not rise too high. To be sure, the government needs to keep on meeting interest payments and rolling the debt over, but it has the financial tools for that.

The specific complaint one commonly hears is that the worsening health of public finance may prompt credit-rating agencies to lower the grade they assign to Japanese government bonds, but there is little chance of that. From an international perspective, Britain, the United States, and France all have fiscal deficits larger than Japan's measured as a percentage of gross domestic product, and Germany's deficit is about the same size. In addition, as Bank of Japan governor Shirakawa Masaaki has acknowledged, the nation has considerable leeway for hiking the consumption tax, which remains at the low level of 5 percent, and this is holding back moves to downgrade government bonds.

What would be more likely is that the government would become unable to issue bonds as a result of turmoil in the financial markets. The recent pattern has been for long-term interest rates to move down whenever stock prices plummet, but rates could instead move up, causing the bond market to crash and obstructing bond flotation. In the current situation, moreover, financial markets are quick to move funds around when even small differentials in interest rates open up. Government bonds could begin being targeted as an asset to avoid, not to acquire, and the authorities would become unable to raise funds.

Generating Robust Public Finances

On June 22 the cabinet approved a fiscal management strategy featuring a scheme to improve the health of public finances. The strategy specifies the target of turning the deficit in the "primary balance"—that is, government expenditures and revenues excluding new bond issues and debt-servicing costs—into a surplus by fiscal 2020 (April 2020 to March 2021). It is unlikely that this plan will progress on schedule, though, on account of likely major changes in factors on which it is premised, such as interest rates, stock prices, and unemployment.

What is important today is not, however, the outstanding public debt or the balance between expenditures and revenues. The key question is how the authorities can secure a sufficient inflow of fiscal resources to sustain the public services that support people's lives even in the event they become unable to raise funds through bond flotation.

Let me illustrate with a concrete example. Suppose that total tax payments amount to about 20 percent of GDP, while total public spending is on the order of 26 percent, leaving a gap of six percentage points. The difference would ordinarily be covered by deficit-financing bonds, and if their issue ran into a roadblock, the public services the government supplies would have to be cut back to the 20 percent level of tax payments. Now suppose that the government strengthens its revenue base, lifting taxes to 26 percent of GDP, and that it also enhances the social security system, causing a six-point increase in its expenditures to 32 percent of GDP. Again, the emergence of obstacles to the issue of government bonds would necessitate cuts in public services, but they would only have to be scaled down to their original 26 percent level.

Prime Minister Kan Naoto has spoken of the need for realizing "robust public finances," and this is what I see as a fiscal setup that could be fairly described as robust. It means, though, that the government must make an adjustment in the burden taxpayers are shouldering. After all, in the general account for FY 2010, taxes are estimated to account for only some 40 percent of total revenue.

At the Toronto summit of the Group of Twenty in June, the advanced countries adopted a declaration committing themselves to cutting their fiscal deficits in half by 2013 (although Japan was exempted in view of its special circumstances). But if the countries of the world move in unison toward austerity budgets, what might the result be?

At the onset of the Great Depression in 1929, John Maynard Keynes warned of the dangers of the "fallacy of composition"; that is, the presumption that what is good for one individual must automatically be good when all individuals behave in the same way. Thus, while each economic actor might see cutting back on spending as the best course of action, the economy would contract if they all reduced their consumption. The fallacy of composition was initially used to illustrate the adverse consequences of identical behavior by actors within a single country, but it also applies to groups of countries, and is a lesson from the past we need to keep in mind. Anyone can appreciate that the fallacy remains a concern, even in the modern world. Paul Krugman, for instance, pointed out in his June 27 column in the *New York Times* that slashing spending in the middle of a downturn will only deepen the depression. In this light, we probably need not take the promise by the advanced countries to cut their deficits in half all that seriously.

In this context as well, we can appreciate that what Japan should do is construct a solid tax-revenue foundation under the fiscal system, especially since financial conditions are so unsettled, with slight differences in interest rates triggering massive fund movements. At this stage, the government probably should not rush off on a quest to attain equilibrium in the primary balance.

Promoting a New Industrial Structure

What, exactly, should the government seek to accomplish? In brief, it should implement fiscal measures to ready the preconditions for the emergence of a new industrial structure.

In the course of the 1920s and 1930s, a period of financial panics and depression, the center of Japan's industrial structure shifted from light industries like textiles to heavy industries like steelmaking and petrochemicals. The shift occurred quite dramatically. Starting from 1929, the consumer price index plummeted by 30 percent in a mere two years. The prices of steel materials also plummeted, but just for a while. On an index with 1928 prices set at 100, steel prices dropped to 60 at the lowest, but then a recovery set in, and by 1933 they had regained their former level. Prices for raw silk, by contrast, failed to bounce back. They dropped to the level of 40 in 1931, recovered some ground by 1933, but then fell back again to about 40. In short, the price mechanism was at work. In the course of the transition in industrial structure, companies in traditional industries that had fallen into decline were forced out of business.

Now the Japanese economy is going through another rough period, but the price mechanism is not functioning effectively. While a deflationary tone is causing prices to decline, steep drops are not occurring. Under the circumstances, the shift in industrial structure will take some time. In the background is the fact that Japan in 1929 was on the gold standard, while today it is not. It might also be observed that governments have now gained wisdom about how they can limit the tragic consequences of a crash that happens all of a sudden.

Inherently, the lead role in the creation of a new industrial structure is played by the financial system. Financial resources need to be deployed from a long-range perspective without being diverted into schemes to make a quick profit. There should be a shift in money flows away from sunset industries and toward new industries that people in the dawning age will require. At the present time, however, Japan's financial system is not yet performing in this capacity. The government should use its fiscal tools to create the necessary conditions accordingly.

The Failure of the Rising-Tide Approach

Ever since the 1980s the authorities have applied a "rising tide" policy to tax cuts based on the reasoning that all will benefit from measures that give help to the wealthy and improve corporate profitability. At the same time, they have intruded into the formerly sacrosanct realm of social security and revised existing systems, limiting the extent of coverage. Let us consider why they opted for this course of action.

The idea was that Japan could boost economic growth by cutting income and corporate taxes, creating a society that rewarded those who made the most effort and unleashing the will to work among all workers. Faster growth would then cause tax revenue to swell, enabling the government to attain a healthy fiscal position without hiking taxes. A trickle-down effect would manifest itself at the same time, it was said, spreading wealth from those who became more affluent to those without much money, thereby limiting the widening of social disparities. The rising-tide argument in this way made economic growth the supreme objective, and anticipated such side effects as a balanced budget and minimal widening of the gap between the rich and the poor.

What actually happened, however, was something else. First, the government's capacity to raise tax revenue declined, and while government spending followed an upward curve on a line graph, the tax revenue curve sloped steeply down, giving the appearance of a yawning alligator. The alligator's mouth opened so wide, in fact, that fiscal deficits mushroomed, and even deeper cuts in social security may become necessary. Second, the tax system's function of redistributing income was impaired, and poverty spread as income disparities widened. Third, the shift in industrial structure was obstructed, and economic development decelerated. That is, the government's policy line led to stagnant growth, falling wages, and unemployment. Although the early years of the new century saw the start of a sustained expansion that lasted longer even than the famed Izanagi boom of the late 1960s, the pace of growth remained at a low level.

Results like these were not unrelated developments; they were linked in a negative chain whose links reinforced each other. We could say that overly large budget deficits arose as a result of the shift to an overly small government.

Taking Action on Three Fronts Simultaneously

How are we to break free of this negative chain created by a policy taking the rising-tide approach to tax cuts? Only if we set off in simultaneous pursuit of two rabbits—economic growth and fiscal rehabilitation—will we be able to overcome the reluctance to rise to the challenge of rebuilding the industrial structure, motivating companies to invest in human resources and move into new fields. This is the positive chain Prime Minister Kan had in mind when he called for the realization of "achieving economic growth, putting public finances on a sound footing, and reforming social security" in an integrated manner.

As I have already explained, public finances will become sound when essential public services can be sustained without depending on borrowing. Once the government is in a strong financial position, it can get to work on providing ample social security. A strong welfare system requires the construction of a safety net composed of livelihood and activity guarantees. This net should not just provide a sense of security but also assist efforts to rise to challenges. If it functions like a trampoline, welfare recipients can use it to jump at chances.

Livelihood guarantees should be provided in a set of cash benefits and services. If, for example, women are to join the labor force, they may need the guarantee of services that support raising children and caring for elderly family members. Activity guarantees should make use of schooling, retraining, and lifelong education, also called "recurrent education," which provides people with the skills for entering the labor market of a new industrial structure. A policy focused on activity guarantees shifts emphasis from the provision of physical infrastructure, such as road and railway networks and the power grid, to the formation of human infrastructure. Labor productivity will increase as workers acquire more abilities, leading to faster economic growth. At the same time, when all members of society are engaged in honing their respective valuable skills, a more equitable distribution of income becomes possible, and social fairness can be realized.

Strong social security provides the foundation for achieving a strong economy. The objective is to generate a qualitative change in the industrial structure, one that will both ensure economic growth and employment and enhance social fairness through equitable income distribution. Once the economy acquires strength, the prospects for robust public finances will steadily improve.

In this trinity of a strong economy, robust public finances, and strong social security, action must proceed on all three fronts at the same time. In the conduct of fiscal management, allocation targets are selected first, and spending amounts are decided after that. In this respect, although the starting point should be seen as the attainment of strong social security, my concern here is the structure of expenditures and revenues in the budget for each year. Since it is the combined effects of the trinity that count, it would make no sense to ask about which element of the trinity to start with or demand that priorities be assigned among the three elements.

The Tax Reform Agenda

Exactly how should the tax system be reformed in order to strengthen public finances? On June 22, the Tax Commission subcommittee that I chair released an interim report on its discussions about revising the tax system. Here, while touching on the ideals lying behind this report, I will present its conclusions in my own words.

A tax system needs to be designed with four sets of principles in mind. One set consists of principles involving fiscal policy, such as the principle of adequacy (whether the tax system is adequate for sustaining public services) and the principle of flexibility (whether it allows for the collection of revenue to be expanded and contracted). Another set is the principles that guarantee equity. Then there are principles for facilitating economic policy and for managing tax administration. The interim report proposes seven agenda items for handling these four sets of principles, determining how revenue sources should be distributed between the central and local governments, and pulling the tax system together.

In the area of fiscal policy, satisfying the adequacy principle means securing sufficient tax revenue to provide public services. In its party platform, the ruling Democratic Party of Japan set the goal of building a society in which people support each other. This goal can be attained through the sharing of resources by means of taxes. This is the first agenda item.

The second is restoring the function of redistribution based on the equity principle. Vertical redistribution, through which the rich share some of their wealth with the poor, is to be enhanced through a reform of income and asset taxes. Third on the agenda is securing stable financial resources for supporting the social security system. Action on this front is related to the flexibility principle of fiscal policy, and it aims to make use of the consumption tax, which serves to accomplish the key tax objective of facilitating horizontal redistribution.

In the area of economic policy principles, the tax system needs to be designed to enable economic growth. What is important, however, is forging a new industrial structure. This is a matter of qualitative change, not just quantitative growth. There is no strong evidence for the assertion that cutting corporate taxes will automatically promote growth. Some economists support this proposition, but others are in disagreement. If moves are made to lower corporate taxes, accordingly, steps should also be taken to broaden the corporate tax base. This is the fourth agenda item.

The fifth item deals with the issue of distributing revenue sources among the central government and the regions, and it seeks to reform the tax system so as to achieve "regional sovereignty."

The proposals in this area would revise the allocation of tax revenue and strengthen local consumption taxes. Japan probably has no choice but to move toward decentralization. In the work of constructing a safety net, the provision of services is a more important concern than the payment of cash benefits, but it is best that these services be fine-tuned as far as possible to match the realities of daily life in each local community.

The principles of tax administration are the concern of the sixth item, which proposes that the tax system be redesigned by shifting it from the "logic of the tax collector" to the "logic of the taxpayer [the people]." In particular, Japan needs a transparent system that can win the consent of taxpayers.

At the end, the interim report pulls all these proposals together in the seventh agenda item, which is to create a tax system with overall coherence. Based on the discussions among its members, the subcommittee believes it necessary to construct a tax system in which income taxes and value-added taxes (the consumption tax) serve in the main role of the two wheels of the cart while other levies, such as property taxes and environmental levies, which are specific taxes, play supplementary roles. In the proposed tax reform, accordingly, the respective components of the tax system—including income, corporate, consumption, and asset taxes—need to be considered not as separate items but as parts of a whole.

Limiting a Consumption Tax Hike

The assumption that the government intends to hike the consumption tax to 10 percent has taken on a life of its own, even though Kan, while campaigning for the July House of Councillors election shortly after he became prime minister, never made a specific pledge to that effect. The report of the Tax Commission's subcommittee also makes no reference to a 10 percent rate. As I noted, the leeway Japan has for lifting the consumption tax to a higher level is helping to persuade credit-rating agencies not to downgrade its government bonds. In this light, perhaps Japan ought to retain room for hiking the tax, since this merit of a low rate would be lost if the government established a new rate at the 10 percent or 20 percent level.

It seems reasonable to say that even if the authorities decide to hike the tax, they ought to limit the extent of the increase as far as they can while reforming the rest of the system so as to secure a more ample supply of revenue from income and other taxes. A call has been made by the Liberal Democratic Party in the opposition for hiking just the consumption tax, setting it at a 10 percent rate, but an equal amount of revenue could be raised through a reform of the tax system overall. If, for instance, the income tax were hiked by two percentage points and maximum tax rates were lifted, the increase in the consumption tax might be held to two points.

Correcting the regressive nature of the consumption tax is another subject of debate. There have been calls, for instance, for introducing a credit for the consumption tax in the income tax system, so that low-income taxpayers would receive a refund for their payments. This, though, would dilute the effect of any hike in the consumption tax. Levying taxes on consumption is by nature a regressive practice, but when the tax applies broadly to the items people consume, it can bring in a large amount of revenue even if it is set at a low rate. There should be no need to remedy the regressive impact of the consumption tax independently, since equity in taxation can be achieved by also taking the income tax, which is progressive in nature, into account. Why turn a simple tax into a complicated one? I fail to understand why some people feel it necessary to resolve the regressive elements within each tax category. We need to pursue a discussion of the whole system, not just of its parts.

Getting Democracy to Work

Finally, I would like to add a word on the government's trustworthiness. This is because the strong popular resistance in Japan to any tax hike is believed to stem partly from the people's lack of trust in the government.

This is an issue that boils down to the question of whether Japanese democracy is functioning as it should. Here we need to learn from the lesson of Germany before World War II. By fanning the flames of popular discontent with the Reichstag (Germany's parliament) and arguing that legislators served no useful purpose, the Nazis attracted an explosively growing political force and succeeded in forcing the Reichstag to pass the Enabling Act, which handed its constitutional functions over to Adolf Hitler. Today in Japan as well, a vicious circle has been set in motion by the poor functioning of the democratic process and the government's failure to supply the kinds of services people desire. This is a very dangerous situation, since opportunities for critics to denounce democracy are being created.

In *The Age of Uncertainty*, John Kenneth Galbraith called attention to the differences between representative democracies, such as the United States and Britain, and direct democracies, such as Switzerland. In a direct democracy, Galbraith pointed out, citizens solve problems by themselves without delegating anyone to act on their behalf. In a representative democracy, by contrast, citizens engage in a search for representatives to act for them. We can find much food for thought in this comment about the proper operation of democracy.

English version originally published in *Discuss Japan—Japan Foreign Policy Forum*, no. 2 (Aug.–Sept. 2010).

Translated from "Keiki kaifuku to zaisei saiken no 'nito' o eru zeisei keikaku" [Tax Reform that Achieves the 'Double Win' of Economic Recovery and Fiscal Consolidation], *Chūō Kōron* (September 2010): 130–37. slightly abridged. (Courtesy of Chūōkōron Shinsha)

VII-(3.2) Stalled Fiscal Consolidation

Government Must Act Soon on Policy Normalization

Ihori Toshihiro

Discuss Japan—Japan Foreign Policy Forum, 2018

This autumn, Prime Minister Abe Shinzō is expected to decide whether or not to proceed with the 10 percent hike in the consumption tax rate scheduled for October 2019. During the House of Representatives election held in October of last year, the ruling party promised to allocate a portion of the revenue increase from the consumption tax hike to educational expenses, such as strengthening preschool education.

Originally, 80 percent of the revenue increase was supposed to be allocated to paying down debt. But that would not benefit the younger working generation, and yet cutting social security spending to fund preschool education would be opposed by the elderly, so that's not an option either. The government has secured a funding source in the budget for the fiscal year ending March 2019 by not paying down debt, but will have to issue deficit bonds to cover the shortfall, meaning that the funding burden will be passed to future generations who have no voting rights.

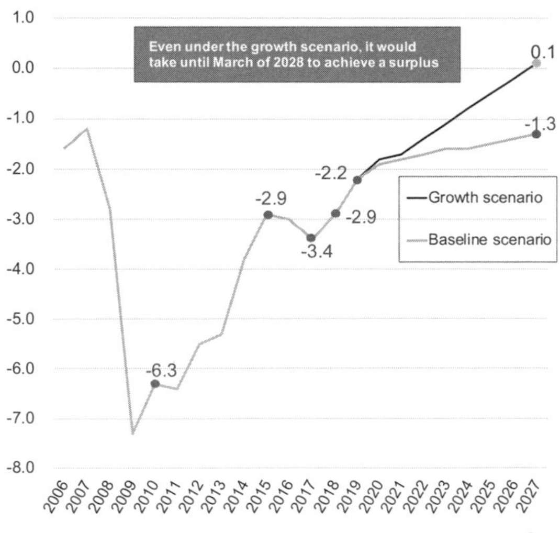

Central and Local Government Primary Balance to GP

Source: Cabinet Office, "Economic and Fiscal Projections for Medium to Long Term Analysis," January 2018.

On the other hand, the opposition parties have come out with promises even more naïve than those of the ruling party in calling for a freeze on increases in the consumption tax while saying that social security could be strengthened and fiscal consolidation achieved even without an increase in the consumption tax.

The House of Representatives has been dissolved before three years have elapsed, and a House of Councilors election takes place every three years. Each time a national election is held, politicians try to offer spending to please all voters and the consumption tax increase is rolled back further, undermining progress on fiscal consolidation. In the national election, the ruling Liberal Democratic Party and the Kōmeitō coalition won an overwhelming victory, but while the political situation may be stable, the will for fiscal consolidation is nowhere to be seen.

* * *

As usual, the government is groping for an aggressive stimulus package, nominally to boost the economy. Social-insurance spending is characterized by inequalities and ineffective policies, but no progress has been made on rectifying these.

As a result, it will be impossible, within the fiscal year ending March 2021, to achieve the fiscal consolidation target of bringing the primary balance into equilibrium. Moreover, most of the revenue increase from the next consumption tax hike will be allocated to government expenditure increases, and the tiered consumption tax system (applying a lower rate on fresh food) will also come into force. Since the tiered system for consumption tax will reduce the tax base, tax revenues will fall. It's as yet uncertain how this revenue shortfall will be made good.

According to Cabinet Office estimates announced in January, even if the consumption tax rate is raised in October of 2019, under the government's growth scenario, the deficit in the primary balance for the year ending March 2021 will swell from the ¥8.2 trillion estimate made in July of last year to over ¥10 trillion. Achievement of an overall surplus will also be pushed back two years to the year ending March 2028 (see figure). According to the baseline scenario, which assumes that the economic growth rate will not recover along the lines projected by the government, the government's fiscal status will become even more severe.

It is also doubtful that it will be possible to achieve the nominal growth rate of 3 to 4 percent as projected under the growth scenario for the 2020s and after. The Olympics will be a major event, but when it is over, there will be a major pullback as the enthusiasm cools. Given the many regulations in Japan which hamper innovation, the rate of economic growth can only slump once the impact of aging and population decline are felt.

As long as talented young workers are not being hired from foreign countries, Japan cannot expect to see very much human capital accumulation. Looking to 2020 and beyond, it is very possible that the real economic growth rate will fall to nearly 0 percent, and it will be very hard even to achieve a nominal growth rate of 3 to 4 percent. Achieving that will by no means be easy, even under the baseline scenario.

* * *

The fiscal consolidation strategy of Abenomics adopts the position that revenues will increase naturally along with economic recovery, but such a leisurely approach means that fiscal consolidation will remain out of reach. When the economy slows from the middle of the 2020s, the baby-boom generation will become late-stage elderly, and social security demand, especially for medical care, will rise dramatically.

Theoretically, if expenditures can be reduced under the optimistic projections of the growth scenario, it would be possible to work out a fiscal consolidation scenario with the consumption tax rate at 10 percent. However, given the trend of rising demand for social security services as the Japanese population ages, it will not be easy to cut expenditures. In the formulation of the budget for the year ending March 2019, the revision of medical treatment remuneration became a focus of debate, and although drug prices were lowered, medical care remuneration itself was increased.

One promising option for reviewing the fiscal consolidation targets is the proposed extension of the targeted date for achieving equilibrium in the primary balance from the year ending March 2021 to the year ending in March of 2028. However, if the target date is postponed seven years or more, investors at home and abroad may doubt the government's resolve to achieve fiscal consolidation, which may lead to market volatility.

According to Cabinet Office estimates, the ratio of outstanding public debt to gross domestic product (GDP) will decline for the present despite the deficit in the primary balance. This will result from the action of the Bank of Japan, which will maintain a policy of massive monetary easing to keep interest rates below the growth rate. For practical purposes, the BOJ's continued buying of Japanese government securities amounts to monetization of the fiscal deficit (or making good the fiscal deficit), and continuing such emergency measures through the 2020s will almost certainly be impossible.

On the whole, Abenomics is an emergency policy package. Since the economy is in a state of emergency, unorthodox measures are being adopted in both monetary and fiscal policy. If the government goes on raising expenditures by expanding public works financed with large supplemental budgets and continues extravagant fiscal spending despite the state of the economic climate, there will be no exit from the complacency of profligate financial policy. Extravagant fiscal spending is not the way to fiscal consolidation.

Abenomics has been underway for five years since the start of the second Abe administration, but it's hard to see when the emergency policies will end. Recently the government's assessment of the economy has been positive, and the economy has been near full employment. The government must now focus on its strategy for fiscal and monetary policy normalization.

* * *

The merits of fiscal consolidation should be judged based on whether economic conditions are better or worse now than they will be in the future. The tax increase must be borne at one time or the other, so debate should focus on whether it is better to ask the present or future generations to bear the burden.

If the tax increase is postponed to a period of economic weakness, the burden will be shifted onto future generations who will be less able to bear the burden. Japan's population will decline in the future, and Japan's existing pay-as-you-go social security system taxes the present working generations to provide benefits to the older generation, so future generations will have to face a heavier burden and fewer benefits in social security. It is very likely that macroeconomic growth will also weaken. One can easily imagine that economic conditions for future generations will be harsh, so it would be preferable for present generations, including the elderly, to share the burden of the tax increase.

When baby boomers become late-stage elderly around 2025, it will become even more difficult politically to reduce the vested interest supporting social security benefits. If macroeconomic conditions are dire at that time, both the government's financial position and the social security system could miscarry. Instead of being obsessed with the next election or current economic trends and postponing solutions to pending issues, the government should change course on the "second arrow" of fiscal stimulus, stress the interests of future generations, and take action on fiscal consolidation and social welfare reforms to attain fiscal sustainability and intergenerational equity.

Health insurance will require massive funding in the near future, so the best option is to build up a fund by identifying funding sources now while there is still time, prepare for the increase in healthcare demand expected in the future, and adopt an individual account-funded system.

For instance, Singapore has adopted a healthcare reserve system based on a self-help approach through compulsory savings in individual accounts. A similar healthcare funded account system has been adopted in the United States. In public pensions, too, it will be important to build a good individual account-funded pension system. Australia has implemented a retirement pension fund system featuring compulsory contributions by business enterprises, and many workers participate in the funded pension system.

Japan's individual type defined contribution pension plan (iDeCo) is a similar system, but its adoption has been slow. If all workers had such accounts by default and elderly savings were strengthened through self-help efforts, it would be possible to streamline the current pay-as-you-go public pension system.

We cannot expect to stimulate the economy if excessive concerns for agricultural and self-employed interests lead to safe and secure policies designed to please everyone. It is important that the government proceed with bold reforms in healthcare, agriculture, distribution, and other fields, adopting a strategy to encourage private-sector creativity and boost the potential growth rate.

While raising the consumption tax in stages, the government must cope with the vested interests of the elderly in such areas as social security, and act boldly to use expenditures more efficiently, restore fiscal discipline, and implement fiscal consolidation over the long term.

English version originally published in *Discuss Japan—Japan Foreign Policy Forum*, no. 45 (Mar. 2018).

Translated by the Japan Journal, Ltd. The article first appeared in the *Keizai kyōshitsu* column of the *Nikkei Shimbun* on February 8, 2018, under the title, "Tōnoku zaisei-kenzenka (I): Hijōji taiō no seijōka isoge" (Stalled Fiscal Consolidation [Part I]: Government Must Act Soon on Policy Normalization). (Courtesy of author)

VII-(3.3) The Nation Needs to Conduct Fiscal Policy Reforms that Correct the Inequity between the Generations

Oguro Kazumasa

Discuss Japan—Japan Foreign Policy Forum, 2011

As society ages, birthrates decline, and the economy globalizes, the Japanese economy and its fiscal situation have continued to stagnate and worsen since the collapse of the bubble economy in 1990. Public debt is about to reach a figure that is some 200 percent of our gross domestic product (GDP). And when the Great East Japan Earthquake hit on March 11, the situation was exacerbated.

While recovering from the quake is important, we must at the same time work on two reforms today to solve the medium- to long-term issues faced by Japan. One is a growth strategy to increase the potential growth rate of the Japanese economy, and the other is correcting the inequity between generations by reforming fiscal policy and social security.

In terms of the latter, politicians are currently split between being pro-tax increase and anti-tax increase, but this is not the real point of this issue. As the term "political aging" suggests, as the population ages, democracy tends to give greater political power to the retiring generation that comprises the greater population volume, and the remaining younger and future generations may see their interests compromised. Accordingly, the real debate in this situation should be between maintaining the status quo, which expands the inter-generational inequities, or correcting the inter-generational inequities. Whether or not the latter occurs depends on how the new government deals with the Plan for the Comprehensive Reform of Social Security and Tax that the ruling party drafted in late June.

Truth be told, the current generation is passing the burden of fiscal and social security onto future generations, as the social security budget is inflating at a rate of ¥1 trillion every year and the national budget deficit is remaining constant (e.g., ¥44 trillion in FY 2011). It is imposing a load on future generations that they cannot possibly bear.

Knowing the Burden Imposed on Future Generations with Generational Accounting–Generational Inequities: ¥120 million

We can see this truth using the method shown in figure 1, called generational accounting, which derives the difference—or generational inequities—between the current generation aged sixty and over (defined at the time of estimate as born up to and including 1945) and future generations (born from 1986 onward; includes people under twenty years of age). According to the results of my estimation, the inequity between current and future generations amounts to ¥120 million per household. Assuming that the lifetime wage of the average businessperson is ¥200 million, the inequity amounts to almost 60 percent of the lifetime wage.

The generational accounting that I used in this estimation is a method of estimating the costs a citizen imposes on the government and the value of the benefits he or she gains from the government throughout his or her lifetime. Specifically, it estimates the lifetime benefits and costs per generation—age groups such as the twenties, thirties, or fifties—and assesses the nation's fiscal policy.

It accounts for the benefits acquired from social capital such as roads and dams and public services such as police, defense, medicine, and nursing, along with the cost burdens such as the tax and insurance premiums the nation requires in order to offer those services. The difference

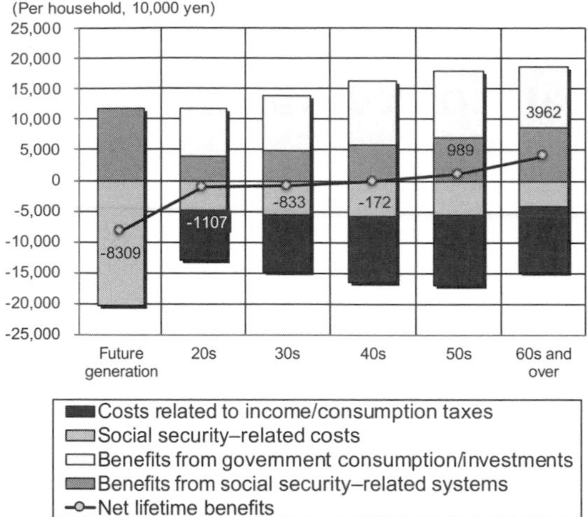

Figure 1. Lifetime Benefits and Costs per Generation
Source: Graph created by author, referring to figures from the Cabinet Office's FY 2005 Annual Report on the Japanese Economy and Public Finance.

between the costs and benefits—the amount derived from subtracting the lifetime benefits (discounted to the present value) from the costs (discounted to the present value) that the current and future generations will pay over their lifetime, assuming the current policy—is called the net cost (discounted to the present value).

According to this method, the net cost for the group aged sixty and over is in negative figures, a benefit of approximately ¥40 million (excess benefit), and the group in their fifties has a benefit of around ¥9.9 million (excess benefit). On the other hand, the net cost for the remaining lower generations is positive, with the future generation at a loss of approximately ¥83 million (excess payment).

The advantage of generational accounting is in making the net cost to future generations visible. Usually, when the government discloses figures on public debt, it only indicates the amount of the debt at that point in time, which reveals nothing of the true cost that future generations will bear. The government could always reduce pension benefits or increase costs to keep the current budget deficit and public debt unchanged and leave the future generation to bear the costs. But by using generational accounting, we can see all that and the entire cost burden.

A Public Pension would Run a Debt of 150 Percent of GDP—A Massive Amount of Unmentioned Debt

With regard to the net cost (discounted to the present value) of each generation as obtained from generational accounting, we can derive the following formula:

> ∑(Net cost of generation j) × (Household population volume of generation j)
> = Current net debt of government
>
> Note: The formula assumes that the benefits acquired from government consumption were distributed to each generation under a fixed rule.

Using data from figure 1, the left-hand side of the formula refers to the total sum of the net cost of the sixties and over generation multiplied by that generation's household population volume, the net cost of the fifties generation multiplied by its household population volume, [. . .] and the net cost of the twenties generation multiplied by its household population volume.

This formula therefore basically explains that the net costs of generation groups work like a zero-sum game. In other words, if the current net debt of the government (>0) is a given, and the net cost of the sixties and fifties groups is a negative

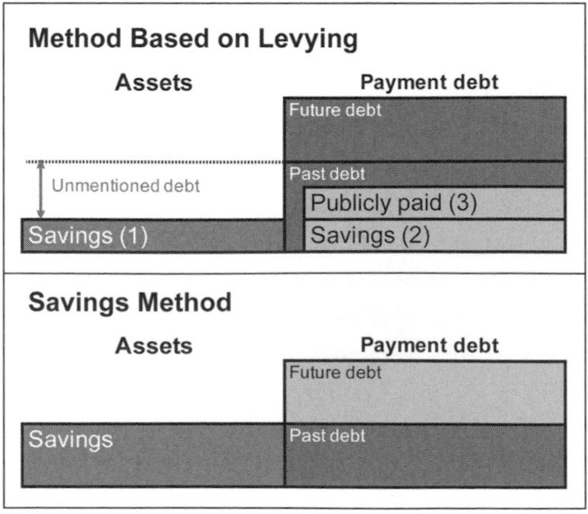

Figure 2. The Concept of Unmentioned Debt
Source: Created by author.

figure (excess benefit), then the net cost of other younger and future generation groups will inevitably be a positive figure (excess payment).

The right-hand side of the formula, the net debt of the government, refers to the government's public and other debts minus its sellable financial assets. However, it is regarding this formula that the government is undergoing debate on the government's balance sheet.

The Cabinet Office, for the first time in ten years, drafted a balance sheet (Government BS) for the general government (State/Regions + Social Security Fund) to be included in the FY 2011 Annual Report on the Japanese Economy and Public Finance (E/F Report) that the Cabinet released in late July. Some people in the Diet and media are claiming that this Government BS "arbitrarily accounts for pension payment debts and certain assets to inflate the government's amount of surplus debt."

This claim does not take the correct view. From the generational accounting perspective, Japan's public pension is estimated to be running an implicit debt of close to 150 percent of GDP (if GDP were ¥500 trillion, it would be ¥750 trillion), and such a claim runs the risk of undervaluing this debt. Implicit debt is defined as "the difference between savings that should have existed if the pension were completely under a funding method, and actual savings." The funding method is the method of saving for one's own retirement, and savings that should have existed if the pension were under a savings method are almost equivalent to the total amount that the senior generation received at no cost back when the pension system commenced. Japan's public pension today, on the other hand, is called *shūsei fuka hōshiki* (pay-as-you-go pension with a partial funding method), under which the current generation is liable for the amount paid to the senior generation, yet saves its own as well, practically. These savings are what is left over from the part of its premiums that was not spent on pension payments.

With regard to public pensions, the government bears the obligation to pay pensions according to the amount of premiums expended by the citizens—or in other words, it bears a payment debt. The savings that should have existed if the pension were under a savings method refers to the area within the Payment Debt in figure 2 that applies to past expenditure, or Past Debt (the amount of payments made to current recipients of the pension plus the amount of future payments [discounted to present value] made to the current generation calculated from the years of pension membership up to this point). And by definition, the difference between Past Debt and Savings (1) in figure 2 is the implicit debt.

Conduct Sweeping Reforms with Government Leadership—Medical and Nursing Care Take the Same Structure

Let us look at the two types of government BS that the Cabinet Office drafted (Cases 1 and 2 in the table below). From the viewpoint of the method based on levying in figure 2, Case 1 accounts for savings (= (1): the amount that the Cabinet BS invests in financial products as part of financial assets) as assets, and ¥181.6 trillion of savings within past debts (= (2): pension savings in the Cabinet BS) as debt. But since (1) and (2) almost cancel each other out, unless the P/L from investing the pension savings does not amount to a massive figure, they do not have a significant impact on the surplus debt (the difference resulting from subtracting assets from debt) of ¥245.3 trillion in the government BS.

Case 2 accounts for savings (1) as assets, and ¥181.6 trillion of savings (2) within past debt and publicly paid ¥273.2 trillion (3) as debt, and records the surplus debt on the government BS as ¥518.5 trillion. Yet in this case as well, what the BS indicates is merely part of the implicit debt in figure 2. The issue of whether or not to include in the government BS all or part of debts (2) or (3) that public pension runs is only secondary; more important is the scale of the implicit debt.

And when the implicit debt is 150 percent (of GDP), the public pension (approximately ¥270 trillion) included as debt in the government BS in Case 2 would apply to the public pension (3) in figure 2 that is part of the implicit debt (¥750 trillion), so when we include the remaining implicit debt (approx. ¥480 trillion) in the government BS, we get a surplus debt of approximately ¥1 quadrillion.

Government BS

Case 1 (Unit: Trillion yen)

Assets	958.8	Debts	1231.20
Non-financial assets	470.1	Government bonds	795.8
Financial assets	515.7	Pension savings	181.6
		Retirement pay	25
		Difference: Assets – Debts	▲245.3

Case 2 (Unit: Trillion yen)

Assets	958.8	Debts	1504.40
Non-financial assets	470.1	Government bonds	795.8
Financial assets	515.7	Pension savings	181.6
		Publicly paid pensions	273.2
		Retirement pay	25.4
		Difference: Assets – Debts	▲518.5

Source: Created by author from the Cabinet Office's FY 2011 Annual Report on Economy and Finance.
Note: ▲ = Negative figures

The presence of this implicit debt could also be explained from the formula mentioned earlier. In doing so, we should consider a case that involves no government expenditure/income other than the public pension to simplify our discussion. To clarify the meaning of implicit debt, we would also assume that the government had no assets or debts when it launched the public pension system. In other words, we will consider generational accounting that limits itself to the public pension. An intuitive image of the formula would be as follows.

> Product of the excess payment (discounted to the present value) of the future and young generations multiplied by the population volume of these generations = Product of the excess benefit (discounted to the present value) of the retiring generation multiplied by its population volume

Strictly speaking, the retiring generation—the right-hand side of this formula—includes the generation that did not pay premiums when the public pension system commenced, and died after receiving only pension benefits. This right-hand side of the formula is itself the implicit debt. This formula therefore explains that unless we compress the excess benefits of the retiring generation, the implicit debt will have to be paid off as excess payments on the part of the younger and future generations.

What is more, there are implicit debts other than what is run by the pension. While the levy-method pension is a system of transferring income from the current generation to the senior generation, medical and nursing care are also fields that see expenditures concentrated in the senior phase of life, and the current generations bear the costs. These systems have a structure that is almost identical to that of the pension, and are also running implicit debts. Some experts estimate that medical and nursing care are running implicit debt amounting to 80 percent of GDP.

We Can Pass the Buck No Longer

As all this shows, the discussion that we really need to be having concerning the government BS is regarding how much the current implicit debt in social security (pension, medical, and nursing care) amounts to, and how the current and future generations should bear its cost.

The most crucial point regarding common discussions on the government BS is the view that we cannot calculate the true burden of future generations. This, I repeat, is because the government could always reduce pension benefits or increase costs to keep the current budget deficit and public debt unchanged and leave the future generations to bear the costs. But generational accounting has ultimately unraveled this, and we now know that the current fiscal policy and social security system are imposing a load on the younger and future generations that they cannot possibly bear.

In any case, Japan today runs about half its annual expenditure as a budget deficit, and its social security budget is inflating by ¥1 trillion every year. This financial state cannot continue forever, and we can clearly see that it is approaching its limit. When it reaches this point, we will only have a limited set of solutions to choose from, and in order to avoid a financial crisis and correct generational inequities, we will have no choice but to conduct fundamental reforms of our fiscal policy and social security while we recover from the earthquake.

Yet whether or not the reform plan mentioned in the beginning will pass in the political proceedings to come is relatively uncertain. The political scene that needs to undertake the reform is utterly confused, due in great part to the twisted parliament, and its prospects are far from clear. Even recently, the ruling and opposing parties staged a battle over the Act on Special Provisions concerning Issuance of Public Bonds to Secure Financial Resources Required for Fiscal Management required for issuing debt-covering bonds. Tactics are always part of politics, but we will not tolerate unproductive conflicts between the ruling and opposing parties in times of emergency. Many still embrace the wishful hope and illusion that Japan will somehow find its way even if it postpones reforms on fiscal policy and social security, and some profess that Japan would be better off facing an economic collapse if it cannot reform anyway.

According to the Medium/Long-Term Projections on Japanese Public Finances released by the government in August, even though the reform plan proposes to increase the consumption tax rate to 10 percent by the year 2015, the rate would have to be set at around 17 percent if the government were to achieve its goal of a profitable standing in terms of basic financial balance by the year 2020. In other words, we should know that the latest reform plan is only the first stage in correcting generational inequities, and the government needs to undertake additional reforms to comprehensively improve fairness.

Now is the time for the government to take a position of leadership in the true sense of the word to improve generational inequities. Commitment to this issue is demanded of the government.

English version originally published in *Discuss Japan—Japan Foreign Policy Forum*, no. 8 (Oct.–Nov. 2011).

Translated from "'Sedaikan kakusa' o zesei suru zaisei kaikaku o" [Fiscal Reforms to Redress the "Intergenerational Divide"], *Shūkan Ekonomisuto* [Weekly Economist] (September 13, 2011): 52–55. (Courtesy of Mainichi Shimbunsha)

VII-(4.1) The Death of Regional Cities

A Horrendous Simulation

Masuda Hiroya

Discuss Japan—Japan Foreign Policy Forum, 2014

The first thing that we need to understand when envisioning the future of a nation is its demographics. Japan, whose population began to decline in 2008, will become a society with a population in full-scale decline. In considering methods to realize an affluent society in such a scenario, it is necessary to look squarely at Japan's current situation.

During my twelve years in office as the governor of Iwate Prefecture, my greatest issue of concern was the declining population and the resulting issue of marginal settlements. When I took office in 1995, the population in Iwate stood at 1,419,000. It was 1,363,000 when I left office in 2007, and by 2012 it had fallen to 1,300,300. A declining population not only reduces the functions of regional communities, but also makes it difficult to maintain services essential for daily life, such as medical care and education. While I was governor, measures I adopted included the introduction of a remote medical system based on the use of information technology, providing subsidies for relocation expenses to those living in villages facing the risk of natural disaster, and promoting the consolidation of such villages. These policies were effective for the purpose of maintaining the functions of regional areas, but they were still passive.

Japan is now facing the crisis of the entire nation becoming marginal municipalities. Our ability to avoid such a crisis and make Japan a sustainable country depends entirely on the choices we make.

The Age of Disappearing Regional Cities Will Arrive

Like a giant wave, declining population will first hit small-scale regional municipalities, and then will rapidly expand to entire regional areas, eventually even swallowing metropolitan areas with its vicious power. If the current pace of decline continues, in thirty years the reproduction potential of the population (details given below) will fall sharply, and there will potentially be a number of regions that, in sequence, will inevitably disappear.

People shocked by these drastic changes wonder why such things are occurring in this way. The phenomenon of the falling birthrate and aging population hid the real picture from us. The declining population due to the falling birthrate has apparently remained unseen because of the continued increase in the number of the elderly as a result of the simultaneous increase in longevity. We will now face an age when even the number of such elderly will start declining in many areas.

People hope that the declining population will be halted sometime in the future, but once it starts, this phenomenon will be unstoppable. With a current total fertility rate of 1.41 in Japan, even if the birthrate gradually rises, the total number of live births will not increase.

Let me explain in more detail (figure 1). The birthrate started to rise in 2005 from 1.26 to 1.41 in 2012. However, the last group of the second baby boomers who were born in 1971–1974 is already hitting thirty-nine years old, while the number of females younger than the generation of this group is dropping. Therefore, even if the birthrate gradually increases in the future, the declining population will not stop, as the number of live births will continue to decline.

Raising a birthrate that has fallen as low as Japan's to a level at which the population can be

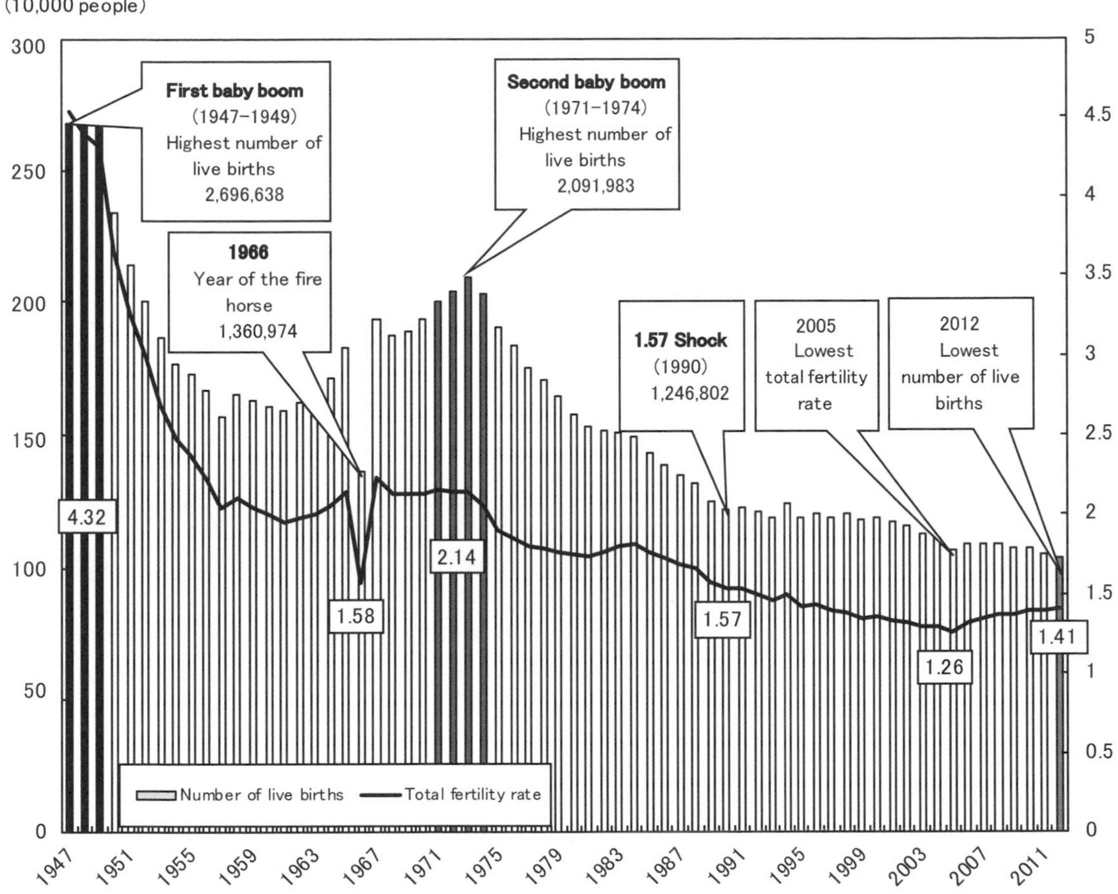

Figure 1. Trends of total fertility rate and number of live births

Sources: "Vital Statistics Survey," Ministry of Health, Labour and Welfare; "Current Population Estimates as of October 1, 2012," Ministry of Internal Affairs and Communications.

sustained (2.1) is thought to be an extremely difficult task.

Still, assuming Japan achieves a birthrate of 2.1 in seventeen years, in 2030, even in this scenario it would be around 2090, sixty years later, when Japan's population would finally stop falling. As if following the law of inertia, a birthrate that has already begun falling will continue to affect Japan over the next several decades. The impact will be felt more severely in regional areas where the pace of population decline is particularly fast. This is the critical situation Japan is facing.

We cannot just stand by, however, as if dumbfounded by this challenge. While calmly accepting the harsh future forecasts, we need to take effective measures as soon as possible.

For example, assuming that recovery of the birthrate to 2.1 as mentioned above is achieved by 2025, five years earlier than 2030, then by around 2090 the population will already be stabilized at 120 million—three million more than when 2.1 is achieved in 2030. On the contrary, if 2.1 is achieved five years later, in 2035, the population will be stabilized at 96 million; three million less than when reaching 2.1 in 2030.

Based on a simple calculation, every five-year delay in the recovery of the birthrate will result in a decline of three million in the future figure for stabilized population. Moreover, if the timing of a recovery is delayed until 2050, the timing of a halt in declining population will be put off to around 2110, while the number of stabilized population will fall to 87 million. Needless to say, as long as the birthrate remains under 2.1, there is no prospect of ending the declining population.

The issue of a declining population is, if compared to illness, a chronic disease. It cannot be fixed easily, but the earlier measures to improve the population constitution are taken, the better the impact will be.

1. Three-Stage Population Decline

Population decline takes place while each population generation makes different progress

First, let's look at how the declining population in Japan will progress in the future.

Table 1 was prepared based on "Population Projections for Japan by Prefecture (March 2013)" issued by the National Institute of Population and Social Security Research. It is estimated that if the current situation prevails, Japan's population of 128 million in 2010 will

Table 1. Future population projection (2012 estimation—Up to 2110)

	Median estimate—Total fertility rate of 1.35				
Total population (10,000 people)	2010	2040	2060	2090	2110
Elderly population (65 and above)	2,948	3,868	3,464	2,357	1,770
Population aging rate (percent)	23.0	36.1	39.9	41.2	41.3
Working-age population (15–64)	8,174	5,787	4,418	2,854	2,126
Young population (0–14)	1,684	1,073	792	516	391

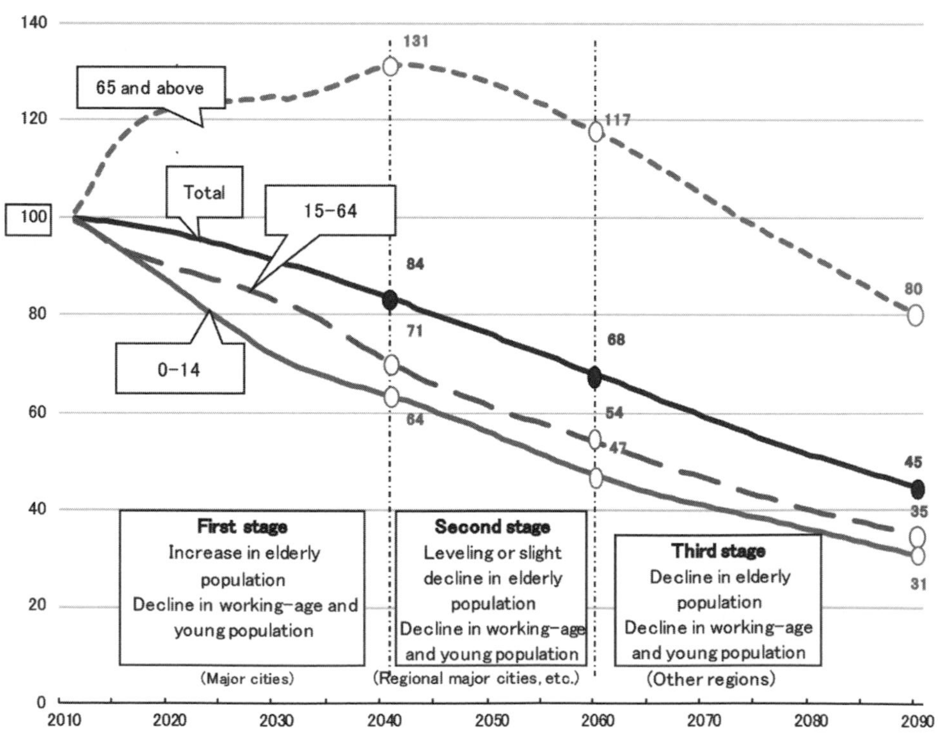

Figure 2. Future population trends—three declining stages

Source: Prepared based on "Population Projections for Japan (January 2012)," National Institute of Population and Social Security Research

Note: Population in each year is presented based on the population in 2010 indexed at 100.

fall below 100 million in 2060, and will stand at below 50 million in 2110, in 100 years.

Figure 2 shows this process of population decline in a simple manner by using an index. In the figure, the young population below fifteen years old and the working-age population of fifteen- to sixty-four-year-olds continue to fall from 2010 to 2090. On the contrary, the elderly population aged sixty-five years old and above will increase until 2040 and then stay almost unchanged for some time before it starts falling in 2060. As a result, Japan's total population will decline at only a moderate rate until around 2040, but then will fall rapidly.

In other words, Japan is expected to experience the three stages of population decline: the first stage will go up to 2040 with a rising elderly population and falling working-age and young population, followed by the second stage in 2040–2060 with a leveling or slightly falling elderly population and a falling working-age and young population, and the third stage in 2060–2090 with a falling elderly population and a falling working-age and young population.

Each region has a significantly different pace of declining population

These population projections show that the pace of population decline will enter full swing from 2040. However, what requires attention is that this process of decline only shows the overall development in Japan as a whole. Observations about each region will show very different pictures. The declining population in big cities and other major cities, such as prefectural capitals, is in the first stage, while in many regional areas the declining population, which is progressing at a pace thirty to fifty years faster than the cities, is already in the second stage, or even entering the third stage.

In other words, the declining population is by no means an issue we will face in the distant future; it is already happening in many regions (see figure 3).

How has this disparity among areas taken place? The population migration particular to Japan has a great deal to do with this development.

Since the end of World War II, Japan has experienced three periods of major population migration from regional areas to large metropolitan

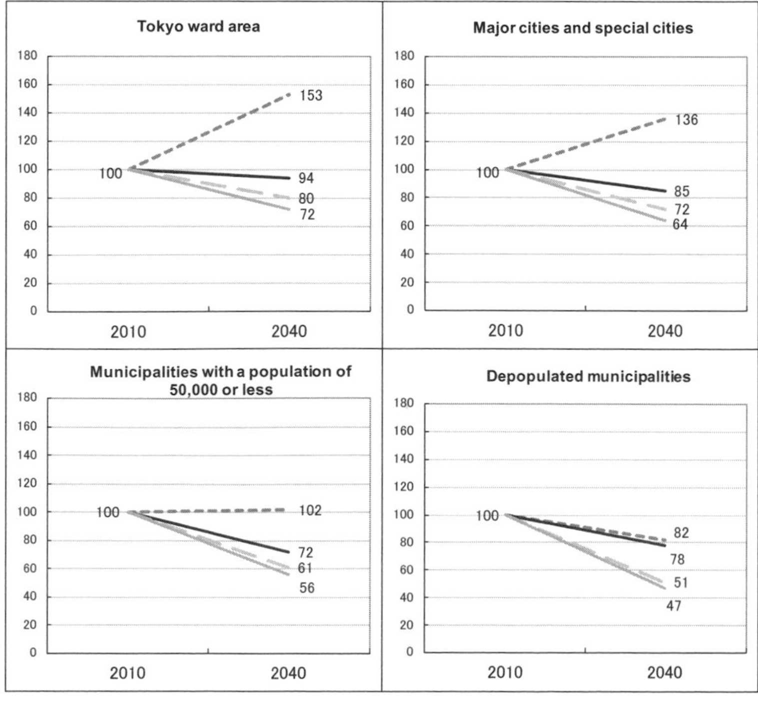

Figure 3. Future population trends that differ in each region

Source: Prepared based on "Population Projections for Japan by Prefecture (March 2013)," National Institute of Population and Social Security Research.
Note: 1. Population in 2040 is presented based on the 2010 population indexed at 100 after calculating the total population for each category.
2. Short dashed line, 65 and above; solid black line, total; long dashed line, 15 to 64; solid grey line, 14 and under.

areas. The first was the period of high growth in 1960–1970. Through mass employment, young people in regional areas migrated as the labor force of the heavy and chemical industries became concentrated in the three major cities (areas close to waterfront regions, suitable for importing and exporting).

The second was the period of the bubble economy in 1980–1993. During this period, industries in the Tokyo area, centered on the service and financial industries, achieved significant growth, while the heavy and chemical industries operating in regional areas faced challenging business conditions due to the strong yen. As a result, a significant proportion of the population migrated to the Tokyo area.

The third period started in 2000. The population migration in this period was prompted by deterioration in the regional economy and employment situation, mainly reflecting damage to the manufacturing industry due to yen appreciation, a fall in the number of public works, and the declining population. With these factors, the migration of people, mainly of the younger generation, from the regional areas to the Tokyo area once again took place (figure 4).

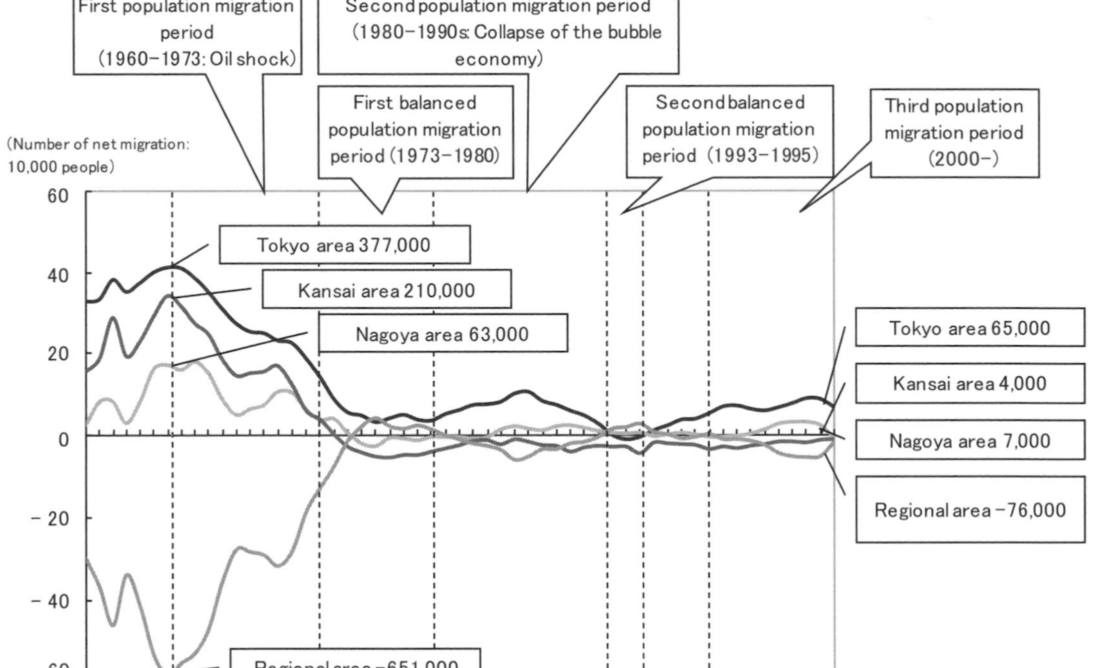

Figure 4. Trend in the social migration of population

Source: "Report on the Internal Migration in Japan Derived from the Basic Resident Registration," Ministry of Internal Affairs and Communication.
Note: The definition of regional classifications used in the figure above is as follows:
Tokyo area: Saitama, Chiba, Tokyo, and Kanagawa
Nagoya area: Gifu, Aichi, and Mie
Kansai area: Kyoto, Osaka, Hyogo, and Nara
Three major city areas: Tokyo, Nagoya, and Kansai areas
Regional area: Areas other than the three major city areas

Migration of young people to big cities has accelerated the population decline

The population migration from regional areas to major metropolitan areas became as large as approximately 11,470,000 between 1954 and 2009. This migration was characterized by the center of the population consistently being the younger generation. If the younger generation that is going to produce children in the future is considered population reproduction capacity, the migration of this generation meant that the regional areas were experiencing not only population decline, but also a significant outflow of population reproduction capacity itself to the big-city areas. The pace of population decline in regional areas increased as a result. These are the reasons why population decline started in regional areas and the pace of population decline in regional areas has been very fast.

On the other hand, the population in major metropolitan areas increased as a result of the influx of young people. But these areas were not necessarily an ideal place for young people to get married and raise children. Surveys and analyses have proven that the birthrate of the younger generation that moved to major metropolitan areas from regional areas has remained low. This is considered to be mainly a result of unstable housing conditions and weak support for childbirth and nursing from families and local communities in the big cities, as well as the development of an environment in which marriage is not encouraged, as indicated in the rising age of first marriages nationwide.

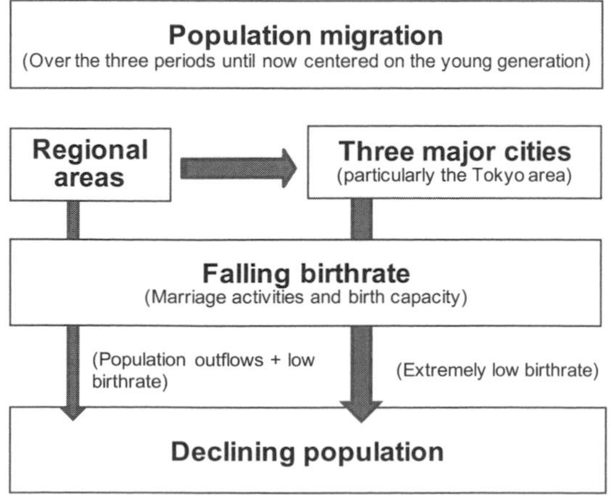

Figure 5. Population migration

The phenomenon of the falling birthrate in big city areas is a common issue reported in many other countries as well as Japan. However, in Japan, the influx of young people, in particular, to the big cities that took place on a massive scale resulted in the acceleration of population decline nationwide (figure 5).

2. The Emergence of a Polarized Society

Areas experiencing rapid decline in the number of young women may disappear in the future

What kinds of indicators can we use to measure the sustainability of an area?

At the present, there are no firm immediate answers to this question. The same applies to the possibility of the disappearance in contrast to the sustainability. The report, the "The Long-Term Outlook of the Country," prepared by the National Land Council of the Ministry of Land, Infrastructure, Transport and Tourism, presents one model of the scale of population that is necessary for maintaining services related to living. However, it does not clearly show the process through which the local social economy and the foundation itself for the residents' living collapse and eventually disappear due to population decline.

For this reason, as a trial, we can look at the reproduction capacity of the population. The indicators that show the population reproduction capacity include the gross reproductive rate, which is the rate at which women of childbearing age reproduce the next generation of girls; the net reproduction rate, which takes into account the mortality rate of girls born; and an indicator that applies the population migration rate to these rates. However, in this report, I will look at a simpler indicator, the population itself of women aged twenty to thirty-nine who play the main role in population reproduction. As long as the population of these women is continually declining, the population reproduction capacity continues to fall, making it impossible to halt the decline of the total population.

The key point is the pace of decline. As in the case when the possibility of a population

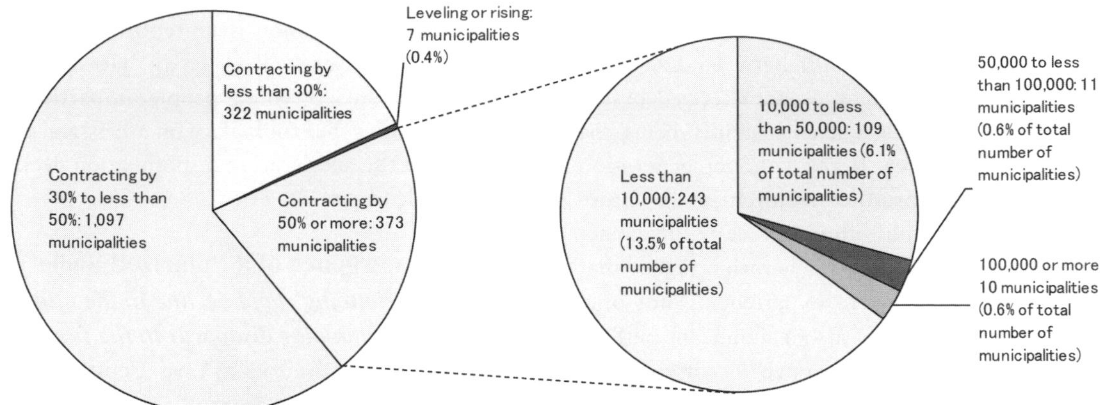

Figure 6. Municipalities whose population of women aged 20–39 years old contracts by 50 percent or more in 2010–2040

Source: Prepared based on "Population Projections for Japan by Prefecture (March 2013)," National Institute of Population and Social Security Research.
Note: The figures were obtained with the wards of twelve major cities counted as individual municipalities; the municipalities of Fukushima Prefecture were not included.

disappearing is high, imagine an area in which, even under the condition that the birthrate immediately recovers to 2.1, the total population will contract by 25 percent or more in thirty years, in 2040, and will halve in fifty years, in 2060. As a result of the recalculation from the perspective of the population of young women, it turns out that an area in which, if the current birthrate continues, the population of young women will halve in thirty years, is applicable to the area mentioned above. In such an area, no matter how much the birthrate increases, population decline will not be halted because the negative impact of the exodus of young women exceeds the effects of the higher birthrate.

Meanwhile, there are also the results of a different calculation, that if the population is to be maintained, the birthrate must immediately increase to between 2.8 and 2.9, which is an unrealistic level.

How many municipalities are there in which the speed of decline of young women is noticeable? Based on a preliminary calculation using the figures in the projection made by the National Institute of Population and Social Security Research, there are as many as 373 municipalities (20.7 percent of the total number of municipalities) whose population of women aged twenty to thirty-nine contracts by more than 50 percent over the thirty years between 2010 and 2040. Of these municipalities, there will be 243 small-scale municipalities (13.5 percent of the total number of municipalities) whose population is below 10,000 in 2040. I cannot help but conclude that these municipalities are very likely to disappear (figure 6).

Population migration will not stabilize

Meanwhile, the projection by the National Institute of Population and Social Security Research is based on the assumption that the population migration rate will stabilize at a certain level in the future. This assumption is not a rational method for projecting the population.

However, will the influx of population to the Tokyo area from regional areas really stabilize? I believe that this influx will never stop. Analysis of the progress of population migration up to the present shows that population inflows to major metropolitan areas (particularly Tokyo) are closely related to the income gap and the

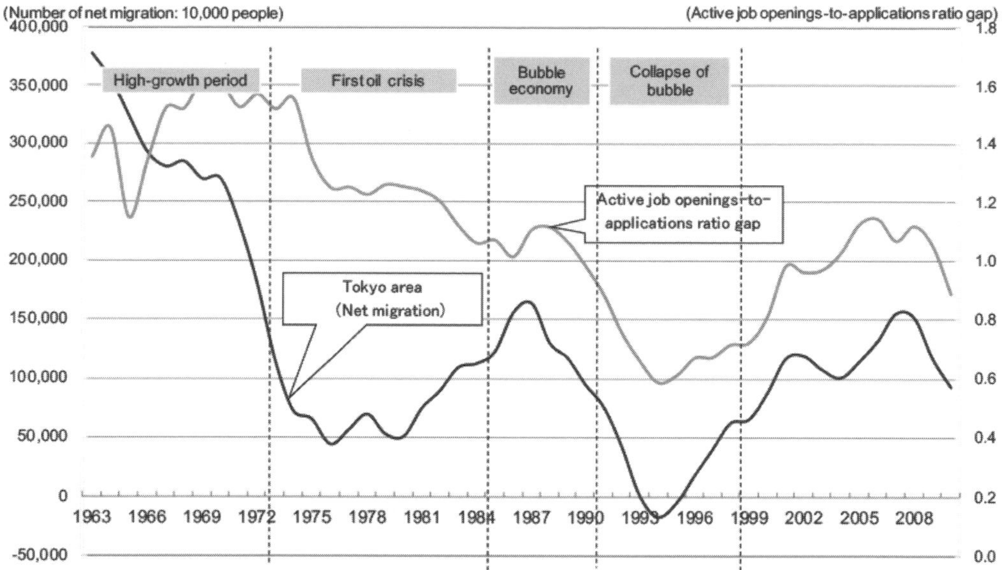

Figure 7. Trends of population migration (net migration) and active job openings-to-application ratio gap

Sources: "Report on Internal Migration in Japan Derived from Basic Resident Registration," Ministry of Internal Affairs and Communication; "Report on Employment Service," Ministry of Health, Labour and Welfare.
Note: The active job openings-to-applications ratio gap used in this figure was calculated by dividing the active job openings-to-applications ratio (active job openings / active applications) in the Tokyo area (Saitama, Chiba, Tokyo, and Kanagawa) by the same ratio in other areas.

employment situation in regional areas and big cities (figure 7). In this aspect, these gaps are unlikely to be narrowed, which is the reason for my statement above.

The key point in this observation is the employment situation in the medical and nursing care sectors in major metropolitan areas. At present, employment in these sectors is halting the decline of employment in regional areas. Because the elderly population in regional areas will remain unchanged or decline, and as a result the situation in medical and nursing care services will remain unchanged or become oversupplied, the ability to absorb employment in these sectors is likely to remain sluggish or decline.

On the other hand, reflecting a time lag in the aging of population by areas, the major urban areas will enter a period when the population that had moved there previously abruptly becomes old. Particularly in the Tokyo area, because the medical and nursing care service foundation is weak, with the number of doctors per 100,000 people and the capacity of nursing care facilities per capita being low, the supply of such services for the elderly will come up significantly short, and the shortage of human resources for medical and nursing care is likely to intensify in the future (see figure 8).

As a result, human resources in the medical and nursing care sectors that have been only supporting employment in regional areas are highly likely to start flowing out of regional areas to the Tokyo area. This development may even cause the complete elimination of employment opportunities for young people in regional areas. Looking at the impact of population migration on the number of employees and the need for medical and nursing care by regional bloc, including the south Kanto bloc (Saitama, Chiba, Tokyo, and Kanagawa), both the working-age population and the number of employees—based on the assumption that the current employment rate will remain unchanged—will fall significantly.

Consequently, if needs for medical and nursing care centered on the Tokyo area continue to increase at the current pace, they could become a factor for a significant population migration by around 2040. We projected what would happen

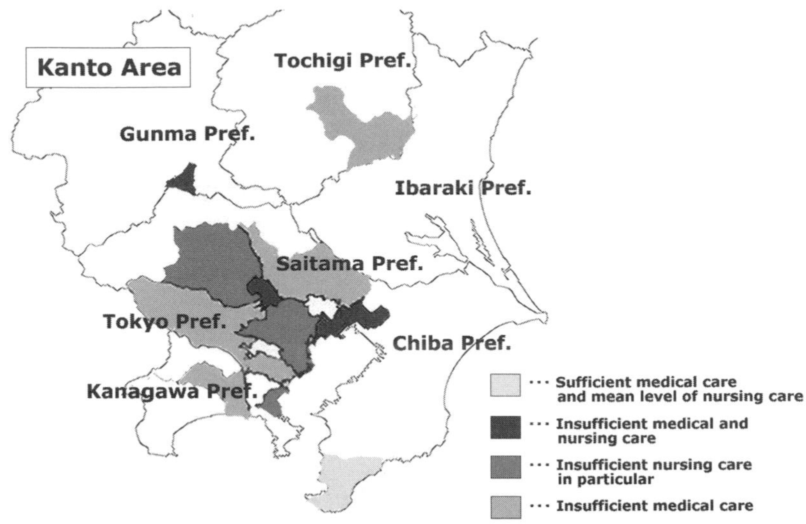

Figure 8. Projection of surplus and shortage in medical and nursing care services in 2040

Source: Documents provided by the 9th National Council on Social Security System Reform (April 19, 2013).

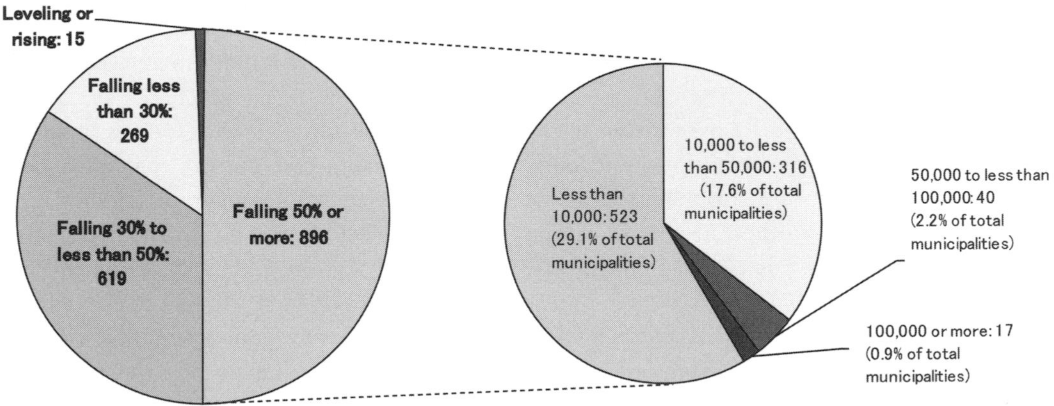

Figure 9. Municipalities whose population of women aged 20–39 will fall 50 percent or more if population migration is not halted

Source: Prepared based on "Population Projections for Japan by Prefecture (March 2013)," of National Institute of Population and Social Security Research, and related data.

Note: 1.Projections based on the assumption that population migration will not be halted were calculated by separately multiplying a positive net migration rate and negative net migration rate, which are prepared by year, gender and age class (up to eighty-four years old), by a certain adjustment rate, in order to make the social net increase of the population (total number of items whose net migration rate is positive) and the social net decrease of the population (total number of items whose net migration rate is negative) in 2010–2015 remain almost at the same level after such years.

2. The figures were obtained with wards of twelve major cities counted as individual municipalities and the municipalities of Fukushima Prefecture not included.

if the population migration continues indefinitely. This projection was made based on the level of population migration in 2010–2015 (inflows of population of around 60,000– 80,000 into major metropolitan areas) projected by the National Institute of Population and Social Security Research remaining almost unchanged.

The number of municipalities whose female population aged twenty to thirty-nine was projected to fall by 50 percent or more during 2010–2040 reached 896, or 49.8 percent, of the total number of municipalities; a noticeable increase compared to the existing projection. As many as approximately half of the municipalities will actually face sharp population declines in the future, should the situation remain the same.

There are five prefectures—Aomori, Iwate, Akita, Yamagata, and Shimane—in which the number of municipalities mentioned above accounts for 80 percent or more of the total number of municipalities in each prefecture. Similarly, there are as many as twenty-four prefectures in which the number of such municipalities accounts for 50 percent or more of the total in each prefecture. On the other hand, it was projected that the population in the Tokyo metropolitan area would also fall, but, given population inflows, the decline would be limited to approximately 10 percent.

Moreover, of these municipalities, those with a population of less than 10,000 in 2040, which are highly likely to disappear in the future, numbered 523, or 29.1 percent, of the overall total. There are seven prefectures—Hokkaido, Aomori, Yamagata, Wakayama, Tottori, Shimane, and Kōchi—in which the number of these municipalities accounted for 50 percent or more of the total number (figure 9).

Population black-hole phenomenon

As a result of inflow of the population of Japan overall into the Tokyo area and other major metropolitan areas, a society in which people are concentrated in limited areas—major urban areas—and live in an extremely dense environment will develop. We call this a polarized society.

The concentration of population in the major metropolitan areas, particularly Tokyo, is conspicuous even compared with other advanced economies. Looking at the trends of the ratio of population in main cities against the total population of each country (figure 10), we can see that (1) Tokyo's share (Tokyo and the three prefectures) of the nation's population grew greatly after World War II in Japan, but such an occurrence did not take place in other advanced economies; (2) the level of Tokyo's share in

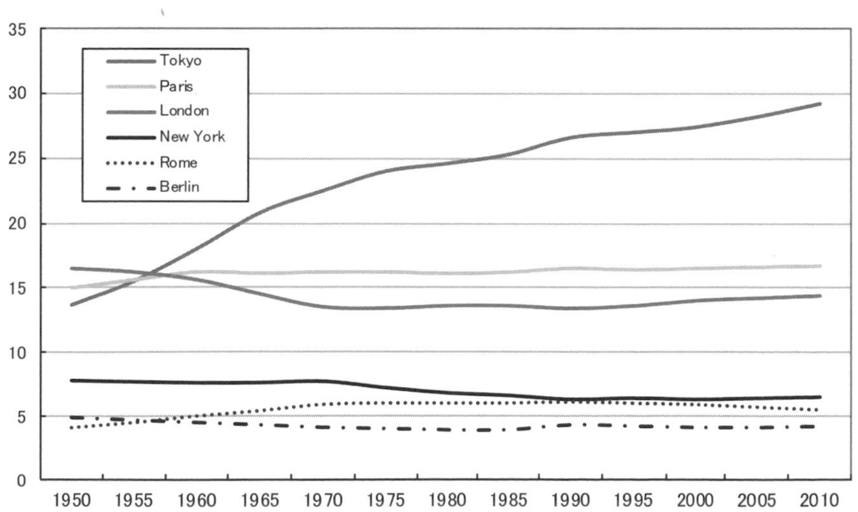

Figure 10. Ratio of the population in main cities against total number of the population of each advanced economy

Source: UN, World Urbanization Prospects, the 2011 Revision.
Note: "Tokyo" implies the population of Tokyo and the three prefectures.

the nation's population is higher than in other advanced economies; and (3) Tokyo's share in the nation's population even now continues to grow.

When considering the phenomenon of over-concentration in the Tokyo area, there is an idea that focuses on the economic merits, such as economies of agglomeration. Of course, if strengthening the major metropolitan areas can ensure the sustainable growth of Japan as a whole, we have a bright future. However, as the declining population has actually started to emerge, such an optimistic view has come to no longer be accepted. While the regional areas that have provided an endless stream of young people are disappearing, the birthrates in major metropolitan areas, with their concentrated population, have been consistently low. Notably, the birthrate in Tokyo is extremely low, at 1.09. Moreover, with a sharp increase in expenses for facilities for the elderly, fiscal resources allocated to countermeasures against the falling birthrate, such as childcare support, will be limited. Consequently, a dramatic improvement in the birthrate cannot realistically be expected. Meanwhile, Kyoto has the second-lowest birthrate (1.23) after Tokyo, and Okinawa has the highest (1.90). Generally speaking, the birthrate is higher in regional areas than in the big cities.

The phenomenon of a low birthrate in areas of concentrated population is also seen in Singapore (1.15) and Hong Kong (1.11). As mentioned above, a declining birthrate as a result of population migration to major metropolitan areas is commonly reported in many countries other than Japan.

If this is true, what can be expected to lie beyond the polarized society in which only major metropolitan areas exist is the acceleration of Japan's overall population decline. As if many stars are being swallowed into a certain point in space, we can see the swallowing of population by the big cities as a "population black hole" phenomenon. To raise Japan's overall birthrate and halt population decline, this major trend of population concentrating in the major metropolitan areas needs to be changed.

There are also a number of issues in a polarized society from the perspective of resistance to changes in economic society. A polarized society is likely to create an economic structure in which integrated effects are pursued. Yet to the contrary, this can be regarded as a singular structure vulnerable to large-scale economic changes. It also has problems in dealing with the risks posed by major disasters. One of the most critical issues that polarized society contains is the possibility of a major disaster occurring in a certain area, such as an earthquake directly beneath the Tokyo metropolitan area, which would paralyze all of Japan. From this viewpoint, it is important for Japan to avoid the advent of polarized society and aim to realize a sustainable society in which regional areas can exert their independent diversity.

3. Necessary National Strategies

Free from macro-policies and the existing decentralization theory

Adopting only macro-policies, such as financial and economic policies, will be inadequate for avoiding a polarized society and achieving a society in which regional areas have sustainability. Further promotion of macro-policies will further strengthen the power in the Tokyo area and have the effect of widening the economic and employment disparities between Tokyo and regional areas, even potentially accelerating the disappearance of regional areas. What is required now is the development of policies that focus on regional areas.

Discussions need to be held to explore matters beyond the existing decentralization theory. The government cannot deny its responsibility for causing the present population decline and concentration in major metropolitan areas. Having said that, the issue still won't be resolved by just transferring the central government to local governments on the assumption that this is a simple struggle between central and local governments. The policy of transferring financial resources to local governments adopted in the so-called triple reform of local finances actually expanded the disparity in tax revenues of municipalities. As this example shows, the simple transfer of authority to local governments might only accelerate population concentration in major metropolitan areas; it will never be able to halt it.

The issue now needing resolution is related to the population that determines the sustainability of a nation and society, and is related to the use of national land—the basis of resource allocation to conduct economic social functions as a nation. Designing a grand plan to solve this issue is a national strategy that the state or a competent central government needs to establish.

However, though a national strategy is required, the scope of the activities in which the central government is involved should be limited to designing the grand plan for the nation as a whole. Needless to say, individual municipalities should prepare specific plans for developing sustainable economic social structures in regional areas.

Japan once tried to establish such national strategies in the Plan for Remodeling the Japanese Archipelago and the Garden City State Concept, but failed to achieve maintenance and increase the regional population. The former, which was announced by Tanaka Kakuei in 1972, proposed the transfer of functions from the Pacific coastal belt zone to regional areas. It would do this mainly by aiming to simultaneously eliminate the negative effects of over- and underpopulation to create a beautiful and comfortable country and society with affluent lifestyles and freedom from future concerns, locating and promoting industries in regional areas in accordance with the development potential of each region, establishing transport networks to support the reallocation of industries, relocating universities to regional areas, raising agricultural productivity, and improving the plans for land use.

After the plan's announcement, public works were expanded and a series of measures to promote the relocation of factories to regional areas took place. However, though these policies achieved a temporary halt in population inflows to Tokyo as a result of the transfer of income to regional areas, they never resulted in the self-sustained expansion of employment and maintenance of population, because all the policies mainly focused on using public spending on development of physical infrastructure.

Meanwhile, the Garden City State Concept, which was announced in 1980 by Prime Minister Ōhira Masayoshi's Research Group on the Garden City State Concept, aimed to revive a vigorous and diversified regional society by realigning the unlimited number of small and large cities scattered like stars all over Japan and the overall network of farming, mountain, and fishing villages. After the announcement, the government introduced a range of policies aimed at developing industry by using regional characteristics. Some of the policies also achieved the minimum impact in each region, but most failed to result in the creation of employment substantial enough to support a population in regional areas.

Parallel implementation of proactive and adjusting strategies

As stated at the beginning of this report, even if measures to maintain or increase the population are immediately implemented, their impact will only become fully visible in thirty to sixty years. Until such time, population declines are unavoidable. Therefore, a national strategy needs to take the vantage point of this timeframe into account. This is to say that, while aiming at maintaining and increasing the population by halting the present declining trend, it is necessary to simultaneously and in parallel implement proactive strategies to develop the structure of the population and national land in which regional areas possess sustainability and adjust strategies to minimize negative effects, such as a contraction in the economic employment scale and an increase in social security expenses resulting from population decline.

In these proactive strategies, it is important to implement policies that pay attention to people. To date, local policies have instead focused on buildings and other physical aspects. From here forward, people themselves will be the axis of the policies.

The first point is to aim at population maintenance and increase. To ensure this at the macro level, comprehensive support for marriage, pregnancy, childbirth, and childcare need to be provided. The second point is population reallocation. Policies need to be introduced targeting reallocation that decisively changes the trends of population inflows into big cities.

The third point is training and acquisition of human resources. In a society with a declining population, improving the abilities of individuals will become even more important. Proactive measures to acquire highly trained human resources from overseas while providing training for developing competent human resources need to be adopted.

Establishing defensive and offensive lines

So, then, what economic social structure will enable regional areas to possess medium- to long-term sustainability? One example proposed here is the structuring of population and national land equipped with defensive and offensive lines that prevent population decline in each wide-area regional bloc and create a unique reproduction structure in each region by fully utilizing its various capabilities.

See figure 11 for clarification of defensive and offensive lines.

This shows what we might call a fractal structure in which each regional area in the lower part plays the role of tying together regions in the part one step higher and supporting them like a tree trunk. Mountain habitats and certain settlements, the area positioned on the top of the structure, are already facing rapid population decline. A polarized society is a society that eventually only has the Tokyo area after this large triangle-shaped figure continues to shrink downward. In this sense, to avoid a polarized society, is it not necessary to develop a defensive line at a certain point? Efforts to achieve that have, in fact, previously been made, but most of them were indecisive and unproductive.

For example, for fear of the disappearance of settlements, efforts were made to stop population decline by improving their infrastructure. But there was insufficient fiscal capacity for taking the same measures for all settlements. Ultimately only small-scale measures that pleased everybody were taken, and these did not work as a defensive line.

Taking measures that are merely an extension of the regional revitalization initiatives currently undertaken may end up repeating the same errors of the past. Forty-seven prefectures doing the same thing is not beneficial. The defense line must have a reproduction structure in which the merit of scale is realized and added value is generated through the concentration of human resources and resources in the structure. The defensive and

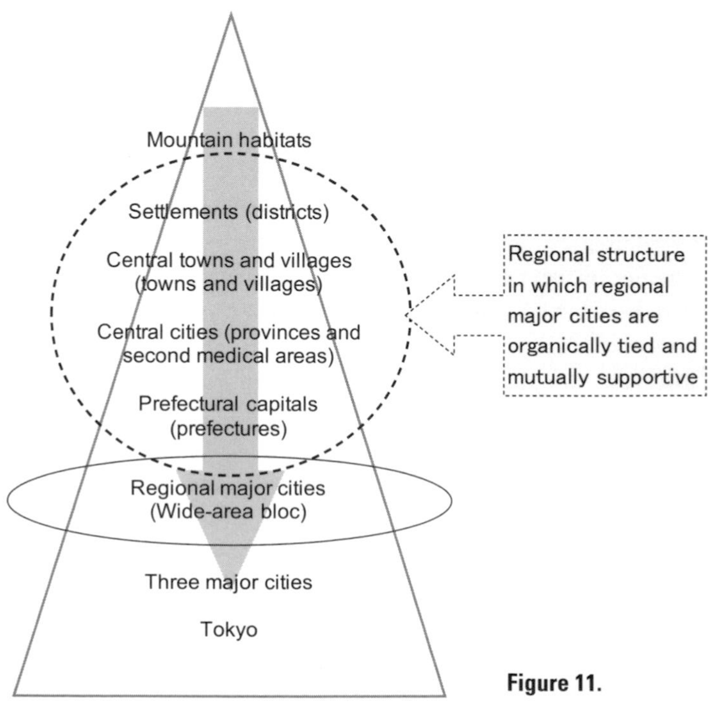

Figure 11.

offensive lines take offensive actions while taking defensive ones. Partly due to the perspective of restriction in fiscal capacity and population, the number of defensive and offensive lines is limited.

From these considerations, it becomes clear that a wide-area bloc unit of regional major cities will play key roles as the final base or the point at which all-out efforts should be made in conducting defensive and offensive measures. Intensively investing resources and taking measures in the regional major cities can create a base in which each region can exert such efforts.

It will take a long time for these proactive strategies to show their effects in full scale. Until then, based on the assumption that the population will decline, adjusting strategies need to be implemented as efforts to minimize the negative impact from the decline. These strategies can be regarded as exit strategies, and great challenges are to be expected in implementing the policies they spawn. "Hemostatic" measures need to be taken promptly to prevent further population outflows, particularly of young people, from regional areas. On this point, it is possible to consider measures such as developing regional industries and decentralizing universities and other educational organizations to regional areas in order to create regional employment.

Streamlining social security also needs to be promoted. Population decline, particularly a significant decline in the working population, will rebound in the form of higher taxes and insurance premiums. Needless to say, social security and other public spending needs to be streamlined to stem the rise of expenditures as much as possible.

In Closing

How can we avoid the crisis of population decline that Japan will face in the near future? Unfortunately, we do not have much time left to come up with solutions, and the choices are limited.

First of all, the situation in which still only certain experts share a sense of crisis about the declining population needs to be rectified. By examining and analyzing the impact of the declining population on various aspects of the social economy on a national scale, all people must together understand the dire prospects at hand. Based on this understanding, by gathering competent human resources in various quarters, national strategies need to be developed and implemented as soon as possible.

To achieve this, the government must establish a command-center-like organization to illustrate basic concepts. Based on these concepts, it is important to draw up specific plans and establish an organization in each wide-area bloc that will act as a regional command center to implement the plans. The issue is grave enough to affect the existence of this nation, but it can be overcome if the Japanese people start dealing squarely with it. We hope the public at various levels will engage in a wide range of discussions.

English version originally published in *Discuss Japan—Japan Foreign Policy Forum*, no. 18 (Jan.–Feb. 2014).

Translated from "Tokushū—Eshisuru chihōtoshi / senritsu no shimyureishon—2040-nen, chihōtoshi shōmetsu; 'Kyokuten shakai' ga tōrai suru" (Feature—The Decline of Regional Cities: A Horrendous Simulation—Regional Cities Will Disappear by 2040; A Polarized Society Will Emerge)," *Chūō Kōron* (December 2013): 18–31. (Courtesy of Chūōkōron Shinsha)

References

Koike Shirō. 2006. "On the Impact of Migration on Fertility." *Jinkō mondai kenkyū* [Journal of Population Problems] 62 (4): 3–19.

Matsutani Akihiko. 2009. *Jinkō ryūdō no chihō saiseigaku* [Exploring the Regeneration of Peripheral Regions by Population Movements]. Tokyo: Nihon Keizai Shimbun Shuppansha.

Motani Kōsuke. 2007. *Jissoku! Nippon no chiiki ryoku* [Measured! Japan's Regional Strength]. Tokyo: Nihon Keizai Shimbun Shuppansha.

———. 2010. *Defure no shōtai: Keizai wa "jinkō no nami" de ugoku* [True Character of Deflation: The Economy Is Driven by "Population Waves"]. Tokyo: Kadokawa.

Yoshida Yoshio and Hiroshima Kiyoshi. 2011. *Jinkō genshō jidai no chiiki seisaku* [Regional Policy in an Age of Population Decline]. Tokyo: Hara Shobō.

VII-(5.1) Declining Population and Sustained Economic Growth

Can They Coexist?

Kōsai Yutaka, Saitō Jun, and Yashiro Naohiro[1]

American Economic Review, 1998

Recently published official population projections suggest a steady decline in the Japanese population after the first decade of the twenty-first century, mainly due to a continuous decline in the fertility rate. Though a declining population and labor force would suggest lower economic growth, the constraint by itself would stimulate efficiency-augmenting technological changes by tightening labor and capital resource constraints. Also, as a result of changes and reforms in the labor market, socioeconomic forces can work to mitigate the decline in fertility. This paper discusses Japan's growth prospects in the twenty-first century, focusing on the endogenous mechanism countering the declining population, and draws lessons from the historical experiences of Japan as well as other countries.

1. Past Economic Development in Japan and East Asia

The celebrated "East Asian Miracle" (World Bank 1993) was intellectually challenged by Paul Krugman (1994). According to his view, the high economic growth in the region was not the result of "gains in efficiency" or total factor productivity (TFP) growth as in many OECD countries, but was instead mainly the result of an "input-driven growth" just like that in the former Soviet Union in the 1960s. Thus, the Asian growth will eventually cease, with its labor endowments being fully employed and its mobilization within the economy coming to an end.

However, this view neglects the possibility that a country might shift from input-driven growth to that associated with gains in efficiency in accordance with changes in the economic environment. It is advantageous for Asian countries to pursue resource-utilizing economic growth as long as they are abundantly endowed with factors of production in the country. Even the United States, according to one estimate, exhibited the input-driven growth pattern at its initial stage of economic development: US GDP growth in the 1820–1870 period was 4.22 percent while the contribution of TFP growth was -0.15 percent (Maddison 1995). The failure of the former Soviet Union in shifting from input-driven growth to that of gains in efficiency was mainly due to its insufficient structural adjustments to changing factor endowments, owing to the centrally planned economic system. Government interventions in most East Asian economies are "market-friendly" ones, in contrast to the market-repressing policies in the former Soviet Union (Itō 1996).

Japan's economic development provides a clue to the transformation of the growth pattern. We divide Japan's economic growth in the last hundred years into four periods. The average rate of economic growth in the prewar period was about 3 percent, and the TFP growth in the period after World War I was slightly higher than in the preceding period. The most significant period came right after World War II. The markedly high economic growth—on average 8 percent for the two decades up to the mid-1970s—was associated with drastic changes in the economy and society preceding the East Asian Miracle (Kōsai 1986). The high-growth era ended with the catching-up of Japan's industry to the level of other OECD countries in the mid-1970s. According to analysis based on the growth-accounting method, the contribution rate of TFP to total GDP growth has steadily risen from 20 percent to 47 percent over the four periods. Thus, Japan's case clearly provides counterevidence to Krugman's hypothesis that resource constraint would put an end to input-driven growth.

2. Causes and Consequences of the Declining Population

A major resource constraint in the coming decades is the declining population. The total fertility rate (average number of children per woman, over her lifetime) in Japan fell from a postwar peak of 4.5 in 1947 to 2.1 in the 1950s, stabilized there for two decades, and then fell again from the mid-1970s to 1.4 in 1996, which is far below the population reproduction rate. The decline in fertility is mainly attributable to an increase in the opportunity cost of women's childrearing. The ratio of self-employed women in total employment fell, while that of women in paid employment rose from 15 percent to close to 40 percent between 1955 and 1996, reflecting rapid economic growth. The improved job opportunities for women increased the trade-off facing them (i.e., between job continuation and childbearing). It is particularly so under the fixed employment practices in Japan, where the reentry of women to good job markets after childrearing is highly restricted. This has led to lower marriage rates, falling from 82 percent to 52 percent at age twenty-five to twenty-nine between 1970 and 1995.

Even with an optimistic assumption that the fertility rate will eventually recover after 2000 to stabilize at 1.6, the population of those between ages fifteen and sixty-four will decline by 17 percent from the 1995 level by 2025. Also, Japan has the highest longevity in the world, reflecting the high level of per capita income and healthcare services. As a result, the ratio of the Japanese elderly in the total Japanese population will be 27.4 percent in 2025, which would be among the highest in OECD countries.

In projecting economic growth in the first half of the twenty-first century, a key issue is how to account for the endogenous mechanisms offsetting the negative impacts of the declining population. Several previous models have derived a negative relationship between fertility and the narrowing male-female wage gap (Galor and Weil 1996).

Nevertheless, a cross-country comparison of major OECD countries shows that those countries where women's wages are closer to men's generally have higher fertility. This implies that fertility rates decline initially with higher wages for women relative to men, and the associated higher opportunity costs for childbearing (substitution effect). But with an increasing scarcity of the labor supply as the result of the declining population, job opportunities and wages between the genders become more equal, and the income effect with respect to the demand for children comes to dominate. Thus, the catching-up of women's wages to men's can coexist with the recovery of fertility beyond a certain point. This is consistent with the observed "U-shaped"

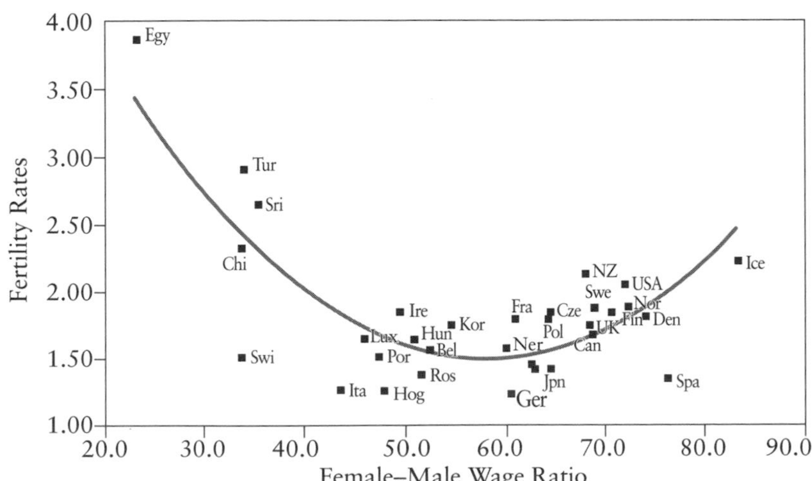

Figure 1. Female-male wage ratio and fertility rates

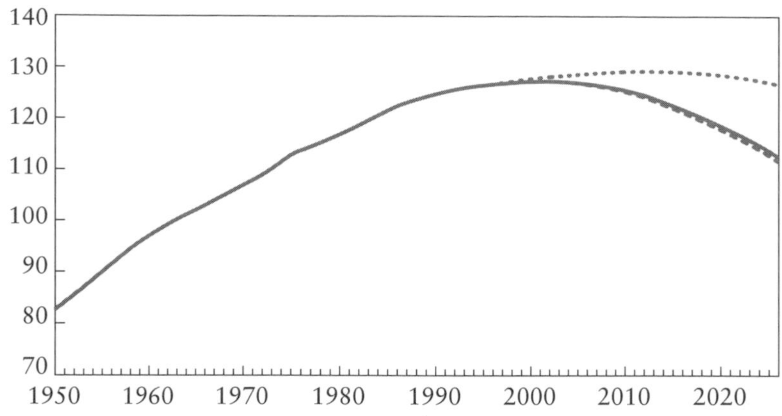

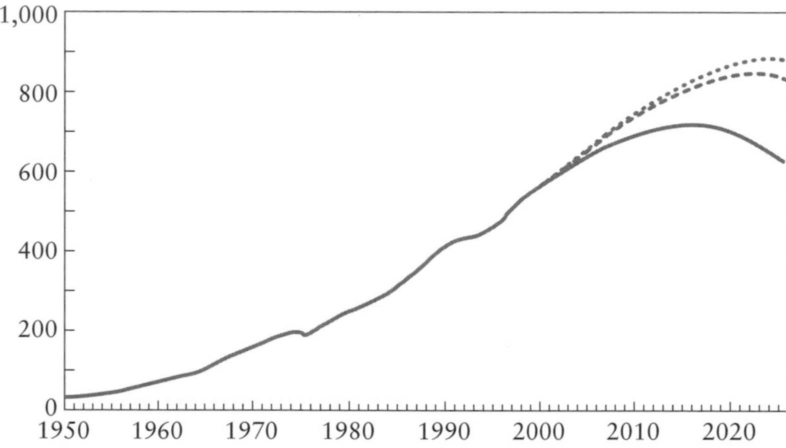

Figure 2. Major simulation results: (A) Population (millions); (B) GDP (trillions of yen, constant prices)

Key: Solid line, baseline; dashed line, simulation case 1; dotted line, simulation case 2.

association between the ratio of women's wages relative to men's and fertility rates when we pool both OECD and developing countries together (figure 1).[2] The U-shaped association between wage disparity and fertility across countries suggests that the differences in factor endowments between the sexes are not innate, but more a matter of social practices, and they become less important with economic and social development as a result of the following three factors: (1) an increase in investment in women's higher education; (2) the lower cost of women's childrearing and other home production by their being shared more equally between men and women; (3) more equal employment opportunities due to the flattening of the wage curve by age and longer maternity leave, as well as better childcare service.[3] Also, economic growth could be sustained even under a declining population if it is supported by an endogenously induced technological progress in the market (i.e., if tightening labor-market conditions tend to stimulate better utilization of scarce resources). Similar tendencies are observed in the OECD countries; those countries with less abundant labor forces tend to have higher labor-productivity growth (Cutler et al. 1990), which could mostly be attributed to TFP growth (Yashiro and Ōishi 1997). The mechanism underlying this endogenous process of TFP growth is interpreted as follows. Accumulation of human capital and a decline in the labor force would raise real wages at a faster pace than in other countries, reflecting the different rates at which the respective societies are aging. It would also increase the return from utilizing human capital and would thereby have the effect of stimulating the development of innovation, which would lead to human capital-intensive technologies (Hayami 1997). These outcomes would also be facilitated by positive external factors; namely, the increasing pool of human capital and the consequent decline in the cost of technological development.

We present a macroeconomic model which incorporates these endogenous mechanisms of the declining population. The estimation is based on the data between 1947 and 1996, and the simultaneously solved results are used to project up to the year 2025.[4] In our macroeconomic model, the fertility rate, which determines population growth, is set as a function of child mortality, the ratio of women's to men's employment (excluding the self-employed), and the availability of childcare services. Both women's and men's employment as ratios to their respective populations are functions of labor productivity. Labor productivity (as well as GDP) is derived from the capital–labor ratio adjusted by the capacity-utilization ratio (exogenous variable); the latter is also used to indicate the efficiency of the market in the simulations. The labor force is derived from population statistics, and capital stocks are derived from the rate of return on capital, which is approximated by the ratio of GDP to capital stocks; the national savings ratio is used as an indicator of financial costs. The national savings ratio is formulated based on the ratio of total employment to total population. Population is derived from fertility and mortality rates (exogenous factor).

We compare the baseline case with the cases where endogenously stimulated counteracting forces are accounted for. In the baseline case, the fertility rate will continue to decline until it stabilizes at quite a low level. An increase in the share of retirees in the total population would be associated with falling ratios of household savings. Also, a declining labor force by itself lowers capital profitability. Thus, both declining capital profitability and higher costs for capital would decrease investment as a proportion of GDP. Per capita GDP will fall slightly beyond the year 2010, mainly because the declining labor force and savings ratio will discourage investment and lower the capital–output ratio. Real GDP in 2025 will be lower than real GDP in 2010 by 10 percent (an average growth of -0.7 percent during the period).

In comparative case 1, we assume that the tightening labor-market conditions, being supported by deregulation and other competition-stimulating measures, would lead to endogenously stimulated gains in efficiency at a level equivalent to the average of the late 1980s. As a result, labor productivity would be higher, and the savings ratio would rise with the increase in employment. This would bring about a slight (0.7 percent) increase in real GDP between 2010 and 2025.

In comparative case 2, we add another assumption to case 1: the negative effect on fertility of increasing employment for women relative to men will be less, mainly due to more participation of men in home production and to labor-market reforms aimed at lowering the barriers for working women with small children to reenter the labor market. These effects are approximated by gradually reducing the parameter of the gender employment gap in the equation explaining fertility rate by one-fourth between the present and 2025. This would help the fertility rate to recover to the level of 2.0, which is close to the level stabilizing the population. Women's employment will be stimulated, with the total employment basically maintained at the same level up to 2025. As a result, the national savings ratio would fall less dramatically than in the baseline, and real GDP growth between 2010 and 2025 would be an annual average of 1.0 percent (figure 2).

3. Conclusion

The negative consequences of population decline can be avoided if endogenously induced mechanisms are sufficiently effective. An increasing scarcity of labor would stimulate more efficient utilization of resources, shifting the economic growth pattern from the "input-drive type" to that of "gains in efficiency." The fertility rate could also recover if it is supported by labor-market reforms that ease the trade-off between women staying on the job and engaging in childrearing. Thus, projecting Japan's long-term economic growth is conditional to the extent that these counteracting forces in the market can be enhanced by policies for liberalizing various regulations in the labor market.

Originally published in *American Economic Review* 88, no. 2 (May 1998): 412–416.

Notes

1. We thank Hugh Patrick and David Weinstein for their helpful comments and JCER for financial support.
2. Similar relationships in terms of male–female labor-force participation cannot be found, mainly due to a high incidence of self-employed in developing countries. Among OECD countries, there is a statistically significant result that a 10 percent difference in women's labor-force participation corresponds to a change of 0.12 in the fertility rate.
3. In Japan, the wage gap between the sexes is mainly attributable to the sharp age–wage profile of men and insufficient mid-career recruitment opportunities of women. With the flattening of the wage profile as a result of the aging of the workforce, employment opportunities for women beyond childrearing age could be expanded, thereby lowering the opportunity cost of leaving the labor market due to childbearing.
4. This is a closed-economy-type model. The expansion of the model into an open-economy type with multiple goods is likely to mitigate the negative impact of declining population.

References

Cutler, David M., James M. Poterba, Louise M. Sheiner, and Lawrence H. Summers. 1990. "An Aging Society: Opportunity or Challenge?" Brookings Paper on Economic Activity 1990 (1): 1–73.

Galor, Oded, and David N. Weil. 1996. "The Gender Gap, Fertility, and Growth." *American Economic Review* 86 (3): 374–87.

Hayami Yūjirō. 1997. *Development Economics: From the Poverty to the Wealth of Nations.* Oxford: Clarendon Press.

Itō Takatoshi. 1996. "Japan and the Asian Economies: A 'Miracle' in Transition." Brookings Paper on Economic Activity 1996 (2): 205–72.

Kōsai Yutaka. 1986. *The Era of High-Speed Growth: Notes on the Postwar Japanese Economy.* Tokyo: University of Tokyo Press.

Krugman, Paul. 1994. "The Myth of Asia's Miracle." *Foreign Affairs* 73 (6): 62–78.

Maddison, Angus. 1995. *Monitoring the World Economy, 1820–1992.* Paris: Organization for Economic Cooperation and Development.

World Bank. 1993. *The East Asian Miracle: Economic Growth and Public Policy.* Oxford: Oxford University Press.

Yashiro Naohiro and Ōishi Akiko. 1997. "Population Aging and the Savings-Investment Balance in Japan." In *The Economic Effects of Aging in the United States and Japan*, edited by Michael D. Hurd and Yashiro Naohiro, 59–88. Chicago: University of Chicago Press.

VII-(5.2) Long-Term Forecast for the Demographic Transition in Japan and Asia

Komine Takao and Kabe Shigesaburō[1]

Asian Economic Policy Review, 2009

The demographic structure of Asia is expected to change rapidly from around 2020 up to around 2050. Following Japan, which is already at an advanced stage of aging and birthrate decline, China, South Korea, Thailand, and Singapore will also witness a further decline in their birthrates and aging of their populations. Next in line will be the remaining countries of the Association of Southeast Asian Nations, as well as India. Such changes, accompanied by a decline in the labor force, will not only adversely affect economic growth, but will also have a major impact on voting structures, savings rates, and social security systems. Moreover, the process of demographic aging in the rest of Asia will be faster than in Japan, and its extent will be substantial, both of which exacerbate the negative effects. On the positive side, these trends will give rise to the emergence of new markets.

1. Introduction

The demographic structure of Asia is expected to change rapidly in the near future, reflecting the high rates of economic growth over the past decades. Following Japan, which is already in an advanced stage of aging and birthrate decline, other Asian countries, such as South Korea and China, will also witness a further decline in their birthrates and the aging of their populations. This raises the question: Taking a long-term perspective, how much will Asian countries' demographic structure have changed in fifty years' time and how large will the impact be? These are the issues that this paper seeks to address.

The most commonly used source regarding projections of the world population is *World Population Prospects* published by the United Nations (2005). We find that these have been quite accurate regarding developing countries. However, for developed countries, where fertility is generally relatively low, the forecasts have tended to overestimate future populations, often by a wide margin. Looking at individual countries, the discrepancies can be quite substantial.[2] The reason behind this difference is that in the *Prospects*, the assumption made was that the total fertility rate (TFR) would converge to 1.85 in 2050 for both high- and low-fertility countries.

At the Japan Center for Economic Research (JCER), we have been interested in the implications for Asian countries for the next fifty years if the above-mentioned assumption does not hold, and, in particular, in the implications of the trend toward low fertility (2007). This paper, based on JCER (2007), aims at obtaining a picture of the future demographic structure in Asia,[3] which will greatly influence economic issues, including social security, politics, and society. In other words, our purpose is to show the general direction of future developments if recent demographic trends in Asia remain as they are and no policy measures to counter these trends are adopted. JCER (2007) was the first study to attempt to gain a comprehensive picture of Asian demographics over the coming fifty years. Therefore, it does not include many factors that could influence fertility, such as retirement age, human-capital investment, or policy interventions. In addition, it must be noted that one of the crucial factors with regard to demographic change, migration, also was not fully taken into consideration. To take migration into consideration would require taking into account both the inflow and the outflow of migrants in each of the respective countries, something that is beyond the scope of this paper.

The remainder of this paper is organized as follows. In the next section, we briefly explain the methodology of our forecasts, and then present our forecasts for the future demographic structure in Asia. Given that Japan is the country in Asia where demographic change has advanced most rapidly, section 3 provides a description of demographic changes and their effects in that country from the 1970s to 2050 as a point of reference. Next, section 4 describes the demographic changes in Asian countries. Finally, section 5, based on the projected trends, discusses appropriate policies to deal with the demographic change in Asian countries and contains our conclusions.

2. Future Demographic Change in Asia

2.1 Characteristics and methodology of the JCER forecast

The forecast conducted by JCER (2007) has two major characteristics. The first is that it simultaneously forecasts population and economic trends, while the second is that it drops the assumption that the TFR of countries will converge to 1.85, the basis of the UN population estimates up to 2050, as mentioned earlier.

In order to take these two mutually influencing forces—population and economic developments—into consideration simultaneously, we used the successive approximation method in making our long-term forecast. This is the method used in making forecasts of business conditions. Treating the economic variables as exogenous variables, we forecast populations based on these economic variables. Using the population figures thus obtained, we then forecast the economic variables. On the basis of the resulting economic variables, we next forecast the populations again. The process was successively repeated. This method, by taking into consideration the cause-and-effect relationships among different variables, allowed us to obtain forecasts of populations and economic trends which were consistent with each other.

Based on the Cobb–Douglas production function and the convergence model developed by Barro and Sala-i-Martin (2004), we then estimated gross domestic product (GDP) per effective labor at time t, y_t using the following equation:

$$y_t=y_{t-1}-(1-e^{-[1-\alpha](n+g+\delta)t})(y_{t-1}-y^*)+u_t,$$

where α represents the capital share, n is the growth rate of the labor-force population, δ is the rate of technological progress, δ is the depreciation rate, and y^* is GDP per effective labor at the steady-state equilibrium, which is calculated by using the investment rate as a proxy for the savings rate. The investment rate is calculated by considering the share of secondary industry[4] in GDP and the dependency ratio[5] based on the life-cycle theory. Meanwhile, the rate of technological progress is calculated by assuming that each country's total factor productivity level converges to that of the US, which is regarded as the technology frontier, because of technology spillovers. (See appendix for a detailed explanation of the variables used.)

We then substitute the resulting GDP data into the population equation. To begin with, we calculate the TFR based on two factors: economic growth and advances in equal gender participation in society as shown in the following equation:

$$TFR_t-TFR_{t-1}=\beta_1[\ln(z_t)-\ln(z_{t-1})]+\beta_2\{[\ln(z_t)]^2-[\ln(z_{t-1})]^2\}$$
$$+\beta_3(MFPR_t-MFPR_{t-1})+\beta_4(MFPR_t^2-MFPR_{t-1}^2)$$

where z is GDP per capita in purchasing power parity (PPP) dollars, and *MFPR* is the ratio of male–female labor-market participation rates for the thirty to thirty-four years age bracket. The resulting TFR is multiplied by the number of women who are able to reproduce (generally, those aged fifteen to forty-nine) to arrive at the total number of children. The resulting number of births calculated in this way is added to the current population for each year to arrive at the future population.[6]

The results of our forecast show substantial differences from those of the UN under its assumption of a convergence in TFRs. For example, in the case of a low-TFR country such as China, the decrease in the TFR becomes relatively steep because of the lack of the moderating effect of convergence. Our estimate shows that China's TFR decreases from 1.78 in 1995–2000 to 1.30 in 2045–2050, with the population peaking in 2025 at 1.419 billion, while the United Nations (2005) assumes that China's TFR in 2045–2050 is 1.85, having been flat since 2015–2020, and that its population peaks at 1.446 billion in 2030.

2.2 Demographic outlook for Asia

Our forecast suggests that in the next fifty years, demographic changes in the countries[7] of Asia will follow the same sequence of demographic changes as in Japan. This sequence is as follows. It begins with (1) a declining TFR, leading to (2) an aging of society, followed by (3) a shrinking of the labor-force population, and finally resulting in (4) a shrinking of the total population. Following Japan, the next countries to experience this sequence will be South Korea, Singapore, Thailand, and China. Let us call these countries "Group 2" countries.

Group 2 countries are already experiencing declining TFRs, and their populations are expected to age rapidly. With a small time lag, they will be followed by the Association of Southeast Asian Nations (ASEAN) countries (excluding Thailand and Singapore) and India ("Group 3" countries). As income levels rise in these countries, their TFRs will decline further and their populations will age from 2025 through 2050 (table 1).

2.3 Demographic changes and economic growth in Asia

The described demographic changes will have a significant impact on the economies of these countries. Our growth forecasts are based on the following considerations. A country's long-term economic growth rate is determined by changes in (1) labor input; (2) capital input; and (3) total factor productivity (technological progress). Demographic changes affect economic growth via two channels. One is changes in the labor force. In Japan, which is ahead of the other Asian countries in terms of demographic developments, the labor-force population is already shrinking. We forecast that the countries in Group 2 will enter this phase of a shrinking labor force in or around 2015–2020, while the countries in Group 3 will see a sharp decline in the rates of increase of their labor force, although labor-force growth rates will not turn negative during the forecast period with the exception of Vietnam. The second channel through which the forecast demographic trends affect economic growth is a slowdown in capital accumulation resulting from a decline in the savings rate. In our forecast, we adopted the life-cycle hypothesis, which states that as a society ages, individuals who draw down their savings outnumber those who increase their savings in preparation for old age, thus depressing the savings rate of the economy as a whole, which, in turn, constrains capital accumulation.

When we forecast long-term economic growth rates by taking these factors into account, we find that Japan will see a gradual fall in its economic growth rate, because its labor force is already declining and is expected to continue to decrease. We forecast that Japan will reach near-zero economic growth in the 2040s. The countries of Group 2 will continue to grow at levels of 3 to 5 percent each year up to around 2020, after which growth will decelerate. The annual economic growth rate of South Korea will fall below 1 percent after 2030. The Chinese labor force will begin to shrink from the 2020s, and the country's annual economic growth rate will decelerate to approximately 1 percent during the 2040s. The labor-force growth of Group 3 countries will also decelerate, although it will not turn negative. Economic growth rates in these countries will fall, but will remain above those of Group 2. The Indian labor force, for example, will continue to increase through 2050, making it possible for that country to maintain an economic growth rate of just under 3 percent per annum even in the 2040s (table 2).

2.4 From demographic bonus to demographic onus

As we have seen, Asian economies will see major changes as a result of demographic trends. Such changes have both economic and social implications that can be interpreted as a shift from a "demographic bonus" to a "demographic onus."

What, then, is a "demographic bonus"? With respect to the relationship between income levels

Table 1. Timing of key events in the population structures of Asian countries

Year	Period when the total fertility rate falls below 2.1	Period when ratio of those aged 65 and over to the total population reaches 14 percent	Period when the labor force begins to decrease	Period when the population begins to decrease
1960–1965	Japan			
1965–1970				
1970–1975				
1975–1980	Singapore			
1980–1985	Hong Kong			
1985–1990	South Korea			
1990–1995	China	Japan		
1995–2000	Thailand			
2000–2005			Japan	
2005–2010	Vietnam			Japan
2010–2015		Hong Kong		
2015–2020	Indonesia	South Korea, Singapore	China, Hong Kong	South Korea
2020–2025	Malaysia		South Korea, Singapore	
2025–2030		China, Thailand		China
2030–2035	India			
2035–2040	Philippines	Vietnam	Thailand, Vietnam	Singapore
2040–2045		Malaysia, Indonesia		Thailand, Vietnam
2045–2050				

Source: JCER (2007).
Notes: 1. Total fertility rate and rates of change of the labor force and the population are measured as five-year averages. The ratios of those aged sixty-five and over are not averages but the levels for the end of a period. For example, if for a particular country the ratio reaches 14 percent in 1995, then the period in which the country is considered to have reached this ratio is 1990–1995. 2. Figures for 2005–2010 and after are based on JCER forecasts.

Table 2. Rates of change of the labor force of Asian countries

	Japan	China	South Korea	Hong Kong	Singapore	Thailand	Malaysia	Philippines	Indonesia	Vietnam	India
1980–1985	1.2	2.8	1.9	2.4	3.0	3.1	2.8	2.6	2.3	2.9	2.4
1985–1990	1.1	2.3	3.1	0.9	3.6	2.7	4.3	2.9	3.8	2.6	2.3
1990–1995	1.2	1.4	2.2	1.6	2.5	0.7	2.9	3.2	2.4	2.5	2.0
1995–2000	0.4	1.0	1.1	1.8	3.4	1.3	3.3	2.3	2.8	2.4	1.9
2000–2005	-0.4	1.0	1.4	1.9	1.4	1.2	2.6	3.8	1.9	2.3	2.0
2005–2010	-0.1	0.8	0.8	1.2	1.4	1.1	2.4	3.1	1.8	2.1	1.8
2010–2015	-0.3	0.3	0.6	0.4	1.0	0.7	2.2	2.6	1.5	1.5	1.7
2015–2020	-0.4	0.0	0.3	-0.4	0.1	0.4	1.9	2.1	1.4	0.9	1.5
2020–2025	-0.6	-0.2	-0.3	-0.6	-0.8	0.3	1.4	1.7	1.1	0.6	1.5
2025–2030	-0.8	-0.5	-0.6	-0.5	-1.1	0.1	1.1	1.4	0.9	0.4	1.3
2030–2035	-1.1	-0.7	-0.8	-0.3	-0.9	0.1	0.8	1.2	0.6	0.2	1.1
2035–2040	-1.4	-0.9	-1.1	-0.2	-0.5	0.0	0.6	1.0	0.4	0.0	0.9
2040–2045	-1.5	-0.9	-1.3	-0.1	-0.4	-0.2	0.5	0.8	0.3	-0.4	0.7
2045–2050	-1.5	-1.1	-1.5	-0.1	-0.7	-0.3	0.4	0.6	0.1	-0.6	0.6

Source: JCER (2007).
Note: Figures after 2006 are based on JCER forecasts.

and population, once infant mortality rates decline at a faster rate than TFRs, countries enter a phase where their population increases. This leads to a subsequent increase in the working-age population, and at around the same time, the TFR starts to decline. At this stage, the percentage of the population that is aged is not yet very high. With the lower TFR, a country then enters a phase of a declining dependency ratio. In other words, the relative size of the productive-age population increases. Since the burden on the working-age population is small, the economy is likely to be energized. This is called the stage of demographic bonus.[8]

Eventually, those born during this phase of population growth, brought about by the rapid decrease in infant mortality rates, will age. Moreover, TFRs will have dropped, and as those born during the phase of declining TFRs reach working age, the dependency ratio will rise to the extent that the decline in young dependents (children) is more than offset by the increase in elderly dependents. As a result, the working-age population as a share of the total population falls. This is the phase of demographic onus where the population share of the labor force declines, the burden on the working generation rises, and demographic trends now are impeding economic growth.

In Japan's case, the years from 1950 through 1970 were a typical period of "demographic bonus." In fact, these were the years of rapid economic growth. Growth of the labor force supported economic growth, and since there was a thick working-age stratum, Japan's savings rates were high. Moreover, since the burden of having an aged population was small, Japan was able to create a generous pay-as-you-go pension system. After 1990, however, Japan entered a typical demographic onus phase.[9] Economic growth was lackluster, the labor force began to shrink, and savings rates declined. Above all else, the burden of pensions and health care on the working generation has increased, and there is greater anxiety about the future.

Let us now apply this concept of demographic bonus and demographic onus to other Asian

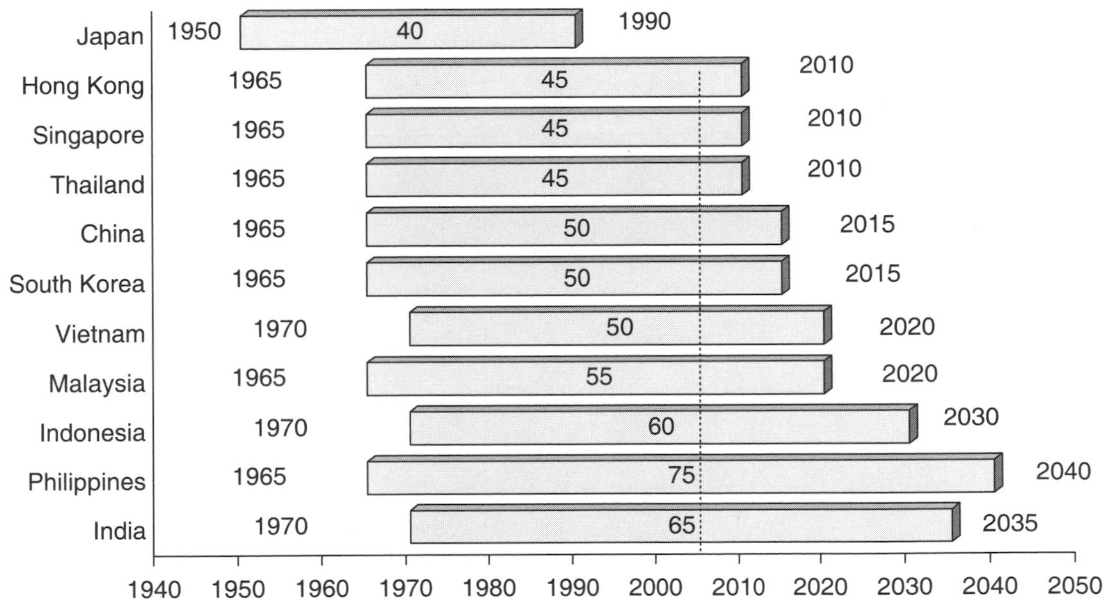

Figure 1. Phases of demographic bonus

Source: JCER (2007).
Notes: 1. The demographic bonus phase is defined as the time when the dependency ratio of a country is decreasing. This is measured at five-year intervals. As for Japan, see footnote 9 in the text.
2. Figures after 2006 are based on JCER forecasts.

countries. Figure 1 shows the periods of demographic bonus for Asian countries based on our estimates of future trends. The figure shows that most of the countries entered the demographic bonus phase between 1965 and 1970, and still remain in it. As in the case of Japan during the high-speed growth era, the other Asian countries are achieving high economic growth rates during the demographic bonus phase. However, for many of these countries, it will not be long until this phase comes to an end, with countries successively moving from the demographic bonus phase to the demographic onus. As indicated in figure 1, the transition will start with Singapore and Thailand from around 2010, followed by China and South Korea from around 2015.

With regard to the discussion of the demographic bonus and onus, however, two things should be noted. First, the demographic bonus does not necessarily result in economic growth, nor does the demographic onus lead to an immediate economic slowdown. For example, some countries may fail to benefit from the demographic bonus in the form of economic growth. Africa and Latin America provide numerous examples. Japan, on the other hand, provides a successful case where a sufficient number of jobs were created to employ a rapidly growing labor force; similarly, many Asian countries, such as South Korea, "have invested their demographic bonus to reinforce the social underpinnings of development" (United Nations Population Fund 1998). In this paper, it is assumed that the demographic bonus will indeed be invested or utilized in such a way that it spurs economic growth.

The second point that needs to be noted with regard to our discussion of the demographic bonus and onus is that migration is not fully considered here, even though it plays an important role. For example, a country with a high dependency ratio can offset the demographic onus through immigration, while emigration may depress the demographic bonus of a country or even lead to a demographic onus.

3. Demographic Changes and Their Impact: The Japanese Case

Japan heads demographic changes in Asia; their impact has already been seen in the Japanese economy, society, and politics. Of course, in terms of demographic trends, each of the Asian countries has its own unique characteristics (which will be described later in section 4), but the present situation in Japan provides a general

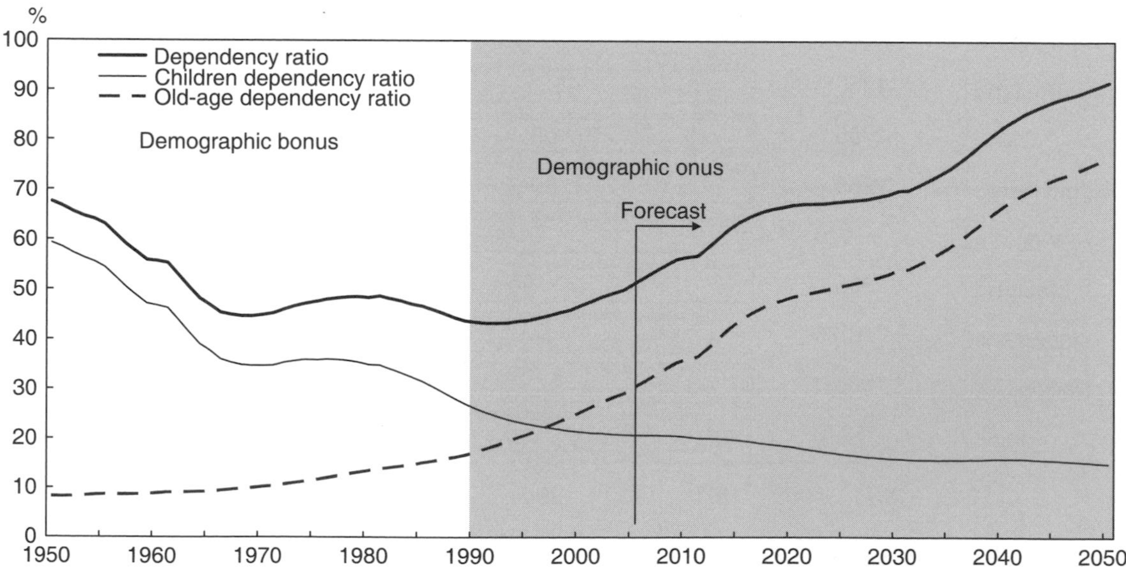

Figure 2. Change in the dependency ratio in Japan: demographic bonus and demographic onus

Source: JCER (2007).

Note: Figures after 2006 are based on JCER forecasts.

illustration of the impact that demographic trends in other Asian countries are likely to have. For Asian countries, the demographic transition will present a number of problems, some of which will be country-specific, while others will be analogous to the Japanese case. This section presents a discussion of demographic changes and their impact as seen in Japan, providing a case study of the implications of low fertility and population aging that other Asian countries will also experience in one form or another.

3.1 Japan's demographic onus and measures to counter its declining TFR

Japan has been in the demographic onus phase since 1990. This demographic onus is illustrated by the very rapid rise in the dependency ratio depicted in figure 2. The ratio increased from 43.5 in 1990 to 51.3 in 2005, and is expected to climb further to 70.1 in 2030 and 91.7 in 2050.

Measures to counter the demographic onus include finding ways in which the demographic onus will not cause problems and eliminating it per se. Raising TFR is a typical example of the latter. However, the Japanese experience is an illustration of the fact that measures to fight a declining birthrate typically come too late. There are two reasons for this: (1) it takes time for society to recognize that a declining TFR is a problem (recognition lag); and (2) it takes time for the effects of the declining birthrate to be felt (effects lag).

Japan's TFR has been below 2.0 since 1975, which means that for more than thirty years, it has been evident that Japan's population would begin to shrink. However, it was only very recently that the problem of the shrinking population was taken up by society as a whole, and it was not until June 2004 that the government tried to adopt a comprehensive policy package to address the continuing decline in birthrates. The level of family-related social spending in Japan is still low, and it cannot be said that resources are invested in earnest in measures to counter the declining birthrate. Also, it is only very recently that businesses have begun to aim at improving employees' "work–life balance" in order to make work and childcare compatible. Even if these measures were effective, it would take twenty to thirty years before they would lead to an increase in the population. Given these considerations, other Asian countries should take a close look at Japan's experience in order to shorten the recognition lag as much as possible with regard to demographic changes.

3.2 Demographic changes and changes in voting structure

Changes in demographics influence the political decision-making process through changes in voting structure. In order to examine this point, let us look at changes in the number of voters by age group. The distribution of voter numbers is determined by two factors. The first is age structure. Looking at the distribution of the population aged twenty years and over (i.e., those eligible to vote), we find that the share of the working generation was high during the demographic bonus phase, but that with the aging of the population, the share of the retiree generation has risen.

The second factor is the voting rate by age group. In Japan, voting rates vary greatly depending on age. For example, in the Lower House election of September 2005, the voting rate for those in the twenty to twenty-four age group was slightly below 50 percent for both men and women. The higher the age of the voter, the higher was the voting rate. For those in their sixties and seventies, the voting rate was approximately 80 percent.

Because of the combined effects of these two factors, the share of elderly voters among total voters is higher than the share of the elderly in the total population. This distortion is expected to intensify rapidly from here on. Figure 3 shows the distribution of voters by age group on the basis of future demographic changes and the voting rate by age group in the 2005 election. Voters are classified into three groups: (1) the early working generation (twenty to forty-nine years); (2) the late working generation (fifty to sixty-four years); and (4) retirees (sixty-five years and over). The percentage of the first group is expected to fall from 41.5 percent in 2008 to 33.2 percent in 2030 and further to 29.3 percent in 2050. The percentage of the second group is expected to increase slightly, from 29.6 percent to 29.8 percent, and then decline to 25.5 percent over the same period, while that of the third group is expected to rise sharply, from 28.9 percent to 37.0 percent and then to 45.2 percent.

Because of these changes in the composition of actual voters, political decision-making is likely to increasingly reflect the will of the retiree generation.[10] This is liable to result in the following: First, since the will of the retiree generation is more likely to be reflected than that of the other generations, the policy focus will tend to be placed on distribution rather than supply-side efficiency.[11] Second, policies that avoid placing a burden on the elderly and that increase the burden on the working generation are likely to be adopted.[12] Third, because the share of young people among actual voters will continue to fall, the likelihood of placing burdens on future generations will increase. In fact, Japan already has huge budget deficits—a problem that urgently needs to be addressed. However, an increase in taxes or other means to raise government revenues (or lower expenditures) are politically unpalatable, rendering the prospect of fiscal rehabilitation uncertain.

3.3 Economic growth under the demographic onus

Adverse demographic changes have an impact on economic growth. Japan is the first country

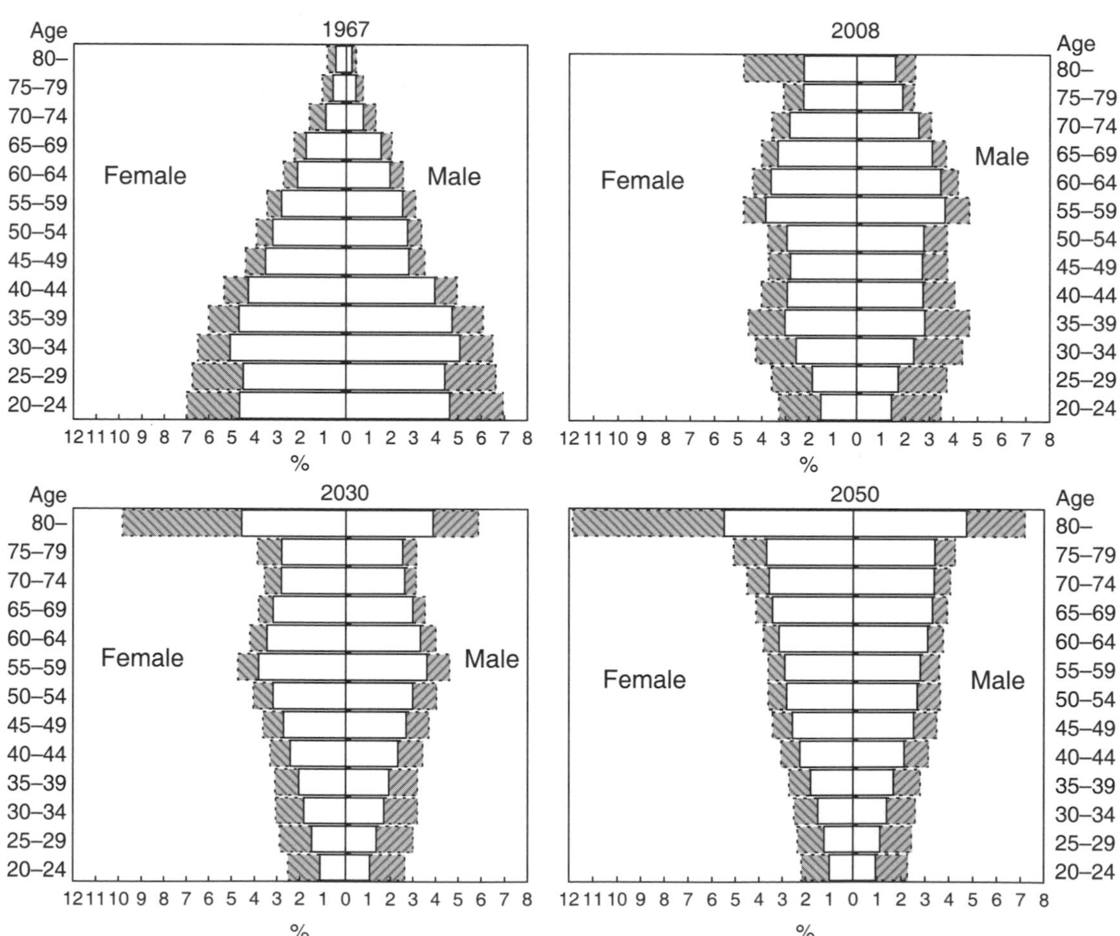

Figure 3. Distribution of eligible and actual voters by age group

Source: Authors' calculations.

Note: The outer dotted lines show the age structure of eligible voters, and the inner solid lines show the age structure of actual voters. Figures indicate the ratio of voters (eligible/actual) by age group to the total eligible voters in each year.

in Asia to experience this impact, with the labor force already shrinking. Japan's working-age population peaked at 87.26 million in 1995, while its labor force peaked at 67.93 million in 1998 and has been declining since.[13] As a result, businesses have recently been finding it difficult to secure needed labor.

Such labor shortages are expected to intensify in the future. According to estimates by the Ministry of Health, Labour and Welfare published in 2005, if there is no significant change in the labor-force participation rate from the present level, the working-age population will decline by as much as 16 percent from 66.42 million in 2004 to 55.97 million in 2030. On the other hand, if we assume that the labor-force participation rates of women and the elderly rise, the working-age population in 2030 will be 61.09 million, which is a decline of 8 percent. In other words, the ministry concludes that if more elderly people and women were utilized in the future, the decline in the labor force might be cut to half of what it would be if no changes were made. Even so, a significant decline in the working-age population will be inevitable.

For the future of Japan, the greatest hopes are pinned on the utilization of the potential female labor force. In Japan, women in the latter half of their twenties and the first half of their thirties tend to quit their jobs on account of marriage or childcare, and return to the labor market after their children reach a certain age. When we examine these exits from and reentries into the labor market in terms of such women's academic background, we find that there are no differences between college graduates and non-college graduates in exits from the labor market, but women who reenter the labor market are mostly non-college-graduates. This means that although many women in Japan receive a level of education as high as men, they leave their jobs because of marriage or childbirth and then remain homemakers. If this latent supply of highly educated women could be tapped, it would not only be an effective way to counter the labor shortage, but would also contribute to improvements in productivity.[14]

Japan's savings rate is also falling. At one time, Japan's savings rate was one of the highest among the industrialized nations. However, it has been declining since the 1990s and is now below that of many other industrialized nations. This can be attributed to the increase in elderly households, which has enlarged the stratum of people who draw down their savings.[15] In the future, Japan must minimize these negative effects of demographic changes and prevent a deceleration of its economic growth.

3.4 Changes in demographic structure and changes in the economic and social structure

Demographic changes force the economic and social structure to change. This is because the structures established without much debate in the demographic bonus phase can place great constraints on growth in the demographic onus phase.

Problems are particularly severe in the social security system, including pensions and health care. The Japanese pension and healthcare systems basically are pay-as-you-go systems, under which workers bear much of the financial burden of pensions and health care for the retiree generation. In the demographic bonus phase, it is easy to create a pay as-you-go social security system. Because the population share of the working generation is high relative to that of the retiree generation, a pay-as-you-go system functions well. In addition, a high economic growth rate means rising tax revenues, providing an environment in which it is easy to lose sight of long-term fiscal discipline. With the arrival of the demographic onus phase, however, a pay-as-you-go system turns into a heavy burden. Since the share of the working generation in the total population declines, a pay-as-you-go system requires either a lowering of benefit levels or an increase in premiums. In either case, it is difficult to obtain a social consensus. This suggests that, even at this early stage, the other countries of Asia need to design their social security systems in preparation for their future demographic onus phase.

4. Characteristics of and Outlook for Asia's Aging

Japan, which heads Asia in terms of population aging, is already grappling with the effects of demographic change. Similar effects are also bound to arise in the rest of Asia, where demographic aging will begin in earnest before long. What is more, this process will display characteristics that are unique to Asia. Specifically, demographic changes in the rest of Asia will be more rapid than those in Japan, and the extent of demographic aging itself will be quite significant.

4.1 Demographic changes faster than Japan's

Let us examine the shift in demographic structure in terms of the speed of aging. Figure 4 shows the number of years it took for the ratio of the population over sixty-five to the total population to rise from 7 percent to 14 percent (i.e., for the share to double). In other words, the figure shows how many years it took or will take for an aging society (where the ratio of those over sixty-five is 7 percent or more) to become an aged society (where the ratio of those over sixty-five is 14 percent or more). In the West, it took societies approximately fifty to a hundred years to become an aged society (e.g., France, 115 years; the US, seventy-three years; the UK, forty-seven years), while in Japan it took only twenty-five years. JCER (2007) forecasts that in other Asian countries, this process will happen as rapidly as it did in Japan, if not faster.[16] The number of years it will take for the ratio of those over sixty-five to the total population to double is twenty-five years (more or less the same as in Japan) for Malaysia, China, Thailand, and Indonesia, but only twenty years for Singapore and South Korea. For Vietnam, it will take only fifteen years.

Compared with Europe, which was able to absorb the impact of aging over a long period of time, Japan has been forced to prepare for an aged society in a relatively short period of time. The time allowed for building a social security system suitable for an aging population is even shorter for other countries of Asia, whose demographic structures are changing fast. The impact of rapid aging will appear in many ways.

First, the time for economic development per

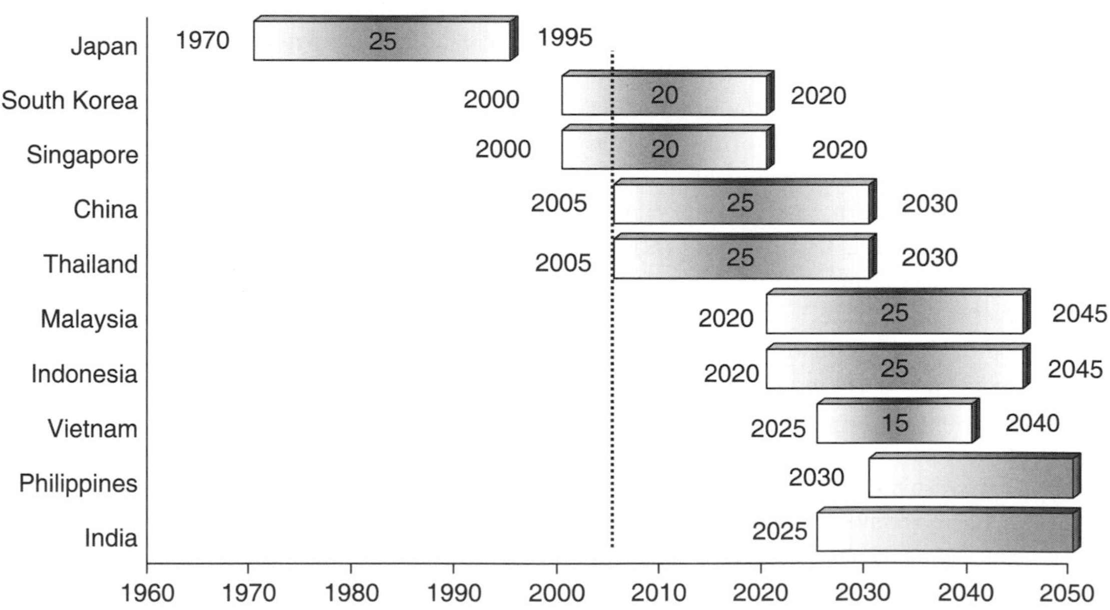

Figure 4. Speed of population aging (period and number of years)

Source: JCER (2007).

Notes: 1. The left-hand end of the band denotes the year when the ratio of the population over sixty-five to the total population reaches 7 percent, while the right-hand end shows the year when this ratio reaches 14 percent. Data are for five-year intervals. In 2050, neither the Philippines nor India will be "aged societies."

2. Figures after 2006 are based on JCER forecasts.

se will be shorter. Let us examine this point from the aspect of income levels. While Japan's per capita GDP in terms of PPP stood at $23,504 in 1990[17] when the demographic bonus ended, our forecasts show that some of the Asian countries whose demographic aging is about to begin will not be able to attain high income levels by the time their demographic bonus ends.[18] While income levels in Hong Kong, Singapore, and South Korea will rise above the Japanese level, those in other countries will remain far below it, in some cases even below the $10,000 mark.

As mentioned earlier, in Europe, the process of the aging of society took a long time. Therefore, those countries were able to attain high income levels, while the impact of aging was absorbed by society as a whole or at personal levels. As a result, Europe was able to sustain mild economic growth. By contrast, in Asia, it is feared that at some point rapid population aging and the stalling of economic growth will begin simultaneously. If aging starts before per capita GDP reaches a reasonably high level, the need of individuals to depend on a social security system will be greater. This could result in greater fiscal burdens on governments compared with countries that have already experienced aging.

Second, rapid aging will make it difficult to take nationwide measures. If the pace of economic development is moderate, income gaps and regional economic gaps within a nation stemming from economic growth may be solved over time. On the other hand, rapid growth requires the problems of economic growth and social harmony to be solved simultaneously. Hence, governments will not have sufficient time to build a fair and inclusive system in response to the needs arising from aging.

In many Asian countries, such as China and India, 60 to 70 percent of the population live in rural areas. If the benefits from economic growth continue to be concentrated in urban areas, where a relatively small proportion of the population lives, the economic gap between rural and urban areas will not diminish, but rather become even greater. If aging progresses under these circumstances, urban areas might be able to take measures for the elderly, but rural areas will not be able to take action. In that case, uniform nationwide measures for the elderly might not be introduced.

At the same time, urban areas themselves have become diverse. Not only megacities like Tokyo, Shanghai, and Seoul, but also midsized cities with populations of up to 500,000 are experiencing rapid increases in their populations (United Nations Population Fund 2007). Midsized or smaller cities are too busy coping with their present population increases to take measures to deal with future aging.

It is certainly desirable that a social security system for future aging should cover an entire nation. However, since countries in Asia are beset with many problems, it might be necessary to contemplate second-best measures; namely, carefully considered regional measures rather than a universal system.

Third, even after measures are introduced, they are bound to be revised. After adopting and improving social security systems, Japan was forced to review its improvements due to changing social conditions.[19] South Korea introduced a universal healthcare insurance system in 1989, and a universal national pension in 1999.[20] However, like Japan, it is being forced to review the universal pension system, as the sources of funds for the national pension are forecast to be exhausted in the 2030s to the 2040s (Moon and Koh 2005; Choi 2008; Jones 2008). Those countries in Asia that are about to start designing and managing their social security systems need to devise them while taking future changes into account. These countries need to be able to modify their systems immediately after or even before their introduction.

Depending on their approach, these countries may benefit from a latecomer advantage in terms of implementation or modification. However, there is also the danger of ending up with a system that is not satisfactory to any generation. This is because rapid changes in the voting structure may hamper the designing of a rational system. Even the best system for the future might not be regarded as the best system if it works against the aged generation, which forms the core of current voters.

4.2 The scale of population aging

The substantial scale of population aging in Asia is symbolized by the fact that by 2050, half of all elderly individuals in the world will be concentrated in Asia. In 1950, Asia's share of the world's over-sixty-five population stood at 36.4 percent, which was more or less the same as that of the West. By 2005, Asia's share had risen to 45.3 percent, and JCER (2007) forecasts that by 2050 it will reach 50.3 percent. These developments are due to the aging of the two countries with the largest populations: China and India.

In aging societies with declining TFRs, low mortality rates are one of the key factors contributing to demographic change, along with low fertility rates. A low mortality rate for adults means a longer life expectancy. Dividing the elderly population over sixty-five into those under seventy-five ("young old") and those over seventy-five ("old old"), JCER (2007) forecasts that by 2050 the latter group will total 682 million around the world, including 175 million in China and 99 million in India. In other words, 52 percent of the world's over-seventy-five population will be concentrated in Asia.

This huge scale of aging suggests that the impact in terms of pressure on government finances and changes in voting structure described in earlier sections will also be significant. On the other hand, an increase in the elderly population may also have a positive impact in two respects. The first is that, domestically, this trend may give birth to new markets and industries. In a society with a high ratio of the elderly, not only will goods and services preferred by seniors play an increasingly prominent role, it is also possible that industries geared to the aged will become new growth industries.

The most promising among these are medical, healthcare, and welfare-related industries. In Japan, for example, the number of workers in the healthcare and welfare fields in 2007 stood at 5.79 million, an increase of 1.05 million from the 2002 level. In terms of the number of workers, health care and welfare together are already the second-largest service industry after wholesale and retailing, which employ 11.13 million. If, with the help of technology and improvements in productivity, the healthcare and welfare industries provide efficient and high-value-added services, then they have the potential to be important growth sectors.[21]

Aging will inevitably have a negative effect on existing industries. However, this does not necessarily mean that this will lead to economic decline. If new growth industries, especially in the secondary or tertiary sector, are nurtured, they can contribute to maintaining economic growth overall. Moreover, new markets may arise within existing sectors to meet the needs of the elderly generation, such as in the areas of clothing, food, housing, education, and leisure.

Another possibility is that, assuming life expectancy continues to increase, workers will try to save more for their retirement by, for example, working for longer periods.[22] In terms of the life-cycle model, we would expect that workers will save more given that their retirement is likely to be longer. Some will try to save more by postponing their retirement. It has even been argued that if workers try to increase their savings instead of depending on their family or public assistance, aging and a declining birthrate will be a boon for economic growth, rather than a drag on it.[23]

5. Conclusion and Outlook for the Future

With Japan at the forefront, China, South Korea, the ASEAN countries, and India will follow the path of aging populations and declining birthrates. From around 2020 through 2050, this will have a negative impact on their long-term growth, and through these processes, the "Asian era" might come to an end. It should be noted, however, that this outlook is for the case in which nothing is done. A decline in growth rates due to demographic change is not predestined.

If appropriate countermeasures are taken, the negative effects of changing demographics can to a great extent be mitigated. Demographic changes have numerous consequences, including labor-force shortages, changes in voting behavior, and falling savings rates. Measures to counter these forces could include (1) with respect to the labor force, a more extensive utilization of women and the aged; (2) being aware of the bias resulting from the voting structure, which will tend to be tipped toward the voices of the elderly; and (3) raising political awareness so that the burden of aging is shared fairly among different generations.

Some European countries that have relatively long experience of low fertility and aging have adopted pro-natal policies not piecemeal but as policy packages that consider families, parents, and especially women who want to both have children and participate in the labor market. Such policy packages that take a comprehensive approach with integrated and mutually supportive policies may provide valuable lessons for countries in Asia that have not yet experienced low fertility and aging, as well as for Japan.

Population aging in the rest of Asia will happen even faster than in Japan, and will be enormous in scale. The rapid demographic changes may make it difficult to take measures on a national scale, and any measures undertaken may have to be revised time and again.

The fact that by 2050, Asia will account for half of the world's aged means that the burden of demographic change will be particularly large; yet, at the same time, such trends also provide opportunities for the development of new markets and industries. Given that life expectancy tends to continually increase, it is conceivable that workers will try to save more, by, for example, working until a later age to prepare for their retirement years.

Courtesy of Japan Center for Economic Research (JCER).

Originally published in *Asian Economic Policy Review* 4, no. 1 (Jun. 2009): 19–38.

Notes

1. The authors would like to thank Marcus Noland, Ogawa Naohiro, the editors of this journal, and the participants of the Asian Economic Policy Review conference held in Tokyo on September 20, 2008, for very useful comments on an earlier draft of this paper. The authors also would like to thank all members of the Long-Term Forecast Team at the Japan Center for Economic Research for their exemplary cooperation in the research and forecasting for this paper.
2. For example, according to the United Nations (2005), Japan's population was expected to continue to grow until 2010 and would still be about 128 million in 2015. In reality, the population of Japan peaked in December 2004 at 128 million.
3. Here, Asia denotes East Asia (Japan, China, South Korea, and Hong Kong SAR), Southeast Asia (the ASEAN countries), and South Asia (India, Pakistan, and Bangladesh).
4. The larger the share of secondary industry in GDP, the more capital is expected to be accumulated because secondary industry is more capital-intensive than primary industry. As a result, the accumulation of capital is expected to be accompanied by a higher investment rate.
5. The dependency ratio is the ratio of the sum of the population aged zero to fourteen and that aged sixty-five and over to the population aged fifteen to sixty-four.
6. In this process, we took account of the trends in mortality rates and the migration assumptions in the United Nations (2005). Based on these migration assumptions, the numbers of net migration of Japan, the ASEAN countries, China, and India will not change after 2020. Therefore, it can be said that in this paper, migration is only partly taken into account.
7. Although Hong Kong, which is included in our analysis, is not a country but a Special Administrative Region, we will omit this distinction in the remainder of the paper for the sake of simplicity.
8. Here, the demographic bonus stage is defined as the period when the ratio of the dependent population is decreasing. This indicator does not consider the number of workers, the number of consumers, or other similar factors, and our definition may therefore be said to be somewhat simplistic. The periods of demographic bonus or onus may therefore differ if more detailed relevant data were considered. However, since the purpose of this paper is to make a cross-country forecast of demographic structures, and to obtain an overall picture of future populations in Asian countries, this simple definition represents a useful first step in this direction.
9. In calculating Japan's demographic bonus (for five-year periods), we marked 1990 as the last year of the demographic bonus phase, because even though the initial postwar downward trend of the dependency ratio came to an end around 1970 and the dependency ratio actually started to increase, it subsequently declined again up around 1990.
10. In the US, a large share of private and public transfers tend to go to the elderly (Preston 1984). While it is not a foregone conclusion that the same will happen in Japan, issues of intergenerational equity are likely to play a prominent role in the political process. What is clear is that the countries examined here, and especially Japan, need to be aware of these latent biases and hold national debates

on how the burden of population aging is to be shared in order to ensure that the burden borne by different generations is not lopsided.

11. In Japan, in recent years, support for the use of public funds for enhancing production-related social capital, such as roads, has weakened, while there have been strong arguments for the correction of social inequalities. This phenomenon may be a result of this tendency.
12. In order to cope with the increase in cost of healthcare for the elderly, the government had decided to reform the healthcare system for seniors so that the elderly would have to shoulder an increased burden themselves. However, due to strong resistance when the measure was put into force, the government had to revise it to reduce the burden on the elderly.
13. In terms of five-year periods, the labor force began to shrink in 2000–2005 (table 1).
14. The prerequisite for this to happen is that various improvements must be made to the social environment, such as the promotion of a better "work–life balance," to make labor-force participation and childrearing more compatible.
15. With respect to the relationship between the demographic structure and economic growth, there is a possibility that the fall in TFR and the increase in average life expectancy will raise the savings rate, thus increasing the depth of capital, which, in turn, will give rise to a second demographic bonus, as will be described in the final section. However, so far, the savings rate in Japan continues to fall amid a declining birthrate and increasing life expectancy.
16. However, some countries, including the Philippines and India, will not become aged societies even by 2050.
17. See footnote 9.
18. Per capita GDP in terms of PPP when the demographic bonus ends in Hong Kong ($32,040 in 2010), Singapore ($30,391 in 2010), and South Korea ($27,724 in 2015) will surpass the Japanese level ($23,504 in 1990), but will remain far below the $10,000 mark in India ($7,758 in 2035), Indonesia ($6,207 in 2030), and Vietnam ($4,763 in 2020).
19. In 1961, Japan implemented a universal health-insurance system and a universal national pension system. In response to the aging of the population, it began to provide free healthcare services for the elderly in 1972 and raised pension benefit levels in 1973 (through the adoption of a sliding clause to offset price increases). However, as a result of population aging, the costs of the health insurance and pension systems have spiraled, making it necessary to raise the eligibility age and increase premiums.
20. The National Pension Scheme, implemented in 1988 and covering workers in the private sector at workplaces with ten or more employees, was expanded to farmers, fishermen, and the self-employed in rural areas, and finally in 1999 to the self-employed in urban areas, to cover almost the entire population.
21. It should be pointed out, however, that an appropriate policy framework needs to be in place to allow such sectors to grow. In Japan, the health and welfare sectors at present are heavily regulated, and in order to fully benefit from the growth opportunities in these fields, deregulation is likely to be necessary. Thus, while the negative effects of changes in demographic structure will materialize automatically, positive effects, such as growth opportunities in new areas, need to be actively fostered.
22. This argument takes account of changes in the behavior of the elderly and states that even if the first demographic bonus has ended, there will be a second demographic bonus (Mason and Lee 2004; Ogawa and Matsukura 2007).
23. However, it should be noted that this argument is based on the assumption that the aged will change their behavior and increase their savings rather than depend on income transfers from their family or the government, fully utilizing financial markets and an investment environment in which individuals can take reasonable risks through investment of their assets.

References

Barro, Robert J., and Xavier I. Sala-i-Martin. 2004. *Economic Growth*. 2nd ed. London: MIT Press.

Choi Young-jun. 2008. "Pension Policy and Politics in East Asia." *Policy and Politics* 36 (1): 127–144.

International Labour Organization. 2006. Economically Active Population Estimates and Projections (EAPEP) dataset, 1980–2020, 5th ed. Bureau of Labor Statistics, Geneva, ILO. Accessed June 28, 2008. http://laborsta.ilo.org/.

Japan Center for Economic Research. 2007. *Long-term Forecast of Global Economy and Population 2006–2050: Demographic Change and the Asian Economy*. Tokyo: JCER. Accessed June 28, 2008. https://www.jcer.or.jp/english/demographic-change-and-the-asian-economy.

Jones, Randall S. 2008. "Public Social Spending in Korea in the Context of Rapid Population Ageing." OECD Economics Department Working Papers, no. 615, OECD, Paris.

Kamps, Christophe. 2004. "New Estimates of Government Net Capital Stocks for 22 OECD Countries 1960–2001." IMF Working Papers, no. 04/67, International Money Fund, Washington, DC.

Mason, Andrew, and Ronald Lee. 2004. "Reform and Support Systems for the Elderly in Developing Countries: Capturing the Second Demographic Dividend." *Genus* 62 (2): 11–35.

Moon Hyung-pyo, and Koh Young-sun. 2005. "The Korean Pension System: Current State and Tasks Ahead." In *A New Paradigm for Social Welfare in the New Millennium*, edited by Cho Lee-jay, Moon Hyungpyo, Kin Yoon-hyung, and Lee Sang-hyop, 229–262. Seoul: Korea Development Institute.

Ogawa Naohiro, and Matsukura Rikiya. 2007. "Ageing in Japan: The Health and Wealth of Older Persons." United Nations Expert Group Meeting on Social and Economic Implications of Changing Population Age Structures. New York: United Nations, 199–220.

Preston, Samuel H. 1984. "Children and the Elderly: Divergent Paths for America's Dependents." *Demography* 21 (4): 435–457.

United Nations. 2005. *World Population Prospects: The 2004 Revision*. New York: UN.

United Nations Population Fund. 1998. *State of World Population 1998*. New York: UNFPA.

United Nations Population Fund. 2007. *State of World Population 2007*. New York: UNFPA.

World Bank. 2006. *World Development Indicators 2006*. CD-ROM. Washington, DC: World Bank.

Appendix

In our population forecast through 2050, the following fifty-one countries are covered: Organization for Economic Co-operation and Development (OECD) countries (excluding the US), newly industrializing economies (NIES) (excluding Taiwan), ASEAN countries (excluding Brunei, Cambodia, Laos, and Myanmar), Brazil, Russia, India, and China (BRIC), and other populous countries (Iran, Uganda, Egypt, Ethiopia, Kenya, Colombia, Sudan, Tanzania, Nigeria, Pakistan, and Bangladesh). These fifty-one countries and regions together account for 80 percent of the world's population. For future populations of the countries and regions not included in our forecast, as well as the US, which was regarded as the benchmark, we used data from the United Nations (2005). Based on the results of the population forecast, we produced a forecast for the economies of these fifty-one countries plus the US.

Countries were divided into three groups: "Group A" (the advanced, industrialized member countries of the OECD, with the exception of Mexico, Turkey, and South Korea, which were included in Group B); "Group B" (newly emerging economies, including those in Asia and the BRIC); and "Group C" (populous developing countries such as Bangladesh and Kenya).

The data for the principal variables are as follows:

Total fertility rate (TFR): For the period between 1980 and 2005, the sources were as follows. For Group A countries, annual data from the World Bank's (2006) *World Development Indicators* (WDI) were used. For Group B and C countries, because it was difficult to obtain annual data, figures recorded at five-year intervals from the United Nations (2005) were used.

GDP and per capita GDP: To calculate GDP and per capita GDP, PPP values in international dollars obtained from the WDI were used.

Indicators of gender equality, working-age population: For the period between 1980 and 2020, data from *Economically Active Population Estimates and Projections* (fifth edition) published by the International Labour Organization (n.d.) were used. The labor-force participation rate of women aged between thirty and thirty-four years was divided by labor-force participation rate of men aged between thirty and thirty-four years.

Capital stock: This was measured in 2000 standard PPP dollars. For the twenty-two OECD nations, estimates were based on the data from Kamps (2004). For other countries, estimates were made using the perpetual inventory method.

Investment ratio: This is defined as the ratio of gross domestic fixed capital formation to GDP. Data from WDI were used.

Ratio of value added of secondary industries to GDP: Data from WDI were used.

Chronology of the Heisei Era

	Date	Event	Prime Minister
1989	Jan. 7	Death of Emperor Shōwa. Crown Prince Akihito enthroned. New era named Heisei.	Takeshita Noboru
	Feb. 24	State funeral for Emperor Shōwa held.	
	Apr. 1	Tax reform implemented, including adoption of 3 percent consumption tax.	
	Jun. 3	Uno Sōsuke designated 75th prime minister; forms cabinet.	Uno Sōsuke
	Aug. 10	Uno cabinet resigns en masse. Kaifu Toshiki named prime minister; forms cabinet.	Kaifu Toshiki
	Sept. 4	Talks for the Structural Impediments Initiative (SII) between Japan and the United States formally begin in Tokyo (to Sept. 5).	
	Nov. 6	Asia Pacific Economic Cooperation (APEC) launched with Japan as one of twelve founding countries.	
	Nov. 9	Berlin Wall falls.	
	Dec. 2	Presidents George H.W. Bush and Mikhail Gorbachev hold summit in Malta. Dec. 3: End of Cold War announced.	
	Dec. 29	Japan's Nikkei stock average finishes the year at an all-time high of ¥38,915.	
1990	Mar. 27	Ministry of Finance limits total bank lending to the real-estate sector.	
	Jun. 28	Final report of the United States and Japan Structural Impediments Initiative (SII) between Japan and the United States issued.	
	Oct. 1	Nikkei Stock Index temporarily falls below ¥20,000.	
1991		Japan's bubble economy bursts.	
	Nov. 5	Kaifu cabinet resigns en masse; Miyazawa Kiichi designated 78th prime minister, forms cabinet.	Miyazawa Kiichi
	Dec. 21	Heads of eleven republics sign CIS protocol; Union of Soviet Socialist Republics ceases to exist. Dec. 25: Gorbachev resigns as president. Soviet Union dissolved.	
1992	Feb. 7	Twelve EC countries sign Maastricht Treaty (Treaty on the European Union).	
	Mar. 27	Official land prices fall for first time in seventeen years.	
	Aug. 28	Japan adopts ¥10.7 trillion program of comprehensive economic measures.	
	Dec. 17	The US, Canada, and Mexico sign the NAFTA (North American Free Trade Agreement). Enters into force January 1, 1994.	
1993	Jan. 1	EC's single European market (giant economic area with twelve participating countries, population of 340 million, and GNP of US$6 trillion) established.	
	Jul. 1	Labor Standards Act and Act on Special Measures for Improvement of Working Hours Arrangements amended. Forty-hour work week is implemented.	
	Aug. 9	Miyazawa cabinet resigns en masse; Japan New Party leader Hosokawa Morihiro elected 79th prime minister, Hosokawa coalition cabinet formed.	Hosokawa Morihiro

	Date	Event	Prime Minister
	Nov. 1	Maastricht Treaty comes into effect, marking start of European Union (EU).	
	Dec. 15	GATT Uruguay Round adopted. Agreement on World Trade Organization (WTO) starts. Japan opens rice markets to foreign imports (*kome kaikoku*).	
1994	Jan. 1	North American Free Trade Agreement (NAFTA) comes into effect. European Economic Area (EEA) established, combining twelve EU member states and three EEA European Free Trade Association (EFTA) states into single market.	
	Mar. 4	Revised Political Reform Act passed, introducing parallel voting system and proportional representation in the House of Representatives.	
	Apr. 28	Hosokawa cabinet resigns en masse; Hata Tsutomu designated 80th prime minister, forms first minority cabinet in thirty-nine years.	Hata Tsutomu
	Jun. 30	Hata cabinet resigns en masse; Murayama Tomiichi designated 81st prime minister. Coalition cabinet formed with LDP's Kōno Yōhei as deputy prime minister and foreign minister and Sakigake's Takemura Masayoshi as minister of finance.	Murayama Tomiichi
	Oct. 7	Basic Plan for Public Investment adopted, committing ¥630 trillion over a ten-year period to public investment.	
1995	Jan. 1	WTO launched.	
	Jan. 17	Great Hanshin-Awaji Earthquake strikes Japan, leaving 6,434 dead or injured.	
	Mar. 20	Tokyo subway sarin gas attacks take place, in which thirteen people are killed and approximately 6,300 injured during a terrorist attack by a radical religious group.	
	Dec. 19	Government approves budget allocation of ¥685 billion to dispose of nonperforming loans held by housing-loan corporations.	
1996	Jan. 11	Murayama cabinet resigns en masse; Hashimoto Ryūtarō elected 82nd prime minister, forms cabinet.	Hashimoto Ryūtarō
	Nov. 7	Second Hashimoto cabinet formed.	
1997	Apr. 1	Consumption tax raised to 5 percent (previously 3 percent), 1 percent of which is designated local consumption tax.	
	Jun. 11	Bank of Japan Act revised. Jun. 13: Advisory panels issue final reports on Japan's "Big Bang" financial reforms.	
	Jul. 2	Bank of Thailand unpegs Thai baht from US dollar and adopts floating exchange rate, leading to currency collapse and triggering Asian financial crisis.	
	Nov. 3	Sanyo Securities, a medium-size security company, fails. Nov. 17: Hokkaido Takushoku Bank, a major commercial bank, fails. Nov. 24: Yamaichi Securities, one of Japan's four largest security houses, fails.	
1998	Feb. 16	Deposit Insurance Law amended; Emergency Measures Law for Stabilization of Financial Functions enacted.	
	Apr. 1	Foreign Exchange and Foreign Trade Law revised.	
	Jun. 22	Financial Supervisory Agency established.	

	Date	Event	Prime Minister
	Jul. 30	Second Hashimoto cabinet resigns en masse; Obuchi Keizō elected 84th prime minister, forms cabinet, calling it "economic revitalization cabinet."	Obuchi Keizō
	Sep. 25	Labor Standards Act amended. Discretionary labor system for planning work introduced.	
	Oct. 12	Financial Reconstruction Law and Financial Strengthening Law enacted. Long-Term Credit Bank of Japan, Ltd. (LTCB) placed under special public management (temporary nationalization).	
	Dec. 13	Nippon Credit Bank, Ltd. placed under special public management (temporary nationalization).	
1999	Jan. 1	Euro adopted as single European currency.	
	Feb. 12	Bank of Japan adopts zero interest-rate policy.	
	Mar. 4	Japan injects ¥7.5 trillion yen worth of public funds into fifteen major Japanese banks.	
	Apr. 1	Resolution and Collection Corporation established.	
	Oct. 5	Kōmeitō (New Kōmeitō) joins coalition government with LDP and Liberal Party, giving coalition majority in House of Representatives. Second reshuffle of Obuchi cabinet takes place with establishment of coalition.	
2000	Apr. 5	Obuchi cabinet resigns en masse after Prime Minister Obuchi suffers stroke, falls into coma. Mori Yoshirō elected 85th prime minister. Mori cabinet formed in coalition with Kōmeitō and Conservative Party.	Mori Yoshirō
	Aug. 11	Bank of Japan ends zero interest-rate policy.	
2001	Jan. 6	In central government shake-up, twenty-two ministries reduced to twelve ministries.	
	Mar. 19	Bank of Japan adopts quantitative easing policy.	
	Apr. 26	Mori cabinet resigns en masse; Koizumi elected 87th prime minister, forms cabinet in coalition with Kōmeitō and Conservative Party.	Koizumi Junichirō
	Dec. 11	China joins WTO.	
2002	Jan. 1	Euro comes into circulation as single currency for twelve European countries.	
	Sept. 30	Koizumi cabinet reshuffled. Takenaka Heizō, minister of state for economic and fiscal policy, also appointed as minister of state for financial services.	
	Oct. 30	Program for Financial Revival announced.	
	Nov. 4	China and ASEAN sign Framework Agreement on ASEAN-China Economic Cooperation.	
2003	Mar. 7	Labour Standards Act amended. Wider range of workplaces brought under the scope of the discretionary labor system for planning work.	
	Mar. 20	Fukui Toshihiko appointed Bank of Japan governor.	
	Apr. 1	Japan Post Public Corporation takes over from Postal Services Agency and starts operations. Prohibition on private-sector involvement relaxed.	
	Jun. 27	Cabinet decides on Basic Policies for Economic and Fiscal Management and Structural Reform 2003 in three-part package (Trinity Reform) reducing national government subsidies, capping total amount of local allocation tax, and using transfer of tax revenue sources for local government finances.	
2004	Jun. 2	Laws relating to privatization of four highway public corporations adopted. Japan Highway Public Corporation and others to be privatized in fiscal year 2005.	

	Date	Event	Prime Minister
	Sept. 10	Cabinet decides Basic Policy on the Privatization of the Japan Post.	
	Sept. 27	Second Koizumi cabinet reshuffled. Non-politician Takenaka Heizō appointed minister for postal system privatization.	
	Nov. 26	Ruling government decides on local financial system reform (Trinity Reform).	
2005	Mar. 31	Major banks achieve target of cutting nonperforming loans by half.	
	Jul. 5	Six bills related to privatization of postal service pass in House of Representatives. Fifty-one LDP members break ranks (thirty-seven voting against, fourteen abstaining).	
	Aug. 8	Six bills for postal service privatization rejected by House of Councillors (thirty LDP members voting against) and killed. House of Representatives dissolved. Shimamura Yoshinobu, minister of agriculture, forestry and fisheries, opposes dissolution and is dismissed. Aug. 11: Shimamura succeeded by Iwanaga Mineichi.	
	Sept. 11	Japan holds 44th general election. LDP wins working majority for first time in fifteen years. Thirteen independents opposed to postal service privatization acquire Diet seats.	
	Oct. 14	Six bills relating to privatization of postal service adopted.	
2006	Sept. 26	Koizumi cabinet resigns en masse; Abe Shinzō elected 90th prime minister, forms LDP–Kōmeitō coalition cabinet.	Abe Shinzō
2007	Apr. 25	China passes US as Japan's largest trading partner in FY 2006.	
	Jul. 29	Japan holds 21st election for House of Councillors. LDP suffers major losses; LDP–Kōmeitō majority overturned by Minshutō, leaving two houses controlled by different parties.	
	Aug. 9	BNP Paribas freezes three US investment funds, the first public acknowledgement of the impending financial crisis.	
	Sept. 25	Abe cabinet resigns en masse; LDP president Fukuda Yasuo becomes 91st prime minister. Sept. 26: Fukuda cabinet formed.	Fukuda Yasuo
	Oct. 1	Japan Post split up and privatized, leading to creation of Japan Post Group and ending government-owned postal monopoly.	
2008	Apr. 9	Shirakawa Masaaki appointed Bank of Japan governor.	
	Sept. 15	(United States) Lehman Brothers records largest-ever bankruptcy. Sept. 16: AIG Insurance bailed out by government. Sept. 25: Washington Mutual records largest bank failure in history. Sept. 29: US government's US$700 billion financial bailout plan, Proposal for Emergency Economic Stabilization Act, defeated; Dow Jones average has worst ever single-day loss, plummeting by 777.68 points. Oct. 3: Revised Emergency Economic Stabilization Act enacted.	
	Sept. 16	Lehman Brothers Japan files for civil rehabilitation proceedings.	
	Sept. 18	Bank of Japan reaches swap agreement with United States and injects dollars into market for first time.	
	Sept. 24	Sept. 24: Fukuda cabinet resigns en masse. LDP cabinet holds majority in House of Representatives; Asō cabinet formed.	Asō Tarō
	Nov. 14	Debut G20 Summit held in Washington, DC, as response to 2007–2008 financial crisis, recognizing need for greater global cooperation.	
	Dec. 5	Labor Standards Act amended. Extra pay rate raised to at least 50% for overtime work in excess of sixty hours in a month.	
2009	Jan. 22	Barack Obama inaugurated as 44th US president.	
	Mar. 10	Nikkei Index closes at post-bubble low of ¥7,054.98.	

	Date	Event	Prime Minister
	Aug. 30	Democratic Party of Japan (DPJ) scores a major victory in the general election.	
	Sept. 16	Asō cabinet resigns en masse; Hatoyama Yukio elected 93rd prime minister, forms coalition cabinet with SDP Japan and People's New Party.	Hatoyama Yukio
	Nov. 20	Kan Naoto, deputy prime minister, minister of finance, and minister of state for economic and fiscal policy, declares the economy has entered deflation.	
	Dec. 30	Cabinet issues New Growth Strategy (Basic Policies) Toward a Radiant Japan.	
2010	Jan. 20	China overtakes Japan as second-largest global economy (GNP).	
	Mar. 31	Heisei wave of great municipal mergers ends. Number of municipalities almost halved to just over 1700.	
	Jun. 4	Hatoyama cabinet resigns en masse. Kan Naoto elected DPJ leader and designated 94th prime minister by Diet. Jun. 8: Kan cabinet formed in coalition with People's New Party.	Kan Naoto
	Jul. 11	Japan holds 22nd election for House of Councillors. DPJ wins, but loses majority, leading to two houses being controlled by different parties.	
	Oct. 5	Bank of Japan begins comprehensive monetary easing.	
2011	Mar. 11	Great East Japan Earthquake occurs, followed by devastating tsunami, leaving 19,747 dead and 2,556 missing (as of March 1, 2021), approx. 470,000 immediate evacuees, and triggering meltdown at Tokyo Electric Power's Fukushima Daiichi Nuclear Plant. Headquarters for Emergency Disaster Response set up and nuclear emergency announced.	
	Aug. 30	Kan cabinet resigns en masse. Sept. 2: Noda Yoshihiko designated 95th prime minister; forms cabinet in coalition with People's New Party.	Noda Yoshihiko
	Nov. 12	Prime Minister Noda attends APEC leaders' meeting in Hawaii (to Nov. 13). Meets with President Obama and announces participation in negotiations for Trans-Pacific Partnership (TPP).	
2012	Apr. 27	Act for Partial Revision of the Postal Service Privatization Act and others passed and enacted. May 8: Act is promulgated. Oct. 1: Japan Post Network Company and Japan Post Service Company merge to become Japan Post.	
	Jun. 15	Democratic Party of Japan, Liberal Democratic Party, and New Kōmeitō reach three-party agreement on bill to increase consumption tax.	
	Nov. 20	Declaration issued marking the launch of negotiations for the Regional Comprehensive Economic Partnership (RCEP) during the 21st ASEAN Summit in Phnom Penh, Cambodia. Jan. 1, 2022: Declaration enters into force.	
	Dec. 26	Noda cabinet resigns en masse. Abe Shinzō designated 96th prime minister; forms second Abe cabinet in coalition with Kōmeitō. Implementation of the "Abenomics" economic strategy.	Abe Shinzō
2013	Jan. 22	Joint Statement of the Government and the Bank of Japan on inflation targeting, in which the Bank of Japan sets "price stability target" (inflation target) at 2 percent.	
	Mar. 20	Kuroda Haruhiko appointed Bank of Japan governor.	
	Apr. 4	BOJ governor Kuroda adopts a new phase of monetary easing.	
	Sept. 7	Tokyo selected to host 2020 Olympic and Paralympic Games.	
2014	Apr. 1	Consumption tax increased to 8 percent (previously 5 percent). First increase in consumption tax in seventeen years.	

Date		Event	Prime Minister
	Oct. 31	Bank of Japan decides on expansion of quantitative and qualitative monetary easing.	
	Nov. 18	Prime Minister Abe postpones raising the consumption tax rate to 10 percent; dissolves House of Representatives.	
	Dec. 14	Japan holds 47th general election. LDP and Kōmeitō gain seats for total of 326, more than two-thirds (317) of total. Dec. 14: 188th special session of Diet held (to Dec. 26). Third Abe coalition cabinet inaugurated.	
2015	Jun. 29	Signing ceremony for Chinese-initiated Asian Infrastructure Investment Bank (AIIB) held in Beijing. Dec. 25: Articles of Agreement come into effect.	
	Oct. 5	Joint meeting of twelve countries considering joining TPP yields statement of agreement on major elements.	
	Dec. 16	Decision made to introduce reduced tax rates.	
2016	Jan. 16	AIIB declared open for business.	
	Jan. 29	Bank of Japan introduces quantitative and qualitative monetary easing with negative interest rates.	
	Feb. 4	Twelve countries (Australia, Canada, Singapore, Chile, Japan, New Zealand, Brunei, USA, Vietnam, Peru, Malaysia, Mexico) sign TPP agreement in Auckland, New Zealand.	
	May 9	International Consortium of Investigative Journalists analyzes "Panama Papers," finds over 210,000 corporations in tax havens located in twenty-one jurisdictions, and releases list of corporations and people involved, including 400 Japanese companies and individuals.	
	May 18	Prime Minister Abe once again postpones planned consumption tax hike.	
	May 21	Prime Minister Abe announces Partnership for Quality Infrastructure at 21st International Conference on the Future of Asia in Tokyo. Japan agrees to provide approx. US$110 billion in Asia in collaboration with Asian Development Bank (ADB) over following five years.	
	Jun. 2	Cabinet approves Japan's Plan for Dynamic Engagement of All Citizens (Nippon ichioku sōkatsuyaku puran), with the aim of achieving the three new target "arrows": "a robust economy that gives rise to hope," "dream-weaving childcare supports," and "social security that provides reassurance."	
	Jun. 23	UK Brexit referendum on leaving EU passes, with 52 percent voting to leave.	
	Sept. 21	Bank of Japan introduces new framework for strengthening monetary easing, named Quantitative and Qualitative Monetary Easing with Yield Curve Control	
2017	Jan. 20	Donald Trump sworn in as 45th US president. Jan. 23: President Trump signs executive order to withdraw from TPP Agreement.	
2018	Mar. 8	TPP11 (Comprehensive and Progressive Agreement for Trans-Pacific Partnership, or CPTPP) signed. Dec. 30: TPP11 enters into force.	
	Jun. 29	Laws relating to workplace reform adopted, including high-level professional system and upper limit regulation penalizing excess overtime.	
2019	Feb. 1	Start of Japan–EU Economic Partnership Agreement. Birth of major trading area accounting for one-third of global GDP and 40 percent of world trade.	
	Apr. 30	Emperor Akihito abdicates, becoming emperor emeritus.	
	May 1	Emperor Naruhito accedes to throne. Era name changes from Heisei to Reiwa.	

About the Supervisor and Editor

Kitaoka Shinichi is professor emeritus of the University of Tokyo and Rikkyo University and special advisor to the president of the Japan International Cooperation Agency (JICA). He received his doctorate in modern Japanese politics and diplomacy from the University of Tokyo and subsequently taught at Rikkyo University and his alma mater. He has held posts as Japan's ambassador extraordinary and plenipotentiary to the United Nations and president of the International University of Japan. He held the post of JICA president from 2015 to 2022. Amongst other English publications, he is the author of *The Political History of Modern Japan: Foreign Relations and Domestic Politics* (London: Routledge, 2018) and *From Party Politics to Militarism in Japan, 1924–1941* (Boulder, CO: Lynne Rienner, 2021), and was supervising editor for *A Western Pacific Union: Japan's New Geopolitical Strategy* (Tokyo: JPIC, 2023).

Komine Takao is professor in the Faculty of Regional Development, Taisho University, senior research fellow at the Japan Center for Economic Research (JCER), and senior research counselor at the Nakasone Peace Institute. He graduated from the University of Tokyo with a BA in economics. He joined the Economic Planning Agency in 1969, going on to serve as director general of the General Research Bureau and director of the Economic Research Institute. His other past posts include serving as director general of the National and Regional Planning Bureau, Ministry of Land, Infrastructure and Transport, and as a professor in the Graduate School of Social Science and the Graduate School of Regional Policy Design at Hosei University. His specialization is in population economy and economic policy.

About the Authors

Fueda-Samikawa Ikuko is principal economist in the Economic Research Department and Financial Research Group director at the Japan Center for Economic Research (JCER). She is also currently a part-time research fellow at Hitotsubashi University. She graduated with an LLB from the University of London's School of Oriental and African Studies and joined Nikkei Inc. as a staff writer in the Editorial Bureau's financial and economic news departments, followed by an assignment to JCER. Prior to her current positions, she worked at the Embassy of Japan in the UK as a senior economic adviser and at Nikkei Inc.'s Global Business Bureau. She specializes in finance and monetary policy.

Fukao Kyōji is president of the Institute of Developing Economies at the Japan External Trade Organization (IDE-JETRO), university professor at the Institute of Economic Research, Hitotsubashi University, and program director and faculty fellow at the Research Institute of Economy, Trade and Industry (RIETI). He received his BA and MA in economics from the University of Tokyo. He is the author of *Japan's Economy and the Two Lost Decades* (Nikkei Publishing Inc., 2012; in Japanese) and co-edited both volumes of *The Cambridge Economic History of the Modern World* (Cambridge University Press, 2021). His research interests include international economics, productivity, and quantitative economic history.

Fukao Mitsuhiro is professor emeritus in the Faculty of Business and Commerce at Keio University and former professor of economics at Musashino University. After graduating from Kyoto University's Faculty of Engineering, he joined the Bank of Japan (BOJ). He has held posts in the BOJ's Institute for Monetary and Economic Studies, the Economic Planning Agency's Research Bureau, the Money and Finance Division within the OECD's Economics and Statistics Department, and the Research and Statistics Department at the BOJ. His primary fields of expertise are international finance, finance, and corporate governance.

Ihori Toshihiro is emeritus professor at the National Graduate Institute for Policy Studies (GRIPS) and the University of Tokyo. He is an academic advisor of the Research Institute of Capital Formation, Development Bank of Japan. He received a BA and MA in economics from the University of Tokyo, and a further MA and PhD in economics from Johns Hopkins University. He has previously held positions including president of the Japanese Economics Association and the Japanese Association of Public Finance, and management board member of the International Institute of Public Finance. His major fields of research are public finance and public economics.

Ikeo Kazuhito (1953–2021) was an economist and professor emeritus of Keio University. He studied at Kyoto University and the Graduate School of Economics, Hitotsubashi University, and obtained his doctoral degree from Kyoto University in 1987. He taught at Okayama, Kyoto, Keio, and Rissho University. He worked for several advisory committees and research institutes for the Bank of Japan, the Financial Services Agency, and the Ministry of Finance, and served as non-executive director to several private financial institutions. He published twenty-three books written in Japanese, most recently *An Introduction to Modern Finance* (Chikuma Shobō, 2010).

Itoh Motoshige is professor of international economics at the Graduate School of Economics, University of Tokyo, and former dean of the graduate school. He received a BA in economics from the University of Tokyo and a PhD in economics from the University of Rochester. He has worked in an advisory role to various ministers and prime ministers in Japan. Currently, he is a member of the Council on Economic and Fiscal Policy. Itoh has published more than forty books on policy issues and his articles have appeared in several economics journals.

Iwata Kazumasa is president of the Japan Center for Economic Research (JCER), professor emeritus at the University of Tokyo, and former deputy governor of the Bank of Japan. He received his BA, MA, and PhD from the University of Tokyo and studied at the Kiel Institute for the World Economy, Kiel University. He has worked for the Economic Planning Agency, Organisation for Economic Co-operation and Development (OECD), and has held academic positions at the University of Tokyo and Yale University. He previously served as president of the Economic and Social Research Institute, Cabinet Office, member of the Council of Economic and Fiscal Policy, and chairman of the Postal Services Privatization Committee.

Iwata Kikuo is emeritus professor in the Faculty of Economics at Sophia University and Gakushūin University. He received his BA in economics and undertook doctoral studies at the University of Tokyo. He has previously been a visiting researcher at the University of California and visiting fellow at the University of Sussex, Australian National University, and University of Otago. At the Bank of Japan he served as deputy governor from 2013 to 2018. His specialization is in economic theory and urban economics.

Jinno Naohiko is emeritus professor at the University of Tokyo, acting chairperson of the Tax Commission, chairman of the Pension Subcommittee of the Social Security Council, and chairman of the Advisory Council on Decentralization Reform. He received his BA and MA from the University of Tokyo, specializing in public finance and local government finance. His career includes posts as assistant professor at Osaka City University, professor at the graduate school of the University of Tokyo's Graduate School of Economics, professor at Kansei Gakuin University, and chairman of the Local Public Finance Council.

Kabe Shigesaburō is senior researcher at Nikkei Inc. His previous role was as senior economist at the Japan Center for Economic research (JCER). He received his PhD in economics from Keio University. He has taught as a part-time lecturer in the Faculty of Management at Atomi University and in the School of Political Science and Economics at Tokai University. Together with Ushiyama Ryūichi, Kinkyō Takuji, and Hamori Shigeyuki, he co-edited *Moving Up the Ladder: Development Challenges for Low and Middle-Income Asia* (World Scientific, 2016). His specialization is in population studies, Asian economics, and human resources development.

Kimura Fukunari is professor in the Faculty of Economics, Keio University, and chief economist at the Economic Research Institute for ASEAN and East Asia (ERIA) in Jakarta, Indonesia. He received a degree in law from the University of Tokyo and an MS and PhD in economics from the University of Wisconsin-Madison. He has worked as assistant professor for the Department of Economics, State University of New York at Albany, and at the Faculty of Economics, Keio University. He specializes in international trade and development economics; his interests include production networks, economic integration, and the digital economy in East Asia.

Kiyota Kōzō is professor of economics at the Keio Economic Observatory and the Keio Graduate School of Economics, Keio University. He received his BA, MA, and PhD in economics from Keio University. Prior to his current employment, he was an associate professor in the College of Business Administration, Yokohama National University. He is also currently a fellow at the Tokyo Center for Economic Research (TCER) and research associate at the Research Institute of Economy, Trade and Industry (RIETI). His research interests are empirical international economics and business data science.

Kōsai Yutaka (1933–2018) was a professor at the Tokyo Institute of Technology and Toyo Eiwa Women's University. He graduated from the University of Tokyo's Faculty of Economics. He served as chief researcher at the Economic Planning Agency's Economic Research Institute and held posts including president of the Japan Center for Economic Research (JCER), research fellow at Hitotsubashi University's Institute of Economic Research, and president of the Cabinet Office Economic and Social Research Institute. He was a recipient of both the Suntory Prize for Social Sciences and Humanities and the Ohira Masayoshi Memorial Prize.

Kuroda Haruhiko is the current governor of the Bank of Japan and former president of the Asian Development Bank. He holds a degree in law from the University of Tokyo and an MPhil in economics from the University of Oxford. He started his career at the Ministry of Finance, going on to hold roles at the International Monetary Fund (IMF) as vice-minister of finance for international affairs. He later served as special advisor to the Koizumi cabinet and has also taught as professor of economics and finance at the Hitotsubashi University Graduate School of Economics.

Masuda Hiroya is director and representative executive officer, president and CEO at Japan Post Holdings. After graduating from the University of Tokyo Faculty of Law, he joined the Ministry of Construction. He was elected as governor of Iwate Prefecture at age forty-three and served for a total of three terms. He went on to serve as a cabinet member under both the Abe and Fukuda administrations. He taught as visiting professor at the University of Tokyo Graduate School of Public Policy until March 2022. His expertise is in local administration.

Matsubara Satoru is professor of economics at Toyo University. He received his doctorate in economics from the University of Tsukuba. He has previously taught as an associate professor at Tōkai University and Toyo University, and is a member of several financial research associations, including the Japan Association for Public Policy Studies and the International Association for Public Economics. Over his career, he has received the Onoe Prize from the International Association for Public Economics, the Japan Association for Public Interest Economics Encouragement Award, and the International Association for Public Economics Award. His research interests include regulatory reform, privatization, and economic policy.

Mireya Solís is director of the Center for East Asia Policy Studies, Philip Knight chair in Japan Studies, and senior fellow in the Foreign Policy Program at the Brookings Institution. An expert in Japan's foreign economic policies, US-Japan relations, international trade policy, and Asia-Pacific economic integration, Solís earned her BA in international relations from El Colegio de México before earning both her PhD in government and MA in East Asian studies from Harvard University. She has previously contributed commentary to the *New York Times*, *Financial Times*, *Washington Post*, *Nikkei*, *Asahi Shimbun*, *Japan Times*, NHK World, Bloomberg, CNN, and BBC.

Murata Keiko is professor in the Faculty of Economics at Rissho University and professor emeritus at Tokyo Metropolitan University. She received her BA in economics from the University of Tokyo and her DPhil in economics from the University of Oxford. At the Cabinet Office she was senior fellow of Economic and Social Research Institute (ESRI), going on to serve as director of Overseas Economies and director of International Affairs. She has held roles as an economist at the Economic Planning Agency and the Organisation for Economic Co-operation and Development (OECD), and senior economist at the Bank of Japan. Her current research interests include consumption and saving in Japan and inequality among elderly households.

Nishizaki Kenji is associate director general of the Bank of Japan's (BOJ) Financial System and Bank Examination Department. He received his BA in economics from the University of Tokyo and MA in economics from the State University of New York at Buffalo. He joined the BOJ in 1994 and served as head of the Policy Studies Division in the Monetary Affairs Department and later head of the Yokohama branch before taking on his current role in 2021. He specializes in macroeconomics, international finance, and the Japanese economy.

Noguchi Yukio is emeritus professor at Hitotsubashi University and a former visiting professor at Stanford University. He has a BS in engineering from the University of Tokyo, an MA in economics from the University of California, and a PhD in economics from Yale University. Before entering academia, he served in the Ministry of Finance from 1964 to 1974. His publications in Japanese include *Kōkyō seisaku* (Public Policy) and *Tochi no keizaigaku* (Economics of Land), amongst others, and have won several prizes including the Suntory Prize for Social Sciences and Humanities and the Yomiuri Yoshino Sakuzo Prize.

Oguro Kazumasa is professor in the Faculty of Economics at Hosei University. He received his BA from Kyoto University and earned his PhD in economics at the Graduate School of Economics at Hitotsubashi University. He was previously senior researcher at the Ministry of Finance's Policy Research Institute and recently served in advisory roles for projects with the Ministry of Health, Labour and Welfare and the Cabinet Secretariat. He continues to serve at the Ministry of Finance Policy Research Institute as well as at the Research Institute of Economy, Trade, and Industry (RIETI) and the Board of Audit of Japan. He specializes in public economics.

Okina Kunio is a specially appointed professor at Otsuma Women's University and honorary fellow of the School of Government at Kyoto University. He has expertise in monetary policy, macroeconomics, and international economics. After graduating from the Faculty of Economics of the University of Tokyo, he joined the Bank of Japan (BOJ). He received his PhD in economics from the University of Chicago. He was previously associate professor and professor at the University of Tsukuba and Kyoto University, and at the BOJ served as head of the Planning and Research Division of the Research and Statistics Department and as director general of the Institute for Monetary and Economic Studies.

Saitō Jun is senior research fellow at the Japan Center for Economic Research (JCER). He received his BA and MA in economics from the University of Tokyo, and MPhil in economics from the University of Oxford. He worked for the Economic Planning Agency, International Monetary Fund (IMF), and JCER before serving in the Cabinet Office as Director General for Economic and Fiscal Analysis. More recently, he has been project professor at Keio University Graduate School of Business and Commerce and visiting professor at International Christian University College of Liberal Arts. He specializes in macroeconomics, the Japanese economy, and economic policy.

Sekine Toshitaka is professor at Hitotsubashi University's Asian Public Policy Program. He received his BA from the University of Tokyo and DPhil from the University of Oxford. Prior to taking up his current position in 2020, he was an economist at the Bank of Japan (BOJ), the Bank for International Settlements (BIS), and the International Monetary Fund (IMF). At the BOJ, he served as director general of the Research and Statistics Department and director general of the Institute for Monetary and Economic Studies. His research includes inflation dynamics, exchange rate pass-through, corporate investment, and bank lending behavior.

Shirakawa Masaaki is distinguished guest professor at Aoyama-Gakuin University, a member of the Group of Thirty, and former governor of the Bank of Japan (BOJ). He studied economics at the University of Tokyo and received his MA from the University of Chicago. He held several key positions at the BOJ before his term as governor, including executive director in charge of monetary policy. He has been professor at the Kyoto University School of Government and served as vice-chairman of the board of directors of the Bank for International Settlements (BIS). His expertise is primarily in monetary policy.

Tachibanaki Toshiaki is professor emeritus at Kyoto University and research fellow at the Institute of Labor Economics (IZA). He received his BA from Otaru University of Commerce, MA from Osaka University, and earned his PhD at Johns Hopkins University. He served as a professor at Osaka University and Kyoto University, a visiting professor at Doshisha University and Kyoto Women's University, and a visiting senior researcher at the Economic Planning Agency. He specializes in labor economics, public economics, and applied econometrics.

Takenaka Heizō is professor emeritus at Keio University and former minister for internal affairs and communications and privatization of postal services of Japan. He received his BA in economics from Hitotsubashi University and his PhD in economics from Osaka University. He has been a visiting scholar at both Harvard University and the University of Pennsylvania, serves on several economic advisory boards and committees, and joined the Foundation Board of the World Economic Forum in 2007. He was an integral part of the Koizumi administration's financial reform plans as minister for economic and fiscal policy. Takenaka's primary research interest is in economic policy.

Tsuru Kōtarō is professor at the Graduate School of Business and Commerce, Keio University, and a faculty fellow and research director at the Research Institute of Economy, Trade and Industry (RIETI). He received his BS in mathematics from the University of Tokyo and holds an MPhil and DPhil in economics from the University of Oxford. His former posts include senior fellow at RIETI and economist at the Bank of Japan, the Organisation for Economic Co-operation and Development (OECD) in Paris, and the Economic Planning Agency. His areas of research include comparative institutional analysis, labor-market institutions, and organizational economics.

Ueda Kazuo is a professor in the Department of Business Studies, Faculty of Business, Kyōritsu Women's University. After postgraduate studies at the University of Tokyo, he received his PhD in economics at the Massachusetts Institute of Technology. He served as assistant professor in the economics departments of the University of British Columbia, Osaka University, and the University of Tokyo before becoming a professor in the University of Tokyo's Faculty of Economics. He has also served as senior economist at the Ministry of Finance's Institute of Fiscal and Monetary Policy and as a member of the Policy Board at the Bank of Japan. His expertise is in macroeconomics and finance.

Ueno Yōichi is chief forecaster at the Japan Center for Economic Research (JCER). He completed his bachelor's degree in the Faculty of Commerce and Management of Hitotsubashi University, going on to complete graduate studies and earn his MBA in the same faculty. He completed his MS in economics at the University of Wisconsin–Madison. He previously worked in the Monetary Affairs Department, Research and Statistics Department, International Department, and Financial Markets Department of the Bank of Japan and has published several papers in English on the Japanese economy and financial markets.

Urata Shūjirō is professor emeritus at Waseda University and senior research advisor at the Economic Research Institute for ASEAN and East Asia. He also serves as faculty fellow at the Research Institute of Economy, Trade and Industry (RIETI), specially appointed fellow at the Japan Center for Economic Research (JCER), and distinguished senior fellow at the Institute of Developing Economies. Urata received his BA in economics from Keio University, and MA and PhD in economics from Stanford University. His former posts include research associate at the Brookings Institution and economist at the World Bank. His specialization is in international economics.

Watanabe Kōta is a researcher at the Canon Institute for Global Studies and the Graduate School of Economics at the University of Tokyo. He completed a doctorate in science at the Interdisciplinary Graduate School of Science and Engineering at the Tokyo Institute of Technology, subsequently receiving a research fellowship from the Japan Society for the Promotion of Science. He worked as an economist in the Bank of Japan's Institute for Monetary and Economic Studies and as an assistant professor in the Faculty of Commerce at Chuo University. His research focuses on economic analysis using large-scale business data and analysis of fluctuations in products and real-estate prices.

Watanabe Tsutomu is professor of economics at the Graduate School of Economics, University of Tokyo. He received his BA from the University of Tokyo and his PhD in economics from Harvard University. Previously he taught as a professor at Hitotsubashi University and worked as a senior economist at the Bank of Japan. He has held visiting positions at several universities, including Kyoto University, Bocconi University, and Columbia University. His main research areas are macroeconomics, international finance, and corporate finance. He is the founder and technical advisor at the data-based financial analysis firm Nowcast, Inc.

Yamashita Kazuhito is research director of the Canon Institute for Global Studies and senior fellow at the Research Institute of Economy, Trade and Industry

(RIETI). He received a degree in law and a PhD in agriculture from the University of Tokyo, and MAs in applied economics as well as public administration from the University of Michigan. At the Ministry of Agriculture, Forestry and Fisheries (MAFF), he held positions including deputy director general of the International Affairs Department and deputy director general of the Rural Development Bureau. His research specialization is in forestry policy, agricultural policy, and trade policy.

Yanagisawa Hakuo is a member of the Liberal Democratic Party (LDP) and has served eight terms as a member of the House of Representatives. He received a degree in law from the University of Tokyo and went on to join the Ministry of Finance. His former positions include director general of the National Land Agency (present-day Ministry of Land, Infrastructure, Transport and Tourism), minister of state for Financial Reconstruction, chairman of the Financial Reconstruction Commission, minister of state for Financial Services, chairperson of the Liberal Democratic Party's Research Commission on the Tax System, minister of Health, Labour and Welfare, and Josai International University president.

Yashiro Naohiro is a specially appointed professor with the Faculty of Global Business at Showa Women's University. He received his BA in liberal arts from International Christian University, his BA in economics from the University of Tokyo, and his PhD in economics from the University of Maryland. He has worked at Japan's Economic Planning Agency and the Organisation for Economic Co-operation and Development (OECD) and served as president of the Japan Center for Economic Research (JCER). He was a member of the Regulatory Reform Committee and the Council on Economic and Fiscal Policy. Yashiro's areas of research include labor economics, social security, and the Japanese economy.

Yoshikawa Hiroshi is professor emeritus at the University of Tokyo and former president of Rissho University. He obtained a BA in economics from the University of Tokyo and a PhD in economics at Yale University. He has taught at the State University of New York, Osaka University, and the University of Tokyo. His area of expertise is macroeconomics and the Japanese economy. His English-language publications include *Population and the Japanese Economy: Longevity, Innovation, and Economic Growth* (JPIC, 2020), *Ashes to Awesome: Japan's 6,000-Day Economic Miracle* (JPIC, 2021), and *Reconstruction of Macroeconomics: Methods of Statistical Physics and Keynes' Principle of Effective Demand* (Springer, 2022).

（英文版）論文集 平成日本を振り返る　第三巻 経済
Examining Heisei Japan, Vol. III: Economy

2023年3月27日　第1刷発行

監　　修　北岡伸一
責任編集・著者　小峰隆夫
著　　者　池尾和人、伊藤元重、井堀利宏、岩田一政、岩田規久男、植田和男、上野陽一、浦田秀次郎、翁 邦雄、小黒一正、可部繁三郎、木村福成、清田耕造、黒田東彦、香西 泰、齋藤 潤、左三川（笛田）郁子、白川方明、神野直彦、関根敏隆、竹中平蔵、橘木俊詔、鶴 光太郎、西崎健司、野口悠紀雄、深尾京司、深尾光洋、増田寛也、松原 聡、ミレヤ・ソリース、村田啓子、八代尚宏、柳沢伯夫、山下一仁、吉川 洋、渡辺広太、渡辺 努（五十音順）
企　　画　公益財団法人日本国際問題研究所
発 行 所　一般財団法人出版文化産業振興財団
〒101-0051 東京都千代田区神田神保町2-2-30
電話　03-5211-7283
ホームページ　https://www.jpic.or.jp/

印刷・製本所　大日本印刷株式会社

Printed in Japan
hardcover ISBN 978-4-86658-227-6
ebook (ePub) ISBN 978-4-86658-228-3